Frommer's®

W9-AVW-222

Oregon
5th Edition

by Karl Samson

Here's what the critics say about Frommer's:

"Amazingly easy to use. Very portable, very complete."

—*Booklist*

"Detailed, accurate, and easy-to-read information for all price ranges."
—*Glamour Magazine*

"Hotel information is close to encyclopedic."

—*Des Moines Sunday Register*

"Frommer's Guides have a way of giving you a real feel for a place."
—*Knight Ridder Newspapers*

WILEY
Wiley Publishing, Inc.

About the Author

Karl Samson lives in Oregon, where he spends his time juggling his obsessions with traveling, gardening, outdoor sports, and wine. Each winter, to dry out his webbed feet, he flees the soggy Northwest to update *Frommer's Arizona*. However, he always looks forward to his return to the land of good espresso. Karl is also the author of *Frommer's Washington, Frommer's Seattle,* and *Frommer's Portable Portland.*

Published by:

Wiley Publishing, Inc.

111 River St.
Hoboken, NJ 07030-5774

ISBN-13: 978-0-471-76388-8
ISBN-10: 0-471-76388-8

Editor: Matthew Brown
Production Editor: Michael Brumitt
Cartographer: Andrew Dolan
Photo Editor: Richard Fox
Production by Wiley Indianapolis Composition Services

Front cover photo: Crater Lake National Scenic Park
Back cover photo: Cascade Mountains: Sparks Lake, fisherman in a canoe

For information on our other products and services or to obtain technical support, please contact our Customer Care Department within the U.S. at 800/762-2974, outside the U.S. at 317/572-3993 or fax 317/572-4002.

Wiley also publishes its books in a variety of electronic formats. Some content that appears in print may not be available in electronic formats.

Manufactured in the United States of America

5 4 3 2 1

Contents

List of Maps   vi

What's New in Oregon   1

1   The Best of Oregon   4

1 The Best Natural Attractions 4
2 The Best Outdoor Activities 5
3 The Best Beaches 6
4 The Best Hikes 6
5 The Best Scenic Drives 7
6 The Best Museums 7
7 The Best Family Attractions 8

8 The Best Historical Sites 8
9 The Best Hotels for Families 9
10 The Best B&Bs 9
11 The Best Small Inns 10
12 The Best Historic Hotels & Lodges . . .11
13 The Best Dining with a View 12
14 The Best Off-the-Beaten-Path
     Restaurants 12

2   Planning Your Trip to Oregon   14

1 The Regions in Brief 14
2 Visitor Information 17
3 Money 17
     Destination: Oregon—
     Red Alert Checklist 18
4 When to Go 19
     Oregon Calendar of Events 20
5 Travel Insurance, Health & Safety . . .22
6 Specialized Travel Resources 24
7 Planning Your Trip Online 26

     Frommers.com: The Complete
     Travel Resource 27
8 The 21st-Century Traveler 28
     Online Traveler's Toolbox 29
9 Getting There 29
10 The Active Vacation Planner 31
     Serious Reservations 32
11 Getting Around 36
12 Tips on Accommodations 38
     Fast Facts: Oregon 39

3   For International Visitors   41

1 Preparing for Your Trip 41
2 Getting to the U.S. 47

3 Getting Around the U.S. 48
     Fast Facts: For the International
     Traveler 49

4   Suggested Oregon Itineraries   54

1 Oregon in 1 Week 54
2 Oregon in 2 Weeks 56
3 Oregon for Families 58

4 A Week in the Willamette
     Valley Wine Country 59
5 Exploring the Oregon Coast 60

5 Portland   62

1 Orientation .63
Did You Know? 66
Portland Neighborhoods in Brief 66
2 Getting Around 67
Fast Facts: Portland 70
3 Where to Stay 72
Family-Friendly Hotels 78
4 Where to Dine 81
Family-Friendly Restaurants 90
5 Seeing the Sights 94
Frommer's Favorite Portland
Experiences 96
Pearls in the Pearl District 99

Great Photo Ops 101
The World's Smallest Park 104
6 Especially for Kids 104
7 Organized Tours 105
8 Outdoor Pursuits 106
9 Spectator Sports 108
10 Day Spas .108
11 Shopping .108
The City of Books 110
12 Portland After Dark 113
Blend Your Own Wine 118
13 A Side Trip to Oregon City 121

6 The Willamette Valley: The Bread (& Wine) Basket of Oregon   122

1 The North Willamette Valley
Wine Country 122
The Twice-a-Year Wineries 126
2 Salem & the Mid-Willamette
Valley 140

Blossom Time 147
3 Corvallis & Albany 149
4 Eugene & Springfield 154
The Bridges of Lane County 156

7 The Oregon Coast   163

1 Astoria 164
2 Seaside 171
Biking the Oregon Coast 172
3 Cannon Beach 175
Cannon Beach Trivia 176
4 Tillamook County 181
5 Lincoln City/Gleneden Beach 188
6 Depoe Bay 195

7 Newport 198
8 Yachats 205
9 Florence & the Oregon Dunes
National Recreation Area 209
10 The Coos Bay Area 215
11 Bandon 219
Stormy Weather 223
12 The Southern Oregon Coast 224

8 The Columbia Gorge   233

1 The Columbia Gorge National
Scenic Area 234
2 Hood River: The Windsurfing
Capital of the Northwest 241

3 The Dalles 248

9 The Cascades 253

1 Mount Hood: Skiing, Hiking
& Scenic Drives 254

2 The Santiam Pass, McKenzie
Pass & McKenzie River 261

3 The Willamette Pass Route 264

4 The North Umpqua–Upper
Rogue River Scenic Byway 266

5 Crater Lake National Park 269

6 The Klamath Falls Area:
Bird-Watching & Native
American Artifacts 271

10 Southern Oregon 275

1 Ashland & the Oregon
Shakespeare Festival 275

2 Jacksonville & Medford:
After the Gold Rush 287

3 Grants Pass & the Rogue
River Valley 294

4 Oregon Caves National Monument
& the Illinois Valley 299

5 The Roseburg Area: Lions &
Tigers & Wineries 302

11 Central Oregon 306

1 North Central Oregon &
the Lower Deschutes River 307

2 The Sisters Area 312

3 Bend & Sunriver: Skiing,
Hiking, Fishing, Mountain
Scenery & More 316

Seeing Stars 318

12 Eastern Oregon 328

1 Pendleton .328

2 La Grande, Baker City &
the Blue Mountains 333

*Chinese History in Eastern
Oregon* 339

3 Joseph, Enterprise & the Wallowa
Mountains .339

"I Will Fight No More Forever" 341

4 Hells Canyon & the Southern
Wallowas 344

5 Ontario & the Owyhee River
Region 346

6 Southeastern Oregon: Land of
Marshes, Mountains & Desert 348

Appendix: Oregon in Depth 350

1 The Natural Environment 350

2 Oregon Today 352

3 Oregon History 101 353

Dateline 353

Did You Know? 356

4 Eat, Drink & Be Merry 359

Index 361

List of Maps

Oregon   15

Oregon in 1 & 2 Weeks   55

More Suggested Itineraries   59

Greater Portland Orientation   63

Where to Stay in Portland   73

Where to Dine in Portland   82

Portland Attractions   95

The Willamette Valley   123

Salem   141

Eugene   155

The Northern Oregon Coast   165

Astoria   167

The Central Oregon Coast   189

The Southern Oregon Coast   217

The Columbia Gorge   235

The Cascades   255

Southern Oregon   277

Ashland   279

Central Oregon & North Central
    Oregon   307

Bend   317

Eastern Oregon   329

An Invitation to the Reader

In researching this book, we discovered many wonderful places—hotels, restaurants, shops, and more. We're sure you'll find others. Please tell us about them, so we can share the information with your fellow travelers in upcoming editions. If you were disappointed with a recommendation, we'd love to know that, too. Please write to:

Frommer's Oregon, 5th Edition
Wiley Publishing, Inc. • 111 River St. • Hoboken, NJ 07030-5774

An Additional Note

Please be advised that travel information is subject to change at any time—and this is especially true of prices. We therefore suggest that you write or call ahead for confirmation when making your travel plans. The authors, editors, and publisher cannot be held responsible for the experiences of readers while traveling. Your safety is important to us, however, so we encourage you to stay alert and be aware of your surroundings. Keep a close eye on cameras, purses, and wallets, all favorite targets of thieves and pickpockets.

Other Great Guides for Your Trip:

Frommer's Portable Portland
Frommer's Washington State
Frommer's Seattle

Frommer's Star Ratings, Icons & Abbreviations

Every hotel, restaurant, and attraction listing in this guide has been ranked for quality, value, service, amenities, and special features using a **star-rating system.** In country, state, and regional guides, we also rate towns and regions to help you narrow down your choices and budget your time accordingly. Hotels and restaurants are rated on a scale of zero (recommended) to three stars (exceptional). Attractions, shopping, nightlife, towns, and regions are rated according to the following scale: zero stars (recommended), one star (highly recommended), two stars (very highly recommended), and three stars (must-see).

In addition to the star-rating system, we also use **seven feature icons** that point you to the great deals, in-the-know advice, and unique experiences that separate travelers from tourists. Throughout the book, look for:

Finds	Special finds—those places only insiders know about
Fun Fact	Fun facts—details that make travelers more informed and their trips more fun
Kids	Best bets for kids and advice for the whole family
Moments	Special moments—those experiences that memories are made of
Overrated	Places or experiences not worth your time or money
Tips	Insider tips—great ways to save time and money
Value	Great values—where to get the best deals

The following **abbreviations** are used for credit cards:

AE	American Express	DISC	Discover	V	Visa
DC	Diners Club	MC	MasterCard		

Frommers.com

Now that you have the guidebook to a great trip, visit our website at **www.frommers.com** for travel information on more than 3,000 destinations. With features updated regularly, we give you instant access to the most current trip-planning information available. At Frommers.com, you'll also find the best prices on airfares, accommodations, and car rentals—and you can even book travel online through our travel booking partners. At Frommers.com, you'll also find the following:

- Online updates to our most popular guidebooks
- Vacation sweepstakes and contest giveaways
- Newsletter highlighting the hottest travel trends
- Online travel message boards with featured travel discussions

What's New in Oregon

The world of travel is always changing. New hotels and museums open. Restaurants and nightclubs close. Establishments move. Oregon is no exception, so, in this book, I've tried to keep tabs on what's new and noteworthy throughout the state. The following are some of the highlights.

PORTLAND Where to Stay Portland has finally begun to get some hip hotels over the past few years. For hipsters on a tight budget, there's the **Jupiter Hotel,** 800 E. Burnside St. (© **877/ 800-0004** or 503/230-9200; www. jupiterhotel.com), which is affiliated with Portland's hottest nightclub, the Doug Fir Lounge.

For hipsters on a bigger budget, downtown's **Hotel Lućia,** 400 SW Broadway (© **877/225-1717** or 503/225-1717; www.hotellucia.com), is the place to stay.

Where to Dine If you want to eat where young foodies are dining, check out the **Gotham Building Tavern,** 2240 N. Interstate Ave. (© **503/235-2294;** www.ripepdx.com), which is accessible from downtown on the MAX light rail.

A deli with it's own bar? Is that kosher? Whether it is or not, that's what you'll find at **Elephant's Deli,** 115 NW 22nd Ave. (© **503/299-6304;** www.elephants-deli.com), a landmark Portland deli that has moved to plush new digs. This is the perfect place to stock up on picnic foods before heading to Washington Park on a sunny day.

Hidden away on a quiet side street in the farther reaches of the Nob Hill neighborhood, **patanegra,** 1818 NW 23rd Place (© **503/227-7282;** www. patanegra-restaurant.com), is a lively neighborhood Spanish restaurant with great tapas. Right next door, you'll find **St. Honoré Boulangerie,** 2335 NW Thurman St. (© **503/445-4342;** www. sainthonorebakery.com), which is currently my favorite bakery in Portland.

Good food, good location, good prices. What's not to like about **Baan-Thai Restaurant,** 1924 SW Broadway (© **503/224-8424**)? Located near Portland State University, this place is a favorite of both professors and students.

Seeing the Sights Fans of modern and contemporary art should be sure to visit the new wing of the **Portland Art Museum,** 1219 SW Park Ave. © **503/226-2811;** www.portlandartmuseum.org).

At the remodeled **World Forestry Center Discovery Museum,** 4033 SW Canyon Rd. (© **503/228-1367;** www. worldforestry.org), across from the Washington Park Zoo, you and your kids can have fun while learning about the importance of forests around the world.

Portland After Dark If you want to catch some live alternative music in Portland's hippest live-music club, descend into the log-cabin chic world of the **Doug Fir Lounge,** 830 E. Burnside St. (© **503/231-9663**). For a great alternative-music scene that isn't driven by the fashionistas, imbibe at **Imbibe,** 2229 SE Hawthorne Blvd. (© **503/239-4002;** www.takeitin.com). For the best and most unusual cocktails in town, search out north Portland's **Mint/820,** 816/820 N. Russell St. (© **503/284-5518**), where you can actually order a beet-infused vodka martini.

THE WILLAMETTE VALLEY The North Willamette Valley Wine Country This region has been booming lately, with new wineries, new inns, and new restaurants. Some of the best Oregon wineries are now open to the public on a regular basis. These include **Archery Summit,** 18599 NE Archery Summit Rd. (© **800/732-8822;** www.archery summit.com); **Domaine Drouhin Oregon,** Breyman Orchards Road (© **503/ 864-2700;** www.domainedrouhin.com); and **Domaine Serene,** 6555 Hilltop Lane (© **866/864-6555** or 503/864-4600; www.domaineserene.com), all of which are just west of Dundee. Other new wineries worth searching out include **August Cellars,** 14000 NE Quarry Rd. (© **503/ 554-6766;** www.augustcellars.com) in Newberg; **Penner-Ash Wine Cellars,** 15771 NE Ribbon Ridge Rd. (© **503/ 554-5545;** www.pennerash.com), near Carlton; and **Soléna Cellars,** 213 S. Pine St. (© **503/852-0082;** www.solena cellars.com), and **Tyrus Evan/The Depot,** 120 N. Pine St. (© **503/852-7010;** www. thecarltondepot.com), both of which are right in Carlton.

For a wine-country room with a view, book a night or two at the **Black Walnut Inn,** 9600 NE Worden Hill Rd., Dundee (© **866/429-4114** or 503/429-4114; www.blackwalnut-inn.com), a Tuscan villa high in the Red Hills of Dundee.

The Yamhill County wine country has seen several excellent restaurants open in the past few years. In Newberg, try the casual **French Bear,** 107 S. College St. (© **503/538-2609**); or the much more formal **Painted Lady,** 201 S. College St. (© **503/538-3850;** www.thepainted ladyrestaurant.com).

In Carlton, you can now accompany your local pinot noir with great French cuisine at the tiny **Cuvée,** 214 W. Main St. (© **503/852-6555**); and in McMinnville, you can pair your wine with Spanish tapas at **La Rambla Restaurant & Bar,** 238 NE Third St. (© **503/435-2126;** www.laramblaonthird.com).

Salem If your travel plans include a stay in Salem, be sure to book your room at the plush new **Phoenix Grand Hotel,** 201 Liberty St. SE (© **877/540-7800** or 503/540-7800; www.phoenixgrandhotel. com). When it's time for dinner, take a drive out into the country to **Wild Pear,** 3635 River Rd. S. (© **503/589-4532;** www.wildpearcatering.com), which has great food and a great location.

Eugene After being closed for a couple of years for renovations, the University of Oregon's **Jordan Schnitzer Museum of Art,** 1430 Johnson Lane (© **541/ 346-3027;** uoma.uoregon.edu), is open once again.

THE OREGON COAST Astoria One of the best waterfront hotels on the Oregon coast isn't on the ocean, it's on the Columbia River. The **Cannery Pier Hotel,** 10 Basin St. (© **888/325-4996** or 503/325-4996; www.cannerypierhotel. com), fits in beautifully with the town's seafaring past yet has great modern amenities.

Fresh from its bicentennial celebrations, the newly designated **Lewis and Clark National and State Historical Park,** off U.S. 101, 5 miles southwest of Astoria (© **503/861-2471;** www.nps.gov/lewi), has a new trail to the Pacific; at press time, the Fort Clatsop replica, burned down in late 2005, was being rebuilt.

Cannon Beach My favorite restaurant in Cannon Beach these days is the **Gower Street Bistro,** 1116 S. Hemlock St. (© **503/436-2729;** www.gowerstreet bistro.com), a European-style charcuterie with loads of character.

Tillamook County In the town of Nehalem, which is little more than a wide spot in the road, the new restaurant **Currents,** 35815 U.S. 101 (© 503/ 368-5557), has great food and a wonderful deck overlooking the Nehalem River. Nearby, the **Nehalem River Inn,** 34910 Hwy. 53 (© 503/368-7708), has been taken over by a young new chef who has cranked the menu up a notch in quality. In Manzanita, be sure to have a glass of wine at **Vino Manzanita,** 387-D Laneda Ave. (© 503/368-VINO).

Lincoln City If you're traveling with Fido, you'll want to bark—I mean *park*—yourself at the **Looking Glass Inn,** 861 SW 51st St. (© 800/843-4940 or 541/996-3996; www.lookingglass-inn. com), a hotel that welcomes dogs with a basket of treats.

Depoe Bay Here at the narrow entrance to the tiniest natural harbor in the country, **Depoe Bay State Park,** 119 U. S. 101 (© 541/764-3304), has a new Whale Watch Center. There are no guarantees about spotting whales, but the displays are informative and the staff and volunteers are helpful.

Newport In Newport's Nye Beach neighborhood, the hippest beachfront community on the coast, you'll find **Panache,** 614 W. Olive St. (© 541/ 265-2929; www.panachenewport.com), a wonderful new restaurant with creative fare. For ultrafresh seafood, visit **Local Ocean Seafoods,** 213 SE Bay Blvd. (© 541/574-7959; www.localocean. net), on the Bayfront.

Florence While you're in town, don't miss the sexy little **Waterfront Depot,** 1252 Bay St. (© 541/902-9100), a restaurant and bar in old town Florence.

Bandon The **Bandon Dunes Golf Resort,** 57744 Round Lake Dr., Bandon (© 888/345-6008 or 541/347-4380; www.bandondunesgolf.com), one of the most highly acclaimed golf resorts in the country, has added a new course.

THE COLUMBIA GORGE Hood River New wineries in the Hood River area include **Pheasant Valley Vineyard & Winery,** 3890 Acree Dr. (© 866/357-WINE or 541/387-3040; www.pheasant-valleywinery.com), and **Mt. Hood Winery,** 3189 Ore. 35 (© 541/386-8333; www.mthoodwinery.com)

Sharing space with a realtors office, the **Oak Street Hotel,** 610 Oak St., Hood River (© 866/386-3845 or 541/ 386-3845; www.oakstreethotel.com), is a pretty little hotel in downtown Hood River. Be sure to have a dinner at **Celilo Restaurant,** 16 Oak St. (© 541/386-5710; www.celilorestaurant.com), which blends urban chic with a Northwest woodsy aesthetic.

SOUTHERN OREGON Jacksonville More wineries in the Applegate Valley, west of historic Jacksonville, are opening to the public, making this one of the best areas in the state to spend an afternoon wine touring. Among my favorite new wineries in the area are Devitt Winery & Vineyards and Wooldridge Creek Vineyard & Wines.

CENTRAL OREGON Sisters The **Lodge at Suttle Lake,** 13300 U.S. 20 (© 541/595-2628; www.thelodgeatsut-tlelake.com), west of Sisters, is a real find. Right in Sisters is **Grand Palace Hotel,** 101 E. Cascade Ave. (© 541/549-2211 or 541/771-7731; www.grandpalacehotel sisters.com), a casual place filled with antique furnishings, many of which are for sale.

Bend A fun, economical place to stay in downtown Bend is **McMenamins Old St. Francis School Hotel,** 700 NW Bond St. (© 877/661-4228 or 541/382-5174; www.mcmenamins.com), and for creative food without the hype, head to **Zydeco Kitchen & Cocktails,** 1085 SE Third St. (© 541/312-2899; www.zydecokitchen.com).

1

The Best of Oregon

You've probably already heard the jokes: Oregonians have webbed feet and they don't tan, they rust. Even people otherwise unfamiliar with Oregon seem to know that it rains a lot here. There's simply no getting around the fact that few states receive as much rain or cloudy weather as Oregon (except Washington, Oregon's northern neighbor). However, Oregon's rainfall no longer seems to have the effect it once did. Sure, it still keeps the landscape green, but it's no longer keeping people from moving here.

Once, Oregon was the promised land of 19th-century pioneers, and today, it is an amalgam of American life and landscapes. Within its boundaries, the state reflects a part of almost every region of the country. Take a bit of New England's rural beauty, its covered bridges, and its steepled churches. Temper the climate with that of the upper South to avoid harsh winters. Now bring in some low, rolling mountains such as the Appalachians; rugged, glaciated mountains such as the Rockies; and Hawaiian-style volcanoes and lava fields. Add a river as large and important as the Mississippi—complete with paddle wheelers—and a coastline as rugged as California's. Of course, there would have to be sagebrush and cowboys and Indians. You could even throw in the deserts of the Southwest and the wheat fields of the Midwest. A little wine country would be a nice touch, and so would some long, sandy beaches. Finally, you'll need a beautiful city, one whose downtown skyscrapers are framed by high, forested hills and whose gardens are full of roses.

To explore such a diverse state takes quite a bit of planning, and knowing ahead of time the best that the state has to offer can make a visit much more enjoyable. After traveling the length and breadth of the state, I've chosen what I feel are the very best attractions, activities, lodgings, and restaurants. These are the places and experiences you won't want to miss. Most are described in more detail elsewhere in this book, but this chapter will give you an overview and get you started.

1 The Best Natural Attractions

- **The Oregon Coast:** Rocky headlands, offshore islands and haystack rocks, natural arches, caves full of sea lions, giant sand dunes, and dozens of state parks make this one of the most spectacular coastlines in the country. The only drawback is that the water is too cold for swimming. See chapter 7.
- **Columbia Gorge National Scenic Area:** Carved by ice-age floodwaters

up to 1,200 feet deep, the Columbia Gorge is a unique feature of the Oregon landscape. Waterfalls by the dozen cascade from the basalt cliffs of the gorge, and highways on both the Washington and the Oregon sides of the Columbia River provide countless memorable views. See p. 234.
- **Mount Hood:** As Oregon's tallest mountain and the closest Cascade

peak to Portland, Mount Hood is a recreational mecca par excellence. Hiking trails, lakes and rivers, and year-round skiing make this one of the most appealing natural attractions in the state. See p. 254.

- **Crater Lake National Park:** At 1,932 feet deep, Crater Lake is the deepest lake in the United States, and its sapphire-blue waters are a bewitchingly beautiful sight when seen from the rim of the volcanic caldera that forms the lake. See p. 269.

- **Central Oregon Lava Lands:** Throughout central Oregon and the central Cascades region, from the lava fields of McKenzie Pass to the obsidian flows of Newberry National Volcanic Monument, you'll find dramatic examples of the volcanic activity that gave rise to the Cascade Range. See chapters 9 and 11.

- **Hells Canyon:** Deeper than the Grand Canyon, this massive gorge along the Oregon-Idaho border is remote and inaccessible, and that is just what makes it fascinating. You can gaze down into it from on high, float its waters, or hike its trails. See p. 344.

2 The Best Outdoor Activities

- **Biking the Oregon Coast:** With U.S. 101 clinging to the edge of the continent for much of its route through Oregon, this road has become one of the most popular cycling routes in the Northwest. The entire coast can be done in about a week, but there are also plenty of short sections that make good day trips. See p. 172.

- **Windsurfing at Hood River:** Winds blast through the Columbia Gorge and whip up white-capped standing waves, and they have turned this area into the windsurfing capital of the United States, attracting windsurfers from around the world. See p. 241.

- **Fly-Fishing for Steelhead on the North Umpqua River:** Made famous by Zane Grey, the North Umpqua is the quintessential steelhead river, and for part of its length it's open to fly-fishing only. The river and the elusive steelhead offer a legendary fishing experience. See p. 267.

- **Rafting the Rogue River:** Of all the state's white-water-rafting rivers, none is more famous than the Rogue. Meandering through remote wilderness in the southern part of the state, this river has been popular with anglers since early in the 20th century and attracted Zane Grey with its beauty and great fishing. Today, you can splash through roaring white water by day and spend your nights in remote lodges that are inaccessible by car. See p. 267.

- **Mountain Biking in Bend:** Outside the town of Bend, in central Oregon, dry ponderosa pine forests are laced with trails that are open to mountain bikes. Routes pass by several lakes, and along the way you'll get great views of the Three Sisters, Broken Top, and Mount Bachelor. See p. 321.

- **Skiing Mount Bachelor:** With ski slopes dropping off the very summit of this extinct volcano, Mount Bachelor ski area, in central Oregon, is the state's premier ski area. Seemingly endless runs of all levels of ability make this a magnet for skiers and snowboarders from around the state, and lots of high-speed quad chairs keep people on the snow instead of standing in line. See p. 319.

3 The Best Beaches

See chapter 7 for details on the beaches listed below.

- **Cannon Beach/Ecola State Park:** With the massive monolith of Haystack Rock rising up from the low-tide line and the secluded beaches of Ecola State Park just north of town, Cannon Beach offers all the best of the Oregon coast. See p. 175.

- **Oswald West State Park:** At this state park south of Cannon Beach, it's a 15-minute walk through the woods to the beach, which keeps the sand from ever getting too crowded. The crescent-shaped beach is on a secluded cove backed by dense forest. This also happens to be a popular surfing spot. See p. 176.

- **Sunset Bay State Park:** Almost completely surrounded by sandstone cliffs, this little beach near Coos Bay is on a shallow cove. The clear waters here get a little bit warmer than unprotected waters elsewhere on the coast, so it's sometimes possible to actually go swimming. See p. 216.

- **Bandon:** It's difficult to imagine a more picturesque stretch of coastline than the beach in Bandon. Haystack rocks rise up from sand and sea as if strewn there by some giant hand. Motels and houses front this scenic beach, which ensures its popularity no matter what the weather. See p. 219.

- **The Beaches of Samuel H. Boardman State Scenic Corridor:** Some of the prettiest, most secluded, and least visited beaches on the Oregon coast are within this remote south-coast state park. Ringed by rocky headlands, the many little crescents of sand in this park provide an opportunity to find *the* perfect beach. See p. 228.

4 The Best Hikes

- **Cape Lookout Trail:** Leading 2.5 miles through dense forests to the tip of this rugged cape on the north Oregon coast, this trail ends high on a cliff above the waters of the Pacific. Far below, gray whales can often be seen lolling in the waves, and the view to the south takes in miles of coastline. See p. 186.

- **John Dellenback Dunes Trail:** If you've ever dreamed of joining the French Foreign Legion or simply want to play at being Lawrence of Arabia, then the Oregon Dunes National Recreation Area is the place for you. Within this vast expanse of sand dunes, you'll find the highest dunes on the Oregon coast—some 500 feet tall. See p. 211.

- **Eagle Creek Trail:** This trail in the Columbia Gorge follows the tumbling waters of Eagle Creek and passes two spectacular waterfalls in the first 2 miles. Along the way, the trail climbs up the steep gorge walls, and in places it is cut right into the basalt cliffs. See p. 237.

- **Timberline Trail:** As the name implies, this trail starts at the timberline, high on the slopes of Mount Hood. Because the route circles Mount Hood, you can start in either direction and make a day, overnight, or multiday hike of it. Paradise Park, its meadows ablaze with wildflowers in July and August, is a favorite for both day hikes and overnight trips. See p. 256.

- **McKenzie River Trail to Tamolitch Pool:** The McKenzie River Trail stretches for 26 miles along the banks of this aquamarine river, but by far the most rewarding stretch of trail is the 2-mile hike to Tamolitch Pool, an astounding pool of turquoise waters formed as the McKenzie River wells up out of the ground after flowing underground for several miles. The trail leads through rugged, overgrown lava fields. See p. 262.

- **Deschutes River Trail:** The Deschutes River, which flows down from the east

side of the Cascades, open ponderosa pin of Bend. Paralleling ing tumultuous way, it is an eas with hikers, mountain bikers, gers. See p. 320.

5 The Best Scenic Drives

- **Gold Beach to Brookings:** No other stretch of U.S. 101 along the Oregon coast is more breathtaking than the segment between Gold Beach and Brookings. This remote coastline is dotted with offshore islands, natural rock arches, sea caves, bluffs, and beaches. Take your time, stop at the many pull-offs, and make this a leisurely all-day drive. See p. 228.

- **Historic Columbia River Highway:** Built between 1914 and 1926 to allow automobiles access to the wonders of the Columbia Gorge, this narrow, winding highway east of Portland climbs up to the top of the gorge for a scenic vista before diving into forests where waterfalls, including the tallest one in the state, pour off of basalt cliffs. See p. 236.

- **The Santiam and McKenzie Passes:** This loop drive, which crosses the

Cascade crest twice, takes in views of half a dozen major Cascade peaks, negotiates a bizarre landscape of lava fields, passes several waterfalls, and skirts aptly named Clear Lake, the source of the McKenzie River. This is one of the best drives in the state for fall color. See p. 261.

- **Crater Lake Rim Drive:** This scenic drive circles the rim of the massive caldera that holds Crater Lake. Along the way are numerous pull-offs where you can admire the sapphire-blue waters and the ever-changing scenery. See p. 270.

- **Cascade Lakes Highway:** This road covers roughly 100 miles as it loops out from Bend along the eastern slope of the Cascades. Views of Broken Top and the Three Sisters are frequent, and along the way are numerous lakes, both large and small. See p. 321.

6 The Best Museums

- **Portland Art Museum:** Although the main focus is on bringing blockbuster, touring shows to town, the Portland Art Museum recently added a new wing for contemporary and modern art. The museum also has respectable collections of Native American artifacts and Northwest contemporary art. See p. 98.

- **Evergreen Aviation Museum** (McMinnville): Looking like a cross between a gigantic airplane hangar and a huge barn, this museum is home to Howard Hughes's "Spruce

Goose," the largest wooden plane ever built. There are also plenty of smaller planes on display to provide a little perspective for this behemoth of the air. See p. 133.

- **Jensen Arctic Museum** (Monmouth): This museum is not very big, but it contains an amazingly diverse collection of artifacts from the Arctic. Even more surprising than the thoroughness of the collection is the fact that the museum is here in Oregon, not in Alaska. See p. 146.

Columbia River Maritime Museum (Astoria): Located near the mouth of the Columbia River, this large modern museum has fascinating exhibits on the Coast Guard and the dangerous waters at the mouth of the river. See p. 166.

- **Favell Museum of Western Art and Indian Artifacts** (Klamath Falls): This museum houses an overwhelming assortment of Native American artifacts, including thousands of arrowheads, spear points, and other stone tools. See p. 272.

- **The Museum at Warm Springs** (Warm Springs Reservation): Set in a remote valley in central Oregon, this modern museum houses an outstanding collection of artifacts from the area's Native American tribes. See p. 309.

- **The High Desert Museum** (Bend): With its popular live-animal exhibits, this is more a zoo than a museum, but exhibits also offer glimpses into the history of the vast and little-known high desert that stretches from the Cascades eastward to the Rocky Mountains. See p. 317.

- **National Historic Oregon Trail Interpretive Center at Flagstaff Hill** (Baker City): The lives of 19th-century pioneers, who gave up everything to venture overland to the Pacific Northwest, are documented at this evocative museum. Set atop a hill in sagebrush country, the museum overlooks wagon ruts left by pioneers. See p. 334.

7 The Best Family Attractions

- **Oregon Museum of Science and Industry** (Portland): With an OMNIMAX theater, a planetarium, a submarine, and loads of hands-on exhibits, this Portland museum is fun for kids and adults alike. See p. 98.

- **Oregon Coast Aquarium** (Newport): This modern aquarium is the biggest attraction on the coast. Tufted puffins and sea otters are always entertaining, while tide pools, jellyfish tanks, sharks, and a giant octopus also contribute to the appeal of this very realistically designed public aquarium. See p. 199.

- **Sea Lion Caves** (north of Florence): This massive cave, the largest sea cave in the country, is home to hundreds of Steller's sea lions that lounge on the rocks beneath busy U.S. 101. See p. 208.

- **West Coast Game Park** (Bandon): The opportunity to pet baby wild animals, including leopards and bears, doesn't come often, so it's hard to pass up this roadside attraction on the southern Oregon coast. See p. 221.

- **Wildlife Safari** (Winston): Giraffes peer in your window and rhinoceroses thunder past your car doors as you drive the family through this expansive wildlife park. The savanna-like setting is reminiscent of the African plains. See p. 302.

8 The Best Historical Sites

- **Lewis and Clark National Historical Park** (Astoria): This new national park comprises numerous historic sites that explorers Lewis and Clark utilized during the winter of 1805–06. The sites are located around the mouth of the Columbia River. During the summer, costumed interpreters bring the history of the fort to life. See p. 166.

- **Jacksonville:** With more than 80 buildings listed on the National Register of Historic Places, this 19th-century gold-mining town is the best-preserved historic community in Oregon. Here you'll also find two inns housed in buildings constructed in 1861, which makes these Oregon's oldest buildings being used as inns. See p. 287.

- **Oregon Trail Wagon Ruts** (Baker City): It's hard to believe that something as seemingly ephemeral as a wagon rut can last more than 150 years, but the path made by the thousands of pioneers who followed the Oregon Trail cut deep into the land. One place you can see ruts is near Baker City's National Historic Oregon Trail Interpretive Center. See p. 334.

- **Kam Wah Chung & Co. Museum** (John Day): This unusual little museum is way off the beaten path but is well worth a visit if you're anywhere in the vicinity. The museum preserves the home, office, and apothecary of a Chinese doctor who ministered to the local Chinese community in the early part of the 20th century. See p. 339.

9 The Best Hotels for Families

- **Embassy Suites** (Portland; ℂ **800/ EMBASSY** or 503/279-9000): Unlike most other Embassy Suites, this is a historic hotel, but it still has those spacious suites that are great for families. Plus, there's a pool and video arcade down in the basement. See p. 76.

- **Hallmark Resort** (Cannon Beach; ℂ **888/448-4449** or 503/436-1566): Set on a bluff with a great view of Cannon Beach's famous Haystack Rock, this is just about the most family oriented hotel in town. There are two indoor pools. See p. 178.

- **Lake of the Woods** (Klamath Falls; ℂ **866/201-4194** or 541/949-8300): This old-fashioned lakefront lodge in the southern Oregon Cascades is a bit like a summer camp for the whole family. There's great swimming and you can rent boats and mountain bikes. See p. 273.

- **Kah-Nee-Ta High Desert Resort & Casino** (Warm Springs; ℂ **800/ 554-4786** or 541/553-1112): This remote resort is centered around a huge warm-springs–fed swimming pool that is a major magnet for vacationing families. You can also go rafting and horseback riding. See p. 311.

- **Black Butte Ranch** (Sisters; ℂ **800/ 452-7455** or 541/595-6211): With stunning views of the Three Sisters peaks, this central Oregon resort has a solid feel of being in the mountains. Four pools, a kayaking lake, horseback riding stables, and bike paths provide plenty of options for keeping the kids entertained. See p. 314.

- **Seventh Mountain Resort** (ℂ **800/ 452-6810** or 541/382-8711): Although this resort is close to the Mount Bachelor ski area and has an ice-skating rink in the winter, it is most popular with families in the summer, when kids flock to the pools, the miniature golf course, the playground, and the basketball court. See p. 324.

- **Sunriver Lodge & Resort** (Sunriver; ℂ **800/801-8765** or 541/593-1000): This resort south of Bend in Oregon's high desert is popular with families for its many miles of bike trails that meander through pine forests. There are also riding stables and canoes and kayaks for rent on the gentle waters of the Deschutes River. See p. 324.

10 The Best B&Bs

- **Heron Haus** (Portland; ℂ **503/ 274-1846**): Located in one of Portland's prettiest neighborhoods, this elegant old mansion is surrounded by lush grounds and has a view over the city. If you want to sample the epitome of bathroom luxury around 1920, ask for the room with the multiple-head shower. See p. 77.

- **Springbrook Hazelnut Farm** (Newberg; ② **800/793-8528** or 503/538-4606): Set in the midst of the Yamhill County wine country, this working hazelnut farm captures the essence of rural Oregon and distills it into a tranquil and restorative retreat. You can opt to stay in the carriage house or a cottage. See p. 135.
- **Black Walnut Inn** (Dundee; ② **866/429-4114** or 503/429-4114): Set high in the hills above Dundee, this inn is designed to resemble a Tuscan villa and is a luxurious retreat amid wine-country vineyards. See p. 135.
- **Willamette Gables Riverside Estate** (Newberg; ② **503/678-2195**): Designed as a replica of a Natchez, Mississippi, plantation home, this modern B&B is set on the banks of the Willamette River and will have you dreaming of Scarlet O'Hara and Rhett Butler. See p. 135.
- **The Secret Garden** (Eugene; ② **888/484-6755** or 541/484-6755): Housed in what was once a sorority house and before that the home of one of Eugene's founding families, this very elegant inn is utterly tasteful. The garden has some very interesting secrets. See p. 160.
- **Arch Cape House** (Cannon Beach; ② **800/436-2848** or 503/436-2800): Patterned after a French château, this mansion-size B&B may seem oddly out of place on the Oregon coast, but no one staying here seems to mind. It could be the huge guest rooms and

castlelike ambience, or it could be the abundance of European antiques and original art. See p. 177.

- **Channel House** (Depoe Bay; ② **800/447-2140** or 541/765-2140): Situated on the cliff above the narrow channel into tiny Depoe Bay, this B&B offers one of the most striking settings on the Oregon coast. The contemporary design includes guest rooms made for romance—a hot tub on the balcony, a fireplace, and an unsurpassed view out the windows. See p. 197.
- **Newport Belle Bed & Breakfast** (Newport; ② **800/348-1922** or 541/867-6290): The rooms at this B&B may not be the most luxurious or the largest, but the fact that they are on a replica paddle wheeler moored in Yaquina Bay near the Oregon Coast Aquarium certainly makes them some of the most unusual. See p. 202.
- **Heceta Head Lightstation** (Yachats; ② 541/547-3696): Ever dreamed of staying at a lighthouse? Well, on the Oregon coast, your dream can come true at this former lighthouse keeper's home. The Victorian B&B, which claims one of the most spectacular locations on the entire coast, is set high on a hill above the crashing waves. See p. 208.
- **Chetco River Inn & Lavender Farm** (Brookings; ② **541/251-0087**): Want to get away from it all without sacrificing luxury and great food? Book a room at this remote B&B on the crystal-clear Chetco River. The setting—in the middle of a national forest—is as tranquil as you could want. See p. 231.

11 The Best Small Inns

- **Cannery Pier Hotel** (Astoria; ② **888/325-4996** or 503/325-4996): Located on a pier 600 feet out in the Columbia River, this new luxury hotel fits in perfectly on the Astoria

waterfront and looks as if it could have been a cannery at one time. See p. 169.
- **Stephanie Inn** (Cannon Beach; ② **800/633-3466** or 503/436-2221):

Combining the look of a mountain lodge with a beachfront setting in Oregon's most artistic town, the Stephanie Inn is a romantic retreat that surrounds its guests with unpretentious luxury. See p. 178.

- **Coast Cabins** (Manzanita; © **503/ 368-7113**): Although not actually an inn or a lodge, this collection of five modern cottages is so thoroughly enchanting that I had to include it here. Beautiful perennial gardens surround the cottages. See p. 182.

- **Sylvia Beach Hotel** (Newport; © **888/795-8422** or 541/265-5428): Taking literature as its theme and decorating its rooms to evoke authors— from Edgar Allan Poe to Dr. Seuss—the Sylvia Beach Hotel is the most original small inn in the Northwest. The fact that it's only a block from the beach is just icing on the cake. See p. 203.

- **Tu Tu Tun Lodge** (Gold Beach; © **800/864-6357** or 541/247-6664): Though some might think of this as a fishing lodge, it's far too luxurious for anglers to keep to themselves. A secluded setting on the lower Rogue River guarantees tranquillity, and

choice guest rooms provide the perfect setting for forgetting about your everyday stresses. See p. 229.

- **Steamboat Inn** (Steamboat; © **800/ 840-8825** or 541/498-2230): Oregon's North Umpqua River is legendary for its steelhead fishing, and this is where you stay if you want to return to elegance and comfort after a day on the water. However, many guests show up with no intention of casting a fly into the river's waters. See p. 268.

- **The Winchester Inn** (Ashland; © **800/972-4991** or 541/488-1113): Located only 2 blocks from the theaters of the Oregon Shakespeare Festival, this place has the feel of a country inn although it's located right in town. Rooms are in three different buildings, including a modern Victorian cottage. See p. 283.

- **Pine Ridge Inn** (Bend; © **800/ 600-4095** or 541/389-6137): This luxurious inn is located on the outskirts of Bend on a bluff overlooking the Deschutes River. With its spacious rooms and suites, antiques, and regional art, it provides both elegance and a Northwest flavor. See p. 322.

12 The Best Historic Hotels & Lodges

- **The Benson** (Portland; © **888/ 523-6766** or 503/228-2000): With its crystal chandeliers, walnut paneling, and ornate plasterwork ceiling in the lobby, this 1912 vintage hotel is Portland's most elegant lodging. See p. 76.

- **Hotel Elliott** (Astoria; © **877/EST-1924** or 503/325-2222): Originally opened in 1924, this hotel retains much of its original character, but now features lots of modern touches and contemporary styling. When it's time to relax, you'll have to choose between the roof-top garden and the cellar wine bar. See p. 169.

- **Columbia Gorge Hotel** (Hood River; © **800/345-1921** or 541/386-5566): Opened in 1921 to handle the first automobile traffic up the Columbia Gorge, this Mission-style hotel commands a stunning view across the gorge and is surrounded by colorful gardens. See p. 245.

- **Timberline Lodge** (Mount Hood; © **800/547-1406** or 503/622-7979): Built by the WPA during the Great Depression, this stately mountain lodge with grand stone fireplace, exposed beams, and wide-plank floors showcases the skills of the craftspeople who created it. See p. 259.

- **Crater Lake Lodge** (Crater Lake National Park; © 541/830-8700): Perched on the rim of the caldera (not crater) that holds the blue waters of Crater Lake, this mountain lodge isn't actually a historic hotel, but it incorporates details from the original lodge that used to stand on this same site. The setting is breathtaking. See p. 270.
- **Ashland Springs Hotel** (Ashland; © 888/795-4545 or 541/488-1700): This historic high-rise hotel was originally built to cash in on Ashland's

mineral springs, but today it is, instead, a superb choice for anyone attending the Oregon Shakespeare Festival. See p. 281.

- **Geiser Grand Hotel** (Baker City; © 888/434-7374 or 541/523-1889): Originally opened in 1889 at the height of the Blue Mountains gold rush, this Baker City grand dame has been completely renovated and succeeds in capturing the feel of a Wild West luxury hotel without sacrificing any modern conveniences. See p. 337.

13 The Best Dining with a View

- **Chart House** (Portland; 503/246-6963): Perched high on a hillside, this restaurant boasts the best view of any restaurant in Portland. The Willamette River is directly below and off in the distance stand Mount Hood and Mount St. Helens. See p. 89.
- **Roseanna's Oceanside Café** (Oceanside; © 503/842-7351): You can expect a long wait to get a table here on a summer weekend, but the view of the haystack rocks just offshore makes this place an absolute legend on the Three Capes Scenic Loop. See p. 187.
- **Pelican Pub & Brewery** (Pacific City; © 503/965-7007): Cheap pub food and good microbrews are usually enough to keep an Oregon brewpub packed, but this one also has a head-on view of Haystack Rock and is right on the beach. See p. 187.
- **Tidal Raves** (Depoe Bay; © 541/765-2995): When the surf's up, you can practically forget about getting a table at this oceanfront restaurant. The windows overlook a rugged

shoreline known for putting on some of the coast's best displays of crashing waves. See p. 198.

- **Saffron Salmon** (Newport; © 541/265-8921): As you dine at this restaurant at the end of a pier on the Newport bayfront, keep an eye out for sea lions and fishermen unloading their catch. See p. 204.
- **Lord Bennett's Restaurant and Lounge** (Bandon; © 541/347-3663): The beach in Bandon is strewn with dozens of huge monoliths that make this one of the most impressive stretches of shoreline in the state, and this restaurant has the perfect view for enjoying sunset over the sand, surf, and giant rocks. See p. 223.
- **Multnomah Falls Lodge** (Columbia Gorge; © 503/695-2376): This historic lodge is at the base of Oregon's tallest waterfall, and although not every table has a view of the waterfall, there are plenty that do, especially in the summer when there is outside seating. See p. 240.

14 The Best Off-the-Beaten-Path Restaurants

- **The Joel Palmer House** (Dayton; © 503/864-2995): Mushrooms are the chef's obsession at this wine-country restaurant, and you'll find

them in almost every dish on the menu. The restaurant is quite formal, housed in an immaculately restored old home. See p. 138.

- **Cascade Dining Room** (Mount Hood; ✆ **503/622-0700**): Located inside the historic Timberline Lodge, the Cascade Dining Room is Oregon's premier mountain-lodge restaurant and has long kept skiers and other hotel guests happy. See p. 260.
- **Log Cabin Inn** (McKenzie Bridge; ✆ **800/355-3432** or 541/822-3432): This place is an Oregon classic and in the past has served the likes of Clark Gable and President Herbert Hoover. Try the venison medallions. See p. 263.
- **Steamboat Inn** (Steamboat; ✆ **800/ 840-8825** or 541/498-2230): Set on the banks of the North Umpqua River, this is ostensibly a fishing-lodge dining room, but the multicourse gourmet meals served here have become the stuff of legends. See p. 268.
- **Kokanee Café** (Camp Sherman; ✆ **541/595-6420**): Located amid the ponderosa pines on the banks of the Metolius River near the Western theme town of Sisters, this rustic restaurant has the look of an upscale fishing lodge, but its clientele is much broader than just the foolish fly anglers who come to test the waters of the Metolius. The trout is, of course, always a good bet. See p. 316.

2

Planning Your Trip to Oregon

When should we go? Are there any fun festivals going on when we plan to be in Oregon? How should we get around? What sorts of activities can we pursue on a vacation in Oregon? This chapter answers these and many other planning questions.

1 The Regions in Brief

Geography and climate play important roles in dividing Oregon into its various regions.

The Willamette Valley This is Oregon's most densely populated region and site of the state's largest cities, including Portland, Eugene, and the state capital of Salem. However, the valley's fabled farmland grows the greatest variety of crops of any region of the United States. These include hops, mint, grass seed, berries, hazelnuts, irises, tulips, Christmas trees, and an immense variety of landscape plants. The Willamette Valley is also one of the nation's finest wine regions, with vineyards cropping up along its entire length.

Summer, when farm stands pop up alongside rural highways, is by far the best time of year to visit the Willamette Valley. If you are interested in wine, though, you might also want to consider October, when vineyards pick and crush their grapes.

The Oregon Coast Stretching for nearly 300 miles, the Oregon coast is one of the most spectacular coastlines in the country. Backed by the Coast Range mountains and alternating sandy beaches with rocky capes and headlands, this mountainous shoreline provides breathtaking vistas at almost every turn of the road. Haystack rocks—large monoliths

just offshore—lend the coast an unforgettable drama and beauty. Along the central coast, huge dunes, some as much as 500 feet tall, have been preserved as the Oregon Dunes National Recreation Area. Small towns, some known as fishing ports and some as artists' communities, dot the coast. Unfortunately, waters are generally too cold for swimming, and a cool breeze often blows even in summer.

Of course, summer is the most popular time of year on the coast, and crowds can be daunting. In Seaside, Cannon Beach, Lincoln City, and Newport, traffic backups try the patience of many vacationers. The north coast, because of its proximity to Portland, is the most visited section of the coast, and it is also one of the most dramatic. The south coast is even more spectacular than the north, and because of its distance from major metropolitan areas it's not nearly as crowded as other stretches of the coast. The central coast, though it boasts the Oregon Dunes National Recreation Area, is less spectacular than the north and south coasts.

The Columbia Gorge Beginning just east of Portland, the Columbia Gorge is a place of immense beauty and natural diversity. Declared a national scenic area, the Gorge is the site of numerous waterfalls, including Multnomah Falls, the fourth highest in the United States. Rising

Oregon

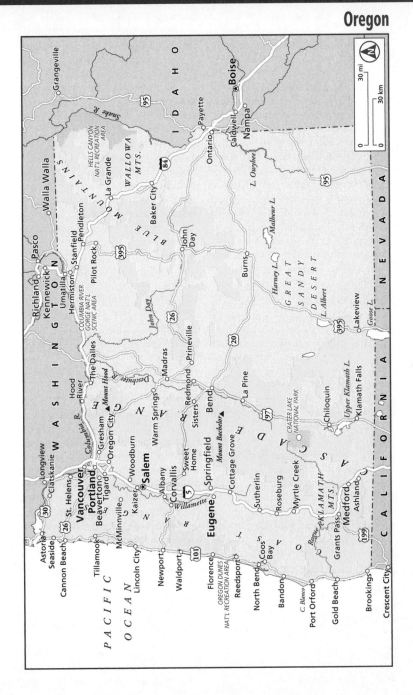

above the waterfalls and basalt cliffs of the Gorge are the snowy slopes of Mount Hood. As the only sea-level gap in the Cascade Range, the Gorge is also something of a wind tunnel, and the winds that regularly blast through the Gorge attract windsurfing enthusiasts from around the world. Consequently, the town of Hood River is now one of the world's top windsurfing spots.

Although the Gorge can be explored in a day or two, if you are an avid hiker or windsurfer, you might want to plan a longer visit. Spring is the best time of year to visit. March through May, countless wildflowers, some of which grow nowhere else but in the Columbia Gorge, burst into bloom, and Gorge wildflower hikes are annual rites of spring for many Oregonians.

The Cascade Range Stretching from the Columbia River in the north to the California state line in the south, this mountain range is a natural dividing line between eastern and western Oregon. Dominated by conical peaks of volcanic origin (all currently inactive), the Cascades are almost entirely encompassed by national forests that serve as both sources of timber and year-round recreational playgrounds. Within these mountains there are several designated wilderness areas in which all mechanized travel is prohibited. Among these, the Mount Hood Wilderness, the Mount Jefferson Wilderness, and the Three Sisters Wilderness are the most scenic. In the southern Cascades, an entire mountain once blew its top, leaving behind a huge caldera that is now filled by the sapphire-blue waters of Crater Lake, Oregon's only national park.

With little private property and few lodges other than rustic (and often run-down) cabin "resorts," the Cascades are primarily a camping destination during the warmer months. In winter, several ski areas and many miles of cross-country ski trails attract skiers and snowboarders.

Southern Oregon Lying roughly midway between San Francisco and Portland, southern Oregon is a jumbled landscape of mountains and valleys through which flow two of the state's most famous rivers. The North Umpqua and the Rogue rivers have been fabled among anglers ever since Zane Grey popularized these waters in his writings. A climate much drier than that of the Willamette Valley to the north gives this region the look of parts of northern California, and, in fact, several towns in the region are very popular with retired Californians. Among these are Ashland, site of the Oregon Shakespeare Festival, and Jacksonville, a historic gold-mining town that is now the site of the Britt Festival, an annual summer festival of music and modern dance. Also in the region are quite a few wineries that take advantage of the warm climate to produce Oregon's best cabernet sauvignon and merlot.

Although summer is the most popular time of year to visit this region, the Oregon Shakespeare Festival runs through much of the spring and fall, which keeps Ashland busy almost year-round.

Central Oregon When the rain on the west side of the Cascades becomes too much to bear, many of the state's residents flee to central Oregon, the drier and sunnier part of the state. Consisting of the east side of the Cascade Range from the Columbia River to just south of Bend, the region spans the eastern foothills of the Cascades and the western edge of the Great Basin's high desert. Known primarily for its lack of rain and proximity to the cities of the Willamette Valley, central Oregon is the state's second-most-popular summer vacation destination (after the coast), with resorts clustered around Sisters and Bend. The biggest and most popular resort is Sunriver, an entire community south of Bend. A volcanic legacy has left the region with some of the most fascinating geology in the state, much of which is preserved in Newberry National Volcanic Monument. Also in this region is the High Desert Museum, a combination museum and zoo that is among the state's most popular attractions.

Although summer is the peak season here, central Oregon is also quite popular in winter—Mount Bachelor ski area provides the best skiing in the Northwest.

Eastern Oregon   Large and sparsely populated, eastern Oregon is primarily high desert interspersed with small mountain ranges. Despite the desert climate, the region is also the site of several large shallow lakes that serve as magnets for a wide variety of migratory birds. In the northeast corner of the region rise the Blue and Wallowa mountains, which are remote, though popular, recreation areas. Carving North America's deepest gorge, and partially forming the border with Idaho, are the Snake River and Hells Canyon. Throughout this region, signs of the Oregon Trail can still be seen.

Because this region is so remote from Portland and the Willamette Valley, it is little visited. However, the breathtaking Wallowa Mountains offer some of the finest backpacking in the state. The town of Joseph, on the north side of these mountains, also happens to be one of the nation's foremost centers for casting bronze sculptures.

2 Visitor Information

Contact the **Oregon Tourism Commission,** 670 Hawthorne ST. SE, Suite 240, Salem, OR 97301 (© **800/547-7842** or 503/378-8850; www.traveloregon.com), or the **Portland Oregon Visitors Association (POVA),** 1000 SW Broadway, Suite 2300, Portland, OR 97205 (© **877/ 678-5263** or 503/275-8355; www.travel portland.com).

Most cities and towns in Oregon have either a tourist office or a chamber of commerce that provides information. When approaching cities and towns, watch for signs along the highway directing you to these information centers. See the individual chapters for addresses.

For Oregon regional websites, try the Oregon Tourism Commission's website at **www.traveloregon.com.** Learn about local Oregon news, sports, and entertainment at **www.oregonlive.com,** *The Oregonian* newspaper's website.

To get information on outdoor recreation in the national forests of Oregon, contact the **Nature of the Northwest Information Center,** 800 NE Oregon St., Room 177, Portland, OR 97232 (© **503/872-2750;** www.naturenw.org). For information on Crater Lake, the only national park in Oregon, contact **Crater Lake National Park,** P.O. Box, Crater Lake, OR 97694 (© **541/594-3100;** www.nps.gov/crla).

For information on camping in Oregon state parks, contact the **Oregon State Park Information Center,** 725 Summers St. NE, Salem, Suite C, OR 97301 (© **800/ 551-6949** or 503/986-0707; www.oregon stateparks.org).

3 Money

ATMs

The easiest and best way to get cash away from home is from an ATM (automated teller machine). The **Cirrus** (© **800/ 424-7787;** www.mastercard.com) and **PLUS** (© **800/843-7587;** www.visa.com) networks span the globe; look at the back of your bank card to see which network you're on, then call or check online for ATM locations at your destination. Be sure you know your personal identification number (PIN) and daily withdrawal limit

Destination: Oregon—Red Alert Checklist

- If you're planning on dining at any of the top-end restaurants in Portland, have you made reservations?
- Have you made theater or day-tour reservations?
- If you purchased traveler's checks, have you recorded the check numbers, and stored the documentation separately from the checks?
- Did you pack your camera, an extra set of camera batteries, and enough film (or memory for your digital camera)?
- Did you bring your ID cards that could entitle you to discounts—such as AAA and AARP cards, and student IDs?
- Do you have the PINs for your credit cards?
- Did you leave a copy of your itinerary with someone at home?

before you depart. *Note:* Remember that many banks impose a fee every time you use a card at another bank's ATM. In addition, the bank from which you withdraw cash may charge its own fee. To compare banks' ATM fees within the U.S., use **www.bankrate.com**.

You can use your credit card to receive cash advances at ATMs. Keep in mind that credit card companies protect themselves from theft by limiting maximum withdrawals outside their home country, so call your credit card company before you leave home. And keep in mind that you'll pay interest from the moment of your withdrawal.

TRAVELER'S CHECKS

Traveler's checks are something of an anachronism from the days before the ATM made cash accessible at any time. Given the fees you'll pay for ATM use at banks other than your own, however, you might be better off with traveler's checks if you're withdrawing money often.

You can get traveler's checks at almost any bank. **American Express** offers denominations of $20, $50, $100, $500, and (for cardholders only) $1,000. You'll pay a service charge ranging from 1% to 4%. By phone, you can buy traveler's checks by calling © **800/807-6233**.

American Express card holders should dial © **800/221-7282**; this number accepts collect calls, offers service in several foreign languages, and exempts Amex gold and platinum cardholders from the 1% fee.

Visa offers traveler's checks at Citibank locations nationwide, as well as at several other banks. The service charge ranges between 1.5% and 2%; checks come in denominations of $20, $50, $100, $500, and $1,000. Call © **800/732-1322** for information. AAA members can obtain Visa checks a $9.95 fee (for checks up to $1,500) at most AAA offices or by calling © **866/339-3378**. **MasterCard** also offers traveler's checks. Call © **800/223-9920** for a location near you.

CREDIT CARDS

Credit cards are another safe way to carry money. They also provide a convenient record of all your expenses, and they generally offer relatively good exchange rates. You can also withdraw cash advances from your credit cards at banks or ATMs, provided you know your PIN. If you don't know yours, call the number on the back of your credit card and ask the bank to send it to you. It usually takes 5 to 7 business days, though some banks will provide the number over the phone if you tell them your mother's maiden name or some other personal information. Keep in mind that many banks now assess a 1% to 3% "transaction fee" on *all* charges you incur abroad (whether you're using the local currency or U.S. dollars). But credit cards still may be the smart way to go when you factor in things like exorbitant ATM fees and the higher exchange rates and service fees you'll pay with traveler's checks.

4 When to Go

Summer is the peak season in Oregon, and during these months, hotel and car reservations are almost essential; the rest of the year, they're highly recommended, but not imperative. If you visit in one of the rainier months between October and May, hotel rates are lower. It will also be easier to get reservations, especially on the coast. However, you will have to bring good rain gear. Whenever you go, keep in mind that you usually get better rates by reserving at least 1 or 2 weeks in advance, whether you're booking a plane, hotel, or rental car. Summer holiday weekends are the hardest times of year to get room reservations, especially on the coast. Book months in advance for Memorial Day, Fourth of July, and Labor Day.

Though Oregon is famous for its gray skies and mild temperatures, the state is actually characterized by a diversity of climates almost unequaled in the United States. For the most part, moist winds off the Pacific Ocean keep temperatures west of the Cascade Range mild year-round. Summers in the Willamette Valley and southern Oregon can see temperatures over 100°F (38°C), but on the coast you're likely to need a sweater or light jacket at night, even in August. The Oregon rains that are so legendary fall primarily as a light, but almost constant, drizzle between October and early July. Sure, there are windows of sunshine during this period, but they usually last no more than a week or so. There are also, unfortunately, occasional wet summers, so be prepared for wet weather whenever you visit. Winters usually include one or two blasts of Arctic air, usually right around Christmas or New Year's, that bring snow and freezing weather to the Portland area. Expect snow in the Cascades any time during the winter, and even some Coast Range passes can get icy.

If you visit the coast, expect grayer, wetter weather than in the Portland area. It can be quite cool here in the summer and is often foggy or rainy throughout the year. In fact, when the Willamette Valley is at its hottest, in July and August, you can be sure that the coast will be fogged in. The best month for the coast is usually September, with good weather often holding on into October.

In the Cascades and eastern Oregon's Blue and Wallowa mountains, snowfall is heavy in the winter and skiing is a popular sport. Summer doesn't come until late in the year here, with snow lingering into July at higher elevations (for instance, the Timberline Lodge area at Mount Hood and the Eagle Cap Wilderness in the Wallowas). At such elevations, late July and on through August are the best times to see the wildflowers in alpine meadows.

The region east of the Cascades is characterized by lack of rain and temperature extremes. This high desert area can be very cold in the winter, and at higher elevations it receives considerable amounts of snow. In summer, the weather can be blazingly hot at lower elevations, though nights are often cool enough to require a sweater or light jacket.

If you're planning to go wine touring, avoid January and February, when most wineries are closed. Also keep in mind that many wineries are open daily during the summer months, but in spring and fall are open only on weekends.

Portland's Average Monthly Temperatures & Rainfall

	Jan	Feb	Mar	Apr	May	June	July	Aug	Sept	Oct	Nov	Dec
Temp. (°F)	40	43	46	50	57	63	68	67	63	54	46	41
Temp. (°C)	4	6	8	10	14	17	20	20	17	12	8	5
Days of Rain	18	16	17	14	12	10	4	5	8	13	18	19

OREGON CALENDAR OF EVENTS

February

The Portland International Film Festival, Portland. Although not one of the country's top film festivals, plenty of interesting foreign films and documentaries are shown. Screenings are held at various theaters around the city. ℗ 503/221-1156; www.nwfilm.org. Last 2 weeks of February.

Oregon Shakespeare Festival, Ashland. The repertory company features about a dozen plays—some by Shakespeare and others by classical and contemporary playwrights—in four theaters. ℗ 541/482-4331; www.osfashland.org. February through October.

Newport Seafood and Wine Festival, Newport. Taste local seafood dishes and wines while shopping for art. ℗ 800/262-7844 or 541/265-8801; www.newportchamber.org/swf. Last full weekend in February.

March

Oregon Dune Mushers' Mail Run, Florence. Think dogs pulling wheeled sleds over the sand of the Florence coastline. This endurance run commemorates routes used before roads were constructed. **www.oregondunemushers.com**. First weekend in March.

Tulip Festival, Woodburn. Bold swaths of color paint the landscape at the Wooden Shoe Bulb Company's annual celebration of tulips. ℗ 800/711-2006 or 503/634-2243; www.woodenshoe.com. Late March to late April.

April

Hood River Valley Blossom Festival, Hood River. Celebrates the blossoming of the orchards outside the town of Hood River. ℗ 800/366-3530 or 541/386-2000; www.hoodriver.org. Third weekend in April.

May

Mother's Day Rhododendron Show, Portland. At Crystal Springs Rhododendron Garden, blooming rhododendrons and azaleas transform the tranquil garden into a mass of blazing color. ℗ 503/771-8386. Mother's Day.

Memorial Day Wine Tastings, throughout the wine country surrounding Portland. This is one of two weekends celebrated by Willamette Valley wineries with special tastings and events. Many wineries not usually open to the public open on this weekend. ℗ 503/646-2985; www.willamettewines.com. Memorial Day weekend.

Boatnik, Grants Pass. Jet boats and hydroplanes race on the Rogue River. There's also a parade and carnival. ℗ 800/547-5927; www.boatnik.com. Memorial Day weekend.

June

Cannon Beach Sand Castle Festival, Cannon Beach. Artistic sand-sculpted creations are created along the beach. ℗ 503/436-2623; www.cannonbeach.org. Early June.

Sisters Rodeo and Parade, Sisters. A celebration of the West in this duded-up Western-theme town near Bend. ℗ 800/827-7522 or 541/549-0121; www.sistersrodeo.com. Second weekend of June.

Portland Rose Festival. From its beginnings back in 1888, the Rose Festival has blossomed into Portland's biggest celebration. The festivities now span nearly a month and include the nation's second-largest all-floral parade, rose queen contest, music festival, art festival, and dragon-boat races. Contact the Portland Rose Festival Association (© **503/227-2681;** www. rosefestival.org) for tickets and information. Most of the events (some of which are free) take place during the middle 2 weeks of June, and hotel rooms can be hard to come by, so plan ahead.

Britt Festivals, Jacksonville. Performing arts festival with world-class jazz, pop, classical, folk, and country music, plus dance and musical theater performances in a beautiful natural setting. © **800/882-7488** or 541/773-6077; www.brittfest.org. June through September.

Oregon Bach Festival, Eugene. One of the biggest Bach festivals in the country. Tickets go on sale in mid-March. © **800/457-1486** or 541/682-5000; www.bachfest.uoregon.edu. Late June to early July.

July

Fourth of July Fireworks, Vancouver, Washington. Vancouver, which is part of the Portland metropolitan area, hosts the biggest fireworks display west of the Mississippi. © **877/600-0800** or 360/750-1553. July 4.

Waterfront Blues Festival, Portland. This is Portland's biggest summer party and takes place in Tom McCall Waterfront Park. Expect lots of big names in blues. © **503/973-FEST;** www.waterfrontbluesfest.com. Fourth of July weekend.

Oregon Country Fair, Eugene. Counterculture craft fair and festival for Deadheads young and old. © **800/ 992-8499** or 541/343-4298; www. oregoncountryfair.org. Second weekend in July.

Sisters Outdoor Quilt Show, Sisters. During the largest outdoor quilt show in the country, the entire town gets decked out in colorful handmade quilts. © **541/549-6061;** www.stitch-inpost.com. Second Saturday of July.

Da Vinci Days, Corvallis. Three-day celebration of science and technology with performances, art, interactive exhibits, children's activities, food, and wine. © **541/757-6363;** www.davinci-days.org. Mid-July.

Salem Arts Festival, Salem. The largest juried art fair in Oregon, under the trees in Bush Park, with musical entertainment and food booths. © **503/581-2228;** www.salemart.org. Third weekend in July.

Oregon Brewers Festival, Tom McCall Waterfront Park. One of the country's largest festivals of independent craft brewers features lots of local and international microbrews and music. © **503/778-5917;** www.oregon brewfest.com. Last weekend in July.

August

Mount Hood Jazz Festival, Gresham (less than 30 min. from Portland). For the jazz fan, this is the most important festival of the summer. © **503/ 491-5950;** www.mthoodjazz.com. Early August.

Oregon State Fair, Salem. A typical agricultural state fair. © **503/947-3247;** www.oregonstatefair.org. The 12 days before and including Labor Day.

Cascade Festival of Music, Bend. Classical and world music in a park setting. © **541/382-8381;** www.cascade music.org. Last week in August.

September

Mt. Angel Oktoberfest, Mount Angel. Biergarten, Bavarian-style oompah bands, food booths. ℰ **503/845-9440**; www.oktoberfest.org. Second weekend after Labor Day.

Shrewsbury Renaissance Faire, Kings Valley (near Corvallis). Go back 500 years to celebrate the age of Elizabeth I and Shakespeare with jousting and period costumes in an Elizabethan village. ℰ **541/929-4897**; www.shrewfaire.com. Second weekend of September.

Pendleton Round-Up and Happy Canyon Pageant, Pendleton. Rodeo, Native American pageant, country-music concert. ℰ **800/457-6336** or 541/276-2553; www.pendletonroundup.com. Mid-September.

Bandon Cranberry Festival, Bandon. Cranberry bog tours, arts and crafts. ℰ **541/347-9616.** Mid-September.

Eugene Celebration, Eugene. Street party celebrating the diversity of the community. Festivities include the crowning of the Slug Queen. ℰ **541/681-4108**; www.eugenecelebration.com. Late September to early October.

October

Hood River Valley Harvest Fest, Hood River. At the Hood River Expo Center, enjoy fruit products of the region, crafts, and entertainment; drive the Fruit Loop to visit farm stands and wineries. ℰ **800/366-3530** or 541/386-2000; www.hoodriver.org. Third weekend in October.

Fall Kite Festival, Lincoln City. Kite carnival including a wide and wild variety of kites, from indoor kites to giant kites. ℰ **800/452-2151**; www.oregoncoast.org. Early October.

November

Stormy Weather Arts Festival, Cannon Beach. Celebration of the rainy season features lots of live music, a gallery walk, and a quick-draw art event in which artists have 1 hour to paint a picture. ℰ **503/436-2623.** www.cannonbeach.org. First weekend in November.

Wine Country Thanksgiving, Willamette Valley. About 30 miles outside of Portland, more than two dozen wineries open their doors for tastings of new releases, usually with food and live music. ℰ **503/646-2985**; www.willamettewines.com. Thanksgiving weekend.

Holiday Lights and Open House at Shore Acres State Park, Charleston. Extravagantly decorated gardens near dramatic cliffs at the Oregon coast. ℰ **541/888-4902.** Thanksgiving to early January.

December

Holiday Festival of Lights, Ashland. Thousands of lights decorate the town. ℰ **541/482-3486**; www.ashlandchamber.com. Month of December.

Holiday Parade of Ships, Willamette and Columbia rivers. Boats decked out in fanciful holiday lights parade and circle on the rivers after nightfall. www.christmasships.org. Mid-December.

5 Travel Insurance, Health & Safety

Check your existing insurance policies and credit card coverage before you buy travel insurance. You may already be covered for lost luggage, canceled tickets, or medical expenses.

The cost of travel insurance varies widely, depending on the cost and length of your trip, your age and health, and the type of trip you're taking, but expect to pay between 5% and 8% of the vacation itself. You can get estimates from various providers through **InsureMyTrip.com**.

TRIP-CANCELLATION INSURANCE Trip-cancellation insurance will help retrieve your money if you have to back out of a trip or depart early, or if your travel supplier goes bankrupt. Permissible reasons for trip cancellation can range from sickness to natural disasters to the State Department declaring a destination unsafe for travel. In this unstable world, trip-cancellation insurance is a good buy if you're purchasing tickets well in advance—who knows what the state of the world, or of your airline, will be in 9 months? Insurance policy details vary, so read the fine print—and make sure that your airline or cruise line is on the list of carriers covered in case of bankruptcy. A good resource is **"Travel Guard Alerts,"** a list of companies considered high-risk by Travel Guard International (see website below). Protect yourself further by paying for the insurance with a credit card—by law, consumers can get their money back on goods and services not received if they report the loss within 60 days after the charge is listed on their credit card statement.

For more information, contact one of the following recommended insurers: **Access America** (✆ 866/807-3982; www.accessamerica.com), **Travel Guard International** (✆ 800/826-4919; www. travelguard.com), **Travel Insured International** (✆ 800/243-3174; www. travelinsured.com), and **Travelex Insurance Services** (✆ 888/457-4602; www.travelex-insurance.com).

MEDICAL INSURANCE   Most health insurance policies cover you if you get sick away from home—but verify that you're covered before you depart, particularly if you're insured by an HMO. If you require additional medical insurance, try **MEDEX Assistance** (✆ 410/453-6300; www.medexassist.com) or **Travel Assistance International** (✆ **800/821-2828;** www.travelassistance.com; for general information on services, call the company's **Worldwide Assistance Services, Inc.,** at ✆ **800/777-8710**).

LOST-LUGGAGE INSURANCE   On domestic flights, checked baggage is covered up to $2,500 per ticketed passenger. On international flights (including U.S. portions of international trips), baggage coverage is limited to approximately $9.07 per pound, up to approximately $635 per checked bag. If you plan to check items more valuable than what's covered by the standard liability, see if your homeowner's policy covers your valuables, get baggage insurance as part of your comprehensive travel-insurance package, or buy Travel Guard's "BagTrak" product. Be sure to take any valuables or irreplaceable items with you in your carry-on luggage, because many valuables aren't covered by airline policies.

If your luggage is lost, immediately file a lost-luggage claim at the airport, detailing the luggage contents. Most airlines require that you report delayed, damaged, or lost baggage within 4 hours of arrival. The airlines are required to deliver luggage, once found, directly to your house or destination free of charge.

STAYING HEALTHY

If you're worried about getting sick while away from home, consider purchasing **medical travel insurance** (see above) and remember to carry your ID card in your purse or wallet at all times. In most cases, your existing health plan will provide the coverage you need.

WHAT TO DO IF YOU GET SICK AWAY FROM HOME

If you get sick, consider asking your hotel concierge to recommend a local doctor—even his or her own. You can also try an urgent-care facility or a local hospital, many of which have walk-in clinics for emergency cases that are not life-threatening. You may not get immediate attention, but you won't pay the high price of an emergency-room visit. Alternatively, search out an urgent-care center. These small medical facilities have doctors on staff who primarily treat walk-in patients who have problems that are not life threatening.

If you suffer from a chronic illness, consult your doctor before your departure. For conditions like epilepsy, diabetes, or heart problems, wear a **MedicAlert identification tag** (✆ **888/633-4298;** www.medicalert.org), which will immediately alert doctors to your condition and give them access to your records through MedicAlert's 24-hour hotline.

Pack **prescription medications** in your carry-on luggage, and carry prescription medications in their original containers, with pharmacy labels—otherwise they won't make it through airport security. Also carry copies of your prescriptions in case you lose your pills or run out. Don't forget an extra pair of contact lenses or prescription glasses.

For domestic trips, most reliable health-care plans provide coverage if you get sick away from home. See "Medical Insurance," above.

6 Specialized Travel Resources

TRAVELERS WITH DISABILITIES

Always mention your disability when making airline reservations. Airline policies differ regarding wheelchairs and Seeing Eye dogs.

Most hotels now offer wheelchair-accessible accommodations, and some of the larger and more expensive properties also offer TDD telephones and other amenities for the hearing and sight impaired.

The public transit systems found in most Oregon cities either have regular vehicles that are accessible for riders with disabilities or offer special transportation services for people with disabilities.

For anyone who is hearing impaired, **Oregon State Parks** has a TT information line (✆ **800/858-9659**) that provides recreation and camping information.

If you plan to visit any of Crater Lake National Park or Lewis & Clark National and State Historical Parks, you can avail yourself of the **Golden Access Passport,** which gives visually impaired persons or those with permanent disabilities (regardless of age) free lifetime entrance to all properties administered by the National Park Service, the U.S. Fish and Wildlife Service, the U.S. Forest Service, the U.S. Army Corps of Engineers, the Bureau of Land Management, and the Tennessee Valley Authority. This may include national

parks, monuments, historic sites, recreation areas, and national wildlife refuges. For more information, go to www.nps.gov/fees_passes.htm or call ✆ **888/467-2757.**

Many travel agencies offer customized tours and itineraries for travelers with disabilities. **Flying Wheels Travel** (✆ **507/451-5005;** www.flyingwheelstravel.com) offers escorted tours and cruises that emphasize sports and private tours in minivans with lifts. **Access-Able Travel Source** (✆ **303/232-2979;** www.accessable.com) offers extensive access information and advice for traveling around the world with disabilities. **Accessible Journeys** (✆ **800/846-4537** or 610/521-0339; www.disabilitytravel.com) caters specifically to slow walkers and wheelchair travelers and their families and friends.

Avis Rent a Car has an "Avis Access" program that offers such services as a dedicated 24-hour toll-free number (✆ **888/879-4273**) for customers with special travel needs; special car features such as swivel seats, spinner knobs, and hand controls; and accessible bus service.

Organizations that offer assistance to travelers with disabilities include **Moss Rehab** (www.mossresourcenet.org), which provides a library of accessible-travel resources online; the **American Foundation for the Blind (AFB;** ✆ **800/232-5463;** www.afb.org), a referral resource for the blind or visually impaired that includes information on traveling with Seeing Eye dogs; and **SATH (Society for Accessible Travel & Hospitality;** ☎ **212/447-7284;** www.sath.org; annual membership fees: $45 adults, $30 seniors and students), which offers a wealth of travel resources for all types of disabilities and informed recommendations on destinations, access guides, travel agents, tour operators, vehicle rentals, and companion services.

For more information specifically targeted to travelers with disabilities, the community website **iCan** (www.ican online.net/channels/travel) has destination guides and several regular columns on accessible travel.

GAYS & LESBIANS

Gay and lesbian travelers visiting Portland should be sure to pick up a free copy of *Just Out* (☎ **503/236-1252;** www. justout.com), a bimonthly newspaper for the gay community. You can usually find copies at **Powell's Books,** 1005 W. Burnside St. Another publication to look for is *Portland's Gay & Lesbian Community Yellow Pages* (☎ **503/230-7701;** www. pdxgayyellowpages.com), which is also usually available at Powell's.

The International Gay and Lesbian Travel Association (IGLTA; ☎ **800/ 448-8550** or 954/776-2626; www.iglta. org) is the trade association for the gay and lesbian travel industry, and offers an online directory of gay- and lesbian-friendly travel businesses; go to their website and click on "Members."

SENIORS

Mention the fact that you're a senior citizen when you make your travel reservations. Although all the major U.S. airlines except America West have canceled their senior discount and coupon book programs, many hotels still offer lower rates for seniors. In most cities, people over the age of 60 qualify for reduced admission to theaters,

museums, and other attractions, and discounted fares on public transportation.

Members of **AARP** (formerly known as the American Association of Retired Persons), 601 E St. NW, Washington, DC 20049 (☎ **888/687-2277;** www.aarp.org), get discounts on hotels, airfares, and car rentals. AARP offers members a wide range of benefits, including *AARP: The Magazine* and a monthly newsletter. Anyone over 50 can join.

The U.S. National Park Service offers a **Golden Age Passport** that gives seniors 62 and older lifetime entrance to most national parks and monuments for a one-time processing fee of $10. It must be purchased in person at any NPS facility that charges an entrance fee. Besides free entry, a Golden Age Passport also offers a 50% discount on federal-use fees charged for such facilities as camping, swimming, parking, boat launching, and tours. For more information, go to www.nps.gov/ fees_passes.htm or call ☎ **888/467-2757.**

Many reliable agencies and organizations target the 50-plus market. **Elderhostel** (☎ **877/426-8056;** www.elder hostel.org) arranges study programs for those aged 55 and over (and a spouse or companion of any age). **ElderTreks** (☎ **800/741-7956;** www.eldertreks.com), restricted to travelers 50 and older, offers small-group tours to off-the-beaten-path or adventure-travel locations.

FAMILY TRAVEL

If you have enough trouble simply getting your kids out of the house in the morning, dragging them thousands of miles away may seem like an insurmountable challenge. But family travel can be immensely rewarding, giving you new ways of seeing the world through smaller pairs of eyes.

To locate those accommodations, restaurants, and attractions that are particularly kid-friendly, refer to the "Kids" icon throughout this guide.

Families traveling in Oregon should be sure to take note of family admission fees at many museums and other attractions. These admission prices are often less than what it would cost for individual tickets for the whole family. At hotels and motels, children usually stay free if they share their parents' room and no extra bed is required, and sometimes they also get to eat for free in the hotel dining room. Be sure to ask.

Recommended family-travel Internet sites include **Family Travel Forum** (www.familytravelforum.com), a comprehensive site that offers customized trip planning; and **Family Travel Network** (www.familytravelnetwork.com), an award-winning site that offers travel features, deals, and tips.

7 Planning Your Trip Online

SURFING FOR AIRFARES

The "big three" online travel agencies, **Expedia.com, Travelocity,** and **Orbitz,** sell most of the air tickets bought on the Internet. (Canadian travelers should try expedia.ca and Travelocity.ca; U.K. residents can go for expedia.co.uk and opodo.co.uk.) **Kayak.com** is also gaining popularity and uses a sophisticated search engine (developed at MIT). Each has different business deals with the airlines and may offer different fares on the same flights, so it's wise to shop around.

Also remember to check **airline websites,** especially those for low-fare carriers such as Southwest and JetBlue, whose fares are often misreported or simply missing from travel-agency websites. Even with major airlines, you can often shave a few bucks from a fare by booking directly through the airline. But you'll get these discounts only by **booking online:** Most airlines now offer online-only fares that even their phone agents know nothing about. For the websites of airlines that fly to and from Washington state, go to "Getting There," p. 29.

Great **last-minute deals** are available through free weekly e-mail services provided directly by the airlines. Most of these are announced on Tuesday or Wednesday and must be purchased online. Most are only valid for travel that weekend, but some (such as Southwest's) can be booked weeks or months in advance. Sign up for weekly e-mail alerts at airline websites or check megasites that compile comprehensive lists of last-minute specials, such as

Smarter Travel (www.smartertravel.com). For last-minute trips, **site59.com** and **lastminutetravel.com** in the U.S. and **lastminute.com** in Europe often have better air-and-hotel package deals than the major-label sites.

If you're willing to give up some control over your flight details, use what is called an **"opaque" fare service** like **Priceline** (www.priceline.com; www.priceline.co.uk for Europeans) or its smaller competitor **Hotwire** (www.hotwire.com). Both offer rock-bottom prices in exchange for travel on a "mystery airline" at a mysterious time of day, often with a mysterious change of planes en route. The mystery airlines are all major, well-known carriers. Your chances of getting a 6am or 11pm flight, however, are still pretty high. Hotwire tells you flight prices before you buy; Priceline usually has better deals than Hotwire, but you have to play their "name our price" game or pick exact flights, times, and airlines from a list of offers. If you're new at this, **BiddingForTravel** (www.biddingfortravel.com) does a good job of demystifying Priceline's prices and strategies.

SURFING FOR HOTELS

Shopping online for hotels is generally done one of two ways: by booking through the hotel's own website or through an independent booking agency (or a fare-service agency like Priceline; see below). Of the "big three" sites, **Expedia.com** offers a long list of special deals and "virtual tours" or photos of available rooms

Frommers.com: The Complete Travel Resource

For an excellent travel-planning resource, we highly recommend **Frommers.com** (www.frommers.com), voted Best Travel Site by *PC Magazine*. We're a little biased, of course, but we guarantee that you'll find the travel tips, reviews, monthly vacation giveaways, bookstore, and online-booking capabilities thoroughly indispensable. Among the special features are our popular **Destinations** section, where you'll get expert travel tips, hotel and dining recommendations, and advice on the sights to see for more than 3,500 destinations around the globe; the **Frommers.com Newsletter,** with the latest deals, travel trends, and money-saving secrets; our **Community** area featuring **Message Boards,** where Frommer's readers post queries and share advice (sometimes even our authors show up to answer questions); and our **Photo Center,** where you can post and share vacation tips. When your research is finished, the **Online Reservations System** (www.frommers.com/book_a_trip) takes you to Frommer's preferred online partners for booking your vacation at affordable prices.

so you can see what you're paying for. **Travelocity** posts unvarnished customer reviews and ranks its properties according to the AAA rating system. **Trip Advisor** (www.tripadvisor.com) is another excellent source of unbiased user reviews of hotels. While even the finest hotels can inspire a misleadingly poor review from a picky or crabby travelers, the body of user opinions is usually a reliable indicator.

Other reliable online booking agencies include **Hotels.com** and **Quikbook.com.** An excellent free program, **TravelAxe** (www.travelaxe.net), can help you search multiple hotel sites at once, even ones you may never have heard of—and conveniently lists the total price of the room, including the taxes and service charges. Another booking site, **Travelweb** (www.travelweb.com), is partly owned by the hotels it represents (including the Hilton, Hyatt, and Starwood chains) and is therefore plugged directly into the hotels' reservations systems. Be sure to **get a confirmation number** and **make a printout** of any online booking transaction.

In the opaque website category, **Priceline** and **Hotwire** are even better for hotels than for airfares; through both, you're allowed to pick the neighborhood and quality level of your hotel before paying. Priceline's hotel product is much better at getting five-star lodging for three-star prices than at finding anything at the bottom of the scale. On the down side, many hotels stick Priceline guests in their least desirable rooms. Be sure to go to the BiddingForTravel website (see above) before bidding on a hotel room on Priceline; it features a fairly up-to-date list of hotels that Priceline uses in major cities.

SURFING FOR RENTAL CARS

For booking rental cars online, the best deals are usually found at rental-car company websites, although all the major online travel agencies also offer rental-car reservations services. Priceline and Hotwire work well for rental cars, too; the only "mystery" is which major rental company you get, and for most travelers the difference between Hertz, Avis, and Budget is negligible.

8 The 21st-Century Traveler

INTERNET ACCESS AWAY FROM HOME

Travelers have any number of ways to check their e-mail and access the Internet on the road. Of course, using your own laptop—or even a PDA (personal digital assistant) or electronic organizer with a modem—gives you the most flexibility. But even if you don't have a computer, you can still access your e-mail and even your office computer from cybercafes.

WITHOUT YOUR OWN COMPUTER

It's hard nowadays to find a city that *doesn't* have a few cybercafes. Although there's no definitive directory for cybercafes—these are independent businesses, after all—two places to start looking are at **www.cybercaptive.com** and **www. cybercafe.com**.

Aside from formal cybercafes, most **public libraries** offer access free or for a small charge.

To retrieve your e-mail, ask your **Internet Service Provider (ISP)** if it has a Web-based interface tied to your existing e-mail account. If your ISP doesn't have such an interface, you can use the free **mail2web** service (www.mail2web.com) to view and reply to your home e-mail. For more flexibility, you may want to open a free, Web-based e-mail account with **Yahoo! Mail** (http://mail.yahoo.com). (Microsoft's Hotmail is another popular option, but Hotmail has severe spam problems.) Your home ISP may be able to forward your e-mail to the Web-based account automatically.

WITH YOUR OWN COMPUTER

More and more hotels, cafes, and retailers are signing on as Wi-Fi (wireless fidelity) "hotspots," from where you can get high-speed connection without cable wires, networking hardware, or a phone line (see below). You can get Wi-Fi connection one of several ways. Many laptops sold in the last year have built-in Wi-Fi capability (an 802.11b wireless Ethernet connection). Mac owners have their own networking technology, Apple AirPort. For those with older computers, you can plug in an 802.11b/**Wi-Fi card** (around $50). You sign up for wireless access service much as you do for cellphone service, through a plan offered by one of several commercial companies that have made wireless service available in airports, hotel lobbies, and coffee shops, primarily in the U.S. (followed by the U.K. and Japan). **T-Mobile Hotspot** (www.t-mobile.com/hotspot) serves up wireless connections at more than 1,000 Starbucks coffee shops nationwide. **Boingo** (www.boingo.com) and **Wayport** (www.wayport.com) have set up networks in airports and high-class hotel lobbies. To locate other hotspots that provide **free wireless networks** go to **www.personaltelco.net/index.cgi/ WirelessCommunities**.

For dial-up access, most business-class hotels offer dataports for laptop modems, and many hotels offer free high-speed Internet access using an Ethernet network cable. **Call your hotel in advance** to see what your options are.

In addition, major Internet Service Providers (ISPs) have **local access numbers,** allowing you to go online by placing a local call. Check your ISP's website for information.

Wherever you go, bring a **connection kit** of the right power and phone adapters, a spare phone cord, and a spare Ethernet network cable—or find out whether your hotel supplies them to guests.

USING A CELLPHONE ACROSS THE U.S.

Just because your cellphone works at home doesn't mean it'll work elsewhere in the country (thanks to our nation's fragmented cellphone system). It's a good bet that your phone will work in major

Online Traveler's Toolbox

Veteran travelers usually carry some essential items to make their trips easier. Following is a selection of handy online tools to bookmark and use:

- **Mapquest** (www.mapquest.com). This best of the mapping sites lets you choose a specific address or destination and, in seconds, returns a map and detailed directions.
- **Visa ATM Locator** (www.visa.com), for locations of PLUS ATMs worldwide, or **MasterCard ATM Locator** (www.mastercard.com), for locations of Cirrus ATMs worldwide.
- **Intellicast** (www.intellicast.com) and **Weather.com** (www.weather.com). Gives weather forecasts for all 50 states and for cities around the world.

cities. But take a look at your wireless company's coverage map on its website before heading out—T-Mobile, Sprint, and Nextel are particularly weak in rural areas. If you need to stay in touch at a destination where you know your phone won't work, **rent** a phone that does from **InTouch USA** (© **800/872-7626;** www.intouchglobal.com) or a rental car location, but beware that you'll pay $1 a minute or more for airtime.

9 Getting There

Portland is the gateway to Oregon. In addition, driving directions throughout this book often use Portland as a reference point, assuming that the traveler will be flying into Portland and then driving to the destination.

BY PLANE

The major carriers to **Portland Airport** (www.flypdx.com) include **Air Canada Jazz** (© 888/247-2262; www.flyjazz.ca), **Alaska Airlines** (© 800/252-7522; www.alaskaair.com), **America West** (© 800/235-9292; www.americawest.com), **American** (© 800/433-7300; www.aa.com), **Continental** (© 800/523-3273; www.continental.com), **Delta** (© 800/221-1212; www.delta.com), **Frontier** (© 800/432-1359; www.frontierairlines.com), **Horizon Air** (© 800/547-9308; www.horizonair.com), **JetBlue Airways** (© 800/JET-BLUE; www.jetblue.com), **Lufthansa** (© 800/645-3880; www.lufthansa.com),

Northwest/KLM (© 800/225-2525; www.nwa.com), **Southwest** (© 800/435-9792; www.southwest.com), and **United** (© 800/864-8331; www.united.com).

For information on flights to the U.S. from other countries, see chapter 3.

GETTING THROUGH THE AIRPORT

With the federalization of airport security, screening procedures at U.S. airports are more stable and consistent than ever. Generally, you'll be fine if you arrive at the airport **1 hour** before a domestic flight and **2 hours** before an international flight.

Bring a **current, government-issued photo ID** such as a driver's license or passport. Keep your ID at the ready to present at check-in, the security checkpoint, and sometimes even the gate. (Children under 18 do not need government-issued photo IDs for domestic flights, but they do for international flights to most countries.)

Passengers with e-tickets, which have made paper tickets nearly obsolete, can beat the ticket-counter lines by using airport **electronic kiosks** or even **online check-in** from their home computers. Online check-in involves logging on to your airlines' website, accessing your reservation, and printing out your boarding pass.

If you have trouble standing for long periods of time, tell an airline employee; the airline will provide a wheelchair. Speed up security by **not wearing metal objects** such as big belt buckles. If you've got metallic body parts, a note from your doctor can prevent a long chat with the security screeners.

Federalization has stabilized **what you can carry on** and **what you can't.** The general rule is that sharp things are out. Bring food in your carry-on rather than checking it, as explosive-detection machines used on checked luggage have been known to mistake food (especially chocolate, for some reason) for bombs. Travelers in the U.S. are allowed one carry-on bag, plus a "personal item" such as a purse, briefcase, or laptop bag. The Transportation Security Administration (TSA) has issued a list of restricted items; check its website (www.tsa.gov/public/index.jsp) for details.

Airport screeners may decide that your checked luggage warrants a hand search. You can now purchase luggage locks that allow screeners to open and relock a checked bag if hand searching is necessary. Look for Travel Sentry–certified locks at luggage or travel shops and Brookstone stores (you can buy them online at www.brookstone.com). Luggage inspectors can open these TSA-approved locks with a special code or key—rather than having to cut them off the suitcase, as they normally do to conduct a hand search. For more information on the locks, visit www.travelsentry.org.

FLY FOR LESS: TIPS FOR GETTING THE BEST AIRFARES

Passengers sharing the same airplane cabin rarely pay the same fare. Travelers who need to purchase tickets at the last minute, change their itinerary at a moment's notice, or fly one-way often get stuck paying the premium rate. Here are some ways to keep your airfare costs down.

If you're flying to Portland from another city in the Western U.S., check with Frontier Airlines, Alaska Airlines, Horizon Airlines, or Southwest. These airlines often have the best fares between western cities.

- Passengers who can book their ticket either **long in advance or at the last minute,** or who **fly midweek** or **at less-trafficked hours** may pay a fraction of the full fare. If your schedule is flexible, say so, and ask if you can secure a cheaper fare by changing your flight plans.

- Keep an eye on local newspapers for **promotional specials** or **fare wars,** when airlines lower prices on their most popular routes. You rarely see fare wars offered for peak travel times, but if you can travel in the off months, you may snag a bargain.

- **Consolidators,** also known as bucket shops, are great sources for international tickets, although they usually can't beat Internet fares within North America. Start by looking in Sunday newspaper travel sections; U.S. travelers should focus on the *New York Times, Los Angeles Times,* and *Miami Herald.* For less-developed destinations, small travel agents who cater to immigrant communities in large cities often have the best deals. Several reliable consolidators are worldwide and available online. **STA Travel** has been the world's lead consolidator for students since purchasing Council

Travel, but their fares are competitive for travelers of all ages. **Air Tickets Direct** (ℂ 800/778-3447; www.airticketsdirect.com) is based in Montreal and leverages the currently weak Canadian dollar for low fares.

• Join **frequent-flier clubs.** Frequent-flier membership doesn't cost a cent, but it does entitle you to better seats, faster response to phone inquiries, and prompter service if your luggage is stolen or your flight is canceled or delayed, or if you want to change your seat.

BY CAR

The distance to Portland from Seattle is 175 miles; from Spokane, 350 miles; from Vancouver, British Columbia, 285 miles; from San Francisco, 640 miles; and from Los Angeles, 1,015 miles.

If you're driving from California, I-5 runs up through the length of the state and continues north toward the Canadian border; it will take you through both Portland and Seattle. If you're coming from the east, I-84 runs from Idaho and points east into Oregon, eventually ending in Portland.

One of the most important benefits of belonging to the **American Automobile Association** (ℂ 800/222-4357; www.aaa.com) is that they supply members with emergency road service. In Portland, AAA is located at 600 SW Market St. (ℂ **503/222-6734;** www.aaaorid.com).

BY TRAIN

Amtrak's (ℂ 800/872-7245; www.amtrak.com) *Coast Starlight* train connects Portland with Seattle, San Francisco, Los Angeles, and San Diego, and stops at historic **Union Station,** 800 NW Sixth Ave. (ℂ **503/273-4860**), about 10 blocks from the heart of downtown Portland. Between Portland and Seattle there are both regular trains and modern European-style Talgo trains, which make the trip in 3½ to 4 hours versus 4½ hours for the regular train. One-way fares on either type of train run $25 to $30. The Talgo train, called *Cascades,* runs between Eugene, Oregon, and Vancouver, British Columbia.

10 The Active Vacation Planner

The abundance of outdoor recreational activities is one of the main reasons people choose to live in and visit Oregon. With both mountains and beaches within an hour's drive of the major metropolitan areas, there are numerous choices for the active vacationer.

OUTDOOR CLASSES & ORGANIZED TRIPS

ACTIVITIES A TO Z

BIKING/MOUNTAIN BIKING The Oregon coast is one of the most popular bicycling destinations in the nation, and each summer attracts thousands of dedicated pedalers. Expect to spend about a week to pedal the entire coast if you're in good shape and are traveling at a leisurely pace. During the summer months, it's best to travel from north to south along the coast because of the prevailing winds. Also keep in mind that many state parks have designated hiker/biker campsites. You can get a free Oregon coast bicycle map, as well as other bicycle maps for the state of Oregon, by calling the Oregon Department of Transportation's **Oregon Bicycle Map Hot Line** (ℂ 503/986-3556).

Other regions growing in popularity with cyclists include the wine country of Yamhill County and other parts of the Willamette Valley. Portland, Salem, Corvallis, Eugene, Cottage Grove, and Central Point all have easy bicycle trails that either are in parks or connect parks. In addition, the region's national forests provide miles of logging roads and single-track trails for mountain biking. Among

Tips Serious Reservations

The days of spontaneous summer weekends are a thing of the past in Oregon. If you want to be assured of getting a room or a campsite at some of the busier destinations, you'll need to make your reservations months in advance, especially if you're going on a weekend.

To be sure that you get the state-park campsite, yurt (circular domed tents with electricity, plywood floors, and beds), cabin, teepee, houseboat, or covered wagon you want, you'll need to make your reservations as much as 9 months in advance (that's the earliest you can reserve) through **ReserveAmerica** (© 800/452-5687; www.reserveamerica.com).

While National Forest Service campgrounds are generally less developed and less in demand than state park campgrounds, many do stay full throughout the summer months, especially those at the beach. For reservations at forest-service campgrounds, call the **National Recreation Reservation Service** (© 877/444-6777 or 518/885-3639; www.reserveusa.com). These sites can be reserved up to 8 months in advance.

The same sort of advance planning also applies to such accommodations as Crater Lake Lodge (Crater Lake National Park does not, however, accept camping reservations), Timberline Lodge, and just about any lodging on the coast on a summer weekend. Making rooms even more difficult to come by are the many festivals scheduled around the state throughout the summer months. Be sure to check whether your schedule might coincide with some popular event.

the most popular mountain-biking areas are the east side of Mount Hood, the Oakridge area southeast of Eugene, the Ashland area, and the Bend and Sisters areas of central Oregon.

If you're interested in a guided bike tour in the state, try **Bicycle Adventures,** P.O. Box 11219, Olympia, WA 98508 (© **800/443-6060** or 360/786-0989; www.bicycleadventures.com). Tour prices range from $1,284 to $2,250 per person including room and meals.

BIRD-WATCHING Oregon offers many excellent bird-watching spots. Malheur National Wildlife Refuge, in central Oregon, is the state's premier bird-watching area and attracts more than 300 bird species yearly. Nearby Summer Lake also offers good bird-watching, with migratory waterfowl and shorebirds most prevalent. There's also good bird-watching on Sauvie Island, outside Portland, where waterfowl, sandhill cranes, and eagles can be seen, and along the coast, where you can see tufted puffins, pigeon guillemots, and perhaps even a marbled murrelet. The Klamath Lakes region of south-central Oregon is well known for its large population of bald eagles, which are best seen in the winter months.

Throughout the year, the National Audubon Society sponsors expeditions and field seminars. For more information, contact the **Audubon Society of Portland** (© 503/292-6855; www.audubon portland.org). For the Rare Bird Report hot line, call © 503/292-0661.

CAMPING Public and private campgrounds abound across Oregon; those along the coast are among the most popular. Campgrounds on lakes also stay busy. During the summer, campground reservations are almost a necessity at most state parks, especially those along the coast. For information on making campsite reservations, see the "Serious Reservations" box, above.

Various state parks also offer a variety of camping alternatives. Tops among these are yurts (circular domed tents with electricity, plywood floors, and beds), which make camping in the rain a bit easier. Yurts, which rent for $27 to $66 a night, can be found at 14 coastal parks, as well as at five inland state parks (Champoeg, Valley of the Rogue, Tumalo, LaPine, and Wallowa Lake).

Log cabins are available at a dozen state parks. Nightly rates range from $20 to $80. A couple of state parks have covered wagons for rent, and others have teepees ($27–$29 per night). On central Oregon's Lake Billy Chinook at The Cove Palisades State Park, you can even rent a houseboat for $995 to $6,995 per week. Contact Cove Palisades Marina (© **541/546-3521;** www.covepalisadesmarina.com).

FISHING   The fish of Oregon enjoy near-legendary status, and although there may be few streams in the region of national importance among anglers, there are still plenty of great rivers. Salmon of half a dozen species, steelhead, sturgeon, wild cutthroat, and rainbow trout are all available, as are mackinaw trout and bass. Offshore fishing for salmon, tuna, and bottom fish is also popular.

The most important thing to know about fishing in Oregon is that the rules are complicated and always in flux. It is essential you know all the regulations for the body of water you are fishing in. To find out what the current regulations are, you'll need to pick up a copy of *Oregon Sport Fishing Regulations.* This publication is free and is available at sporting goods stores and bait-and-tackle shops. Alternatively, order copies by contacting

the **Oregon Department of Fish and Wildlife,** 3406 Cherry Ave. NE, Salem, OR 97303 (© **800/720-ODFW** or 503/947-6000; www.dfw.state.or.us).

GOLF   Oregon has hundreds of private and public golf courses, including numerous resort courses, most of which are in the Portland and Bend-Redmond areas. There are also quite a few excellent courses along the coast. However, the courses at the Bandon Dunes Golf Resort, on the central Oregon coast, are the state's most celebrated fairways.

HIKING & BACKPACKING   Oregon is a hiker's paradise. The state has thousands of miles of hiking trails, including the Pacific Crest Trail, which runs along the spine of the Cascades from the Columbia River to the California line (and onward all the way to both Canada and Mexico). The state's hiking trails are concentrated primarily in national forests, especially in wilderness areas, in the Cascade Range. Along the length of the Pacific Crest Trail are such scenic hiking areas as the Mount Hood Wilderness, the Mount Jefferson Wilderness, the Three Sisters Wilderness, the Diamond Peak Wilderness, the Mount Thielsen Wilderness, and the Sky Lakes Wilderness. Many state parks also have extensive hiking-trail systems.

The Oregon Coast Trail is a designated route that runs the length of the Oregon coast. In most places it travels along the beach, but in other places it climbs up and over capes and headlands through dense forests and windswept meadows. The longest stretches of the trail are along the southern coast in Samuel H. Boardman State Park. There's also a long beach stretch in the Oregon Dunes National Recreation Area.

Other coastal parks with popular hiking trails include Saddle Mountain State Park, Ecola State Park, Oswald West State Park, and Cape Lookout State Park. Silver Falls State Park, east of Salem, is another of my favorite hiking spots. The many trails of the Columbia Gorge National Scenic Area are also well trodden, with Eagle Creek Trail being a longtime favorite. The trails leading out from Timberline Lodge on Mount Hood lead through forests and meadows at the tree line and, unfortunately, can be very crowded on summer weekends. For a quick hiking fix, Portlanders often head for the city's Forest Park.

If you'd like to do your hiking with a guide, contact Joe Whittington at **Oregon Peak Adventures,** P.O. Box 25576, Portland, OR 97298 (② **877/965-5100** or 503/297-5100; www.oregonpeakadventures.com). Whittington leads hikes in the Columbia Gorge, on the Oregon coast, and on Mount St. Helens and Mount Adams. Prices start at around $35 per person for a half-day hike.

KAYAKING & CANOEING While Puget Sound, up in Washington, is the sea kayaking capital of the Northwest, Oregonians have also taken to this sport. However, sea kayaks in Oregon very rarely make it to the sea, where waters are usually far too rough for kayaks. But there are numerous protected bays along the Oregon coast that are popular paddling spots. Also, the Lewis & Clark National Wildlife Refuge on the Columbia River not far from Astoria offers miles of quiet waterways to explore.

White-water kayaking is popular on many of the rivers that flow down out of the Cascade Range in Oregon, including the Deschutes, the Clackamas, the Molalla, and the Sandy. Down in southern Oregon, the North Umpqua and the Rogue provide plenty of white-water action.

Sundance River Center (② **888/777-7557** or 541/479-8508; www.sundanceriver.com), which is located near Grants Pass, is one of the premier kayaking schools in the country. They offer a 9-day beginner's program ($1,950) that does a 4-day trip down the wild-and-scenic section of the Rogue River after several days of initial instruction.

Canoeing is popular on many of Oregon's lakes. Some of the best are Hosmer and Sparks lakes west of Bend, Clear Lake south of Santiam Pass, Waldo Lake near Willamette Pass southeast of Eugene, and Upper Klamath Lake (where there's a canoe trail).

MOUNTAINEERING Mount Hood and several other Cascades peaks offer challenging mountain climbing and rock climbing for both the novice and the expert. If you're interested in learning some mountain-climbing skills or want

---

(Tips) Travel Tip

Before heading out to a national forest anywhere in Oregon, be sure to get a Northwest Forest Pass. Most national-forest trailhead parking areas in the state now require such a permit, and though they can sometimes be purchased from machines at the most popular trailheads, it's better to have one before heading out. To find out if you need a pass for your particular destination, contact the **Nature of the Northwest Information Center,** 800 NE Oregon St., Room 177, Portland, OR 97232 (② **503/872-2750;** www.naturenw.org). Passes are available at national-forest ranger stations throughout the state and also at many outdoors supply stores, such as REI. Day passes cost $5 and annual passes are $30. In some cases such passes are required not just for trailheads but for other national forest recreational areas as well.

to hone your existing skills, contact **Timberline Mountain Guides,** P.O. Box 1167, Bend, OR 97709 (*©* **541/ 312-9242;** www.timberlinemtguides. com), a company that offers snow-, ice-, and rock-climbing courses. They also lead summit climbs on Mount Hood. A 2-day Mount Hood mountaineering course with summit climb costs $390.

ROCK CLIMBING   Smith Rock State Park, near Redmond in central Oregon, is a rock-climbing mecca of international renown, and many climbers claim that sport climbing got its American start here. Smith Rock abounds in climbing routes, some of which are among the toughest in the world. If you're a serious climber, pick up a copy of Alan Watts's *Climber's Guide to Smith Rock* (Chockstone Press, 1992), an exhaustive guide to the many climbing routes here. On the Web, check out **www.smithrock.com**.

SKIING   Because the winter weather in Oregon is so unpredictable, the state is not known as a ski destination. Most of the state's ski areas are relatively small and cater primarily to local skiers. Mount Bachelor, in central Oregon outside of Bend, is the one exception. Because of its high elevation and location on the drier east side of the Cascades, it gets a more reliable snowpack and isn't as susceptible to midwinter warming spells, which tend to bring rain to west-side ski slopes with irritating regularity.

Ski areas in Oregon include Mount Hood Meadows, Mount Hood Ski Bowl, Timberline Ski Area, Cooper Spur Ski Area, and Summit Ski Area, all of which are on Mount Hood outside Portland. Farther south, there are Hoodoo Ski Bowl (east of Salem), Willamette Pass (east of Eugene), and Mount Bachelor (outside Bend). In the eastern part of the state, Anthony Lakes and Spout Springs provide a bit of powder skiing. Down in the south, Ski Ashland is the only option.

Many downhill ski areas also offer groomed **cross-country ski trails.** Cross-country skiers will find an abundance of trails up and down the Cascades. Teacup Lake and Mount Hood Meadows, on Mount Hood, offer good groomed trails. Near Mount Bachelor, there are also plenty of groomed trails. Crater Lake is another popular spot for cross-country skiing. Backcountry skiing is also popular in the Wallowa Mountains in eastern Oregon.

WHALE-WATCHING   Gray whales, which can reach 45 feet in length and weigh up to 35 tons, migrate annually between Alaska and Baja California, and pass close by the Oregon coast between December and May. However, with more and more whales stopping to spend the summer off the Oregon coast, it is now possible to see them just about any month of the year.

Depoe Bay, north of Newport, is not only the smallest harbor in the world, but also a home port for several whale-watching boats that head out throughout the year to look for gray whales. It's also possible to whale watch from shore, with Cape Meares, Cape Lookout, Cape Kiwanda, Devil's Punchbowl, Cape Perpetua, Sea Lion Caves, Shore Acres State Park, Face Rock Wayside (in Bandon), Cape Blanco, Cape Sebastian, and Harris Beach State Park being some of the better places from which to watch.

WHITE-WATER RAFTING   Plenty of rain and snowmelt and lots of mountains combine to produce dozens of good white-water-rafting rivers in Oregon, depending on the time of year and water levels. Central Oregon's Deschutes River and southern Oregon's Rogue River are the two most popular rafting rivers. Other popular rafting rivers include the Clackamas outside Portland, the McKenzie outside Eugene, and the North Umpqua outside Roseburg. Out in the southeastern corner, the remote Owyhee River provides adventurers with still more white water. See the respective regional chapters for information on rafting companies operating on these rivers.

WINDSURFING & KITE BOARDING The Columbia River Gorge is one of the most renowned windsurfing and kite-boarding spots in the world. As the winds whip up the waves, skilled sailors rocket across the water and launch themselves skyward to perform aerial acrobatics. On calmer days and in spots where the wind isn't blowing so hard, there are also opportunities for novices to learn the basics. Summer is the best sailing season, and the town of Hood River is the center of the boarding scene, with plenty of windsurfing and kite-boarding schools and rental companies. The southern Oregon coast also has some popular spots, including Floras Lake just north of Port Orford and Meyers Creek in Pistol River State Park, south of Gold Beach.

11 Getting Around

BY CAR

A car is by far the best way to see Oregon. There just isn't any other way to get to the more remote natural spectacles or to fully appreciate such regions as the Oregon coast or eastern Oregon.

The major car-rental companies are all represented in Portland and have desks at Portland International Airport, which is the most convenient place to pick up a car. There are also many independent and smaller car-rental agencies listed in the Portland Yellow Pages. Currently, weekly rates for an economy car in July (high-season rates) are around $150 with no discounts. Expect lower rates in the rainy months.

At Portland International Airport on the ground floor of the airport parking deck, across the street from the baggage-claim area, you'll find the following companies: **Avis** (© 800/831-2847 or 503/249-4950; www.avis.com), **Budget** (© 800/527-0700 or 503/249-4556; www.budget.com), **Dollar** (© 800/800-3365 or 503/249-4793; www.dollar.com), **Enterprise** (© 800/261-7331 or 503/692-8400; www.enterprise.com); and **Hertz** (© 800/654-3131 or 503/249-8216; www.hertz.com). Outside the airport, but with desks adjacent to the other car-rental desks, are **Alamo** (© 800/327-9633 or 503/249-4901; www.goalamo.com), **National** (© 800/227-7368 or 503/249-4900; www.nationalcar.com), and **Thrifty** (© 800/847-4389 or 503/254-6563; www.thrifty.com).

For the best deal on a rental car, make your reservation at least a week in advance. It also pays to shop around and call the same companies a few times over the course of a couple of weeks. If you decide on the spur of the moment to rent a car, check to see whether any weekend or special rates are available. If you're a member of a frequent-flier program, be sure to mention it; you might get mileage

---

⟨Value⟩ Driving a Bargain in Oregon

If there's any way you can arrange to pick up your car somewhere other than the airport, you can save the 10% airport concession fee. If you can pick up your car in Beaverton or Hillsboro (western suburbs of Portland), you can also avoid the 12.5% Multnomah County tax that applies at the airport and at downtown Portland car-rental offices.

Finds Cruising the Columbia River

Paddle-wheel steamboats played a crucial role in the settling of Oregon, shuttling people and goods up and down the Columbia River before railroads came to the region. Today, the *Queen of the West* and the *Empress of the North,* two paddle-wheel cruise ships operated by the **American West Steamboat Company,** 2101 Fourth Ave., Suite 1150, Seattle, WA 98121 (© **800/434-1232;** www.columbiarivercruise.com), cruise the Columbia offering a luxury never before known in Columbia River paddle wheelers. Fares for the 7-night cruise range from $1,239 to $5,133 per person.

If you'd rather cruise aboard a smaller vessel, consider a trip with **Cruise West** (© **888/851-8133;** www.cruisewest.com), which offers an 8-day cruise from Portland on the Columbia and Snake rivers. Fares range from $1,799 to $5,149 per person. Similar trips, though with naturalists and historians on board, are offered by **Lindblad Expeditions** (© **800/397-3348** or 212/765-7740; www.expeditions.com), which charges $2,490 to $3,940.

---

credit for renting a car. Always ask about special promotions and try different combinations of where to pick up and drop off your car.

GASOLINE   Oregon is an anachronism when it comes to gas stations; there are no self-service gas stations in the state. So, when you pull into a gas station, just sit back and let the attendant fill your tank. Also, keep in mind that Oregon is a big state, so keep your gas tank as full as possible when traveling in the mountains or on the sparsely populated east side of the Cascades.

MAPS   Maps are available at most highway tourist information centers, at the tourist information offices listed earlier in this chapter and throughout this book, and at gas stations throughout the region. For a map of Oregon, contact the **Oregon Tourism Commission** (© **800/ 547-7842**). Members of AAA can get detailed road maps of Oregon by calling their local AAA office.

SPECIAL DRIVING RULES   You may turn right on a red light after a full stop, and if you are in the far-left lane of a one-way street, you may turn left into the adjacent left lane of a one-way street

at a red light after a full stop. Everyone in a moving vehicle is required to wear a seat belt.

BREAKDOWNS/ASSISTANCE   In the event of a breakdown, stay with your car, lift the hood, turn on your emergency flashers, and wait for a police patrol car. *Do not leave your vehicle.*

DRIVING TIMES   It takes about 1½ hours to drive from Portland to Canon Beach on the Oregon coast; from Portland to Mount Hood, about 1 hour; and from Portland to Bend, about 3 hours. Portland to Seattle is about a 3½-hour trip, depending on traffic conditions.

BY PLANE

Although there are airports with regular commercial service in Redmond, Eugene, and Medford, flying isn't usually a very appropriate way to get around Oregon. However, if you are heading to the central or southern Oregon coast, you might want to consider flying into either the Eugene or the Medford Airport. If you are headed to Bend or Sunriver, flying into Redmond might work for you. If you are headed to Ashland for some Shakespeare, you could consider the Medford airport.

BY RECREATIONAL VEHICLE (RV)

An economical way to tour Oregon is with a recreational vehicle. If you're considering renting an RV, look under "Recreational Vehicles—Rent and Lease" in the Yellow Pages of your local phone book. They can be rented for a weekend, a week, or longer. In Portland, you might try **Cruise America,** 8400 SE 82nd Ave. (© **800/671-8042** or 503/777-9833; www.cruiseamerica.com). If you're going to be traveling in the peak season of summer, it's important to make reservations for your RV at least 2 months ahead of time. The rest of the year, a couple of weeks' lead time is usually sufficient.

12 Tips on Accommodations

It's always a good idea to make hotel reservations as soon as you know your trip dates. Reservations usually require a deposit of one night's payment. Portland and the Oregon coast are particularly busy during summer months, and hotels book up in advance—especially on holiday and festival weekends. If you do not have reservations, it is best to look for a room in the midafternoon because hotels may be filled by evening. Major downtown hotels, which cater primarily to business travelers, commonly offer weekend discounts of as much as 50% to entice vacationers to fill up the empty rooms. However, resorts and hotels near tourist attractions tend to have higher rates on weekends.

For information on B&Bs in Oregon, contact the **Oregon Bed and Breakfast Guild,** P.O. Box 3187, Ashland, OR 97520 (© **800/944-6196;** www.obbg.org).

TIPS FOR SAVING ON YOUR HOTEL ROOM

The **rack rate** is the maximum rate that a hotel charges for a room. It's the rate you'd get if you walked in off the street and asked for a room for the night. Hardly anybody pays these prices, however, and there are many ways around them.

- **Don't be afraid to bargain.** Most rack rates include commissions of 10% to 25% for travel agents, which some hotels may be willing to reduce if you make your own reservations and haggle a bit. Always ask whether a room less expensive than the first one quoted is available, or whether any special rates apply to you. You may qualify for corporate, student, military, senior, or other discounts. Be sure to mention membership in AAA, AARP, frequent-flier programs, or trade unions, which may entitle you to special deals as well. Find out the hotel policy on children—do kids stay free in the room or is there a special rate?

- **Dial direct.** When booking a room in a chain hotel, compare the rates offered by the hotel's local line with that of the toll-free number. Also check with an agent and online. A hotel makes nothing on a room that stays empty, so the local hotel reservations desk may be willing to offer a special rate unavailable elsewhere.

- **Remember the law of supply and demand.** Resort hotels are most crowded and therefore most expensive on weekends, so discounts are usually available for midweek stays. Business hotels in downtown locations are busiest during the week, so you can expect big discounts over the weekend. Avoid high-season stays whenever you can: Planning your vacation just a week before or after official peak season can mean substantial savings.

- **Avoid excess charges.** Ask whether your hotel charges for parking. Find out about surcharges imposed on local and long-distance calls—many hotels charge a fee just for dialing out on the phone in your room. Finally, ask about local taxes and service charges (common at guest ranches and high-end resorts), which could increase the cost of a room by 25% or more.

- **Consider a suite.** If you're traveling with your family or another couple, you can pack more people into a suite (which usually comes with a sofa bed), and thereby reduce your per-person rate. Remember that some places charge for extra guests.

FAST FACTS: **Oregon**

American Express **Azumano Travel,** 400 SW Stark St. (© 800/777-2018 or 503/294-2000), is an **American Express Travel Services Representative.** For card member services, phone © 800/528-4800. Call © 800/AXP-TRIP or go to **www.americanexpress.com** for other locations or general information.

Area Codes Currently, Oregon has three area codes. In the Portland area, where 10-digit dialing is required for local calls, 503 is the main area code. However, you may occasionally encounter the 971 area code. Outside of the northwest corner of the state (roughly Mount Hood and Portland to the coast and south to Salem), the area code is 541.

ATM Networks Automatic teller machines (ATMs) (with Star, Cirrus, PLUS, Accel, and the Exchange networks widely available) are nearly ubiquitous throughout Oregon, so you can get cash as you travel; some small-town banks still do not have ATMs, though.

Business Hours The following are general hours; specific establishments may vary. Banks are open Monday through Friday from 9am to 5pm (some also on Sat from 9am–noon). Stores are open Monday through Saturday from 10am to 6pm and Sunday from noon to 5pm (malls usually stay open until 9pm Mon–Sat). Bars generally open around 11am, but are legally allowed to be open Monday through Saturday from 6am to 1am and Sunday from 10am to 1am.

Car Rentals See "Getting Around," earlier in this chapter.

Climate See "When to Go," earlier in this chapter.

Driving Rules See "Getting Around," earlier in this chapter.

Drugstores **Rite-Aid** (© 800/748-3243; www.riteaid.com for locations) and Walgreens (© 800/WALGREENS for locations) are two large pharmacy chains found in the Northwest.

Embassies & Consulates See chapter 3.

Emergencies Call © 911 for fire, police, and ambulance.

Holidays See "Oregon Calendar of Events," earlier in this chapter.

Information See "Visitor Information," earlier in this chapter.

Liquor Laws The legal minimum drinking age in Oregon is 21. Bars can legally stay open until 2am. Beer and wine can often be purchased in supermarkets, but liquor can be purchased only in state-licensed liquor stores, of which there are very few, and a handful of grocery stores.

Lost & Found Be sure to tell all of your credit card companies the minute you discover your wallet has been lost or stolen, and file a report at the nearest police precinct. Your credit card company or insurer may require a police-report number or record of the loss. Most credit card companies have an emergency toll-free number to call if your card is lost or stolen; they may be able to wire you a cash advance immediately or deliver an emergency credit card in a day or two. Visa's U.S. emergency number is ℭ 800/847-2911 or 410/581-9994. American Express cardholders and traveler's check holders should call ℭ 800/221-7282. MasterCard holders should call ℭ 800/307-7309 or 636/722-7111. For other credit cards, call the toll-free number directory at ℭ 800/555-1212.

Maps See "Getting Around," earlier in this chapter.

Pets Some hotels and motels in Oregon accept small, well-behaved pets. However, a small fee often is charged to allow them into guest rooms. Many places, in particular bed-and-breakfasts, don't allow pets at all. (Policies can change frequently, so always be sure to confirm.) On the other hand, many bed-and-breakfasts have their own pets, so if you have a dog or cat allergy, be sure to mention it when making a B&B reservation. Pets are usually restricted in national parks for their own safety, so call each park's ranger station to check before setting out.

Police To reach the police, dial ℭ 911.

Smoking Many restaurants in Oregon are nonsmoking establishments.

Taxes Oregon is a shopper's paradise—there's no sales tax.

Time Zone With the exception of far-eastern Oregon near Ontario, the state is on Pacific Standard Time (PST) and observes daylight saving time from the first Sunday in April to the last Sunday in October, making it consistently 3 hours behind the East Coast.

3

For International Visitors

Whether it's your 1st visit or your 10th, a trip to the United States may require advance planning. This chapter will provide you with essential information, helpful tips, and advice for the more common problems that international visitors may encounter while vacationing in Oregon.

1 Preparing for Your Trip

ENTRY REQUIREMENTS

Check at any U.S. embassy or consulate for current information and requirements. You can also obtain a visa application and other information online at the **U.S. State Department**'s website, at **www.travel.state.gov**.

VISAS The U.S. State Department has a **Visa Waiver Program** allowing citizens of the following countries (at press time) to enter the United States without a visa for stays of up to 90 days: Andorra, Australia, Austria, Belgium, Brunei, Denmark, Finland, France, Germany, Iceland, Ireland, Italy, Japan, Liechtenstein, Luxembourg, Monaco, the Netherlands, New Zealand, Norway, Portugal, San Marino, Singapore, Slovenia, Spain, Sweden, Switzerland, and the United Kingdom. Citizens of these nations need only a valid passport and a round-trip air or cruise ticket upon arrival. If they first enter the United States, they may also visit Mexico, Canada, Bermuda, and/or the Caribbean islands and return to the United States without a visa. Further information is available from any U.S. embassy or consulate. Canadian citizens may enter the United States without visas; they need only proof of residence.

Citizens of all other countries must have (1) a valid passport that expires at least 6 months later than the scheduled end of their visit to the United States, and (2) a tourist visa, which may be obtained without charge from any U.S. consulate.

To obtain a visa, the traveler must submit a completed application form, with a 1½-inch-square photo, and demonstrate binding ties to a residence abroad. Usually you can obtain a visa at once or within 24 hours, but it may take longer during the summer rush from June through August. If you cannot go in person, ask the nearest U.S. embassy or consulate about applying by mail. Your travel agent or airline office may also be able to provide you with visa applications and instructions. The U.S. consulate or embassy that issues your visa will determine whether you will be issued a multiple- or single-entry visa and any restrictions regarding the length of your stay.

British subjects can obtain up-to-date visa information by calling the **U.S. Embassy Visa Information Line** (© **0891/200-290**) or by visiting the "Visas to the U.S." section of the American Embassy London's website at www.usembassy.org.uk.

Irish citizens can obtain up-to-date visa information through the **Embassy of the USA Dublin,** 42 Elgin Rd., Dublin 4, Ireland (© **353/1-668-8777;** or by checking the "Consular Services" section of the website at http://dublin.usembassy.gov).

Australian citizens can obtain up-to-date visa information from the **U.S. Embassy Canberra,** Moonah Place, Yarralumla, ACT 2600 (✆ **02/6214-5600**) or by checking the U.S. Diplomatic Mission's website at http://usembassy-australia.state.gov/consular.

Citizens of **New Zealand** can obtain up-to-date visa information by contacting the **U.S. Embassy New Zealand,** 29 Fitzherbert Terrace, Thorndon, Wellington (✆ **644/472-2068**), or get the information directly from the "For New Zealanders" section of the website at http://usembassy.org.nz.

MEDICAL REQUIREMENTS　Unless you're arriving from an area known to be suffering from an epidemic (particularly cholera or yellow fever), inoculations or vaccinations are not required for entry into the United States. If you have a medical condition that requires **syringe-administered medications,** carry a valid signed prescription from your physician—the Federal Aviation Administration (FAA) no longer allows airline passengers to pack syringes in their carry-on baggage without documented proof of medical need. If you have a disease that requires treatment with **narcotics,** you should also carry documented proof with you—smuggling narcotics aboard a plane is a serious offense that carries severe penalties in the U.S.

For **HIV-positive visitors,** requirements for entering the United States are somewhat vague and change frequently. According to the latest publication of *HIV and Immigrants: A Manual for AIDS Service Providers,* the Immigration and Naturalization Service (INS) doesn't require a medical exam for entry into the United States, but INS officials may stop individuals because they look sick or because they are carrying AIDS/HIV medicine. For up-to-the-minute information, contact **AIDSinfo**

(✆ **800/448-0440** or 301/519-6616 outside the U.S.; www.aidsinfo.nih.gov) or the **Gay Men's Health Crisis** (✆ **212/367-1000;** www.gmhc.org).

DRIVER'S LICENSES　Foreign driver's licenses are usually recognized in the U.S., but you should get an international one if your home license is not in English.

PASSPORT INFORMATION

Safeguard your passport in an inconspicuous, inaccessible place like a money belt. Make a copy of the critical pages, including the passport number, and store it in a safe place, separate from the passport itself. If you lose your passport, visit the nearest consulate of your native country as soon as possible for a replacement. Passport applications are downloadable from the websites listed below.

Note: The International Civil Aviation Organization has recommended a policy requiring that *every* individual who travels by air have a passport. Many countries are now requiring that even children have their own passports to travel internationally.

FOR RESIDENTS OF CANADA

You can pick up a passport application at any of 28 regional passport offices or most travel agencies. Canadian children who travel must have their own passport. However, if you hold a valid Canadian passport issued before December 11, 2001, that bears the name of your child, the passport remains valid for you and your child until it expires. Passports cost C$87 for those 16 years and older (valid 5 years), C$37 children 3 to 15 (valid 5 years), and C$22, children under 3 (valid 3 years). Applications, which must be accompanied by two identical passport-sized photographs and proof of Canadian citizenship, are available at travel agencies throughout Canada or from the central **Passport Office,** Department of Foreign Affairs and International Trade, Ottawa, ON K1A 0G3 (✆ **800/567-6868;**

www.fac-aec.gc.ca/menu-en.asp). Processing takes 5 to 10 days if you apply in person, or about 3 weeks by mail.

FOR RESIDENTS OF THE UNITED KINGDOM

To pick up an application for a standard 10-year passport (5-year passport for children under 16), visit the nearest passport office, major post office, or travel agency. You can also contact the **United Kingdom Passport Service** at ℂ **0870/571-0410** or visit its website at www.passport.gov.uk. Passports are £42 for adults and £25 for children under 16, with another £30 fee if you apply in person at a passport office. Processing takes about 2 weeks (1 week if you apply at the passport office).

FOR RESIDENTS OF IRELAND

You can apply for a 10-year passport (€57), at the **Passport Office,** Setanta Centre, Molesworth Street, Dublin 2 (ℂ **01/671-1633;** www.irlgov.ie/iveagh). Those under age 18 and over 65 must apply for a €12 3-year passport. You can also apply at 1A South Mall, Cork (ℂ **021/272 525**) or over the counter at most main post offices.

FOR RESIDENTS OF AUSTRALIA

You can get an application from your local post office or any branch of Passports Australia, but you must schedule an interview at the passport office to present your application materials. Call the **Australian Passport Information Service** at ℂ **131-232,** or visit the government website at www.passports.gov.au. Passports for adults are A$150 and for those under 18 are A$75.

FOR RESIDENTS OF NEW ZEALAND

You can pick up a passport application at any New Zealand Passports Office or download it from their website. Contact the **Passports Office** at ℂ **0800/225-050** in New Zealand or 04/474-8100, or log on to www.passports.govt.nz. Passports for adults are NZ$71 and for children under 16 NZ$36.

CUSTOMS
WHAT YOU CAN BRING IN

Every visitor more than 21 years of age may bring in, free of duty, the following: (1) 1 liter of wine or hard liquor; (2) 200 cigarettes, 100 cigars (but not from Cuba), or 3 pounds of smoking tobacco; and (3) $100 worth of gifts. These exemptions are offered to travelers who spend at least 72 hours in the United States and who have not claimed them within the preceding 6 months. It is altogether forbidden to bring into the country foodstuffs (particularly fruit, cooked meats, and canned goods) and plants (vegetables, seeds, tropical plants, and the like). Foreign tourists may carry in or out up to $10,000 in U.S. or foreign currency with no formalities; larger sums must be declared to U.S. Customs on entering or leaving, which includes filing form CM 4790. For details regarding U.S. Customs and Border Protection, consult your nearest U.S. embassy or consulate, or **U.S. Customs** (ℂ **202/927-1770;** www.customs.ustreas.gov).

WHAT YOU CAN TAKE HOME

U.K. citizens returning from a non-E.U. country have a customs allowance of: 200 cigarettes; 50 cigars; 250g of smoking tobacco; 2 liters of still table wine; 1 liter of spirits or strong liqueurs (over 22% volume); 2 liters of fortified wine, sparkling wine or other liqueurs; 60cc (ml) perfume; 250cc (ml) of toilet water; and £145 worth of all other goods, including gifts and souvenirs. People under 17 cannot have the tobacco or alcohol allowance. For more information, consult **HM Customs & Excise** at ℂ **0845/010-9000** (from outside the U.K., 020/8929-0152), or http://customs.hmrc.gov.uk.

For a clear summary of **Canadian** rules, request the booklet *I Declare,* from the **Canada Customs and Revenue Agency** (© 800/461-9999 in Canada, or 204/983-3500; www.cbsa-asfc.gc.ca/E/pub/cp/rc4044). Canada allows its citizens a C$750 exemption, and you're allowed to bring back duty-free 1 carton of cigarettes, 1 can of tobacco, 40 imperial ounces of liquor, and 50 cigars. Canadian citizens under 18 or 19, depending on their province, cannot have the tobacco or alcohol allowance. In addition, you're allowed to mail gifts to Canada valued at less than C$60 a day, if they're unsolicited and don't contain alcohol or tobacco (write on the package "Unsolicited gift, under $60 value"). All valuables should be declared on the Y-38 form before departure from Canada, including serial numbers of valuables you already own, such as expensive foreign cameras. *Note:* The C$750 exemption can only be used once a year and only after an absence of 7 days.

The duty-free allowance in **Australia** is A$900 or, for those under 18, A$450. Citizens age 18 and over can bring in 250 cigarettes or 250 grams of loose tobacco, and 2.25 liters of alcohol. If you're returning with valuables you already own, such as foreign-made cameras, you should file form B263. A helpful brochure available from Australian consulates or Customs offices is *Know Before You Go.* For details, consult the **Australian Customs Service** at © 1300/363-263 or www.customs.gov.au.

The duty-free allowance for **New Zealand** is NZ$700. Citizens over 17 can bring in 200 cigarettes, 50 cigars, or 250 grams of tobacco (or a mixture of all three if their combined weight doesn't exceed 250g); plus 4.5 liters of wine and beer, or 1.125 liters of liquor. New Zealand currency does not carry import or export restrictions. Fill out a certificate of export, listing the valuables you are taking out of the country; that way, you can bring them back without paying duty.

Most questions are answered in a free pamphlet available at New Zealand consulates and Customs offices: *New Zealand Customs Guide for Travellers, Notice no. 4.* For more information, contact **New Zealand Customs,** The Customhouse, 17–21 Whitmore St., Box 2218, Wellington (© 0800/428-786 or 04/473-6099; www.customs.govt.nz).

HEALTH INSURANCE

Although it's not required of travelers, health insurance is highly recommended. Unlike many European countries, the United States does not usually offer free or low-cost medical care to its citizens or visitors. Doctors and hospitals are expensive, and in most cases will require advance payment or proof of coverage before they render their services. Policies can cover everything from the loss or theft of your baggage and trip cancellation to the guarantee of bail in case you're arrested. Good policies will also cover the costs of an accident, repatriation, or death. Packages such as **Europ Assistance's "Worldwide Healthcare Plan"** are sold by European automobile clubs and travel agencies at attractive rates. **Worldwide Assistance Services, Inc.** (© 800/777-8710; www.worldwide assistance.com) is the agent for Europ Assistance in the United States.

Though lack of health insurance may prevent you from being admitted to a hospital in nonemergencies, don't worry about being left on a street corner to die: The American way is to fix you now and bill the living daylights out of you later.

INSURANCE FOR BRITISH TRAVELERS Most big travel agents offer their own insurance and will probably try to sell you their package when you book a holiday. Think before you sign. **Britain's Consumers' Association** recommends that you insist on seeing the policy and reading the fine print before buying travel insurance. **The Association of British Insurers** (© 020/7600-3333;

www.abi.org.uk) gives advice by phone and publishes *Holiday Insurance,* a free guide to policy provisions and prices. You might also shop around for better deals: Try **Columbus Direct** (© 0870/033-9988; www.columbusdirect.net).

INSURANCE FOR CANADIAN TRAVELERS Canadians should check with their provincial health plan offices or call **Health Canada** (© 866/225-0709; www.hc-sc.gc.ca) to find out the extent of their coverage and what documentation and receipts they must take home in case they are treated in the United States.

MONEY

CURRENCY The U.S. monetary system is very simple: The most common **bills** are the $1 (a "buck"), $5, $10, and $20 denominations. There are also $2 bills (seldom encountered), $50 bills, and $100 bills (the last two are usually not welcome as payment for small purchases). All the paper money was recently redesigned, making the faces on them disproportionately large, but the old-style bills are still legal tender.

Coins come in seven denominations: 1¢ (1 cent, or a penny); 5¢ (5 cents, or a nickel); 10¢ (10 cents, or a dime); 25¢ (25 cents, or a quarter); 50¢ (50 cents, or a half dollar); the gold-colored Sacagawea coin, worth $1; and the rare silver dollar.

Note: The "foreign-exchange bureaus" so common in Europe are rare even at airports in the U.S., and nonexistent outside major cities. It's best not to change foreign money (or traveler's checks denominated in a currency other than U.S. dollars) at a small-town bank, or even a branch in a big city; in fact, leave any currency other than U.S. dollars at home—it may prove a greater nuisance to you than it's worth.

TRAVELER'S CHECKS Traveler's checks are widely accepted, but make sure that they're denominated in U.S. dollars; foreign-currency checks are often difficult to exchange. The three traveler's checks that are most widely recognized—and least likely to be denied—are **Visa, American Express,** and **Thomas Cook.** Be sure to record the numbers of the checks, and keep that information in a separate place in case they get lost or stolen. Some Oregon businesses in tourist destinations are good about taking traveler's checks, but you're better off cashing them in at a bank (in small amounts, of course) and paying in cash. *Remember:* You'll need identification, such as a driver's license or passport, to change a traveler's check.

CREDIT CARDS & ATMs Credit cards are the most widely used form of payment in the United States: **Visa** (Barclaycard in Britain), **MasterCard** (Euro-Card in Europe, Access in Britain, Chargex in Canada), **American Express, Diners Club,** and **Discover.** There are, however, a handful of stores and restaurants in Oregon that do not take credit cards, so be sure to ask in advance. Most businesses display a sticker near their entrance to let you know which cards they accept. (*Note:* Businesses may require a minimum purchase, usually around $10, to use a credit card.)

It's highly recommended that you bring at least one major credit card. You must have one to rent a car, and hotels and airlines usually require a credit card imprint as a deposit against expenses. And in an emergency, a credit card is invaluable.

You'll find automated teller machines (ATMs) in just about every town in Oregon, and on every block in the business districts of the big cities. Some ATMs will allow you to draw U.S. currency against your bank and credit cards. Check with your bank before leaving home, and remember that you will need your personal identification number (PIN) to do so. Most accept Visa, MasterCard, and

Travel Tip

Keep a copy of all your travel papers separate from your wallet or purse, and leave a copy with someone at home in case of an emergency.

American Express, as well as ATM cards from other U.S. banks. Expect to be charged up to $3 per transaction, however, if you're not using your own bank's ATM.

One way around these fees is to ask for "cash back" at grocery stores that accept ATM cards and don't charge usage fees. Of course, you'll have to purchase something first. The same is true at most U.S. post offices.

ATM cards with major credit card backing, known as "debit cards," are now a commonly acceptable form of payment in most stores and restaurants. Debit cards draw money directly from your checking account. Some stores enable you to receive cash back on your debit-card purchases as well.

SAFETY

GENERAL SUGGESTIONS   Although Oregon's tourist spots are generally safe, U.S. urban areas tend to be less safe than those in Europe or Japan. You should always stay alert. This is particularly true of large American cities. If you're in doubt about which neighborhoods are safe, don't hesitate to make inquiries with the hotel front desk staff or the local tourist office.

Avoid deserted areas, especially at night, and don't go into public parks after dark unless there's a concert or similar occasion that will attract a crowd.

Avoid carrying valuables with you on the street, and keep expensive cameras or electronic equipment bagged up or covered when not in use. If you're using a map, try to consult it inconspicuously—or, better yet, study it before you leave your room. Hold on to your pocketbook, and place your billfold in an inside pocket. In theaters, restaurants, and other public places, keep your possessions in sight.

Always lock your room door—don't assume that once you're inside the hotel you are automatically safe and no longer need to be aware of your surroundings.

DRIVING SAFETY   Driving safety is important, too, and carjacking is not unprecedented. Question your rental agency about personal safety and ask for a traveler-safety brochure when you pick up your car. Obtain written directions—or a map with the route clearly marked—from the agency showing how to get to your destination. (Many agencies now offer the option of renting a cellphone for the duration of your car rental; check with the rental agent when you pick up the car. Otherwise, contact **InTouch USA** at ✆ **800/872-7626** or www.intouchusa.com for short-term cellphone rental.) And, if possible, arrive and depart during daylight hours.

If you drive off a highway and end up in a dodgy-looking neighborhood, leave the area as quickly as possible. If you have an accident, even on the highway, stay in your car with the doors locked until you assess the situation or until the police arrive. If you're bumped from behind on the street or are involved in a minor accident with no injuries, and the situation appears to be suspicious, motion to the other driver to follow you. Never get out of your car in such situations. Go directly to the nearest police precinct, well-lit service station, or 24-hour store.

Park in well-lit, busy areas when possible. Always keep your car doors locked, even if the vehicle is attended. Never leave any packages or valuables in sight. If someone attempts to rob you or steal your car, don't try to resist the thief/carjacker. Report the incident to the police department immediately by calling ✆ **911.**

2 Getting to the U.S.

BY PLANE

AIRLINES   In addition to the domestic U.S. airlines listed in chapter 2, many international carriers serve LAX and other U.S. gateways. These include, among others: **Aer Lingus** (© 01/886-8888 in Dublin; www.aerlingus.ie), **Air Canada** (© 800/776-3000; www.aircanada.ca), **British Airways** (© 0845/7733-377 in the U.K.; www.british-airways.com), **Canadian Airlines** (© 800/426-7000), **Japan Airlines** (© 0354/89-1111 in Tokyo; www.jal.co.jp), **Qantas** (© 13-13-13 in Australia; www.qantas.com.au), and **Virgin Atlantic** (© 01293/747-747 in the U.K.; www.fly.virgin.com). British Airways and Virgin Atlantic offer direct flights to San Francisco and Los Angeles from London. **Air New Zealand** (© 73-7000 in New Zealand; www.airnewzealand.co.nz) also flies direct to California.

AIRLINE DISCOUNTS   Smart travelers can reduce the price of a plane ticket by shopping around. Overseas visitors, for example, can take advantage of the APEX (Advance Purchase Excursion) reductions offered by all major U.S. and European carriers. For more money-saving airline advice, see "Getting There," in chapter 2. For the best rates, compare fares and be flexible with the dates and times of travel.

BY TRAIN

Although **Amtrak** (© 800/872-7245; www.amtrak.com) offers service from Vancouver, British Columbia, to Portland, a trip that should take only 8 or 9 hours, you have to overnight in Seattle unless you want to take the Amtrak bus between Vancouver and Seattle. One-way fares from Vancouver are usually between $44 and $54 if you book in advance.

IMMIGRATION & CUSTOMS CLEARANCE   Visitors arriving by air, no matter what the port of entry, should cultivate patience and resignation before setting foot on U.S. soil. Clearing immigration control can take as long as 2 hours, especially on summer weekends, so carry this guidebook or other reading material. This is especially true in the aftermath of the September 11, 2001, terrorist attacks, when U.S. airports have considerably beefed up security clearances. People traveling by air from Canada, Bermuda, and certain Caribbean countries can sometimes clear Customs and Immigration at the point of departure, which is much faster.

In contrast, travelers arriving by car, by ferry, or by rail from Canada will find border-crossing formalities somewhat more streamlined, though not nearly as easy as they were before the September 11, 2001, terrorist attacks.

Tips Prepare to Be Fingerprinted

As of January 2004, many international visitors traveling on visas to the United States will be photographed and fingerprinted at Customs in a new program created by the Department of Homeland Security called **US-VISIT**. Non-U.S. citizens arriving at airports and on cruise ships must undergo an instant background check as part of the government's efforts to deter terrorism by verifying the identity of incoming and outgoing visitors. Exempt from the extra scrutiny are visitors entering by land or those who don't require a visa for short-term visits (mostly from Europe; see p. 41). For more information, go to the Homeland Security website at **www.dhs.gov/dhspublic**.

3 Getting Around the U.S.

For specific information on traveling to and around Oregon, see "Getting There" and "Getting Around," in chapter 2.

BY PLANE   Some large airlines offer transatlantic or transpacific passengers special discount tickets under the name **Visit USA,** which allows mostly one-way travel from one U.S. destination to another at very low prices. Unavailable in the U.S., these discount tickets must be purchased abroad in conjunction with your international fare. This system is the easiest, fastest, cheapest way to see the country. Obtain information well in advance from your travel agent or the airline, since the conditions attached to these discount tickets can be changed without advance notice.

BY TRAIN   International visitors (excluding Canadians) can also buy a **USA Rail Pass,** good for 15 or 30 days of unlimited travel on **Amtrak** (© **800/USA-RAIL;** www.amtrak.com). The pass is available through many overseas travel agents. Prices valid for travel across the United States in 2005 for a 15-day pass were $295 off-peak, $440 peak; a 30-day pass costs $385 off-peak, $550 peak. Fares are significantly cheaper, however, within particular regions. See Amtrak's website for the cost of travel within the western, eastern, or northwestern United States. With a foreign passport, you can also buy passes direct from some Amtrak locations, including San Francisco, Los Angeles, Chicago, New York, Miami, Boston, and Washington, D.C. Reservations are generally required and should be made as early as possible. Regional rail passes are also available.

BY BUS   Bus travel is often the most economical form of public transit for short hops between U.S. cities, but it can also be slow and uncomfortable—certainly not an option for everyone

(particularly when Amtrak, which is far more luxurious, offers similar rates). **Greyhound/Trailways** (© **800/231-2222;** www.greyhound.com), the sole nationwide bus line, offers an **International Ameripass** that must be purchased before coming to the United States, or by phone through the Greyhound International Office at the Port Authority Bus Terminal in New York City (© **212/971-0492**). The pass can be obtained from foreign travel agents or through Greyhound's website (order at least 21 days before your departure to the U.S.) and costs less than the domestic version. 2005 passes cost as follows: 4 days ($179), 7 days ($239), 10 days ($289), 15 days ($349), 21 days ($419), 30 days ($479), 45 days ($529), or 60 days ($639). You can get more info on the pass at the website, or by calling © **402/330-8552.** In addition, special rates are available for seniors, students, and children.

BY CAR   The most cost-effective way to travel the United States is by car. The interstate highway system connects cities and towns all over the country, with an extensive network of federal, state, and local highways and roads as well. Some of the national car-rental companies with offices in Oregon include **Alamo** (© 800/462-5266; www.alamo.com), **Avis** (© 800/230-4898; www.avis.com), **Budget** (© 800/527-0700; www.budget.com), **Dollar** (© 800/800-3665; www.dollar.com), **Hertz** (© 800/654-3131; www.hertz.com), and **National** (© 800/227-7368; www.nationalcar.com).

If you plan to rent a car in the United States, you probably won't need the services of an additional automobile organization. If you're planning to buy or borrow a car, automobile-association membership is recommended. **AAA,** the **American Automobile Association** (© **800/222-4357;** http://travel.aaa.com), is the country's largest auto club and supplies its members with maps, insurance, and, most important, emergency road service. The cost of joining runs from $63 for singles to $87 for two members, but if you're a member of a foreign auto club with reciprocal arrangements, you can enjoy free AAA service in America. See "Getting There" in chapter 2 for more information.

FAST FACTS: For the International Traveler

Automobile Organizations Auto clubs will supply maps, suggested routes, guidebooks, accident and bail-bond insurance, and emergency road service. The **American Automobile Association (AAA)** is the major auto club in the United States. If you belong to an auto club in your home country, inquire about AAA reciprocity before you leave. You may be able to join AAA even if you're not a member of a reciprocal club; to inquire, call AAA (© **800/222-4357**). AAA is actually an organization of regional auto clubs, so look under "AAA Automobile Club" in the White Pages of the telephone directory. AAA has a nationwide emergency road service telephone number (© **800/AAA-HELP**).

Business Hours Offices are usually open weekdays from 9am to 5pm. Banks are open weekdays from 9am to 3pm or later and sometimes Saturday mornings. Stores typically open between 9 and 10am and close between 5 and 6pm from Monday through Saturday. Stores in shopping complexes or malls tend to stay open late: until about 9pm on weekdays and weekends, and many malls and larger department stores are open on Sundays.

Currency & Currency Exchange See "Entry Requirements" and "Money" under "Preparing for Your Trip," earlier.

Drinking Laws The legal age for purchase and consumption of alcoholic beverages is 21; proof of age is required and often requested at bars, nightclubs, and restaurants, so it's always a good idea to bring ID when you go out. Supermarkets and convenience stores in California sell beer, wine, and liquor.

Do not carry open containers of alcohol in your car or any public area that isn't zoned for alcohol consumption. The police can fine you on the spot. And nothing will ruin your trip faster than getting a citation for DUI ("driving under the influence"), so don't even think about driving while intoxicated.

Electricity Like Canada, the United States uses 110 to 120 volts AC (60 cycles), compared to 220 to 240 volts AC (50 cycles) in most of Europe, Australia, and New Zealand. If your small appliances use 220 to 240 volts, you'll need a 110-volt transformer and a plug adapter with two flat parallel pins to operate them here. Downward converters that change 220–240 volts to 110–120 volts are difficult to find in the United States, so bring one with you.

Embassies & Consulates All embassies are located in the nation's capital, Washington, D.C. Some consulates are located in major U.S. cities, and most nations have a mission to the United Nations in New York City. If your country isn't listed below, call for directory information in Washington, D.C. (© **202/555-1212**) or log on to **www.embassy.org/embassies**.

The embassy of **Australia** is at 1601 Massachusetts Ave. NW, Washington, DC 20036 (② 202/797-3000; www.austemb.org). There are consulates in New York, Honolulu, Houston, Los Angeles, and San Francisco.

The embassy of **Canada** is at 501 Pennsylvania Ave. NW, Washington, DC 20001 (② 202/682-1740; www.canadianembassy.org). Other Canadian consulates are in Buffalo (New York), Detroit, Los Angeles, New York, and Seattle.

The embassy of **Ireland** is at 2234 Massachusetts Ave. NW, Washington, DC 20008 (② 202/462-3939; www.irelandemb.org). Irish consulates are in Boston, Chicago, New York, San Francisco, and other cities. See website for complete listing.

The embassy of **Japan** is at 2520 Massachusetts Ave. NW, Washington, DC 20008 (② 202/238-6700; www.embjapan.org). Japanese consulates are located in many cities, including Atlanta, Boston, Detroit, New York, San Francisco, and Seattle.

The embassy of **New Zealand** is at 37 Observatory Circle NW, Washington, DC 20008 (② 202/328-4800; www.nzemb.org). New Zealand consulates are in Los Angeles, Salt Lake City, San Francisco, and Seattle.

The embassy of the **United Kingdom** is at 3100 Massachusetts Ave. NW, Washington, DC 20008 (② 202/588-7800; www.britainusa.com). Other British consulates are in Atlanta, Boston, Chicago, Cleveland, Houston, Los Angeles, New York, San Francisco, and Seattle.

Emergencies Call ② **911** to report a fire, call the police, or get an ambulance anywhere in the United States. This is a toll-free call (no coins are required at public telephones).

If you encounter traveler's problems, call the Los Angeles chapter of the **Traveler's Aid Society** (② 310/646-2270; www.travelersaid.org), a nationwide, nonprofit, social service organization that helps travelers in difficult straits. Its services might include reuniting families separated while traveling, providing food and/or shelter to people stranded without cash, and even emotional counseling.

Gasoline (Petrol) Petrol is known as gasoline (or simply "gas") in the United States, and petrol stations are known as both gas stations and service stations. At press time, the cost of gasoline in the U.S. is abnormally high ($3 a gallon) and fluctuating drastically, on the rise. Taxes are already included in the printed price. One U.S. gallon equals 3.8 liters or .85 imperial gallons.

Holidays Banks, government offices, post offices, and many stores, restaurants, and museums are closed on the following legal national holidays: January 1 (New Year's Day), the third Monday in January (Martin Luther King, Jr., Day), the third Monday in February (Presidents' Day), the last Monday in May (Memorial Day), July 4 (Independence Day), the first Monday in September (Labor Day), the second Monday in October (Columbus Day), November 11 (Veterans' Day/Armistice Day), the fourth Thursday in November (Thanksgiving Day), and December 25 (Christmas). The Tuesday after the first Monday in November is Election Day, a federal government holiday in presidential-election years (held every 4 years, and next in 2008).

Legal Aid If you are "pulled over" for a minor infraction (such as speeding), never attempt to pay the fine directly to a police officer; this could be construed as attempted bribery, a much more serious crime. Pay fines by mail, or directly into the hands of the clerk of the court. If accused of a more serious offense, say and do nothing before consulting a lawyer. Here the burden is on the state to prove a person's guilt beyond a reasonable doubt, and everyone has the right to remain silent, whether he or she is suspected of a crime or actually arrested. Once arrested, a person can make one telephone call to a party of his or her choice. Call your embassy or consulate.

Mail If you aren't sure what your address will be in the United States, mail can be sent to you, in your name, c/o General Delivery at the main post office of the city or region where you expect to be. (Call © **800/275-8777** for information on the nearest post office.) The addressee must pick up mail in person and must produce proof of identity (driver's license, passport, etc.). Most post offices will hold your mail for up to 1 month, and are open Monday to Friday from 8am to 6pm, and Saturday from 9am to 3pm.

Generally found at intersections, mailboxes are blue with a red-and-white stripe and carry the inscription U.S. MAIL. If your mail is addressed to a U.S. destination, don't forget to add the five-digit postal code (or zip code), after the two-letter abbreviation of the state to which the mail is addressed. This is essential to prompt delivery.

At press time, domestic postage rates were 24¢ for a postcard and 39¢ for a letter. For international mail, a postcard to Mexico or Canada is 55¢, 75¢ to the rest of the world; an airmail letter is 63¢ to Mexico or Canada for the first ounce, 84¢ to the rest of the world.

Measurements See the chart on the inside front cover of this book for details on converting metric measurements to U.S. equivalents.

Taxes The United States has no value-added tax (VAT) or other indirect tax at the national level. Every state, county, and city may levy its own local tax on all purchases, including hotel and restaurant checks and airline tickets. These taxes will not appear on price tags. There is no sales tax in Oregon. Hotel tax applies to the room tariff only (which is not subject to sales tax); it's set by the city, ranging from 7% to 16% throughout Oregon.

Telephone, Telegraph, Telex & Fax Private corporations run the telephone system in the U.S., so rates can vary widely, especially for long-distance service and operator-assisted calls. Generally, hotel surcharges on long-distance and local calls are astronomical, so you're better off using a **public pay telephone,** which you'll find clearly marked in most public buildings and private establishments, as well as on the street. Convenience grocery stores and gas stations almost always have them. Many convenience groceries and packaging services sell **prepaid calling cards** in denominations up to $50; these can be the least expensive way to call home. Many public phones at airports now accept American Express, MasterCard, and Visa credit cards. **Local calls** made from public pay phones in most locales cost either 25¢ or 35¢. Pay phones do not accept pennies, and few will take anything larger than a quarter.

You may want to look into leasing a cellphone for the duration of your trip.

Most long-distance and international calls can be dialed directly from any phone. **For calls within the United States and to Canada,** dial 1 followed by the area code and the seven-digit number. **For other international calls,** dial 011 followed by the country code, city code, and the number you are calling.

Calls to area codes **800, 888, 877,** and **866** are toll-free. However, calls to area codes **700** and **900** (chat lines, bulletin boards, "dating" services, and so on) can be very expensive—usually a charge of 95¢ to $3 or more per minute, and they sometimes have minimum charges that can run as high as $15 or more.

For **reversed-charge or collect calls,** and for person-to-person calls, dial the number 0 then the area code and number; an operator will come on the line, and you should specify whether you are calling collect, person-to-person, or both. If your operator-assisted call is international, ask for the overseas operator.

For **local directory assistance** ("information"), dial 411; for long-distance information, dial 1, then the appropriate area code and 555-1212.

Telegraph and telex services are provided primarily by Western Union. You can bring your telegram to the nearest Western Union office or dictate it by phone (© **800/325-6000**). You can also telegraph money, or have it telegraphed to you, very quickly over the Western Union system, but this service can cost as much as 15% to 20% of the amount sent.

Most hotels have **fax machines** available for guest use (be sure to ask about the charge to use it). Many hotel rooms are even wired for guests' fax machines. A less expensive way to send and receive faxes may be at stores such as **The UPS Store** (formerly Mail Boxes Etc.), a national chain of retail packing service shops. (Look in the Yellow Pages directory under "Packing Services.")

The U.S. has two kinds of telephone directories. The **White Pages** list private households and business subscribers in alphabetical order. The inside front cover lists emergency numbers for police, fire, ambulance, poison-control center, crime-victims hot line, and so on. The first few pages will tell you how to make long-distance and international calls, complete with country codes and area codes. Government numbers are usually printed on blue paper within the White Pages. Printed on yellow paper, the so-called **Yellow Pages** list all local services, businesses, industries, and houses of worship according to activity with an index at the front or back. (Drugstores/pharmacies and restaurants are also listed by geographic location.) The Yellow Pages also include city plans or detailed area maps, postal zip codes, and public transportation routes.

Time The continental United States is divided into **four time zones:** Eastern Standard Time (EST), Central Standard Time (CST), Mountain Standard Time (MST), and Pacific Standard Time (PST). Alaska and Hawaii have their own zones. For example, when it's 9am in Portland (PST), it's 7am in Honolulu (HST),10am in Denver (MST), 11am in Chicago (CST), noon in New York City (EST), 5pm in London (GMT), and 2am the next day in Sydney.

Daylight saving time takes effect at 2am the first Sunday in April until 2am the last Sunday in October, except in Arizona, Hawaii, the U.S. Virgin Islands, and Puerto Rico. (Indiana will begin observing daylight saving time in Apr 2006.) Daylight savings moves the clock 1 hour ahead of standard time. (A new law will extend daylight saving in 2007; clocks will change the second Sun in Mar and the first Sun in Nov.)

Tipping Tips are a very important part of certain workers' income, and gratuities are the standard way of showing appreciation for services provided. (Tipping is certainly not compulsory if the service is poor!) In hotels, tip **bellhops** at least $1 per bag and tip the **chamber staff** $1 to $2 per day (more if you've left a disaster area for him or her to clean up). Tip the **doorman** or **concierge** only if he or she has provided you with some specific service (for example, calling a cab for you or obtaining difficult-to-get theater tickets). Tip the **valet-parking attendant** $1 every time you get your car.

In restaurants, bars, and nightclubs, tip **service staff** 15% to 20% of the check, tip **bartenders** 10% to 15%, tip **checkroom attendants** $1 per garment, and tip **valet-parking attendants** $1 per vehicle.

As for other service personnel, tip **cab drivers** 15% of the fare; tip **skycaps** at airports at least $1 per bag; and tip **hairdressers** and **barbers** 15% to 20%.

Toilets You won't find public toilets or "restrooms" on the streets in most Oregon cities, but they can be found in hotel lobbies, bars, restaurants, museums, department stores, railway and bus stations, and service stations. Large hotels and fast-food restaurants are often the best bet for clean facilities. If possible, avoid the toilets at parks and beaches, which tend to be dirty; some may be unsafe. Restaurants and bars in resorts or heavily visited areas may reserve their restrooms for patrons. Some establishments display a notice indicating this. You can ignore this sign or, better yet, avoid arguments by paying for a cup of coffee or a soft drink, which will qualify you as a patron.

4

Suggested Oregon Itineraries

Where should I go? What should I see? What's the best route? How do I maximize my time? I know all these questions well. I've asked them myself when I've been planning vacation itineraries, and I've been asked them by other people planning trips to Oregon. This chapter should help you answer those questions. I'm not going to get down to the nitty-gritty details like where to get gas, but I do mention below the occasional not-to-be-missed or out-of-the-way restaurant or lodge.

If you read through all these itineraries, you'll notice a bit of overlap. Indeed, there are some destinations and attractions that just should not be missed on any visit to the state. For example, a trip to Oregon should include at least a day in Portland, and, to really get a sense of about the state, you have to explore both the coast and the mountains.

1 Oregon in 1 Week

Oregon is a big state, so don't expect to see it all in a week's vacation. However, if your vision of Oregon includes everything from forests of towering trees to snow-capped volcanic peaks and waves crashing on rugged shores, you're in luck: You can take in all of these, plus plenty of the state's famous wineries and brewpubs, during a 7-day visit—if you're willing to drive quite a bit. The following 1-week itinerary will allow you to experience many of the state's highlights.

Day ❶: Portland ✦✦
Start your visit in Portland, Oregon's largest city and a model of livability. Head to Washington Park to visit the **Japanese Garden** (p. 102) and the **International Rose Test Garden** (p. 101). Hang out in a cafe, wine bar, or brewpub to find out how Portland relaxes. Ride the MAX or the Portland Streetcar (they're both free downtown) to visit some outlying neighborhoods. Wander around the Pearl District and stop by the **Saturday Market** (p. 100) if it happens to be the weekend. Stroll through **Tom McCall Waterfront Park** (p. 98) on the banks of the Willamette River.

Day ❷: The Mount Hood Loop ✦✦✦
On your second day, head east from Portland through the Columbia River Gorge and around Mount Hood. In the Gorge, drive the **Historic Columbia River Highway** (p. 236) and try to avoid straining your neck while gazing up at **Multnomah Falls** (p. 236). Have lunch in Hood River, a town that has become one of the world's premier windsurfing and kiteboarding spots. As you loop around snow-capped Mount Hood, Oregon's tallest peak, stop at the historic **Timberline Lodge** (p. 259). Go for a short hike.

**Oregon
in 1 Week**

**Oregon
in 2 Weeks**

Day ❸: Astoria ⭐⭐

Next head west to the Oregon coast. Starting at the mouth of the Columbia River, you can explore **Astoria** (p. 164), a historic river port and home to the **Lewis and Clark National Historical Park** (p. 166). This town is still an active shipping and fishing port and has loads of character. The **Columbia River Maritime Museum** (p. 166) is one of the state's best museums.

Day ❹: Cannon Beach to the Three Capes Scenic Loop ⭐⭐⭐

The next day, head south from Astoria to **Cannon Beach** (p. 175), the most charming town on the coast and home to the impressive **Haystack Rock.** Just north of town, visit the rugged beaches of **Ecola State Park** (p. 176) and south of

town, stop at **Hug Point and Arcadia waysides** (p. 176) as well as **Oswald West State Park** (p. 176). At this latter park, a short trail leads to one of the prettiest beaches in the state. Longer trails lead up onto rugged headlands. South of here, mellow out in **Manzanita** (p. 182) before continuing south to the **Three Capes Scenic Loop** (p. 185), which takes in Cape Meares, Cape Lookout, and Cape Kiwanda.

Day ❺: Newport ⭐⭐

Continue driving south, through miles of congestion in Lincoln City, to **Depoe Bay** (p. 195), where you'll find not only the smallest natural harbor on the coast but, south of town, the **Otter Crest Scenic Loop** (p. 196) and **Devil's Punchbowl State Natural Area** (p. 196).

Continuing south you'll come to **Newport** (p. 198), another of the coast's popular family-vacation destinations. The big attraction here is the **Oregon Coast Aquarium** (p. 199). On the **Newport Bayfront** (p. 200), you'll find fish-packing plants and souvenir shops. Here in Newport, you can also visit the **Yaquina Bay Lighthouse** (p. 199) and the **Yaquina Head Lighthouse** (p. 199).

Day ❻: Crater Lake National Park ✿✿✿

Today is your longest drive, so get an early start and spend some time at **Cape Perpetua Scenic Area** (p. 205), **Heceta Head Lighthouse State Scenic Viewpoint** (p. 208), and **Sea Lion Caves** (p. 208). Head inland at the historic river town of **Florence** (p. 209), perhaps after grabbing some lunch on the waterfront. Follow the beautiful blue waters of the North Umpqua River from Roseburg to **Crater Lake National Park** (p. 269). If you reach the national park early enough, drive the scenic road that circles the lake.

Day ❼: Ashland ✿✿

This morning, take a **boat tour** (p. 270) on Crater Lake, and then head down out of the mountains to the town of **Ashland** (p. 275), which is the home of the **Oregon Shakespeare Festival** (p. 276). It runs from February to October and is the state's premier performing arts festival. Ashland has loads of great shops and restaurants. The next day either drive back to Portland or fly out of Medford.

2 Oregon in 2 Weeks

Plan on spending 2 weeks in Oregon and you'll get a much better sense of this state's diverse landscapes. You'll also get to spend more time exploring the great outdoors and taking interesting tours.

Days ❶–❷: Portland ✿✿

Start your Oregon vacation in Portland, where parks and gardens are the main attractions. Downtown, stroll through **Tom McCall Waterfront Park** (p. 98) and visit the **Portland Classical Chinese Garden** (p. 99). In Washington Park, visit the **Japanese Garden** (p. 102) and the **International Rose Test Garden** (p. 101). If you're the outdoorsy type, go for a hike in **Forest Park** (p. 100) or paddle the Willamette River in a sea kayak. Alternatively, do a jet-boat tour with **Willamette Jetboat Excursions** (p. 105). Go shopping in the Pearl District or on Nob Hill, and check out the **Portland Art Museum** (p. 98). Spend some time in a brewpub, wine bar, or cafe.

Days ❸–❹: The Mount Hood Loop ✿✿✿

Spend the next 2 days circling snow-covered Mount Hood by way of the Columbia River Gorge. Drive the **Historic Columbia River Highway** (p. 236) and stop at **Multnomah Falls** (p. 236) and other waterfalls. Hike the **Eagle Creek Trail** (p. 237), and then relax on a river cruise aboard the sternwheeler *Columbia Gorge* (p. 238). As you loop around snow-capped Mount Hood, Oregon's tallest peak, stop at the historic **Timberline Lodge** (p. 259) for the night. Go for a hike, perhaps at **Cooper Spur** (p. 256), on the northeast side of Moun Hood.

Days ❺–❻: Bend ✿✿

From Mount Hood, head south into central Oregon's high desert and ponderosa-pine landscapes. This region gets more sunshine than the west side of the Cascades and consequently has several golf resorts. Near the town of Bend, you can explore the old lava fields, cinder cones, and a volcanic crater of **Newberry National Volcanic Monument** (p. 318); go **whitewater rafting** (p. 321); and hike beneath the jagged peaks of the **Three Sisters** (p. 312). In winter, go skiing and snowboarding at **Mount Bachelor** (p. 319).

Day ❼: Crater Lake National Park ✿✿✿

Continue south from the Bend area to **Crater Lake National Park** (p. 269), which preserves the deepest lake in the United States. Drive the scenic road around the lake and take a **boat tour** (p. 270). Do one or two short hikes to high points along the rim of the caldera that forms this gorgeous blue lake, and stay at **Crater Lake Lodge** (p. 270).

Days ❽–❾: Ashland & Jacksonville ✿✿

If you're a fan of Shakespeare, you'll want to spend a couple of days in the hip retirement town of Ashland, where the **Oregon Shakespeare Festival** (p. 276) stages the Bard's works from February to October. Plenty of other playwrights also get equal time. When you aren't at the theater, shop the great boutiques, do a little wine touring, and eat out at the best restaurants in southern Oregon. Drive over to the historic town of Jacksonville, which is also home to the **Britt Festivals** (p. 287), a summer-long series that brings in great musicians and dance troupes.

Days ⓫–⓬: The Southern Oregon Coast ✿✿✿

From Ashland, head to the southern Oregon coast (the highway will take you briefly into the redwood country of northern California). The most scenic stretch of the coast is between Brookings and Gold Beach. Most of this area is preserved as the **Samuel H. Boardman State Scenic Corridor** (p. 228), which has lots of overlooks and also includes many stretches of the **Oregon Coast Trail** (p. 228). In Gold Beach, take a **jet-boat tour** (p. 227) up the Rogue River. Spend a night in **Bandon** (p. 219), where the beach is littered with haystack rocks.

Day ⓬: The Central Coast ✿✿✿

North of Bandon, there is a trio of state parks—**Cape Arago, Sunset Bay,** and **Shore Acres** (p. 216)—that should not be missed. North of Coos Bay, you drive through the **Oregon Dunes National Recreation Area** (p. 210), where some sand dunes are 500 feet tall. There are lots of hiking trails through the Sahara-like landscape. Stop for lunch in the historic river town of **Florence** (p. 209). North of Florence, the mountains once again meet the sea. Stop at **Sea Lion Caves** (p. 208) and the picturesque **Heceta Head Lighthouse** (p. 208) before exploring the rugged shoreline of **Cape Perpetua Scenic Area** (p. 205). Stay in **Yachats** (p. 205).

Day ⓭: The Three Capes Loop ✿✿✿

From Yachats, drive north to Newport and visit the **Oregon Coast Aquarium** (p. 199). Then work your way through the traffic congestion and sprawl of Lincoln City to reach the little fishing town of Pacific City and the start of the Three Capes Scenic Loop. Climb the giant sand dune at **Cape Kiwanda State Park** (p. 186), then drive north to **Cape Lookout State Park** (p. 186), and, if you have time, hike out to the end of the cape. The last stop on this loop is **Cape Meares State Park** (p. 186).

Day ⓮: Astoria ✿✿

Continue north, stopping in **Manzanita** (p. 182) and artsy **Cannon Beach** (p. 175) to see two of my favorite Oregon-coast towns. Also be sure to take the short hike to the beach at **Oswald West State Park** (p. 176). Finish your tour in **Astoria** (p. 164), a working port town with lots of grand old Victorian homes. Just outside of town, you'll find **Lewis and Clark National Historical Park** (p. 166), which commemorates the explorers who spent the winter of 1805–06 here at the mouth of the Columbia River. The next day, head back to Portland.

3 Oregon for Families

While Oregon doesn't have a major amusement park to attract families, it does have lots of great child-oriented museums in Portland, and there are several other children's attraction in nearby Salem. Plus, the state does has loads of the great outdoors, including wild ocean beaches, a dormant volcano with snow-skiing all summer, and an extinct volcano that really blew its top.

Days ❶–❷: Portland 🎠🎠

Start your Oregon family vacation in Portland, where you and the kids have lots of options for fun activities. For example, you can spend a whole day in Washington Park. Here you'll find the **Oregon Zoo** (p. 102), the **World Forestry Center Discovery Museum** (p. 103), and the **Portland Children's Museum** (p. 104). The next day, head to the **Oregon Museum of Science and Industry** (p. 98), where you can watch an IMAX movie, see a planetarium show, and explore a submarine. Afterwards, you can head out on the Willamette River on a high-speed **jet-boat ride** (p. 105). If you've got young kids, don't miss a chance to eat at **Peanut Butter & Ellie's** (p. 89).

Days ❸–❺: The Northern Oregon Coast 🎠🎠

From Portland, head west to the coast. Although the waters on the Oregon coast are too cold for most adults, children don't seem to mind the chilly temperatures at all. However, you'll be better off buying some kites and spending your time on the beach rather than in the water. **Seaside** is the north coast's premier family beach town and is full of arcades, saltwater-taffy stores, and places where you can rent unusual cycles (beach trikes, four-wheel surreys, tandems). I recommend staying in Cannon Beach, a much prettier town, and day tripping to Seaside. In Cannon Beach, you can explore the tide pools at the base of Haystack Rock. There are also several nearby state parks. Alternatively, you can base yourself in **Lincoln City,** the coast's other main family beach town.

Day ❻: Salem 🎠

After you've built enough sand castles, head back inland to the state capital of Salem, which has a great waterfront park that's home to **Salem's Riverfront Carousel** (p. 144), the fun **A. C. Gilbert Discovery Village** (p. 144), and the *Willamette Queen* (p. 144) paddle wheeler. A few miles south of town, you'll find **Enchanted Forest** and **Thrill-Ville USA** (p. 144), two more great children's attractions.

Day ❼: Crater Lake National Park 🎠🎠🎠

Although it's a long drive from Salem to **Crater Lake National Park** (p. 269), you shouldn't miss the opportunity to visit this amazing natural attraction that was created when a large volcano blew its top. If your kids can hike a mile downhill (and back up), or if you don't mind carrying the little ones, be sure to take the boat ride around the lake.

Days ❽–❾: Bend & Sunriver 🎠🎠

Next, head north to central Oregon, which is the state's favorite sunshine destination. Here, near Bend and Sunriver, you'll find several family resorts that are geared toward keeping families entertained. There are big swimming pools, bikes, and lots of scheduled activities for kids of all ages. The short **white-water rafting trips** (p. 321) on the Deschutes River just outside Bend are always a big hit with kids. The other must-visit attraction in the area is the **High Desert Museum** (p. 317), which is as much a zoo as it is a museum. You can also stop at

Oregon for Families

Exploring the Oregon Coast

Newberry National Volcanic Monument (p. 318) and the **Lava Lands Visitor Center** (p. 318).

Day ⑩: Mount Hood ⚜⚜⚜
Finally, head up to Mount Hood and try to stay at the historic **Timberline Lodge** (p. 259), where you just might bump into the lodge's St. Bernard mascot. In the winter, this is a popular family ski area; in summer, you can do a little summer skiing or snowboarding at **Timberline Ski Area** (p. 257), or check out all the fun rides and activities at the **Mt. Hood Ski-Bowl Action Park** (p. 257) in Government Camp. The trail to Mirror Lake is an easy hike that's popular with families.

4 A Week in the Willamette Valley Wine Country

Here's an itinerary for serious oenophiles. If the sleeper hit movie *Sideways* got you curious about pinot noir, then you definitely need to spend a week in wine country. Because there are so many wineries in Oregon's Willamette Valley, and because there are only so many wineries you can visit in a day, a week of tasting can easily lead to your having a fabulous cellar full of Oregon wines.

Day ❶: Portland

Start your wine tour in Portland. Here you should spend some time at **Oregon Wines on Broadway** (p. 113), a combination wine bar and wine shop specializing in Oregon wines. On any given day, you can sample 30 different Oregon pinot noirs and get an idea of which wineries you might want to visit. If you plan your trip just right, you can also attend a wine-blending class at **Urban Wineworks** (p. 118).

Day ❷: Dundee & the Red Hills

From Portland, it is less than 45 minutes to the start of wine country. **August Cellars** (p. 126) and **Rex Hill Vineyards** (p. 128), just east of Newberg, are the first wineries you'll come to. A few miles farther on Ore. 99W, you'll come to Dundee, which is the heart of the wine country. The Red Hills north of town are covered with vineyards and there are numerous wineries within a few miles of town. **Lange Estate Winery and Vineyards** (p. 127) and **Torii Mor** (p. 128) are a couple of my favorite area wineries. Have dinner at one of Dundee's great restaurants.

Day ❸: West of Dundee

Today, explore the hills west of Dundee, where you'll find some of the most highly regarded pinot noir producers in the state. **Archery Summit** (p. 126), **Domaine Drouhin Oregon** (p. 126), and **Domaine Serene** (p. 127) should not be missed. Also in this area, you'll find **Sokol Blosser Winery** (p. 128). Don't pass up the opportunity to stop at some of the area's fruit stands. In the morning, you might want to visit the historic town of Aurora (p. 134) and do a little antiques shopping.

Days ❹–❺: Carlton 𝒜𝒜

The little town of Carlton is home to some of Oregon's best wineries and deserves a couple of days of wine tasting. You won't want to miss the **Carlton Winemakers Studio** (p. 129), **Cuneo Cellars** (p. 129), **Penner-Ash Wine Cellars** (p. 129), **Soléna** (p. 129), **Tyrus Evan** (p. 129), and **Willakenzie Estate** (p. 130). One morning, visit the **Evergreen Aviation Museum** (p. 133), which is home to Howard Hughes's "Spruce Goose." Plan to have dinner at **Cuvée** (p. 139), Carlton's delightful little French restaurant; the next night, head to McMinnville for dinner.

Days ❻–❼: The Eola Hills & the West Valley 𝒜𝒜

South of McMinnville lie the Eola Hills and lots of good wineries. Be sure to visit **Amity Vineyards** (p. 131), one of the state's oldest wineries. Other wineries worth searching out include **Bethel Heights Vineyards** (p. 132), **Kristin Hill Winery** (p. 132), **Cristom Vineyards** (p. 132), **Mystic** (p. 132), **Stangeland Vineyards** (p. 132), **Witness Tree Vineyard** (p. 133), and **Yamhill Valley Vineyards** (p. 128). One morning, visit the interesting little **Jensen Arctic Museum** (p. 146) or drive in to Salem to the **Hallie Ford Museum of Art** (p. 142). The next morning, start out at the **Lawrence and Fire's Eye galleries** (p. 134), which are next door to the Oregon Wine Tasting Room. If you like chocolate, be sure to visit the **Brigittine Monastery** (p. 134) to buy some fudge.

5 Exploring the Oregon Coast

While inland Oregon has loads to offer visitors, it is the coast that is the state's crown jewel. To be sure, Oregon's beaches are not the lounge-chair and margarita beaches of Mexico and the Caribbean, but this coast is one of the most dramatic shorelines in America. Hiking, kite flying, and exploring tide pools are the top recreational activities on the Oregon coast, so come prepared for an active vacation.

Day ❶: Astoria 🎭🎭

Start your Oregon coast vacation by flying into Portland and driving down the Columbia River to Astoria. You will be following the route of explorers Lewis and Clark, who spent the winter of 1805–06 near present-day Astoria. Visit the **Lewis and Clark National Historical Park** (p. 166), then head to **Fort Stevens State Park** (p. 166) at the mouth of the Columbia River. Also be sure to visit the **Columbia River Maritime Museum** (p. 166).

Day ❷: Cannon Beach 🎭🎭

Head south down the coast to the arts community of **Cannon Beach** (p. 175), which lies on the south side of Tillamook Head. Check out all the galleries, and marvel at the massive **Haystack Rock,** which rises up from the beach in the middle of town. Just north of Cannon Beach, you can hike the trails of **Ecola State Park** (p. 176). To escape the crowds, head south of town to **Arcadia** or **Hug Point wayside** (p. 176) or the larger **Oswald West State Park** (p. 176).

Day ❸: The Three Capes Scenic Loop 🎭🎭🎭

Drive around Tillamook Bay to the **Three Capes Scenic Loop.** The first cape you'll come to on this drive is **Cape Meares State Scenic Viewpoint** (p. 185), which is a good place from which to spot gray whales. Further south is **Cape Lookout State Park** (p. 186), where there is a trail through the forest to the end of the cape. The southernmost of the three capes is **Cape Kiwanda State Natural Area** (p. 186), where a giant sand dune rises up from the beach and a rocky island stands just offshore. Here at Cape Kiwanda you'll find a great hotel and brewpub.

Days ❹–❺: Newport & Yachats 🎭🎭🎭

Continue south through the sprawl and congestion of Lincoln City to Newport. En route, be sure to drive the **Otter Crest Scenic Loop** (p. 196), just north of Depoe Bay, and stop to marvel at the **Devil's Punchbowl** (p. 196). Newport's main attraction is the not-to-be-missed **Oregon Coast Aquarium** (p. 199). Outside of town, you can also visit the **Yaquina Bay Lighthouse** (p. 199) and the **Yaquina Head Lighthouse** (p. 199). South of Newport 24 miles is Yachats, one of the prettiest stretches of the central coast. Hike the rocky shoreline here, and visit **Cape Perpetua Scenic Area** (p. 205), **Heceta Head Lighthouse** (p. 208), and **Sea Lion Caves** (p. 208).

Days ❻–❼: Oregon Dunes National Recreation Area to Bandon 🎭🎭🎭

South of Cape Perpetua, you leave the mountains behind and drive through 50 miles of forests, lakes, and giant sand dunes that have been preserved as the **Oregon Dunes National Recreation Area** (p. 210). In the middle of dune country, stop for lunch in historic **Florence** (p. 209), then continue on to visit **Sunset Bay, Shore Acres,** and **Cape Arago state parks** (p. 216) outside Coos Bay. Finish the day amid the dramatic boulders and haystack rocks that litter the beach at **Bandon** (p. 219).

Days ❽–❾: The Southern Oregon Coast 🎭🎭🎭

This is the remotest and least developed section of the coast, and it has numerous state parks and waysides. Wander the headlands at **Cape Blanco** (p. 225) and **Cape Sebastian** (p. 228). Explore the beach and Battle Rock in **Port Orford** (p. 225). In Gold Beach, take a **jet-boat tour** (p. 227) up the wild Rogue River. South of Gold Beach, stop to marvel at the monoliths at **Pistol River State Scenic Viewpoint** (p. 228) and hike segments of the Oregon Coast Trail within the **Samuel H. Boardman State Scenic Corridor** (p. 228). From Brookings, drive back north and then west to reach I-5, which is the fastest route back to Portland.

5

Portland

Situated at the confluence of the Willamette and Columbia rivers, Portland, Oregon, with a metropolitan population of roughly two million, is a city of discreet charms. That it claims a rose garden as one of its biggest attractions should give you an idea of just how laid-back this city is. Sure, Portlanders are just as attached to their cellphones and PDAs as residents of other urban areas, but this is the City of Roses, and people still take time to stop and smell the flowers. Spend much time here, and you, too, will likely feel the leisurely pace seeping into your bones.

While nearby Seattle, Washington, has zoomed into the national consciousness, Portland has, until recently, managed to dodge the limelight and the problems that come with skyrocketing popularity. For many years now Portland has looked upon itself as a small, accessible city, vaguely European in character. *Clean* and *friendly* are the two most common descriptors of the city. However, as word has spread about overcrowding in Seattle, people looking for the good life and affordable housing have turned to Portland, which is now experiencing the same sort of rapid growth that Seattle began going through more than a decade ago.

Portland does not have any major tourist sights. Instead, it is a city of quiet charms that must be searched for and savored—the shade of the stately elms in the South Park Blocks, the tranquillity of the Japanese Garden, the view from the grounds of Pittock Mansion, the miles of hiking trails in Forest Park. Sure, there's a good art museum and a world-class science museum, but these are not nearly as important to the locals as the many parks and public gardens. Not only does Portland claim beautiful rose gardens, the most authentic Japanese Garden in North America, and the largest classical Chinese garden in the country, but it also has both the world's smallest city park and the largest forested urban park in the country.

The city is also the nation's microbrew capital. Espresso may be the beverage that gets this town going in the morning, but it is microbrewed beer that helps the city maintain its mellow character. There are so many brewpubs here in Portland that the city has been nicknamed Munich on the Willamette. Wine bars are also popular hangouts, which shouldn't come as a surprise, considering how close the city is to the Willamette Valley wine country.

Portland itself may be short on things for visitors to do, but the city's surroundings certainly are not. Within a 1½- to 2-hour drive from Portland, you can be strolling a Pacific Ocean beach, walking beside a waterfall in the Columbia Gorge, hiking on Mount Hood (a dormant volcano as picture perfect as Mt. Fuji), driving through the Mount St. Helens blast zone, or sampling world-class pinot noirs in the Oregon wine country. It is this proximity to the outdoors that makes Portland a great city to use as a base for exploring some of the best of the Northwest.

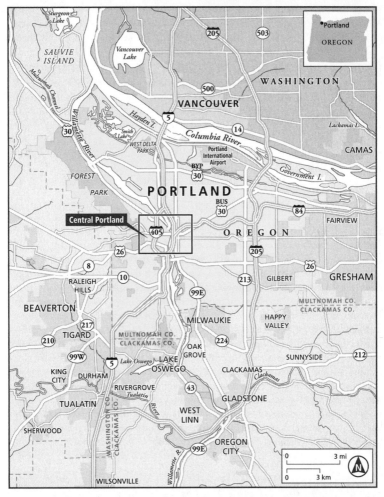

1 Orientation

ARRIVING

BY PLANE

Portland International Airport (PDX) (☎ **877/739-4636** or 503/460-4234; www.portlandairportpdx.com) is located 10 miles northeast of downtown Portland, adjacent to the Columbia River. There's an information booth by the baggage-claim area where you can pick up maps and brochures and find out about transportation into the city. Many hotels near the airport provide courtesy shuttle service to and from the airport; be sure to ask when you make a reservation.

GETTING INTO THE CITY BY CAR If you've rented a car at the airport and want to reach central Portland, follow signs for downtown. These signs will point you first to I-205 and then I-84 west, which brings you to the Willamette River. Take the Morrison Bridge exit to cross the river. The trip takes about 20 minutes and is entirely on interstates. For more information on renting a car, see section 2 of this chapter, "Getting Around," below.

GETTING INTO THE CITY BY TAXI, SHUTTLE, BUS, OR LIGHT RAIL If you haven't rented a car at the airport, the best way to get into town is to take the **Airport MAX (Red Line)** light-rail system. This light-rail line operates daily roughly every 15 minutes between 5am and midnight and the trip from the airport to Pioneer Courthouse Square in downtown Portland takes approximately 35 minutes. (All but one or two of the downtown hotels lie within 4 or 5 blocks of the square; plan on walking since taxis in Portland don't generally cruise for fares. Folks arriving with a lot of luggage will be better off taking a cab or shuttle van from the airport.) The fare is between $1.65 and $1.95. For information on this service, contact **TriMet** (© **503/238-7433;** www.trimet.org).

A taxi to downtown generally costs between $30 and $35.

BY TRAIN/BUS

Amtrak trains stop at the historic **Union Station,** 800 NW Sixth Ave. (© **800/872-7245** or 503/273-4860; www.amtrak.com), about 10 blocks from the heart of downtown Portland. Taxis are usually waiting to meet trains and can take you to your hotel. Alternatively, you might be able to get your hotel to send a van to pick you up, or, if you are renting a car from a downtown car-rental office, the agency will usually pick you up at the station. Public buses stop in the block south of the station (toward downtown) and are free within the downtown area.

The **Greyhound Bus Lines** station is at 550 NW Sixth Ave. (© **800/231-2222** or 503/243-2310; www.greyhound.com) on the north side of downtown near Union Station. As with getting into downtown from the train station, there is no charge to ride any public city bus if you catch it outside the Greyhound terminal, which is within Portland's Fareless Square area (see below).

Although you could easily walk from the station into the heart of downtown, you have to pass through a somewhat rough neighborhood for a few blocks. This area is currently undergoing a renaissance and is not nearly as bad as it once was.

VISITOR INFORMATION

The **Portland Oregon Visitors Association (POVA) Information Center,** 701 SW Sixth Ave. (© **877/678-5263** or 503/275-8355; www.travelportland.com), is in Pioneer Courthouse Square in downtown Portland. There's also an information booth by the baggage-claim area at the Portland Airport.

CITY LAYOUT

Portland is in northwestern Oregon at the confluence of the Columbia and Willamette rivers. To the west are the West Hills, which rise to more than 1,000 feet. Some 90 miles west of the West Hills are the spectacular Oregon coast and the Pacific Ocean. To the east are rolling hills that extend to the Cascade Range, about 50 miles away. The most prominent peak in this section of the Cascades is Mount Hood (11,235 ft.), a dormant volcanic peak that looms over the city on clear days. From many parts of Portland it's also possible to see Mount St. Helens, a volcano that erupted violently in 1980.

With about two million people in the entire metropolitan area, Portland remains a relatively small city. This is especially evident when you begin to explore the compact downtown area. Nearly everything is accessible on foot, and the city authorities do everything they can to encourage walking.

MAIN ARTERIES & STREETS   I-84 (**Banfield Fwy. or Expwy.**) enters Portland from the east. East of the city is **I-205,** which bypasses downtown Portland and runs past the airport. **I-5** runs through on a north-south axis, passing along the east bank of the Willamette River directly across from downtown. **I-405** circles around the west and south sides of downtown. **U.S. 26 (Sunset Hwy.)** leaves downtown heading west toward Beaverton and the coast. **Oregon Highway 217** runs south from U.S. 26 in Beaverton.

The most important artery within Portland is **Burnside Street.** This is the dividing line between north and south Portland. Dividing the city from east to west is the **Willamette River,** which is crossed by eight bridges in the downtown area. From north to south these bridges are the Fremont, Broadway, Steel, Burnside, Morrison, Hawthorne, Marquam, and Ross Island. Additional bridges beyond the downtown area include the Sellwood Bridge, located between downtown and Lake Oswego, and the St. John's Bridge, which connects Northwest Portland with north Portland.

For the sake of convenience, we have defined downtown Portland as the 300-block area within the **Fareless Square.** This is the area (shaded in on the map on p. 73) in which you can ride for free on the city's public buses, the MAX light-rail system, and the Portland Streetcar. In downtown, the Fareless Square is bounded by I-405 on the west and south, by Irving Street on the north, and by the Willamette River on the east. A Fareless Square extension also allows transit riders to travel free between downtown Portland and both the Oregon Convention Center and Lloyd Center Mall. There is no charge to ride either the MAX light-rail trolleys or any of the buses that connect downtown with the Rose Quarter and Lloyd District across the Willamette River in northeast Portland.

FINDING AN ADDRESS   Finding an address in Portland can be easy. Almost all addresses in Portland, and for miles beyond, include a map quadrant—NE (northeast), SW (southwest), and so forth. The dividing line between east and west is the Willamette River; between north and south it's Burnside Street. Any downtown address will be labeled either SW (southwest) or NW (northwest). An exception to this rule is the area known as North Portland, which is the area across the Willamette River from downtown going toward Jantzen Beach. Streets here have a plain "North" designation. Also, Burnside Street is designated either "East" or "West."

Avenues run north–south and streets run east–west. Street names are the same on both sides of the Willamette River. Consequently, there is a SW Yamhill Street and a SE Yamhill Street. In Northwest Portland, street names are alphabetical going north from Burnside to Wilson. Naito Parkway is the street nearest the Willamette River on the west side, and Water Avenue is the nearest on the east side. Beyond these are numbered avenues. On the west side you'll also find Broadway and Park Avenue between Sixth Avenue and Ninth Avenue. With each block, the addresses increase by 100, beginning at the Willamette River for avenues and at Burnside Street for streets. Odd numbers are generally on the west and north sides of the street, and even numbers on the east and south sides.

Here's an example: You want to go to 1327 SW Ninth Ave. Because it's in the 1300 block, you'll find it 13 blocks south of Burnside and, because it's an odd number, on the west side of the street.

Fun Fact **Did You Know?**

- The flasher in the famous "Expose Yourself to Art" poster is none other than Bud Clark, the former mayor of Portland.
- Portland is the only city in the United States with an extinct volcano within the city limits (Mount Tabor).
- Matt Groening, creator of *The Simpsons,* got his start in Portland.
- More Asian elephants have been born in Portland (at the Oregon Zoo) than in any other city in North America.
- Twenty downtown water fountains were a gift to the city from teetotaling early-20th-century timber baron Simon Benson, who wanted his mill workers to have something other than alcohol to drink during the day.

STREET MAPS   Stop by the **Portland Oregon Visitors Association Information Center,** 701 SW Sixth Ave., Suite 1 (*©* **877/678-5263** or 503/275-9750; www.travel portland.com), in Pioneer Courthouse Square in downtown Portland for a free map of the city.

Powell's City of Books, 1005 W. Burnside St. (*©* **866/201-7601** or 503/228-4651), has an excellent free map of downtown that includes a walking-tour route and information on many of the sights you'll pass along the way.

Members of the **American Automobile Association (AAA)** can get a free map of the city at the AAA offices at 600 SW Market St. (*©* **503/222-6734;** www. aaaorid.com).

PORTLAND NEIGHBORHOODS IN BRIEF

Portland's neighborhoods are mostly dictated by geography. The Willamette River forms a natural dividing line between the eastern and western portions of the city, while the Columbia River forms a boundary with the state of Washington on the north. The West Hills, comprising Portland's prime residential neighborhoods, are a beautiful backdrop for this attractive city. Covered in evergreens, the hills rise to a height of 1,000 feet at the edge of downtown. Within these hills are the Oregon Zoo, the International Rose Test Garden, the Japanese Garden, and several other attractions.

For a map of Portland neighborhoods, turn to the "Portland Attractions" map on p. 95.

DOWNTOWN This term usually refers to the business and shopping district south of Burnside and north of Jackson Street between the Willamette River and 13th Avenue. Here you'll find a dozen or more high-end hotels, dozens of restaurants of all types, and loads of shopping (including the major department stores). Within downtown's **Cultural District** (along Broadway and the South Park blocks), are most of the city's performing arts venues and a couple of museums.

SKIDMORE HISTORIC DISTRICT Also known as Old Town, this is Portland's original commercial core and centers around SW Ankeny Street and SW First Avenue. Many of the restored buildings have become retail stores, but despite the presence of the **Saturday Market,** the neighborhood has never become a popular shopping district, mostly because of its welfare hotels, missions, street people, and drug dealing. However, with its many clubs and bars, it is the city's main nightlife district. The neighborhood is safe during the day, but visitors should exercise caution at night.

CHINATOWN Portland has had a Chinatown almost since its earliest days. This small area, with its numerous Chinese groceries and restaurants, is wedged between the Pearl District and the Skidmore Historic District and is entered through the colorful Chinatown Gate at West Burnside Street and Fourth Avenue. The neighborhood's main attraction is the impressive **Portland Classical Chinese Garden.** Because of its proximity to bars on West Burnside Street and the homeless missions and welfare hotels in Old Town, this is not a good neighborhood to explore late at night.

THE PEARL DISTRICT This neighborhood of galleries, residential and business lofts, cafes, breweries, and shops is bounded by the North Park blocks, Northrup Street, I-405, and Burnside Street. Crowds of people come here on **First Thursday** (the first Thurs of every month) when the galleries and other businesses are open late. This is Portland's hip urban loft scene and one of the city's main upscale-restaurant neighborhoods.

NORTHWEST/NOB HILL Located along NW 23rd and NW 21st avenues, this is one of Portland's two most fashionable neighborhoods. Here you'll find many of the city's best restaurants (mostly along NW 21st Ave.), as well as lots of cafes, boutiques, and national chain stores. Surrounding

the two main business streets of the neighborhood are blocks of restored Victorian homes on shady tree-lined streets. This is where you'll find the city's liveliest street scene.

IRVINGTON Though neither as attractive nor as large as the Northwest/Nob Hill neighborhood, Irvington, centered around Broadway in northeast Portland, is almost as hip. For several blocks along Broadway (around NE 15th Ave.) you'll find interesting boutiques and numerous good, inexpensive restaurants.

HAWTHORNE/BELMONT DISTRICT This enclave of southeast Portland is full of eclectic boutiques, moderately priced restaurants, and hip college students from nearby **Reed College.** Just south of Hawthorne Boulevard, beginning at SE 12th Avenue, you'll find the interesting **Ladd's Addition** neighborhood, which has five rose gardens and a great pastry shop. Belmont Street, just north of Hawthorne Boulevard, and Division Street, to the south, are two of the city's up-and-coming hip neighborhoods.

SELLWOOD/WESTMORELAND Situated in southeast Portland, this is the city's antiques district and contains many restored Victorian houses. Just north of the Sellwood antiques district, surrounding the intersection of SE Milwaukie Avenue and SE Bybee Boulevard, you'll find the heart of the Eastmoreland neighborhood, home to numerous good restaurants.

2 Getting Around

BY PUBLIC TRANSPORTATION

FREE RIDES   Portland is committed to keeping its downtown uncongested, and to this end has invested heavily in its public transportation system. The single greatest innovation—as well as the best reason to ride the TriMet public buses, the MAX light-rail system, and the Portland Streetcar—is that they're free within an area known as the **Fareless Square.** That's right, free!

There are 300 blocks of downtown included in the Fareless Square, and as long as you stay within the boundaries, you don't pay a cent. The Fareless Square covers the area between I-405 on the south and west, Hoyt Street on the north, and the Willamette River on the east. The Fareless Square extension also makes it possible to take public transit (either the bus or the MAX light-rail trolley) between downtown Portland and both the Rose Quarter (site of the Oregon Convention Center) and the Lloyd District (site of the Lloyd Center Mall), which are both across the Willamette River in northeast Portland.

BY BUS   TriMet buses operate daily over an extensive network. You can pick up the *TriMet Guide,* which lists all the bus routes with times, or individual route maps and time schedules, at the **TriMet Customer Assistance Office,** behind and beneath the waterfall fountain at Pioneer Courthouse Square (© **503/238-7433;** www.trimet.org). The office is open Monday through Friday from 8:30am to 5:30pm. Bus and MAX passes and transit information are also available at area Fred Meyer, Safeway, and most Albertson grocery stores. Nearly all TriMet buses pass through the Transit Mall on SW Fifth Avenue and SW Sixth Avenue.

Outside the Fareless Square, adult fares on TriMet buses, MAX light-rail trains, and Portland Streetcars are $1.65 or $1.95, depending on how far you travel. Seniors 65 years and older pay 80¢ with valid proof of age; children 7 through 17 pay $1.30. You can also make free transfers between the bus and both the MAX light-rail system and the Portland Streetcar. All-day tickets costing $4 are good for travel to all zones and are valid on buses, MAX, and streetcars. These tickets can be purchased from any bus driver or at MAX stops.

BY LIGHT RAIL   The **Metropolitan Area Express (MAX)** is Portland's above-ground light-rail system that connects downtown Portland with the airport, the eastern suburb of Gresham, the western suburbs of Beaverton and Hillsboro, and North Portland. MAX is basically a modern trolley, but there are also replicas of vintage trolley cars (© **503/323-7363**). Between March and December these operate between downtown Portland and the Lloyd Center on Sundays; year round, they operate along the Portland Streetcar line on Saturdays and Sundays. One of the most convenient places to catch the MAX is at Pioneer Courthouse Square. The MAX light-rail system crosses the Transit Mall on SW Morrison Street and SW Yamhill Street. Transfers to the bus are free.

As with the bus, MAX is free within the Fareless Square, which includes all the downtown area. A Fareless Square extension also makes it possible to ride the MAX between downtown Portland and both the Rose Quarter (site of the Oregon Convention Center) and the Lloyd District (site of the Lloyd Center Mall). Both are across the Willamette River in northeast Portland. If you are traveling outside of the Fareless Square, be sure to buy your ticket and stamp it in the time-punch machine on the platform before you board MAX. There are ticket-vending machines at all MAX stops that tell you how much to pay for your destination; these machines also give change. The MAX driver cannot sell tickets. Fares are the same as on buses. There are ticket inspectors who randomly check to make sure passengers have stamped tickets.

The **Portland Streetcar** (© **503/238-RIDE;** www.portlandstreetcar.org) operates between RiverPlace, on the waterfront at the south end of downtown, through the Pearl District to the Nob Hill neighborhood. The route takes in not only the attractions of the Cultural District but also all the restaurants and great shopping in the Pearl District and along NW 21st and 23rd avenues, which makes this streetcar a great way for visitors to get from downtown (where most of the hotels are located) to the neighborhoods with the greatest concentrations of restaurants. On Saturdays and Sundays, vintage streetcars operate free of charge (donations are encouraged). Streetcar fares for trips outside the Fareless Square are $1.50 for adults, $1.20 for youths, and 70¢ for seniors.

BY CAR

CAR RENTALS   Portland is a compact city, and public transit will get you to most attractions within its limits. However, if you are planning to explore outside the city—and Portland's greatest attractions, such as Mount Hood and the Columbia River Gorge, lie not in the city itself but in the countryside within an hour of the city—you'll definitely need a car.

The major car-rental companies are all represented in Portland and have desks at Portland International Airport, which is the most convenient place to pick up a car. There are also many independent and small car-rental agencies listed in the Portland Yellow Pages. Currently, weekly rates for an economy car in July (high-season rates) are around $150 with no discounts. Expect lower rates in the rainy months.

On the ground floor of the airport parking deck, across the street from the baggage-claim area, you'll find the following companies: **Avis** (© 800/831-2847 or 503/249-4950; www.avis.com), **Budget** (© 800/527-0700 or 503/249-4556; www.budget.com), **Dollar** (© 800/800-3365 or 503/249-4793; www.dollar.com), **Enterprise** (© 800/261-7331 or 503/692-8400; www.enterprise.com); and **Hertz** (© 800/654-3131 or 503/249-8216; www.hertz.com). Outside the airport, but with desks adjacent to the other car-rental desks, are **Alamo** (© 800/327-9633 or 503/249-4901; www.goalamo.com), **National** (© 800/227-7368 or 503/249-4900; www.nationalcar.com), and **Thrifty** (© 800/847-4389 or 503/254-6563; www.thrifty.com).

PARKING   Throughout most of downtown Portland and the Pearl District, you won't find any parking meters on the streets. However, in the middle of every block, you will find an electronic parking meter that takes coins, credit cards, and debit cards. These machines issue little parking receipts that you then have to tape in the curbside window of your car. Although a bit inconvenient, this system allows you to buy time while parked in one space and still use your remaining time if you move your car to another space. In most parts of town, you don't have to feed the meters after 7pm or on Sunday.

The best parking deal in town is at the **Smart Park** garages, where the cost is 95¢ per hour for the first 4 hours (but after that the hourly rate jumps to $3, so you'd be well advised to move your car), $2 for the entire evening after 6pm, or $5 to $6 all day on the weekends. Look for the red, white, and black signs featuring Les Park, the friendly parking attendant. You'll find Smart Park garages at First Avenue and Jefferson Street, Fourth Avenue and Yamhill Street, 10th Avenue and Yamhill Street, Third Avenue and Alder Street, O'Bryant Square, and Naito Parkway and Davis Street. More than 200 downtown merchants also validate Smart Park tickets for 2 hours if you spend at least $25, so don't forget to take your ticket along with you.

SPECIAL DRIVING RULES   You may turn right on a red light after a full stop, and if you are in the far left lane of a one-way street, you may turn left into the adjacent left lane of a one-way street at a red light after a full stop. Everyone in a moving vehicle is required to wear a seat belt.

BY TAXI

Because most everything in Portland is fairly close, getting around by taxi can be economical. Although there are almost always taxis waiting in line at major hotels, you won't find them cruising the streets—you'll have to phone for one. **Broadway Cab** (✆ **503/227-1234**) and **Radio Cab** (✆ **503/227-1212**) charge $2.50 for the first mile, $2 for each additional mile, and $1 for additional passengers.

ON FOOT

City blocks in Portland are about half the size of most city blocks elsewhere, and the entire downtown area covers only about 13 blocks by 26 blocks. This makes Portland a very easy place to explore on foot. The city has been very active in encouraging people to get out of their cars and onto the sidewalks downtown. The sidewalks are wide and there are many fountains, works of art, and small parks with benches.

FAST FACTS: Portland

AAA The **American Automobile Association** (✆ 800/222-4357; www.aaaorid. com) has a Portland office at 600 SW Market St. (✆ 503/222-6734), which offers free city maps to members.

Airport See "Getting There," in chapter 2 and "Arriving," in section 1 of this chapter.

American Express **Azumano Travel,** 400 SW Stark St. (✆ 800/777-2018 or 503/294-2000), is an **American Express Travel Services Representative.** For card member services, phone ✆ 800/528-4800. Call ✆ 800/AXP-TRIP or go to www.americanexpress.com for other locations or general information.

Area Codes The Portland metro area has two area codes—503 and 971—and it is necessary to dial all 10 digits of a telephone number, even when making local calls.

Babysitters If your hotel doesn't offer babysitting services, call **Northwest Nannies** (✆ 503/245-5288).

Car Rentals See section 2, "Getting Around," earlier in this chapter.

Climate See section 4, "When to Go," in chapter 2.

Dentist Contact the **Multnomah Dental Society** (✆ 503/513-5010) for a referral.

Doctor If you need a physician referral while in Portland, contact the **Medical Society of Metropolitan Portland** (✆ 503/222-0156).

Emergencies For police, fire, or medical emergencies, phone ✆ 911.

Eyeglass Repair Check out **Binyon's Master Eye Associates,** 803 SW Morrison St. (✆ 503/226-6688).

Hospitals Three conveniently located area hospitals are **Legacy Good Samaritan,** 1015 NW 22nd Ave. (✆ 503/413-7711); **Providence Portland Medical Center,** 4805 NE Glisan St. (✆ 503/215-1111); and the **Oregon Health & Sciences University Hospital,** 3181 SW Sam Jackson Park Rd. (✆ 503/494-8311), which is just southwest of the city center and has a drop-in clinic.

Information See "Visitor Information," in section 1 of this chapter.

Internet Access If you need to check e-mail while you're in Portland, first check with your hotel, or, if you have your own laptop with a wireless card, find a cafe with Wi-Fi access. Otherwise, visit a **FedEx Kinko's.** There's one downtown at 221 SW Alder St. (① **503/224-6550**) and northwest at 950 NW 23rd Ave. (① **503/222-4133**). You can also try the **Multnomah County Library,** 801 SW 10th Ave. (① **503/988-5123**), which is Portland's main library and offers online services.

Liquor Laws The legal minimum drinking age in Oregon is 21. Aside from on-premise sales of cocktails in bars and restaurants, hard liquor can only be purchased in liquor stores. Beer and wine are available in convenience stores and grocery stores. Brewpubs tend to sell only beer and wine, but some also have licenses to sell hard liquor.

Maps See "City Layout," in section 1 of this chapter.

Newspapers/Magazines Portland's morning daily newspaper is *The Oregonian.* For arts and entertainment information and listings, consult the "A&E" section of the Friday *Oregonian* or pick up a free copy of *Willamette Week* at Powell's Books and other bookstores, convenience stores, or cafes.

Pharmacies Convenient to most downtown hotels, **Central Drug,** 538 SW Fourth Ave. (① **503/226-2222**), is open Monday through Friday from 9am to 6pm, Saturday from 10am to 4pm.

Photographic Needs **Wolf Camera,** 220 SW Main St. (① **503/224-2365**), offers 1-hour film processing. **Camera World,** 400 SW Sixth Ave. (① **503/241-7979**), is the largest camera and video store in the city.

Police To reach the police, call ① **911.**

Post Offices The most convenient downtown post office is University Station, 1505 SW Sixth Ave. (① **503/274-1362**), open Monday through Friday from 7am to 6pm, Saturday from 10am to 3pm. For more information, call ① **800/275-8777.**

Restrooms There are public restrooms underneath Starbucks coffee shop in Pioneer Courthouse Square, in downtown shopping malls, and in hotel lobbies.

Safety Because of its relatively small size and progressive emphasis on keeping the downtown alive and growing, Portland is still a relatively safe city. Take extra precautions, however, if you venture into the entertainment district along West Burnside Street and in Chinatown at night. If you plan to go hiking in Forest Park, don't leave anything valuable in your car. This holds true in the Skidmore Historic District (Old Town) as well.

Smoking Although many of the restaurants listed in this book are smoke-free, many Portland restaurants allow smoking. At most high-end restaurants, the smoking area is usually in the bar/lounge, and although many restaurants have separate bar menus, most will serve you off the regular menu even if you are eating in the bar. There are a few nonsmoking bars in Portland.

Taxes Portland is a shopper's paradise—there's no sales tax. However, there is a 12.5% tax on hotel rooms within the city and a 12.5% tax on car rentals (plus an additional airport-use fee if you pick up your rental car at the airport; this additional fee is anywhere from around 10% to around 16%). Outside the city, the room tax varies.

Taxis See section 2, "Getting Around," earlier in this chapter.

Time Zone Portland is on Pacific time, 3 hours behind the East Coast. In the summer, daylight saving time is observed and clocks are set forward 1 hour.

Transit Info For bus, MAX, and Portland Streetcar information, call the **TriMet Customer Assistance Office** (© **503/238-7433**).

Weather If it's summer, it's sunny; otherwise, there's a chance of rain. This almost always suffices, but for specifics, call the Portland Oregon Visitor Association's **weather information hot line** (© **503/275-9792**). If you want to know how to pack before you arrive, check **www.cnn.com/weather** or **www.weather.com**.

3 Where to Stay

Whether you're looking for a downtown corporate high-rise, a restored historic hotel, a hip boutique hotel, a romantic B&B, or just something relatively inexpensive, you'll find it in Portland. You even have a couple of good choices for riverfront hotels.

If your budget won't allow for a first-class downtown business hotel, try near the airport or elsewhere on the outskirts of the city (Troutdale and Gresham on the east side; Beaverton and Hillsboro on the west; Wilsonville and Lake Oswego in the south; and Vancouver, Washington, in the north), where you're more likely to find inexpensive to moderately priced motels.

You'll find the greatest concentration of bed-and-breakfasts in the Irvington neighborhood of northeast Portland. This area is close to downtown and is generally quite convenient even if you are here on business.

In the following listings, price categories are based on the rate for a double room in high season. (Most hotels charge the same for a single or double room.) Keep in mind that the rates listed do not include local room taxes, which vary between 7% and 11.5%.

For comparison purposes, we list what hotels call "rack rates," or walk-in rates—but you should never have to pay these highly inflated prices. Various discounts (AAA, senior, corporate, and Entertainment Book) often reduce these rates, so be sure to ask (and check each hotel's website for Internet specials). In fact, you can often get a discounted corporate rate simply by flashing a business card (your own, that is). At inexpensive chain motels, there are almost always discounted rates for AAA members and seniors.

You'll also find that room rates are almost always considerably lower October through April (the rainy season), and large downtown hotels often offer weekend discounts of up to 50% throughout the year. Some of the large, upscale hotel chains have now gone to an airline-type rate system based on occupancy, so if you call early enough, before a hotel books up, you might get a really good rate. On the other hand, call at the last minute and you might catch a cancellation and still be offered a low rate. However, it's always advisable to make reservations as far in advance as possible if you're planning to visit during the busy summer months. Also be sure to ask about special packages (romance, golf, or theater), which most of the more expensive hotels usually offer.

Most hotels offer nonsmoking rooms, and most bed-and-breakfasts are exclusively nonsmoking. The majority of hotels also offer wheelchair-accessible rooms.

Where to Stay in Portland

Avalon Hotel & Spa **13**
The Benson **6**
Embassy Suites **10**
Four Points by Sheraton Portland Downtown **11**
Governor Hotel **5**
The Heathman Hotel **9**
Heron Haus **2**
Hotel Lucia **7**
Hotel Vintage Plaza **8**
Jupiter Hotel **14**
Inn @ Northrup Station **3**
The Lion and the Rose **15**
Mallory Hotel **4**
Portland's White House **16**
RiverPlace Hotel **12**
Silver Cloud Inn Portland Downtown **1**

Information
Post Office
Fareless Square

HELPING HANDS

If you're having trouble booking a room, try the **Portland Oregon Visitors Associa-tion (POVA),** 701 SW Sixth Ave., Portland, OR 97205 (© **877/678-5263** or 503/275-8355; www.travelportland.com), which offers a reservation service for the Portland metro area.

For information on **bed-and-breakfasts** in the Portland area, call the POVA or contact the **Oregon Bed and Breakfast Guild,** P.O. Box 3187, Ashland, OR 97520 (© **800/944-6196;** www.obbg.org).

DOWNTOWN

EXPENSIVE

Avalon Hotel & Spa 🏨🏨🏨 This hotel sits right on the banks of the Willamette River just south of downtown. Although this location is a bit inconvenient for explor-ing the city on foot, there is a riverside bike path right in front of the hotel, making this a good bet if you're a jogger or like to take leisurely walks. The Avalon's contem-porary decor makes it one of the most stylish hotels in the city, and the riverfront rooms, most of which have balconies, provide good views and a chance to breath in fresh air while soaking up life on the Willamette. The hotel's stylish restaurant boasts the same great river views and walls of glass to make the most of the setting. The full-service spa just off the lobby gives this luxurious boutique hotel the feel of a much larger resort.

0455 SW Hamilton Court, Portland, OR 97239. © **888/556-4402** or 503/802-5800. Fax 503/802-5820. www. avalonhotelandspa.com. 99 units. $155–$215 double; $285–$650 suite. Children under 18 stay free in parent's room. AE, DC, DISC, MC, V. Valet parking $10. **Amenities:** Restaurant (New American); lounge; health club; day spa; Jacuzzi; sauna; concierge; courtesy car; business center; 24-hr. room service; massage; laundry service; dry cleaning. *In room:* A/C, TV, dataport, coffeemaker, hair dryer, iron, safe, high-speed Internet access, Wi-Fi.

Governor Hotel 🏨🏨🏨 This plush historic hotel is located right on the Portland Streetcar line in downtown and has a very classic and masculine ambience. The huge lobby abounds in marble and has gilded plasterwork ceilings reminiscent of the royal palaces of Europe. Accommodations vary considerably in size but are all attractively decorated with vaguely Art Deco styling. The least expensive rooms are rather small but are nevertheless quite comfortable. Still, I'd opt for one of the deluxe guest rooms. Unfortunately, bathrooms are, in general, quite cramped by today's standards and lack counter space. Suites, on the other hand, are spacious and some even have huge patios overlooking the city. Be sure to check out the hotel's restaurant—Jake's Grill—which has a beautiful mural commemorating the Lewis and Clark expedition.

614 SW 11th Ave., Portland, OR 97205. © **800/554-3456** or 503/224-3400. Fax 503/241-2122. www.govhotel.com. 100 units. $169–$189 double; $239–$500 suite. AE, DC, DISC, MC, V. Valet parking $21. **Amenities:** Restaurant (American); lounge; concierge; business center; 24-hr. room service; massage; laundry service; dry cleaning. *In room:* A/C, TV, dataport, minibar, coffeemaker, hair dryer, iron, safe, high-speed Internet access, Wi-Fi.

The Heathman Hotel 🏨🏨 The Heathman has long been considered one of Port-land's top hotels, but in many ways this hotel suffers from an identity crisis. An incon-gruous beefeater doorman ushers guests into a minimalist lobby that is adjacent to an utterly traditional "tea court," which itself is adjacent to the hotel's French restaurant, which is owned by the McCormick and Schmick's restaurant chain and is decorated with Andy Warhol prints. Guest rooms, all recently redecorated, are theatrically done in a vaguely Art Deco motif that seems cluttered. All the table-top amenities and abundant pillows tend to make the rooms feel even smaller than they actually are, and the basic rooms are definitely small. If you decide to give this place a try, you'll get to choose your bed—feather bed, pillow-top, or Tempur-Pedic.

1001 SW Broadway, Portland, OR 97205. © 800/551-0011 or 503/241-4100. Fax 503/790-7110. www.heathman hotel.com. 150 units. $199–$249 double; $249–$1,000 suite. Children under 13 stay free in parent's room. AE, DC, DISC, MC, V. Parking $26. Pets accepted ($25). **Amenities:** Restaurant (French/Northwest); lounge; exercise room and access to nearby health club; concierge; 24-hour room service; laundry service; dry cleaning. *In room:* A/C, TV, dataport, minibar, French-press coffeemaker, hair dryer, iron, high-speed Internet access.

Hotel Lućia ĞĞ

Portland may not have a W Hotel, but it does have the Lućia, which is just as hip. Located across from the prestigious and very traditional Benson hotel, the Lućia is the Portland address of choice for young business travelers with a taste for contemporary style. There's a big emphasis on the visual arts here, with paintings by Northwest artists on the lobby walls, and black-and-white photos by famed White House photographer David Hume Kennerly throughout the hotel. Guest rooms are some of the prettiest in the city, with great beds and bathrooms that have lots of chrome and frosted-glass counters. Drawbacks here include paper-thin walls in some rooms, a young inexperienced staff, and a slow elevator (despite the stylish makeover, this is an old building). Try to get a discounted rate to make up for these shortcomings.

400 SW Broadway, Portland, OR 97205. © 877/225-1717 or 503/225-1717. Fax 503/225-1919. www.hotellucia. com. 128 units. $149–$255 double; $265–$625 suite. Children under 18 stay free in parent's room. AE, DC, DISC, MC, V. Parking $23. **Amenities:** Restaurant (Thai); lounge; exercise room; concierge; business center; 24-hr. room service; laundry service; dry cleaning. *In room:* A/C, TV, dataport, minibar, hair dryer, iron, safe, Wi-Fi.

Hotel Vintage Plaza ĞĞ

This hotel, which was built in 1894 and is on the National Register of Historic Places, is *the* place to stay in Portland if you are a wine lover. A wine theme predominates in the hotel's decor, and there are complimentary evening tastings of Northwest wines. There are a wide variety of room types here, and though the standard rooms are worth recommending, the starlight rooms and bi-level suites are the real scene stealers. The starlight rooms in particular are truly extraordinary. Though small, they have greenhouse-style windows that provide very romantic views at night and let in floods of light during the day. The bi-level suites, some with Japanese soaking tubs, are equally attractive spaces. **Pazzo Ristorante** is a dark, intimate trattoria.

422 SW Broadway, Portland, OR 97205. © 800/243-0555 or 503/228-1212. Fax 503/228-3598. www.vintageplaza.com. 107 units. $129–$259 double; $149–$399 suite. Children under 18 stay free in parent's room. AE, DC, DISC, MC, V. Valet parking $25. Pets accepted. **Amenities:** Restaurant (Italian); lounge; exercise room, access to nearby health club; concierge; business center; 24-hr. room service; massage; laundry service; dry cleaning. *In room:* A/C, TV, dataport, minibar, fridge, coffeemaker, hair dryer, iron, high-speed Internet access, Wi-Fi.

RiverPlace Hotel ĞĞĞ

With the Willamette River at its back doorstep and the sloping lawns of Waterfront Park to one side, the RiverPlace is Portland's only downtown waterfront hotel. This alone would be enough to recommend the hotel, but its quiet boutique-hotel atmosphere would make it an excellent choice even if it weren't on the water. In general, furnishings are neither as elegant nor as luxurious as at The Benson, but more than half the rooms are suites, some of which have wood-burning fireplaces and whirlpool baths. There are also condominiums for long stays, but the riverview standard king rooms are the best deal. The hotel's restaurant overlooks the river, and there's also a comfortable bar with a patio overlooking the river. All in all, what you're paying for here is the waterfront locale, which is fine by me.

1510 SW Harbor Way, Portland, OR 97201. (C) **800/227-1333** or 503/228-3233. Fax 503/295-6161. www.riverplace hotel.com. 84 units. $169–$219 double; $169–$219 junior suite; $199 and up for a suite. AE, DC, DISC, MC, V. Valet parking $23. Pets accepted ($45 nonrefundable cleaning fee). **Amenities:** Restaurant (Northwest); lounge; access to nearby health club; day spa; Jacuzzi; sauna; concierge; business center; 24-hr. room service; massage; laundry service; dry cleaning. *In room:* A/C, TV/DVD, dataport, fridge, hair dryer, iron, Wi-Fi.

MODERATE

The Benson *★★★*   Built in 1912, The Benson exudes old-world sophistication and elegance. In the French baroque lobby, walnut paneling frames a marble fireplace, Austrian crystal chandeliers hang from the ornate plasterwork ceiling, and a marble staircase allows for grand entrances. These are the poshest digs in Portland, and guest rooms are luxuriously furnished in a plush Euro-luxe styling. Rooms vary considerably in size, and most of the deluxe kings are particularly spacious. However, the corner junior suites, which are large and have lots of windows, are the hotel's best deal. All the guest rooms have Tempur-Pedic mattresses. Bathrooms, unfortunately, are small and have little shelf space. The hotel's **London Grill** is well known for its Sunday brunch. Just off the lobby, there's El Gaucho steakhouse; in the Lobby Bar, there's live jazz in the evenings.

309 SW Broadway, Portland, OR 97205. (C) **888/523-6766** or 503/228-2000. Fax 503/471-3920. www.bensonhotel.com. 287 units. $124–$229 double; $199–$299 junior suite; $400–$1,000 suite. AE, DC, DISC, MC, V. Valet parking $25. Pets accepted ($75). Children under 18 stay free in parent's room. **Amenities:** 2 restaurants (Northwest/Continental, steaks); lounge; exercise room; access to nearby health club; concierge; business center; 24-hr. room service; babysitting; laundry service; dry cleaning. *In room:* A/C, TV, dataport, minibar, coffeemaker, hair dryer, iron, Wi-Fi.

Embassy Suites *★★* *Kids* *Value*   Located in the restored former Multnomah Hotel, which originally opened in 1912, the Embassy Suites has a beautiful large lobby that is a masterpiece of gilded plasterwork. The accommodations here are primarily two-room suites, with the exception of a handful of studio suites. In keeping with the historic nature of the hotel, the suites have classically styled furnishings. What's much more important, though, is that they give you lots of room to spread out, a rarity in downtown hotels. The hotel's Portland Steak and Chophouse has a classic dark and woody steakhouse decor as well as a large bar. There's a nightly complimentary evening manager's reception.

319 SW Pine St., Portland, OR 97204. (C) **800/EMBASSY** or 503/279-9000. Fax 503/497-9051. www.embassy portland.com. 276 units. $139–$209 double. Rates include full breakfast. Children 18 and under stay free in parent's room. AE, DC, DISC, MC, V. Valet parking $22; self-parking $15. **Amenities:** Restaurant (steak); lounge; indoor pool; exercise room; access to nearby health club; day spa; Jacuzzi; sauna; concierge; car-rental desk; courtesy van; business center; room service; massage; babysitting; laundry service; dry cleaning. *In room:* A/C, TV, dataport, fridge, coffeemaker, hair dryer, iron, Wi-Fi.

Four Points by Sheraton Portland Downtown *★★* *Value*   Overlooking Waterfront Park and located on the MAX light-rail line, this 1960s vintage hotel is nondescript from the outside, but the inside has a contemporary look that makes it surprisingly stylish for a budget hotel. You are only steps from the Willamette River (although not actually on the water), and are also close to businesses, fine restaurants, and shopping. Guest rooms are comfortable and have a modern styling.

50 SW Morrison St., Portland, OR 97204-3390. (C) **800/368-7764** or 503/221-0711. Fax 503/274-0312. www.four points.com/portlanddowntown. 140 units. $99–$150 double. AE, DC, DISC, MC, V. Parking $11. Pets accepted. **Amenities:** Restaurant (American/International); lounge; exercise room; access to nearby health club; business center; room service; dry cleaning. *In room:* A/C, TV, dataport, coffeemaker, hair dryer, iron, high-speed Internet access, Wi-Fi.

Mallory Hotel 🏨 *(finds)*   The Mallory, which is right on the west-side Max line, has long been a favorite of Portland visitors who want the convenience of staying downtown but don't have an endless expense account. This is an older hotel, and the lobby, with its ornate gilt plasterwork trim and crystal chandeliers, has a certain classic (and faded) grandeur. Time seems to have stood still here. (There's a lounge straight out of the 1950s.) At press time, the rooms were scheduled for a complete makeover that will give the hotel a glamorous 1940s Hollywood feel. The dining room continues the lobby's grand design, with heavy drapes and faux-marble pillars.

729 SW 15th Ave., Portland, OR 97205. ☎ **800/228-8657** or 503/223-6311. Fax 503/223-0522. www.malloryhotel.com. 130 units. $125–$199 double; $139–$379 suite. Rates include continental breakfast. Children under 18 stay free in parent's room. AE, DC, DISC, MC, V. Free parking. Pets accepted ($25). **Amenities:** Restaurant (American); lounge; exercise room; game room; business center; room service; laundry service; dry cleaning. *In room:* A/C, TV, dataport, fridge, coffeemaker, hair dyer, iron, high-speed Internet access, Wi-Fi.

NOB HILL & NORTHWEST PORTLAND
EXPENSIVE

Heron Haus 🏨🏨   A short walk from the bustling Nob Hill shopping and dining district of Northwest Portland, the Heron Haus B&B offers outstanding accommodations, spectacular views, and tranquil surroundings. Surprisingly, the house still features some of the original plumbing. In most places this would be a liability, but not here, since the same man who plumbed Portland's famous Pittock Mansion (p. 102) did the plumbing here. Many of that building's unusual bathroom features are also found at the Heron Haus—one shower has *seven* showerheads. In another room there's a modern whirlpool spa with excellent views of the city. All the rooms have fireplaces.

2545 NW Westover Rd., Portland, OR 97210. ☎ **503/274-1846.** Fax 503/248-4055. www.heronhaus.com. 6 units. $135–$350 double. Rates include continental breakfast. MC, V. Free parking. *In room:* A/C, TV, dataport, hair dryer, iron, high-speed Internet access.

MODERATE

Inn @ Northrup Station 🏨🏨 *(finds)*   Colorful, hip, retro. That about sums up this hotel in the trendy Nob Hill neighborhood. On top of this high style, the hotel has large rooms with kitchens or kitchenettes, and the Portland Streetcar stops right outside the hotel, which makes this a convenient hotel for exploring the city's most interesting neighborhoods. The colorful retro decor really sets this all-suite hotel apart from more cookie-cutter corporate hotels around town, and if you appreciate bright colors and contemporary styling, this should be your first choice in town. Lots of the rooms here have balconies, and there's a roof-top terrace. The hotel's location in a quiet residential neighborhood is another plus, and several of Portland's top restaurants are within a short walk.

2025 NW Northrup St., Portland, OR 97209. ☎ **800/224-1180** or 503/224-0543. Fax 503/273-2102. www.northrup station.com. 70 units. $99–$199 double. Rates include continental breakfast. Children under 12 stay free in parent's room. AE, DC, DISC, MC, V. Free parking. **Amenities:** Laundry service; dry cleaning. *In room:* A/C TV, dataport, fridge, coffeemaker, hair dryer, Wi-Fi.

Silver Cloud Inn Portland Downtown 🏨   This hotel is on the edge of Portland's trendy Nob Hill neighborhood, and though it's also near an industrial area, it is still a very attractive and comfortable place (ask for a room away from Vaughn St.). Reasonable rates are the main draw here, but the rooms are also well designed. The minisuites have wet bars, microwave ovens, and separate seating areas, but the king minisuites with whirlpool tubs are my favorites. The best thing about the hotel is its

Kids Family-Friendly Hotels

Embassy Suites (p. 76)   Located in the center of the city, this renovated historic hotel offers spacious rooms (mostly two-room suites). You and the kids will have room to spread out and can hang out by the indoor pool when you tire of exploring Portland.

Homewood Suites by Hilton Vancouver/Portland (p. 80)   This hotel is on the north side of the Columbia River, in Vancouver, Washington. A paved riverside trail, a fun family restaurant, and a brewpub—not to mention its location right across the street from the river—all add up to convenience for families. That you'll get a one- or two-bedroom apartment with a full kitchen just makes life on vacation that much easier.

The Lakeshore Inn (p. 80)   This reasonably priced inn is right on the shore of the lake, and it also has a pool. The big rooms with kitchenettes are great for families; for more space, opt for a one- or two-bedroom suite.

location within a 5-minute drive (or 15-min. walk) of a half dozen of the city's best restaurants. To find the hotel, take I-405 to Ore. 30 west and get off at the Vaughn Street exit.

2426 NW Vaughn St., Portland, OR 97210. ✆ **800/205-6939** or 503/242-2400. Fax 503/242-1770. www.silver cloud.com. 82 units. $99–$139 double. Rates include continental breakfast. Children under 18 stay free in parent's room. AE, DC, DISC, MC, V. Free parking. **Amenities:** Exercise room; business center; guest laundry; laundry service; dry cleaning. *In room:* A/C, TV, dataport, coffeemaker, hair dryer, iron, free local calls, high-speed Internet access.

THE ROSE QUARTER, IRVINGTON & SOUTHEAST PORTLAND
EXPENSIVE

The Lion and the Rose 🐾🐾   This imposing Queen Anne–style Victorian inn is located in the Irvington District, a fairly quiet residential neighborhood 1 block off Northeast Broadway. It's a good choice if you want to keep your driving to a minimum. Restaurants, cafes, eclectic boutiques, and a huge shopping mall are all within 4 blocks. Even without the splendid location, the inn would be a gem. Guest rooms each have a distinct decor. In the Lavonna Room, there are bright colors and a turret sitting area, while in the deep green Starina Room you'll find an imposing Edwardian bed and armoire. Both the Garden Room and the Lavonna Room have claw-foot tubs in their bathrooms; other bathrooms are cramped but attractive. If you have problems climbing stairs, ask for the ground floor's Rose Room, which has a whirlpool tub. Breakfasts are sumptuous affairs, great for lingering.

1810 NE 15th Ave., Portland, OR 97212. ✆ **800/955-1647** or 503/287-9245. Fax 503/287-9247. www.lionrose.com. 6 units. $120–$175 double. No children under 10. AE, DISC, MC, V. **Amenities:** Concierge. *In room:* A/C, TV, dataport, hair dryer, iron, free local calls, Wi-Fi.

Portland's White House 🐾🐾   With massive columns framing the entrance, a semicircular driveway, and, in the front garden, a bubbling fountain, this imposing Greek-revival mansion bears a more than passing resemblance to its namesake in Washington, D.C. Behind the mahogany front doors, a huge entrance hall with original hand-painted wall murals is flanked by a parlor and the formal dining room, where the large breakfast is served beneath sparkling crystal chandeliers. A double staircase leads past a large stained-glass window to the second-floor accommodations. Canopy-and-brass queen beds, antique furnishings, and bathrooms with claw-foot tubs further the feeling of classic luxury here. Request the balcony room, and you can gaze out past the Greek columns and imagine you're in the Oval Office. There are also three rooms in the restored carriage house.

1914 NE 22nd Ave., Portland, OR 97212. ℂ 800/272-7131 or 503/287-7131. Fax 503/249-1641. www.portlands whitehouse.com. 8 units. $125–$225 double. Rates include full breakfast. AE, DISC, MC, V. *In room:* A/C, TV, dataport, Wi-Fi.

INEXPENSIVE

Jupiter Hotel 🔊 *Finds*   Although this place calls itself a boutique hotel, it's actually a boutique motel. The Jupiter has had an extreme makeover and is now an überhip address for the Portland arts crowd and those in town to participate in the city's hip scene. With its glowing blue wall panels, piped in music in the courtyard, and log-cabin swank Doug Fir Lounge, the Jupiter has enough going on to keep the party going all night long, so don't plan on getting much sleep if you stay here. Platform beds, fuzzy pillows, photo-murals on the walls, retro accents, and dim lighting (or is it supposed to be romantic lighting?) provide guest rooms with plenty of retro-hip styling for young travelers on a tight budget.

800 E. Burnside St., Portland, OR 97214. ℂ 877/800-0004 or 503/230-9200. www.jupiterhotel.com. 80 units. $89–$99 double. AE, DISC, MC, V. **Amenities:** Restaurant (New American); lounge; massage. *In room:* A/C, TV, data-port, hair dryer, Wi-Fi.

McMenamins Kennedy School 🔊 *Finds*   The Kennedy School, which was an elementary school from 1915 to 1975, is owned by the same folks who turned Portland's old poor farm into the most entertaining and unusual B&B in the state (see the listing for McMenamins Edgefield in chapter 8, on p. 239). In the guest rooms you'll still find the original blackboards and great big school clocks (you know, like the one you used to watch so expectantly). However, the classroom/guest rooms here now have their own bathrooms, so you won't have to raise your hand or walk down the hall. On the premises you'll also find a restaurant, a beer garden, a movie theater pub, a cigar bar, and a big hot soaking pool. The Kennedy School is located well north of stylish Irvington neighborhood in an up-and-coming part of the city that dates from the early years of the 20th century.

5736 NE 33rd Ave., Portland, OR 97211. ℂ 888/249-3983 or 503/249-3983. www.mcmenamins.com. 35 units. $84–$99 double. Children 6 and under stay free. AE, DC, DISC, MC, V. **Amenities:** Restaurant (American); 4 lounges; soaking pool; massage. *In room:* Wi-Fi.

VANCOUVER, WASHINGTON

Located just across the Columbia River from Portland, Vancouver, Washington, is an economical and convenient area from which to explore Portland.

MODERATE

The Heathman Lodge 🔊🔊 *Value*   Mountain lodge meets urban chic at this suburban Vancouver hotel adjacent to the Vancouver Mall. Located 20 minutes by car from downtown Portland, the hotel is well placed for exploring both the Columbia Gorge and Mount St. Helens. With its log, stone, and cedar-shingle construction, this hotel conjures up the Northwest's historic mountain lodges. As at Timberline Lodge on Oregon's Mount Hood, this hotel is filled with artwork and embellished with rugged Northwest-inspired craftwork, including totem poles, Eskimo kayak frames, and Pendleton blankets. Guest rooms feature a mix of rustic pine and peeled-hickory furniture as well as rawhide lampshades and Pendleton-inspired bedspreads. Most rooms also have Tempur-Pedic mattresses.

7801 NE Greenwood Dr., Vancouver, WA 98662. © **888/475-3100** or 360/254-3100. Fax 360/254-6100. www.heathmanlodge.com. 142 units. $79–$149 double; $159–$350 suite. AE, DC, DISC, MC, V. **Amenities:** Restaurant (Northwest); lounge; indoor pool; exercise room; Jacuzzi; sauna; concierge; business center; room service; guest laundry; laundry service; dry cleaning. *In room:* A/C, TV, dataport, fridge, coffeemaker, hair dryer, iron, Wi-Fi.

Homewood Suites by Hilton Vancouver/Portland *Kids* Located across the street from the Columbia River, this modern suburban all-suite hotel is a great choice for families. The hotel charges surprisingly reasonable rates for large apartmentlike accommodations that include full kitchens. Rates include not only a large breakfast, but afternoon snacks as well (Mon–Thurs). These snacks are substantial enough to pass for dinner if you aren't too hungry. The hotel is right across the street from both a beach-theme restaurant and a brewpub. Across the street, you'll also find a paved riverside path that's great for walking or jogging. The only drawback is that it's a 15- to 20-minute drive to downtown Portland.

701 SE Columbia Shores Blvd., Vancouver, WA 98661. © **800/CALL-HOME** or 360/750-1100. Fax 360/750-4899. www.homewoodsuites.com. 104 units. $99–$179 double. Rates include full breakfast. AE, DC, DISC, MC, V. Free parking. Pets accepted ($25 1st day, $10 subsequent days). **Amenities:** Outdoor pool; sports court; exercise room; Jacuzzi; business center; coin-op laundry; laundry service; dry cleaning. *In room:* A/C, TV, dataport, kitchen, fridge, coffeemaker, hair dryer, iron, free local calls, high-speed Internet access.

THE AIRPORT AREA & TROUTDALE

Moderately priced hotels abound in the airport area, which makes this a good place to look for a room if you arrive with no reservation.

INEXPENSIVE

Silver Cloud Inn Portland Airport *Value* Conveniently located right outside the airport, this hotel has one of the best backyards of any hotel in the Portland area. A lake, lawns, and trees create a tranquil setting despite the proximity of both the airport and a busy nearby road. Rooms are designed primarily for business travelers, but even if you aren't here on an expense account, they are a good value, especially those with whirlpool tubs. Some suites have gas fireplaces. Best of all, with the exception of two suites, every room has a view of the lake. An indoor pool is another big plus. To find this hotel, take the complimentary airport shuttle or head straight out of the airport, drive under the I-205 overpass, and watch for the hotel sign ahead on the left.

11518 NE Glenn Widing Dr., Portland, OR 97220. © **800/205-7892** or 503/252-2222. Fax 503/257-7008. www.scinns.com. 102 units. $109–$129 double; $119–$149 suite. Rates include continental breakfast. Children under 19 stay free in parent's room. AE, DC, DISC, MC, V. Free parking. **Amenities:** Indoor pool; exercise room; Jacuzzi; courtesy airport shuttle; business center; guest laundry; dry cleaning. *In room:* A/C, TV, dataport, fridge, coffeemaker, hair dryer, iron, free local calls, high-speed Internet access.

LAKE OSWEGO
INEXPENSIVE

The Lakeshore Inn *Finds Kids* Considering that the town of Lake Oswego is Portland's most affluent bedroom community, this motel is quite reasonably priced. It's right on the shore of the lake, and there's a pool on a deck built on the water's edge, making it a great place to stay in summer. Rooms have standard motel furnishings but are large and have kitchenettes. There are also one- and two-bedroom suites. The 7-mile drive into downtown Portland follows the Willamette River and is quite pleasant. There are several restaurants and cafes within walking distance.

210 N. State St., Lake Oswego, OR 97034. © **800/215-6431** or 503/636-9679. Fax 503/636-6959. www. thelakeshoreinn.com. 33 units. $69–$99 double; $89–$139 suite. Rates include continental breakfast. AE, DC, DISC, MC, V. **Amenities:** Outdoor pool; coin-op laundry. *In room:* A/C, TV, dataport, kitchenette, coffeemaker, hair dryer, iron, free local calls, Wi-Fi.

4 Where to Dine

The Portland restaurant scene is jumping and the city has developed a reputation to rival Seattle's when it comes to great restaurants. Several distinct dining districts are full of upscale spots, and though you aren't likely to choose to eat at one of these places on the spur of the moment (reservations are usually imperative), their proximity allows you to check out a few places before making a decision later.

The Pearl District's renovated warehouses currently house the trendiest restaurants, while Nob Hill's NW 21st Avenue boasts half a dozen terrific establishments within a few blocks. The Sellwood and Westmoreland neighborhoods of southeast Portland make up another of the city's hot restaurant districts, and for good inexpensive food, it's hard to beat the many offerings along NE Broadway in the Irvington neighborhood, and along North Mississippi Avenue in north Portland.

Dinner in Portland isn't complete without an Oregon wine; pinot noir and pinot gris in particular receive widespread acclaim. However, they can be more expensive than other domestic wines.

DOWNTOWN (INCLUDING THE SKIDMORE HISTORIC DISTRICT & CHINATOWN)
EXPENSIVE
The Heathman Restaurant and Bar 🏵🏵🏵 NORTHWEST/FRENCH   This grande dame of Northwest-style restaurants serves Northwest cuisine with a French accent. Philippe Boulot, a James Beard Foundation Award winner, changes his menu seasonally, but one thing remains constant: The ingredients used are the freshest of Oregon and Northwest seafood, meat, wild game, and produce. The interior is Art Deco inspired, the atmosphere bistrolike. An extensive wine list spotlights Oregon wines. The Heathman Hotel has an extensive collection of classic and contemporary art, and on the restaurant walls you'll find Andy Warhol's *Endangered Species* series.

In the Heathman Hotel, 1001 SW Broadway. © **503/790-7752.** Reservations highly recommended. Main courses $8.50–$18 lunch, $17–$30 dinner. AE, DC, DISC, MC, V. Mon–Thurs 6:30–11am, 11:30am–2pm, and 5–10pm; Fri 6:30–11am, 11:30am–2pm, and 5–11pm; Sat 7am–2pm and 5–11pm; Sun 7am–2pm.

Higgins 🏵🏵🏵 NORTHWEST/MEDITERRANEAN   Higgins strikes a perfect balance between contemporary and classic in both decor and cuisine. The menu, which changes frequently, explores contemporary culinary horizons, while the decor in the tri-level dining room opts for wood paneling and elegant place settings. Despite all this, the restaurant remains unpretentious, and portions can be surprisingly generous for a high-end restaurant. Flavors change with the season, but are often both subtle and earthy. The honey-and-chile-glazed pork loin, which comes with seasonal side dishes such as rosemary-roasted potatoes, highlights the restaurant's ability to balance creativity with familiarity. Be sure to leave room for dessert, and if you happen to be a beer lover, you'll be glad to know that Higgins has one of the most interesting beer selections in town (and plenty of good wine, too).

1239 SW Broadway. © **503/222-9070.** Reservations recommended. Main courses $8–$16 lunch, $19–$30 dinner. AE, DC, MC, V. Mon–Fri 11:30am–2pm and 5–10:30pm; Sat–Sun 5–10:30pm; bistro menu served in the bar daily until midnight.

Where to Dine in Portland

PGE Park

NORTHWEST

NOB HILL

Japanese Garden ■

■ International Rose Test Garden

WASHINGTON PARK

TUNNEL

Main Post Office ✉

Pioneer Courthouse Square ■

DOWNTOWN

PORTLAND STATE UNIVERSITY

Fremont Bridge

ⓘ Information
✉ Post Office
▨ Fareless Square

DINING ◆
Assagio **47**
Ban-Thai Restaurant **26**
Bijou Café **34**
bluehour **16**
Caffe Mingo **4**
Caprial's Bistro & Wine **48**
Carafe Bistro **25**
Castagna **44**
Chart House **27**
Daily Café in the Pearl **11**
Elephant's Deli **9**
Esparza's Tex-Mex Café **38**
Fong Chong **35**
Fratelli **14**

Genoa **41**
Good Dog/Bad Dog **20**
Gotham Building Tavern **36**
The Heathman Restaurant & Bar **23**
Higgins **24**
Huber's **32**
Jake's Famous Crawfish **18**
Ken's Place **43**

McCormick & Schmick's Harborside Restaurant **29**
Newport Bay Restaurant **30**
Nicholas's **39**
Patanegra **1**
Paley's Place **3**
Pambiche **37**
Peanut Butter & Ellie's **28**
Pho Van **15**

CAFES, COFFEE BARS AND TEA ROOMS ●
Ken's Artisan Bakery **7**
Moonstruck Chocolate Café **21**
Palio Dessert House **46**
Papa Haydn **5**
Pearl Bakery **17**
Peet's Coffee **19**
Pix Patisserie **45**
Rimsky-Korsakoffee House **42**
St. Honoré Boulangerie **1**
Stumptown Coffee Roasters **33**
World Cup **14**

Pizzicato Gourmet Pizza **6**
Piazza Italia **12**
Ringside Downtown **10**
Salvador Molly's **40**
Southpark Seafood Grill
& Wine Bar **22**
Typhoon! **8**
Veritable Quandary **31**
Wildwood **2**

Portland
OREGON

Veritable Quandary ✿✿ NEW AMERICAN   Located in an old brick building just a block off Tom McCall Waterfront Park, this restaurant is a must for summer meals. The restaurant's garden patio, the prettiest in town, faces a small park. The menu changes daily, but keep an eye out for the grilled prawns, and don't pass up the *osso buco*. The chef here pulls in all kinds of influences, so don't be surprised if you find bacon-wrapped dates stuffed with goat cheese or springs rolls filled with duck confit, shiitakes, and Chinese cabbage (served with a side of wasabi-ginger sauce).

1220 SW First Ave. © 503/227-7342. www.veritablequandary.com. Reservations recommended. Main courses $12–$15 lunch, $16–$29 dinner. AE, DC, DISC, MC, V. Mon–Fri 11:30am–3pm and 5–10pm; Sat–Sun 9:30am–3pm and 5–10pm.

MODERATE

There's an outpost of **Typhoon!** at 410 SW Broadway (© **503/224-8285**), in the Hotel Lucía. See the complete review on p. 75.

Carafe Bistro ✿✿ FRENCH   With its small zinc bar, wicker patio chairs, and warm interior hues, Carafe feels just the way you'd expect a neighborhood bistro in Paris to feel. The menu is simple bistro fare (everything from baked escargot to *croque monsieur*), and there are economical nightly three-course prix-fixe dinners for $20. With many appetizers, salads, and side dishes, you can easily assemble a thoroughly Gallic meal. On top of all this, Carafe is right across the street from Keller Auditorium.

200 SW Market St. © 503/248-0004. Main courses $7.50–$13 lunch, $14–$20 dinner. AE, DC, DISC, MC, V. Mon–Thurs 11am–9pm; Fri 11am–10pm; Sat 5–10pm.

Huber's ✿ *Finds* AMERICAN   Huber's, Portland's oldest restaurant, first opened its doors to the public in 1879 and is tucked inside the Oregon Pioneer Building down a quiet hallway. The main room has a vaulted stained-glass ceiling, Philippine mahogany paneling, and the original brass cash register. Turkey dinner with all the trimmings is the house specialty, but you can also gobble stir-fried turkey and prawns, turkey pot pie, and even turkey picatta. Another specialty is Spanish coffee made with rum, Kahlua, Triple Sec, coffee, and cream. The preparation, which involves flaming the rum in a wine glass, is a very impressive tableside production. Because Huber's bar is quite popular, you'll probably enjoy your meal more if you come for lunch instead of dinner. Be sure to ask for a table in the old vaulted room.

411 SW Third Ave. © 503/228-5686. www.hubers.com. Reservations recommended. Main courses $7–$25. AE, DC, DISC, MC, V. Mon–Thurs 11:30am–4pm and 5–10pm; Fri 11:30am–4pm and 5–11pm; Sat noon–4pm and 5–11pm.

Jake's Famous Crawfish ✿✿ SEAFOOD   Jake's has been a Portland institution since 1909, and the back bar came all the way around Cape Horn in 1880. Much of the rest of the decor looks just as old and well worn as the bar and therein lies this restaurant's charm. But it's the great seafood at reasonable prices that makes this place a real winner. There's a daily menu listing a dozen or more specials, but there's really no question about what to eat at Jake's: crawfish, which is always on the menu and served several different ways. Monday through Friday from 3 to 6pm, bar appetizers are only $1.95. The noise level after work, when local businesspeople pack the bar, can be high, and the wait for a table can be long if you don't make a reservation. Don't let these obstacles put you off, though.

401 SW 12th Ave. © 503/226-1419. www.jakesfamouscrawfish.com. Reservations recommended. Main courses $6–$15 lunch, $12–$32 dinner. AE, DC, DISC, MC, V. Mon–Thurs 11am–11pm; Fri–Sat 11am–midnight; Sun 3–11pm.

McCormick and Schmick's Harborside at the Marina 🐟🐟 SEAFOOD
Anchoring the opposite end of RiverPlace Esplanade from the RiverPlace hotel, this
large, glitzy restaurant serves up a view of the Willamette, not to mention excellent
seafood. Four dining levels assure everyone a view of the river and marina below, and,
in summer, customers head out to tables on the sidewalk. Because it's so popular, the
place tends to be noisy and the help can sometimes be a bit harried; this doesn't detract
from the fine food, though. Seafood (such as tombo tuna with port wine and cranberries, or salmon and halibut sautéed with forest mushrooms, hazelnuts, and berries) is
the main attraction here, but the menu is quite extensive. The clientele is mostly
upscale, especially at lunch and during the after-work hours.

0309 SW Montgomery St. ✆ **503/220-1865.** www.mccormickandschmicks.com. Reservations recommended. Main
courses $12–$27. AE, DC, DISC, MC, V. Sun–Thurs 11am–10pm; Fri–Sat 11am–11pm.

Newport Bay Restaurant 🐟 (Kids) SEAFOOD   Though there are Newport Bay
restaurants all over the Portland area, this one has by far the best location—floating on
the Willamette River. Located in the marina at Portland's RiverPlace shopping-and-din-
ing complex, the Newport Bay provides excellent views of the river and the city skyline,
especially from the deck. Popular with young couples, families, and boaters, this place
exudes a cheery atmosphere, and service is efficient. Nearly everything on the menu has
some sort of seafood in it, even the sandwiches, salads, and pastas. Entrees are straightforward and well prepared—nothing too fancy. Sunday brunch is a very good deal.

0425 SW Montgomery St. ✆ **503/227-3474.** www.newportbay.com. Reservations recommended. Main courses
$8–$22. AE, DC, DISC, MC, V. Mon–Thurs 11am–11pm; Fri–Sat 11am–midnight; Sun 10am–11pm. Closes 1 hr. earlier
Oct–May.

Southpark Seafood Grill & Wine Bar 🐟🐟 (Value) MEDITERRANEAN/
SEAFOOD   With its high ceiling, long heavy drapes, and interesting wall mural, the
wine bar here is a contemporary interpretation of late-19th-century Paris, and the
main dining room is both comfortable and classy. For a starter, don't pass up the fried
calamari, rock shrimp, and vegetables served with spicy aioli. Equally delicious is the
butternut squash and ricotta-filled ravioli with toasted hazelnuts, which comes in a
rich Marsala wine sauce that begs to be sopped up with the crusty bread. An extensive
wine list presents some compelling choices, and the desserts are consistently excellent.

901 SW Salmon St. ✆ **503/326-1300.** www.southpark.citysearch.com. Reservations recommended. Main courses
$8.50–$15 lunch, $14–$24 dinner. AE, MC, V. Mon–Thurs 11:30am–3pm and 5–10pm; Fri 11:30am–3pm and
5–11pm; Sat 11am–3pm and 5–11pm; Sun 11am–3pm and 5–10pm.

INEXPENSIVE

Baan-Thai Restaurant 🐟 (Finds) THAI   Everyone in Portland seems to have a
favorite Thai restaurant, and, while Baan-Thai may not show up on local "Best of
Portland" lists, it should. It's cheap, it's casual, and it's pretty conveniently located.
And best of all: This place does awesome fish dishes. Try the Niagara fish (a whole
fried fish topped with spicy lime sauce) or the Panang salmon in creamy curry sauce.
The volcano chicken, which is actually a whole game hen baked and then fried and
served with Thai barbecue sauce, is another must-have.

1924 SW Broadway. ✆ **503/224-8424.** Main courses $6–$15. MC, V. Mon–Sat 11am–10pm.

Bijou Café 🐟 (Kids) NATURAL FOODS   The folks who run the Bijou take both
food and health seriously. They'll serve you a bowl of steamed brown rice and raisins
for breakfast, but you can also get delicious fresh oyster hash or brioche French toast.

The real hits here are the sautéed potatoes and the muffins, which come with full breakfasts; don't leave without trying them. Local and organic products are used as often as possible at this comfortably old-fashioned, yet thoroughly modern cafe.

132 SW Third Ave. ⓒ **503/222-3187.** Breakfast and lunch $6.50–$13. MC, V. Mon–Fri 7am–2pm; Sat–Sun 8am–2pm.

Fong Chong ⨕ CHINESE   This place may not look like much from the outside (or from the inside, for that matter), but the throngs of people crowding the tables in the middle of the day should give you an idea that this place does good dim sum. This traditional Chinese midday meal of small plates is ordered off of carts that are wheeled around the dining room and is served daily between 10:30am and 3pm. With lots of steamed dumplings, pot stickers, and shrimp balls, it's easy to order more than you can eat. Pace yourself. Located 2 blocks from the Portland Classical Chinese Garden, this is a great place to stick with the Chinese theme after a visit to the gardens.

301 NW Fourth Ave. ⓒ **503/228-6868.** Main courses $6–$12; dim sum $3–$6. MC, V. Daily 10:30am–10pm.

NORTHWEST PORTLAND (INCLUDING THE PEARL DISTRICT & NOB HILL)
EXPENSIVE
bluehour ⨕ FRENCH/ITALIAN   Restaurateur Bruce Carey has long dominated the Portland restaurant scene, and at this high-style restaurant, he continues to woo and wow the local trendsetters. Located in a converted warehouse that serves as head-quarters for Portland advertising giant Wieden+Kennedy, bluehour has a very theatri-cal atmosphere. With sophisticated menu items such as seared foie gras and American sturgeon caviar, as well as with superb service, it's obvious that bluehour is Portland's most haute restaurant—though this is also the sort of place where being seen by the right people is as important as the food.

250 NW 13th Ave. ⓒ **503/226-3394.** www.bluehouronline.com. Reservations highly recommended. Main dishes $20–$49. AE, DISC, MC, V. Tues–Thurs 5:30–10pm; Fri–Sat 5:30–10:30pm.

Paley's Place ⨕⨕ NORTHWEST/FRENCH   Located in a Victorian-era house, Paley's is a favorite of Portland foodies. Chef Vitaly Paley continues to receive acco-lades year after year, and in 2005 won a James Beard Foundation Award. The menu relies extensively on the freshest local organic ingredients (often stacked in baskets on the front porch) and ranges from traditional bistro fare to dishes with complex flavors and a hint of Northwest inspiration. Whether you're in the mood for spit-roasted suckling pit or corn-and-crab risotto, you'll certainly find something that appeals to you. If you've never tried sweetbreads, this is the place to do so, and the signature *frites,* with a mustard aioli, are not to be missed. Big on wines, Paley's offers wine tast-ing on Wednesdays. For dessert, I can't pass up the warm chocolate soufflé with out-rageously rich house-made ice cream. Inside, the restaurant is small and stylishly comfortable but can be quite noisy.

1204 NW 21st Ave. ⓒ **503/243-2403.** www.paleysplace.citysearch.com. Reservations highly recommended. Main courses $21–$35. AE, MC, V. Mon–Thurs 5:30–10pm; Fri–Sat 5:30–11pm; Sun 5–10pm.

RingSide Downtown ⨕ STEAK   Despite the location on a rather unattractive stretch of West Burnside Street, RingSide has long been a favorite Portland steak-house. Boxing may be the main theme of the restaurant, but the name is a two-fisted pun that also refers to the incomparable onion rings that are an essential part of any meal here. Have your rings with a side order of one of their perfectly cooked steaks for a real knockout meal. The three-course prix-fixe dinners are only $25 if you order before 5:45pm or after 9pm.

2165 W. Burnside St. © **503/223-1513.** www.ringsidesteakhouse.com. Reservations highly recommended. Steaks $26–$38; other main courses $18–$47; prix-fixe dinner $25–$35. AE, DISC, MC, V. Mon–Sat 5pm–midnight; Sun 4–11:30pm.

Wildwood *⋒⋒* NEW AMERICAN   With a menu that changes daily and a spare, elegant interior decor straight out of *Architectural Digest,* Wildwood has for many years been one of Portland's best restaurants. If you love creative cuisine, be sure to give this place a try. Fresh seasonal ingredients combined into simple-yet-imaginative dishes are the hallmark of chef Cory Schreiber's cooking, and often there are no more than a handful of ingredients in a dish so as to let each of the flavors shine through. I can never get enough chanterelle mushrooms, so on a recent evening I couldn't pass up an appetizer pizza made with chanterelles and lobster mushrooms and an entree of sturgeon with chanterelles and fried lemons. This is the only non-Indian restaurant I know of that has a tandoor oven, and you can usually count on the meat dishes that are roasted in this oven. Salads and sorbets are exceptionally good, too. If you can't get a reservation, you can usually get served in the bar.

1221 NW 21st Ave. © **503/248-9663.** www.wildwoodrestaurant.com. Reservations highly recommended. Main courses $12–$14 lunch, $18–$37 dinner. AE, MC, V. Mon–Thurs 11:30am–2:30pm and 5:30–9pm; Fri–Sat 11:30am–2:30pm and 5:30–10pm; Sun 5–8:30pm.

MODERATE

Caffe Mingo *⋒⋒ Finds* ITALIAN   This intimate little neighborhood restaurant has terrific food, an interior as attractive as that of any other upscale restaurant here on Northwest Portland's restaurant row, and relatively low prices. If there's any problem with this immensely popular place it's that you almost always have to wait for a table, and they only take reservations for large parties. The solution? Get here as early as possible. The menu is short, and focuses on painstakingly prepared Italian comfort food. Just about all the items on the menu are winners, from the antipasto platter, which might include roasted fennel, fresh mozzarella, and roasted red pepper, to an unusual penne pasta dish with tender beef braised in chianti and espresso. The *panna cotta* dessert ("cooked cream" with fruit) is reason enough to come back here again and again, even if you have to wait in the rain to get a seat.

807 NW 21st Ave. © **503/226-4646.** Reservations accepted only for parties of 6 or more. Main courses $10–$20. AE, DC, DISC, MC, V. Sun–Thurs 5–10pm; Fri–Sat 5–10:30pm.

Fratelli *⋒⋒* REGIONAL ITALIAN   In this rustic-yet-chic restaurant, cement walls provide a striking contrast to dramatic draperies and candles that drip casually onto the tabletops. Dishes are consistently good, with surprisingly moderate prices for the Pearl District. There's excellent olive oil to go with your bread and an antipasto plate that might include spring beans with arugula and octopus, chicken wrapped in prosciutto, rabbit *crepinette* (a sort of sausage), or a luscious savory *panna cotta.* The polenta with wild mushrooms and the seared chicken wrapped in prosciutto are longtime favorites here. This restaurant's aesthetic and menu are similar to Caffe Mingo's (see above), but at Fratelli you can make reservations.

1230 NW Hoyt St. © **503/241-8800.** Reservations recommended. Main courses $13–$20. AE, DC, MC, V. Sun–Thurs 4:30–9:30pm; Fri–Sat 4:30–10:30pm.

patanegra ★★ *Finds* SPANISH   Located next door to one of my favorite bakeries, this Spanish restaurant is the reincarnation of one of Portland's first tapas places. And tapas occupy most of the menu here, but patanegra also serves a few different types of paella. Still, I can't ever get past all the flavor-packed little tapas plates. The best way to approach this rather exotic menu is to just start ordering whatever sounds most interesting and then order more if your first round doesn't fill you up. Let me warn you, though, that the tapas menu is heavy on proteins and starches and a bit light on veggies. Oh well, you can always have a salad tomorrow.

1818 NW 23rd Place. ✆ 503/227-7282. www.patanegra-restaurant.com. Main courses $19; tapas $6–$10. AE, MC, V. Tues–Fri 11:30am–11pm; Sat 5–11pm.

Pho Van ★★ VIETNAMESE   If you think of Formica tables and fluorescent lights when you think of Vietnamese restaurants, think again. This is one of the most stylish restaurants in town, with decor drawing on a modern Asian aesthetic. The prices, however, are extremely reasonable. As the name implies, you can get flavorful *pho* soup (a Vietnamese staple), but I prefer the dishes from the grill and the other more substantial entrees, as well as the crispy crepes filled with shrimp, scallops, and vegetables.

1012 NW Glisan St. ✆ 503/248-2172. Reservations recommended. Main courses $8–$15 lunch, $8.50–$19 dinner. AE, DISC, MC, V. Mon–Sat 11am–3pm and 5–10pm.

Piazza Italia ★★ ITALIAN   Portland has more than its fair share of good Italian restaurants, but none feels as much like a trip to Italy as this one. The staff speaks Italian most of the time and the TV over the bar is tuned to Italian soap operas and soccer matches. Just inside the front door is a glass case full of the imported meats, cheeses, and olives that go into the antipasto plate. This place is small and has a very limited menu, but it's always bustling. Try the simple linguine *squarciarella,* made with eggs, prosciutto, onions, and Parmesan cheese. During the summer, the tables on the sidewalk are the in-demand seats.

1129 NW Johnson St. ✆ 503/478-0619. www.piazzaportland.com. Main courses $9.50–$14. AE, DISC, MC, V. Mon–Sat noon–10pm; Sun noon–8pm.

Typhoon! ★ THAI   Located just off NW 23rd Avenue, this trendy spot is a bit pricey for a Thai restaurant, but the unusual menu offerings generally aren't available at other Portland Thai restaurants. Be sure to start a meal with the *miang kum,* which consists of dried shrimp, tiny chilies, ginger, lime, peanuts, shallots, and toasted coconut drizzled with a sweet-and-sour sauce and wrapped up in a spinach leaf. The burst of flavors on your taste buds is absolutely astounding. (I first had this in Thailand and waited years to get it in the United States.) The whole front wall of the restaurant slides away for Thai-style open-air dining in the summer. There is an extensive tea list.

There's another **Typhoon!** at 410 SW Broadway (✆ **503/224-8285**), in the Hotel Lućia.

2310 NW Everett St. ✆ 503/243-7557. www.typhoonrestaurants.com. Reservations recommended. Main courses $9–$18. AE, DC, DISC, MC, V. Mon–Thurs 11:30am–2pm and 4:30–9pm; Fri 11:30am–2pm and 4:30–10pm; Sat noon–3pm and 4:30–10pm; Sun noon–3pm and 4:30–9pm.

INEXPENSIVE
Daily Café in the Pearl ★ AMERICAN/SANDWICHES   Healthy, flavorful breakfasts and creative sandwiches are the mainstays of this hip-yet-casual urban cafe

in the heart of the Pearl District. On sunny days, take your meal out onto the converted loading dock and ogle all the buff people coming and going from the area's gym. Although grilled vegetarian panini and wasabi tuna salad may better sum up the culinary aesthetics here, they also do a mean bacon cheeseburger. This is primarily a lunch spot, but dinners are also served.

902 NW 13th Ave. © 503/242-1916. Main courses $4–$6.50. MC, V. Mon–Tues 7am–5pm; Wed–Sat 7am–9:30pm; Sun 9am–2pm.

Elephant's Deli ⊛ DELI   This is definitely not your corner deli and it pushes the boundaries of what can even be considered a deli. Elephant's is a behemoth, which of course makes the name appropriate, and it's mouthwateringly diverse in its food offerings. Whether you want some pastrami to go or a full gourmet meal, you can get it here—this is the best place in town to put together a picnic before heading up to Washington Park. Want a cocktail? Elephant's has a full bar and plenty of good appetizers to accompany the drinks. Now, don't you wish you had one of these pachyderms in your town?

115 NW 22nd Ave. © 503/299-6304. www.elephantsdeli.com. Reservations not accepted. Main courses $5–$15. AE, MC, V. Mon–Sat 7am–8:30pm; Sun 9:30am–6:30pm.

SOUTHWEST PORTLAND
EXPENSIVE

Chart House ⊛⊛ SEAFOOD   Although this place is a part of a chain with lots of outposts all over California and the rest of the West, it also happens to boast the best view of any restaurant in Portland. On top of that, it serves the best New England clam chowder in the state. While you savor your chowder, you can marvel at the views of the Willamette River, Mount Hood, Mount St. Helens, and nearly all of Portland's east side. Fresh fish—either grilled, baked, or blackened—is the house specialty. You'll also find a selection of excellent steaks for the problem diner in your group who just won't eat seafood. No dinner here is complete without the hot chocolate lava cake, which has to be ordered at the start of your meal if you want it to be ready when you are. I recommend coming here for lunch or the early-bird dinner specials, which cost $15 to $17 and are available Sunday through Thursday between 5 and 6:30pm.

The Chart House is in an out-of-the-way spot about a 10-minute drive from downtown Portland; be sure to call ahead and get driving directions.

5700 SW Terwilliger Blvd. © 503/246-6963. www.chart-house.com. Reservations recommended. Main courses $8–$25 lunch, $17–$40 dinner. AE, DC, DISC, MC, V. Mon–Fri 11:30am–2:30pm and 5–10pm; Sat–Sun 5–10pm.

INEXPENSIVE

Peanut Butter & Ellie's ⊛ (Finds) (Kids) AMERICAN   This cozy, colorful spot in an upscale southwest Portland neighborhood takes the term "kid-friendly" to the extreme. This place is exclusively for children, though their parents are welcome if they are well behaved. The menu features, you guessed it, peanut-butter-and-jelly sandwiches (some topped with grapes, raisins, or even shredded carrots). Okay, so there are soups, salads, chicken sandwiches, grilled-cheese sandwiches, and a few other offerings, but the peanut butter-constructions are the real highlights. Most of the tables are kid-size, but there are a few for adults. Oh, and by the way, the peanut butter is organic and made right here.

4405 SW Vermont St. © 503/282-1783. www.peanutbutterellies.com. Main courses $4.50–$8.50. MC, V. Daily 9am–8pm.

NORTH & NORTHEAST PORTLAND
EXPENSIVE
Gotham Building Tavern &&& NEW AMERICAN/ITALIAN   You won't meet Batman here, and this is definitely no tavern—so you can forget about swilling Pabst Blue Ribbon. This is one of Portland's best new restaurants and has crafted a thoroughly modern menu and dining space. The walls are stacked with big slabs of woods that lend the dining room a hint of log-cabin chic, and count yourself lucky if you get a table in the section of the dining room that looks like a giant wooden basket. The menu takes simple ingredients and makes them into memorable dishes—porchetta and white beans, for example, which was as good as any porchetta I had on my last trip to Italy. Even a simple dish such as bavette pasta with cheese and black pepper can be absolutely delicious in its simplicity. The owners of this restaurant also operate Clarklewis at 1001 SE Water St., and a special reservation-only family-style dining room that is in the same building as the Gotham Building Tavern.

2240 N. Interstate Ave. © 503/235-2294. www.ripepdx.com. Reservations recommended. Main courses $17–$21. AE, MC, V. Tues–Thurs 8am–2:30pm and 5–9pm; Fri 8am–2:30pm and 5–10pm; Sat 9am–2pm and 5–10pm; Sun 9am–2pm and 5–9pm.

MODERATE
Pambiche & *Finds* CUBAN   Driving past this tiny hole-in-the-wall neighborhood eatery, you'd never guess that it's one of Portland's most popular restaurants. But you can't pass the tropical hot pink building without giving it a glance. Don't just gawk—get in there! The food is straight out of Havana, with taro-root fritters, codfish-and-potato croquettes, fried yucca root, and fried bananas. And that's just on the appetizer list. Don't fill up on all those tasty little tropical treats, though; the main dishes, such as shrimp Creole, Cuban-style beef hash, and oxtail braised in red wine, are all served in huge portions.

2811 NE Glisan St. © 503/233-0511. Main courses $6.50–$10 lunch, $8–$18 dinner. MC, V. Sun–Thurs 11am–10pm; Fri–Sat 11am–midnight.

SOUTHEAST PORTLAND
VERY EXPENSIVE
Genoa &&& REGIONAL ITALIAN   This has long been the best Italian restaurant in Portland, and with fewer than a dozen tables, it's also one of the smallest. Everything,

---

Kids Family-Friendly Restaurants

Bijou Cafe (p. 85)   Parents who care about the food their children eat will want to bring the family to this cozy old-fashioned diner that serves great breakfasts made with organic ingredients.

Newport Bay Restaurant (p. 85)   A cheery atmosphere, straightforward meals, and a great location on the Willamette River make this a good family pick.

Peanut Butter & Ellie's (p. 89)   This place isn't just family friendly, it's designed exclusively for kids, and, of course, the various peanut-butter-and-jelly sandwiches are big hits with the little ones.

from the breads to the luscious desserts, is made fresh in the kitchen with the best local seasonal ingredients. This is an ideal setting for a romantic dinner, and service is attentive—the waiter explains dishes in detail as they are served, and dishes are magically whisked away as they're finished. The fixed-price menu changes every 3 weeks, but a typical dinner might start with a little pork-stuffed crepe topped with warm apple-quince sauce and onion marmalade. Follow that with butternut-squash soup, a wild-mushroom pasta, and a pear salad before arriving at the main course, which might be something like medallions of monkfish in a red wine reduction sauce or duck breast with a port wine–and-peppercorn sauce. It takes Herculean restraint to choose among chocolate and nut tortes, fresh berry tarts, or liqueur-infused desserts.

2832 SE Belmont St. (C) 503/238-1464. www.genoarestaurant.com. Reservations required. Fixed-price 4-course dinner $60; 7-course dinner $75. AE, DC, DISC, MC, V. Daily 5:30–9:30pm (4-course dinner limited to 5:30 and 6pm seatings only).

EXPENSIVE

Caprial's Bistro & Wine ⊀⊀ NORTHWEST   If you're a foodie, you're probably already familiar with celebrity chef Caprial Pence, who helped put the Northwest on the national restaurant map and has since gone on to write several cookbooks and host TV and radio food shows. That her eponymous restaurant is a fairly casual place tucked away in a quiet residential neighborhood in southeast Portland may come as a surprise. The menu changes monthly and is limited to four or five main dishes and about twice as many appetizers. Entrees combine perfectly cooked meat and seasonal seafood dishes with vibrant sauces. Desserts are usually rich without being overly sweet. There is also a wine bar offering a superb selection of wines at reasonable prices.

7015 SE Milwaukie Ave. (C) 503/236-6457. www.caprial.com. Reservations highly recommended. Main courses $7.75–$12 lunch, $18–$28 dinner. AE, MC, V. Tues–Thurs 11:30am–2:30pm and 5–9pm; Fri–Sat 11:30am–2:30pm and 5–9:30pm.

Castagna ⊀⊀ FRENCH/ITALIAN   Located on a rather nondescript stretch of Hawthorne Boulevard and much removed from the bustle of this boulevard's central commercial area, Castagna is a magnet for Portland foodies. Considering the less-than-stylish location and minimalist (though thoroughly designed) interior, it's obvious that the food's the thing here. Dishes tend toward simple preparations that allow the freshness of the ingredients to express themselves. Entrees such as the black cod with parsnip-sunchoke purée, porcini mushrooms, and pea shoots sum up the dominant culinary aesthetic at this restaurant. In addition to the main dining room, there is an inexpensive cafe serving much simpler fare.

1752 SE Hawthorne Blvd. (C) 503/231-7373. www.castagnarestaurant.com. Reservations highly recommended. Main dishes $18–$28; cafe main courses $11–$19. AE, DISC, MC, V. Main restaurant Wed–Thurs 5:30–9:30pm, Fri–Sat 5:30–10:30pm; cafe Mon–Thurs 5:30–10pm, Fri–Sat 5:30–11pm, Sun 5–9:30pm.

MODERATE

Assaggio ⊀⊀ RUSTIC ITALIAN   This trattoria in the Sellwood neighborhood focuses on pastas and wines; the menu lists lots of pastas, and the wine list includes dozens of Italian wines, some of which are rarely encountered in the U.S. The atmosphere in this tiny place is theatrical, with indirect lighting, dark walls, and the likes of Mario Lanza playing in the background. Don't be surprised if after taking your first bite, you suddenly hear a Verdi aria. The pastas, with surprisingly robust flavors, are the main attraction. *Assaggio* means a sampling or a taste, and that is exactly what you get if you order pasta Assaggio-style—a sampling of several dishes, all served family-style. This is especially fun if you're here with a group.

7742 SE 13th Ave. ℂ **503/232-6151.** www.assaggiorestaurant.com. Reservations recommended. Main courses $11–$19. AE, MC, V. Mon–Thurs 11am–2:30pm and 5–9:30pm; Fri–Sat 11am–2:30pm and 5–10pm; Sun 5–9:30pm.

Ken's Place 🖈 *Value* AMERICAN REGIONAL   It's just a tiny retro diner with framed crocheted potholders on the walls, but chef/owner Ken Gordon turns out dishes here that would do justice to the best restaurants in town. On any given night, there may only be half a dozen entrees, but these economically priced dishes might include chianti-braised pork leg with raisins and olives or an Asian-style pork chop with ginger applesauce. There are always plenty of side dishes with which to fill out a meal. Desserts such as chewy caramel pecan tart should not be missed. This casual neighborhood place is the absolute antithesis of Portland's chic restaurants, but the food is every bit as good. Desserts are stacked on a desk just inside the front door, so you'll know what you're saving room for.

1852 SE Hawthorne Blvd. ℂ **503/236-9520.** Reservations not accepted. Main courses $9.25–$20. MC, V. Tues–Sat 5:30–9:30pm.

INEXPENSIVE

Esparza's Tex-Mex Café 🖈 *Kids* TEX-MEX   With red-eyed cow skulls on the walls and marionettes, model planes, and stuffed iguanas and armadillos hanging from the ceiling, the decor here can only be described as Tex-eclectic, a description that is just as appropriately applied to the menu. Sure there are enchiladas and tamales and tacos, but they might be filled with ostrich or buffalo. Rest assured Esparza's also serves standard ingredients such as chicken and beef. Main courses come with some pretty good rice and beans, and if you want your meal hotter, they'll toss you a couple of jalapeño peppers. The *nopalitos* (fried cactus) are worth a try, and the margaritas are some of the best in Portland. While you're waiting for a seat (there's almost always a wait), check out the vintage tunes on the jukebox.

2725 SE Ankeny St. ℂ **503/234-7909.** Reservations not accepted. Main courses $8.50–$18. AE, DC, DISC, MC, V. Mon–Sat 11:30am–10pm (in summer Fri–Sat until 10:30pm).

Nicholas's *Finds* MIDDLE EASTERN   This little hole-in-the-wall on an unattractive stretch of Grand Avenue is usually packed at mealtimes, and it's not the decor or ambience that pulls people in. The big draw is the great food and cheap prices. In spite of the heat from the pizza oven and the crowded conditions, the customers and wait-staff still manage to be friendly. Our favorite dish is the *Manakish,* Mediterranean pizza with thyme, oregano, sesame seeds, olive oil, and lemony-flavored sumac. Also available are a creamy hummus, baba ghanouj, kabobs, falafel, and gyros.

318 SE Grand Ave. (between Pine and Oak sts.). ℂ **503/235-5123.** www.nicholasrestaurant.com. Reservations not accepted. Main courses $4.75–$11. No credit cards. Mon–Sat 11am–9pm; Sun noon–9pm.

Salvador Molly's 🖈 *Finds* CARIBBEAN   With lots of colorful mismatched tables and chairs and a funky, tropical decor, this Caribbean restaurant is a real hot spot. Flavors are in your face, servings are big, and prices are low. Best of all, this self-styled pirate cookin' is a surefire antidote to a gray winter day. What's not to love? With lots of spicy starters, this is also a great spot for a light meal. Be forewarned, however, that the food here can be fiery. There's even a "Wall of Flame" for people who can survive

Salvador Molly's habanero-spiked great balls of fire. For tamer tastes, try the *arepas* (Venezuelan corn cakes), the oyster taco, or tamales steamed in banana leaves.

3350 SE Morrison St. (C) 503/234-0896. www.salvadormollys.com. Main courses $8.25–$14. AE, DISC, MC, V. Mon–Thurs 4:30–10pm; Fri 4:30–midnight; Sat noon–midnight; Sun noon–10pm.

COFFEE, TEA, BAKERIES & PASTRY SHOPS
CAFES

If you'd like to sample some cafes around Portland that serve the full range of coffee drinks and that are atmospheric, we recommend the following:

With an upscale Starbucks-style interior decor, a social conscience, and a Pearl District location, **World Cup,** 721 NW Ninth Ave. (© **503/546-7377**), is a coffee haven for the politically correct. It's even located in an unusual environmentally friendly "green" building that has a rooftop terrace. Other World Cups are located inside Powell's City of Books, 1005 W. Burnside St. (© **503/228-4651**, ext. 234), and in the Nob Hill neighborhood at 1740 NW Glisan St. (© **503/228-4152**).

Many a Portlander swears by the coffee at **Stumptown Coffee Roasters,** 128 SW Third Ave. (© **503/295-6144**), a big, trendy cafe with an art-school aesthetic. Whether you go for the French press or a double shot of espresso, you're sure to be satisfied. Over on the east side of the Willamette River are Stumptown's two original cafes: 3377 SE Division St. (© **503/230-7797**) and 3356 SE Belmont St. (© **503/232-8889**), which both tend to attract a young, hip clientele.

If hot chocolate, not coffee, is your cup of choice, then be sure to stop by **Moonstruck Chocolate Café,** 608 SW Alder St. (© **503/241-0955**), where you can chooses from a wide variety of hot chocolate drinks. There's another Moonstruck in the Nob Hill neighborhood at 526 NW 23rd Ave. (© **503/542-3400**).

BAKERIES & PASTRY SHOPS

Pearl Bakery ✿✿, 102 NW Ninth Ave. (© **503/827-0910**), in the heart of the Pearl District, is famous in Portland for its breads and European-style pastries. The gleaming bakery cafe is also good for sandwiches, such as a roasted eggplant and tomato pesto on crusty bread.

Say the words "Papa Haydn" to a Portlander, and you'll see a blissful smile appear. What is it about this little bistro that gets locals gushing superlatives? The desserts. The lemon chiffon torte, raspberry gâteau, black velvet, and tiramisu at **Papa Haydn West** ✿✿, 701 NW 23rd Ave. (© **503/228-7317**), are legendary. There's another location at 5829 SE Milwaukie Ave. (© **503/232-9440**) in Sellwood.

Also in the Nob Hill neighborhood, you'll find **Ken's Artisan Bakery,** 338 NW 21st Ave. (© **503/248-2202;** www.kensartisan.com), which doesn't do a wide variety of pastries. But what it does do, it does very well. Yum! Try the fruit tarts. My current favorite bakery in the neighborhood is the utterly Gallic **St. Honoré Boulangerie,** 2335 NW Thurman St. (© **503/445-4342;** www.sainthonorebakery.com); not only does this place turn out awesome pastries and breads, but you can read *Le Monde,* while eating your croissant.

Located in Ladd's Addition, an old neighborhood full of big trees and craftsman-style bungalows, **Palio Dessert House** ✿, 1996 SE Ladd Ave. (© **503/232-9412**), is a very relaxed place with a timeless European quality. To get there, take Hawthorne Boulevard east to the corner of 12th and Hawthorne, then go diagonally down Ladd Avenue.

The **Rimsky-Korsakoffee House** ⊛, 707 SE 12th Ave. (© **503/232-2640**), a classic old-style coffeehouse (complete with mismatched chairs), has been Portland's favorite dessert hangout for more than a decade. Live classical music and great desserts keep patrons loyal. (The mocha fudge cake is small but deadly.) It's open from 7pm to midnight on Sunday through Thursday and until 1am on Fridays and Saturdays.

We've saved the best for last: **Pix Patisserie,** 3402 SE Division St. (© **503/232-4407**), makes by far the most decadent pastries in Portland. Every sweet little jewel here is a work of art, and it can sometimes be a real challenge to desecrate these creations with a fork. Go ahead; take a bite. You won't soon forget the experience!

If it's hot out and nothing will do but something cold and creamy, check out one of Portland's gelaterias. These Italian-style frozen-dessert parlors have taken Portland by storm. In the Nob Hill neighborhood, there's **Alotto Gelato,** 931 NW 23rd Ave. (© **503/228-1709**), and over in northeast Portland, just off East Burnside Street, there's **Staccato Gelato,** 232 NE 28th Ave. (© **503/231-7100**).

QUICK BITES & CHEAP EATS

If you're just looking for something quick, cheap, and good to eat, there are lots of great options around the city. Downtown, at **Good Dog/Bad Dog,** 708 SW Alder St. (© **503/222-3410**), you'll find handmade sausages. The bratwurst with kraut and onions is a good deal.

Designer pizzas topped with anything from roasted eggplant to wild mushrooms to Thai peanut sauce can be had at **Pizzicato Gourmet Pizza** ⊛. Find them downtown at 705 SW Alder St. (© **503/226-1007**); in Northwest Portland at 505 NW 23rd Ave. (© **503/242-0023**); and in southeast Portland at 2811 E. Burnside (© **503/236-6045**).

5 Seeing the Sights

Most American cities boast about their museums and historic buildings, shopping, and restaurants; Portland, as always, is different. Ask a Portlander about the city's must-see attractions, and you'll probably be directed to the Japanese Garden, the International Rose Test Garden, and the Portland Saturday Market.

This isn't to say that the Portland Art Museum, which specializes in blockbuster exhibits, isn't worth visiting or that there are no historic buildings around. It's just that Portland's gardens, thanks to the weather here, are some of the finest in the country. What's more, all the rain seems to keep artists indoors creating beautiful art and crafts for much of the year, work that many artists sell at the Portland Saturday Market.

Gardening is a Portland obsession, and there are numerous world-class public gardens and parks within the city. Visiting all the city's gardens alone can take up 2 or 3 days of touring, so leave plenty of time in your schedule if you have a green thumb.

Once you've seen the big attractions, it's time to start learning why everyone loves living here so much. Portlanders for the most part are active types, who enjoy skiing on Mount Hood and hiking in the Columbia Gorge just as much as they enjoy going to art museums, so no visit to Portland would be complete without venturing out into the Oregon countryside. Within 1½ hours you can be skiing on Mount Hood, walking beside the chilly waters of the Pacific, sampling pinot noir in wine country, or hiking beside a waterfall in the Columbia Gorge. But for those who prefer urban activities, the museums and parks listed below should satisfy.

Portland Attractions

Berry Botanic Garden **17**
Crystal Springs
Rhododendron Garden **15**
Elk Rock Garden of
the Bishop's Close **18**
International Rose Test
Garden **3**
Jamison Square **10**
Japanese Garden **2**
Mill Ends Park **13**
Oaks Park
Amusement Center **16**
Oregon Historical
Society Museum **7**
Oregon Museum of Science
& Industry (OMSI) **14**
Pioneer Courthouse Square **9**
Pittock Mansion **1**
Portland Art Museum **6**
Portland Childen's Museum **5**
Portland Classical
Chinese Garden **11**
Portlandia &
the Portland Building **8**
Portland Sunday Market **12**
Washington Park **4**
World Forestry Center
Discovery Museum **5**

Frommer's Favorite Portland Experiences

- **Strolling the Grounds at the Japanese Garden.** This is the best Japanese garden in the United States, perhaps the best anywhere outside of Japan. Our favorite time to visit is in June when the Japanese irises are in bloom. There's no better stress reducer in the city.
- **Beer Sampling at Brewpubs.** They may not have invented beer here in Portland, but they've certainly turned it into an art form. Whether you're looking for a cozy corner pub or an upscale taproom, you'll find a brewpub where you can feel comfortable sampling what local brewmeisters are concocting.
- **Kayaking Around Ross Island.** Seattle may be the sea-kayaking capital of the Northwest, but Portland's not a bad spot for pursuing this sport either. You can paddle on the Columbia or Willamette rivers, but our favorite easy outing is around Ross Island in the Willamette River. You can even paddle past the submarine at the Oregon Museum of Science and Industry and pull out at Tom McCall Waterfront Park.
- **Mountain Biking the Leif Erickson Road.** Forest Park is the largest forested city park in the country, and running its length is unpaved Leif Erickson Road. The road is closed to cars and extends for 12 miles. Along the way, there are occasional views of the Columbia River. This is a long but relatively easy ride, without any strenuous climbs.
- **Hanging Out at Powell's.** They don't call Powell's the City of Books for nothing. This bookstore, which sells both new and used books, is so big you have to get a map at the front door. No matter how much time I spend here, it's never enough. A large cafe makes it all that much easier to while away the hours.

DOWNTOWN PORTLAND'S CULTURAL DISTRICT

Any visit to Portland should start at the corner of Southwest Broadway and Yamhill Street on **Pioneer Courthouse Square.** The brick-paved square is an outdoor stage for everything from flower displays to concerts to protest rallies, but not too many years ago this beautiful area was nothing but a parking lot. The parking lot had been created in 1951 (in the days before historic preservation) when the Portland Hotel, an architectural gem of a Queen Anne–style château, was torn down.

Today the square, with its waterfall fountain and freestanding columns, is Portland's favorite gathering spot, especially at noon, when the **Weather Machine** ✦, a mechanical sculpture, forecasts the weather for the next 24 hours. Amid a fanfare of music and flashing lights, the Weather Machine sends up clouds of mist and then either a sun (clear weather), a dragon (stormy weather), or a blue heron (clouds and drizzle) appears.

Keep your eyes on the square's brick pavement, too. Every brick contains a name (or names) or statement, and some are rather curious. Also on the square, you'll find the **Portland Oregon Visitor Association Information Center** and a Starbucks. Unfortunately, you'll also find plenty of street kids hanging out here all hours of the day and night, so don't be surprised if they ask you for spare change.

- **Free Rides on the Vintage Trolleys.** TriMet buses, MAX light-rail trolleys, and Portland Streetcars are all free within a large downtown area known as the Fareless Square. That alone should be enough to get you on some form of public transit while you're in town, but if you're really lucky, you might catch one of the vintage trolley cars that operate on the MAX and Portland Streetcar lines on weekends from March through December. There aren't any San Francisco–style hills, but the trolleys are still fun to ride.

- **An Afternoon at the Portland Saturday Market.** This large arts-and-crafts market is an outdoor showcase for hundreds of the Northwest's creative artisans. You'll find one-of-a-kind clothes, jewelry, kitchenwares, musical instruments, and much, much more. The food stalls serve up some great fast food, too.

- **Summertime Concerts at the Washington Park Zoo.** Summertime in Portland means partying with the pachyderms. Throughout the summer you can catch live music at the zoo's amphitheater. Musical styles include blues, rock, bluegrass, folk, Celtic, and jazz. Sometimes for nothing more than the regular zoo admission, you can catch the concert and tour the zoo (if you arrive early enough). Picnics are encouraged, and beer and wine are for sale during concerts.

- **First Thursday Art Walk.** On the first Thursday of every month, Portland goes on an art binge. People get dressed up and go gallery hopping from art opening to art opening. There are usually hors d'oeuvres and wine available, and sometimes there's even live music. The galleries stay open until 9pm.

Also not to be missed in this neighborhood are *Portlandia* ⊛⊛ and the **Portland Building,** 1120 SW Fifth Ave. Symbol of the city, *Portlandia* is the second-largest hammered bronze statue in the country (the largest is the Statue of Liberty). The massive kneeling figure holds a trident in one hand and reaches toward the street with the other. This classically designed figure perches incongruously above the entrance to the controversial Portland Building, considered to be the first postmodern structure in the United States. Today, anyone familiar with the bizarre constructions of Los Angeles architect Frank Gehry would find it difficult to understand how such an innocuous and attractive building could have ever raised such a fuss, but it did just that in the early '80s.

Oregon Historical Society Museum ⊛   In the middle of the 19th century, the Oregon Territory was a land of promise and plenty. Thousands of hardy individuals set out along the Oregon Trail, crossing a vast and rugged country to reach the fertile valleys of this region. Others came by ship around Cape Horn. If you'd like to learn about the people who discovered Oregon before you, visit this well-designed museum. Fascinating exhibits chronicle Oregon's history from before the arrival of the first Europeans to well into the 20th century. Museum docents, with roots stretching back to the days of the Oregon Trail, are often on hand to answer questions. You can't miss this museum—look for the eight-story-high trompe l'oeil mural stretching across the front.

1200 SW Park Ave. (©) **503/222-1741.** www.ohs.org. Admission $10 adults, $8 students and seniors, $5 children 6–18, free for children under 6. Mon–Sat 10am–5pm; Sun noon–5pm. Bus: 6 or 8. MAX: Library Station. Portland Streetcar: Art Museum (northbound); 11th Ave. and Jefferson St. (southbound).

Portland Art Museum   This is the oldest art museum in the Northwest, and in October 2005 a new wing that gave the museum lots more space for displaying its collection of modern and contemporary art. This collection begins with European Impressionist and moves right up to the present. Although the museum has respectable collections of European, Asian, and American art, the best reason to visit is to see the extensive collection of Native American art and artifacts. There's also a good collection of Northwest contemporary art that includes a fascinating two-story wall of "artifacts" by glass artist William Morris. The Portland Art Museum is frequently the Northwest stop for touring blockbuster exhibits. There's also a small sculpture court. October through April, on Wednesday nights from 5:30 to 7:30pm, the Museum After Hours program presents live music (admission is $8–$10 if you aren't a museum member). Between November 5, 2006, and March 4, 2007, there will be an exhibit of ancient Egyptian treasures.

1219 SW Park Ave. (©) **503/226-2811.** www.portlandartmuseum.org. Admission $10–$15 adults, $9–$13 seniors and students, $6 children 5–18, free for children under 5. Tues–Wed and Sat 10am–5pm; Thurs–Fri 10am–8pm; Sun noon–5pm. Bus: 6. MAX: Library Station. Portland Streetcar: Art Museum (northbound); 11th Ave. and Jefferson St. (southbound).

SKIDMORE HISTORIC DISTRICT, CHINATOWN & THE WILLAMETTE RIVER WATERFRONT

If Pioneer Courthouse Square is the city's living room, **Tom McCall Waterfront Park,** along the Willamette River, is the city's front-yard play area. There are acres of lawns, shade trees, sculptures, and fountains, and the paved path through the park is popular with in-line skaters and joggers. This park also serves as the site of numerous festivals each summer. Also in the park is the Japanese-American Historical Plaza, dedicated to Japanese Americans who were sent to internment camps during World War II.

Just north of this plaza, a pedestrian walkway crosses the Steel Bridge to the east side of the Willamette River and the **Eastbank Esplanade,** which stretches for about 1½ miles along the east bank of the river. Although this paved multiuse path gets a lot of traffic noise from the adjacent freeway, it offers great views of the Portland skyline. Along the route there are small parks and gardens, interesting sculptures, and benches for sitting and soaking up the view. The highlight of this path is a section that floats right on the river and is attached to pilings in much the same way that a floating dock is constructed. You can access the Eastbank Esplanade by way of the pedestrian pathway on the Steel Bridge. This bridge is at the north end of Waterfront Park.

Oregon Museum of Science and Industry (OMSI) ⓡ *Kids*   Located on the east bank of the Willamette River across from the south end of Waterfront Park, this modern science museum has six huge halls, and both kids and adults find the exhibits fun and fascinating. This is a hands-on museum, and everyone is urged to get involved with displays, from a discovery space for toddlers to physics and chemistry labs for older children. Simulated earthquakes and tornadoes are perennial favorites. There's plenty of pure entertainment at an **OMNIMAX theater** and the **Murdock Sky Theater,** which features laser-light shows and astronomy presentations. The USS *Blueback*

Pearls in the Pearl District

The Pearl District has become Portland's hottest neighborhood, and in addition to all the restaurants, wine bars, and boutiques, there are some fun works of public art and a beautiful little park that looks like a small park in Paris.

Stroll through the tree-shaded parks of the North Park blocks, which form the eastern edge of the Pearl District; at the Burnside Street end of these parks you'll see a huge Chinese bronze elephant that was a gift from one of Portland's sister cities. A couple of blocks north of this elephant, watch for a bronze dog-bowl water fountain set in a checkerboard floor of stone. This odd sculpture was created by William Wegman, famous for his humorous photos of his dogs.

Right in the heart of the Pearl District, at the corner of NW Johnson Street and NW 10th Avenue, you'll find Jamison Square, a park with an unusual wall-like cascading waterfall that fills a shallow pool. Around the graveled areas of the park, you'll find bistro chairs where you can sit and enjoy a latte from a nearby espresso bar. Be sure to notice the totem-pole–inspired sculptures along the western edge of the park.

submarine (used in the film *The Hunt for Red October*) is docked here, and tours are given daily.

A paved pathway runs beside OMSI and heads north to the Eastbank Esplanade and south 3 miles to Oaks Bottom amusement park. Along the pathway beside the museum, there are several interesting informational plaques about the history of Portland and its relationship to the Willamette River. OMSI is also the departure point for several different boat cruises up and down the Willamette River.

1945 SE Water Ave. Ⓒ **800/955-6674** or 503/797-6674. www.omsi.edu. Museum or OMNIMAX $9 adults, $7 seniors and children 3–13; $5.50 submarine tours, planetarium shows, and matinee laser-light shows; $7.50 evening laser shows; discounted combination tickets available. Thurs 2pm until closing all tickets are 2 for 1. Mid-June to Labor Day daily 9:30am–7pm; Labor Day to mid-June Tues–Sun 9:30am–5:30pm. Closed Thanksgiving and Christmas. Bus: 4, 14, or 33.

Portland Classical Chinese Garden 🎃🎃   This classically styled Chinese garden takes up an entire city block and is the largest of its type outside of China. The walls surrounding these gardens in Portland's Chinatown separate the urban 21st century from the timeless Chinese landscape within. The landscape is designed to evoke the wild mountains of China and to create a tranquil oasis within an urban setting. The gardens are centered around a small pond, which, at one end, has a rock wall meant to conjure up the sort of images often seen in Chinese scroll paintings. Numerous pavilions, a small bridge, and a winding pathway provide ever-changing views of the gardens. With its many paved paths and small viewing pavilions, this garden has a completely different feel from the Japanese Garden. Try to visit as soon as the gardens open in the morning; when the crowds descend and the guided tours start circulating—well, so much for tranquillity. On the other hand, if you want to learn more about the garden, you can join a guided tour at noon or 1pm. Be sure to stop and have a cup of tea and maybe a snack in the garden's tearoom.

NW Everett St. and NW Third Ave. ℭ **503/228-8131.** www.portlandchinesegarden.org. Admission $7 adults, $6 seniors, $5.50 students and children 6–18, free for children 5 and under. Apr–Oct daily 9am–6pm; Nov–Mar daily 10am–5pm. Bus: 1, 4, 5, 8, 10, 16, 33, 40, or 77. MAX: Old Town/Chinatown Station.

Portland Saturday Market 𝒜   The Portland Saturday Market (actually held on both Saturday and Sunday) is arguably the city's best-loved event. For years the Northwest has attracted artists and craftspeople, and every Saturday and Sunday nearly 300 of them can be found selling their creations here. In addition to the dozens of crafts stalls, you'll find ethnic and unusual foods and lots of free entertainment. This is one of the best places in Portland to shop for one-of-a-kind gifts. The atmosphere is always cheerful and the crowds colorful. Located at the heart of the Skidmore District, Portland Saturday Market makes an excellent starting or finishing point for a walk around Portland's downtown historic neighborhood. On Sunday, on-street parking is free.

Underneath the west end of the Burnside Bridge between SW First Ave. and SW Naito Pkwy. ℭ **503/222-6072.** www.portlandsaturdaymarket.com. Free admission. 1st weekend in Mar to Christmas Eve Sat 10am–5pm and Sun 11am–4:30pm. Bus: 12, 19, or 20. MAX: Skidmore Fountain Station.

WASHINGTON PARK & PORTLAND'S WEST HILLS

Portland is justly proud of its green spaces, and foremost among them are **Washington Park** and **Forest Park.**

Within Washington Park, you'll find the **Japanese Garden** and **International Rose Test Garden,** which are adjacent to one another on the more developed east side of the park (see the listings below). On the west side of the park (farther from the city center), you'll find not only the Hoyt Arboretum but also the Oregon Zoo, World Forestry Center Discovery Museum, and the Portland Children's Museum.

The 185-acre **Hoyt Arboretum** (ℭ **503/865-8733;** www.hoytarboretum.org) 𝒜 is planted with 1,100 species of trees and shrubs from temperate regions around the world and has several miles of hiking trails. Between April and October, there are free 1-hour guided tours of the arboretum on the first Saturday of the month at 10am. At the south end of the arboretum, adjacent to the World Forestry Center Discovery Museum and the Oregon Zoo, is the **Vietnam Veterans Living Memorial.** At the Visitor Center, 4000 SW Fairview Blvd. (Mon–Fri 9am–4pm and Sat 9am–3pm), you can pick up maps and guides to the arboretum. The arboretum can be reached either from the Oregon Zoo/World Forestry Center Discovery Museum/Portland Children's Museum area or by following the arboretum signs from West Burnside Street.

To the north of Hoyt Arboretum is **Forest Park** 𝒜𝒜 (ℭ **503/823-PLAY**), which, with more than 5,000 acres of forest, is the largest forested city park in the United States. Within the park, there are more than 74 miles of trails and old fire roads for hiking, jogging, and mountain biking. More than 100 species of birds call this forest home, making it a great spot for urban bird-watching. Along the forest trails, you can see huge old trees and find quiet picnic spots tucked away in the woods. One of the most convenient park access points is at the top of NW Thurman Street (just keep heading uphill until the road dead-ends). You can also park at the Hoyt Arboretum Visitor Center (see above) or the Audubon Society (see below), pick up a map of Forest Park, and head out from either of these locations.

Adjacent to Forest Park, you'll also find the **Portland Audubon Society,** 5151 NW Cornell Rd. (ℭ **503/292-6855;** www.audubonportland.org), which has a couple of miles of hiking trails on its forested property. In keeping with its mission to promote enjoyment, understanding, and protection of the natural world, these nature trails are

Great Photo Ops

If you've seen a photo of Portland with conical snow-covered Mount Hood looming in the background and you want to snap a similar photo while you're in town, there are several places to try. Most popular are probably the terraces of the International Rose Test Garden and from behind the pavilion at the Japanese Garden. Another great view can be glimpsed from the grounds of the Pittock Mansion. All three of these places are described in detail elsewhere in this chapter.

One other vista is located atop Council Crest, a hilltop park in Portland's West Hills. To reach this park, take the Sylvan exit off U.S. 26 west of downtown Portland, turn south and then east (left) on Humphrey Boulevard, and then follow the signs. Alternatively, you can follow SW Broadway south out of downtown Portland and follow the signs. This road winds through attractive hillside neighborhoods for a ways before reaching Council Crest.

open to the public. You can also visit the Nature Store or Wildlife Care Center here. To find this facility from downtown Portland, first drive to NW 23rd Avenue, and then head uphill on NW Lovejoy Street, which becomes NW Cornell Road. (*Warning:* Car break-ins are commonplace at the parking area just down the road from the Audubon Society, so don't leave anything of value in your car.)

By car, the easiest route to the Washington Park attractions from downtown Portland is to take SW Jefferson Street west, turn right onto SW 18th Avenue, left on SW Salmon Street, right on SW King Street, and then left onto SW Park Place. Although this sounds confusing, you'll find most of the route well marked with "Scenic Drive" signs. Alternatively, you can drive west on West Burnside Street and watch for signs to the arboretum, or take the zoo exit off U.S. 26. All of these attractions can also be reached via Bus 63. You can also take the MAX line to the Washington Park Station, which is adjacent to the Oregon Zoo, World Forestry Center Discovery Museum, Portland Children's Museum, and Hoyt Arboretum. From here, it is possible (in the summer months) to take a bus shuttle to the Japanese Garden and International Rose Test Garden. There's also a miniature train that runs from the zoo to a station near the two public gardens. However, to ride this train, you must first pay zoo admission.

International Rose Test Garden ✿✿ Covering more than 5 acres of hillside in the West Hills above downtown Portland, these are among the largest and oldest rose test gardens in the United States and are the only city-maintained test gardens to bestow awards on each year's best roses. The gardens were established in 1917 by the American Rose Society and are used as a testing ground for new varieties of roses. Though you will probably see some familiar roses in the Gold Medal Garden, most of the 400 varieties on display are new hybrids being tested before marketing. Among the roses in bloom from late spring to early winter, you'll find a separate garden of miniature roses. There's also a Shakespeare Garden that includes flowers mentioned in the bard's works. After seeing these acres of roses, you'll understand why Portland is known as the City of Roses and why the Rose Festival in June is the city's biggest annual celebration. The small Rose Garden Store (© **503/227-7033**) is packed with rose-inspired products.

400 SW Kingston Ave., Washington Park. © **503/823-3636**. Free admission (donations accepted). Daily dawn–dusk. Bus: 63.

The Japanese Garden 🎋🎋🎋

Considered the finest example of a Japanese garden in North America, Portland's Japanese Garden should not be missed. Not only are there five different styles of Japanese gardens scattered over 5½ acres, but there's also a view of volcanic Mount Hood, which has a strong resemblance to Mount Fuji.

Although Japanese gardens are traditionally not designed with colorful floral displays, this garden definitely has its seasonal highlights. In early spring there are the cherry trees, in mid-spring there are the azaleas, in late spring a huge wisteria bursts into bloom, and in early summer, large Japanese irises color the banks of a pond. Among the gardens, there's a beautiful and very realistic waterfall.

> **All Aboard!**
> The **Washington Park and Zoo Railway** travels between the zoo and the International Rose Test Garden and Japanese Garden. Tickets for the miniature railway are $3.50 for adults, $2.75 for seniors and children 3 to 11, and free for children under 3. There's also a shorter route that just loops around the zoo.

This is a very tranquil spot and is even more peaceful on rainy days, when the crowds stay away, so don't pass up a visit just because of inclement weather. Also, on the third Saturday of each of the summer months, there's a demonstration of the Japanese tea ceremony in the garden's teahouse.

611 SW Kingston Ave. (in Washington Park). © **503/223-1321**. www.japanesegarden.com. Admission $6.75 adults, $5 seniors, $4 students and children 6–17, free for children under 6. Apr–Sept Mon noon–7pm and Tues–Sun 10am–7pm; Oct–Mar Mon noon–4pm and Tues–Sun 10am–4pm. Closed Thanksgiving, Christmas, and New Year's Day. Bus: 63. MAX: Washington Park Station (then, in summer months, take the shuttle bus or the zoo train).

Oregon Zoo 🎋 *Kids*

The Oregon Zoo is perhaps best known for its elephants and has the largest breeding herd of elephants in captivity. However, in recent years, the zoo has been adding new exhibits and branching out beyond the world of pachyderms. The Africa exhibit, which includes a very lifelike rainforest and a savanna populated by zebras, rhinos, giraffes, hippos, and other animals, is one of the most realistic habitats you'll ever see at a zoo. Equally impressive is the Alaskan tundra exhibit, with grizzly bears, wolves, and musk oxen. The Cascade Crest exhibit includes mountain goat habitat, and in the Steller Cove exhibit, you can watch the antics of Steller's sea lions and sea otters. Don't miss the bat house or the Amazon Flooded Forest exhibit.

In the summer, there are **outdoor concerts** in the zoo's amphitheater; admission prices vary.

4001 SW Canyon Rd., Washington Park. © **503/226-1561**. www.oregonzoo.org. Admission $9.50 adults, $8 seniors, $6.50 children 3–11, free under age 2; $2 admission for all 2nd Tues of each month. Apr 15–Sept 15 daily 9am–6pm; Sept 16–Apr 14 daily 9am–4pm. Closed Christmas. Bus: 63. MAX: Washington Park Station.

Pittock Mansion 🎋

At nearly the highest point in the West Hills, 1,000 feet above sea level, stands the most impressive mansion in Portland. Once slated to be torn down to make way for new housing, this grand château, built by the founder of Portland's *Oregonian* newspaper, is fully restored and open to the public. Built in 1914 in a French Renaissance style, the mansion featured many innovations, including a built-in vacuum system and amazing multiple showerheads in the baths. Today it's furnished with 18th- and 19th-century antiques, much as it might have been at the time the Pittocks lived here. With an expansive view over the city to the Cascade Range, the lawns surrounding the mansion are great for picnics. You can also access Forest Park's Wildwood Trail from here.

3229 NW Pittock Dr. (Ⓒ) 503/823-3624. www.pittockmansion.org. Admission $6 adults, $5 seniors, $3 children 6–18. June–Aug daily 11am–4pm; Sept–May daily noon–4pm. Closed 4 days in late Nov, Christmas, and the month of Jan.

World Forestry Center Discovery Museum   Although Oregon depends less and less on the timber industry with each passing year, this museum is still busy educating visitors about the importance of forest resources around the world. Step inside the huge wooden main hall, and you come face to bark with several large and very lifelike trees. Press a button at its base and you can pilot a video camera around the tree's branches. Pay an extra few dollars, and you can climb into a chairlift that lets you explore these same trees. In another exhibit, you can practice being a smoke jumper (firefighter), while in another area, you can go on a video raft ride. There are also interesting temporary exhibits staged here throughout the year, from photographic exhibits to displays of the woodworker's art.

4033 SW Canyon Rd. (Ⓒ) 503/228-1367. www.worldforestry.org. Admission $7 adults, $6 seniors, $5 children 5–18, free for children under 6. Daily 10am–5pm. Closed Thanksgiving, Christmas Eve, and Christmas. Bus: 63. MAX: Washington Park Station.

PORTLAND'S OTHER PUBLIC GARDENS

For Portland's two best-loved public gardens, the **International Rose Test Garden** and the **Japanese Garden,** see "Washington Park & Portland's West Hills," above.

If roses are your passion, you'll also want to check out the **Peninsula Park Rose Garden** at the corner of North Portland Boulevard and North Albina Avenue (take the Portland Blvd. exit off I-5 and go 2 blocks east), which has even more rose bushes than the International Rose Test Garden.

The Berry Botanic Garden 𝄞   Originally founded as a private garden, the Berry Botanic Garden is now one of Portland's favorite public gardens. Among the highlights is a large, forestlike collection of mature rhododendron shrubs. There are also rock gardens with unusual plants, a native plant trail, and a fern garden. The garden is open by reservation only.

11505 SW Summerville Ave. (Ⓒ) 503/636-4112. www.berrybot.org. Adults $5. Open daylight hours by appointment. Bus: 35.

Crystal Springs Rhododendron Garden 𝄞   Nowhere do rhododendrons do better than in the cool, rainy Northwest, and nowhere in Portland is there a more impressive planting of rhodies than at Crystal Springs. Eight months out of the year, this is a tranquil garden, with a waterfall, a lake, and ducks to feed. But when the rhododendrons and azaleas bloom from March to June, it becomes a spectacular mass of blazing color. The Rhododendron Show and Plant Sale is held here on Mother's Day weekend.

SE 28th Ave. (1 block north of SE Woodstock Blvd.). (Ⓒ) 503/771-8386. Admission $3 Mar 1 to Labor Day Thurs–Mon 10am–6pm; free at other times. Open year-round daily dawn to dusk. Bus: 19.

Elk Rock Garden of the Bishop's Close 𝄞   Set on a steep hillside above the Willamette River between Portland and Lake Oswego, this was once a private garden but was donated to the local Episcopal bishop of Oregon on the condition that it be

The World's Smallest Park

Don't blink as you cross the median strip on Naito Parkway at the corner of Southwest Taylor Street, or you might just walk right past **Mill Ends Park**, the smallest public park in the world.

Covering a whopping 452 square inches of land, this park was the whimsical creation of local journalist Dick Fagen. After a telephone pole was removed from the middle of Naito Parkway (then known as Front Ave.), Fagen dubbed the phone pole hole Mill Ends Park (Mill Ends, a lumber mill term, was the name of Fagen's newspaper column). The columnist, whose office looked down on the hole in the middle of Front Avenue, peopled the imaginary park with leprechauns and would often write of the park's goings-on in his column. On St. Patrick's Day 1976, it was officially designated a Portland city park. Rumor has it that despite its diminutive size, the park has been the site of several weddings (although the parks department has never issued a wedding permit for it).

opened to the public. The mature gardens are at their best through the spring and early summer. There's also an excellent view of Mount Hood from the grounds.

11800 SW Military Lane. ℂ **800/452-2562** or 503/636-5613. www.diocese-oregon.org/theclose. Free admission. Daily 8am–5pm. Bus: 35.

6 Especially for Kids

In addition to the attractions listed below, the kids will especially enjoy the **Oregon Museum of Science and Industry** (p. 98), which has lots of hands-on exhibits, and the **Oregon Zoo** (p. 102). From inside the zoo, it's possible to take a small train through Washington Park to the International Rose Test Garden, below which there is the **Rose Garden Children's Park,** a colorful play area for younger children. The **Salmon Street Springs fountain,** in downtown's Tom McCall Waterfront Park (at SW Naito Pkwy. and SW Salmon St.), is another fun place to take the kids. During hot summer months, there are always lots of happy kids playing in the jets of water that erupt from the pavement here. There are also big lawns in **Waterfront Park,** so the kids can run off plenty of excess energy. There's also a splashy play-pond at Jamison Square in the Pearl District.

Portland Children's Museum *Kids*   Located across the parking lot form the Oregon Zoo, this large, modern children's museum includes exhibits for children ages 6 months to 13 years. Kids can act out fairy tales, play in a magical forest, or go shopping in a kid-size grocery store. However, it is the Water Works exhibit that is likely to make the biggest splash with your kids. There are also six studios with changing exhibits and opportunities for exploring the visual, literary, and performing arts. Combined with the nearby zoo, this museum makes for an easy all-day kid-oriented outing.

4015 SW Canyon Rd. ℂ **503/223-6500.** www.portlandcm2.org. Admission $6 adults and children, $5 seniors, free for children under 1 yr. Tues–Sat 9am–5pm; Sun 11am–5pm. Closed some national holidays. Bus: 63. MAX: Washington Park Station.

Oaks Park Amusement Center *(Kids)*   What would summer be without the screams of happy thrill seekers risking life and limb on a roller coaster? Covering more than 44 acres, this amusement park first opened in 1905 to coincide with the Lewis and Clark Exposition. Beneath the shady oaks for which the park is named, you'll find waterfront picnic sites, miniature golf, music, and plenty of thrilling rides. Check out the largest wood-floored roller-skating rink in the West, where an organist still plays the Wurlitzer for the skaters.

East end of the Sellwood Bridge. (C) 503/233-5777. www.oakspark.com. Free admission; individual-ride tickets $1.75, limited-ride bracelet $11, deluxe-ride bracelet $14. Rides open Apr to early Oct; skating rink open year-round. Hours vary seasonally; call for details. Bus: 40.

7 Organized Tours

CRUISES

With two large rivers winding through the city, Portland is a town that needs to be seen from the water. Try the ***Portland Spirit*** ((C) 800/224-3901 or 503/224-3900; www.portlandspirit.com), a 75-foot yacht that specializes in dinner cruises. Lunch, brunch, and dinner cruises feature Northwest cuisine with views of the city skyline. There are also basic sightseeing cruises, and on Friday nights July through September, there are also Friday afternoon cocktail cruises with a live band. Call for reservations and schedule. Prices range from $16 to $60 for adults and $11 to $55 for children. This company also operates jet-boat tours that go up the Columbia River to the Bonneville Dam and down the Columbia to Astoria.

For high-speed tours up the Willamette River, there are the **Willamette Jetboat Excursions** *(R)* ((C) 888/538-2628 or 503/231-1532; www.willamettejet.com). These high-powered open-air boats blast their way from downtown Portland to the impressive Willamette Falls at Oregon City. The 2-hour tours, which start at OMSI, are $29 for adults and $19 for children 4 to 11, free for children under 4. Tours are offered from late April to early October. There are also less expensive 1-hour tours, but these do not go upriver to the falls.

BUS TOURS

If you want to get a general overview of Portland, **Gray Line** ((C) 888/684-3322 or 503/243-6789; www.grayline.com) offers several half-day and full-day tours. One itinerary takes in the International Rose Test Garden and Pittock Mansion; another stops at the Portland Classical Chinese Garden and the Pearl District. There are also tours to see the waterfalls in the Columbia Gorge, to Mount Hood, and to the Oregon coast. Tour prices range from $34 to $75 for adults, and from $17 to $38 for children.

RAIL EXCURSIONS

While Portland is busy reviving trolleys and streetcars as a viable mass transit option, the **Willamette Shore Trolley** *(R)* ((C) **503/697-7436;** www.trainweb.org/oerhs/wst.htm) offers scenic excursions along the Willamette River in historic trolley cars (including a double-decker) from the early part of this century. The old wooden trolleys rumble over trestles and through a tunnel as they cover the 7 miles between Portland and the upscale suburb of Lake Oswego (a 40-min. trip). Along the way, you pass through shady corridors with lots of views of the river and glimpses into the yards of posh riverfront homes. In Lake Oswego, the trolley station is on State Street, between A Avenue and Foothills Road. In Portland, the station is about 1 mile south of downtown in an industrial area off Macadam Avenue at the corner of Moody Avenue and Bancroft Street. The round-trip fare is $10 for adults, $9 for seniors, and $6 for children 3 to 12. Call for a schedule.

WALKING TOURS

Peter's Walking Tours of Portland (© 503/665-2558; www.walkportland.com), led by Peter Chausse, are a great way to learn more about Portland. The walking tours of downtown last 3 hours and take in the city's fountains, parks, historic places, art, and architecture. Tours are by reservation and cost $15 for adults and $5 teens (free for children under 8 with a paying adult).

Two to three times a year, Sharon Wood Wortman, author of *The Portland Bridge Book,* offers a **Bridge Tour** that explores several Portland bridges. These tours are offered through the Outdoor Recreation Program of **Portland Parks and Recreation** (© 503/823-5132; www.portlandparks.org). Many other walking tours are also available through Portland Parks and Recreation.

The seamy underbelly of history is laid bare on **Portland Underground Tours** (© 503/622-4798; www.members.tripod.com/cgs-mthood), which head down below street level in the historic Old Town neighborhood. On these unusual tours, which are only for those who are steady on their feet and able to duck under pipes and joists and such, you'll hear tales of the days when Portland was known as one of the most dangerous ports on the Pacific Rim. Sailors were regularly shanghaied from bars and brothels in this area and a vast network of tunnels and underground rooms was developed to support the shanghaiing business. Tours cost $12 for adults and $7 for children under 12 and are offered by reservation only.

8 Outdoor Pursuits

If you're planning ahead for a visit to Portland, contact **Metro,** 600 NE Grand Ave., Portland, OR 97232-2736 (© 503/797-1850; www.metro-region.org/parks), for its *Metro GreenScene* publication that lists tours, hikes, classes, and other outdoor activities and events being held in the Portland metro area.

BIKING

Portland is a very bicycle-friendly city, and you'll notice plenty of cyclists on the streets. There are also miles of paved bike paths around the city, and some good mountain biking areas as well. For mountain-bike rentals, head to **Fat Tire Farm,** 2714 NW Thurman St. (© 503/222-3276), where bikes go for $25 to $50 a day. Straight up Thurman Street from this bike shop, you'll find the trail head for **Leif Erickson Drive,** an old gravel road that is Forest Park's favorite route for cyclists and runners (the road is closed to motor vehicles); the trail is 12 miles long.

If you'd like to explore Portland's riverfront bike paths, stop in at **Waterfront Bicycle Rentals,** 0315 SW Montgomery St., Suite 360 (© 503/227-1719), where you can rent a bike for $7.50 to $13 per hour or $26 to $35 per half-day. From here head through Tom McCall Waterfront Park, cross the Steel Bridge, and ride down the Eastbank Esplanade path. This trail leads 4 miles south to the upscale Sellwood neighborhood.

GOLF

If you're a golfer, don't forget to bring your clubs along on a trip to Portland. There are plenty of public courses around the area, and greens fees at municipal courses range from $23 to $40 for 18 holes. Municipal golf courses operated by the Portland Bureau of Parks and Recreation include **Redtail Golf Course,** 8200 SW Scholls Ferry

Rd. ((C) **503/646-5166**); **Eastmoreland Golf Course,** 2425 SE Bybee Blvd. ((C) **503/ 775-2900**), which is the second-oldest golf course in the state (this one gets our vote for best municipal course); **Heron Lakes Golf Course,** 3500 N. Victory Blvd. ((C) **503/289-1818**), which has two courses designed by Robert Trent Jones; and **Rose City Golf Course,** 2200 NE 71st Ave. ((C) **503/253-4744**), on the site of a former country club. For more information, log on to **www.parks.ci.portland.or.us/Parks/ golf.htm**.

If you want to tee off where the pros play, head west from Portland 20 miles to **Pumpkin Ridge Golf Club** ⚘⚘, 12930 NW Old Pumpkin Ridge Rd., North Plains ((C) **503/647-4747;** http://pumpkinridge.nemexinc.com), a 36-hole course that has hosted the U.S. Women's Open. Greens fees range from $30 to $150 on the one course that is open to the public.

Also west of the city, on the south side of Hillsboro, you'll find **The Reserve Vineyards and Golf Club** ⚘⚘, 4805 SW 229th Ave., Aloha ((C) **503/649-8191;** www. reservegolf.com). Greens fees range from $40 to $85 depending on time of year and day of the week.

HIKING

Hiking opportunities abound in the Portland area. For shorter hikes, you don't even have to leave the city, just head to **Forest Park.** Bordered by West Burnside Street on the south, Newberry Road on the north, St. Helens Road on the east, and Skyline Road on the west, this is the largest forested city park in the country. Within this urban wilderness, you'll find more than 50 miles of trails. One of our favorite access points is at the top of NW Thurman Street in Northwest Portland. (After a hike, you can stop by a neighborhood brewpub, an espresso bar, or bakery along NW 23rd Ave. or NW 21st Ave. for a post-exercise payoff.) The Wildwood Trail is the longest trail in the park and along its length offers lots of options for loop hikes. For a roughly 2.5-mile hike, head up Leif Erickson Drive to a left onto the Wild Cherry Trail to a right onto the Wildwood Trail to a right onto the Dogwood Trail, and then a right on Leif Erickson Drive to get you back to the trail head. There are also good sections of trail to hike in the vicinity of the Hoyt Arboretum. To reach the arboretum's visitor center, 4000 SW Fairview Blvd. (open Mon–Fri 9am–4pm and Sat 9am–4pm), drive west on West Burnside Street from downtown Portland and follow signs to the arboretum. You can get a trail map here at the visitor center.

About 5 miles south of downtown, you'll find **Tryon Creek State Park** on Terwilliger Boulevard. This park is similar to Forest Park and is best known for its displays of trillium flowers in the spring. There are several miles of walking trails within the park, and a bike path to downtown Portland starts here.

You can buy or rent camping equipment from **REI Co-Op,** 1405 NW Johnson St. ((C) **503/221-1938**). This huge outdoor recreation supply store also sells books on hiking in the area.

SEA KAYAKING

If you want to check out the Portland skyline from water level, arrange for a sea kayak tour through the **Portland River Company** ⚘⚘, 0315 SW Montgomery St., Suite 330 ((C) **888/238-2059** or 503/229-0551; www.portlandrivercompany.com), which operates out of the RiverPlace Marina at the south end of Tom McCall Waterfront Park. A 2½-hour tour that circles nearby Ross Island costs $43 to $47 per person. This company also rents sea kayaks (to experienced paddlers) for $10 to $20 per hour.

9 Spectator Sports

Tickets to most games, including those of the Trail Blazers and the Portland Beavers, are sold through **Ticketmaster** (© **503/224-4400;** www.ticketmaster.com).

Tickets to events at the Rose Garden arena and Memorial Coliseum are also sold through the **Rose Quarter** box office (© **503/797-9617;** www.rosequarter.com). The Rose Garden arena is home to the Portland Trail Blazers and is the main focal point of Portland's **Rose Quarter.** This sports and entertainment neighborhood includes the Rose Garden, Memorial Coliseum, and several restaurants and bars. To reach the Rose Garden or adjacent Memorial Coliseum, take the Rose Quarter exit off I-5. Parking is expensive, so you might want to consider taking the MAX light-rail line from downtown Portland (the Rose Quarter stop is in the Fareless Square).

AUTO RACING   Portland International Raceway, West Delta Park, 1940 N. Victory Blvd. (© **503/823-RACE;** www.portlandraceway.com), hosts road races, drag races, motorcross and other motorcycle races, go-kart races, and even vintage-car races. February through October are the busiest months here.

BASEBALL   The Portland Beavers Baseball Club (© **503/553-5400** or 503/224-4400 for tickets; www.portlandbeavers.com), the AAA affiliate of the San Diego Padres, plays minor-league ball at PGE Park, SW 20th Avenue and Morrison Street. Tickets are $7 to $12.

BASKETBALL   The NBA's Portland Trail Blazers (© **503/231-8000** or 503/797-9619; www.nba.com/blazers) do well enough each year to have earned them a very loyal following. Unfortunately, they have a habit of not quite making it all the way to the top. The Blazers pound the boards at the Rose Garden arena. Call for current schedule and ticket information. Tickets are $10 to $131. If the Blazers are doing well, you can bet that tickets will be hard to come by.

10 Day Spas

If you'd rather opt for a massage than for a hike in the woods, consider spending a few hours at a day spa. These facilities typically offer massages, facials, seaweed wraps, and the like. Portland day spas include the **Avalon Hotel & Spa,** 0455 SW Hamilton Ct. (© **503/802-5800**); **Aveda Lifestyle Store and Spa,** 5th Avenue Suites Hotel, 500 Washington St. (© **503/248-0615**); and **Salon Nyla—The Day Spa,** adjacent to the Embassy Suites hotel at 327 SW Pine St. (© **503/228-0389;** www.salonnyla.com). However, the most unusual day spas in town are in the Pearl District. **Nirvana Apothecary & Day Spa,** 736 NW 11th Ave. (© **503/546-8155;** www.nirvana dayspa.com), is done up sort of like a Moroccan palace, while **Aequis,** 419 SW 11th Ave. (© **503/223-7847;** www.aequisspa.com), is an Asian-inspired retreat that follows Ayurvedic principles. Expect to pay about $85 or $95 for a 1-hour massage and $200 to $450 for a multi-treatment spa package.

11 Shopping

Portland has no sales tax, making it a popular shopping destination for Washingtonians, who cross the Columbia River to avoid paying their state's substantial sales tax.

THE SHOPPING SCENE

The **blocks around Pioneer Courthouse Square** are the heartland of upscale shopping in Portland. It's here that you'll find Nordstrom, NIKETOWN, Saks Fifth

Avenue, Tiffany, Pioneer Place shopping mall, and numerous upscale boutiques and shops.

However, Portland's hippest shopping districts are the **Pearl District** and **Nob Hill/Northwest,** both of which are in Northwest Portland. Most of the Pearl District's best shopping is along NW 10th and 11th avenues going north from West Burnside Street. Here you'll find all kinds of trendy boutiques, art galleries, and home-furnishing stores. The best Nob Hill shopping is along NW 23rd Avenue going north from West Burnside Street. Both neighborhoods have block after block of interesting, hip boutiques, and, along NW 23rd Avenue, a few national chains such as Gap, Urban Outfitters, and Pottery Barn.

For shops with a more down-to-earth, funky flavor, head out to the **Hawthorne District,** which is the city's counterculture shopping area (lots of tie-dye and imports).

Most small stores in Portland are open Monday through Saturday from 9 or 10am to 5 or 6pm. Shopping malls are usually open Monday through Friday from 9 or 10am to 9pm, Saturday from 9 or 10am to between 6 and 9pm, and Sunday from 11am until 6pm. Many department stores stay open past 6pm. Most art galleries and antiques stores are closed on Monday.

SHOPPING A TO Z
ANTIQUES
The **Sellwood** neighborhood (south of downtown at the east end of the Sellwood Bridge) is Portland's main antiques-shopping district, with about 30 antiques shops and antiques malls along 12 blocks of SE 13th Avenue. With its old Victorian homes and 19th-century architecture, Sellwood is an ideal setting for these shops. There are plenty of good restaurants in the area in case it turns into an all-day outing.

You'll also find three more large antiques malls (all under the same ownership) nearby on Milwaukie Boulevard: **Stars,** at 6717 SE Milwaukie Blvd. (© **503/ 235-9142**), and at 7027 SE Milwaukie Blvd. (© **503/239-0346**); and **Star & Splendid,** 7030 SE Milwaukie Blvd. (© **503/235-5990**).

ART GALLERIES
On the **first Thursday of the month,** galleries in downtown Portland schedule coordinated openings in the evening. Stroll from one gallery to the next, meeting artists and perhaps buying an original work of art. On the last Thursday of each month, galleries in the NE Alberta Street neighborhood stage a similar event. This latter event tends to attract a very culturally diverse crowd and has become the hottest art scene in the city. To find NE Alberta Street, drive north from downtown Portland on I-5 and watch for the NE Alberta Street exit.

A guide listing dozens of Portland galleries is available at galleries around the city.

General Art Galleries
Augen Gallery   When it opened nearly 20 years ago, the Augen Gallery focused on internationally recognized artists such as Jim Dine, Andy Warhol, and David Hockney. Today, the gallery has expanded its repertoire to regional contemporary painters and printmakers as well. 817 SW Second Ave. © **503/224-8182.** www.augengallery.com.

Blackfish Gallery   Artist-owned since 1979, the Blackfish is a large space featuring contemporary images. Since this gallery is a cooperative, it doesn't have the same constraints as a commercial art gallery and thus can present more cutting-edge and thought-provoking work. 420 NW Ninth Ave. © **503/224-2634.** www.blackfish.com.

The Laura Russo Gallery   The focus here is on Northwest contemporary artists, showcasing talented emerging artists as well as the estates of well-known regional artists. Laura Russo has been on the Portland art scene for a long time and is highly respected. 805 NW 21st Ave. ℂ 503/226-2754. www.laurarusso.com.

Pulliam Deffenbaugh Gallery   This gallery represents a long list of both talented newcomers and masters from the Northwest. Solo shows and salon-style group shows are held here. 929 NW Flanders St. ℂ 503/228-6665. www.pulliamdeffenbaugh.com.

Quintana Galleries   This large, bright space is virtually a small museum of Native American art, selling everything from Northwest Indian masks to contemporary paintings and sculptures by various Northwest coast Indian and Inuit artists. They also carry a smattering of Northwest and Southwest Indian antiquities. The jewelry selection is outstanding. Prices, however, are not cheap. 120 NW Ninth Ave. ℂ 800/321-1729 or 503/223-1729. www.quintanagalleries.com.

Art Glass

The Bullseye Connection Gallery   Located in the Pearl District, the Bullseye Connection Gallery is Portland's premier art-glass gallery and shows work of internationally acclaimed glass artists. 300 NW 13th St. ℂ 503/227-0222. www.bullseyeconnection gallery.com.

BOOKS

Major chain bookstores in Portland include **Barnes & Noble,** 1720 Jantzen Beach Center (ℂ 503/283-2800), and **Borders,** 708 SW Third Ave. (ℂ 503/220-5911). For information on Portland's massive Powell's City of Books, see the box below.

The City of Books

Portland's own **Powell's City of Books,** 1005 W. Burnside St. (ℂ 503/228-4651 or 866/201-7601; www.powells.com), is the bookstore to end all bookstores. Powell's, which covers an entire city block three floors deep, claims to be the world's largest bookstore. At any given time, the store has roughly three-quarters of a million books on the shelves. Both new and used books are shelved side by side, which is why browsing is what Powell's is all about.

Once inside the store, be sure to pick up a store map, which will direct you to the color-coded rooms. Serious book collectors won't want to miss a visit to the Rare Book Room.

One warning: If you haven't got at least an hour of free time, enter at your own risk. It's so easy to lose track of time at Powell's that many customers miss meals and end up in the store's in-house cafe.

Believe it or not, City of Books is even bigger than what you see here; it has several satellite stores, including **Powell's Technical Books,** 33 NW Park St. (ℂ 503/228-3906); **Powell's Books for Cooks and Gardeners,** 3747 SE Hawthorne Blvd. (ℂ 503/235-3802); **Powell's Books on Hawthorne,** 3723 SE Hawthorne Blvd. (ℂ 503/238-1668); and **Powell's Books at PDX,** Portland International Airport (ℂ 503/249-1950).

CRAFTS

For the largest selection of local crafts, visit the **Portland Saturday Market** (see "Markets," below), which is a showcase for local crafts.

Contemporary Crafts Museum & Gallery In business since 1937, and located in a residential area between downtown and the John's Landing neighborhood, this is the nation's oldest not-for-profit art gallery. It shows only works of clay, glass, fiber, metal, and wood. The bulk of the large gallery is filled with glass and ceramic pieces in ongoing thematic exhibitions. There are also several cabinets of jewelry. 3934 SW Corbett Ave. © 503/223-2654. www.contemporarycrafts.org.

Hoffman Gallery The Hoffman Gallery is on the campus of the Oregon College of Art and Craft, one of the nation's foremost crafts education centers since 1906. The gallery hosts installations and group shows by local, national, and international artists. The adjacent gift shop has a good selection of handcrafted items. The grounds are serene and relaxing, and there is also a cafe. 8245 SW Barnes Rd. © 503/297-5544.

The Real Mother Goose This is Portland's premier fine crafts shop and one of the top such shops in the United States. It showcases only the very best contemporary American crafts, including imaginative ceramics, colorful art glass, intricate jewelry, exquisite wooden furniture, and sculptural works. Hundreds of craftspeople and artists from all over the United States are represented here. 901 SW Yamhill St. © 503/223-9510. www.therealmothergoose.com. Also at Portland International Airport, Main Terminal (© 503/284-9929).

Twist This large store has quite a massive selection of wildly colorful and imaginative furniture, crockery, glassware, and lamps, and also a limited but impressive selection of handmade jewelry from artists around the United States. 30 NW 23rd Place © 503/224-0334. www.twistonline.com. Also at Pioneer Place, 700 SW Fifth Ave. (© 503/222-3137).

DEPARTMENT STORES

Meier and Frank Meier and Frank is a Portland institution and has been doing business here for more than 100 years. The flagship store on Pioneer Courthouse Square was built in 1898 and, with 10 stories, was at one time the tallest store in the Northwest. Today those 10 floors of consumer goods and great sales still attract crowds of shoppers. Prices are lower than at nearby Nordstrom. 621 SW Fifth Ave. © 503/223-0512. Also at 1100 Lloyd Center (© 503/281-4797) and 9300 SW Washington Square Rd. in Tigard (© 503/620-3311).

Nordstrom Directly across the street from Pioneer Courthouse Square and a block away from Meier and Frank, Nordstrom is a top-of-the-line department store that originated in Seattle and takes great pride in its personal service and friendliness. 701 SW Broadway. © 503/224-6666. Also at 1001 Lloyd Center (© 503/287-2444) and 9700 SW Washington Square Rd. in Tigard (© 503/620-0555).

FASHION

Sportswear

Columbia Sportswear Company This flagship store is surprisingly low-key, given that the nearby Nike flagship store and REI in Seattle are designed to knock your socks off. Displays showing Columbia Sportswear's well-made outdoor clothing and sportswear are rustic, with lots of natural wood. The most dramatic architectural feature of the store is the entryway, in which a very wide tree trunk seems to support the roof. 911 SW Broadway. © 503/226-6800.

Columbia Sportswear Company Factory Outlet Store *(Value)*   This outlet store in the Sellwood neighborhood south of downtown and across the river sells remainders and past-season styles from the above-mentioned sportswear company, which is one of the Northwest's premiere outdoor clothing manufacturers. You'll pay 30% to 50% less here than you will at the downtown flagship store. 1323 SE Tacoma St. ℂ **503/238-0118.**

Nike Factory Company Store *(Value)*   The Nike outlet is one season behind the current season at NIKETOWN (see below), selling swoosh-brand running, aerobic, tennis, golf, basketball, kids, and you-name-it sports clothing and accessories at discounted prices. 2650 NE Martin Luther King Jr. Blvd. ℂ **503/281-5901.**

NIKETOWN Portland   Sure, you may have a NIKETOWN back home, but this one is the closest to Nike's headquarters in nearby Beaverton, which somehow makes it just a little bit special. A true shopping experience. 930 SW Sixth Ave. ℂ **503/221-6453.**

Men's & Women's

Langlitz Leathers   This family-run shop produces the Rolls Royce of leather jackets. Even though there may be a wait (the shop turns out only six handmade jackets a day), motorcyclists ride their Harleys all the way from the East Coast to be fitted. 2443-A SE Division St. ℂ **503/235-0959.**

Norm Thompson   Known throughout the country for its mail-order catalogs, Norm Thompson is a mainstay of the well-to-do in Portland. Classic styling for men and women is the name of the game here. 1805 NW Thurman St. ℂ **503/221-0764.** Also at Portland International Airport (ℂ **503/249-0170**). www.normthompson.com.

Portland Outdoor Store   In business since 1919, this westernwear store is a Portland institution that feels little changed from decades ago. The big neon sign out front and the old general store atmosphere is enough to pull in even people who aren't into playing cowboy or cowgirl. 304 SW Third Ave. ℂ **800/222-1051** or 503/222-1051.

The Portland Pendleton Shop   Pendleton wool is as much a part of life in the Northwest as forests and salmon. This company's fine wool fashions for men and women define the country-club look in the Northwest and in many other parts of the United States. Pleated skirts and tweed jackets are de rigueur here, as are the colorful blankets that have warmed generations of Northwesterners through long chilly winters. 900 SW Fifth Ave. (entrance is actually on Fourth Ave. between Salmon and Taylor). ℂ **800/241-9665** or 503/242-0037.

Women's Clothing

Changes   This shop specializes in handmade clothing, including handwoven scarves, jackets, shawls, handpainted silks, and other wearable art. 927 SW Yamhill St. ℂ **503/223-3737.**

FOOD

The **Made in Oregon** shops offer the best selection of local food products. See "Gifts & Souvenirs," below, for details.

GIFTS & SOUVENIRS

For unique locally made souvenirs, your best bet is the **Portland Saturday Market** (see "Markets," below, for details).

Made in Oregon   This is your one-stop shop for all manner of made-in-Oregon gifts, food products, and clothing. Every product sold is either grown, caught, or made in Oregon. You'll find smoked salmon, filberts, jams and jellies, and Oregon wines. All branches are open daily, but hours vary from SW Morrison St. (in the Galleria). (C) **800/828-9673** or 503/241-3630. www.ma Portland International Airport ((C) **503/282-7827**); and in Lloyd Center mall, S Broadway ((C) **503/282-7636**).

JEWELRY

For some of the most creative jewelry in Portland, visit **Twist**, the **Hoffman Gallery,** the **Contemporary Crafts Gallery,** and the **Real Mother Goose.** See "Crafts," above.

MALLS & SHOPPING CENTERS

Pioneer Place   Just a block from Pioneer Courthouse Square, this is Portland's most upscale shopping center. Anchored by a Saks Fifth Avenue, Pioneer Place is filled with stores selling designer fashions and expensive gifts. 700 SW Fifth Ave. (between Third and Fifth aves.). (C) **503/228-5800**. www.pioneerplace.com.

MARKETS

Portland Saturday Market   The Portland Saturday Market (held on both Sat and Sun) is a Portland tradition. Every weekend nearly 300 artists and craftspeople can be found selling their creations at this open-air market beneath the Burnside Bridge. In addition to the dozens of crafts stalls, you'll find ethnic and unusual foods, and lots of free entertainment. This is one of the best places in Portland to shop for one-of-a-kind gifts that are small enough to fit into your suitcase. On Sunday, on-street parking is free. The market is open from the first weekend in March to Christmas Eve Saturdays 10am to 5pm and Sundays 11am to 4:30pm. Under the west end of the Burnside Bridge (between SW First Ave. and SW Naito Pkwy.). (C) **503/222-6072**. www.portlandsaturdaymarket.com.

TOYS

Finnegan's Toys and Gifts   This is the largest toy store in downtown Portland and appeals to the kid in all of us. It'll have your inner child kicking and screaming if you don't buy that silly little toy you never got when you were young. 922 SW Yamhill St. (C) **503/221-0306**.

WINE

Oregon Wines on Broadway   This cozy wine bar/shop is located diagonally across from the Hotel Vintage Plaza in downtown Portland. Here you can taste some of Oregon's fine wines, including 30 different pinot noirs, as well as chardonnays, Gewürztraminers and Washington State cabernet sauvignons, merlots, and Syrahs. 515 SW Broadway. (C) **800/943-8858** or 503/228-4655. www.oregonwinesonbroadway.com.

12 Portland After Dark

Portland is the Northwest's number-two cultural center (after Seattle, of course). The city's symphony orchestra, ballet, and opera are all well regarded, and the many theater companies offer classic and contemporary plays. In summer, festivals move the city's cultural activities outdoors.

To find out what's going on during your visit, pick up a copy of *Willamette Week,* Portland's free weekly arts-and-entertainment newspaper. The *Oregonian,* the city's daily newspaper, also publishes lots of entertainment-related information in its Friday "A&E" section and also in the Sunday edition of the paper.

FORMING ARTS

e most part, the Portland performing-arts scene revolves around the **Portland ~~ter~~ for the Performing Arts (PCPA),** 1111 SW Broadway (© **503/248-4335;** ~~/ww~~.pcpa.com), which comprises five performance spaces in three buildings. The **Arlene Schnitzer Concert Hall,** Southwest Broadway and Southwest Main Street, known locally as the Schnitz, is an immaculately restored 1920s movie palace that still displays the original Portland theater sign and marquee out front and is home to the Oregon Symphony. This hall also hosts popular music performers, lecturers, and many other special performances. Directly across Main Street from the Schnitz, at 1111 SW Broadway, is the sparkling-glass jewel box known as the **New Theater Building.** This building houses both the **Newmark** and **Dolores Winningstad theaters** and **Brunish Hall.** The Newmark Theatre is home to Portland Center Stage, while the two theaters together host stage productions by local and visiting companies. Free tours of all three of these theaters are held Wednesdays at 11am, Saturdays every half-hour between 11am and 1pm, and the first Thursday of every month at 6pm.

A few blocks away from this concentration of venues is the 3,000-seat **Keller Auditorium,** SW Third Avenue and SW Clay Street, the largest of the four halls and the home of the Portland Opera and the Oregon Ballet Theatre. The auditorium was constructed shortly after World War I and completely remodeled in the 1960s. In addition to the resident companies mentioned above, these halls host numerous visiting companies each year, including touring Broadway shows.

The PCPA's box office is open for ticket sales Monday through Saturday from 10am to 5pm. Tickets to PCPA performances, and also performances at many other venues around the city, are also sold through either **Ticketmaster** (© **503/224-4400;** www.ticketmaster.com), which has outlets at area G.I. Joe's and Fred Meyer stores, or **Tickets West** (© **800/992-8499** or 503/224-8499; www.ticketswest.com), which has outlets at area Safeway stores. The PCPA does, however, have a **Half-Price Ticket Hotline** (© **503/275-8358**) that sells day-of-show, half-price tickets to theater performances by some of the area's smaller companies.

One other performing arts venue worth checking out is **The Old Church,** 1422 SW 11th Ave. (© **503/222-2031;** www.oldchurch.org). Built in 1883, this wooden Carpenter Gothic church is a Portland landmark. It incorporates a grand traditional design, but was constructed with spare ornamentation. Today the building serves as a community facility, and every Wednesday at noon it hosts free lunchtime organ recitals on the church's 1883 organ. There are also many other performances held here throughout the year.

OPERA & CLASSICAL MUSIC

Founded in 1896, the **Oregon Symphony** (© **800/228-7343** or 503/228-1353; www.orsymphony.org), which performs at the Arlene Schnitzer Concert Hall, 1111 SW Broadway (see above), is the oldest symphony orchestra on the West Coast, and is currently under the baton of conductor Carlos Kalmar. Each year between September and June, the symphony stages several series, including classical, pops, Sunday matinees, and children's concerts. Ticket prices range from $7 to $85 (seniors and students may purchase half-price tickets 1 hr. before concerts).

Each season, the **Portland Opera** (© **866/739-6737** or 503/241-1802; www.portlandopera.org), which performs at Keller Auditorium, SW Third Avenue and SW Clay Street (see above), offers five different productions that include both grand opera and light opera. The season runs November through May. Ticket prices range from $37 to $145.

Summer is the time for Portland's annual chamber music binge. **Chamber Music Northwest** (© 503/294-6400; www.cmnw.org) is a 5-week-long series that starts in late June and attracts the world's finest chamber musicians. Performances are held at Reed College and Catlin Gable School (tickets $21–$40).

THEATER

Portland Center Stage (© 503/274-6588; www.pcs.org), which holds performances at the Portland Center for the Performing Arts, 1111 SW Broadway (see above), is Portland's largest professional theater company. They stage a combination of six to seven classic and contemporary plays during their September-to-April season (tickets $20–$51).

Portland's other main theater company, **Artists Repertory Theatre,** 1516 SW Alder St.(© 503/241-1278; www.artistsrep.org), often stages more daring plays. They can be hit or miss, but they're frequently very thought-provoking. The season often includes a world premiere. Tickets run $15 to $40.

If it's musicals you want, you've got a couple of options in Portland. At the Keller Auditorium, you can catch the **Broadway in Portland** series (© 503/241-1802; www.broadwayacrossamerica.com). Tickets range from around $30 to $135.

DANCE

Although the **Oregon Ballet Theatre** (© 888/922-5538 or 503/222-5538; www.obt. org), which performs at the Keller Auditorium and the Newmark Theatre (see above), is best loved for its performances each December of *The Nutcracker.* The rest of each season includes performances of classic and contemporary ballets (tickets $13–$66).

Fans of modern dance should be sure to check to see what's being staged by **White Bird** (© 503/245-1600; www.whitebird.org). This organization brings in such celebrated companies as Twyla Tharp Dance, the Merce Cunningham Dance Company, the Paul Taylor Dance Company, and the Alvin Ailey American Dance Theater.

Also keep an eye out for performances by **Imago Theatre,** 17 SE Eighth Ave. (© 503/231-9581; www.imagotheatre.com), which, though it is also a live theater company, is best known for its wildly creative productions of *Frogz* and *Big Little Things,* both of which are fanciful dance performances that appeal to both adults and children. **Do Jump! Extremely Physical Theatre** (© 503/231-1232; www.dojump. org), is another highly creative dance company worth watching for. Their performances incorporate dance, acrobatics, aerial work, and plenty of humor.

PERFORMING ARTS SERIES

The **Museum After Hours** series at the **Portland Art Museum,** 1219 SW Park Ave. (© 503/226-2811; www.portlandartmuseum.org), is a great place to catch some of the best local jazz, blues, rock, and folk bands. Performances are held October through April on Wednesday nights from 5:30 to 7:30pm, and admission is $8 if you aren't a museum member.

When summer hits, Portlanders like to head outdoors to hear music. The city's top outdoor music series is held at **Washington Park Zoo,** 4001 SW Canyon Rd. (© 503 226-1561; www.oregonzoo.org), which brings in the likes of the Indigo Girls, C' Kings, Pink Martini, and John Hiatt. Ticket prices range from $9.50 to $26.

THE CLUB & MUSIC SCENE
ROCK, BLUES & FOLK

Aladdin Theater   This former movie theater now serves as one of Portland's main venues for touring performers such as Richard Thompson, Bruce Cockburn, Judy Collins, and They Might Be Giants. The very diverse musical spectrum represented includes blues, rock, ethnic, country, folk, and jazz. 3017 SE Milwaukie Ave. © 503/233-1994. Tickets $10–$35. www.aladdin-theater.com.

Berbati's Pan   Located in Old Town, this has long been one of Portland's best and most popular rock clubs. A wide variety of acts play here, primarily the best of the local rock scene and bands on the verge of breaking into the national limelight. Be sure to check out the back bar, which is 150 years old. 10 SW Third Ave. © 503/226-2122. Cover $5–$15.

Crystal Ballroom   The Crystal Ballroom first opened before 1920, and since then has seen performers ranging from early jazz musicians to James Brown, Marvin Gaye, and the Grateful Dead. The McMenamin Brothers (of local brewing fame) renovated the Crystal Ballroom several years back and refurbished its dance floor, which, due to its mechanics, feels as if it's floating. The ballroom now hosts a variety of performances and special events nearly every night of the week. **Lola's Room,** a smaller version of the Ballroom, is on the second floor and also has a floating dance floor. You'll find **Ringlers Pub** (a colorful brewpub) on the ground floor. 1332 W. Burnside St. © 503/225-0047. www.danceonair.com. Cover free–$30.

Doug Fir Lounge   With a no-smoking policy and shows that are usually over by midnight, this bar may not sound like too much fun, but it is, in fact, the hottest club in Portland. The decor is an incongruous blend of log cabin and Swedish modern, but somehow it all works. 830 E. Burnside St. © 503/231-9663. Cover $5–$20.

Roseland Theater & Grill   The Roseland Theater, though it isn't all that large, is currently one of Portland's two or three main venues for performances by touring national rock acts. Be sure to check the schedule; you never know who might be playing. 8 NW Sixth Ave. © 503/224-2038. Cover $5–$35.

JAZZ

Imbibe 🎔   With live jazz and other types of adult music most nights of the week, this bar/dinner club is one of the most enjoyable places in Portland to take in some live music. The musical bookings are very eclectic, so be sure to check the schedule when you're in town. 2229 SE Hawthorne Blvd. © 503/239-4002. www.takeitin.com. Cover free–$5.

Jimmy Mak's   This small Pearl District club is one of Portland's last remaining jazz clubs. *Downbeat* magazine even ranked it as one of the top 100 jazz clubs in the country. Monday through Saturday nights, there's live music. Okay, so sometimes it's blues music, but I won't hold that against them. 300 NW 10th Ave. © 503/295-6542. Cover

Hands down the most elegant old-world bar in Portland, the [c]ity's most luxurious hotel. The Circassian walnut paneling and definitely put you in the mood for a martini or single malt. [?], there's live jazz in the evening. In the Benson Hotel, 309 SW Broad-

CABARET

Darcelle's XV   In business since 1967 and run by Portland's best-loved cross-dresser, this cabaret is a campy Portland institution with a female-impersonator show that has been a huge hit for years. There are shows Wednesday through Saturday. 208 NW Third Ave. ℂ **503/222-5338**. www.darcellexv.com. Cover $10. Reservations recommended.

DANCE CLUBS

See also the listing for **Saucebox,** below, under "Bars"; this restaurant and bar becomes a dance club after 10pm, when a DJ begins spinning tunes.

Andrea's Cha-Cha Club   Located in the Grand Cafe and open Wednesday through Saturday nights, this is Portland's premier dance spot for fans of Latin dancing. Whether it's cha-cha, salsa, or the latest dance craze from south of the border, they'll be doing it here. Lessons are available Wednesday and Friday nights at 9pm. 832 SE Grand Ave. ℂ **503/230-1166**. Cover $2–$3.

THE BAR & PUB SCENE

BARS

Bartini   Located just off NW 21st Avenue, this dark little bar specializes in, you guessed it, martinis. In fact, they've got a list of more than 100 martinis on offer. Good happy hour. 2108 NW Glisan St. ℂ **503/224-7919**.

The Brazen Bean   This hip cocktail and cigar bar in an old Victorian home in Northwest Portland has a cool *fin de siècle* European elegance that makes it a very classy place to sip a martini. This is mainly a man's domain, but cigar-puffing women will appreciate it as well. 2075 NW Glisan St. ℂ **503/294-0636**.

Jake's Famous Crawfish   In business since 1892, Jake's is a Portland institution and should not be missed (see the full review on p. 84). The bar is one of the busiest in town when the downtown offices let out. 401 SW 12th Ave. ℂ **503/226-1419**. www.jakes famouscrawfish.com.

McCormick and Schmick's Harborside Pilsner Room   Located at the south end of Tom McCall Waterfront Park overlooking the Willamette River and RiverPlace Marina, this restaurant/bar is affiliated with Hood River's Full Sail brewery and keeps plenty of Full Sail brews on tap (plus other area beers as well). The crowd is upscale, the view one of the best in town. (See p. 85 for a review of the restaurant.) 0309 SW Montgomery St. ℂ **503/220-1865**. www.mccormickandschmicks.com.

Mint/820   Mixologist Lucy Brennan, owner of this swanky place, has single-handedly turned Portland into a town full of cocktail connoisseurs. Using fresh fruit juices, purées, and other unusual ingredients, Brennan has reinvented the cocktail. How about a beet-infused martini or a creamy avocado cocktail? 816/820 N. Russell St. ℂ **503/284-5518**.

¡Oba!   One of the trendiest bars in Portland, this big Pearl District bar/nuevo Latino restaurant has a very tropical feel despite the warehouse district locale. After work, the bar is always packed with the stylish and the upwardly mobile taking advantage of great happy hour deals. Don't miss the tropical-fruit margaritas! 555 NW 12th Ave. ℂ **503/228-6161**. www.obarestaurant.com.

Portland City Grill   Located way up on the 30th floor, this restaurant/bar has the best view in downtown Portland. Come for the great happy hour so you can catch the sunset, or stop by later in the night to catch some live jazz and check out the upscale singles scene. Unico/U.S. Bank Tower, 111 SW Fifth Ave. ℂ **503/450-0030**. www.portlandcitygrill.com.

Saucebox   Popular with the city's dressed-in-black scene makers, this recently remodeled downtown restaurant/bar is a large, dramatically lit dark box that can be very noisy. If you want to talk, you'd better do it before 10pm, when the DJ arrives to transform this place from restaurant/bar into dance club. They serve great cocktails. 214 SW Broadway. ℂ 503/241-3393. www.saucebox.com.

Vault Martini   No need for a combination or secret code to get into this Vault, but it does help to dress the part when drinking at this trendy Pearl District bar. The decor is sleek and stylish, and the cocktail menu is lengthy. 226 NW 12th Ave. ℂ 503/224-4909.

WINE BARS

Bar Pastiche   This tiny little wine bar is attached to an upscale grocery store and is known for its diverse array of tiny tapas plates. While other tapas places around town feed you big little plates, this place serves little, little plates, but boy are they creative. The desserts, from Pix Patisserie, are works of art. 3731 SE Hawthorne Blvd. ℂ 503/236-4760.

Noble Rot   With a garage door for a front wall, this stylish little wine bar opens up to the fresh air whenever the weather is conducive. You can get various wine flights (selections of 2-oz. tastings), and there are plenty of Oregon wines available. The wine bar also serves excellent food. By the way, *noble rot* is a type of grape fungus that is utilized in the production of sweet dessert wines. 2724 SE Ankeny St. ℂ 503/233-1999. www.noblerot.biz.

Oregon Wines on Broadway   With just a handful of stools at the bar and a couple of cozy tables, this tiny place is the best spot in Portland to learn about Oregon wines. On any given night there will be 30 Oregon pinot noirs available by the glass, and plenty of white wines as well. 515 SW Broadway. ℂ 800/943-8858 or 503/228-4655. www.oregonwinesonbroadway.com.

Southpark Seafood Grill & Wine Bar   With its high ceiling, long heavy drapes, halogen lights, and lively wall mural, the wine bar at Southpark (see the full dining review on p. 85) is a contemporary interpretation of a Parisian cafe from the turn of the last century. Very romantic. 901 SW Salmon St. ℂ 503/326-1300.

Vino Paradiso   Located in the heart of the Pearl District, this is currently Portland's swankiest wine bar and has live music as well as lots of good wines. There are also some tasty menu items to go with your wine. 417 NW 10th Ave. ℂ 503/295-9536.

Blend Your Own Wine

Tired of wines that just don't do it for you? Always looking for a little more fruit and a little less tannin? Why not bottle up your own personal *cuvée*? At **Urban Wineworks**, 407 NW 16th Ave. (ℂ 503/226-9797; www.urban wineworks.com), at the corner of NW Flanders Street, that's exactly what you get to do on Tuesday evenings between 6:30 and 7:30pm. You don't get to ferment the wine or manage the vineyard, but blending your own wine is both fun and educational. This winery also has a tasting room and wine bar, and on the first Thursday of every month between 5:30 and 8:30pm, they have artists paint an original work of art on the end of a wine barrel.

BREWPUBS

Although brewpubs have now become commonplace throughout much of the country, here in Portland, they're still brewing beers the likes of which you won't taste in too many other places on this side of the Atlantic. This is the heart of the Northwest craft-brewing explosion, and if you're a beer connoisseur, you owe it to yourself to go directly to the source.

Brewpubs have become big business in Portland, and there are now glitzy upscale pubs as well as funky warehouse-district locals. No matter what vision you have of the ideal brewpub, you're likely to find your dream come true. Whether you're wearing bike shorts or a three-piece suit, there's a pub in Portland where you can enjoy a handcrafted beer, a light meal, and a convivial atmosphere.

With almost three dozen brewpubs in the Portland metropolitan area, the McMenamins chain is Portland's biggest brewpub empire. The owners of this empire think of themselves as court jesters, mixing brewing fanaticism with a Deadhead aesthetic. Throw in a bit of historic preservation and a strong belief in family-friendly neighborhood pubs and you'll understand why these joints are so popular.

Downtown

McMenamin's Ringlers Pub   With mosaic pillars framing the bar, Indonesian antiques, and big old signs all around, this cavernous place is about as eclectic a brewpub as you'll ever find. A block away (at 1223 SW Stark St.) are the two associated pubs of Ringlers Annex, which is in a flat-iron building. One of these pubs is below street level with a beer-cellar feel, and the other has walls of multipaned glass. These three pubs get my vote for most atmospheric alehouses in town. 1332 W. Burnside St. ℂ 503/225-0627. www.mcmenamins.com.

Northwest Portland

MacTarnahan's Tap Room   With huge copper fermenting vats proudly displayed and polished to a high sheen, this is by far the city's most ostentatious, though certainly not its largest, brewpub. This pub's flagship brew, Mac's Scottish-style amber ale, has some very loyal local fans. 2730 NW 31st Ave. ℂ 503/228-5269.

Rogue Ales Public House   This Pearl District pub is an outpost of a popular microbrewery headquartered in the Oregon coast community of Newport. Rogue produces just about the widest variety of beers in the state, and, best of all, keeps lots of them on tap at this pub. If you're a fan of barley-wine ale, don't miss their Old Crustacean. 1339 NW Flanders St. ℂ 503/222-5910.

Southeast

The Lucky Labrador Brew Pub   With a warehouse-size room, industrial feel, and picnic tables on the loading dock out back, this brewpub is a classic of southeast Portland. The crowd is young, and dogs are welcome. (They don't even have to be Labs.) 915 SE Hawthorne Blvd. ℂ 503/236-3555. www.luckylab.com.

Northeast & North Portland Pubs

Alameda Brewhouse   With its industrial chic interior, this high-ceilinged neighborhood pub brews up some of the most unusual beers in Portland. How about a rosepetal bock, a juniper berry porter, or a heather-flower ale made without hops? Some work, some don't, but fans of craft beers have to appreciate the willingness to experiment. 4765 NE Fremont St. ℂ 503/460-9025. www.alamedabrewhouse.com.

Moments **A Portland Original: The Theater Pub**

Portland brewpub magnates the McMenamin brothers have a novel way to sell their craft ales—in movie pubs. Although it's often hard to concentrate on the screen, it's always a lot of fun to attend a show. The movies are usually recent releases that have played the main theaters but have not yet made it onto DVD. Theaters include the **Bagdad Theater,** 3702 SE Hawthorne Blvd. (② 503/ 236-9234), a restored classic Arabian Nights movie palace; the **Mission Theater,** 1624 NW Glisan St. (② 503/223-4527), which was the first McMenamins theater pub; the **Kennedy School Theater,** 5736 NE 33rd Ave. (② 503/249-3983), in a former elementary school; and the **Edgefield Theater,** 2126 SW Halsey St., Troutdale (② 503/669-8610). You can also have beer and pizza with your movie at the **Laurelhurst Theater,** 2735 E. Burnside St. (② 503/232-5511; www.laurel hursttheater.com), which is not a McMenamins establishment.

Amnesia Brewing Company   With the look of an old warehouse and a "beer garden" in the parking lot, this little north Portland brewpub is another of Portland's old-school brewpubs, which means laid back in the extreme. The beers are good, but the food is pretty limited. 832 N. Beech St. ② 503/281-7708.

McMenamin's Kennedy School   Never thought they'd ever start serving beer in elementary school, did you? However, in the hands of the local McMenamins brewpub empire, an old northeast Portland school is now a sprawling complex complete with brewpub, beer garden, movie-theater pub, and even a bed-and-breakfast inn. Order up a pint and wander the halls checking out all the cool artwork. 5736 NE 33rd Ave. ② 503/249-3983. www.mcmenamins.com.

Widmer Brewing and Gasthaus   Located on the edge of a rapidly reviving industrial area just north of the Rose Garden arena, this place has the feel of a classic blue-collar pub. This is the brewery for Portland's largest craft brewing company, which is best known for its hefeweizen. German and American foods are served. On the MAX Yellow Line. 955 N. Russell St. ② 503/281-3333. www.widmer.com.

THE GAY & LESBIAN NIGHTLIFE SCENE
A DANCE CLUB
The Embers Avenue   Though primarily a gay disco, Embers is also popular with straights. There are always lots of flashing lights and sweaty bodies until the early morning. Hip-hop and '90s pop are the current DJ faves. Look for drag shows several nights a week. 110 NW Broadway. ② 503/222-3082. Cover–$2–$5.

BARS
The area around the intersection of **SW Stark Street and West Burnside Street** has the largest concentration of gay bars in Portland.

C.C. Slaughters Nightclub & Lounge   Popular with a young crowd, this Old Town bar spins disco sounds most nights, with a night of country music each week. 219 NW Davis St. ② 503/248-9135. www.ccslaughterspdx.com.

Crush Bar   This big, hip bar is over in southeast Portland and attracts a very diverse crowd that includes not only gay men but lesbians and straights as well. There are three distinct settings within the walls of this place, including a comfortable lounge,

My, what an inefficient way to fish.

Ring toss, good. Horseshoes, bad.

Faster! Faster! Faster!

We take care of the fiddly bits, from providing over 43,000 customer reviews of hotels, to helping you find our best fares, to giving you 24/7 customer service. So you can focus on the only thing that matters. Goofing off.

travelocity
You'll never roam alone.™

a room for dining and dancing, and a room where smoking is allowed. DJs spin dance tunes most nights. 1400 SE Morrison St. ℭ **503/235-8150**. www.crushbar.com.

Eagle Bar   If leather and Levi's are your uniform, then you'll feel right at home at this bar. Loud rock and DJ dance music plays most nights, and Sunday's are currently leather night. 1300 W. Burnside St. ℭ **503/241-0105**. www.portlandeagle.com.

Scandal's & The Otherside Lounge   In business for more 25 years, this bar/restaurant is at the center of the gay bar scene. There always seems to be some special event going on here. Try to get a window seat so you can keep an eye on passersby on the sidewalk. 1038 SW Stark St. ℭ **503/227-5887**.

13 A Side Trip to Oregon City

When the first white settlers began crossing the Oregon Trail in the early 1840s, their destination was Oregon City and the fertile Willamette Valley. At the time, Portland had yet to be founded, and Oregon City, set beside powerful Willamette Falls, was the largest town in Oregon. However, with the development of Portland and the shifting of the capital to Salem, Oregon City began to lose its importance. Today it is primarily an industrial town, though one steeped in Oregon history and worth a visit. To get here from downtown Portland, drive south on SW First Avenue and continue on SW Macadam Avenue, which is Ore. 43. Follow this road for roughly 12 miles to reach Oregon City. (It should take 30–45 min.) You can also take I-5 south to I-205 east.

Once in Oregon City, your first stop should be just south of town at the **Willamette Falls overlook** ✺ on Ore. 99E. Though the falls have been much changed by industry over the years, they are still an impressive sight.

End of the Oregon Trail Interpretive Center ✺   With its three Paul Bunyan–size wagons parked in the middle of Abernethy Green (the official end of the Oregon Trail), this interpretive center is impossible to miss. Inside the first of the giant wagons you'll find an exhibit hall, hands-on area, and gift shop. After looking around this first wagon, you'll then be led through the next one by costumed interpreters who explain the difficulties of provisioning for the overland trek. The third wagon houses a multimedia presentation based on three Oregon Trail diaries.

1726 Washington St., Oregon City. ℭ 503/657-9336. www.endoftheoregontrail.org. Admission $7 adults, $5 children 5–12, free for children under 5. Memorial Day to Labor Day Mon–Sat 9:30am–5:30pm, Sun 10:30am–5:30pm; Nov–Feb Wed–Sat 11am–4pm, Sun noon–4pm; Mar–May and Sept–Oct Mon–Sat 9:30am–5pm, Sun 10:30am–5pm. Tour hours vary by day and season. Closed Thanksgiving, Christmas Eve, Christmas, and New Year's Day.

McLoughlin House   Oregon City's most famous citizen, retired Hudson's Bay Company chief factor John McLoughlin, helped found this mill town on the banks of the Willamette River in 1829. By the 1840s, immigrants were pouring into Oregon, and McLoughlin provided food, seeds, and tools to many. Upon retirement in 1846, McLoughlin moved to Oregon City, where he built what was at that time the most luxurious home in Oregon. Today McLoughlin's house is a National Historic Site and is furnished as it would have been when McLoughlin lived there. Many of the pieces on display are original to the house.

713 Center St., Oregon City. ℭ 503/656-5146. www.mcloughlinhouse.org. Admission $4 adults, $3 seniors, and $2 children 6–17, free for children under 6. Wed–Sat 10am–4pm; Sun 1–4pm. Closed Dec 22–Jan 31 and major holidays.

6

The Willamette Valley: The Bread (& Wine) Basket of Oregon

For more than 150 miles, from south of Eugene to the Columbia River at Portland, the Willamette River (pronounced Wih-*lam*-it) flows between Oregon's two major mountain ranges. Tempered by cool moist air from the Pacific Ocean, yet protected from winter winds by the Cascade Range to the east, the Willamette Valley enjoys a mild climate that belies its northerly latitudes. It was because of this relatively benign climate and the valley's rich soils that the region's first settlers chose to put down roots here. Today, the valley is home to Oregon's largest cities, its most productive farmlands, the state capital, and the state's two major universities.

Despite the many hardships, families were willing to walk 2,000 miles across the continent for a chance at starting a new life in the Willamette Valley. The valley very quickly became the breadbasket of the Oregon country, and today, it still produces an agricultural bounty unequaled in its diversity. Throughout the year, you can sample the produce of this region at farms, produce stands, and wineries. In spring, commercial fields of tulips and irises paint the landscape with bold swaths of color. In summer, there are farm stands near almost every town, and many farms will let you pick your own strawberries, raspberries, blackberries, peaches, apples, cherries, and plums. In the autumn, you can sample the filbert and walnut harvest, and at any time of year, you can do a bit of wine tasting at dozens of wineries.

1 The North Willamette Valley Wine Country

McMinnville: 38 miles SW of Portland, 26 miles NW of Salem

Were it not for Prohibition, wine connoisseurs might be comparing California wines to those of Oregon rather than vice versa. Oregon wines had already gained a national reputation back in the days when Oregon became one of the earliest states to vote in Prohibition. It would be a few years before more liberal California would outlaw alcohol, and, in the interim, the Golden State got the upper hand. When Prohibition was rescinded, California quickly went back to wine production, but no one bothered to revive Oregon's wine-producing potential until the 1970s. However, by then, Napa Valley had popped the cork on its wine dominance. Perhaps some day Willamette Valley wineries will be as well known as those in California, and for fans of pinot noir, those days have already arrived. Oregon's pinot noirs have gained such international attention that even some French wineries have planted vineyards here and begun producing their own Oregon wines. Forget what you learned in the movie *Sideways;* America's best pinot noirs are made in Oregon, not California.

The north Willamette Valley wine country begins in the town of Newberg and extends south to the Salem area. The majority of the region's wineries flank Ore. 99W, and a drive down this rural highway will turn up dozens of blue signs pointing to wineries within a few miles of the road. To the south of Salem, there are more wineries in the Corvallis and Eugene areas, which are dealt with in the appropriate sections of this chapter. To the north of Ore. 99W, there are still more wineries in Washington County, which is actually in the drainage of the Tualatin River, which flows into the Willamette. These latter wineries are included in this section.

The most important wine-growing areas within this region, and the areas that produce the best wines, are the Red Hills above the town of Dundee, the slopes outside the town of Carlton, and the Eola Hills northwest of Salem. In Dundee, you'll find the greatest concentration of good restaurants, while in McMinnville, the largest town in the area, you'll find plenty of hotel rooms and more good restaurants.

ESSENTIALS

GETTING THERE　You'll find the heart of wine country between Newberg and McMinnville along Ore. 99W, which heads southwest out of Portland.

VISITOR INFORMATION　Contact the **McMinnville Area Chamber of Commerce,** 417 NW Adams St., McMinnville, OR 97128 (© **503/472-6196;** www.mcminnville.org), or the **Chehalem Valley Chamber of Commerce,** 415 E. Sheridan St., Newberg, OR 97132 (© **503/538-2014;** www.chehalemvalley.org). The **Willamette Valley Visitors Association,** 553 NW Harrison Blvd., Corvallis, OR 97330 (© **866/548-5018;** www.oregonwinecountry.org), is another good source of information on this area.

FESTIVALS　The most prestigious festival of the year is the **International Pinot Noir Celebration,** P.O. Box 1310, McMinnville, OR 97128 (© **800/775-4762** or 503/472-8964; www.ipnc.org), held each year on the last weekend in July or first weekend in August. The 3-day event includes tastings, food, music, and seminars. Registration forms are mailed out in February each year and tickets are currently $795 per person. Passport to Pinot, a separate event held during the celebration, is only $125.

TOURING THE WINERIES

Forget pretentiousness, grand villas, celebrity wineries, snobbish waiters, or high prices for tastings—this is not the Napa Valley. Oregon wineries are, for the most part, still small establishments. Even the new wineries that have been opening up right on Ore. 99W (and that seem calculated to provide beach-bound vacationers with a bit of distraction and some less-than-impressive wine for the weekend) are still small affairs compared to the wineries of Napa Valley. Although in recent years more and more "corporate" wineries have been opening with the sole purpose of producing high-priced pinot noir, many of the region's wineries are still family-owned and -operated and produce moderately priced wines.

　Now forget about cabernet sauvignon, merlot, and zinfandel. The Willamette Valley just isn't hot enough to produce these varietals. With the exception of southern Oregon wineries and a few Willamette Valley wineries that buy their grapes from warmer regions (the Columbia Gorge, southern Oregon, California, and Washington's Yakima Valley), Oregon wineries have, thankfully, given up on trying to produce cabs and zins to compete with those of California. The wines of the Willamette Valley are primarily the cooler climate varietals traditionally produced in Burgundy, Alsace, and Germany. Pinot noir is the uncontested leader of the pack, with pinot gris running a close second. However, Gewürztraminer and Riesling are also produced, and, with the introduction of early ripening Dijon-clone chardonnay grapes, the region is finally beginning to produce chardonnays that can almost compete with those of California. Other wines you'll likely encounter in this area include Müller-Thurgau (a usually off-dry white wine), muscats (dessert wines), and sparkling wines (often made from pinot noir and chardonnay grapes).

　Wine country begins only a few miles west and southwest of Portland. Approaching the town of Newberg on Ore. 99W, you leave the urban sprawl behind and enter the rolling farm country of Yamhill County. These hills form the western edge of the Willamette Valley and provide almost ideal conditions for growing wine grapes. The views from these hills take in the Willamette Valley's fertile farmlands as well as the snowcapped peaks of the Cascades.

Between Newberg and Rickreall, you'll find dozens of wineries and tasting rooms that are open on a regular basis. There are concentrations of wineries in Dundee's Red Hills and in the Eola Hills northwest of Salem, and if you head north from Ore. 99W, you'll find another dozen or so wineries near Carlton, Yamhill, Hillsboro, and Forest Grove. Each of these groupings of wineries makes a good day's tasting route and have been organized here so that you can easily link them together as such.

Most, but not all, wineries maintain tasting rooms that are usually open between 11am or noon and 5pm. During the summer, most tasting rooms are open daily, but in other months they may be open only on weekends or by appointment. Wineries located right on Ore. 99W are usually open throughout the year. Many wineries also have a few picnic tables, so if you bring some goodies with you and then pick up a bottle of wine, you'll be set for a great picnic.

Tips **Taster's Tip**

Although few Oregon wineries have regularly scheduled winery tours, if you're interested and there is someone on hand to show you around, you're usually welcome to tour the facilities.

For anyone simply interested in tasting a little Oregon wine, the wineries along the highway are a good introduction. If you have more than a passing interest in wine, you'll want to explore the wineries that are located a few miles off Ore. 99W.

Many of the best wineries, however, are only open by appointment or on Memorial Day and Thanksgiving weekends. If you're serious about your wine, you might want to make appointments to visit some of these smaller wineries or plan a visit to coincide with Thanksgiving or Memorial Day. Oenophiles, especially pinot noir fans, are likely to uncover some rare gems and discover a few new favorite wineries this way.

At some wineries, you'll be asked to pay a tasting fee. However, most Oregon wineries do not charge for tastings unless they are offering reserve vintages or older "library" wines. Many wineries have celebrations, festivals, music performances, and picnics throughout the summer, and during these celebrations there is sometimes a fee to cover the cost of the appetizers and wine that are served. The Memorial Day and Thanksgiving weekend tastings usually carry a fee of between $5 and $15.

For more information about the Oregon wine scene, including a calendar of winery events, pick up a copy of *Oregon Wine Press Magazine,* a monthly newspaper (available at area wine shops and wineries), or contact the **Oregon Wine Magazine,** 644 SE 20th Ave., Portland, OR 97214 (© **503/232-7607;** www.oregonwinepress.com). The **Willamette Valley Wineries Association,** P.O. Box 25162, Portland, OR 97298 (© **503/646-2985;** www.willamettewines.com), publishes a free map and guide to the local wineries. You can pick up copies at almost any area winery.

NEWBERG & DUNDEE AREA WINERIES

To sample wines from several small area wineries, stop by **Wine Etc.,** 1174 SW Ore. 99W, Dundee (© **503/538-9878;** www.dundeewinetasting.com). Sandwiches and salads are also available here at lunch.

Adelsheim Vineyard If you're from out of state and you're at all familiar with Oregon pinot noir, you've probably had some Adelsheim wine. This winery has been around since the 1970s and consistently produces well-regarded pinots. The single-vineyard wines here are the standouts. If you'd like to tour a winery, this is the one to tour; call ahead to arrange your tour ($10).

The Twice-a-Year Wineries

Harvest season aside, Memorial Day weekend and Thanksgiving weekend are the two most important times of the year in wine country. On these weekends, wineries often introduce their new releases and sometimes offer barrel tastings of wines that haven't yet been bottled. Many wineries offer live music, and most offer some sort of food, often exotic cheeses, to accompany the wines they are tasting.

Many of the area's best boutique wineries are open to the public *only* on these two weekends. So, if you're serious about wine, you won't want to pass up a Willamette Valley wine tour on one or the other of these holidays.

For information on what wineries will be open, contact the **Willamette Valley Wineries Association**, P.O. Box 25162, Portland, OR 97298 (② **503/646-2985**; www.willamettewines.com) or the **Convention & Visitors Bureau of Washington County**, 5075 SW Griffith Dr., Suite 120, Beaverton, OR 97075 (② **800/537-3149** or 503/644-5555; www.wcva.org).

16800 NE Calkins Lane, Newberg. ② **503/538-3652**. www.adelsheim.com. Tasting fee $5. May–Dec Wed–Sun 11am–4pm; Jan–Apr Thurs–Sat 11am–4pm.

Archery Summit ☽☽   With big wines, a big winery, and a big reputation, Archery Summit is one of Oregon's premier producers of pinot noir. Only pinot noir is produced, and the grapes all come from Archery Summit's own 100-acre estate. Wines are aged almost exclusively in new-oak barrels and spend time in some of the only barrel-aging caves in the state. Prices are in the $40 to $75 range.

18599 NE Archery Summit Rd., Dayton. ② **800/732-8822**. www.archerysummit.com. Daily 10am–4:30pm. Tasting fee $10. West of Dundee on Ore. 99W, turn right on Archery Summit Rd.

Argyle Winery   Located right on the highway in Dundee, this winery specializes in sparkling wines and chardonnay. Although wines can be purchased here for less than $20, most are in the $20 to $30 range, with pinot noirs in the $30 to $50 range. Most of the wines here seem overpriced. Due to traffic congestion in Dundee, this winery is best visited when heading east on Ore. 99W.

691 Ore. 99W, Dundee. ② **888/4-ARGYLE** or 503/538-8520. www.argylewinery.com. Daily 11am–5pm.

August Cellars   This is the first winery you'll come to along Ore. 99W as you reach the Yamhill County wine country. The big new winemaking facility here is just off the highway and is actually home to several small wineries.

14000 NE Quarry Rd., Newberg. ② **503/554-6766**. www.augustcellars.com. May–Sept daily 11am–5pm; Oct–Apr Sat–Sun 11am–5pm. Just off Ore. 99W east of Newberg.

Domaine Drouhin Oregon ☽☽☽   When France first heard that Oregon wineries were making pinot noir years ago, most scoffed. Not Maison Joseph Drouhin of Burgundy; they bought land in the Red Hills of Dundee and planted vines. Today, the Burgundian-style wines of Domaine Drouhin Oregon are superb examples of old-world winemaking—silky, seductive, and well balanced.

Breyman Orchards Rd., Dayton. ✆ **503/864-2700**. www.domainedrouhin.com. Tasting fee $5. Wed–Sun 11am–4pm. West of Dundee on Ore. 99W, turn right on McDougall Rd. and right again onto Breyman Orchards Rd.

Domaine Serene   Located across the road from Domaine Drouhin Oregon, this is another of Oregon's top wineries, with an impressive winemaking facility and impressive prices ($40–$60) to prove it. Great ratings from *Wine Spectator* have made these wines some of the most sought after in the state. Pinot noir, chardonnay, and Syrah are produced here.

6555 Hilltop Lane, Dayton. ✆ **866/864-6555** or 503/864-4600. www.domaineserene.com. Tasting fee $15. Apr–Nov Thurs–Sun 11am–4pm. West of Dundee on Ore. 99W, turn right on McDougall Rd. and right again onto Breyman Orchards Rd.

Duck Pond Cellars   With its strategic location right on the highway, large parking lot, and tasting room full of gourmet food products and wine accessories, this winery aims to snag beach-bound traffic, and on summer weekends the tasting room is often too crowded. Because they're so convenient to the highway, you might as well drop by and see if anything strikes your fancy.

23145 Ore. 99W, Dundee. ✆ **800/437-3213** or 503/538-3199. www.duckpondcellars.com. May–Sept daily 10am–5pm; Oct–Apr daily 11am–5pm.

Erath Vineyards   In business since 1972, Erath Vineyards, set high in the Red Hills of Dundee, was founded by Dick Erath, one of the pioneers of modern Oregon winemaking. A wide variety of wines is produced here and you can usually sample 10 or more during your visit to the tasting room. There's a pretty little public park, just right for a picnic, at the foot of the winery's driveway.

9409 NE Worden Hill Rd., Dundee. ✆ **800/539-9463** or 503/538-3318. www.erath.com. Daily 11am–5pm. In Dundee, go north on Ninth St., which becomes Worden Hill Rd.

Lange Estate Winery & Vineyards ⭐⭐   Superb pinot noirs are the hallmark of this small winery. The estate wines produced here are among the best pinot noirs in the state and tend to be priced from $30 to $40. Lange also produces a few wines (mostly pinot gris and chardonnay) in the $15-to-$20 range.

18380 NE Buena Vista Rd., Dundee. ✆ **503/538-6476**. www.langewinery.com. Daily 11am–5pm. Tasting fee $5. In Dundee, go north on Ninth St. and follow signs.

Pinot Station Tasting Room ⭐   This tasting room right in Dundee pours the wines of both Torii Mor and Dobbes Family Estate. This latter winery is owned by Joe Dobbes, one of Oregon's top winemakers. The "Wine by Joe" label wines are the best deals here. In addition to pinot noir and pinot gris, Dobbes Family Estate produces Viognier and Syrah.

240 SE Fifth St., Dundee. ✆ **503/538-7100**. www.dobbesfamilyestate.com. Tasting fee $5. Daily 11am–6pm. Just off Ore. 99W.

Ponzi Vineyards/Ponzi Wine Bar ⭐   Ponzi Vineyards was one of the Oregon wine pioneers, and though it has its winery north of here near Beaverton, this tasting room/wine bar is a more convenient place to sample Ponzi wines. Expect excellent pinot gris and chardonnay and be sure to sample the Arneis, an Italian varietal dry white wine that is aged in oak and is rarely planted in this area. Also don't miss the Vino Gelato, a dessert wine made from frozen grapes.

100 SW Seventh St., Dundee. ✆ **503/554-1500**. www.ponziwinebar.com. Daily 11am–5pm.

Rex Hill Vineyards One of the oldest and largest wineries in Oregon, Rex Hill's setting is impressive and its tasting room would seem right at home in Napa Valley. Inside the tasting room, you'll find antiques, contemporary art, and a large fireplace. Pinot noirs are the main focus here, but Rex Hill also does respectable pinot gris and chardonnay.

30835 N. Hwy. 99W., Newberg. © 800/739-4455. www.rexhill.com. Daily 11am–5pm; in summer, Mon–Thurs 11am–5pm, Fri–Sun 10am–5pm.

Sokol Blosser Winery Another of the big Oregon wineries, Sokol Blosser sits high on the slopes above the west end of Dundee. Off-dry whites are a strong point here, and the Evolution No. 9, a blend of 10 different grapes, shouldn't be missed. Pinot noirs, on the other hand, tend to be overpriced and overrated in my opinion. A walk-through showcase vineyard provides an opportunity to learn about the growing process.

5000 Sokol Blosser Lane, Dundee. © 800/582-6668 or 503/864-2282. www.sokolblosser.com. Tasting fee $5. Daily 11am–5pm. West of Dundee off Ore. 99W.

Torii Mor Winery ✦ With the Japanese-inspired name (*torii* means "gate" in Japanese) and gardens, you might expect this winery to produce sake, but, instead, they limit their production primarily to high-end pinot noir. Their better pinot noirs tend to be in the $40 range.

18325 NE Fairview Dr., Dundee. © 503/538-2279. www.toriimorwinery.com. Tasting fee $5. Daily 11am–5pm. In Dundee, go north on Ninth St. (which becomes Worden Hill Rd.), and turn right on Fairview Rd.

MCMINNVILLE AREA WINERIES

For a selection of area wines (several of which can be tasted on any given day), visit **Noah's–A Wine Bar,** 525 NE Third St., McMinnville (© 503/434-2787). West of McMinnville on Ore. 18, at the **Oregon Wine Tasting Room & Bellevue Market,** 19690 SW Ore. 18, McMinnville (© 503/843-3787), you can sample wines from numerous area wineries. This tasting room is open daily from 11am to 6pm. There's also a gourmet market here that is a great place to get picnic supplies.

Panther Creek Cellars ✦✦ To find out just how different pinot noirs from different vineyards can be, stop in at Panther Creek's facility in downtown McMinnville. In any given year, this winery usually produces eight vineyard-designate pinot noirs, and some of these wines have been rated among the best in the world.

455 N. Irvine St., McMinnville. © 503/274-8080. www.panthercreekcellars.com. Tasting fee $2. May–Nov Wed–Sun noon–5pm.

Yamhill Valley Vineyards ✦ Located west of McMinnville near Sheridan, this winery is set on a 150-acre estate in the foothills of the Coast Range. Pinot noirs are the strong point here, and prices for younger pinots are often quite reasonable (under $20). Good pinot gris, pinot blanc, and dry Riesling are also produced. Many of the wines have a pronounced mineral character.

16250 SW Oldsville Rd., McMinnville. © 800/825-4845. www.yamhill.com. Mid-Mar to Memorial Day weekend Sat–Sun 11am–5pm; Memorial Day weekend through Thanksgiving weekend daily 11am–5pm; first 3 weekends Dec Sat–Sun 11am–5pm. West of McMinnville 5 miles on Ore. 18, turn north on Oldsville Rd.

THE YAMHILL & CARLTON AREA

In the town of Carlton, you'll find **The Tasting Room,** 105 W. Main St. (© 503/852-6733; www.pinotnoir.com), which specializes in wines from wineries that are not usually open to the public; indeed, this an absolute must if you can't be around on Memorial Day or Thanksgiving weekend. Most wines featured here are from wineries in the immediate vicinity of Carlton. Also here in Carlton, you'll find the **Carlton Winemakers Studio,** 801 N. Scott St. (© **503/852-6100;** www.winemakersstudio.com), which represents numerous wineries, including Andrew Rich Wines, Hamacher Wines, and Domaine Meriwether. This tasting room is open daily from 11am to 5pm.

Anne Amie Vineyards   Set amid nearly 100 acres of vines and located high on a hill with one of the best views in the area, this winery has a large tasting room and does quite a few respectable white wines, most of which sell for less than $20. The winery produces good chardonnay and several vineyard-designate pinot noirs.

6580 NE Mineral Springs Rd., Carlton. © 800/248-4835. www.anneamie.com. Daily 10am–5pm. Take Ore. 99W to Lafayette and go north on Mineral Springs Rd.

Cuneo Cellars 🕸🕸   Big reds are the specialty of this winery. Winemaker Gino Cuneo's Cana's Feast cabernet-merlot blend is a favorite. Cabernet sauvignon, pinot noir, and even Nebbiolo all get the same treatment. If you like assertive red wines, don't miss this small winery.

750 Lincoln St., Carlton. © 503/852-0002. www.cuneocellars.com. Daily noon–5pm. Located just off Ore. 47 on the north side of town.

Laurel Ridge Winery 🕸🕸   With its wide variety of wines, Laurel Ridge is a sure-fire spot to please a carload of different wine palates. Laurel Ridge has long been known for its excellent sparkling wines and sauvignon blanc, but also does some good inexpensive pinot noirs. A couple of different ports are also available.

13301 NE Kuehne Rd., Carlton. © 503/852-7050. Daily 11am–5pm. From Carlton, drive east on Main St., which becomes Hendricks Rd. and then curves around to the north to become Kuehne Rd.

Penner-Ash Wine Cellars 🕸🕸   Although winemaker Lynn Penner-Ash has been on the Oregon wine scene for years, she only built her own winery in 2005, and a very impressive facility it is. Set high on a hill with a stupendous view, it would be worth a visit even if Penner-Ash didn't produce excellent wines. The pinot noirs and Syrahs here are some of the best in the state.

15771 NE Ribbon Ridge Rd., Newberg. © 503/554-5545. www.pennerash.com. Fri–Sun 11am–5pm. From Ore. 240 between Newberg and Yamhill, drive north on NE Ribbon Ridge Rd.

Soléna Cellars 🕸   Can you say inky? I knew you could. Highly extracted pinot noirs that look more like Syrah than pinot are the hallmark of this husband-and-wife winery. Along with that deep, dark color comes plenty of tannin, which means these are wines for your cellar. In addition to the usual Willamette Valley varietals, this winery also produces merlot, zinfandel, and Syrah from southern Oregon grapes and cabernet sauvignon from Washington grapes.

213 S. Pine St., Carlton. © 503/852-0082. www.solenacellars.com. Thurs–Sun noon–5pm.

Tyrus Evan/The Depot 🕸   Located in Carlton's old railroad depot and operated by the celebrated Ken Wright Cellars winery, Tyrus Evan specializes in bordeaux blends (here referred to as clarets) and Syrahs. These wines tend to be big and juicy and the winery is a must for anyone who is not a fan of pinot noir.

120 N. Pine St., Carlton. © 503/852-7010. www.thecarltondepot.com. Tasting fee $5. Thurs–Mon 11am–6pm.

Willakenzie Estate ⚘   Situated on a 400-acre estate above the Chehalem Valley, this winery produces primarily pinot noir, pinot gris, pinot blanc, and pinot meunier, plus a bit of chardonnay in its gravity-fed facility. There's a nice picnic area with good views. This is one of the prettiest spots in all of wine country, and the wines are excellent.

19143 NE Laughlin Rd., Yamhill. ✆ 888/953-9463 or 503/662-3280. www.willakenzie.com. May–Oct daily noon–5pm; Nov–Apr Fri–Sun noon–5pm. From Ore. 240 just east of Yamhill, drive north on NE Laughlin Rd.

THE HILLSBORO & BEAVERTON AREA

Cooper Mountain Vineyards   Now nearly surrounded by wealthy suburbs, this mountaintop winery is one of the few in the state that uses only organic grapes. The pinot gris is moderately priced and quite tasty, as are the chardonnays, which go light on the oak. Pinot noirs are decent and for those who like a light wine, there is a pinot blanc that makes a great picnic wine.

9480 SW Grabhorn Rd., Beaverton. ✆ 503/649-0027. www.coopermountainwine.com. Daily noon–5pm. From Ore. 217 on the west side of Portland, take Ore. 210 (Scholls Ferry Rd.) west approximately 5 miles, turn right on Tile Flat Rd. and right again on Grabhorn Rd.

Oak Knoll Winery   Although the only grape they actually grow here is a Niagara, from which they make a fruity but very drinkable wine, Oak Knoll manages each year to acquire some of the best grapes from area vineyards, and from these the winery usually succeeds in producing some good wines. Oak Knoll's Frambrosia is an ambrosial raspberry dessert wine.

29700 SW Burkhalter Rd., Hillsboro. ✆ 800/625-5665 or 503/648-8198. www.oakknollwinery.com. May–Sept daily Mon–Fri 11am–6pm, Sat–Sun 11am–5pm; Oct–Apr daily 11am–5pm. From Hillsboro, go south on Ore. 219 and turn left on Burkhalter Rd.

Ponzi Vineyards   Although Ponzi's tasting room/wine bar on Ore. 99W in Dundee is more convenient for most people touring wine country, it is also possible to taste wines here at the winery. Though there are no views here, the quiet setting and old shade trees make this an ideal spot for a picnic. See the listing above for information on wines produced by this pioneering Oregon winery.

14665 SW Winery Lane, Beaverton. ✆ 503/628-1227. www.ponziwines.com. Reserve wines tasting fee $5. Daily 11am–5pm. From Ore. 217 on the west side of Portland, take Ore. 210 (Scholls Ferry Rd.) west 4½ miles to a left on Vandermost Rd.

THE GASTON & FOREST GROVE AREA

David Hill Winery   This winery, up a gravel road, overlooks the forested foothills of the Coast Range and has its tasting room in a picturesque farmhouse. Here you'll usually find more than a dozen wines available for tasting. The sparkling wine and dessert wines (including a port) are particularly noteworthy. For the most part, wines here are very reasonably priced ($10–$15 range).

46350 David Hill Rd., Forest Grove. ✆ 877/992-8545 or 503/992-8545. www.davidhillwinery.com. Tues–Sun noon–5pm. West of Forest Grove off Ore. 8.

Elk Cove Vineyards ⚘   In business since 1974 and located in an idyllic setting in the hills above the community of Gaston, this is another of the state's larger wineries. Pinot noir and pinot gris make up the bulk of the wine produced here, and the Roosevelt pinot noir, although expensive, can be very good. The Ultima dessert wines are delicious.

27751 NW Olson Rd., Gaston. ✆ 877/ELK-COVE or 503/985-7760. www.elkcove.com. Daily 10am–5pm; closed Thanksgiving, Christmas Eve, Christmas, and New Year's Day. From Ore. 47 in Gaston, go west on Olson Rd.

Kramer Vineyards   Located a little farther along the same road as Elk Cove Vineyards, this small family-run winery usually does a decent chardonnay. Prices are fairly reasonable. There are numerous special events here throughout the year.

26830 NW Olson Rd., Gaston. ℂ **503/662-4545**. www.kramerwine.com. June–Sept daily noon–5pm; Mar–May and Oct–Dec Fri–Sun noon–5pm; closed Jan–Feb and Easter, Thanksgiving, and Christmas. From Ore. 47 in Gaston, go west on Olson Rd.

Montinore Vineyards ⚶   This is another of Oregon's big wineries, and as at other large Oregon wineries, the wines are often somewhat lacking. Exceptions include reasonably priced pinot noirs, chardonnays, and their late-harvest Riesling. The vineyard setting, with an old farmhouse that seems straight out of the antebellum South, is quite picturesque.

3663 SW Dilley Rd., Forest Grove. ℂ **503/359-5012**. www.montinore.com. Daily 11am–5pm; closed major holidays. South of Forest Grove off Ore. 47 at Dilley.

Shafer Vineyard Cellars ⚶   Small enough that the owners still work the tasting room but large enough to have a dozen or more wines available for tasting on any given day, this winery is strong on white wines, which it sells at very reasonable prices. Expect good Müller-Thurgaus and Gewürztraminers, and the Rieslings are also very consistent.

6200 NW Gales Creek Rd., Forest Grove. ℂ **503/357-6604**. www.shafervineyardcellars.com. Feb–Dec daily 11am–5pm; Jan Sat–Sun 11am–5pm. From Forest Grove, go 4½ miles west on Ore. 8.

Tualatin Estate Vineyards   Under the same ownership as the huge Willamette Valley Vineyards, this off-the-beaten-path winery is worth seeking out. Although Tualatin Estate does a respectable pinot noir, the winery is best known for its semi-sparkling muscat dessert wine. You can also expect good late-harvest Gewürztraminer.

10850 NW Seavey Rd., Tualatin. ℂ **503/357-5005**. Mar to mid-Dec Sat–Sun noon–5pm; closed mid-Dec to Feb. From Forest Grove, go west on Ore. 8, turn north on Thatcher Rd. and then west on Clapshaw Hill Rd.

THE EOLA HILLS AREA

Some people claim the best pinot noirs in Oregon come from the Eola Hills northwest of Salem. Why not decide for yourself?

Amity Vineyards ⚶   This was one of the earliest wineries in Oregon and is one of the few wineries in the state producing gamay noir wine. Amity also produces unsulfited pinot noir from organically grown grapes. Pinot noirs are usually in the $30 range and are often excellent. Its late-harvest and dessert wines are delicious. Amity also operates the Oregon Wine Tasting Room & Bellevue Market (see above).

Finds **Saké It to Me, Baby**

When you've had it with peppery pinot noir, crisp pinot gris, and oaky chardonnay, why not try a little sake? In Forest Grove you'll find **Saké One Brewery**, 820 Elm St. off Ore. 47 (ℂ **800/550-SAKE** or 503/357-7056; www.sakeone.com), which is one of North America's few sake breweries and produces premium sakes that are meant to be served cold. Saké One also bottles fruit-flavored sakes that are made with Asian pear and raspberry flavoring. Think sake latte and you've got a pretty good idea of what these latter wines are like. The tasting room is open daily from noon to 5pm, excluding major holidays.

18150 Amity Vineyards Rd., Amity. © **888/264-8966** or 503/835-2362. www.amityvineyards.com. Reserve wines tasting fee $4. June–Sept daily 11am–5pm; Oct–May noon–5pm. In Amity, go east on Rice Lane.

Bethel Heights Vineyards 𝕽 Set high on a hill and surrounded by more than 50 acres of grapes, Bethel Heights primarily produces chardonnays and pinot noirs. Even their least expensive pinot noirs usually start around $25, and while their best chardonnays are also around $25, they can be very good.

6060 Bethel Heights Rd. NW., Salem. © **503/581-2262**. www.bethelheights.com. June–Aug Tues–Sun 11am–5pm; Mar–May and Sept–Nov Sat–Sun 11am–5pm; closed Dec–Feb. From Ore. 221 in Lincoln, take Zena Rd. west and turn right on Bethel Heights Rd.

Cristom Vineyards 𝕽 With a beautiful setting high in the Eola Hills, this winery is an ideal place for a picnic. The chardonnays, from both estate-grown grapes and grapes grown elsewhere in the region, are quite good and fall in the $25 price range. Cristom is one of the few wineries in the region producing Viognier from estate-grown grapes. They have also planted some Syrah grapes.

6905 Spring Valley Rd. NW., Salem. © **503/375-3068**. www.cristomwines.com. Mid-Apr to Memorial Day and Labor Day to Thanksgiving Sat–Sun 11am–5pm; Memorial Day to Labor Day Wed–Sun 11am–5pm; closed Dec to mid-Apr. From Ore. 221 in Lincoln, take Zena Rd. west and turn right on Spring Valley Rd., or take Spring Valley Rd. west from Ore. 221 north of Lincoln.

Eola Hills Wine Cellars Well known in the area for its Sunday brunches, this winery on the outskirts of Rickreall offers everything from cabernet sauvignon to zinfandel—almost all at reasonable prices. While many of the wines here seem to be crafted for the grocery-store market, there are the occasional gems.

501 S. Pacific Hwy., Rickreall. © **800/291-6730** or 503/623-2405. www.eolahillswinery.com. Daily 11am–5pm; closed Thanksgiving and Christmas. On Ore. 99W between Rickreall and Monmouth.

Kristin Hill Winery "Méthode champenoise" sparkling wines are a specialty here and make this small family-run winery well worth a visit. The Fizzy Lizzy, a cherry-infused dry sparkling wine, is one of Kristin Hill's most popular wines.

3330 SE Amity-Dayton Hwy., Amity. © **503/835-0850**. Mar–Dec daily noon–5pm; Jan–Feb Sat–Sun noon–5pm. Just north of Amity at the junction with Ore. 233.

Mystic Wines 𝕽𝕽 This little winery on the north side of the Eola Hills bucks the Oregon pinot noir trend by producing excellent Syrah, zinfandel, cabernet sauvignon, and merlot with grapes that come primarily from near the Oregon town of The Dalles. Prices are mostly in the $20 to $30 range.

11931 Hood View Rd. NW, Amity. © **503/581-2769**. http://mysticwine.com. May–Nov Sat–Sun noon–5pm; closed Dec to Memorial Day. Off Ore. 221 about 1 mile north of Hopewell.

Stangeland Vineyards 𝕽 With an attractive stone-walled tasting room, this small family-owned winery north of Salem is a good place to start a wine tour of the Eola Hills. Stangeland produces some excellent fruit-forward pinot noirs in a variety of price ranges and has won numerous national and international awards.

8500 Hopewell Rd. NW, Salem. © **800/301-9482** or 503/581-0355. www.stangelandwinery.com. June–Dec Sat–Sun noon–5pm; Jan–May open 1st weekend of each month Sat–Sun noon–5pm or by appointment. From West Salem, go north on Ore. 221 for 9 miles and turn left on Hopewell Rd.

Van Duzer Vineyards 𝕽 Producing primarily pinot noir, pinot gris, and chardonnay in the Burgundian style, this winery is built on the side of an oak-shaded knoll

Tips **The Grape Escape**

If you're interested in learning more about Oregon wines, contact **Grape Escape** (© **503/283-3380;** www.grapeescapetours.com), which offers in-depth winery tours of the Willamette Valley. All-day tours include stops at several wineries, appetizers, lunch, and dessert, and pickup and drop-off at your hotel ($95–$165 per person). For people with less time, there are half-day afternoon trips that take in two or three wineries ($75–$125 per person).

with a commanding view across the valley to the Eola Hills. The tasting room is small and only a few wines are available at any given time.

11975 Smithfield Rd., Dallas. © **503/623-6420.** www.vanduzer.com. Mar–Dec daily 11am–5pm. North of Rickreall off Ore. 99W; take graveled Smithfield Rd. 3 miles west.

Witness Tree Vineyard 🖈 Named for a tree used by surveyors in the 19th century, this unpretentious winery produces estate-grown chardonnays and pinot noirs. In a region of high-priced pinots, Witness Tree is noteworthy for offering very drinkable bottles at around $25 (though they also produce pricier vintage select pinots that are often very good).

7111 Spring Valley Rd. NW., Salem. © **888/GR8T-PNO** or 503/585-7874. www.witnesstreevineyard.com. June–Aug Tues–Sun 11am–5pm; Mar–May and Sept–Dec Sat–Sun 11am–5pm; limited hours and dates Jan–Feb. From Ore. 221 in Lincoln, take Zena Rd. west and turn right on Spring Valley Rd. or take Spring Valley Rd. west from Ore. 221 north of Lincoln.

OTHER WINE COUNTRY ACTIVITIES
THE SPRUCE GOOSE
Evergreen Aviation Museum 🖈🖈 The middle of wine country may seem an odd landing place for Howard Hughes's famous "Spruce Goose" flying boat, but that's exactly what you'll find in this massive, barnlike museum. Although designed during World War II as a flying troop transport that wouldn't have to worry about attacks from German U-boats, the "Spruce Goose" wasn't completed until 1947, at which point it was no longer needed. The plane flew only one time, with Howard Hughes at the controls. The massive wooden plane rests in the company of many smaller planes. Among these are an SR-71 Blackbird spy plane, a Ford Trimotor, a P-51 Mustang, a Spitfire, and a replica of the Wright Brothers' 1903 plane. By the way, the term "Spruce Goose" is actually a misnomer; most of the plane is made of birch.

500 NE Capt. Michael King Smith Way, McMinnville. © **503/434-4180.** www.sprucegoose.org. Admission $11 adults, $10 seniors, $7 students, free for children 5 and under. Daily 9am–5pm; closed Thanksgiving, Christmas, New Year's Day, and Easter. On Ore. 18 (the McMinnville bypass).

GETTING OUTDOORS IN WINE COUNTRY
You can see the wine country from the air on a hot-air balloon ride with **Vista Balloon Adventures** (© **800/622-2309** or 503/625-7385; www.vistaballoon.com), which charges $179 per person for a 1-hour flight (with hot breakfast and sparkling wine). Alternatively, between March and October, you can opt for a flight over the region in a glider. Contact **Cascade Soaring,** McMinnville Airport (© **503/472-8805**), which offers a variety of flights ranging in duration from 15 to 55 minutes and in price from $50 to $170. Gliders carrying one or two passengers are used.

Seven miles south of Newberg off Ore. 219, on the banks of the Willamette River, is **Champoeg State Park** (pronounced Sham-*poo*-ee) (© **503/678-1251**). The park includes a campground, a bike path, a picnic area, a historic home, a log cabin, and a visitor center that traces Champoeg's history from its days as a Native American village up through its pioneer farming days. Park admission is $3.

THE AURORA COLONY

An interesting chapter in Oregon pioneer history is preserved 13 miles south of Oregon City in the town of Aurora, which was founded in 1855 as a Christian communal society. Similar to such better-known communal experiments as the Amana Colony and the Shaker communities, the Aurora Colony lasted slightly more than 20 years. Today Aurora is a National Historic District and the large old homes of the community's founders have been restored. Many of the old commercial buildings now house antiques stores. You can learn the history of Aurora at the **Old Aurora Colony Museum,** Second and Liberty streets (© **503/678-5754;** www.auroracolonymuseum.com). February through December, the museum is open Tuesday through Saturday from 11am to 4pm and on Sunday from noon to 4pm. The museum is closed in January. Admission is $3.50 for adults, $3 for seniors, and $1.50 for children under 18.

SHOPPING IN THE AREA

If you're interested in picking up some local art or crafts, there are several places worth visiting. Seven miles west of McMinnville near Sheridan, you'll find the **Lawrence Gallery,** Ore. 18 (© **800/894-4278** or 503/843-3633; www.lawrencegallery.net). This large art gallery features regional artists and has a sculpture garden and a water garden. Right across the street, you'll find the **Fire's Eye Gallery,** Ore. 18 (© **503/843-9797;** www.fireseyegallery.com), with more whimsical, colorful artwork than the Lawrence Gallery.

If you enjoy shopping for antiques and collectibles, check out the **Lafayette Schoolhouse Antique Mall,** 784 Ore. 99W, Lafayette (© **503/864-2720**), housed in a 1910 schoolhouse and filled with more than 100 dealers. Lafayette is 6 miles east of McMinnville on Ore. 99W.

To stock up on local jams, wines, and other gourmet food items, visit **Your Northwest,** Ore. 99W and Seventh Street, Dundee (© **888/252-0699** or 503/554-8101; www.yournw.com). This little shop is crammed full of all manner of foods and Northwest crafts. **Firestone Farms,** 18400 N. Hwy. 99W, Dayton (© **503/864-2672**), just west of Dundee, also sells a wide selection of local produce, wines, and gourmet foods. For fresh produce spring through fall, stop at **Farmer John's Produce & Nursery,** 15000 SW Oldsville Rd., McMinnville (© **503/474-3514;** www.farmerjohns produce.com), which is located southwest of McMinnville off Ore. 18. For fresh local fruit, don't miss **Sweet Oregon Berry Farm** (© **503/864-2897**), which is at the junction of Ore. 18 and Ore. 99W, between Dundee and Lafayette. Dried flowers, herbs, soaps, and other garden-related gifts can also be found at the beautiful **Red Ridge Farms,** 5510 NE Breyman Orchards Rd., Dayton (© **503/864-8502;** www.redridge farms.com), a nursery and gift shop high in the hills west of Dundee. Call for directions and hours.

If you like chocolate, head to Amity and stop in at the **Brigittine Monastery,** 23300 Walker Lane (© **503/835-8080;** www.brigittine.org), which is known for its heavenly fudge. The fudge and truffles are for sale at the guest reception area, which is open Monday through Saturday from 9am to 5:30pm and Sunday from 1:30 to 5:30pm.

WHERE TO STAY
THE NEWBERG & DUNDEE AREA

Avellan Inn ⌘ The Avellan Inn is a small country inn that has just two guest rooms. From the outside, the inn resembles an old barn, complete with weathered cedar board-and-batten siding. Inside, however, it is nothing like a barn. Big walls of glass illuminate the breakfast area and a wood stove keeps the room nice and cozy in cooler months. Emily's Room, my personal favorite here, has a private entrance and a huge covered deck that, when the weather is clear, has a view of Mount Hood. When you stay here, you'll be within a 5- to 10-minute drive of several good wineries.

16900 NE Ore. 240, Newberg, OR 97132. ✆ **503/537-9161.** www.avellaninn.com. 2 units. $125–$145 double. Rates include full breakfast. DISC, MC, V. *In room:* A/C, hair dryer, free local calls.

Black Walnut Inn ⌘⌘ Perched high in the Red Hills of Dundee with a view that seems to take in all of Oregon wine country, this inn looks for all the world as though it had been transported here from Tuscany. Although guest rooms don't have the same Tuscan feel, they are comfortably homey. Some have antique furnishings and some are more contemporary, so there's a room that's just right for nearly anyone. Some rooms have a soaking tub and all have a balcony or patio. The gardens and patios here are the perfect place to sip a glass of wine at sunset.

9600 NE Worden Hill Rd., Dundee, OR 97115. ✆ **866/429-4114** or 503/429-4114. Fax 503/538-4194. www.black walnut-inn.com. 7 units. $180–$575 suite. Rates include full breakfast. Children 12 and older accepted. AE, MC, V. **Amenities:** Concierge; massage. *In room:* A/C, TV/DVD/VCR, hair dryer, free local calls, high-speed Internet access.

Red Ridge Farm Suite ⌘⌘ There's only one huge suite available at this luxurious little place, and it is such a quintessential wine-country retreat that you should make this your first choice if you're looking for a romantic hideaway in the hills. The suite takes up the entire second floor of a gorgeous building that has a garden-oriented gift shop on the ground floor. Access is via a spiral staircase up the building's turret (in which lavender hangs to dry in summer). The modern styling, big windows, and wine-country views make this the sort of place you'd see in *Sunset* magazine.

5510 NE Breyman Orchards Rd., Dayton, OR 97114. ✆ **503/864-8502.** Fax 503/864-8391. www.redridgefarms.com. 1 unit. $185 double. MC, V. *In room:* A/C, TV/VCR, kitchen, fridge, coffeemaker, hair dryer, iron. Closed Dec–Mar.

Springbrook Hazelnut Farm ⌘⌘ Located only 20 miles from Portland, this 70-acre working farm is a convenient rural getaway for anyone who craves a slow-paced vacation. The four craftsman-style buildings are listed on the National Register of Historic Places and include the main house, a carriage house, and a cottage. Original artwork abounds in the boldly decorated, colorful main house. Both of the main buildings overlook the farm's pond and lovely back garden, and there are also tennis courts and a swimming pool. Through the hazelnut orchard is Rex Hill Vineyards, and there's also a small winery operating here on the farm. The little white cottage, with its antique fireplace mantle, fir floors, and tiled bathroom, overlooks the farm's pond and a meadow that's filled with daffodils in the spring.

30295 N. Ore. 99W, Newberg, OR 97132. ✆ **800/793-8528** or 503/538-4606. www.nutfarm.com. 2 units. $225 cottage or carriage house. Rates include full breakfast. AE, DC, DISC, MC, V. **Amenities:** Outdoor pool; tennis court. *In room:* Kitchen, fridge, coffeemaker, hair dryer, iron, no phone.

Willamette Gables Riverside Estate ⌘⌘ *Finds* The banks of Oregon's Willamette River may not be where you'd expect to find a Southern plantation home, but, nonetheless, here it is. Designed as a reproduction of a home in Natchez, Mississippi, this secluded and tranquil B&B is authentic in almost every detail and is as elegant an inn as you'll find anywhere in the region. The views of the river from the breakfast room will start your day out just right. The inn is close to Champoeg State Park, about midway between Aurora and Newberg.

10323 Schuler Rd., Aurora, OR 97002. ⓒ **503/678-2195.** Fax 503/678-6309. www.willamettegables.com. 5 units. $145–$175 double. Rates include full breakfast. MC, V. *In room:* No phone.

Wine Country Farm ⚗   Located high in the hills between Dundee and Lafayette, this B&B has one of the best views in the area, a wine tasting room, and 5 acres of grapevines. When this 1910 farmhouse was renovated and converted into a B&B, the owners even gave the facade the look of a French farmhouse. Two of the rooms have good views, as do the breakfast room and the deck that runs the entire length of the house. Some rooms have TVs and VCRs. A croquet lawn and horseshoe pit provide traditional rural recreational activities when guests aren't out wine tasting.

6855 Breyman Orchards Rd., Dayton, OR 97114. ⓒ **800/261-3446** or 503/864-3446. Fax 503/864-3109. www.winecountryfarm.com. 9 units. $125–$185 double. Rates include full breakfast. Children 12 and older accepted. MC, V. **Amenities:** Jacuzzi; bikes; massage; laundry service. *In room:* A/C.

THE MCMINNVILLE AREA

Mattey House ⚗   This restored 1892 Queen Anne Victorian farmhouse sits on 10 acres of farmland behind 1½ acres of grapevines. This is a grand old house, and up on the second floor, you'll find a tiny balcony overlooking the vineyard. It's the perfect spot for a glass of wine in the afternoon. Guest rooms are decorated in country Victorian style, with antique beds. The Riesling Room, with its claw-foot bathtub, is my favorite. Innkeepers Jack and Denise Seed are always glad to help you plan your day's explorations.

10221 NE Mattey Lane, McMinnville, OR 97128. ⓒ **503/434-5058.** Fax 503/434-6667. www.matteyhouse.com. 4 units. $100–$135 double. Rates include full breakfast. Children 10 and older welcome. MC, V. *In room:* Hair dryer, no phone.

McMenamins Hotel Oregon ⚗   This restored historic hotel in downtown McMinnville is operated by a Portland-based chain of brewpubs, nightclubs, and unusual hotels that are all filled with interesting artwork. Guest rooms here are done in a simple, classic style, with antique and reproduction furniture. The corner kings with private baths and big windows on two sides are the nicest rooms; most rooms here have shared bathrooms. Offsetting this inconvenience is the hotel's genuinely historic feel. The ground-floor brewpub/dining room, cellar bar, and rooftop bar and deck overlooking McMinnville and the Yamhill Valley all help make the Hotel Oregon eminently recommendable. There are also a couple of good restaurants within a few blocks.

310 NE Evans St., McMinnville, OR 97128. ⓒ **888/472-8427** or 503/472-8427. www.mcmenamins.com. 42 units (6 with private bathroom). $50–$95 double with shared bathroom; $80–$110 double with private bath. Rates include full breakfast. Children 6 and under stay free in parent's room. AE, DC, DISC, MC, V. **Amenities:** Restaurant (American); 3 lounges. *In room:* A/C.

Youngberg Hill Inn ⚗⚗   Set on a 50-acre farm that includes pinot noir vineyards, this is the quintessential wine-country inn. A mile-long gravel driveway leads to the inn, which sits atop a hill with commanding views of the Willamette Valley, snow-capped Cascades peaks, and the Coast Range. Large decks wrap around both floors of the inn, and some of the rooms have their own fireplaces. Big breakfasts get visitors off to a good start each morning. Pull up a chair on the porch, pour a glass of the inn's own pinot noir, gaze out over the rolling hills, and you'll probably start thinking about cashing in the mutual funds to start a vineyard of your own.

10660 SW Youngberg Hill Rd., McMinnville, OR 97128. © 888/657-8668 or 503/472-2727. Fax 503/472-1313. www.youngberghill.com. 7 units. $149–$179 double; $199–$249 suite. Rates include full breakfast. Children over 4 are welcome. MC, V. **Amenities:** Massage. *In room:* A/C, hair dryer, iron, free local calls, Wi-Fi.

THE FOREST GROVE AREA

McMenamins Grand Lodge ✿   Housed in a former Masonic retirement home, this sprawling lodge is part of a local microbrewery chain and has a decidedly countercultural feel. Although only five of the rooms here have a private bath, there are plenty of well-appointed bathrooms, and most rooms do have sinks. There's also lots of colorful artwork incorporated into the design of the building. However, the principal attractions here are the brewpub, beer garden, and numerous small lounges scattered around the main building. The lodge is surrounded by huge lawns and has its own disc golf course, wine bar, and movie theater.

3505 Pacific Ave., Forest Grove, OR 97116. © 877/922-9533 or 503/992-9533. www.thegrandlodge.com. 77 units (5 with private bathroom). $45–$85 double with shared bathroom; $95–$185 double with private bathroom. Rates include full breakfast. Children 6 and under stay free in parent's room. AE, DC, DISC, MC, V. **Amenities:** 2 restaurants (American); 4 lounges; soaking pool; day spa; massage. *In room:* No phone, Wi-Fi.

THE EOLA HILLS

Bethel Heights Farm Bed & Breakfast ✿   Set high on a hill overlooking the Willamette Valley and the Coast Range, this inn is in the middle of a 20-acre farm and vineyard. Outside the front door are a rock garden, small pond, and gazebo, while down the hill and into the oak woods, you'll find a much larger farm pond. Inside, all is spotless and modern. The two rooms have outstanding views west to the Coast Range. One has a patio, the other a balcony. The gourmet breakfasts include homemade jams and syrups and homemade pastries. If you're in the area specifically to do a bit of wine touring, there is no better location than this contemporary inn in the middle of the Eola Hills wine region.

6055 Bethel Heights Rd. NW, Salem, OR 97304. © 503/364-7688. www.oregon-b-and-b.com. 2 units. $105 double. DISC, MC, V. *In room:* No phone.

WHERE TO DINE
THE NEWBERG & DUNDEE AREA

If wine tasting has made you sleepy and you need a good latte, head to the **Coffee Cottage,** 808 E. Hemlock St., Newberg (© **503/538-5126**).

The Dundee Bistro ✿✿ NORTHWEST   Located in the same building as the Ponzi Wine Bar and the Your Northwest gift shop, this chic eatery would be right at home in Portland's trendy Pearl District. The bistro's hip, urban style, however, also epitomizes a modern wine-country aesthetic, which makes this place quite popular with people touring the area wineries. The menu is relatively short and changes on a regular basis to reflect the region's best seasonal ingredients, which translates into the likes of smoked salmon carpaccio with orange, olive tapenade, capers, and shaved fennel; pork loin with Parmesan polenta and chanterelle mushrooms; beef shoulder with cannelloni beans and spinach, and truffled foie gras butter. The wine list focuses on area wines.

100-A SW Seventh St., Dundee. © 503/554-1650. www.dundeebistro.com. Reservations recommended. Main courses $12–$24. AE, MC, V. Sun–Thurs 11:30am–8:30pm; Fri–Sat 11:30am–9pm.

The French Bear ✿ NORTHWEST   This casual restaurant in downtown Newberg is popular with local winemakers and is a good spot for breakfast or lunch before a day of wine touring. Meals are creative and utilize fresh, local ingredients but you won't spend a fortune. If you like crab, try the crab cakes or crab soufflé. Even the simple chicken pot pie here gets a Northwest spin here with chanterelle mushrooms. Although dinner is also served here and can be very good, I tend to think of the French Bear as a breakfast and lunch spot. There are plenty of local wines available.

107 S. College St., Newberg. © 503/538-2609. Reservations recommended. Main courses $14–$18. AE, DC, DISC, MC, V. Mon–Wed 7am–6pm; Thurs–Sat 7am–9pm.

The Painted Lady ☆☆ FRENCH/NORTHWEST   Located just off Ore. 99W in a restored Victorian home in downtown Newberg, this dinner house is the latest high-end restaurant to take root in wine country. With credentials that include study at the Culinary Institute of America, chef/owner Allen Routt brings sophistication and creativity to a town that has long thought of Chinese and Mexican as exotic foods. The menu is strictly prix fixe, and the three-course dinner ($39) offers plenty of choices. The menu changes with the seasons, but a recent night featured roasted-red-pepper soup with crab and horseradish cream; halibut with corn and chanterelle-mushroom fricassee; stuffed pheasant breast with wild-mushroom risotto; and rice pudding with pinot-noir-soaked currants. If you'd rather trust the decision making to the chef, opt for the seven-course grand tasting menu ($55).

201 S. College St., Newberg. © 503/538-3850. www.thepaintedladyrestaurant.com. Reservations highly recommended. Prix fixe menus $39 and $55. AE, DISC, MC, V. Wed–Sun 5–10pm.

Red Hills Provincial Dining ☆☆ FRENCH/CONTINENTAL/NORTHWEST   Housed in a 1920s craftsman bungalow, this restaurant sums up the Oregon wine-country appeal with both its setting and its food. The dinner menu changes regularly, and you can be sure it will always include plenty of fresh local produce, as well as Northwest meats and seafoods. The menu draws on a variety of European influences and can be counted upon to feature the likes of chicken breast with Marcona almonds, figs, and pastis; *delicata* squash alfredo, filet mignon with pinot noir demi-glace, or lamb shanks braised in pinot noir. There's a very good selection of wines available (local wines are featured), and dishes are calculated to pair well with the wines of the region.

276 Ore. 99W, Dundee. © 503/538-8224. Reservations recommended. Main courses $20–$30. AE, DISC, MC, V. Tues–Sun 5–8 or 9pm.

Tina's ☆☆ CONTINENTAL/NORTHWEST   Despite its rather small and nondescript building right on the highway in Dundee, Tina's has long been one of the Yamhill County wine country's premier restaurants, and with its contemporary menu and decor, it's my favorite place to eat in the area. The menu changes regularly and usually has no more than half a dozen entrees and fewer of appetizers. However, a balance between the traditional (grilled rib-eye steak with portobello mushrooms and hand-cut fries) and the less familiar (pan-roasted duck breast with corn soufflé and green-peppercorn sauce), keeps diners content. There are usually almost as many desserts available as there are entrees, and the wine selection, of course, emphasizes local wines.

760 Ore. 99W. © 503/538-8880. www.tinasdundee.com. Reservations recommended. Main courses $8–$10 lunch, $22–$30 dinner. AE, DISC, MC, V. Tues–Fri 11:30am–2pm and 5–9pm; Sat–Sun 5–9pm.

THE AMITY & DAYTON AREA
The Joel Palmer House ☆☆☆ FRENCH/NORTHWEST   If you love mushrooms in all their earthy guises, then in this downtown Dayton restaurant you will find your culinary nirvana. Chef/owner Jack Czarnecki is a man obsessed with mushrooms, and

nearly every dish has mushrooms in it. Start your meal with the extraordinary wild-mushroom soup made with suillis mushrooms, then move on to the filet mignon with pinot-noir sauce and wild mushrooms or the beef Stroganoff with Oregon white truffles. The rack of lamb with a pinot-hazelnut sauce, although it lacks mushrooms, is a quintessential wine-country entree. Mushroom lovers will be in good hands if they opt for the "Jack's Mushroom Madness" prix-fixe dinner. The extensive wine list features Oregon wines. The restaurant is in a house built in the 1850s and is quite formal.

600 Ferry St., Dayton. ℭ 503/864-2995. www.joelpalmerhouse.com. Reservations highly recommended. Main courses $18–$28; prix fixe $55. AE, DC, DISC, MC, V. Tues–Sat 5–9pm; closed mid-Feb to mid-Mar.

THE MCMINNVILLE & CARLTON AREA

For casual and inexpensive meals, try the **McMenamins Pub,** Hotel Oregon, 310 NE Evans St. (ℭ **503/472-8427**), which serves decent pub fare, plus good microbrews and regional wines. More pub fare, microbrews, and local wines can also be had at the **Golden Valley Brewery & Pub,** 980 E. Fourth St. (ℭ **503/472-2739;** www.golden valleybrewery.com). For espresso, drop by **Union Block Coffee,** 403 NE Third St. (ℭ **503/472-0645**).

Bistro Maison ⟡ FRENCH   This cozy little spot in an old house in downtown McMinnville is a casual French restaurant with great food. The husband-and-wife owners bring loads of experience to the restaurant, including time spent at famed New York restaurants the Russian Tea Room and Tavern on the Green. The menu offers such French standards as escargot and coq au vin, but whatever you order for an entree, be sure to start with the mussels or the very authentic fondue. There are daily *plats du jour,* with Sundays featuring a good cassoulet. Although the service here can be hit or miss, the food is good enough to overlook most shortcomings on the part of the waitstaff. In summer, ask for a table on the tree-shaded patio.

729 NE Third St. ℭ 503/474-1888. www.bistromaison.com. Reservations recommended. Main courses $9–$12 lunch, $16–$18 dinner. MC, V. Wed–Thurs 11:30am–2pm and 5–8pm; Fri 11:30am–2pm and 5–9pm; Sat 5–9pm; Sun noon–8pm.

Cuvée ⟡⟡ FRENCH   Chef/owner Gilbert Henry had long established himself as one of the top toques in Portland before moving recently to the small town of Carlton in the heart of the wine country. Here Henry's classic French cuisine is the perfect foil for fine wines from Carlton-area wineries. The boeuf bourguignon is the perfect dish to go with a local pinot, but there's also usually a lamb dish (perhaps cassoulet or lamb chops) on the menu. Be sure to start your meal with some oysters or sautéed mushrooms and local pinot gris or chardonnay. Attached to the restaurant is a cute little shop—**Lulu** (ℭ **503/852-6777**)—that sells hand-picked imports from France.

214 W. Main St., Carlton. ℭ 503/852-6555. Reservations highly recommended. Main courses $18–$23. AE, DISC, MC, V. Wed–Sat 5:30–9:30pm; Sun 4–8pm.

The Fresh Palate Cafe ⟡ SEAFOOD/NORTHWEST   This casual spot is popular both with people touring the wine country and those headed to or from the coast. The crab cakes here are a must-have, and are best accompanied by a local pinot gris. Other good choices include a sandwich made with hazelnut-crusted salmon and wild-mushroom ravioli. There are usually a half dozen or so daily specials. Because this is the best place for miles around, there is usually a wait for a table on summer weekends. If the weather is nice, try to get a table on the deck.

19706 SW Ore. 18 (between McMinnville and Sheridan). © **503/843-4400.** www.freshpalatecafe.com. Reservations recommended on weekends. Main courses $10–$19. AE, MC, V. Daily 11am–3pm (Nov–Apr Fri–Sat 5–8pm).

La Rambla Restaurant & Bar ✿✿ SPANISH   First came the Italian restaurants, then the French, now Oregon's Willamette Valley wine country has a very classy Spanish restaurant. Located right in downtown McMinnville, La Rambla has a gorgeous dining room with a long bar down one side. I like sitting at the bar, sipping wine and noshing on tapas such as grilled eggplant stuffed with goat cheese, mussels with caramelized onions and Jerez wine, and Andalusian gypsy stew. However, if you're more inclined to a format dinner, they've got a few good choices as well.

238 NE Third St., McMinnville. © **503/435-2126.** www.laramblaonthird.com. Reservations recommended. Main courses $14–$34; tapas $3–$12. AE, MC, V. Mon–Thurs 11am–2pm and 5–9pm; Fri 11am–2pm and 5–10pm; Sat 11am–10pm; Sun 11am–9pm.

Nick's Italian Café ✿✿ NORTHERN ITALIAN   Despite its unpretentious exterior, this restaurant in downtown McMinnville serves some of the best meals in the region. Each evening, there's a fixed-price five-course dinner that might start with prosciutto-wrapped figs and melon, followed by minestrone soup and a salad of greens with a huckleberry vinaigrette and toasted walnuts and filberts. From there you'll move on to a pasta dish and then the entree, which might be salt-crusted salmon with chanterelle-mushroom cream sauce; rib-eye steak with Gorgonzola butter; or prosciutto-stuffed chicken with fontina sauce and shaved black truffles. If you still have room after all that, be sure to try the chocolate-hazelnut brandy torte.

521 NE Third St., McMinnville. © **503/434-4471.** www.nicksitaliancafe.com. Reservations recommended. 5-course fixed-price dinner $42. AE, MC, V. Tues–Thurs 5:30–9pm; Fri–Sat 5:30–10pm; Sun 5–8pm.

IN THE GASTON & FOREST GROVE AREA
You can get decent pub food at the **Ironwork Grill,** McMenamins Grand Lodge, 3505 Pacific Ave. (© **503/992-9533**), in Forest Grove. This hotel also has a beer garden in the summer.

EN ROUTE TO THE BEACH
It used to be almost impossible to get beach-bound traffic on Ore. 18 west of McMinnville to stop for anything, but that was before the **Spirit Mountain Casino** (© **800/760-7977;** www.spiritmountain.com) opened in the town of Grand Ronde and became the most popular casino in Oregon. These days a lot of the traffic on this highway isn't even going to the beach, it's headed straight to this large, glitzy temple of luck.

2 Salem & the Mid-Willamette Valley

47 miles S of Portland, 40 miles N of Corvallis, 131 miles W of Bend, 57 miles E of Lincoln City

Although it's the state capital, the third largest city in the state, and home to Willamette University, Salem feels more like a small Midwestern college town than a Pacific Rim capital. Founded by a Methodist missionary, the city still wears its air of conservatism like a minister's collar. No one has ever accused Salem of being too raucous or rowdy. Even when both the school and the legislature are in session, the city barely seems charged with energy. The quiet conservatism does, however, give the city a certain charm that's not found in the other cities of the Willamette Valley. Though there are some interesting museums and the state capitol building to be visited here, it is the countryside surrounding Salem that is the real attraction. Within 20 to 25 miles of Salem, you'll find the Oregon Garden, Silver Falls State Park (one of the most

Salem

ATTRACTIONS ●
A.C. Gilbert Discovery Village **3**
Bush Barn Art Center **9**
Bush House Museum **10**
Hallie Ford
   Museum of Art **11**
Historic Deepwood Estate **16**
Honeywood **17**
Mission Hill Museum **14**
Oregon State Capitol **12**
Salem's Riverfront Carousel **2**
St. Innocent Winery **4**

ACCOMMODATIONS ■
A Creekside Garden Inn **13**
Phoenix Grand Hotel **7**

DINING ◆
The Beanery **6**
Court Street Dairy Lunch **5**
Gerry Frank's Konditorei **8**
Morton's Bistro Northwest **1**
Ram Restaurant &
   Big Horn Brewery **15**
Wild Pear **1**

beautiful state parks in Oregon), wineries, commercial flower fields, and several quaint small towns (Silverton, Mt. Angel, Independence, and Monmouth) that conjure up the Willamette Valley's pioneer past.

Salem's roots date from 1834, when Methodist missionary Jason Lee, who had traveled west to convert the local Indians, founded Salem, making it the first American settlement in the Willamette Valley. In 1842, 1 year before the first settlers crossed the continent on the Oregon Trail, Lee founded the Oregon Institute, the first school of higher learning west of the Rockies. In 1857, the first textile mill west of the Mississippi opened here, giving Salem a firm industrial base. However, despite all these historic firsts, Oregon City and Portland grew much faster and quickly became the region's population centers. Salem seemed doomed to backwater status until the year 1859, when Oregon became a state and Salem was chosen its capital.

ESSENTIALS
GETTING THERE   Salem is on I-5 at the junction of Ore. 22, which heads west to connect with Ore. 18 from Lincoln City and southeast to connect with U.S. 20 from Bend.

Amtrak has passenger rail service to Salem. The station is at 13th Street between Leslie and Bellevue streets.

VISITOR INFORMATION   Contact the **Salem Convention & Visitors Association,** 1313 Mill St. SE, Salem, OR 97301 (© **800/874-7012** or 503/581-4325; www.travelsalem.com). For more information on the Silverton area, contact the **Silverton Chamber of Commerce,** P.O. Box 257, Silverton, OR 97381 (© **503/873-5615;** www.silvertonor.com).

FESTIVALS   Two of the biggest events of the year in Salem are the **Oregon State Fair** (© **503/947-3247;** www.fun-oregon.com), which is held from late August to Labor Day, and the **Salem Arts Festival** (© **503/581-2228;** www.salemart.org/fair), which is the largest juried art fair in Oregon and is held the third weekend in July.

Each year on the second weekend after Labor Day, the town of Mt. Angel is the site of the huge **Mt. Angel Oktoberfest** ☆ (© **503/845-9440;** www.oktoberfest.org). With polka bands from around the world, beer and wine gardens, German food, and dancing in the streets, this is just about the biggest party in the state.

SALEM
SEEING THE SIGHTS
Though it is sometimes easy to forget, Salem is a river town. On the western edge of downtown, you'll find Salem's Riverfront Park, which features a state-of-the-art playground, amphitheater, carousel, and meandering pathways. It is also home to the A.C. Gilbert Discovery Village (see below). The park also is where you'll find the dock for the *Willamette Queen* (© **503/371-1103;** www.willamettequeen.com), a paddle wheeler that cruises the Willamette River. Cruises range from basic 1-hour outings to lunch, brunch, dinner, and even murder-mystery cruises. Prices range from $10 ($5 for children 12 and under) for a 50-minute cruise to $35 for a 2-hour dinner or brunch cruise ($21 for children 12 and under). Seniors receive a 10% discount. Reservations are required.

Bush Barn Art Center ☆   The Salem Art Association's Bush Barn Art Center includes a sales gallery as well as exhibition spaces that feature changing art exhibits. The focus is on local and regional artists, and the quality is quite high. Each year on the third weekend in July, Bush's Pasture Park is the site of the Salem Art Fair and Festival, one of the most popular art festivals in the Northwest.

Bush and High sts. © 503/581-2228. www.salemart.org. Free admission. Tues–Fri 10am–5pm; Sat–Sun noon–5pm; closed major holidays.

Bush House Museum ☆   Set at the top of a shady hill in the 100-acre Bush's Pasture Park, this imposing Italianate Victorian home dates back to 1878. Inside, you can see the original furnishings, including 10 fireplaces and the original wallpaper. At the time it was built, this home had all the modern conveniences—indoor plumbing, gaslights, and central heating. Also on the grounds is Oregon's oldest greenhouse conservatory.

600 Mission St. SE. © 503/363-4714. www.salemart.org. Admission $4 adults, $3 students and seniors, $2 children 6–12. May–Sept Tues–Sun noon–5pm; Oct–Apr Tues–Sun 2–5pm; closed major holidays.

Hallie Ford Museum of Art ☆☆   This is the second-largest art museum in Oregon and features collections of Native American baskets and Northwest, European, and Asian art. The first-floor galleries are devoted to contemporary art and feature changing exhibitions. Upstairs, you'll find one gallery filled with more than 70 Native American baskets, the finest collection of such baskets in the state. Other galleries contain artifacts ranging from an ancient Egyptian coffin mask to 19th-century Chinese porcelain.

700 State St. ℂ **503/370-6855**. www.willamette.edu/museum_of_art. Admission $3 adults, $2 seniors and students; free admission Tues. Tues–Sat 10am–5pm. Closed July 4, Thanksgiving, and Dec 25–Jan 1.

Historic Deepwood Estate ☞ Set on 5½ acres of English-style gardens and woodlands, this Queen Anne Victorian home is a delicate jewel box of a house. Although the house, with its many stained-glass windows, golden-oak moldings, and numerous lightning rod–topped peaked roofs and gables, was built in 1894, the gardens weren't added until the 1930s and were designed by the Northwest's first women-owned landscape architecture firm.

1116 Mission St. SE. ℂ **503/363-1825**. www.oregonlink.com/deepwood. Admission $4 adults, $3 seniors and students, $2 children 6–12. Grounds daily dawn–dusk; guided house tours May–Sept Sun–Fri noon–5pm, Oct–Apr Tues–Sat noon–5pm.

Mission Mill Museum ☞☞ The sprawling red Thomas Kay Woolen Mill, a water-powered mill built in 1889, is one of the most fascinating attractions in Salem. (The Salem Visitors Information Center on site also makes this the best place to start a tour of the state capital.) The restored buildings house exhibits on every stage of the wool-making process, and in the main mill building, the water-driven turbine is still in operation, producing electricity for the buildings. Also on these neatly manicured grounds are several other old structures (including the Jason Lee House, which was built by Salem's founder in 1841 and is the oldest frame house in the Northwest), a cafe, and a collection of interesting shops. The Marion County Historical Society Museum (ℂ **503/364-2128**), also on the grounds, houses exhibits on the history of the area with a particularly interesting section on the local Kalapuya Indians.

1313 Mill St. SE. ℂ **503/585-7012**. www.missionmill.org. Admission $7 adults, $6 seniors, $4 children 6–18. Mon–Sat 10am–5pm; closed major holidays.

Oregon State Capitol Where's the dome? That's the first thing that strikes most visitors to the Oregon State Capitol, which looks as if builders forgot to complete the building. However, it was actually designed without a dome, and, consequently, the building, which opened in 1938, has a stark appearance (not unlike that of a mausoleum). If you look closer, though, you'll recognize the pared down lines of Art Deco design aesthetics in this building. *The Oregon Pioneer*, a 23-foot-tall gilded statue, tops the building, which is faced with white Italian marble. Outside the building, there are numerous sculptures and attractive gardens; inside, there are murals of historic Oregon scenes. Tours of the capitol are available during the summer. There are also changing art exhibits and videos about the history of the building and the state.

900 Court St. NE. ℂ **503/986-1388**. www.leg.state.or.us. Free admission. Building Mon–Fri 7:30am–5:30pm, Sat 9am–4pm; tours offered Mon–Sat 9am–3pm. Closed national holidays.

A NEARBY STATE PARK & TWO WILDLIFE REFUGES

North of Salem 8 miles you'll find **Willamette Mission State Park** (ℂ **503/393-1172;** www.oregonstateparks.org), which preserves the site of the first settlement in the Willamette Valley. It was here that Methodist missionary Jason Lee and four assistants established their first mission in 1834. Today, there are 8 miles of walking, biking, and horseback-riding paths through the park, which is also home to the largest black cottonwood tree in the country.

If it's bird-watching that interests you, there are two national wildlife refuges in the area that are excellent places to observe ducks, geese, swans, and raptors. Ankeny National Wildlife Refuge is 12 miles south of Salem off I-5 at exit 243. Basket Slough

National Wildlife Refuge is northwest of the town of Rickreall on Ore. 22, which passes through the north end of downtown Salem. Fall through spring is the best time of year for birding here. For more information, contact the **Willamette Valley National Wildlife Refuge Complex** (© 541/757-7236; http://pacific.fws.gov/WillametteValley).

ESPECIALLY FOR KIDS

In addition to the two attractions listed below, the younger ones will likely enjoy a ride on **Salem's Riverfront Carousel** ⊛, 101 Front St. NE (© 503/540-0374; www.salemcarousel.org), which is a modern carousel with 42 hand-carved horses. The carousel has its own building in Riverfront Park and is within walking distance of A.C Gilbert Discovery Village.

April through September, the carousel operates Monday through Thursday from 10am to 7pm, Friday and Saturday from 10am to 9pm, and Sunday from 11am to 6pm; other months the carousel closes 1 to 2 hours earlier. Rides are $1.25.

A.C. Gilbert Discovery Village ⊛ (Kids)
Known as the "man who saved Christmas," Salem's A. C. Gilbert may not be familiar to most people, but the toy he invented, the Erector Set, certainly is. Erector Sets have inspired generations of budding engineers, and it was during World War I that Gilbert saved Christmas. It seems Congress wanted to turn his toy factory into a munitions factory, but after taking Erector Sets to Congress, he convinced the solons that America needed to prime its next generation of inventors just as much as it needed to prime its war machine. Here, in two Queen Anne Victorian homes, a few other small historic buildings, and a half-acre outdoor play/recreation center, the 21st century's inventors can let loose their own creative energies. Among the many interactive exhibits here, there are plenty of Erector Set constructions, a bubble room, and an ancient forest.

116 Marion St. NE. © 503/371-3631. www.acgilbert.org. Admission $5 adults and children over 3, $3.50 seniors, free for children under 3. Mon–Sat 10am–5pm; Sun noon–5pm. Closed Easter, Thanksgiving, Christmas, and New Year's Day.

Enchanted Forest (Kids)
Classic children's stories come to life at this amusement park for kids. In addition to Storybook Lane, Old Europe Village, and Western Town, there's a haunted house, a bobsled run, a log-flume ride, and a comedy theater. Rides cost extra. Adjacent to Enchanted Village is **Thrill-Ville USA** (© 503/363-4095; www.thrillvilleusa.homestead.com), a small amusement park with the world's biggest slide, plus a roller coaster, water slides, and other rides and activities. It's open in summer daily from 11am to 6pm; rides cost $2 to $3 and an all-day waterslide pass is $10.

8462 Enchanted Way SE, Turner. © 503/363-3060 or 503/371-4242. www.enchantedforest.com. Admission $8.50 adults, $8 seniors, $7.50 children 3–12, free for children under 3. Mar 15–31 daily 9:30am–6pm; Apr and Sept Sat–Sun 9:30am–6pm; May to Labor Day daily 9:30am–6pm. Closed Oct–Mar 14. Take I-5 7 miles south of Salem to Exit 248.

SILVERTON

Set in the foothills of the Cascade Range, Silverton is a quaint community on the banks of Silver Creek. The creek-side setting gives the town something of the feel of an old New England mill town, and although the area's major attractions are Silver Falls State Park and The Oregon Garden, the downtown, where a pedestrian-covered bridge leads to a pleasant, shady park, is also worth a stroll.

WATERFALLS & DISPLAY GARDENS

The Oregon Garden 🏵🏵   The Oregon Garden is one of the largest public display gardens in the Northwest. It was created to showcase the state's horticultural heritage and the wide variety of plants grown in Oregon's commercial plant nurseries. All the gardens are quite impressive. In addition to an incredible array of plantings, the numerous display gardens include several water features and ponds, terraced gardens, a sensory garden, a children's garden, and a native oak grove. During the summer months, concerts are held in the garden's amphitheater. The Oregon Garden is also home to the Gordon House, a small Frank Lloyd Wright home that was moved to this site and is open for tours.

879 W. Main St., Silverton. ⓒ 877/674-2733 or 503/874-8100. www.oregongarden.org. Admission: May–Sept $8 adults, $7 seniors, $6 students 8–17; Oct–Apr $5 adults, $4 seniors and students 8–17; Gordon House admission $2 self-guided ground-floor tour, $5 guided tour of whole house. May–Sept daily 10am–6pm; Oct–Apr daily 10am–4pm. Closed Thanksgiving, Christmas Eve, Christmas, and New Year's Day.

Silver Falls State Park 🏵🏵   Located 26 miles east of Salem on Ore. 214, this is the largest state park in Oregon and one of the most popular. Hidden in the lush canyons and dark old-growth forests of this park are 10 silvery waterfalls ranging in height from 27 to 177 feet. The trails are some of the most enjoyable in the state and can usually be hiked any time of year. Although the best hike is the 7-mile loop trail that links all the falls, shorter hikes are also possible. You can even walk behind the South, Lower South, and North falls. You can spend an afternoon or several days exploring the park. Camping (for reservations, call **Reservations Northwest** ⓒ **800/452-5687**), swimming, picnicking, bicycling, and horseback riding are all popular activities. Guided **horseback rides** are available from Memorial Day to Labor Day ($27 for a 1-hr. ride). For reservations, call ⓒ **503/873-3890.**

15 miles southeast of Silverton on Ore. 214. ⓒ 503/873-8681. www.oregonstateparks.org. Admission $3 per car. Daily dawn–dusk.

OTHER AREA ATTRACTIONS & ACTIVITIES

While in Silverton, be sure to wander around town and admire the many murals. Local artists who display their work at the **Lunaria Gallery,** 113 N. Water St. (ⓒ **503/873-7734;** www.lunariagallery.com), painted some of these. Also worth a visit is the **Silver Creek Gallery,** 119A N. Water St. (ⓒ **503/873-6767**), featuring works by regional artists and jewelry designed by the gallery's owners.

WHERE TO STAY

Water Street Inn 🏵   Located in downtown Silverton in an 1890 vintage Victorian home, this inn is the ideal place to stay if you want to take extra time for exploring the Oregon Gardens and nearby Silver Falls State Park. This old house has some of the most attractive B&B rooms in the Willamette Valley. Most of the rooms are quite spacious and two have double whirlpool tubs. Rooms 1 and 5 are my favorites.

421 N. Water St., Silverton, OR 97381. ⓒ 866/873-3344 or 503/873-3344. www.thewaterstreetinn.com. 5 units. $95–$165 double. Children over 12 are accepted. AE, MC, V. **Amenities:** Massage; guest laundry. *In room:* A/C, TV/VCR, dataport, hair dryer, iron, free local calls, Wi-Fi.

WHERE TO DINE

For a quick pick-me-up, try the **Silver Creek Coffee House,** 111 N. Water St. (ⓒ **503/874-9600**), which has a deck overlooking Silver Creek.

Silver Grille Cafe & Wines ★★ BISTRO FRENCH   This classy little restaurant in an old storefront is a welcome outpost of urban culinary aesthetics in this small town. The menu, which changes frequently, emphasizes fresh local produce and hormone-free meats, but you might find a carpaccio of Oregon buffalo marinated in sherry vinegar and olive oil or a cherry-tomato bisque with basil foam. Among the entrees, there are always good pastas, such as penne pasta with local chanterelle mushrooms. As the wine bottles around the dining room, the wine quotes on the front windows, and the small wine shop would indicate, wine is a very important part of a meal here.

206 E Main St. ⓒ 503/873-4035. www.silvergrille.com. Main courses $16–$21. AE, MC, V. Wed–Sun 5–9:30pm.

MT. ANGEL

Mt. Angel is best known as the site of Oregon's most popular Oktoberfest celebration, but should you be here any other time of year besides the second weekend after Labor Day, you might want to visit the **Mount Angel Abbey** (ⓒ 503/845-3303; www.mtangel.edu), which stands atop a 300-foot bluff on the edge of town and has peaceful gardens, an architecturally interesting library designed by famous Finnish architect Alvar Aalto, and a collection of rare books. Established by Benedictine monks in 1882, the abbey has a gift shop and offers tours by appointment. The abbey is also the site of the annual **Abbey Bach Festival** (ⓒ 503/845-3321), which takes place each year on the last Wednesday, Thursday, and Friday in July, and usually sells out shortly after tickets go on sale in March. However, last-minute tickets are sometimes available.

MONMOUTH

Jensen Arctic Museum ★★ (Finds   Although Monmouth may seem an unlikely location for a museum dedicated to the natural and cultural history of the Arctic, it is here that the museum's founder lived while working with Alaskan Eskimo peoples. The core of the museum's exhibits is Dr. Jensen's personal collection, but over the years, the museum has become a repository for more than 60 other collections. Though small, this museum has fascinating displays, including a parka made from cormorant feathers, salmon-skin mukluks, a waterproof seal-intestine jacket, and woven-baleen baskets.

590 W. Church St., Monmouth. ⓒ 503/838-8468. www.wou.edu/jensenmuseum. Admission $2 adults, $1 children. Wed–Sat 10am–4pm.

BROOKS

Antique Powerland Museum   Dedicated to the preservation of old farm equipment and related items, this sprawling open-air museum is home to lots of old tractors and steam-driven mills. For the kids, there's a miniature railroad. This museum is best known as the site of the annual Great Oregon Steamup, held each year on the last weekend in July and the first weekend in August. Also on the grounds is the **Pacific Northwest Truck Museum** (ⓒ 503/463-8701; www.pacificnwtruckmuseum.org), open on weekends April through September.

3995 Brooklake Rd. NE, Brooks. ⓒ 503/393-2424. Admission $2. May–Sept Tues–Sat 10am–5pm, Sun noon–5pm; Mar–Apr and Oct–Nov Tues–Sun 11am–4pm.

WINE TOURING

For information on the many wineries west and northwest of Salem, see "The North Willamette Valley Wine Country" section earlier in this chapter.

Ankeny Vineyard   Located south of Salem not far from Willamette Valley Vineyards, this small family-run winery overlooks a national wildlife area and is surrounded by neighboring vineyards. Pinot noir and pinot gris are the specialties here, but they also produce Marechal Foch. Prices are generally quite reasonable.

2565 Riverside Rd. S., Salem. (C) **503/378-1498.** www.ankenyvineyards.com. Wed–Sun noon–5pm. From Salem, drive south on I-5, take exit 243 and continue 5 miles west.

Honeywood   This winery, which dates back to 1933, is the oldest in Oregon. The winery specializes in sweet fruit-wines, which they do very well. The raspberry, boysenberry, and marionberry wines are all great accompaniments to chocolate desserts.

1350 Hines St. SE, Salem. (C) **800/726-4101** or 503/362-4111. www.honeywoodwinery.com. Mon–Fri 9am–5pm; Sat 10am–5pm; Sun 1–5pm. Between Mission and 13th sts. in southeast Salem.

St. Innocent Winery ✿   This winery produces very drinkable white wines as well as some good pinot noirs. It is also one of the few wineries in the state to produce sparkling wines.

1360 Tandem St. NE Salem. (C) **503/378-1526.** www.stinnocentwine.com. Sat–Sun noon–5pm. Call for directions.

Willamette Valley Vineyards ✿   Willamette Valley Vineyards, one of the largest wine producers in the state, sits high on a hill overlooking the Willamette Valley, and with its huge facility and fabulous views, it's about as close to a Napa Valley wine-tasting

---

Blossom Time

Each year between mid-May and early June, the countryside around Salem bursts into color as commercial iris fields come into bloom. During blossom time, the two biggest growers open up their farms to the public. **Cooley's Gardens,** 11553 Silverton Rd. NE, Silverton ((C) **503/873-5463;** www.cooleys gardens.com), with approximately 200 acres and millions of irises, is the world's largest bearded-iris grower. This farm is open daily from 8am to 7pm between mid-May and late May. To reach the gardens, take the Market Street exit and drive east to Lancaster Drive; at Lancaster, turn left and drive north to Silverton Road, where you make a right turn. It's less than 10 miles on Silverton Road. **Schreiner's Iris Gardens,** 3625 Quinaby Rd. NE, Salem ((C) **800/ 525-2367;** www.schreinersgardens.com), the nation's largest retail iris grower, has more than 200 acres of irises and is an equally impressive sight. To reach Schreiner's, take the Chemawa exit (exit 260) off I-5 north of Salem, drive west on Chemawa Road, turn right once you're west of the freeway and follow signs to Volcano Stadium. Continue north past the stadium and turn right on Quinaby Road. Also in the area are **Adelman Peony Gardens,** 5690 Brooklake Rd. NE ((C) **503/393-6185;** www.peonyparadise.com), which has more than 300 varieties of peonies in bloom between early May and mid-June. They're open daily from 9am to 7pm during blossom time. From the Brooks exit, go east on Brooklake Road.

From late March to late April, you can see more than 90 acres of tulips in bloom at **Wooden Shoe Bulb Company,** 33814 S. Meridian Rd., Woodburn ((C) **800/711-2006** or 503/634-2243; www.woodenshoe.com). Throughout the blossom season, there are wooden shoe–making seminars, steam-tractor demonstrations, live music, and lots of other activities.

experience as you'll find in Oregon. With nearly 20 wines usually available for tasting and several separate labels available, Willamette Valley manages to produce wines to please almost every palate. Be sure to try the reserve wines, for which there is a $5 tasting fee.

8800 Enchanted Way SE, Turner. ✆ **800/344-9463** or 503/588-9463. www.wvv.com. Daily 11am–6pm. Take exit 248 or 244 off I-5.

WHERE TO STAY

A Creekside Garden Inn ✰ *Value*   This B&B is located on a narrow lane in a quiet residential neighborhood and has Mill Creek running through the backyard. The gardens here are the highlight, and the guest rooms take their themes from the flowers and greenery that surround the inn. Among the rooms are the Greenhouse, Picket Fences, the Arbor, all of which are decorated with plenty of floral motifs.

333 Wyatt Ct. NE, Salem, OR 97301. ✆ **800/949-0837** or 503/391-0837. Fax 503/391-1713. www.salembandb.com. 5 units (3 with private bathroom). $65 double with shared bathroom; $80–$100 double with private bathroom. Rates include full breakfast. Children over 14 welcome. MC, V. *In room:* A/C.

Phoenix Grand Hotel ✰✰   From the moment you drive into the slate-walled portico at this big new downtown conference hotel, it's obvious that this is by far the best hotel in Salem; the Phoenix Grand is primarily a place for conference attendees to stay, though the rooms here are just too nice to be left to the business travelers. With beautiful leather couches and chairs in the large guest rooms and suites, this place is not your standard corporate hotel. Although the huge lobby might make you wonder when the crowds are going to descend, the Phoenix Grand is often a very laid-back and relaxed place.

201 Liberty St. SE, Salem, OR 97301. ✆ **877/540-7800** or 503/540-7800. Fax 503/540-7830. www.phoenixgrand hotel.com. 193 units. $119 double; $139–$399 suite. Rates include continental breakfast. AE, DC, DISC, MC, V. **Amenities:** Restaurant (New American); lounge; indoor pool; exercise room; Jacuzzi; business center; laundry service; dry cleaning. *In room:* A/C, TV, dataport, fridge, coffeemaker, hair dryer, iron, high-speed Internet access.

WHERE TO DINE

SALEM

If you have a sweet tooth, you won't want to miss **Gerry Frank's Konditorei,** 310 Kearney St. SE (✆ **503/585-7070**), which has an amazing selection of extravagant cakes and pastries. For a good cup of espresso (or a sandwich), head to **The Beanery,** 220 Liberty St. NE (✆ **503/399-7220**). If you're looking for a microbrew and a burger, try **Ram Restaurant & Big Horn Brewery,** 515 12th St. SE (✆ **503/363-1904**). For Sunday brunch, consider **Eola Hills Wine Cellars,** 501 S. Pacific Hwy., Rickreall (✆ **800/291-6730** or 503/623-2405; www.eolahillswinery.com), which serves gourmet omelets, pan-fried oysters, pasta, Belgian waffles, sparkling wine, and more for $20. Reservations recommended.

Court Street Dairy Lunch *Finds* BURGERS   In business since the 1920s, the Court Street Dairy Lunch is the quintessential small-town diner and a Salem institution. Burgers and sandwiches "just like Mom used to make" are the attraction. The specialties of the house are the ranch burger and ranch dog, marionberry pie, and chocolate malts.

347 Court St. NE. ✆ **503/363-6433.** Meals $3–$8. AE, DISC, MC, V. Mon–Fri 6am–2pm.

Morton's Bistro Northwest ✰✰ AMERICAN REGIONAL   This romantic little bistro, across the river from downtown Salem, serves up the most imaginative meals in town. The menu changes regularly, depending on the whim of the chef, the availability of ingredients, and even the weather, but flavors might range from the subtle scents of prawns with saffron, clams, Spanish chorizo sausage, and couscous to the fiery flavors of penne diablo made with Dungeness crab and andouille sausage. Be sure to order the superb Caesar salad for two (if it's not on the menu, just ask). Instead of a wine list, Morton's has a wine wall for diners to peruse.

1128 Edgewater St. NW. (C) 503/585-1113. www.mortonsbistronw.com. Reservations recommended. Main courses $17–$27. MC, V. Tues–Sat 5–9 or 10pm.

Wild Pear ☞ NEW AMERICAN   On a winding country road 2 miles west of Salem is an adorable little roadhouse that serves some of the freshest and most flavorful food in Salem. The restaurant, housed in an old country store, is decorated in a sort of country-cottage chic. Wild Pear is casual but the menu is sophisticated. You might start with steak quesadilla made with cambazola cheese or a smoked chicken-and-spinach salad. The entree list is fairly long, with several steaks, as well as the likes of porcini-mushroom ravioli with white-truffle cream sauce. There's a smaller Wild Pear downtown at 372 State St. (**(C) 503/378-7515**), which is open between 10am and 5 or 6pm.

3635 River Rd. S. (C) 503/589-4532. www.wildpearcatering.com. Reservations recommended. Main courses $10–$25. MC, V. Tues–Thurs 10am–3pm and 5–9pm; Fri 10am–3pm and 5–10pm; Sat Fri 8:30am–3pm and 5–10pm.

SALEM AFTER DARK

There are regularly scheduled performances by touring companies at the historic **Elsinore Theater,** 170 High St. SE (**(C) 503/375-3574** or 503/581-8810; www.elsinore theatre.com). Since 1954, **Pentacle Theatre,** 324 52nd Ave. NW (**(C) 503/364-7200;** www.pentacletheatre.org), located in the West Salem hills, has been bringing live theater to the state capital.

3 Corvallis & Albany

40 miles S of Salem, 45 miles N of Eugene, 55 miles E of Newport

In Latin, Corvallis means "heart of the valley," and that is exactly where this college town is located. Set in the middle of the Willamette Valley and surrounded by farmlands, Corvallis is home to Oregon State University (OSU), a noted center for agricultural research. Life in this town revolves around the university, but the lively downtown, with its riverfront setting, makes this a pleasant base for exploring nearby wine country and the historic town of Albany. Numerous walking and bicycling paths add to the appeal of a stay here.

   In addition to being home to OSU, Corvallis is at the center of the Willamette Valley's grass-seed fields. Area farms produce much of the nation's grass-seed crop. Visitors should note that in late summer, after the seed has been harvested, the remaining stubble has traditionally been burned off. The field burnings can blanket the valley with dense black smoke, making driving quite difficult along certain roads. So, don't be too alarmed if you encounter smoky skies in the area in August.

   Nearby Albany, 13 miles northeast, was a prosperous town in territorial days. Located on the banks of the Willamette River, the town made its fortune as a shipping point in the days when the river was the main transportation route for the region. More than 500 historic homes make Albany the best-preserved historic town in the state, but, owing to the big mill on the outskirts of town, the city has never really been able to cash in on its historic character.

ESSENTIALS

GETTING THERE   Albany is on I-5 at the junction with U.S. 20, which heads east to Bend and west to Newport. Corvallis is 12 miles west of I-5 at the junction of U.S. 20, Ore. 99W, and Ore. 34.

VISITOR INFORMATION   Contact **Corvallis Tourism,** 553 NW Harrison St., Corvallis, OR 97330 (© **800/334-8118** or 541/757-1544; www.visitcorvallis.com), or the **Albany Visitors Association,** 250 Broadalbin St. NW, Suite 110, Albany, OR 97321 (© **800/526-2256** or 541/928-0911; www.albanyvisitors.com).

GETTING AROUND   Public bus service around the Corvallis area is provided by the **Corvallis Transit System** (© **541/766-6916;** www.ci.corvallis.or.us/pw/cts). Adult fare is 75¢.

FESTIVALS   DaVinci Days (© **541/757-6363;** www.davinci-days.org), held each year in mid-July, is Corvallis's most fascinating festival. The highlight of this celebration of art, science, and technology is the **Kinetic Sculpture Race** in which competitors race homemade, people-powered vehicles along city streets, through mud and sand, and down the Willamette River. Prizes are given for engineering and artistry. Another offbeat celebration, the **Shrewsbury Renaissance Faire** (© **541/929-4897;** www.shrewfaire.com), is held each year in the community of Kings Valley (north of nearby Philomath) in early September.

EXPLORING OFF-CAMPUS CORVALLIS

The tree-shaded streets of downtown Corvallis are well worth a wander. Here you'll find lots of interesting shops, as well as the stately **Benton County Courthouse,** 120 NW Fourth Street, built in 1888 and still in use today. A few blocks away, you'll find the **Corvallis Arts Center,** 700 SW Madison Ave. (© **541/754-1551;** www.art centric.org), which is housed in an old church and schedules rotating exhibits of works by regional artists. The gift shop has a good selection of crafts. The center is open Tuesday through Sunday from noon to 5pm; admission is free.

Corvallis's pretty Riverfront Commemorative Park stretches for 10 blocks along the Willamette River in downtown Corvallis, and includes walkways and lawns, river-viewing decks and plazas, sculptures, and a fountain that doubles as a map of the region's rivers. On Saturday mornings from spring through the fall, the park is also the site of the Corvallis Saturday Farmers Market. The park's pathways connect to Corvallis's extensive network of biking paths, one of which crosses a covered bridge. If you'd like to explore these pathways, you can rent a bike at **Bike n' Hike,** 401 SW Third St. (© **541/753-2912;** www.bikenhike.com).

EXPLORING HISTORIC ALBANY

Albany is a hidden jewel right on I-5 that is often overlooked because the only thing visible from the interstate is a smoke-belching wood-pulp mill. Behind this industrial

---

Tips Beaver Believers

If you're a "Beaver Believer"—in other words, a fan of Oregon State University's NCAA football team—you can find out about getting game tickets by contacting the **OSU Beaver Ticket Office** (© **800/GO-BEAVS** or 541/737-4455; www. osubeavers.com).

screen lies a quiet town that evokes days of starched crinolines and straw boaters. Throughout the mid- to late 19th century, Albany prospered, shipping agricultural and wood products down river to Oregon City and Portland. Though every style of architecture popular during that period is represented in downtown Albany's historic districts, it is the town's many elegant Victorian homes that are the most compelling. Each year, on the last Saturday of July, many of the historic homes are opened to the public for a **Historic Interior Homes Tour,** and on the third Sunday in December, homes are opened for a **Christmas Parlour Tour.** For a guide to the historic buildings, and information on the tours, contact the **Albany Visitors Association.**

Among the town's more noteworthy buildings are two sparkling white 1890s churches—the **Whitespires Church** and **St. Mary's Church**—both built in the Gothic revival style. The **Monteith House,** 518 Second Ave. SW (© **541/928-0911**), built in 1849, is the town's oldest frame building. The house is open from mid-June to mid-September Wednesday through Saturday from noon to 4pm; admission is free. To learn more about Albany's past, stop in at the **Albany Regional Museum,** 136 Lyon St. SW (© **541/967-7122;** www.armuseum.com). It's open Monday through Saturday from noon to 4pm. Admission is by donation. While touring the historic districts, you can stop in at more than a dozen antiques stores, most of which are on First and Second avenues downtown.

WINE TOURING

In downtown Corvallis, across the street from Riverfront Commemorative Park, check out **Sahalie Wine Cellars,** 151 Monroe St., Suite 101 (© **541/754-7457;** www. sahaliewine.com), a big basement wine bar and tasting room with cozy couches and live music. You can taste Sahalie and other Corvallis-area area wines. The tasting room is open Tuesday through Saturday from 1 to 10:30pm (the wine bar opens at 5pm).

Airlie Winery   This winery is quite a distance from the main wine-touring routes, but its setting in a narrow valley surrounded by forested hills is idyllic. There's a large pond and a covered picnic area, making it a good place to stop for a picnic lunch. They produce a wide variety of wines, but their Müller-Thurgaus and Gewürztraminers are highlights.

15305 Dunn Forest Rd., Monmouth. © 503/838-6013. www.airliewinery.com. Mar–Dec Sat–Sun noon–5pm; closed Jan–Feb. From Ore. 99W between Corvallis and Monmouth, go 7 miles west on Airlie Rd., turn left on Maxfield Creek Rd. and continue another 3 miles.

Benton-Lane Winery   This winery has a big reputation in Oregon and it is well worth searching out the off-the-beaten-path winery and tasting room. Benton-Lane focuses primarily on pinot noir and does a superb job. The wide range of prices means there's a pinot for every budget. The valley views from the tasting room are great.

23924 Territorial Hwy. © 541/847-5792. www.benton-lane.com. May–Nov daily noon–5pm; Dec–Apr Mon–Fri noon–4:30pm. From Corvallis, drive south on Ore. 99W to Monroe and fork right onto Territorial Rd.

Springhill Cellars ★★   This small family-run winery produces excellent pinot noir and pinot gris, both of which are priced at under $20. They also do an unusual pinot noir rosé. This is one of my favorite small wineries in the state.

2920 NW Scenic View Dr., Albany. © 541/928-1009. www.springhillcellars.com. Memorial Day to Thanksgiving Sat–Sun 1–5pm. Take Ore. 20 east 8 miles, turn left on Scenic Dr. and continue just over 2 miles north.

Tyee Wine Cellars ★   The Tyee Wine Cellars tasting room is in an old milking barn from the days when this was a dairy farm. Although Tyee usually does a decent pinot noir, their real strength lies in the consistency of their whites—pinot gris, pinot blanc, chardonnay, and Gewürztraminer all tend to be dry and light. Be sure to walk the 1½-mile trail through farm and forest.

26335 Greenberry Rd., Corvallis. ⟨C⟩ 541/753-8754. www.tyeewine.com. Apr to mid-June and early Sept to Dec Sat–Sun noon–5pm; mid-June to Labor Day daily noon–5pm; closed Jan–Mar. From Corvallis, go 7 miles south on Ore. 99W and then 2⅓ miles west on Greenberry Rd.

A COVERED BRIDGE TOUR

If you're a fan of covered bridges, you won't want to pass up an opportunity to drive the back roads east of Albany. Here you'll find nine wooden covered bridges dating mostly from the 1930s. For a map to these covered bridges, contact the **Albany Convention & Visitors Association.** A 10th covered bridge, the Irish Bend Bridge, can be found in Corvallis on a pedestrian/bicycle path on the west side of the university campus.

OUTDOOR ACTIVITIES

If you're a bird-watcher, the **William L. Finley National Wildlife Refuge** (⟨C⟩ 541/ 757-7236), 12 miles south of Corvallis on Ore. 99W, is a good place to add a few more to your list. This refuge has three short, easy hiking trails that provide the region's best glimpse of what the Willamette Valley looked like before the first settlers arrived.

For superb views of the valley and a moderately strenuous hike, head west 16 miles from Corvallis on Ore. 34 to **Mary's Peak,** the highest peak in the Coast Range. A road leads to the top of the mountain, but there is also a trail that leads from the campground up through a forest of old-growth noble firs to the meadows at the summit. For more information, contact the **Siuslaw National Forest,** 4077 SW Research Way (P.O. Box 1148) Corvallis, OR 97339 (⟨C⟩ **541/750-7000;** www.fs.fed.us/r6/siuslaw).

WHERE TO STAY

IN CORVALLIS

Hanson Country Inn 𝄞   Situated atop a knoll on the western edge of town and surrounded by fields and forests, this B&B feels as if it's out in the country, yet is within walking distance of the university. The Dutch colonial-style farmhouse was built in 1928 and features loads of built-in cabinets, interesting woodwork, and lots of windows. Plenty of antiques fill the rooms and lend the inn a feeling appropriate to its age. Two of the rooms have large balconies. The two-bedroom cottage, ideal for families, sits behind the main house and is tucked back in the trees.

795 SW Hanson St., Corvallis, OR 97333. ⟨C⟩ 541/752-2919. www.hcinn.com. 4 units (including a cottage). $145–$165 double. Rates include full breakfast. AE, DISC, MC, V. Take Western Blvd. to West Hills Rd.; Hanson St. is on the right just past the fork onto West Hills Rd. **Amenities:** Guest laundry. *In room:* A/C, TV, dataport.

Super 8 Motel 𝄞   It may seem hard to believe that a Super 8 Motel could be one of the best accommodations in town, but Corvallis just doesn't have too many places to stay. This budget motel has a great location on the bank of the Willamette River only a few blocks from downtown.

407 NW Second St., Corvallis, OR 97330. ⟨C⟩ **800/800-8000** or 541/758-8088. Fax 541/758-8267. 101 units. $48–$77 double. Rates include continental breakfast. AE, DC, DISC, MC, V. **Amenities:** Indoor pool; Jacuzzi; coin-op laundry. *In room:* A/C, TV, dataport, free local calls.

WHERE TO DINE
IN CORVALLIS

When you just have to have a jolt of java and a pastry, drop by **The Beanery,** 500 SW Second St. (© 541/753-7442), or **New Morning Bakery,** 219 SW Second St. (© 541/754-0181). For great breakfasts, head to **Sunnyside Up,** 116 NW Third St. (© 541/758-3353). If you're looking for some picnic fare stop by **Great Harvest Bread Co.,** 134 SW First St. (© 541/754-9960). On hot summer days, head to **Francesco's Gelato Caffe,** 208 SW Second St. (© 541/752-1326), for creamy gelato. For microbrews and pub fare, try **The Fox & Firkin,** 202 SW First St. (© 541/753-8533), which serves an astonishing number of good beers on tap.

Big River Restaurant ๙๙ INTERNATIONAL   Housed in a renovated warehouselike space across the street from the Willamette River, this big, lively place serves everything from designer brick-oven pizzas to Asian-inspired pastas to Cuban pork loin to various smoked chicken dishes. The owners of the restaurant have a commitment to fresh local produce (often organic), local wines, Oregon-caught seafood (when possible), and organic meats. The rustic breads are baked here on the premises. Though this is a big space, you probably won't be able to miss the case full of tempting desserts. Be forewarned that this place is very noisy.

101 NW Jackson St. © **541/757-0694.** Call ahead wait list. Main courses $14–$22. AE, DC, MC, V. Mon–Fri 11am–2pm and 5–9:30pm; Sat 5pm–9:30pm.

Intaba's Wood Fired Eatery ๙ *Finds* INTERNATIONAL   This place is just so Oregon it should not be missed. The menu is eclectic, the ingredients are usually organic, and the wood-fired oven and patio are made of mud! Actually, the owners of the restaurant like to call it earth, not mud. If you're intrigued, come by for a meal and order something from the earth oven, which, by the way, is named Maya. Offerings include lots of creative pizzas and such exotic dishes as Ethiopian Berbere tempeh, fire-grilled ginger-infused salmon, and fire-grilled organic chicken marinated in tequila and lime juice.

1115 SE Third St. © **541/754-6958.** www.intabas.com. Reservations recommended. Main courses $11–$23. MC, V. Tues–Sat 11:30am–2:30pm and 5–9pm; Sun 10am–2pm and 5–9pm.

Iovino's Ristorante ๙๙ ITALIAN   Urban chic meets small-town prices at this stylish Italian restaurant facing Corvallis's Riverfront Commemorative Park. The converted warehouse space has a minimalist quality you'd expect to find in Portland's trendy Pearl District. Portions are big and there are good salads. If you see the grilled polenta topped with sun-dried tomato pesto and house-made mascarpone cheese on the menu, get it. Yum! On warm summer days, hold out for a sidewalk table. Be sure to ask about the martini of the day.

126 SW First St. © **541/738-9015.** Reservations recommended. Main courses $15–$22. AE, MC, V. Mon–Thurs 11:30am–3pm and 5–9pm; Fri 11:30am–3pm and 5–10pm; Sat 5–10pm; Sun 5–9pm.

Le Bistro ๙๙ *Finds* FRENCH   This minimally decorated restaurant focuses on country French preparations, and with surprisingly low prices, manages to attract students as well as professors and local high-tech employees. Although there are daily specials, the main menu offers no surprises, just down-home French country cooking. Among other dishes, you'll find coq au vin and pork medallions with a light mustard *velouté.* The restaurant is only half a block from the river and the Riverfront Commemorative Park.

150 SW Madison Ave. (© **541/754-6680.** www.lebistro.com. Reservations recommended. Main courses $12–$21. MC, V. Tues–Sat 4:30–9:30pm.

IN ALBANY

For a good cup of coffee, try **Boccherini's Coffee & Tea House,** 208 SW First Ave. (© **541/926-6703**). If it's a good pint of ale and some pub food you crave, check out **Wyatt's Eatery & Brewhouse,** 211 SW First Ave. (© **541/917-3727;** www. wyattseatery.com).

4 Eugene & Springfield

40 miles S of Salem, 71 miles N of Roseburg, 61 miles E of Florence

Although Eugene, with more than 100,000 residents, is the second-largest city in Oregon, tie-dyed T-shirts are more common than silk ties on downtown streets. This laid-back character is due in large part to the presence of the University of Oregon, the state's liberal arts university. On the university's tree-shaded 250-acre campus you'll find both a recently renovated and expanded art museum and a natural-history museum. Adding to the city's diverse cultural scene is the grandiose, glass-gabled **Hult Center for the Performing Arts.**

Eugene has for years been home to liberal-minded folks who adopted alternative lifestyles. At the **Saturday Market,** a weekly outdoor craft market, you can see the works of many of these colorful and creative spirits.

Throw in a couple of beautiful riverfront parks with miles of bike paths, numerous excellent restaurants, brewpubs, nearby wineries, and proximity to both mountains and coast, and you have a great base for exploring a good chunk of the state.

ESSENTIALS

GETTING THERE   Eugene is located just off I-5 at the junction with I-105, which connects Eugene and Springfield, and Ore. 126, which leads east to Bend and west to Florence. Ore. 58 leads southeast from Eugene to connect with U.S. 97 between Klamath Falls and Bend. Ore. 99W is an alternative to I-5.

The **Eugene Airport,** 28855 Lockheed Dr. (© **541/682-5430;** www.eugene airport.com), is 9 miles northwest of downtown off Ore. 99W. America West Airlines, Delta Air Lines, Horizon Air, and United fly here. There's nonstop service to Portland, Seattle, San Francisco, Los Angeles, Las Vegas, Denver, Salt Lake City, and Phoenix.

Amtrak (© **800/USA-RAIL**) passenger trains stop in Eugene. The station is at East Fourth Avenue and Willamette Street.

VISITOR INFORMATION   Contact the **Convention & Visitors Association of Lane County Oregon,** 754 Olive St., Eugene, OR 97401 (© **800/547-5445** or 541/484-5307; www.visitlanecounty.org).

GETTING AROUND   Car rentals are available at the Eugene airport from **Avis, Budget, Enterprise,** and **Hertz.** If you need a taxi, contact **Oregon Taxi** (© **541/ 434-TAXI**). **Lane Transit District (LTD)** (© **541/687-5555;** www.ltd.org) provides public transit throughout the metropolitan area and out to a number of nearby, towns including McKenzie Bridge; some routes do not run on Sunday. You can pick up bus-route maps and other information at the **LTD Customer Service Center** at the corner of 11th Avenue and Willamette Street. LTD fares are $1.25 for adults, 60¢ for seniors and youths 6 to 18.

Eugene

←①

ACCOMMODATIONS ■
The Campbell House **7**
Hilton Eugene &
  Conference Center **11**
The Secret Garden **20**
Valley River Inn **2**

DINING ◆
Adam's Place **16**
The Broadway **14**
Marché **9**
Metropol Bakery **9**
Palace Bakery **12**
Sweet Basil **17**
Sweet Life **5**
Zenon Café **13**

ATTRACTIONS ●
Alton Baker Park **18**
Hult Center for the Performing Arts **10**
Jordan Schnitzer Museum of Art **19**
Oregon Air & Space Museum **1**
Oregon Wine Warehouse **15**
Owen Memorial Rose Garden **3**
Shelton-McMurphey-Johnson House **8**
Skinner Butte Park **6**
Territorial Vineyards & Wine Company **4**
University of Oregon Museum of Natural History **21**

FESTIVALS   Eugene's two biggest and most important music festivals are the **Oregon Bach Festival** (📞 **800/457-1486** or 541/682-5000; www.oregonbachfestival. com) and the **Oregon Festival of American Music** (📞 **800/248-1615** or 541/ 687-6526; www.ofam.net). The former is just what its name implies and is held the last week in June and the first week in July. The latter is a celebration of everything from blues to gospel to jazz and is held in August. The **Eugene Celebration** (📞 **541/681-4108;** www.eugenecelebration.com), held at the end of September, is a 3-day celebration that includes a wacky parade and the crowning of the annual Slug Queen. In mid-July, all the region's hippies, both young and old, show up in nearby Veneta for the **Oregon Country Fair** 🏵🏵 (📞 **541/343-4298;** www.oregoncountry fair.org), a showcase for alternative music and unusual crafts. Also of note is **Junction City's Scandinavian Festival** (📞 **541/998-9372;** www.scandinavianfestival.com), which celebrates the region's Scandinavian heritage and is held each year on the second weekend in August. Junction City is 14 miles northwest of Eugene.

SEEING THE SIGHTS
MUSEUMS & HISTORIC BUILDINGS
Oregon Air and Space Museum   This museum focuses on the history of aviation in Oregon. Numerous aircraft, including a World War I Fokker triplane, an F-4 Phantom, an F-86 Sabre, a Japanese Zero replica, and a Russian YAK-50, are on display.

90377 Boeing Dr. ℂ 541/461-1101. Admission $5 adults, $4 seniors, $3 children 13–18, $2 children 6–12, free for children under 6. Wed–Sun noon–4pm.

Jordan Schnitzer Museum of Art ⚘⚘ An extensive Asian arts collection and exhibits of contemporary art are the main focus of this large art museum on the campus of the University of Oregon. Among the highlights of the Asian arts collection are a small jade pagoda, silk Chinese imperial robes, a suit of 18th-century Japanese armor, and a 19th-century Japanese palanquin. Keep an eye out for the exhibit on foot-binding in China. You'll also find a small exhibit of paintings by Northwest artist Morris Graves. This museum reopened in 2005 after an extensive renovation.

1430 Johnson Lane. ℂ 541/346-3027. http://uoma.uoregon.edu. Admission $5 adults, $3 seniors and students, free for children 13 and under (free for all on 1st Fri of each month). Thurs–Sun 11am–5pm; Wed 11am–8pm. Closed July 4, Thanksgiving, Christmas, New Year's Day. East of 14th Ave. and Kincaid St. on the U of O campus.

Shelton-McMurphey-Johnson House ⚘ Built in 1888, this ornate Queen Anne Victorian home stands on the south slope of Skinner Butte on the north edge of downtown Eugene and was long referred to as the Castle on the Hill. Tours of the beautiful old home focus on the families that lived here over the century that it was a private residence.

303 Willamette St. ℂ 541/484-0808. www.smjhouse.org. Admission $5 adults, $2 children under 12. Tues–Fri 10am–1pm; Sat–Sun 1–4pm.

University of Oregon Museum of Natural History ⚘ This small museum is housed in a building designed to vaguely resemble a traditional Northwest Coast Indian longhouse. The ancient peoples and even more ancient animals that once roamed the Northwest are the main focus of the museum's exhibits. Geology, botany, and archaeology topics also get plenty of display space here.

1680 E. 15th Ave. ℂ 541/346-3024. http://natural-history.uoregon.edu. Admission $3 adults; $2 seniors and youths 3–18. Tues–Sun 11am–5pm.

The Bridges of Lane County

There are more than 50 covered bridges in Oregon. The oldest is the Drift Creek Bridge near Lincoln City, which dates from 1914, and the newest (a pedestrian bridge in Silverton) dates to as recently as 2000. Built of wood and covered to protect them from the rain and extend their life, the covered bridges of Oregon are found primarily in the Willamette Valley, where early farmers needed safe river and stream crossings to get their crops to market. The highest concentration of covered bridges is found in Lane County, which stretches from the crest of the Cascade Range all the way to the Pacific Ocean and is home to 20 covered bridges.

You can get a map and guide to Lane County's covered bridges from the **Convention & Visitors Association of Lane County Oregon**, 754 Olive St., Eugene, OR 97401 (ℂ **800/547-5445** or 541/484-5307; www.visitlanecounty. org).

PARKS & GARDENS

Alton Baker Park, on the north bank of the Willamette River, is Eugene's most popular park and offers jogging and biking trails. Across the river, **Skinner Butte Park,** on the north side of downtown Eugene, has more paved paths. Nearby are the **Owen Memorial Rose Garden.** At the **Mount Pisgah Arboretum,** 34901 Frank Parrish Rd. (© 541/747-3817; www.efn.org/~mtpisgah), south of town, you can hike 7 miles of trails through meadows and forests. There are good views along the way, but watch out for poison oak. Set beneath towering fir trees high on a hill overlooking the city, **Hendricks Park and Rhododendron Garden,** 1800 Skyline Blvd. (© 541/682-5324), is one of the prettiest parks in the city, especially in the spring when the rhododendrons bloom. There are free public tours of the garden on Sundays at 1pm between early April and late May. You'll find this park in southeast Eugene off Franklin Boulevard (U.S. 99). Take Walnut Street to Fairmount Boulevard and then turn east on Summit Avenue. If you're crazy about rhododendrons (as so many Northwesterners are), be sure to schedule a visit to **Greer Gardens,** 1280 Goodpasture Island Rd. (© 800/548-0111 or 541/686-8266; www.greergardens.com), one of the Northwest's most celebrated nurseries.

WINE TOURING

Eugene is at the southern limit of the Willamette Valley wine region, and there are half a dozen wineries within 30 miles of the city. For a good introduction to the wines of the region, stop in at the **Oregon Wine Warehouse,** 943 Olive St. (© 541/342-8598; www.oregonww.com), which is open Tuesday through Friday from 3 to 8pm and Saturday from noon to 8pm.

Chateau Lorane ♠ Chateau Lorane produces a greater variety of wines than just about any other winery in the state, and many of these you won't find at other Oregon wineries. Several are also made from organic grapes. Some of the more unusual wines include Huxelrebe, Marechal Foch, and several meads.

27415 Siuslaw River Rd., Lorane. © **541/942-8028.** www.chateaulorane.com. June–Sept daily noon–5pm; Oct–May Sat–Sun noon–5pm. Take Ore. 126 west to Veneta and go south through Crow to Lorane.

King Estate ♠ Set in an idyllic valley southwest of Eugene, this is one of the largest wineries in the state. The winery, part of an 820-acre estate, is surrounded by 250 acres of certified-organic vineyards and features a huge, châteaulike facility. If you want to tour a winery, this is one of the best to visit.

80854 Territorial Rd. © **800/884-4441** or 541/942-9874. www.kingestate.com. Daily noon–5pm. Take Ore. 126 west to Veneta and go south through Crow almost to Lorane.

LaVelle Vineyards ♠ Consistently good white wines (fruity but not too sweet) are the hallmark here. The pinot gris and Riesling are usually quite good. LaVelle also has a tasting room/wine bar/bistro in downtown Eugene at the Fifth Street Public Market, 296 E. Fifth Ave. (© 541/338-9875). This latter facility is a good place to start a wine tour of the area.

89697 Sheffler Rd., Elmira. © **541/935-9406.** www.lavelle-vineyards.com. Vineyard: Memorial Day to Labor Day daily noon–5pm; Labor Day to Memorial Day Sat–Sun noon–5pm. Eugene Tasting Room: Sun–Mon noon–6pm; Tues–Sat noon–10pm. Closed Thanksgiving, Christmas, and New Year's Day. Off Ore. 126 west of Eugene.

Secret House Vineyards Winery ♠ This small winery is known for its sparkling wines, but chardonnay, pinot noir, and Riesling wines are also produced. There's the big Wine and Blues Festival here each year in late August.

88324 Vineyard Lane, Veneta. ⟨ℭ⟩ **800/497-1574** or 541/935-3774. www.secrethousewinery.com. Daily 11am–5pm. West of Eugene 15 miles on Ore. 126.

Silvan Ridge/Hinman Vineyards 𝒢 If you happen to enjoy sweet wines, you'll definitely want to drop by this winery. The semi-sparkling muscat here is outstanding, the perfect dessert wine. Hinman also does respectable merlots and cabernet sauvignons with grapes from southern Oregon, and the pinot gris can be quite good. All in all, one of the most reliable wineries in the state. Most wines are under $20.

27012 Briggs Hill Rd., Eugene. ⟨ℭ⟩ **866/5-SILVAN.** www.silvanridge.com. Daily noon–5pm; closed all major holidays. Take Ore. 126 west to Bertelsen Rd. and go south to Spencer Creek Rd.; turn right and continue for 2 miles; turn left on Briggs Hill Rd. and continue 3½ miles.

Territorial Vineyards & Wine Company This is another of Eugene's in-town wineries and has a swanky tasting room that's open 2 days a week. The winery produces pinot gris, chardonnay, and several pinot noirs.

907 W. Third Ave. ⟨ℭ⟩ **541/684-9463.** www.territorialvineyards.com. Fri–Sat 2–7pm.

OUTDOOR ACTIVITIES

Eugene has long been known as Tracktown, USA, and if you want to follow in the footsteps of Steve Prefontaine, there are plenty of routes around town for doing some running. At the Convention & Visitors Association of Lane County Oregon (see above), you can pick up a map of area running trails. These jogging routes include the popular **Pre's Trail,** a 3.87-mile system of loops in Alton Baker Park, which is just across the Willamette River from downtown Eugene. When the university's track team isn't practicing, it's also possible to run the track at the University of Oregon's **Hayward Field,** where Pre and other Eugene runners have trained. You'll find Hayward Field off Agate Street in the southeast corner of the campus. Runners may also want to drop by the **Nike Store,** Fifth Street Public Market, 248 E. Fifth Ave. (⟨ℭ⟩ **541/ 342-5155**), which has an interesting exhibit about Steve Prefontaine, Bill Bowerman, and Phil Knight, who together laid the foundations for Nike's success.

With two rivers, the McKenzie and the Willamette, flowing through the area, it isn't surprising that Eugene has quite a few water-oriented activities. You can rent canoes and kayaks at **Oregon River Sports,** 3400 Franklin Blvd. (⟨ℭ⟩ **888/790-PADL** or 541/334-0696; www.oregonriversports.com), which has its canoe-rental facility in Alton Baker Park. Rates range from $8 to $10 per hour or $25 to $60 per day. See the "The Santiam Pass, McKenzie Pass & McKenzie River" section of chapter 9 for information on rafting the nearby McKenzie River.

SHOPPING

You can shop for one-of-a-kind crafts at Eugene's **Saturday Market** (⟨ℭ⟩ **541/ 686-8885;** www.eugenesaturdaymarket.org), which covers more than 2 downtown blocks beginning at the corner of Eighth Avenue and Oak Street. The bustling market was founded in 1970 and is something of a bastion of hippie crafts. There are also

Go Ducks!

Fans of the University of Oregon's Ducks football team can try to buy tickets by contacting the **UO Athletic Ticket Office** (⟨ℭ⟩ **800/WEB-FOOT** or 541/346-4461; www.goducks.com).

food vendors, fresh produce, and live music. The market, held April through mid-November, takes place on Saturdays between 10am to 5pm.

Other days of the week, you can explore the **Market District,** a 6-block area of restored buildings that houses unusual shops, galleries, restaurants, and nightclubs. The **Fifth Street Public Market,** 296 E. Fifth St. (🕐 541/484-0383; www.5thstreet market.com), at the corner of Fifth Avenue and High Street, is the centerpiece of the area. In this shopping center, you'll find **New Twist** (🕐 541/342-8686), selling fine crafts and wildly artistic jewelry; **French Quarter** (🕐 541/343-8904), selling fine linens; **Destinations** (🕐 541/302-0787), a travel store; and **Nike** (🕐 541/342-5155). Directly across Fifth Avenue is the **5th & Pearl building,** which houses a couple of restaurants and a few more shops. Also nearby is **Down to Earth,** 532 Olive St. (🕐 541/342-6820; www.down-to-earth.com), a fascinating garden and housewares shop housed in an old granary building.

If you're interested in art, there is a monthly **First Friday Artwalk** during which downtown art galleries have openings and stay open late. For information, contact the **Lane Arts Council,** 99 W. 10th Ave., Suite 100 (🕐 **541/485-2278;** www.lanearts.org).

WHERE TO STAY

The Campbell House 🕐🕐   Located only 2 blocks from the Market District and set at the base of Skinner's Butte overlooking the city, this large Victorian home was built in 1892 and now offers luxury, convenience, and comfort. The guest rooms here vary considerably in size and price, but you're sure to find something you like in your price range. Several of the guest rooms on the first floor have high ceilings, and on the lower level there's a pine-paneled room with a fishing theme and another with a golf theme. The upstairs rooms have plenty of windows, and in the largest room you'll find wood floors and a double whirlpool tub. A separate carriage house contains some of the inn's most luxurious and most thoughtfully designed rooms. Breakfasts are served in a room with a curving wall of glass.

252 Pearl St., Eugene, OR 97401. 🕐 **800/264-2519** or 541/343-1119. Fax 541/343-2258. www.campbellhouse.com. 19 units. $119–$349 double. Children under 2 stay free in parent's room. AE, DC, DISC, MC, V. Rates include full breakfast. **Amenities:** Restaurant (New American); access to nearby health club; concierge; business center; room service; massage; babysitting; laundry service; dry cleaning. *In room:* A/C, TV, dataport, fridge, hair dryer, iron, free local calls, Wi-Fi.

Hilton Eugene & Conference Center 🕐🕐   This is Eugene's only downtown corporate high-rise convention hotel, and it caters primarily to business travelers and conventioneers. However, with the Hult Center for the Performing Arts next door and dozens of restaurants and cafes within a few blocks, it's also a good choice if you want to take in a show or explore downtown Eugene on foot. Try to get a room on an upper floor so you can enjoy the views. The restaurant just off the lobby features a Northwest fishing theme and serves moderately priced meals.

66 E. Sixth Ave., Eugene, OR 97401. 🕐 **800/HILTONS** or 541/342-2000. Fax 541/342-6661. www.eugene.hilton.com. 272 units. $99–$179 double; $330–$395 suite. Children under 18 stay free in parent's room. AE, DC, DISC, MC, V. Valet parking $7. Pets accepted ($25). **Amenities:** Restaurant (Northwest); lounge; indoor pool; exercise room; Jacuzzi; sauna; bike rentals; concierge; car-rental desk; courtesy airport shuttle; salon; room service; laundry service; dry cleaning; concierge-level rooms. *In room:* A/C, TV, dataport, coffeemaker, hair dryer, iron, high-speed Internet access, Wi-Fi.

McKenzie View 🕐🕐 *Finds*   This country inn is set on 6 acres of woodlands outside of Springfield, and overlooks the McKenzie River. Beautiful perennial and cutting gardens surround the inn, and there are decks and a gazebo. The inn itself is an expansive contemporary home that is comfortably furnished (neither overdone nor so full of antiques that guests feel uncomfortable). Three of the rooms are quite large (two are suites) and have views of the river through large windows. The smallest room doesn't have a river view, but it is quite economical. Avid gardeners will love this place. The inn is about a 15- to 20-minute drive from downtown Eugene.

34922 McKenzie View Dr., Springfield, OR 97478. © **888/MCK-VIEW.** Fax 541/726-6968. www.mckenzie-view.com. 4 units. Apr–Oct $90–$250 double; Nov–Mar $75–$200 double. Rates include full breakfast. MC, V. **Amenities:** Access to nearby health club. *In room:* A/C, dataport, hair dryer.

The Secret Garden ★★ *Finds* This B&B is housed in a former sorority house, which had previously been the home of Eugene pioneer Alton Baker. Today, the large inn features European and Asian art and antiques, and guest rooms that are beautifully and tastefully decorated. One of our favorites is the Scented Garden, which has floor lamps made from Tibetan horns and a gorgeous sitar on display. And yes, there is a secret garden, a unique outdoor room with living walls concealing a whirlpool tub.

1910 University St., Eugene, OR 97403. © **888/484-6755** or 541/484-6755. Fax 541/431-1699. www.secret gardenbbinn.com. 10 units. May–Oct $125–$245 double; Nov–Apr $115–$225 double. Rates include full breakfast. AE, MC, V. **Amenities:** Access to nearby health club; Jacuzzi. *In room:* A/C, TV/VCR, fridge, hair dryer, iron.

Valley River Inn ★★ Although this lushly landscaped low-rise hotel boasts an enviable location on the bank of the Willamette River, the rates are aimed at those with expense accounts, not at vacationers. However, if you can get any sort of substantial discount, this might be a good choice. The hotel is only a few minutes' drive from downtown and the university, and is adjacent to Eugene's largest shopping mall. All the rooms are large and have a balcony or patio, but the riverside rooms have the best views. Sweetwater's Restaurant has a long wall of glass overlooking the river and serves primarily Northwest cuisine.

1000 Valley River Way, Eugene, OR 97401. © **800/543-8266** or 541/743-1000. Fax 541/683-5121. www.valley riverinn.com. 269 units. $180–$225 double; $200–$350 suite. AE, DC, DISC, MC, V. Pets accepted. **Amenities:** Restaurant (Northwest); lounge; outdoor pool; exercise room, access to nearby health club; Jacuzzi; sauna; bike rental; concierge; courtesy airport shuttle; room service; laundry service; dry cleaning. *In room:* A/C, TV, dataport, coffeemaker, hair dryer, iron, high-speed Internet access.

WHERE TO DINE

For rustic breads, breakfast pastries, and desserts, drop by the **Palace Bakery,** 844 Pearl St. (© **541/484-2435**), which is an offshoot of the popular Zenon Café. For good baked goods and quick lunches, stop by **Metropol Bakery,** Fifth Street Public Market, 296 E. Fifth Ave. (© **541/687-9370**). For gourmet food to go, perhaps for a picnic at a winery, drop by **The Broadway,** 200 W. Broadway (© **541/685-0790**), which is a sort of gourmet deli, grocery store, wine shop, and cafe all rolled into one. If you've got a sweet tooth, don't miss out on **Sweet Life,** 755 Monroe St. (© **541/ 683-5676**), which bakes the best pastries in Eugene.

EXPENSIVE

Adam's Place ★★ NORTHWEST Located downtown on the pedestrian mall, Adam's Place's interior conjures up an old English inn and is one of the most elegant dining establishments in the city. The menu is short, changes frequently, and relies heavily on fresh local produce. On a recent autumn evening the appetizer menu included creamy cambazola fondue and a halibut ceviche Napoleon. Entree flavors tend to be simple yet creative. Seared duck breast might be served with roasted mission figs and onions, and cedar-planked halibut might be topped by lentils with squid ink. In the summer, you can dine under the stars out on the patio. Several nights each week there is live jazz in the adjacent Luna nightclub.

30 E. Broadway. (C) **541/344-6948.** www.adamsplacerestaurant.com. Reservations recommended. Main courses $19–$26. AE, MC, V. Tues–Thurs 4:30–10pm; Fri–Sat 4:30–midnight.

Marché *&* MEDITERRANEAN   Marché, located in the Fifth Street Public Market, is the quintessential urban American bistro, and, with its hip decor, tiny (but popular) bar, patio, and display kitchen with a few settings for solo diners, the restaurant pulls in a wide range of customers, from couples on dates to pretheater parties and even families. The menu is as creative as you'll find in Eugene and preparations are fairly reliable. As often as possible, ingredients are organic and non-GMO (genetically modified). There's an extensive list of reasonably priced wines, plus plenty of wines by the glass.

296 E. Fifth Ave. (C) **541/342-3612.** www.marcherestaurant.com. Reservations recommended. Main courses $9.50–$15 lunch, $18–$32 dinner. AE, DC, DISC, MC, V. Mon–Thurs 11:30am–11pm; Fri–Sat 11:30am–midnight; Sun 10am–11pm.

MODERATE

Zenon Café *&&* INTERNATIONAL   Zenon has long been the city's top outpost for cutting-edge cookery. If you've read about it in the latest issue of *Gourmet* or *Bon Appétit,* you'll probably find it on the menu here. The setting is fairly stark, though with some raw wood for warmth, but the menu, which changes daily, is long and includes plenty of small plates as well as full-size entrees. You're almost assured of finding something you've never tried before. Before you ever reach your table, though, you'll have to run the gauntlet of the dessert case, which usually flaunts about 20 irresistible cakes, pies, tortes, and other pastries.

898 Pearl St. (C) **541/343-3005.** Main courses $9–$15 lunch, $12–$23 dinner. MC, V. Sun–Thurs 8am–11pm; Fri–Sat 8am–midnight.

INEXPENSIVE

Sweet Basil *&* *(Value* THAI   With its chic urban decor, zesty flavors, artful presentation, and reasonable prices, this upscale Thai restaurant has seriously raised the bar for Thai restaurants in the state. This is some of the best Thai food I've had in Oregon, and the *pad phet gai* (chicken and vegetables with homemade curry sauce) is a riot of vibrant flavors. They even do a good job with the *pad thai,* a dish that can often be rather insipid at some Thai restaurants. On sunny days, try to get a sidewalk table. Lunches are one of the best deals in Eugene.

941 Pearl St. (C) **541/284-2944.** Reservations recommended. Main courses $6.25 lunch, $8–$21 dinner. AE, DC, DISC, MC, V. Mon–Thurs 11:30am–3pm and 5–9pm; Fri 11:30am–3pm and 5–10pm; Sat noon–4pm and 5–10pm; Sun noon–4pm and 5–9pm.

EUGENE AFTER DARK

With its two theaters and nonstop schedule, the **Hult Center for the Performing Arts,** One Eugene Center, Seventh Avenue and Willamette Street ((C) **541/682-5000;** www.hultcenter.org), is the heart and soul of this city's performing arts scene. The center's huge glass gables are an unmistakable landmark, and each year this sparkling temple of the arts puts together a first-rate schedule of performances by the Eugene Symphony, the Eugene Ballet Company, the Eugene Opera, and other local and regional companies, as well as visiting companies and performers. During the summer, the center hosts the Oregon Bach Festival. Also be sure to see what the **Shedd Institute for the Arts,** East Broadway and High Street ((C) **541/687-6526;** www.theshedd.org), has scheduled at its Jaqua

Concert Hall. Summer concerts with the likes of Jackson Browne and Crosby, Stills, and Nash are also held at the **Cuthbert Amphitheater** in Alton Baker Park.

To find out what's happening, pick up a copy of the free *Eugene Weekly,* which is available at restaurants and shops around town.

BREWPUBS

In addition to the places listed below, you'll find plenty of microbreweries in Eugene. These include the **High Street Brewery & Cafe,** 1243 High St. (© **541/345-4905;** www.mcmenamins.com); the **East 19th Street Cafe,** 1485 E. 19th St. (© **541/ 342-4025;** www.mcmenamins.com); **Steelhead Brewing Co.,** 199 E. Fifth Ave. (© **541/686-2739**); and **Eugene City Brewery,** 844 Olive St. (© **541/345-4155;** www.rogue.com). This latter pub is operated by Rogue Brewing in Newport.

NIGHTCLUBS & BARS

Luna ⚜ This downtown restaurant and bar is best known around town as the classiest jazz spot in Eugene. But you can also catch blues, Latin, hip hop, and even Middle Eastern and other types of music. This is also Eugene's favorite spot for a martini. 30 E. Broadway. © **541/434-LUNA**. www.lunajazz.com.

Jo Federigo's Café & Bar ⚜ Housed in a historic granary building, this basement club and restaurant has live music nightly. The lineup usually includes jazz several nights a week. 259 E. Fifth Ave. © **541/343-8488**.

Oregon Electric Station ⚜⚜ This building dates from 1914, and with a wine cellar in an old railroad car, lots of oak, and a back bar that requires a ladder to access all the various bottles of premium spirits, it's the poshest bar in town. 27 E. Fifth Ave. © **541/ 485-4444**.

WOW Hall ⚜⚜ The historic Woodmen of the World Hall now serves as a sort of community center for the performing arts and hosts an eclectic array of concerts and performances by alternative bands. 291 W. Eighth Ave. © **541/687-2746**. www.wowhall.org.

7

The Oregon Coast

Extending from the mouth of the Columbia River in the north to California's redwood country in the south, the Oregon coast is a shoreline of jaw-dropping natural beauty. Yes, it's often rainy or foggy, and, yes, the water is too cold and rough for swimming, but the coastline more than makes up for these shortcomings with its drama and grandeur. Wave-pounded rocky shores; dense, dark forests; lonely lighthouses; rugged headlands—these all set this shoreline apart.

In places, the mountains of the Coast Range rise straight from the ocean's waves to form rugged, windswept headlands that still bear the colorful names given them by early explorers—Cape Foulweather, Cape Blanco, and Cape Perpetua. With roads and trails that scale these heights, these capes provide ideal vantage points for surveying the wave-washed coast. Between these rocky headlands stretch miles of sandy beaches. In fact, on the central coast there's so much sand that dunes rise as high as 500 feet.

Wildlife viewing opportunities along the Oregon coast are outstanding. From the beaches and the waters just offshore rise countless haystack rocks, rocky islets, monoliths, and other rock formations that serve as homes to birds, sea lions, and seals. Harbor seals loll on isolated sand spits, and large colonies of California sea lions lounge on rocks and docks, barking incessantly and entertaining people with their constant bickering. The best places to observe sea lions are on the Newport waterfront, at Sea Lion Caves north of Florence and at Cape Arago State Park outside of Coos Bay. Hundreds of gray whales also call these waters home, and each year thousands more can be seen during their annual migrations. Twice a year, in late winter and early spring, gray whales migrate between the Arctic and the waters off Baja California. They pass close by the coast and can be easily spotted from headlands such as Tillamook Head, Cape Meares, Cape Lookout, and Cape Blanco. In coastal meadows, majestic elk graze contentedly, and near the town of Reedsport, the Dean Creek meadows have been set aside as an elk preserve. It's often possible to spot 100 or more elk grazing here. The single best introduction to the aquatic flora and fauna of the Oregon coast is Newport's Oregon Coast Aquarium, where you can learn more about the myriad animals and plants that inhabit the diverse aquatic environments of the Oregon coast.

Rivers, bays, and offshore waters are also home to some of the best **fishing** in the country. The rivers, though depleted by a century of overfishing, are still home to salmon, steelhead, and trout, most of which are now hatchery raised. Several charter-boat marinas up and down the coast offer saltwater-fishing for salmon and bottom fish. Few anglers return from these trips without a good catch. **Crabbing** and **clamming** are two other productive coastal pursuits that can turn a trip to the beach into a time for feasting.

To allow visitors to enjoy all the beauties of the Oregon coast, the state has

---

Value The Cost of the Coast

State parks, county parks, national-forest recreation areas, outstanding natural areas—along the Oregon coast, there are numerous state and federal access areas that now charge day-use fees. You can either pay these fees as you encounter them or purchase an Oregon Coast Passport for $10. These passes are good for 5 days, and get you into all state and federal parks and recreation areas along the coast. (However, you'll still have to pay campsite fees.) A $35 annual pass is also available. Passports are available at most state parks that charge a day-use fee. For more information contact **Oregon State Parks Information Center** (© 800/551-6949).

---

created nearly 80 state parks, waysides, recreation areas, and scenic viewpoints between Fort Stevens State Park in the north and McVay Rock State Recreation Site in the south. Among the more popular activities at these parks are kite flying and beachcombing (but not swimming; the water is too cold).

As I've already mentioned, it rains a lot here. Bring a raincoat, and don't let a little moisture prevent you from enjoying one of the most beautiful coastlines in the world. In fact, the mists and fogs add an aura of mystery to the coast's dark, forested mountain slopes. Contrary to what you might think, the hot days of July and August are not always the best time to visit. When it's baking inland, the coast is often shrouded in fog. The best months to visit tend to be September and early October, when the weather is often fine and the crowds are gone.

1 Astoria

95 miles NW of Portland; 20 miles S of Long Beach, WA; 17 miles N of Seaside

Astoria, situated on the banks of the Columbia River just inland from the river's mouth, is the oldest American community west of the Mississippi. More a river town than a beach town, Astoria's greatest attraction lies in its hillsides of restored Victorian homes and the scenic views across the Columbia to the hills of southwestern Washington. The combination of historical character, scenic vistas, a lively arts community, and some interesting museums make this one of the most intriguing communities on the Oregon coast. Although it still has seamy sections of waterfront, the town has been busy over the past few years developing something of a tourist-oriented waterfront character.

Astoria's Euro-American history got its start in the winter of 1805 to 1806 when Lewis and Clark built a fort near here and established an American claim. Five years later, in 1811, fur traders working for John Jacob Astor arrived at the mouth of the Columbia River to set up a fur-trading fort that was named Fort Astoria. During the War of 1812, the fort was turned over to the British, but by 1818 it reverted to American hands. When the salmon-canning boom hit in the 1880s, Astoria became a bustling little city—the second largest in Oregon—and wealthy merchants began building the ornate, Victorian-style homes that today give Astoria its historic character.

ESSENTIALS
GETTING THERE   From Portland, take U.S. 30W. From the north or south, take U.S. 101.

The Northern Oregon Coast

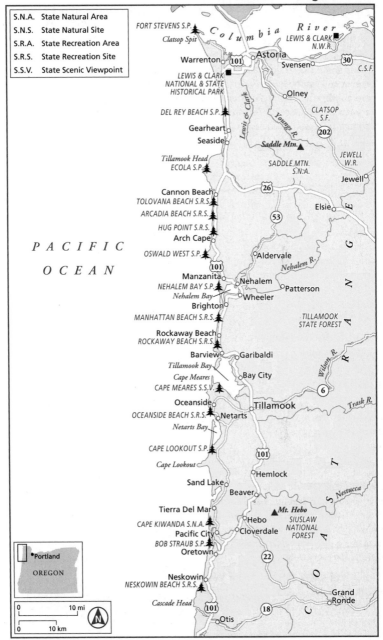

S.N.A.   State Natural Area
S.N.S.   State Natural Site
S.R.A.   State Recreation Area
S.R.S.   State Recreation Site
S.S.V.   State Scenic Viewpoint

FORT STEVENS S.P.
Clatsop Spit
LEWIS & CLARK
N.W.R.
Columbia River
Warrenton
Astoria
Svensen
C.S.F.
LEWIS & CLARK
NATIONAL & STATE
HISTORICAL PARK
Olney
CLATSOP
S.F.
DEL REY BEACH S.P.
Gearheart
Seaside
Lewis & Clark
Youngs R.
Saddle Mtn.
JEWELL
W.R.
Tillamook Head
ECOLA S.P.
SADDLE.MTN.
S.N:A.
Jewell
Cannon Beach
TOLOVANA BEACH S.R.S.
ARCADIA BEACH S.R.S.
HUG POINT S.R.S.
Arch Cape
OSWALD WEST S.P.
Elsie
Aldervale
Nehalem R.
PACIFIC
OCEAN
Manzanita
NEHALEM BAY S.P.
Nehalem Bay
Brighton
MANHATTAN BEACH S.R.S.
Rockaway Beach
ROCKAWAY BEACH S.R.S.
Barview
Nehalem
Wheeler
Patterson
TILLAMOOK
STATE FOREST
Garibaldi
Tillamook Bay
Cape Meares
CAPE MEARES S.S.V.
Oceanside
OCEANSIDE BEACH S.R.S.
Netarts
Netarts Bay
Bay City
Tillamook
Wilson R.
Trask R.
CAPE LOOKOUT S.P.
Cape Lookout
Hemlock
Sand Lake
Beaver
Nestucca
Tierra Del Mar
CAPE KIWANDA S.N.A.
Pacific City
BOB STRAUB S.P.
Oretown
Mt. Hebo
Hebo
Cloverdale
SIUSLAW
NATIONAL
FOREST
COAST
RANGE
Neskowin
NESKOWIN BEACH S.R.S.
Cascade Head
Otis
Grand
Ronde

Portland
OREGON

0   10 mi
0   10 km
N

165

VISITOR INFORMATION   Contact the **Astoria-Warrenton Area Chamber of Commerce,** 111 W. Marine Dr. (P.O. Box 176), Astoria, OR 97103 (✆ **800/ 875-6807** or 503/325-6311; www.oldoregon.com).

FESTIVALS   The **Astoria Regatta** (www.astoriaregatta.org), held each year in early August, is the city's biggest festival and includes lots of sailboat races. You've probably heard of cowboy poetry, but have you heard of fisher poetry? Astoria's annual **Fisher Poets Gathering** (www.clatsopcc.edu/fisherpoets), held in late February, celebrates the poetry of commercial fishermen and women.

DELVING INTO ASTORIA HISTORY

Columbia River Maritime Museum 🕅🕅   The Columbia River, the second-largest river in the United States, was the object of centuries of exploration in the Northwest, and, since its discovery in 1792, it has been essential to the region. This boldly designed museum, built to resemble waves on the ocean, tells the story of the river's maritime history. High seas and constantly shifting sands make this one of the world's most difficult rivers to enter; displays of shipwrecks, lighthouses, and historical lifesaving missions testify to the danger. The Coast Guard, fishing, navigation, and naval history are also subjects of museum exhibits, with a dramatic Coast Guard motor lifeboat display a highlight of the museum. Docked beside the museum and open to visitors is the lightship *Columbia,* the last seagoing lighthouse ship to serve on the West Coast. This is one of the best museums in the state.

1792 Marine Dr. ✆ 503/325-2323. www.crmm.org. Admission $8 adults, $7 seniors, $4 children 6–17. Daily 9:30am–5pm. Closed Thanksgiving and Christmas.

Flavel House Museum 🕅   The Flavel House, owned and operated by the Clatsop County Historical Society, is the grandest and most ornate of Astoria's many Victorian homes. This Queen Anne–style Victorian mansion was built in 1885 by Capt. George Flavel, who made his fortune operating the first pilot service over the Columbia River Bar and was Astoria's first millionaire. When constructed, this house was the envy of every Astoria resident. The high-ceilinged rooms are filled with period furnishings that accent the home's superb construction, and throughout the house there is much ornate woodwork.

441 Eighth St. ✆ 503/325-2203. Admission $5 adults, $4 seniors and students, $2 children 6–17. Apr–Oct daily 9:30am–5pm; Nov–Mar daily 11am–4pm.

Heritage Museum   Housed in Astoria's former city hall, this small museum chronicles the history of Astoria and surrounding Clatsop County. The main exhibits consist of Native American and pioneer artifacts, as well as historic photos, and there is also an exhibit on the many saloons that filled this town in the late 19th century.

1618 Exchange St. ✆ 503/325-2203. Admission $3 adults, $2 seniors, $1 children 6–17. Apr–Oct daily 10am–5pm; Nov–Mar Tues–Sat 11am–4pm.

Lewis and Clark National and State Historical Park 🕅🕅   During the winter of 1805–06, Meriwether Lewis, William Clark, and the other members of the Corps of Discovery camped at a spot near the mouth of the Columbia River. They built a log stockade and named their encampment Fort Clatsop after the local Clatsop Indians who had befriended them. In the 1950s, a reproduction of that fort was constructed, but in the fall of 2005, as the fort's big bicentennial celebration approached, the fort burned down. At press time, there were hopes that reconstruction would begin soon, so by the time you read this, there may already be a new Fort Clatsop to

COLUMBIA RIVER

Astoria
Portland
OREGON

ACCOMMODATIONS ■
Cannery Pier Hotel **1**
Clementine's Bed and
  Breakfast **6**
Hotel Elliott **16**
Rosebriar Hotel **18**

DINING ◆
Baked Alaska **10**
The Cellar on 10th **8**
Columbian Café **9**
Flying Barney's Rusty Cup
  Coffee House & Beanery **17**
Gunderson's Cannery Cafe **4**
Josephson's **2**
Silver Salmon Grille **13**
T. Paul's Urban Café **14**

ATTRACTIONS ●
Astoria Column **23**
Astoria Visual Arts **7**
Columbia River Maritime
  Museum **22**
Flavel House Museum **5**

Fort Astoria **19**
Heritage Museum **21**
Let It Rain **12**
Lunar Boy Gallery **15**
RiverSea Gallery **11**
Shallon Winery **20**
Sixth Street Viewing Dock **3**

0   1/8 mi
0   1/8 km

visit. As part of the 2005 bicentennial celebration, the new 6-mile Fort to Sea Trail
was constructed and several sites in Washington state were made part of this new
national park. Over on the Washington side of the Columbia, there are new sculptures, including one by celebrated artist Maya Lin. From late spring to Labor Day,
park rangers clad in period clothing give demonstrations of activities such as flintlock
use, buckskin preparation, and candle making. In the visitor center you can learn
more about the history of the area. During the summer, shuttle buses link this park
with several state parks and other significant Lewis and Clark sites.

Off U.S. 101, 5 miles southwest of Astoria. ℭ **503/861-2471.** www.nps.gov/lewi. Admission $3–$5 adults. Labor
Day to mid-June daily 9am–5pm; mid-June to Labor Day daily 9am–6pm. Closed Christmas.

OTHER ASTORIA ACTIVITIES & ATTRACTIONS

Atop Coxcomb Hill, which is reached by driving up 16th Street and following the
signs and painted COLUMN markings on the road, you'll find the **Astoria Column.**
Built in 1926, the column was patterned after Trajan's Column in Rome and stands
125 feet tall. On the exterior wall, a mural depicts the history of the area. There are
164 steps up to the top of the column, and on a clear day the view makes the climb
well worth the effort. The column is open daily from dawn to dusk and admission is
free. On the way to the Astoria Column, stop by **Fort Astoria,** on the corner of 15th

and Exchange streets. A log blockhouse and historical marker commemorate the site of the trading post established by John Jacob Astor's fur traders.

There are several places in downtown where you can linger by the riverside atop the docks that once made up much of the city's waterfront. Stop by the **Sixth Street Viewing Dock,** where there is a raised viewing platform as well as a fishing dock. From here you can gaze out at the massive Astoria-Megler Bridge, stretching for more than 4 miles across the mouth of the river. Also keep an eye out for sea lions. The best way to see the waterfront is aboard the restored 1913 streetcar operated by **Astoria Riverfront Trolley.** This trolley operates daily from Memorial Day to Labor Day and on a limited schedule other months. Rides are $1.

Right in downtown Astoria, you'll find one of the most unusual wineries in the state. **Shallon Winery,** 1598 Duane St. (© 503/325-5978; www.shallon.com), specializes in fruit wines, but it is the unique whey wines that are winemaker Paul van der Veldt's greatest achievement. The Cran du Lait, made with local cranberries and whey from the Tillamook cheese factory, is surprisingly smooth and drinkable. Also look for the amazing chocolate-orange wine, a thick nectar that will make a chocoholic of anyone.

If you'd like to see what local artists are up to, stop by the gallery of **Astoria Visual Arts,** 160 10th St. (© 503/325-4589; www.astoriavisualarts.org), a not-for-profit arts organization. For more regional art, visit the **RiverSea Gallery,** 1160 Commercial St. (© 503/325-1270). At **Lunar Boy Gallery,** 1133 Commercial St. (© 503/325-1566; www.lunarboygallery.com), you'll find a truly bizarre selection of art derived from the worlds of graphic design, cartoons, and animated films. Should you find yourself in need of an umbrella, stop by **Let It Rain,** 1124 Commercial St. (© 800/998-0773 or 503/325-7728), which has one of the largest selections of umbrellas in the Northwest.

OUTDOOR ACTIVITIES

Fort Stevens State Park (© 503/861-1671), 8 miles from Astoria at the mouth of the Columbia, preserves a fort that was built during the Civil War to protect the Columbia River and its important port cities. Though Fort Stevens had the distinction of being the only mainland military reservation to be fired on by the Japanese, the fort was deactivated after World War II. Today the fort's extensive grounds include historic buildings and gun emplacements, and the **Fort Stevens Museum** (© 503/861-2000). Throughout the summer, the museum operates tours of the fort in a military surplus truck. There are also miles of bicycle paths, beaches, a campground, and a picnic area. Admission is $3. At the north end of the park, you can climb to the top of a viewing tower and get a good look at the South Jetty, which was built to make navigating the mouth of the Columbia easier. Also within the park you can see the wreck of the *Peter Iredale,* one ship that did not make it safely over the sandbars at the river's mouth. Each year over Labor Day weekend, there is a Civil War reenactment here at the park. You can rent bikes from **Bikes & Beyond,** 1089 Marine Dr. (© 503/325-2961), for $8 per hour, $15 for a half-day, or $25 for a full day.

A few miles south of Fort Stevens on U.S. 101, you'll find **Sunset Beach State Recreation Area;** it provides beach access and is the western end of the 6-mile-long Fort to Sea Trail, which stretches from here to Fort Clatsop in Lewis and Clark National Historical Park.

Several charter-fishing boats operate out of nearby Warrenton. Arrange trips through **Tiki Charters** (© 503/325-7818) and **Charlton Deep Sea Charters** (© 503/861-2429). Expect to pay $85 to $110 per person.

A few miles east of town on Ore. 30, bird-watchers will find a roadside viewing platform overlooking the marshes of the **Twilight Creek Eagle Sanctuary.** Take Burnside Road off Ore. 30 between the John Day River and Svenson.

WHERE TO STAY

Cannery Pier Hotel 🐡🐡 This luxurious hotel is one of my favorite lodgings on the Oregon coast, although it is actually on the Columbia River, not on the Pacific Ocean. In fact, this hotel isn't just on the waterfront, it's *in* the river. Built 600 feet out in the river on an old cannery pier, this hotel is a completely new construction that fits in perfectly with old wooden waterfront buildings around Astoria. Guest rooms are exceedingly comfortable, with window seats, little balconies, gas fireplaces, and superplush beds. In the bathrooms, you'll find a claw-foot tub, from which you can gaze out at the river while you soak. Your view will take in not only the waters of the mighty Columbia River but also the impressive Astoria-Megler Bridge looming high overhead—and tankers and cruise ships rumble up and down the river. Want a better look? Check out the telescope in the lobby.

10 Basin St., Astoria, OR 97103. ✆ **888/325-4996** or 503/325-4996. Fax 503/325-8350. www.cannerypierhotel.com. 46 units. Summer $169–$199 double; $299–$525 suite; other months $139–$179 double; $249–$525 suite. Rates include continental breakfast. AE, DISC, MC, V. **Amenities:** Exercise room; full-service spa; Jacuzzi; sauna; bikes; coin-op laundry. *In room:* TV, dataport, fridge, coffeemaker, hair dryer, iron, high-speed Internet access, Wi-Fi.

Clementine's Bed and Breakfast 🐡🐡 Located in downtown Astoria across the street from the Flavel House Museum, this eclectic little inn built in 1888 in the Italianate Victorian style is filled with Asian arts and antiques and is surrounded by beautiful flower gardens. Rooms vary considerably in size. Two have their own little balconies, and several have expansive views of the river and town. The two suites are quite large and are great for families. With backgrounds in music and river guiding on the Colorado River, innkeepers Judith and Cliff Taylor keep guests informed about what there is to see and do in the area.

847 Exchange St., Astoria, OR 97103. ✆ **800/521-6801** or 503/325-2005. www.clementines-bb.com. 8 units. $75–$115 double; $115–$160 suite. Rates include full breakfast. DISC, MC, V. 2-night minimum on summer weekends. Pets accepted in suites ($15). **Amenities:** Jacuzzi; concierge. *In room:* Hair dryer, no phone, Wi-Fi.

Hotel Elliott 🐡🐡 Historic hotels are few and far between on the Oregon coast, but even if they were a dime a dozen, this would be the best. The hotel was reopened in 2003 after a complete restoration and is now absolutely beautiful. The restoration kept the vintage feel of the hotel while giving it thoroughly modern interior decor. Rooms have lots of nice touches, including heated tile floors in the bathrooms, handblown glass globes on reading lights, regional artwork, furniture with comfortable contemporary styling, plush feather-top beds, and, in suites, granite-topped wet bars. Down in the cellar, there's a cigar-and-wine bar, and up on the roof, there's a roof-top garden with fire pits and grand views.

357 12th St., Astoria, OR 97103. ✆ **877/EST-1924** or 503/325-2222. www.hotelelliott.com. 32 units. $105–$160 double; $135–$650 suite. Rates include continental breakfast. AE, DISC, MC, V. Pets accepted ($25). **Amenities:** Access to nearby health club; concierge; 24-hour room service; babysitting; laundry service; dry cleaning. *In room:* TV, dataport, minibar, coffeemaker, hair dryer, iron.

Rosebriar Hotel 🐡 Originally built as a private home in 1902, the Rosebriar became a convent in the 1950s, then was renovated and turned into a small 1920s-style hotel in the 1990s. Ornate wainscoting, scrollwork ceilings, and lots of wood

---

Tips **Plan Ahead—Campground Reservations**

For information on **camping** in area state parks, call the state parks information line at © **800/551-6949**. To make a camping reservation, contact **ReserveAmerica** (© **800/452-5687**; www.reserveamerica.com).

---

trim show the quality of workmanship that went into this home. The grand old Georgian mansion sits high above the river and the street, with commanding views from the two front rooms. The carriage-house cottage has its own fireplace, whirlpool tub, and private patio.

636 14th St., Astoria, OR 97103. © **800/487-0224** or 503/325-7427. www.rosebriar.net. 12 units. June–Sept $75–$169 double, $250 suite; Oct–May $69–$139 double, $219 suite. Rates include full breakfast. 2-night minimum on weekends. AE, DISC, MC, V. *In room:* TV.

CAMPGROUNDS

Fort Stevens State Park, on the beach at the mouth of the Columbia River, is one of the largest and most popular state park campgrounds on the Oregon coast. For reservations, contact **ReserveAmerica** (© **800/452-5687**; www.reserveamerica.com).

WHERE TO DINE

In addition to the restaurants listed below, you should be sure to stop by **Josephson's,** 106 Marine Dr. (© **800/772-3474** or 503/325-2190; www.josephsons.com), a local seafood-smoking company that sells smoked salmon by the pound and has a take-out deli counter with clam chowder, smoked seafood on rolls, and more. If you're looking for some local ale, stop by **The Wet Dog Cafe,** 144 11th St. (© **503/325-6975**), the town's only brewpub. If it's wine you're after, stop by **The Cellar on 10th,** 1004 Marine Dr. (© **503/325-6600;** www.thecellaron10th.com), a well-stocked wine shop that has weekly tastings and occasional winemaker dinners. For espresso, a quick lunch, or a light dinner, head to **T. Paul's Urban Café,** 1119 Commercial St. (© **503/ 338-5133**). You can also get good espresso at **Flying Barney's Rusty Cup Coffee House & Beanery,** 1213 Commercial St. (© **503/325-8265**).

Baked Alaska *Finds* NORTHWEST   Built on a pier in downtown Astoria, this restaurant isn't just on the waterfront, it's over the waves. Not only are there great views (keep an eye out for sea lions), but the menu includes both comfort food and creative dishes. This place started out as a mobile soup trailer in Alaska, and when the chef/owner and his wife decided to settle down in one place, he picked Astoria. Begin with the soup in a sourdough bread bowl—it's what got this place started. Beyond soup, try the campfire salmon, blackened New York steak, or the unusual thundermuck tuna (seared tuna dusted with ground coffee).

1 12th St. © 503/325-7414. Reservations recommended. Main courses $8–$12 lunch, $17–$21 dinner. AE, DC, DISC, MC, V. Daily 11am–9pm.

Columbian Café *Finds* VEGETARIAN/SEAFOOD   With offbeat and eclectic decor, this tiny place looks a bit like a cross between a college hangout and a seaport diner, and, indeed, the clientele reflects this atmosphere. There are only a handful of booths and a lunch counter, and the cafe's reputation for good vegetarian fare keeps the seats full. Crepes are the house specialty and come with a variety of fillings, including avocado, tomato, and cheese, or curried bananas. Dinner offers a bit more variety, with an emphasis on seafood, and there are always lots of specials. Even the condiments here, including pepper jelly and garlic jelly, are homemade. Next door, and affiliated with the cafe, are the Voodoo Room nightclub and the Columbian Theater movie theater.

1114 Marine Dr. ⓒ **503/325-2233.** Breakfast or lunch $5–$12; dinner $12–$22. No credit cards. Mon–Tues 8am–2pm; Wed–Thurs 8am–2pm and 5–9pm; Fri 8am–2pm and 5–10pm; Sat 9am–2pm and 5–10pm; Sun 9am–2pm. (Dining hours may change with the season.)

Gunderson's Cannery Cafe ⚡ SEAFOOD/NORTHWEST   Housed in a former salmon cannery, this casual restaurant offers creative food and great views. You might even spot sea lions while you're dining. For nightly specials, the chef draws upon world cuisines for inspiration; and on the main menu, you'll also find international influences in such dishes as pan-Asian salmon and Mediterranean halibut. The crab and shrimp cakes are perennial favorites. Lunches are mostly sandwiches (the panini are my favorites), salads, and good chowder.

Sixth St. on the Columbia River. ⓒ **503/325-8642.** www.cannerycafe.com. Reservations recommended. Main courses lunch $7.50–$15, dinner $14–$26. AE, DISC, MC, V. Mon 11am–8pm; Tues–Thurs and Sun 8am–8pm; Fri–Sat 8am–9pm.

Silver Salmon Grille ⚡ SEAFOOD/NORTHWEST   Astoria also has good restaurants that don't have river views, and this is one of my favorites. With its beautiful cherry-wood back bar, which came around Cape Horn in the 1880s and once graced an Astoria brothel, the Silver Salmon manages to capture a bit of local history. As the name implies, this restaurant celebrates salmon and offers it in more than half a dozen ways, from smoked-salmon crepes to salmon-and-shrimp piccata. Okay, so maybe you aren't a fan of salmon; try the London broil or chateaubriand instead. This is the most formal restaurant in town.

1105 Commercial St. ⓒ **503/338-6640.** www.silversalmongrille.com. Main courses $6–$14 lunch, $13–$35 dinner. AE, DISC, MC, V. Daily 11am–10pm.

ASTORIA AFTER DARK

If you're here in the summer, try to catch a performance of *Shanghaied in Astoria,* a musical melodrama that is staged each year by the **Astor Street Opry Company,** 279 W. Marine Dr. (ⓒ **503/325-6104;** www.shanghaiedinastoria.com). Performances are usually held from mid-July to mid-September. Also be sure to check the schedule of the **Liberty Theater,** 12th and Commercial streets (ⓒ **503/325-5922;** www.liberty-theater.org), a beautifully restored 1920s movie palace.

2 Seaside

17 miles S of Astoria, 79 miles W of Portland, 7 miles N of Cannon Beach

Seaside is the northern Oregon coast's favorite family vacation destination. The town is one of the oldest beach resorts on the coast (dating from 1899) and is filled with quaint historic cottages and tree-lined streets. However, it is better known for its miniature golf courses, bumper boats, video arcades, and souvenir shops.

This is not the sort of place most people imagine when they dream about the Oregon coast, and if you're looking for a quiet, romantic weekend getaway, Seaside is *not* the place. As one of the closest beaches to Portland, crowds and traffic are a way of life on summer weekends. The town is also a very popular conference site, and several of the town's largest hotels cater primarily to this market (and have the outrageous rates

Biking the Oregon Coast

The Oregon coast is one of the nation's best-known bicycle tour routes, ranking right up there with the back roads of Vermont, the Napa Valley, and the San Juan Islands. Cyclists will find breathtaking scenery, interesting towns, parks and beaches to explore, wide shoulders, and well-spaced places to stay. You can stay in campgrounds (all state-park campgrounds have hiker/biker campsites) or in hotels. If you can afford it, an inn-to-inn pedal down this coast is the way to go; as you slowly grind your way up hill after hill, you'll appreciate not having to carry camping gear.

The entire route, from Astoria to California, covers between 368 and 378 miles (depending on your route) and includes a daunting 16,000 total feet of climbing. Although most of the route is on U.S. 101, which is a 55-mph highway for most of its length, the designated coast route leaves the highway for less crowded and more scenic roads whenever possible.

During the summer, when winds are generally out of the northwest, you'll have the wind at your back if you ride from north to south. In the winter (when you'll likely get very wet), you're better off riding from south to north to take advantage of winds out of the southwest. Planning a trip along the coast in winter is not advisable; even though there is less traffic, winter storms frequently blow in with winds of up to 100 mph.

For a map and guide to bicycling the Oregon coast, contact the **Oregon Department of Transportation** (© **503/986-3555;** www.odot.state.or.us/techserv/bikewalk). You might also want to get a copy of the *Umbrella Guide to Bicycling the Oregon Coast* (Umbrella Books, 1990), by Robin Cody.

to prove it). However, the nearby community of Gearhart, which has long been a retreat for wealthy Portlanders, is as quiet as any town you'll find on this coast.

ESSENTIALS

GETTING THERE   Seaside is on U.S. 101 just north of the junction with U.S. 26, which connects to Portland.

VISITOR INFORMATION   Contact the **Seaside Chamber of Commerce,** 7 N. Roosevelt St., Seaside, OR 97138 (© **888/306-2326** or 503/738-3097; www.seasideor.com).

FESTIVALS   The weekend before Labor Day weekend, the **Hood to Coast Run** celebration is held in Seaside.

ENJOYING THE BEACH & SEASIDE'S OTHER ATTRACTIONS

Seaside's centerpiece is its 2-mile-long beachfront **Promenade** (or Prom), built in 1921. At the west end of Broadway, the Turnaround divides the walkway into the North Prom and the South Prom. Here a bronze statue marks the official end of the trail for the Lewis and Clark expedition. South of this statue on Lewis & Clark Way between the Promenade and Beach Drive, 8 blocks south of Broadway, you'll find the **Lewis and Clark Salt Works,** a reconstruction of a fire pit used by members of the famous expedition. During the winter of 1805–06, while the expedition was camped at Fort Clatsop, near present-day Astoria, Lewis and Clark sent several men southwest 15 miles to a good spot for making salt from seawater. It took three men nearly 2 months to produce 4 bushels of salt for the return trip east. Five kettles were used for boiling seawater, and the fires were kept stoked 24 hours a day.

History is not what attracts most people to Seaside, though. Rather, it's the miles of **white-sand beach** that begin just south of Seaside at the foot of the imposing Tillamook Head and stretch north to the mouth of the Columbia River. Though the waters here are quite cold and only a few people venture in farther than knee-deep, there are lifeguards on duty all summer, which is one reason Seaside is popular with families. At the south end of Seaside beach is one of the best surf breaks on the north coast. You can rent a board and wetsuit at **Cleanline Surf,** 719 First Ave. (© 503/ 738-7888; www.cleanlinesurf.com). A complete rental package runs $35 a day. You can also rent body boards here.

But because of the cold water, kite flying, beach cycling, and other nonaquatic activities prove far more popular than swimming or surfing. All over town there are places that rent four-wheeled bicycles, called surreys, and three-wheeled cycles (funcycles) for pedaling on the beach. The latter are the most popular and the most fun, but can really be used only when the tide is out and the beach is firm enough to pedal on. Cycles go for between $10 and $15 an hour, and multipassenger surreys rent for between $20 and $40 an hour. Try **Wheel Fun Rentals,** 407 S. Holladay Dr. (© 503/ 738-8447; www.wheelfunrentals.com), which has a second location at 153 Avenue A.

If you prefer hiking to cycling, head south of town to the end of Sunset Boulevard, where you'll find the start of the **Tillamook Head Trail,** which leads 6 miles over the headland to Indian Beach in **Ecola State Park.** This trail goes through shady forests of firs and red cedars with a few glimpses of the Pacific along the way.

Golfers can play a round at the 9-hole **Seaside Golf Club,** 451 Ave. U (© 503/ 738-5261), which charges $10 to $12 for 9 holes; another 9-hole course, **The Highlands at Gearhart,** 1 Highlands Rd. (© 503/738-5248), also charges $12 for 9 holes. However, the area's best course is the **Gearhart Golf Links,** on North Marion Street in Gearhart (© 800/547-0115 or 503/738-3538; http://gearhartgolflinks.com), where you'll pay $45 to $55 for 18 holes. This course was established in 1892, which makes it the oldest golf course in Oregon.

The **Seaside Aquarium,** 200 N. Promenade (© 503/738-6211; www.seaside aquarium.com), where you can feed seals, is popular. Admission is $7 for adults, $5.75 for seniors, and $3.50 for children ages 6 to 13. In a big case visible from outside the aquarium, there is a 36-foot-long gray whale skeleton. Kids will also enjoy the gaudily painted **carousel** at the Seaside Town Center Mall at 300 Broadway.

WHERE TO STAY
IN SEASIDE

The Gilbert Inn 𝕲𝕲   One block from the beach and 1 block south of Broadway, on the edge of both the shopping district and one of Seaside's old residential neighborhoods, the Gilbert Inn is a big yellow Queen Anne–style Victorian house with a pretty little yard. Alexander Gilbert, who had this house built in 1892, was once the mayor of Seaside, and he built a stately home worthy of someone in such a high position. Gilbert made good use of the area's plentiful fir trees; the interior walls and ceilings are constructed of tongue-and-groove fir planks. The inn is decorated in country French decor that enhances the Victorian ambience.

341 Beach Dr., Seaside, OR 97138. © 800/410-9770 or 503/738-9770. Fax 503/717-1070. www.gilbertinn.com. 10 units. $89–$115 double; $105–$125 suite. 2-night minimum on weekends, 3-night on minimum on holiday weekends. Rates include full breakfast. AE, DISC, MC, V. *In room:* TV/DVD, hair dryer, iron, free local calls, Wi-Fi.

Inn of the Four Winds ⊹   You'll find this little oceanfront hotel up at the north end of the Promenade, away from all the activity in the center of town but still only a short walk from good restaurants. Most guest rooms have balconies, ocean views, and gas fireplaces. There are also large suites. All the rooms have a vaguely Italianate style, though it's obvious the decorator was on a tight budget. Some suites have kitchens. Keep in mind that although this hotel is right on the beach, it's a very wide beach.

820 N. Promenade, Seaside, OR 97138. © 800/818-9524 or 503/738-9524. http://innofthefourwinds.com. 14 units. $109–$179 double. AE, DC, DISC, MC, V. **Amenities:** Massage. *In room:* TV/DVD, fridge, coffeemaker, hair dryer.

IN GEARHART

Gearhart Ocean Inn ⊹ *Value*   This old motor-court-style motel offers modest and economical accommodations that have been renovated with the sort of care usually reserved for historic homes. A taupe exterior with blue-and-white trim gives the two rows of wooden buildings a touch of sophistication, and roses, Adirondack chairs, and little pocket gardens add character to the grounds. The rooms all have lots of character and have been decorated in a mix of country cute and casual contemporary. Some rooms have kitchens and/or fireplaces.

67 N. Cottage St. (P.O. Box 2161), Gearhart, OR 97138. © 800/352-8034 or 503/738-7373. Fax 503/717-8008. www.gearhartoceaninn.com. 12 units. $55–$135 double. Children under 2 stay free in parent's room. AE, DC, DISC, MC, V. Pets accepted ($15 fee). **Amenities:** Access to nearby health club; bikes; guest laundry. *In room:* TV/VCR, fridge, coffeemaker, free local calls.

WHERE TO DINE
IN SEASIDE

If you're looking for a quick meal, some picnic food, or something to take back and cook in your room, drop by the old-timey **Bell Buoy Crab Co.**, 1800 S. Roosevelt St. (© **503/738-6348**), which sells not only cooked Dungeness crabs, but award-winning chowder, smoked salmon, fresh seafood, and shrimp or crab melts. For good coffee and baked goods, head south of downtown Seaside to **Corpenny's Coffee House & Bakery**, 2281 Beach Dr. (© **503/738-7353**).

Goose Hollow at the Cove ⊹ *Finds* AMERICAN   The neon sign in the front window proclaims "the best Reuben in the universe," and if you've ever had the Reuben at the original Goose Hollow in Portland, you know enough not to argue with this claim. This casual south Seaside restaurant is hands-down my favorite lunch spot in the area. In fact, I would drive miles to have one of those awesome Reubens.

220 Ave. U. © 503/717-1940. Main courses $6.25–$13. AE, DISC, MC, V. Sun–Thurs 11:30am–10pm; Fri–Sat 11:30am–11pm.

Lil' Bayou ⊹ CAJUN   If cool damp weather has you craving some warming, spicy food, hit the Bayou. I like the crawfish étouffée and the crawfish pie, but you can also get good jambalaya and gumbo. If you like oysters, try the Rockefella oyster stew, but be sure to save room for the sweet-potato pecan pie. The adjacent Magnolia Lounge likes to keep a Mardi Gras spirit going all year round.

20 N. Holladay Dr. © 503/717-0624. www.lilbayou.com. Reservations recommended. Main courses $13–$28. MC, V. Sun–Mon and Tues–Thurs 11:30am–3:30pm and 4:30–9pm; Fri–Sat 11:30am–3:30pm and 4:30–10pm.

Vista Sea Café *&* PIZZA/SANDWICHES   Whether you're in the mood for pizza or soup and a sandwich, you can't go wrong here. High-backed antique booths and big windows that let in plenty of sunshine in the summer make this a cheerful spot. Whatever you do, don't leave without trying the clam chowder, which is served with delicious homemade beer bread. On the pizza menu you'll find creations such as a tasty pesto pizza and bay shrimp pizza.

150 Broadway. *☎* **503/738-8108.** Pizzas $12–$24; sandwiches $6.25–$8.50. AE, DISC, MC, V. Summer daily 11:30am–8pm (open fewer days and shorter hours in winter).

IN GEARHART
Pacific Way Cafe and Bakery *&* *Finds* SANDWICHES/NORTHWEST   This former mom-and-pop grocery store is in the center of Gearhart and has such a classic old-fashioned Cape Cod–style beach feel that it's well worth searching out. The vintage interior of the restaurant harkens to the 1930s. At lunch, there are appetizing sandwiches and salads. In the evening, try the wild mushroom macaroni and cheese or the prosciutto-wrapped scallops, if either is on the menu. There's an adjacent bakery open Saturday and Sunday from 7am to 1pm.

601 Pacific Way. *☎* **503/738-0245.** Main dishes $9–$13 lunch, $13–$27 dinner. MC, V. Thurs–Mon 11am–3:30pm and 5–9pm.

3 Cannon Beach *★★★*

7 miles S of Seaside, 112 miles N of Newport, 79 miles W of Portland

When most people dream of a vacation on the Oregon coast, chances are they're thinking of a place such as **Cannon Beach:** weathered cedar-shingle buildings, picket fences behind drifts of nasturtiums, quiet gravel lanes, interesting little art galleries, and massive rock monoliths rising from the surf just off the wide sandy beach. If it weren't for all the other people who think Cannon Beach is a wonderful place, this town would be perfect. However, Cannon Beach is suffering from its own quaintness and the inevitable upscaling that ensues when a place begins to gain national recognition. Once the Oregon coast's most renowned artists' community, Cannon Beach is now going the way of California's Carmel—lots of upscale shopping tucked away in utterly tasteful little plazas along a neatly manicured main street. Despite the crowds, it still has a village atmosphere, and summer throngs and traffic jams can do nothing to assault the fortresslike beauty of the rocks that lie just offshore.

ESSENTIALS
GETTING THERE   Cannon Beach is on U.S. 101 just south of the junction with U.S. 26.

VISITOR INFORMATION   Contact the **Cannon Beach Chamber of Commerce,** 207 N. Spruce St. (P.O. Box 64), Cannon Beach, OR 97110 (*☎* **503/ 436-2623;** www.cannonbeach.org).

GETTING AROUND   The **Cannon Beach Shuttle,** which provides free van service up and down the length of town, operates daily with seasonal hours. Watch for signed shuttle stops. Donations for the ride are accepted.

FESTIVALS   Each year in late April, the **Puffin Kite Festival** fills the skies over Cannon Beach with colorful kites and features stunt kite-flying exhibitions. In early June, the **Sand Castle Day** contest turns the beach into one vast canvas for sand sculptors

> (*Fun Fact* **Cannon Beach Trivia**
>
> • Cannon Beach was named for a cannon that washed ashore after the U.S. Navy schooner *Shark* wrecked on the coast north of here in 1846.
> • Cannon Beach's Haystack Rock, which rises 235 feet above the water, is the most photographed monolith on the Oregon coast.
> • The offshore rocks are protected nesting grounds for sea birds. Watch for tufted puffins, something of a Cannon Beach mascot.
> • Tillamook Rock is the site of the **Tillamook Rock Lighthouse** (aka "Terrible Tilly"), which was subject to huge storm waves that occasionally sent large rocks crashing through the light, 133 feet above sea level. The lighthouse was decommissioned in 1957 and is now used as a columbarium (a vault for the interment of the ashes of people who have been cremated).

from all over the region, and in early November, the **Stormy Weather Arts Festival** celebrates the arrival of winter storms.

HITTING THE BEACH

Ecola State Park ⊛⊛ (© 800/551-6949 or 503/436-2844), just north of the town of Cannon Beach, marks the southernmost point that Lewis and Clark explored on the Oregon coast. The park offers the most breathtaking vantage point from which to soak up the view of Cannon Beach, Haystack Rock, and the Tillamook Rock Lighthouse. The park also has several picnic areas perched on bluffs high above the crashing waves and a trail that leads 6 miles over Tillamook Head to Seaside. The 1-mile stretch of trail between the main bluff-top picnic area and Indian beach is particularly rewarding, passing through old-growth forests and offering good views of the ocean and beaches far below. There's also the 2.5-mile Clatsop Loop Trail, which leads through dense forest to a viewpoint high on Tillamook Head. The day-use fee is $3 per vehicle.

Kite flying and beachcombing are the most popular Cannon Beach pastimes. But you can also enjoy the beach a variety of other ways, too. Between mid-May and Labor Day, guided horseback rides to Cove Beach and Haystack Rock are offered by **Sea Ranch Stables,** 415 Fir St. (© 503/436-2815; www.cannon-beach.net/searanch), which is at the north entrance to Cannon Beach. Rides cost $45 to $80, and you must drop by the stables and make a reservation.

Another great way to see the beach is from a funcycle, a three-wheeled beach cycle. These cycles enable you to ride up and down the beach at low tide. Funcycles can be rented from **Mike's Bike Shop,** 248 N. Spruce St. (© 800/492-1266 or 503/436-1266; www.mikesbike.com) for $10 for an hour and a half. Mountain bikes and road bikes are also available for rent from Mike's.

Three miles south of town is **Arcadia Beach Wayside** ⊛, one of the prettiest little beaches on the north coast; and another mile farther south you'll find **Hug Point State Recreation Site** ⊛, which has picnic tables, a sheltered beach, and the remains of an old road that was cut into the rock face of this headland. **Oswald West State Park** ⊛⊛, 10 miles south of Cannon Beach, is one of my favorites of all the parks on the Oregon coast. A short paved trail leads to a driftwood-strewn cobblestone beach on a small cove. Headlands on either side of the cove can be reached by hiking trails that offer splendid views. The waves here are popular with surfers, and there's a walk-in campground.

EXPLORING THE TOWN

For many Cannon Beach visitors, **shopping** is the town's greatest attraction. In the heart of town, along Hemlock Street, you'll find dozens of densely packed small shops and galleries offering original art, fine crafts, unusual gifts, and casual fashions. Galleries worth seeking out include **Northwest by Northwest,** 232 N. Spruce St. (© **800/494-0741** or 503/436-0741; http://nwbynwgallery.com), which features works by established Northwest artists; **White Bird Gallery,** 251 N. Hemlock St. (© **503/436-2681;** www.whitebirdgallery.com), a good gallery for colorful contemporary art and fine crafts. **Icefire Glassworks,** 116 E. Gower St. (© **503/436-2359**), a glassblowing studio south of downtown; and **Cannon Beach Gallery,** 1064 S. Hemlock St. (© **503/436-0744;** www.cannonbeacharts.org), which is across the street from Icefire and is operated by a local arts organization and mounts shows in a wide variety of styles not usually seen in other Cannon Beach galleries (which tend to be heavy on beach landscapes). On the surface, Cannon Beach may not look as though it has much history, but from Lewis and Clark's visit to the cannon that washed up on shore and gave the town its name, there is a bit to learn about this town's past. Visit the **Cannon Beach Historical Society,** 1387 S. Spruce St. (© **503/436-9301;** www.cbhistory.org), where modern, well-designed exhibits tell the story of the town's past, including the history of tourism here.

Want to turn a Cannon Beach getaway into a truly relaxing escape? Book a massage or a skin or hydrotherapy treatment at the **Cannon Beach Spa,** 232-b N. Spruce St. (© **888/577-8772** or 503/436-8772; www.cannonbeachspa.com). Prices run around $85 for an hour massage.

WHERE TO STAY

If you're heading here with the whole family or plan to stay awhile, consider renting a house, a cottage, or an apartment. Offerings range from studio apartments to large luxurious oceanfront houses, and prices span an equally wide range. Contact **Cannon Beach Property Management** (© **877/386-3402** or 503/436-2021; www.cbpm.com) for more information.

EXPENSIVE

Arch Cape House 🏖️🏖️ *Finds*   If you can't find time in your schedule for that trip to France this year, a stay at St. Bernard's will provide a reasonable facsimile. Although the setting, just off U.S. 101 between Cannon Beach and Manzanita, won't convince you that you're in Provence, the building itself is as grand a manor house as any in France. Incorporating elements from castles and châteaux, it's straight out of a fairy tale. European antiques, original art, and an abundance of tapestry-cloth furnishings fill the house. Each of the rooms fulfills a different fantasy of the perfect romantic escape. There is the circular Tower Room, with its own soaking tub; the Gauguin, filled with reproductions of paintings by you-know-who; and the Tapestry Room, with a stained-glass ceiling and an ocean view from the soaking tub. Lavish, three-course breakfasts are served in the conservatory. So luxurious is this place that the fact that you aren't right on the beach doesn't even seem to matter.

31970 E. Ocean Lane, Arch Cape, OR 97102. © **800/436-2848** or 503/436-2800. Fax 503/436-1206. www.archcape house.com. 8 units. $129–$209 double. Rates include full breakfast and evening wine social hour. AE, DISC, MC, V. **Amenities:** Sauna; concierge. *In room:* TV/VCR, fridge, dataport, hair dryer, iron.

The Ocean Lodge 🐟🐟🐟   Located right next door to the luxurious Stephanie Inn, this lodge is every bit as deluxe, but boasts a more laid-back, vintage Northwest feel. The lobby has huge rough-cut timber beams and warm wood tones. All rooms are spacious suites with fireplaces and decks, most have in-room Jacuzzis, and some boast good views of Haystack Rock—if you can afford the premium, the views are well worth requesting. Ground-floor oceanfront rooms also have direct access to the beach. The lodge's beach bungalows are across the street and some are up two flights of stairs.

2864 S. Pacific St. P.O. Box 1037, Cannon Beach, OR 97110. © **888/777-4047** or 503/436-2241.www.theocean lodge.com. 45 units. Late June to mid-Oct $219–$299 double; lower rates other months. Rates include continental breakfast. AE, DC, DISC, MC, V. Pets accepted ($15). **Amenities:** Access to nearby health club. *In room:* TV/DVD, dataport, fridge, coffeemaker, hair dryer, iron.

Stephanie Inn 🐟🐟🐟   The Stephanie Inn is the most classically romantic inn on the Oregon coast—the perfect place for an anniversary or other special weekend away. With flower boxes beneath the windows and neatly manicured gardens by the entry, the inn is reminiscent of New England's country inns, but the beach out the back door is definitely of Pacific Northwest origin. Inside, the lobby feels warm and cozy with its river-rock fireplace, huge wood columns, and beamed ceiling. The guest rooms, all individually decorated, are equally cozy, and most have double whirlpool tubs and gas fireplaces. The higher you go in the three-story inn, the better the views and the more spacious the outdoor spaces (patios, balconies, and decks). A bounteous breakfast buffet is served each morning, and there is also a complimentary afternoon wine gathering. Creative four-course prix-fixe dinners ($44) are served in the evening (reservations are required).

2740 S. Pacific St. (P.O. Box 219), Cannon Beach, OR 97110. © **800/633-3466** or 503/436-2221. www.stephanie-inn. com. 50 units. $199–$399 double; $409–$469 suite. Rates include full breakfast. Children over 12 are welcome. AE, DC, DISC, MC, V. **Amenities:** Restaurant (Northwest); access to nearby health club; courtesy shopping shuttle; room service; massage. *In room:* A/C, TV/DVD, coffeemaker, hair dryer.

MODERATE

Cannon Beach Hotel Lodgings 🐟   Although not in the town's best location (there are parking lots all around), this hotel manages to capture Cannon Beach's spirit economically. A white picket fence, green shutters, and cedar-shingle siding give the hotel plenty of character, while inside you'll find attractively furnished rooms that vary in size and price. The best rooms are those with fireplaces and whirlpool tubs, and two of these have partial ocean views. Rooms are also available in three nearby buildings, with some of these rooms being more luxurious than those in the main hotel.

1116 S. Hemlock St. (P.O. Box 943), Cannon Beach, OR 97110. © **800/238-4107** or 503/436-1392. Fax 503/ 436-1396. www.cannonbeachhotel.com. 37 units. Mid-July to Sept $69–$230 double; Oct–Nov and Mar to mid-June $45–$160 double; Dec–Feb $40–$140 double. Rates include continental breakfast (for rooms in hotel only). Children 10 and under stay free in parent's room. AE, DC, DISC, MC, V. Pets accepted in 1 building ($15 per night). **Amenities:** Restaurant (Northwest); room service. *In room:* TV, free local calls.

Hallmark Resort 🐟 *Kids*   Situated on a bluff with a head-on view of Haystack Rock, the Hallmark appeals primarily to families, and a wide range of rates reflects the variety of rooms available. The lowest rates are for nonview standard rooms, and the highest rates are for oceanfront two-bedroom suites. Between these extremes are all manner of rooms, studios, and suites. The best values are the limited-view rooms, many of which have fireplaces and comfortable chairs set up to take in what little view there might be. Some rooms also have kitchens.

1400 S. Hemlock St. (P.O. Box 547), Cannon Beach, OR 97110. ✆ **888/448-4449** or 503/436-1566. Fax 503/ 436-0324. www.hallmarkinns.com. 142 units. $79–$219 double; $134–$229 suite. AE, DC, DISC, MC, V. Pets accepted ($20). **Amenities:** 2 indoor pools; exercise room; 3 Jacuzzis; concierge; massage; coin-op laundry. *In room:* TV/VCR, fridge, coffeemaker, hair dryer, iron, free local calls, high-speed Internet access.

The Waves/The Argonauta Inn/White Heron Lodge ✿✿ Variety is the name of the game in eclectic Cannon Beach, and The Waves plays the game better than any other accommodation in town. This lodge, only a block from the heart of Cannon Beach, consists of more than four dozen rooms, suites, cottages, and beach houses. The Garden Court rooms (with no ocean views) are the least expensive. My favorites, however, are the cottages of The Argonauta Inn. Surrounded by beautiful flower gardens in the summer, these old oceanfront cottages capture the spirit of Cannon Beach. For sybarites and romantics, there are fireplaces in some rooms and whirlpool spas overlooking the ocean. If you want to get away from the crowds, ask for an apartment at the recently renovated White Heron Lodge. The Waves itself offers contemporary accommodations, some of which are right on the beach and have great views.

188 W. Second St. (P.O. Box 3), Cannon Beach, OR 97110. ✆ **800/822-2468** or 503/436-2205. Fax 503/436-1490. www.thewavesmotel.com. 55 units. The Waves $84–$199 double $179–399 suite; White Heron Lodge $199–$279; Argonauta: $89–399 suite. 3-night minimum July–Aug; 2-night minimum on weekends Sept–June. Children under 6 stay free in parent's room. DISC, MC, V. **Amenities:** Jacuzzi; massage; coin-op laundry. *In room:* TV/VCR, dataport, kitchen, fridge, coffeemaker, hair dryer, iron, free local calls.

CAMPGROUNDS

Despite the fact that **Oswald West State Park,** which is south of Cannon Beach, is the only area state park campground with walk-in campsites, the sites are closer together than those at most car campgrounds. Don't say I didn't warn you if the guy in the next campsite keeps you up all night with his snoring. At the north end of town, the **Sea Ranch R.V. Park & Stables,** 415 Fir St. (P.O. Box 214), Cannon Beach, OR 97110 (✆ **503/436-2815;** www.cannon-beach.net/searanch), offers sites for RVs and tents. The campground is green and shady and is right across the street from the road to Ecola State Park. Rates range from $23 to $27 per night. There are also some small cabins for rent for $70 to $80 per night. You can also try **Wright's for Camping,** P.O. Box 213, Cannon Beach, OR 97110 (✆ **503/436-2347;** www.wrightsforcamping.com), which is set back in the trees on the inland side of the road at the second Cannon Beach exit off U.S. 101 and charges $20 for campsites. At either of these, you'll need to make reservations at least a month in advance for summer weekends.

WHERE TO DINE

For good locally brewed beer, visit **Bill's Tavern & Brewhouse,** 188 N. Hemlock St. (✆ 503/436-2202). For good espresso, try **Bella Espresso,** 231 Hemlock St. (✆ 503/ 436-2595; www.bella-espresso.com), or **Sleepy Monk Coffee,** 1235 S. Hemlock St. (✆ 503/436-2796; http://sleepymonkcoffee.com), which specializes in organic coffee. For cookies, head to the **Cannon Beach Cookie Co.,** 239 Hemlock St. (✆ 503/436-1129). If you just want a sandwich, try **Café Acajou,** 255 N. Hemlock St., Suite A2 (✆ 503/436-1116). If you're looking for some wine for your romantic weekend, stop in at **The Wine Shack,** 124 Hemlock St. (✆ 503/436-1100; www.beachwine.com), or **Laurel's Cannon Beach Wine Shop,** 263 N. Hemlock St. (✆ 503/436-1666).

Bistro Restaurant ☆☆ NORTHWEST   If you're looking for atmosphere and good food, this is the place. Bistro Restaurant is set back a bit from the street behind a small garden and down a brick walkway. Step through the door and you'll think you've just walked into a French country inn. Stucco walls, old prints of flowers, and fresh flowers on the tables are the only decor this tiny place can afford without growing cramped. Dining choices here include exquisitely prepared seafood dishes such as pan-fried oysters, crab cakes, and seafood stew. There's live music on weekend evenings, and even a tiny bar.

263 N. Hemlock St. ☎ 503/436-2661. Reservations highly recommended. Main courses $14–$24. MC, V. Daily 5–9:30pm or 10pm; closed Tues–Wed in off season.

Café Mango ☆ ECLECTIC   Upstairs from some shops and galleries at the sound end of downtown Cannon Beach, you'll find a wonderful little cafe that's a great spot for breakfast or lunch. Buckwheat crepes are the specialty here and come in both sweet and savory varieties. The smoked salmon and feta cheese crepe is one of my favorites. At breakfast, you can also get scones and croissants. Just in case you're wondering, mangos do indeed show up on the menu here. If you're not in the mood for crepes, you can get Mexican breakfasts and burritos. Dinners are also served and can be very creative. Try the salmon with mango salsa.

123 S. Hemlock St. ☎ 503/436-2393. www.cafe-mango.com. Main courses $4–$11 breakfast, $14–$28 dinner. Reservations recommended for dinner. MC, V. Summer daily 9am–10pm; other months Thurs and Sun–Mon 9am–2:30pm, Fri–Sat 9am–2:30pm and 5–9pm.

Gower Street Bistro ☆☆ NEW AMERICAN   This little restaurant is positively adorable. The white-tile floors, wicker chairs, white wainscoting, pressed-tin ceiling, and display case full of imported meats and cheese all set the scene for superb food. The quiches (served at breakfast, lunch, and dinner) are big, fat works of art that should not be missed, although I can never pass up the pulled-pork sandwich, which is the best I've had outside of North Carolina. At dinner, start with a charcuterie or cheese plate and then go for the 40-clove chicken with calvados or the down-home meatloaf.

1116 S. Hemlock St. ☎ 503/436-2729. www.gowerstreetbistro.com. Reservations recommended. Main courses $9–$13 lunch, $10–$30 dinner. AE, DISC, MC, V. Summer daily 8am–10pm; other months daily 9am–9pm.

EN ROUTE TO OR FROM PORTLAND

If you'd like to see a large herd of **Roosevelt elk,** watch for the Jewell turnoff about 37 miles before reaching Cannon Beach on U.S. 26. From the turnoff, continue 10 miles north following the wildlife-viewing signs to the **Jewell Meadows Wildlife Area** ☆☆ (☎ 503/755-2264; www.dfw.state.or.us/wildlifearea/jewellmeodows.htm) where there's a large meadow frequented in the cooler months by up to 300 elk. Although November through March are the best months to see the elk, September and October are rutting season and, at this time, big bulls can often be heard bugling and seen locking antlers. Summer is not usually a reliable time for seeing the elk, but in June, you may see elk cows with calves. During the winter, the elk are provided with supplemental hay to keep the herd healthy, and it is possible to assist in the daily feeding. Participants are taken out into the meadows on a flatbed trailer loaded with hay, which is then tossed out to the expectant elk. To participate, however, you'll need to call on the morning of December 1 to make your reservation. (Weekends fill up the fastest.)

Twelve miles past the U.S. 26 turnoff for Jewell, you'll find **Saddle Mountain State Natural Area** ☆☆, which is a favorite day hike in the area. A strenuous 2.5-mile trail leads to the top of Saddle Mountain, from which there are breathtaking views up and down the coast. In the spring, rare wildflowers are abundant along this trail. The trail is steep and rocky, so wear sturdy shoes or boots and carry water.

WHERE TO DINE

Camp 18 Restaurant ⚓ AMERICAN   There is no better place than this combination restaurant and logging museum to learn how logging was done in the days before clear-cutting. The restaurant is in a huge log lodge with lots of chain-saw art, axes for door handles, and a hollowed-out stump for a hostess desk. The restaurant's 85-foot-long ridge pole, the log beam that runs along the inside of the peak of the roof, is the largest of its kind in the country, and weighs 25 tons. There are also stone fireplaces and lots of old logging photos. After tucking into logger-size meals (don't miss the marionberry cobbler), you can wander the grounds studying old steam logging equipment. A gift shop sells logging-oriented souvenirs. Oh, and the food? Basic steak and seafood, mostly fried, with a few pasta and chicken dishes thrown in.

42362 U.S. 26 (Milepost 18, 22 miles east of Seaside). ℭ **800/874-1810** or 503/755-1818. Main courses $5–$12 lunch, $14–$23 dinner. AE, DISC, MC, V. Sun–Thurs 7am–8pm; Fri–Sat 7am–9pm.

4 Tillamook County

75 miles W of Portland, 51 miles S of Seaside, 44 miles N of Lincoln City

Although this is one of the closest stretches of coast to Portland, it is not a major destination because there are no large beachfront towns in the area. The town of Tillamook, which lies inland from the Pacific at the south end of Tillamook Bay, is the area's commercial center, but it is the surrounding farmland that has made Tillamook County famous in Oregon. Ever since the first settlers arrived in Tillamook in 1851, dairy farming has been the mainstay of the economy, and today large herds of contented cows graze in the area's odiferous fields. With no beaches to attract visitors, the town of Tillamook has managed to turn its dairy industry into a tourist attraction. No, this isn't the cow-watching capital of Oregon, but the town's cheese factory is now one of the most popular stops along the Oregon coast. Most of the milk produced by area cows goes to the Tillamook County Creamery Association's cheese factory, which turns out a substantial share of the cheese consumed in Oregon.

Although Tillamook town has no beaches, there are a few beachside hamlets in the area that offer a variety of accommodations, activities, and dining options. Tillamook is also the starting point for the scenic Three Capes Loop, which links three state parks and plenty of great coastal scenery. By the way, Tillamook is a mispronunciation of the word *Killamook,* which was the name of the Native American tribe that once lived in this area. The name is now applied to a county, a town, and a bay.

ESSENTIALS

GETTING THERE   Tillamook is on U.S. 101 at the junction with Ore. 6, which leads to Portland.

VISITOR INFORMATION   For more information on the area, contact the **Tillamook Chamber of Commerce,** 3705 U.S. 101 N., Tillamook, OR 97141 (ℭ **503/ 842-7525;** www.tillamookchamber.org); or the **Nehalem Bay Area Chamber of Commerce,** P.O. Box 601, Wheeler, OR 97147 (ℭ **877/368-5100;** www.nehalembay chamber.com).

MANZANITA

As the crowds have descended on Cannon Beach, people seeking peace and quiet and a slower pace have migrated south to the community of Manzanita. Located south of Neahkanie Mountain, Manzanita enjoys a setting similar to Cannon Beach but without the many haystack rocks. There isn't much to do here except walk on the beach and relax, which is exactly why most people come here.

The beach at Manzanita stretches for 5 miles from the base of Neahkanie Mountain to the mouth of the Nehalem River and is a favorite of both surfers and windsurfers. The latter have the option of sailing either in the oceanfront waves or in the quieter waters of Nehalem Bay, which is just across Nehalem Spit from the ocean. Access to both the bay and the beach is provided at **Nehalem Bay State Park** (© **503/368-5154**), which is just south of Manzanita and encompasses all of Nehalem Spit. The park, which includes a campground (and an airstrip), has a 2-mile paved bike path, a horse camp, and horse trails. The day-use fee is $3. During the summer, horseback rides are usually available here in the park. Out at the south end of the spit, more than 50 harbor seals can often be seen lounging on the beach. To reach the seal area requires a 5-mile round-trip hike. Alternatively, you can take a brief seal-watching boat excursion through **Jetty Fishery** (see below).

If you absolutely must do something while you're here, you could play a round of golf on the meandering fairways of the 9-hole **Manzanita Golf Course,** Lake View Drive (© **503/368-5744**), which charges $15 for 9 holes.

WHERE TO STAY

If you want to rent a vacation house in Manzanita, contact **Manzanita Rental Company,** 686 Manzanita Ave. (P.O. Box 162), Manzanita, OR 97130 (© **800/579-9801** or 503/368-6797; www.manzanitarentals.com).

Coast Cabins 🐾🐾 *(Finds)*   These five modern cabins are set back a ways from the beach but are the most impressive cabins on the entire coast. Done in a sort of modern interpretation of Scandinavian cabins, these accommodations are designed as romantic getaways for couples. Two of the cabins are tall, two-story structures, and the second-floor bedrooms have walls of windows. The cabin interiors are well designed and artfully decorated, with such touches as Tibetan carpets, original art, and unusual lighting fixtures. Now, imagine the burnished glow of the cabins' cedar exteriors accented by lovely terraced perennial gardens, and you'll have an idea of just how the perfect getaway on the Oregon coast should look.

635 Laneda Ave., Manzanita, OR 97130. © **503/368-7113.** www.coastcabins.com. 5 units. $110–$295 double. 2-night minimum on weekends and throughout the summer. AE, MC, V. Pets accepted ($25). *In room:* TV/VCR, kitchen, fridge, coffeemaker, hair dryer, iron, free local calls, Wi-Fi.

The Inn at Manzanita 🐾🐾   Searching for an unforgettably romantic spot for a weekend getaway? This is it. Right in the heart of Manzanita, the Inn at Manzanita is a great place to celebrate a special event. All the rooms have double whirlpool tubs and fireplaces, and most rooms have balconies that look out through the pine trees to the ocean. The weathered cedar-shingle siding blends unobtrusively with the natural vegetation, and the grounds are planted with beautiful flowers for much of the year.

67 Laneda Ave. (P.O. Box 243), Manzanita, OR 97130. © **503/368-6754.** Fax 503/368-5941. www.innatmanzanita. com. 13 units. $120–$170 double (lower off-season midweek rates available). 2-night minimum on weekends and July 1 to Labor Day; 3 nights on some holidays. MC, V. No children accepted. **Amenities:** Bike rental; concierge. *In room:* TV/DVD, fridge, coffeemaker, hair dryer, free local calls, Wi-Fi.

WHERE TO DINE

Do not visit Manzanita without buying some bread, pastries, or gourmet food to go from **Bread and Ocean,** 387 Laneda Ave. (© **503/368-5823**). This little hole-in-the-wall is the perfect place to put together a picnic for the beach. For lattes and the latest news, head to **Manzanita News & Espresso,** 500 Laneda Ave. (© **503/368-7450**). For fresh and smoked seafood to go, or for a light meal, stop in at **Manzanita Seafood & Chowder House,** 519 Laneda Ave. (© **503/368-CRAB**). At the end of the day, wind down at **Vino Manzanita,** 387-D Laneda Ave. (© **503/368-VINO**), a very hip little wine bar.

WHEELER

Located on Nehalem Bay, this wide spot in the road has long been popular for crabbing and fishing. However, in recent years it has also become a favorite sea-kayaking locale. The marshes of the bay provide plenty of meandering waterways to explore, and several miles of the Nehalem River can also be easily paddled if the tides are in your favor. You can rent a sea kayak at **Wheeler Marina** (© **503/368-5780**), right on the waterfront in Wheeler or at adjacent **Wheeler on the Bay Lodge & Marina,** 580 Marine Dr. (© **800/469-3204** or 503/368-5858). Rates range from around $15 to $28 per hour and from $28 to $50 per day; higher rates are for double kayaks.

If you're interested in trying your hand at crabbing, contact **Jetty Fishery** (© **800/821-7697** or 503/368-5746; www.jettyfishery.com), located just south of Wheeler at the mouth of the Nehalem River. They rent boats and crab rings and offer dock crabbing. The folks here also offer a ferry service ($6 per person) across the river to Nehalem Bay State Park, where you can often see dozens of harbor seals lying on the beach. You can also sometimes see seals close up if you sit on the jetty rocks at nearby Neadonna, which is just south of Jetty Fishery.

WHERE TO STAY

The Nehalem River Inn ⋆ *Finds*   The Oregon coast is not just about beaches and rocky headlands; it's also about meandering tidal rivers, and this country inn is set on just such a river. Situated a couple of miles off U.S. 101 between Nehalem and Wheeler, the inn is a hideaway par excellence. Accommodations have been redone by young new owners. You can now choose between a room with classic, old-fashioned styling (plus a whirlpool tub beside the bed) and plush contemporary styling. The inn has an excellent restaurant and rents kayaks to guests.

34910 Ore. 53, Nehalem, OR 97131. © 503/368-7708. www.nehalemriverinn.com. 5 units. Summer $99–$150 double; other months $79–$120 double. MC, V. Pets accepted ($50). **Amenities:** Restaurant (Northwest); lounge; Jacuzzi; kayak rentals; concierge; room service. *In room:* TV/VCR, coffeemaker, hair dryer, high-speed Internet access, Wi-Fi.

Wheeler on the Bay Lodge & Marina ⋆   Located right on the shore of Nehalem Bay, this is a great spot for a romantic weekend. One of my favorite rooms on the coast, the Honeymoon Room, has walls of glass looking onto the bay, a private deck, a fireplace, and, best of all, a whirlpool tub with great views. Six of the rooms have spas, and most of these have water views. All the rooms sport distinctive decor.

580 Marine Dr. (P.O. Box 580), Wheeler, OR 97147. © 800/469-3204 or 503/368-5858. Fax 503/368-4204. www.wheeleronthebay.com. 10 units. $80–$145 double. Children 15 and under stay free in parent's room. MC, V. Pets accepted ($10 per night). **Amenities:** Kayak rentals; massage. *In room:* TV/VCR/DVD, dataport, fridge, coffeemaker, hair dryer, iron, free local calls.

CAMPGROUNDS

At **Nehalem Bay State Park,** there are yurts as well as plenty of campsites. To make reservations, contact **ReserveAmerica** (© 800/452-5687; www.reserveamerica.com).

WHERE TO DINE

If you like smoked salmon, don't miss **Karla's Smokehouse** ↗, 2010 U.S. 101 N. (© 503/355-2362), which is at the north end of nearby Rockaway Beach and sells some of the best smoked fish and oysters on the coast. At press time, Karla was talking of retiring, so you may have missed out on the chance to sample her smoked fish by the time you visit the area. For the best breakfasts in Tillamook County, head to **Wanda's Café & Bakery** (© 503/368-8100), which is right on U.S. 101 in Nehalem (watch for it on the left as you come down the hill from Manzanita).

Currents ↗ NORTHWEST The creative food here alone would make this one of my favorite north coast restaurants, but in addition to having great food, Currents has a wonderfully relaxing deck overlooking the Nehalem River. From start to finish, offerings here are exceedingly complex, with flavors running rampant on your taste buds. Start with shrimp-and-squash bisque with truffle crème fraîche, smoked rockfish, and crispy prosciutto or perhaps Moroccan crab cakes. Next, I recommend the braised beef short ribs with truffle-fig tapenade or the grilled rockfish with a crab, fennel, and marscapone crepe. Think sunset dinner, and you'll have an unforgettable meal. Currents is also a fun destination to paddle to if you rented a kayak in nearby Wheeler.

35815 U.S. 101, Nehalem. © 503/368-5557. Main courses $6–$8 lunch, $15–$23 dinner. MC, V. Wed–Sun noon–3pm and 6–9pm.

Nehalem River Inn ↗↗ *Finds* FRENCH/NORTHWEST Set on the banks of the Nehalem River, this restaurant, part of a secluded little country inn, serves some of the best food on the Oregon coast. The menu is contemporary, and although it changes with the seasons, you might start your meal with kabocha squash soup or a salad topped with roast quail and pears. For an entree, try the succulent filet mignon, which might be accompanied by truffled macaroni. The hidden-away location and high caliber of the meals make this restaurant a real find.

34910 Ore. 53 (less than 3 miles off U.S. 101). © 503/368-7708. Reservations highly recommended. Main courses $21–$28. MC, V. Fri–Sat 5:30–8:30pm; Sun–Mon 5:30–8pm. No children allowed.

GARIBALDI

Named (by the local postmaster) in 1879 for Italian patriot Giuseppi Garibaldi, this little town is at the north end of Tillamook Bay and is the region's main sportfishing and crabbing port. If you've got an urge to do some salmon or bottom fishing, this is the place to book a trip. Try **Kerri Lin Charters** (© 503/355-2439) or **Garibaldi Charters** (© 800/900-HOOK or 503/322-0007; www.garibaldicharters.com). Rates are between $75 and $95 for a full day of salmon fishing. Deep-sea halibut fishing will run you about $150 per day. **Whale-watching** and **bird-watching** trips are also offered. At the **Garibaldi Marina,** 302 Mooring Basin Rd. (© 800/383-3828 or 503/322-3312; www.garibaldimarina.com), you can rent boats, tackle, and crab rings, if you want to do some fishing or crabbing on your own.

Garibaldi is also where you'll find the depot for the *Oregon Coast Explorer* (© 800/685-1719 or 503/842-8206; www.potb.org/oregoncoastexplorer.htm), an excursion train that runs along some of the most scenic portions of this section of coast. The train usually runs weekends during the summer. Call to see if it's on track when you visit. The round-trip fare is $13 for adults and $7 for children under 11.

TILLAMOOK

Tillamook has long been known as one of Oregon's foremost dairy regions, and Tillamook cheese is ubiquitous in the state. So it's no surprise that the **Tillamook Cheese Factory,** 4175 Hwy. 101 N. (© **800/542-7290** or 503/815-1300; www. tillamookcheese.com), located just north of Tillamook, is the most popular tourist attraction in town. Visitors can observe the cheese-making process (cheddars are the specialty), and there's also a large store where all manner of cheeses and other edible gifts are available. The factory is open daily from 8am to 8pm from mid-June to Labor Day, and 8am to 6pm from Labor Day to mid-June.

If the Tillamook Cheese Factory seems too crowded for you, head back toward town a mile and you'll see the **Blue Heron Cheese & Wine Company,** 2001 Blue Heron Dr. (© **800/275-0639** or 503/842-8281; www.blueheronoregon.com), which is on the same side of U.S. 101 as the Tillamook Cheese Factory. Located in a big old dairy barn with a flagstone floor, this store stocks the same sort of comestibles as the Tillamook Cheese Factory, though the emphasis here is on brie (which, however, is not made locally). Farm animals make this a good stop for kids. Blue Heron is open daily from 8am to 8pm in summer and 9am to 5pm in winter.

A hangar built during World War II for a fleet of navy blimps is 2 miles south of town off U.S. 101 and lays claim to being the largest freestanding wooden building in the world. Statistics bear this out: It's 250 feet wide, 1,100 feet long, and 170 feet high. The blimp hangar now houses the **Tillamook Air Museum,** 6030 Hangar Rd. (© **503/842-1130;** www.tillamookair.com), which contains more than 30 restored vintage planes, including a P-51 Mustang, a B-25 Mitchell, an F4U-7 Corsair, and a F-14A Tomcat. In summer, the museum is open daily from 9am to 6pm; other months, it's open daily from 10am to 5pm. Admission is $11 for adults, $9.50 for seniors, and $6 for youths 6 to 17.

You can go up in a small plane to see this section of the coast, and you may even see whales. Contact **Tillamook Scenic Air Tours** (© **503/842-1942**), which offers tours in a restored 1942 Stinson Reliant V-77 plane and a 1928 Travel Air open cockpit two-passenger biplane. Flights start at around $50 per person.

Anglers interested in going after salmon or steelhead in Tillamook Bay or area rivers should contact **Fishing Oregon** (© **503/842-5171;** www.fish-oregon.com).

WHERE TO DINE

If you need to stock up your larder for the beach house or are on your way back from a weekend at the beach, don't miss an opportunity to stop in at **Bear Creek Artichokes** (© **503/398-5411**), which is located 11 miles south of Tillamook on U.S. 101. This is one of the few commercial artichoke farms in Oregon and usually has fresh artichokes throughout the summer and fall. The farm stand has lots of other great produce, as well as jams, mustards, and salsas.

THE THREE CAPES SCENIC LOOP

The **Three Capes Scenic Loop** begins just west of downtown Tillamook and leads past Cape Meares, Cape Lookout, and Cape Kiwanda. Together these capes offer some of the most spectacular views on the northern Oregon coast. All three capes are state parks, and all make great whale-watching spots in the spring or storm-watching spots in the winter. To start the loop, follow Third Street out of town and watch for the right turn for Cape Meares State Scenic Viewpoint. This road will take you along the shore of Tillamook Bay and around the north side of Cape Meares, where the resort town of Bayocean once stood. Built early in the 20th century by developers with a dream to create the Atlantic City of the West, Bayocean was constructed at the end of a sand spit that often felt the full force of winter storms. When Bayocean homes began falling into the ocean, folks realized that this wasn't going to be the next Atlantic City. Today there's no sign of the town, but the long sandy beach along the spit is a great place for a walk and a bit of bird-watching.

Just around the tip of the cape, you'll come to **Cape Meares State Scenic Viewpoint,** which is the site of the **Cape Meares Lighthouse.** The lighthouse is open to the public and houses a small museum. The views from atop this rocky headland are superb. Continuing around the cape, you come to the residential community of **Oceanside,** from where you have an excellent view of the **Three Arch Rocks** just off-shore. The beach at Oceanside is a popular spot and is often protected from the wind in the summer. At the north end of the beach, a pedestrian tunnel leads under a headland to a secluded beach. Oceanside is a popular lunch stop for people doing the Three Capes Loop.

Three miles south of Oceanside, you'll come to tiny **Netarts Bay,** which is known for its excellent clamming and crabbing. Continuing south, you come to **Cape Lookout State Park** ✺✺ (© **503/842-4981**), which has a campground, picnic areas, beaches, and several miles of hiking trails. The most breathtaking trail leads 2.5 miles out to the end of Cape Lookout, where, from several hundred feet above the ocean, you can often spot gray whales in the spring and fall. There is a $3 day-use fee here.

Cape Kiwanda ✺✺, which lies just outside the town of Pacific City, is the last of the three capes and is preserved as Cape Kiwanda State Natural Area. At the foot of the cape's sandstone cliffs, you'll find sand dunes and tide pools, and it's possible to scramble up a huge sand dune to the top of the cape for dramatic views of this rugged piece of shoreline. At the base of the cape is the staging area for Pacific City's beach-launched dory fleet. These flat-bottomed commercial fishing boats are launched from the beach and plow through crashing breakers to get out to calmer waters beyond. When the day's fishing is done, the dories roar into shore at full throttle and come to a grinding stop as high up on the beach as they can. This is Oregon's only such fishing fleet and is celebrated each year during the annual Dory Derby on the third weekend in July. If you'd like to go out in one of theses dories and fish for salmon or albacore tuna, contact **Haystack Fishing** (© **866/965-7555;** haystackfishing.com), which charges anywhere from $130 to $250 for a day of fishing.

WHERE TO STAY
In Pacific City
Inn at Cape Kiwanda ✺✺ *Finds*   Although it's across the street from the beach (and Cape Kiwanda State Natural Area), this modern cedar-shingled three-story hotel has one of the best views on the Oregon coast: Directly offshore rises Haystack Rock, a huge jug-handled monolith. Since a great view isn't quite enough, the hotel was designed with luxurious, contemporary rooms, all of which have balconies and fireplaces. A few have whirlpool tubs, and there is also a very luxurious suite. The corner rooms are my favorites. The inn is affiliated with the Pelican Pub & Brewery, which is right across the street, and on the inn's ground floor there is an art gallery, salon with massage services, and an espresso bar that also sells wine and books.

33105 Cape Kiwanda Dr., Pacific City, OR 97135. © **888/965-7001** or 503/965-7001. Fax 503/965-7002. www.innat capekiwanda.com. 35 units. $109–$249 double; $199–$309 suite. 2-night minimum on holidays, and weekends July–August. Children under 18 stay free in parent's room. AE, DISC, MC, V. Pets accepted ($20). **Amenities:** Restaurant (brewpub); lounge; exercise room; bike rentals; business center; room service; massage; coin-op laundry. *In room:* TV/DVD, fridge, coffeemaker, hair dryer, free local calls, Wi-Fi.

CAMPGROUNDS

Cape Lookout State Park is the largest campground along the Three Capes Loop. For reservations, contact **ReserveAmerica** (© 800/452-5687; www.reserveamerica.com). **Whalen Island County Park,** on the south side of Sand Lake just off Sand Lake Road, is a smaller and less crowded alternative (though it's not right on the ocean).

WHERE TO DINE
In Oceanside

Roseanna's Oceanside Café ☞ SEAFOOD/INTERNATIONAL   Roseanna's is such a Scenic Loop legend that people come from miles around to eat here and don't seem to mind long waits to get a table. What brings them are the views of the beach and offshore rocks, the long list of desserts, and the reliable meals. Lunch prices are reasonable, with such offerings as a full-flavored cioppino soup or oyster sandwich. Angels on horseback (oysters wrapped in bacon and broiled) is one of my favorite appetizers. Entrees include a choice of shellfish or fish with a choice of sauces (apricot-ginger glaze, aioli, or spicy garlic-chile, for example). The wait for a table can be long, so if you just want a quick snack, there are bar stools at the front counter.

1490 Pacific Ave. © 503/842-7351. Main courses $7.25–$13 lunch, $14–$18 dinner. MC, V. Daily 10:30am–9pm (may close 1 hr. earlier in winter).

In Pacific City

For tasty baked goods and lunches, stop in at **The Grateful Bread Bakery & Restaurant,** 34805 Brooten Rd. (© 503/965-7337), with tables both inside and out on a deck. If you enjoy good books and good coffee you'll appreciate **Migrations,** 33105 Cape Kiwanda Dr. (© 503/965-4661), which is located on the ground floor of the Inn at Cape Kiwanda.

Pelican Pub & Brewery ☞ PUB FOOD   With massive Haystack Rock looming just offshore and the huge dune of Cape Kiwanda just up the beach, this brewpub claims the best view of any pub in Oregon. The Pelican is right on the beach and even has its own beach volleyball court. There's a good selection of brews, including Tsunami Stout and my personal favorite, the Doryman's Dark Ale. Sandwiches, burgers, fabulous fish and chips, and pizzas are the menu mainstays here. The steamed clams served with barley bread made from beer grain are divine. Kids are welcome, and the beach location makes this a great spot for lunch or dinner if you're hanging out on the beach all day.

33180 Cape Kiwanda Dr. © 503/965-7007. www.pelicanbrewery.com. Main courses $9–$20. AE, DISC, MC, V. Sun–Thurs 8am–9pm; Fri–Sat 8am–10pm (closes 1 hr. later in summer).

The Riverhouse ☞ AMERICAN   This tiny place is built on the bank of the Nestucca River and has great river views out its many windows. With casual, friendly atmosphere, this place has the feel of someplace that time and contemporary fads have passed by. Although burgers and sandwiches are the order of the day at lunch, the dinner menu features prawns in a creamy wine sauce; fresh fish amandine; halibut basted with butter, lemon pepper, and dill; filet mignon, and crepes Florentine. Be sure to check out the photos of the 1999 flood that caused this restaurant to be raised up to the second floor.

Brooten Rd. © 503/965-6722. Main courses $7.50–$25. MC, V. Daily 11am–9pm (11am–8pm in winter).

NESKOWIN

The quaint little community of Neskowin is nestled at the northern foot of Cascade Head, 12 miles north of Lincoln City. Inland families have spent their summers in these tiny cottages and tree-lined lanes for decades. Quiet vacations are the norm in Neskowin, where you'll find only condominiums and rental houses. The beach is accessible at **Neskowin Beach State Recreation Site,** which faces Proposal Rock, a tree-covered haystack rock bordered by Neskowin Creek. On the beach, keep an eye out for the stumps of trees that died hundreds of years ago when an earthquake lowered the shoreline in this area.

If you're interested in art, check out the **Hawk Creek Gallery,** 48460 U.S. 101 S. (© **503/392-3879**), which features the paintings of Michael Schlicting, a master watercolorist.

Just to the south of Neskowin is rugged, unspoiled **Cascade Head.** Rising 1,770 feet from sea level, this is one of the highest headlands on the coast. Lush forests of Sitka spruce and windswept cliff-top meadows thrive here and are home to such diverse flora and fauna that the Nature Conservancy purchased much of the headland. Trails onto Cascade Head start about 2 miles south of Neskowin. The Nature Conservancy's preserve has been set aside primarily to protect the habitat of the rare Oregon silverspot butterfly; the upper trail is closed from January 1 to July 15 due to the timing of the butterflies' life cycles. However, a lower trail, reached from Three Rocks Road (park at Knight Park and walk up Savage Rd. to the trailhead) is open year-round.

On the south side of Cascade Head, you'll find the **Sitka Center for Art and Ecology,** P.O. Box 65, Otis, OR 97368 (© **541/994-5485;** www.sitkacenter.org), which runs summer classes on subjects such as writing, painting, ecology, and ceramics.

WHERE TO STAY

In addition to the condominium resort listed here, there are numerous vacation cottages and beach houses for rent in Neskowin. Contact **Sea View Vacation Rentals,** 6335 Pacific Ave. (P.O. Box 1049), Pacific City, OR 97135 (© **888/701-1023** or 503/965-7888; www.seaview4u.com), or **Grey Fox Vacation Rentals,** P.O. Box 364, Neskowin, OR 97149 (© **888/720-2154** or 503/392-4355; www.oregoncoast.com/greyfox).

Neskowin Resort ⊀   All the units at this condominium resort have views of Proposal Rock, and the views, combined with the tranquillity of Neskowin, set this place apart from hotels in nearby Lincoln City. All the units also have kitchens, making it a popular choice with families. Hawk Creek runs along the back of the resort, and just across the parking lot is a good little cafe. The views from the rooms here are among the best on the Oregon coast. Be sure to request one of the remodeled condos.

48990 U.S. 101 S. (P.O. Box 447), Neskowin, OR 97149. © **503/392-4850.** Fax 503/392-4264. www.neskowin vacationrentals.com. 20 condos. July 1–Sept 15 $109–$129 double, $139–$159 suite, $209–$345 suite; lower rates mid-Sept to June. No credit cards. Pets accepted. **Amenities:** Restaurant (American); coin-op laundry. *In room:* TV, kitchen, fridge, coffeemaker.

5 Lincoln City/Gleneden Beach

88 miles SW of Portland, 44 miles S of Tillamook, 25 miles N of Newport

Lincoln City is the Oregon coast's number-one family destination, and, despite the name, it is not really a city at all. It's a collection of five small towns that grew together over the years and that now stretch for miles along the coast. Today there's no specific downtown, and though there may be more motel rooms here than anywhere else on

The Central Oregon Coast

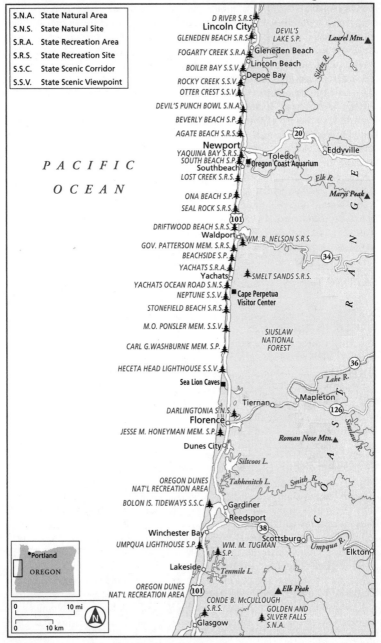

S.N.A.   State Natural Area
S.N.S.   State Natural Site
S.R.A.   State Recreation Area
S.R.S.   State Recreation Site
S.S.C.   State Scenic Corridor
S.S.V.   State Scenic Viewpoint

PACIFIC

OCEAN

D RIVER S.R.S.
Lincoln City
GLENEDEN BEACH S.R.S.
DEVIL'S LAKE S.P.
Laurel Mtn.
FOGARTY CREEK S.R.A.   Gleneden Beach
BOILER BAY S.S.V.   Lincoln Beach
Depoe Bay
ROCKY CREEK S.S.V.
OTTER CREST S.S.V.
DEVIL'S PUNCH BOWL S.N.A.
BEVERLY BEACH S.P.
AGATE BEACH S.R.S.
Newport
YAQUINA BAY S.R.S.
Toledo
Eddyville
SOUTH BEACH S.P.
Southbeach   Oregon Coast Aquarium
LOST CREEK S.R.S.
Elk R.
Marys Peak
ONA BEACH S.P.
SEAL ROCK S.R.S.
DRIFTWOOD BEACH S.R.S.
Waldport
WM. B. NELSON S.R.S.
GOV. PATTERSON MEM. S.R.S.
BEACHSIDE S.P.
YACHATS S.R.A.
Yachats   SMELT SANDS S.R.S.
YACHATS OCEAN ROAD S.N.S.
NEPTUNE S.S.V.   Cape Perpetua
Visitor Center
STONEFIELD BEACH S.R.S.
M.O. PONSLER MEM. S.S.V.
SIUSLAW NATIONAL FOREST
CARL G. WASHBURNE MEM. S.P.
HECETA HEAD LIGHTHOUSE S.S.V.
Lake R.
Sea Lion Caves
Tiernan   Mapleton
DARLINGTONIA S.N.S.
Florence
Roman Nose Mtn.
JESSE M. HONEYMAN MEM. S.P.
Dunes City
Siltcoos L.
OREGON DUNES
NAT'L RECREATION AREA
Tahkenitch L.   *Smith R.*
BOLON IS. TIDEWAYS S.S.C.
Gardiner
Reedsport
Winchester Bay
Scottsburg
UMPQUA LIGHTHOUSE S.P.
WM. M. TUGMAN
S.P.
Umpqua R.
Elkton
Lakeside   *Tenmile L.*
OREGON DUNES
NAT'L RECREATION AREA
CONDE B. McCULLOUGH
S.R.S.
Elk Peak
GOLDEN AND
SILVER FALLS
S.N.A.
Glasgow

Portland
OREGON

0   10 mi
0   10 km

N

the Oregon coast, there's little to distinguish most of the thousands of rooms. However, families looking for a long beach and steady winds for flying kites will likely enjoy Lincoln City. Motel rates here, though often high for what you get, are generally better than those in beach towns that are longer on charm, and you'll find an abundance of vacation homes for rent, too. Likewise, restaurants catering to big families and small pocketbooks are the norm. Such restaurants purvey hot meals rather than haute cuisine, and you can eat your fill of seafood without going broke.

Once referred to as "20 miracle miles," Lincoln City is no longer the miracle it once was. Miracle miles have become congested sprawl, and a summer weekend in Lincoln City can mean coping with bumper-to-bumper traffic. Not surprisingly, many have come to think of this as "20 miserable miles." If at all possible, come during the week or during the off-season to avoid the crowds.

Once you get off U.S. 101, though, Lincoln City has neighborhoods as charming as any on the coast, and at the south end of town, in the Taft District, the city has been working hard to bring back a historical character and provide an attractive, pedestrian-friendly area. In Gleneden Beach just south of Lincoln City, you'll find the coast's most prestigious resort. Also in the Lincoln City area are some of Oregon's best art galleries and some interesting artists' studios.

ESSENTIALS

GETTING THERE   Ore. 22 from Salem merges with Ore. 18 before reaching the junction with U.S. 101. From Portland, take Ore. 99W to McMinnville and then head west on Ore. 18.

VISITOR INFORMATION   For more information on the area, contact the **Lincoln City Visitor and Convention Bureau,** 801 SW U.S. 101, Lincoln City, OR 97367 (© **800/452-2151** or 541/996-1274; www.oregoncoast.org).

FESTIVALS   Annual **kite festivals** include the Summer Kite Festival in late June and the Fall Kite Festival in early October. In addition, Lincoln City hosts the annual **Cascade Head Music Festival** (www.cascadeheadmusic.org) in mid- to late June, and in August there's the annual **Sandcastle Building Contest.** On the nearby Siletz Indian Reservation, the **Nesika Illahee,** the annual Siletz Pow Wow takes place on the second weekend in August.

ENJOYING THE BEACH & THE OUTDOORS

Lincoln City's 7½-mile-long **beach** is its main attraction. However, cold waters and constant breezes conspire to make swimming a pursuit for Polar Bear Club members only. The winds, on the other hand, make this beach the best kite-flying spot on the Oregon coast. If you didn't bring your own kite, you can buy one at **Catch the Wind,** 266 SE U.S. 101 (© **541/994-9500;** www.catchthewind.com). Among the better beach-access points are the D River State Wayside, on the south side of the river, and the Road's End State Wayside, up at the north end of Lincoln City. Road's End is also a good place to explore some tide pools. You'll find more tide pools on the beach at Northwest 15th Street and at Southwest 32nd Street.

Adding to the appeal of Lincoln City's beach is **Devil's Lake,** which drains across the beach by way of the D River, the world's shortest river. Formerly called Devil's River, the D River is only 120 feet long, flowing from the outlet of Devil's Lake, under U.S. 101, and across the beach to the Pacific Ocean. Boating, sailing, water-skiing, windsurfing, swimming, fishing, and camping are all popular Devil's Lake activities.

Access points on the west side of the lake include **Devil's Lake State Recreation Area (West),** NE Sixth Street (© 541/994-2002), which has a campground, and **Regatta Grounds Park** and **Holmes Road Park,** both of which are off West Devil's Lake Road and have boat ramps and picnic tables. On the east side you'll find **Devil's Lake State Park (East)** 2 miles east on East Devil's Lake Road, and **Sand Point Park** on View Point Lane near the north end of East Devil's Lake Road. Both of these parks have picnic tables and swimming areas. If you don't have your own boat, you can rent canoes, kayaks, paddleboats, aquabikes, and various motorboats at **Blue Heron Landing,** 4008 W. Devil's Lake Rd. (© 541/994-4708). Rates range from $10 an hour for a kayak up to $90 for a 2-hour personal watercraft rental. You'll also find bumper boats here at Blue Heron Landing.

If you're a gardener or enjoy visiting public gardens, schedule time to visit the **Connie Hansen Garden,** 1931 NW 33rd St. (© 541/994-6338; www.conniehansen garden.com). This cottage garden was created over a 20-year period and abounds in primroses, irises, and rhododendrons, making it a great place to visit in the spring. The gardens are open daily from 9am to 5pm. Call for directions.

Golfers have two options. The top choice is the Scottish-inspired (though solidly Northwestern in character) **Salishan Golf Links** ☞, 7760 U.S. 101, Gleneden Beach (© 800/890-0387 or 541/764-3632; www.salishan.com), which charges $55 to $95 for 18 holes. This resort course is a longtime Oregon coast favorite. The town's other main course is the **Chinook Winds Golf Resort,** 3245 NE 50th St. (© 541/994-8442; www.chinookwindscasino.com), which is affiliated with Chinook Winds Casino and is undergoing a major upgrading. This course charges $37 to $49 for 18 holes.

If you want to challenge the waves, you can rent a wetsuit, surfboard, or body board down at the south end of town at the **Lincoln City Surf Shop,** 4792 SE U.S. 101 (© 541/996-7433); or the **Oregon Surf Shop,** 4933 SW U.S. 101 (© 541/996-3957).

Hikers should head inland approximately 10 miles to **Drift Creek Falls Trail** ☞, which leads through coastal forest to a 240-foot-long suspension bridge above a 75-foot-tall waterfall. From the bridge you have a bird's-eye view not only of the falls but of the treetops as well. It's a 1.3-mile hike to the bridge and the route is moderately difficult. To find the trail head (Northwest Forest Pass is required), head east from U.S. 101 on Drift Creek Road, which is just north of Salishan lodge at the south end of Lincoln City. Turn right onto South Drift Creek Road and then left onto Forest Road 17 (not Anderson Creek Rd.) and continue 10 miles on this single-lane road.

Sharing a name with this hiking trail is a historic covered bridge—the **Drift Creek Bridge.** Completely restored a few years back, this covered bridge was built in 1914 and is 66 feet long. To find the bridge, drive U.S. 101 south from Lincoln City toward Gleneden Beach and Salishan Resort. Turn east on Drift Creek Road, and in about 2 miles, turn right at a sign for the bridge and continue a half mile.

INDOOR PURSUITS

These days the hottest thing in town is the **Chinook Winds Casino,** 1777 NW 44th St. (© 888/CHINOOK or 541/996-5825; www.chinookwindscasino.com), a massive gambling casino run by the Confederated Tribes of Siletz Indians and located right on the beach at the north end of town. The casino offers bingo, blackjack, poker, slot machines, and keno. There's plenty of cheap food, as well as a video-game room

---

Fun Fact **Finders Keepers**

Each year between mid-October and the end of May, Lincoln City hides more than 2,000 art-glass balls, similar to the much-prized Japanese handblown glass fishing floats that sometimes drift ashore on this coast. Look above the high-tide line for the colorful globes of glass. Some are hidden each week.

---

for the kids. Big-name entertainers help attract folks who might not otherwise consider visiting a casino.

You can catch live jazz at **Eden Hall,** 6675 Gleneden Beach Loop Rd., Gleneden (© **541/764-3826;** www.edenhall.com), a big club and restaurant just south of the Salishan Lodge.

The casino may actually be second in popularity to the **Tanger Outlet Center,** 1500 SE East Devils Lake Rd. (© **541/996-5000;** www.tangeroutlet.com), which is on the corner of U.S. 101. Among the many expected name-brand shops here, you'll find Chateau Benoit winery tasting room.

Lincoln City has a surprising number of interesting art galleries and artists' studios. At the north end of town, the first gallery you'll come to is the **Ryan Gallery,** 4270 N. U.S. 101 (© **541/994-5391**). Right in the heart of Lincoln City's main business strip, watch for the **Earthworks Gallery,** 620 NE U.S. 101 (© **541/557-4148**), which emphasizes ceramic and glass art, but also carries a variety of other fine crafts.

South of Lincoln City proper, you'll find the impressive **Freed Gallery,** 6119 SW U.S. 101 (© **541/994-5600;** www.freedgallery.com), which has an excellent selection of art glass and ceramic work, as well as sculptures and paintings in a wide variety of styles. Just off U.S. 101, north of Salishan Lodge, you'll find **Alder House III,** 611 Immonen Rd. (no phone; www.alderhouse.com), the oldest glassblowing studio in Oregon. The shop and studio are open daily from 10am to 5pm between mid-March and November. Nearby, you'll also find **Mossy Creek Pottery,** 483 Immonen Rd. (© **541/996-2415;** www.mossycreekpottery.com), with an eclectic selection of porcelain and stoneware by Oregon potters.

WHERE TO STAY

In addition to the town's many hotels and motels, Lincoln City has plenty of vacation rental houses and apartments offering good deals, especially for families. For information, contact **Horizon Rentals** (© **800/995-2411** or 541/994-2226; www.horizonrentals. com) or **Pacific Retreats** (© **800/473-4833** or 541/994-4833; www.pacificretreats. com). Rates generally range from around $100 up to $400 nightly for houses for anywhere from 4 to 12 people.

EXPENSIVE

The Inn at Spanish Head 🕰🕰 Located toward the south end of Lincoln City, this is one of the only high-rise hotels on the Oregon coast, but you'd never know it from the parking lot. From the entry, the hotel appears to be only two stories tall. What isn't readily apparent is that, due to the fact that the hotel is built into a steep cliff that rises up from the beach, the lobby is on the ninth floor (there are eight stories below the parking-lot level). This is a condominium resort and all the rooms are individually owned, which means there's a different decor in every room. However, the furnishings are reliably comfortable. All the rooms have an ocean view, and there are large suites for families. Some rooms, however, are very cramped. The hotel's restaurant and lounge, on the 10th floor, provides a dizzying view and serves fresh seafood.

4009 SW U.S. 101, Lincoln City, OR 97367. ⓒ 800/452-8127 or 541/996-2161. Fax 541/996-4089. www.spanishhead. com. 120 units. $175–$195 double; $289 suite; lower rates in winter. Children under 16 stay free in parent's room. AE, DC, DISC, MC, V. **Amenities:** Restaurant (seafood); lounge; outdoor pool; exercise room; Jacuzzi; 2 saunas; room service; massage; coin-op laundry. *In room:* TV/VCR, dataport, kitchen/kitchenette, fridge, coffeemaker, hair dryer, iron, free local calls.

The O'dysius Hotel 🏨🏨 Although it seems a bit out of place, this hotel offers the sort of luxury you would expect from a downtown Portland historic hotel but with a beach right across the street. Traditional European styling dominates, and the lobby, with its antique furniture, has the feel of a very luxurious living room. It's here that the hotel serves its complimentary afternoon wine. Guest rooms have lots of nice touches, including slate entries, down comforters, Art Nouveau lamps, gas fireplaces, and VCRs. All the rooms have ocean views, and some have balconies. If you enjoy luxury but aren't into the golf-resort scene, this is definitely the place for you. For the best view, ask for a room on the fifth floor.

120 NW Inlet Court, Lincoln City, OR 97367. ⓒ **800/869-8069** or 541/994-4121. Fax 541/994-8160. www. odysius.com. 30 units. $155–$195 double; $227–$309 suite. Rates include continental breakfast. AE, DISC, MC, V. Children 12 and older welcome. Pets accepted. **Amenities:** Concierge; massage. *In room:* TV/VCR, dataport, coffeemaker, hair dryer, iron.

Salishan Spa & Golf Resort 🏨🏨🏨 *Kids* The largest and most luxurious resort on the coast, Salishan Lodge is nestled amid towering evergreens on a hillside at the south end of Siletz Bay. However, because the resort is almost half a mile from the beach and on the inland side of U.S. 101, it's more of a golf resort than a beach resort. An extensive network of walking paths meanders through the 760-acre grounds, and there are plenty of activities for kids. Guest rooms come in three sizes. Whichever size you opt for, try to get a second-floor room. Most of these have cathedral ceilings and stone fireplaces. For breathtaking views, you'll have to shell out top dollar for a deluxe or premier room. The Salishan Dining Room is the most upscale restaurant on the entire coast and has a superb wine collection. In the past few years, this resort has undergone a thorough renovation.

7760 U.S. 101 N. (P.O. Box 118), Gleneden Beach, OR 97388. ⓒ **888/SALISHAN** or 541/764-2371. Fax 541/764-3663. www.salishan.com. 205 units. May to late Oct $139–$199 double; late Oct to Apr $115–$175 double. AE, DC, DISC, MC, V. Pets accepted ($25). **Amenities:** 3 restaurants (Northwest, American); lounge; indoor pool; 18-hole golf course; 1 outdoor and 3 indoor tennis courts; exercise room; full-service spa; Jacuzzi; sauna; 24-hr. room service; massage; babysitting; laundry service; dry cleaning. *In room:* TV, dataport, fridge, coffeemaker, hair dryer, iron, high-speed Internet access.

MODERATE

Looking Glass Inn 🏨 While most hotels that claim to be pet-friendly simply tolerate dogs, this hotel welcomes dogs with open arms. Bring your pooch with you, and your canine companion will get a basket with a water bowl and doggy treats at check in. Okay, you, too, will be welcomed and will likely enjoy this recently remodeled hotel even more than Fido does. Located in the historic Taft District across the street from Siletz Bay, the Looking Glass, with its cedar shingles and white trim, has a classic Cape Cod feel. Rooms are available with whirlpool tubs, balconies, or gas fireplaces.

861 SW 51st St., Lincoln City, OR 97367. ⓒ **800/843-4940** or 541/996-3996. www.lookingglass-inn.com. 36 units. July to Labor Day $89–$169 double; Labor Day to June $59–$119 double. Rates include continental breakfast. AE, DISC, MC, V. Pets accepted ($10). *In room:* TV/VCR, dataport, fridge, coffeemaker, hair dryer.

Siletz Bay Lodge ✆ Located at the south end of Lincoln City right on Siletz Bay, this modern motel is a particularly good choice for families and but is also a good option for couples. Although the motel isn't on the ocean, it is on a driftwood-strewn beach that has quiet waters that are perfect for kids, and across the bay you can often see harbor seals lounging on the beach. About half of the standard rooms have balconies. Spa rooms and spa suites are also available if you happen to be in town for a romantic getaway.

1012 SW 51st St. (P.O. Box 952), Lincoln City, OR 97367. ✆ **888/430-2100** or 541/996-6111. Fax 541/996-3992. www.siletzbaylodge.com. 44 units. Summer $108–$155 double; $155 suite. Off season $59–$115 double; $130 suite. Rates include continental breakfast. 3-night minimum on holidays. Children under 12 stay free in parent's room. AE, DC, DISC, MC, V. **Amenities:** Jacuzzi. *In room:* TV, dataport, fridge, coffeemaker, hair dryer.

CAMPGROUNDS

There's a campground at **Devil's Lake State Recreation Area,** just off U.S. 101 north of the D River. To make reservations, contact **ReserveAmerica** (✆ **800/452-5687;** www.reserveamerica.com).

WHERE TO DINE

If you're looking for some good smoked salmon or smoked oysters, stop by **Mr. Bill's Village Smokehouse,** 2981 SW U.S. 101 (✆ **888/MR-BILLS** or 503/994-4566; www.mrbillsvillagesmokehouse.com).

EXPENSIVE

Bay House ✆✆ NORTHWEST With a big wall of glass overlooking Siletz Bay and Salishan Spit, the Bay House, between Lincoln City and Gleneden Beach, provides fine dining and dramatic sunsets (and good bird-watching if you're interested). There are snowy linens on the tables, and service is gracious. The menu here changes seasonally but always shows influences from Asia (shellfish curry) and the Mediterranean (halibut Parmesan), and sometimes a blend of the two (pan-roasted salmon with fig-fennel chutney). Don't pass up the delicious pan-seared scallops with chardonnay pan sauce if they're on the menu.

5911 SW Hwy. 101. ✆ **541/996-3222.** www.bayhouserestaurant.com. Reservations recommended. Main courses $19–$35. AE, DISC, MC, V. Wed–Fri and Sun 5:30–9pm; Sat 5–9pm.

MODERATE

Blackfish Café ✆✆ SEAFOOD Located near the north end of Lincoln City, this restaurant has a big reputation for such a casual and unpretentious spot. This is likely because at both lunch and dinner, care is taken with all the preparations. The grilled prawn "martini" and Dungeness crab "margarita" (basically just seafood cocktails) make great starters. The menu includes everything from fish and chips to citrus-marinated breast of duck and sea bass with olive-pepper butter. Keep an eye out for any dish served with the Asian slaw, which is probably the most unusual slaw you'll ever taste. Lunches just might be the best on the entire coast.

2733 NW U.S. 101. ✆ **541/996-1007.** www.blackfishcafe.com. Reservations recommended. Main courses $9.50–$18. AE, DISC, MC, V. Wed–Thurs and Sun–Mon 11:30am–9pm; Fri–Sat noon–10pm.

Kyllo's Seafood Grill ✆ SEAFOOD Providing a lively "beach party" atmosphere on a family-oriented beach, Kyllo's is housed in an architecturally unusual contemporary building with curved walls that make the restaurant impossible to miss. Inside, you'll find a big copper fireplace, plenty of deck space, and a facade of glass to take in the view of the D River and the ocean. If all this sounds like you're going to be paying for the atmosphere, think again. Prices for such dishes as large and tasty crab cakes, halibut with lemon-garlic butter, or pan-fried oysters are quite reasonable. But you'll probably have to wait for a table if you come here on a summer evening.

1110 NW First Court. ℂ 541/994-3179. Main courses $8.50–$26. AE, DISC, MC, V. Sun–Thurs 11:30am–9pm; Fri–Sat 11am–10pm (closes 1 hr. earlier in winter).

INEXPENSIVE

Otis Café ℛ (Finds AMERICAN   If you've ever seen the determination with which urbanites flock to the beach on summer weekends, you can understand what a feat it is to get cars to stop before they have sand in the treads of their tires. This tiny roadside diner, 5 miles north of Lincoln City and 4 miles shy of the beach, manages to do just that with its black bread, cinnamon rolls, and fried red potatoes. The homemade mustard and killer salsa are also favorites. Pies—marionberry, strawberry/rhubarb, or walnut—have crusts to be savored only by people unconcerned with cholesterol and are memorable even in a region of numerous perfect pies. Expect a line out the screen door.

1259 Salmon River Hwy. (Ore. 18), Otis. ℂ 541/994-2813. Breakfast, lunch, and dinner $5–$14. AE, DISC, MC, V. Sun–Thurs 7am–8pm; Fri–Sat 7am–9pm.

6 Depoe Bay

13 miles S of Lincoln City, 13 miles N of Newport, 70 miles W of Salem

Depoe Bay calls itself the smallest harbor in the world, and though the tiny harbor covers only 6 acres, it's home to more than 100 fishing boats. These boats must all enter the harbor through a narrow rock-walled channel, little more than a crack in the coastline's solid rock wall. During stormy seas, it's almost impossible to get in or out of the harbor safely.

Shell mounds and kitchen middens around the bay indicate that Native Americans long ago called this area home. In 1894, the U.S. government deeded the land surrounding the bay to a Siletz Indian known as Old Charlie Depot, who had taken his name from an army depot at which he had worked. Old Charlie later changed his name to DePoe, and when a town was founded here in 1927, it took the name Depoe Bay. Though most of the town is a bit off the highway, you'll find a row of garish souvenir shops right on U.S. 101, which sadly mar the beauty of this rocky section of coast. Among these shops are several family restaurants and charter-fishing and whale-watching companies.

ESSENTIALS

GETTING THERE   From the north, the most direct route is Ore. 99W/18 to Lincoln City, and then south on U.S. 101. From the south take U.S. 20 from Corvallis to Newport, and then go north on U.S. 101.

VISITOR INFORMATION   Contact the **Depoe Bay Chamber of Commerce,** 70 NE U.S. 101 (P.O. Box 21), Depoe Bay, OR 97341 (ℂ **877/485-8348** or 541/765-2889; www.depoebaychamber.org).

FESTIVALS   Memorial Day is time for the **Fleet of Flowers,** during which local boats carry flower wreaths out to sea in memory of loved ones. In mid-September, the town holds its annual **Salmon Bake,** which is a great opportunity to enjoy some traditionally prepared salmon. Contact the chamber of commerce for details.

DEPOE BAY ACTIVITIES & ATTRACTIONS

Aside from standing on the highway bridge watching the boat traffic passing in and out of the world's smallest harbor, the most popular activity here, especially when the seas are high, is watching the **spouting horns** across U.S. 101 from Depoe Bay's souvenir shops. Spouting horns, which are similar to blowholes, can be seen all along the coast, but nowhere are they more spectacular than here. These geyserlike plumes occur in places where water is forced through narrow channels in basalt rock. As the channels become more restricted, the water shoots skyward under great pressure and can spray 60 feet into the air. If the surf is really up, the water can carry quite a ways, and more than a few unwary visitors have been soaked.

Be sure to stop in at **Depoe Bay State Park,** 119 U.S. 101 (© **541/764-3304),** which is located on the cliff above the entrance to the harbor and consists of a couple of picnic tables and a Whale Watch Center perched on the rocks above the ocean. There are also lots of displays about whales, and rangers and volunteers are on hand to point out gray whales if they happen to be visible. Hours vary with the seasons.

At **Fogarty Creek State Recreation Area,** a couple of miles north of Depoe Bay, you'll find a beautiful little cove with basalt cliffs at one end and a creek flowing across the beach. The parking area is on the east side of U.S. 101. There is a $3 day-use fee here. **Boiler Bay State Scenic Viewpoint,** a mile north of Depoe Bay, is a good picnic spot from which to look for gray whales. There are also tide pools among the rocks in some small coves here. Although the beach itself is not accessible from the state park pull-off, about midway between Boiler Bay and Fogarty Creek, a mile north of here, there's a trail that leads down to the beach.

South of Depoe Bay, U.S. 101 winds through scenes of rugged splendor, passing several small, picturesque coves. Just south of town, **Rocky Creek State Scenic Viewpoint,** with windswept lawns, picnic tables, and great views of buff-colored cliffs and spouting horns, is a good picnic spot. In a few more miles you'll come to the **Otter Crest State Scenic Loop,** which leads to Cape Foulweather. Named by Capt. James Cook in 1778, the cape was his first glimpse of land after leaving the Sandwich Islands (Hawaii). The cape frequently lives up to its name, with winds often gusting to more than 100 miles per hour. However, the views are quite stupendous. Keep an eye out for the sea lions that sun themselves on offshore rocks near Cape Foulweather. A historic building now used as a gift shop provides a protected glimpse of the sea from atop Cape Foulweather.

At the south end of the Otter Crest Scenic Loop, you'll find an overlook at **Devil's Punchbowl State Natural Area** ☞☞. The overlook provides a glimpse into a collapsed sea cave that during high tides or stormy seas becomes a churning cauldron of foam. Adjacent to Devil's Punchbowl, in a small cove, you'll find numerous tide pools that can be explored at low tide. From this cove, you can also explore inside the Devil's Punchbowl. South of Devil's Punchbowl State Natural Area lies **Beverly Beach State Park** (© **541/265-9278),** which has a large campground and is a popular surfing spot. Here at the Devil's Punchbowl, you'll also find a **Mo's Chowder House** (© **541/ 765-2442)** and the **Flying Dutchman Winery** (© **541/765-2553;** www.dutchman winery.com).

If you're interested in **sportfishing** or **whale-watching** ☞☞, contact **Tradewinds Charters** (© **800/445-8730** or 541/765-2345), at the north end of the bridge or **Dockside Charters** (© **800/733-8915** or 541/765-2545; www.docksidedepoebay.com), down by the marina. Whale-watching trips run $15 to $35, depending on the type of boat you go out on and how long you stay out. Fishing trips run from $65 for 5 hours to $160 for a day of halibut or tuna fishing. For a more exciting style of whale-watching, head out with **Zodiac Tours of Depoe Bay** (© 888/445-9410 or 541/765-2804), which takes out up to six passengers at a time on their small Zodiac boat. A 1-hour trip is $25 and a 2-hour trip is $45.

WHERE TO STAY

Channel House 😊😊   Perched above the narrow, cliff-bordered channel into tiny Depoe Bay is the Channel House, one of the coast's most luxurious and strikingly situated small inns. A contemporary building with lots of angles and windows, the Channel House has large rooms, and the gas fireplaces and private decks with whirlpool tubs make it one of the most romantic inns on the coast. You can sit and soak as fishing boats navigate their way through the channel below you.

35 Ellingson St. (P.O. Box 56), Depoe Bay, OR 97341. © 800/447-2140 or 541/765-2140. Fax 541/765-2191. www. channelhouse.com. 12 units. Apr–Oct $100–$255 double, $275–$310 suite; Nov–Mar (Sun–Thurs) $100–$191 double, $206–$233 suite. Rates include continental breakfast. AE, DISC, MC, V. No children accepted. **Amenities:** Concierge. *In room:* TV, fridge, hair dryer, free local calls, Wi-Fi.

Inn at Arch Rock 😊 *Finds*   You just won't find a better view from any hotel on the Oregon coast. This collection of renovated Cape Cod–style buildings sits above the cliffs on the north side of Depoe Bay, and you can sit in your room and watch the waves crashing against the rocks. When you want to get your feet wet in the summer, follow the flight of stairs that leads down to a tiny beach. Guest rooms have a simple cottage decor, and some have kitchens or fireplaces. Out on the lawns overlooking the ocean you'll find white Adirondack chairs and a fire pit. The inn also rents out some adjacent condominiums and is just around the corner from the Tidal Raves restaurant.

70 NW Sunset St. (P.O. Box 1516), Depoe Bay, OR 97341. © 800/767-1835 or 541/765-2560. www. innatarchrock.com. 13 units. $69–$169 double; $139–$259 suite/cottage; lower rates in winter. Rates include continental breakfast. Children 3 and under stay free in parent's room. AE, DISC, MC, V. Pets accepted ($10 per night). *In room:* TV/VCR, fridge, coffeemaker, free local calls.

Inn at Otter Crest 😊😊   Few hotels on the Oregon coast boast as spectacular a setting as the Inn at Otter Crest, one of the region's top resorts. If you want to get away from it all and enjoy a bit of forest seclusion on the beach, there's no better spot. The inn's numerous weathered-cedar buildings are surrounded by 35 acres of forests and beautifully landscaped gardens on a rocky crest above a secluded cove. Trails meander through the woods and lead down to the nearby Devil's Punchbowl and Beverly Beach State Park. Most rooms have excellent ocean views through a wall of glass that opens onto a balcony. My favorites are the loft suites, which have fireplaces, kitchens, and high ceilings. Service is rather casual, and you'll have to leave your car in a parking lot that's somewhat removed from the guest rooms. (Staff will shuttle you around in golf carts.)

301 Otter Crest Loop Rd., Otter Rock, OR 97369. © 800/452-2101 or 541/765-2111. Fax 541/765-2047. www.innat ottercrest.com. 130 units. $79–$169 double; $109–$199 suite. 2-night minimum on holidays, and weekends July–Aug. AE, DISC, MC, V. **Amenities:** Restaurant (American); lounge; outdoor pool; 2 tennis courts; exercise room; Jacuzzi; sauna; guest laundry. *In room:* TV, fridge, coffeemaker, hair dryer, iron, free local calls, high-speed Internet access, Wi-Fi.

The Surfrider 😊   Though it has been around for many years and is nothing fancy, this low-rise motel, just north of Depoe Bay, claims an enviable location and view, and has long been a family favorite. It's hidden from the highway, which gives it a secluded feel, and there are great views from the open bluff-top setting. You can choose between basic motel rooms and rooms with fireplaces, kitchens, or whirlpool tubs. At the foot of a long staircase is the wide beach of Fogarty Creek State Recreation Area, which is on a pretty little cove. The dining room and lounge have great views of this cove.

3115 NW U.S. 101 (P.O. Box 219), Depoe Bay, OR 97341. © 800/662-2378 or 541/764-2311. Fax 541/764-4634. www.surfriderresort.com. 55 units. Memorial Day weekend, June weekends, and July–Sept $114–$134 double, $139–$189 suite, $399 house; lower rates in off season. Children under 13 stay free in parent's room. AE, DC, DISC, MC, V. **Amenities:** Restaurant (American); lounge; indoor pool; Jacuzzi; sauna; massage; coin-op laundry. *In room:* TV/VCR, dataport, fridge, coffeemaker, hair dryer, Wi-Fi.

WHERE TO DINE

Oceanus ✦ ECLECTIC   While Depoe Bay isn't a very large town, it manages to have two very good restaurants that boast some of the best views on the coast. Oceanus, though small, has big walls of glass to take in the view. The menu here is almost exclusively seafood; the steamed clams, cioppino, and hazelnut-and-citrus-crusted halibut are all good choices. Most of the entrees served in the evening are also available at lunch in smaller portions and at lower prices.

177 U.S. 101. © 541/765-4553. Reservations recommended. Main courses $8–$15 lunch, $16–$24 dinner. DISC, MC, V. Sun and Tues–Thurs 11am–3pm and 4–8pm; Fri–Sat 11am–3pm and 4–9pm.

Tidal Raves ✦✦ (Finds) SEAFOOD   With bright, uncluttered decor and big windows for taking in the wave-carved sandstone cliffs outside, Tidal Raves, located at the north end of Depoe Bay's strip of tourist shops, is the most dramatically situated restaurant on the Oregon coast. This place has had folks raving for years now, and on days when the surf is up, it's hard to take your eyes off the wave-pounded cliffs outside the window and concentrate on your food. The menu offers plenty of straightforward seafood, but it also includes some creative preparations such as oysters Santa Fe and Thai grilled tiger shrimp. For light eaters, there are small portions of many menu favorites.

279 NW U.S. 101. © 541/765-2995. Reservations highly recommended. Main courses $7.50–$21. MC, V. Daily 11am–9pm.

7 Newport

23 miles S of Lincoln City, 58 miles W of Corvallis, 24 miles N of Yachats

As Oregon coast towns go, Newport has a split personality. Dockworkers unloading fresh fish mingle with vacationers licking ice-cream cones, and both fishing boats and pleasure craft ply the waters of the bay. The air smells of fish and shrimp, and free-loading sea lions doze on the docks while they wait for their next meal from the processing plants along the waterfront. Directly across the street, art galleries and souvenir shops stand side by side. Across Yaquina Bay from the waterfront, you'll find the Oregon Coast Aquarium (the coast's top tourist attraction) and the Hatfield Marine Science Center. If you're looking for a balance of the old and the new on the Oregon coast, Newport is the place.

Newport got its start in the late 1800s as both an oystering community and one of the earliest Oregon beach resorts, and many of the old cottages and historic buildings can still be seen in the town's Nye Beach neighborhood. Although Nye Beach has the feel of a 19th-century resort, the downtown bayfront is, despite its souvenir shops, galleries, and restaurants, still a working port and home to the largest commercial fishing fleet on the Oregon coast. Oysters are also still important to the local economy and are raised in oyster beds along Yaquina Bay Road, east of town.

Though in recent years it has come close to matching the overdevelopment of Lincoln City, this fishing port on the shore of Yaquina Bay still manages to offer a balance of industry, history, culture, beaches, and family attractions.

ESSENTIALS

GETTING THERE   Newport is on U.S. 101 at the junction with U.S. 20, which leads to Corvallis.

VISITOR INFORMATION   Contact the **Greater Newport Chamber of Commerce,** 555 SW Coast Hwy., Newport, OR 97365 (© **800/262-7844** or 541/ 265-8801; www.newportchamber.org).

FESTIVALS   In late July each year, the music of composer Ernest Bloch, who once lived in this area, is celebrated during the **Ernest Bloch Music Festival** (© **541/ 765-3142**). In February, there's the **Seafood and Wine Fest;** contact the Newport Chamber of Commerce for information.

FINS & FLIPPERS

Hatfield Marine Science Center ⚘ *Kids*   Before the Oregon Coast Aquarium was built, Newport was already known as a center for marine science research. This facility, though primarily a university research center, also contains displays that are open to the public. Exhibits, although not quite as impressive as those at the Oregon Coast Aquarium, highlight current topics in marine research and include an octopus aquarium and a "touch" tank. Interpretive exhibits explain life in the sea. A worthwhile adjunct to a visit to the Oregon Coast Aquarium.

2030 Marine Science Dr. © **541/867-0100.** http://hmsc.oregonstate.edu. Admission by donation. Memorial Day to Sept daily 10am–5pm; Oct 1 to Memorial Day Thurs–Mon 10am–4pm. Closed Thanksgiving, Christmas.

Oregon Coast Aquarium ⚘⚘⚘ *Kids*   Considered one of the top aquariums in the country, the Oregon Coast Aquarium focuses primarily on sea life native to the Oregon coast. There are so many fascinating displays that it's easy to spend the better part of a day here. The stars are the playful sea otters, but the clown-faced tufted puffins, which are kept in a walk-through aviary, are big favorites as well. The sea lions sometimes rouse from their naps to put on impromptu shows, and the lucky visitor even gets a glimpse of a giant octopus with an arm span of nearly 20 feet. Artificial waves surge in a tank that reproduces, on a speeded-up scale, life in a rocky intertidal zone. And so far, you haven't even made it to the indoor aquarium displays. One of the most fascinating exhibits here is a walk-through deep-sea shark tank featuring a 200-foot-long acrylic walkway. There are examples of sandy beaches, rocky shores, salt marshes, kelp forests, and the open ocean. Because this is the most popular attraction on the Oregon coast, lines to get in can be very long. Arrive early if you're visiting on a summer weekend.

2820 SE Ferry Slip Rd. © **541/867-3474.** www.aquarium.org. Admission $12 adults, $10 seniors, $7 children 3–12; Behind the Scenes Tours $7.75 adults, $4.75 children ages 3–12. Memorial Day to Labor Day daily 9am–6pm; Labor Day to Memorial Day daily 10am–5pm. Closed Christmas.

SEEING THE LIGHTS

Newport is home to two historic lighthouses, which are just 3 miles apart. The **Yaquina Bay Lighthouse** began operation in 1871 but in 1874 was replaced by the **Yaquina Head Lighthouse.** The latter was supposed to be built on Cape Foulweather, farther to the north, but heavy seas made it impossible to land there. Instead, the light was built on Yaquina Head, and so powerful was the light that it supplanted the one at Yaquina Bay.

At 93 feet tall, the **Yaquina Head Lighthouse,** 3 miles north of Newport, is the tallest lighthouse on the Oregon coast and is still a functioning light. The lighthouse lies within the **Yaquina Head Outstanding Natural Area** (© **541/574-3100**), and adjacent to the lighthouse, you'll find the **Yaquina Head Interpretive Center,** which houses displays covering everything from the life of lighthouse keepers and their families to the sea life of tide pools. Cormorants and pigeon guillemots can be seen roosting on the steep slopes, and harbor seals lounge on the rocks. In early winter and spring, you may spot gray whales migrating along the coast. On the cobblestone beach below the lighthouse, you can explore tide pools at low tide, and there is even a wheelchair-accessible tide-pool trail in a cove that once was the site of a rock quarry. In summer, the interpretive center is open daily from 10am to 5pm and the lighthouse is open daily from 10am to 4pm; in other months, the interpretive center is open from 10am to 4pm or 5pm and the lighthouse is open from noon to 4pm. Admission to Yaquina Head is $5 per car.

The older of the two lighthouses, **Yaquina Bay Lighthouse,** is now part of Yaquina Bay State Park, 846 SW Government St. (© **800/551-6949** or 541/265-5679), which can be found just north and west of the Yaquina Bay Bridge. This 1871 lighthouse is the oldest building in Newport, and it is unusual in that the light is in a tower atop a two-story wood-frame house. The building served as both home and lighthouse, and supposedly is haunted. The lighthouse is open from Memorial Day weekend to the end of September daily from 11am to 5pm; from October to Memorial Day weekend, it's open daily from noon to 4pm. Entrance is free.

BEACHES

Beaches in the Newport area range from tiny rocky coves to long, wide stretches of sand perfect for kite flying. Right in town, north and west of the Yaquina Bay Bridge, you'll find **Yaquina Bay State Recreation Site,** which borders on both the ocean and the bay. North of Newport is **Agate Beach,** which was once known for the beautiful agates that could be found there. However, sand now covers the formerly rocky beach, hiding the stones from rock hunters. This beach has a stunning view of Yaquina Head. Two miles south of Newport, you'll find **South Beach State Park** (© **541/867-4715**), a wide sandy beach with picnic areas and a large campground (that also rents yurts).

Six miles south of Newport, you'll find **Ona Beach State Park,** a sandy beach with a picnic area under the trees. Beaver Creek, a fairly large stream, flows through the park and across the beach to the ocean. The state park offers guided kayak tours on Beaver Creek. For information or reservations, call © **541/867-6590.** Another 2 miles south will bring you to **Seal Rock State Recreation Site,** where a long wall of rock rises from the waves and sand and creates numerous tide pools and fascinating nooks and crannies to explore.

For an unusual way to experience Newport area beaches, contact Guy DiTorrice, the **Oregon Fossil Guy** (© **541/961-2489;** www.oregonfossilguy.com), who leads tours to coastal fossil sites and explains Oregon's fascinating coastal geology. Tours start at $29 per person.

THE BAYFRONT

The Bayfront is tourist central for Newport. Here you'll find ice-cream parlors, saltwater-taffy stores, chowder houses, and souvenir shops. The Bayfront is also home to commercial fishermen, seafood processing plants, and art galleries, and in its waters are numerous sea lions, which love to sleep on the floating docks adjacent to Undersea Gardens. From the adjacent pier, you can observe the sea lions at close range. Their bickering and barking makes for great free entertainment.

As one of the coast's most popular family vacation spots, Newport has all the tourist traps one would expect. Billboards up and down the coast advertise the sorts of places that kids have to visit. Tops on this list are **Ripley's Believe It or Not** and the **Wax Works Museum.** Across the street from these you'll find **Undersea Gardens,** where a scuba diver feeds fish in a large tank beneath a boat moored on the Bayfront. All three attractions are on the Bayfront and share the same address and phone number: Mariner Square, 250 SW Bay Blvd. (© 541/265-2206; www.marinersquare.com). Admission for each is $8.95 for adults, $4.95 for children 5 to 12; or $18 for adults and $9.95 for children to visit all three attractions.

Adults will likely be more interested in the Bayfront's numerous art galleries. **Breach the Moon Gallery,** 434 SW Bay Blvd. (© 541/265-9698; www.breachthe moon.com), features art glass and art with ocean and whale themes. Nearby is **Oceanic Arts,** 444 SW Bay Blvd. (© 541/265-5963), which sells interesting crafts, including wind chimes and lots of ceramics. The **Wood Gallery,** 818 SW Bay Blvd. (© 800/359-1419 or 541/265-6843; www.woodgalleryonline.com), specializes in wooden items, including boxes and musical instruments.

The Bayfront is also the place to arrange **whale-watching tours** and **fishing trips.** Two-hour whale-watching tours are offered throughout the year by **Marine Discovery Tours,** 345 SW Bay Blvd. (© 800/903-BOAT or 541/265-6200; www.marine discovery.com), which charges $30 for adults, $28 for seniors, and $15 for kids age 4 to 13. You can charter a fishing boat on the Bayfront at **Newport Tradewinds,** 653 SW Bay Blvd. (© 800/676-7819 or 541/265-2101; www.newporttradewinds.com). Salmon, tuna, halibut, and bottom fish can all be caught off the coast here depending on the season. Fishing trips cost anywhere from $60 to $165.

Newport claims to be the Dungeness crab capital of the world, and if you'd like to find out if this claim is true, you can rent crab rings and boats at **Sawyer's Landing,** 4098 Yaquina Bay Rd. (© 541/265-3907), for $45 for 3 hours or $65 for the whole day.

NYE BEACH

Newport was one of the earliest beach vacation destinations in Oregon, and it was in Nye Beach that the first hotels and vacation cottages were built. Today this neighborhood, north of the Yaquina Bay Bridge along the beach, is slowly being renovated and has both historic and hip hotels, good restaurants, some interesting shops, and, of course, miles of sandy beach. There's public parking at the turnaround on Beach Drive.

The works of local and regional artists are showcased at the **Newport Visual Arts Center,** 777 NW Beach Dr. (© 541/265-6540). The center is open Tuesday through Sunday from 11am to 6pm. Just a few blocks away, the **Newport Performing Arts Center,** 777 W. Olive St. (© 541/265-ARTS; www.coastarts.org/pac), hosts local and nationally recognized performers.

At the **Nye Beach Gallery,** 715 NW Third St. (© 541/265-3292), you'll find the nature-oriented sculptures of Lon Bruselback, as well as an interesting selection of wines and specialty cheeses for sale. A block away, **Toujours,** 704 NW Beach Dr. (© 541/574-6404), sells natural-fiber women's clothes. On this same street, you'll find several other interesting gift shops.

OTHER NEWPORT ACTIVITIES & ATTRACTIONS

If you'd like to delve into local history, stop by the **Oregon Coast History Center,** 545 SW Ninth St. (© **541/265-7509**), which consists of two historic buildings—the Burrows House and the Log Cabin. The Burrows House was built in 1895 as a boardinghouse and now contains exhibits of Victorian household furnishings and fashions. The Log Cabin houses Siletz Indian artifacts from the area, as well as exhibits on logging, farming, and maritime history. The museum is open Tuesday through Sunday, June through September from 10am to 5pm and October through May from 11am to 4pm. Admission is free.

In the community of Seal Rock, 10 miles south of Newport, you'll find **Triad Gallery,** 5667 NW U.S. 101 (© **541/563-5442**), which has an eclectic array of fine arts and crafts and is the most strikingly designed art gallery on the Oregon coast.

Take a drive east from the bayfront along scenic Yaquina Bay Road and you'll come to **Toledo,** a small town that is slowly becoming something of an art community. In downtown Toledo, you'll find several artists' studios and galleries. For more information, contact the **Toledo Chamber of Commerce** (© **541/336-3183;** www.visittoledo oregon.com).

WHERE TO STAY
EXPENSIVE
Starfish Point 🌟🌟 Located north of town in a grove of fir trees on the edge of a cliff, the Starfish Point condominiums are my favorite rooms in the area. Each of the six condos has two bedrooms and two baths spaced over two floors. Between the two floors you'll find a cozy sitting area in an octagonal room that's almost all windows. This little sunroom is in addition to the spacious living room with its fireplace and stereo. The bathrooms here are extravagant, with two-person whirlpool tubs and skylights or big windows. A path leads down to the beach, and to the north is Yaquina Head, one of the coast's picturesque headlands. You're a ways out of town here, so you might want to cook your own meals and savor the solitude.

140 NW 48th St., Newport, OR 97365. © **800/870-7795** or 541/265-3751. Fax 541/265-3040. www.starfishpoint.com. 6 units. $165–$190 double; lower rates in off season. 2-night minimum on weekends. AE, DC, DISC, MC, V. Pets accepted ($10). *In room:* TV/VCR/DVD, kitchen, fridge, coffeemaker.

MODERATE
Elizabeth Street Inn 🌟 Located in the Nye Beach area and within walking distance of Yaquina Bay State Park, this oceanfront hotel, with its stone foundation wall, cedar-shingle facade, and white trim, has a classic beachy feel. There's nautical theme throughout and all rooms have ocean views, balconies, and fireplaces; some also have whirlpool tubs. The hotel is perched up on a bluff above the beach, and there are several good restaurants within walking distance.

232 SW Elizabeth St. (P.O. Box 1342), Newport, OR 97365. © **877/265-9400** or 541/265-9400. Fax 541/265-9551. www.elizabethstreetinn.com. 74 units. $159–$199 double, $229 suite; lower rates Nov–Mar. Rates include continental breakfast. AE, DISC, MC, V. **Amenities:** Indoor pool; exercise room; Jacuzzi. *In room:* TV, fridge, coffeemaker, hair dryer.

Newport Belle Bed & Breakfast 🌟🌟 *Finds* This 100-foot-long modern sternwheeler is one of the most unusual B&Bs on the Oregon coast and is docked in the Newport Marina in Yaquina Bay not far from the Oregon Coast Aquarium. The guest rooms (staterooms) here are small, as you'd expect on any boat, but they all have big windows, private bathrooms, and wood floors. A parlor on the main deck serves as a gathering space.

P.O. Box 685, South Beach, OR 97366. ② 800/348-1922 or 541/867-6290. Fax 541/867-6291. www. newportbelle.com. 5 units. $125–$145 double. Rates include full breakfast. 2-night minimum on weekends and during summer. AE, DC, DISC, MC, V. Children over 7 accepted. *In room:* No phone.

Sylvia Beach Hotel ✺✺ *(Finds)* This eclectic four-story cedar-shingled hotel pays homage to literature and is one of the Oregon coast's most famous lodgings. The guest rooms are named for different authors, and in each you'll find memorabilia, books, and decor that reflect their lives, times, and works. The Agatha Christie Room, the hotel's most popular, seems full of clues, while in the Edgar Allan Poe Room, a pendulum hangs over the bed and a stuffed raven sits by the window. Among the writers represented are Tennessee Williams, Colette, Ernest Hemingway, Mark Twain, Jane Austen, F. Scott Fitzgerald, Emily Dickinson, and even Dr. Seuss. The Tables of Content restaurant downstairs is a local favorite (p. 204).

267 NW Cliff St., Newport, OR 97365-3707. ② 888/795-8422 or 541/265-5428. www.sylviabeachhotel.com. 20 units. $68–$178 double. Rates include full breakfast. 2-night minimum on weekends. AE, MC, V. **Amenities:** Restaurant (Northwest). *In room:* No phone.

Tyee Lodge ✺✺ Located just south of Yaquina Head, this oceanfront bed-and-breakfast sits atop a high bluff surrounded by tall trees. Guest rooms are large and all have good ocean views, as do the living and dining rooms. There are gas fireplaces in all the rooms, and the house has a modern look with Native American accents. In the breakfast room, you'll find a telescope for whale-watching, and on cooler days, a fireplace warms the living room. A private trail leads down to the beach, and an outdoor hot tub looks out to the ocean.

4925 NW Woody Way, Newport, OR 97365. ② 888/553-8933 or 541/265-8953. www.tyeelodge.com. 5 units. $110–$160 double. Rates include full breakfast. AE, DISC, MC, V. **Amenities:** Concierge; business center. *In room:* Hair dryer, free local calls, Wi-Fi.

CAMPGROUNDS

North of Newport you'll find **Beverly Beach State Park,** which is known for its good surfing and has campsites and yurts. South of town, at the mouth of Yaquina Bay, is **South Beach State Park** (② 541/867-4715), one of the biggest state-park campgrounds on the coast (it also has yurts). However, I prefer Beverly Beach. To make reservations at either campground, contact **ReserveAmerica** (② 800/452-5687; www.reserveamerica.com).

WHERE TO DINE

For an espresso, a slice of pizza, or a good panino sandwich, drop by **Panini Bakery,** 232 NW Coast St. (② 541/265-5033), which is in the Nye Beach neighborhood. For pastries and artisan breads, search out **La Maison Bakery & Cafe,** 35 SW Ninth St. (② 541/265-8812), which is just off U.S. 101. On a hot summer day, nothing tastes better than a pint of microbrewed ale at **Rogue Ales Public House,** 748 SW Bay Blvd. (② 541/265-3188; www.rogue.com). There's a second pub over near the Oregon Coast Aquarium at 2320 OSU Dr. (② 541/867-3660). For coffee, grab a table on the deck at **The Coffee House,** 156 SW Bay Blvd. (② 541/265-6263), and you'll have front-row seat for watching all the action on the bayfront.

MODERATE

April's at Nye Beach ✺✺ MEDITERRANEAN Located in the historic Nye Beach neighborhood, this restaurant provides an alternative to the Tables of Content restaurant across the street. Popular with the hip crowd, as well as with patrons of the nearby Newport Center for the Performing Arts, the restaurant dishes up good contemporary Italian fare amid artistic surroundings. The afternoon light here is fabulous, so try to schedule your dinner for sunset (and ask for a table with an ocean view). There's an excellent selection of regional wines at reasonable prices.

749 NW Third St. ☎ **541/265-6855.** Reservations recommended. Main courses $15–$21. DISC, MC, V. Wed–Sun 5–8:45pm. Closed in Jan.

Panache ☙ NORTHWEST   Big and bright, this restaurant brings a highly refined dining experience to the area, and may be the wave of the future for the once-funky Nye Beach neighborhood. Located across the street form the Performing Arts Center, this elegant restaurant is the perfect spot for a pretheater dinner. Start your meal with the "pink martini" shrimp cocktail and then move on to the unusual savory seafood cheesecake. The menu usually also includes a couple of vegetarian entrees. The lunch menu is primarily sandwiches, but you can get a slice of the seafood cheesecake, too.

614 W. Olive St. ☎ **541/265-2929.** www.panachenewport.com. Reservations recommended. Main courses $7–$10 lunch, $16–$29 dinner. AE, DISC, MC, V. Tues–Sat 11am–2pm and 5–9pm; Sun 10am–2pm.

Saffron Salmon ☙☙ NORTHWEST   With its walls of glass, bold contemporary styling, and location at the end of a pier on the bayfront, this restaurant is my favorite restaurant in Newport. As you dine on saffron-scented salmon, you'll watch commercial fishermen unloading their catch just outside the window. Fish just doesn't get any fresher than this. Keep an eye out for sea lions, too. At lunch, go for the saffron salmon sandwich.

859 SW Bay Blvd. ☎ **541/265-8921.** Reservations recommended. Main courses $4–$17 lunch, $10–$27 dinner. AE, MC, V. Thurs–Tues 11:30am–2:30pm and 5–8:30pm.

Tables of Content ☙☙ *Finds* INTERNATIONAL   Located in the Sylvia Beach Hotel, this restaurant serves delicious and very reasonably priced four-course dinners. Although on any given night you'll have limited choices, if you enjoy creative cookery and eclectic combinations, you'll leave happy. Expect dishes such as mushroom sauté, Greek salad, salmon dijonnaise, and black-bean cakes.

Sylvia Beach Hotel, 267 NW Cliff St. ☎ **541/265-5428.** www.sylviabeachhotel.com. Reservations required. Fixed-price 4-course dinner $20. AE, MC, V. Seatings Sun–Thurs 7pm; Fri–Sat 6 and 8:30pm.

INEXPENSIVE

Lighthouse Deli & Fish Company ☙ DELI   If you're looking for the best fish and chips on the Oregon coast, be sure to sample the offerings at this little roadside stand near the Oregon Coast Aquarium. You can get salmon and chips, halibut and chips, oysters and chips, shrimp and chips, or the basic house fish and chips, which is made with whatever fresh inexpensive fish is available that day. Okay, so the chips aren't the best, but the fish is very lightly battered, which lets its flavor shine through. They also do smoked salmon and tuna.

3640 SW U.S. 101. ☎ **541/867-6800.** www.lighthousedeli.com. Main dishes $5–$11. DISC, MC, V. Daily 7am–9pm.

Local Ocean Seafoods ☙ SEAFOOD   If you want fresh, sustainably harvested seafood, this casual fish-market-style eatery is the place. The modern space, with its big windows, is located directly across the street from the water, so you can watch fishing boats coming and going and know that the fish on your plate was caught only hours ago. The fish tacos and the albacore tuna kabobs are excellent, but you can also get a simple whole crab or a crab po' boy. There are also plenty of oyster and shrimp dishes as well.

213 SE Bay Blvd. ☎ **541/574-7959.** www.localocean.net. Main courses $6–$18. MC, V. Daily 11am–8:30pm.

Mo's ⚲ SEAFOOD   Established in 1942, Mo's has become such an Oregon coast institution that it has spawned five other restaurants up and down the coast. Clam chowder is what made Mo's famous, and you can get it by the bowl, by the cup, or family style. *Be forewarned, though:* Some people think this clam chowder is the best and others think it's awful. (We'd put it somewhere in between the two extremes.) Basic seafood dinners are fresh, large, and inexpensive, and the seafood-salad sandwiches are whoppers. There are also such dishes as cioppino, oyster stew, and slumgullion (clam chowder with shrimp). Expect a line out the door.

657 SW Bay Blvd. ⓒ 541/265-2979. www.moschowder.com. Complete dinner $4–$13. AE, DISC, MC, V. Daily 11am–9pm.

8 Yachats

24 miles S of Newport, 26 miles N of Florence, 138 miles SE of Portland

Located on the north side of 800-foot-high Cape Perpetua, the village of Yachats (pronounced *Yah*-hots) is something of an artists' community that also attracts a good number of counterculture types. When you get your first glimpse of the town's setting, you, too, will likely agree that there's more than enough beauty here to inspire anyone to artistic pursuits. Yachats is an Alsi Indian word meaning "dark waters at the foot of the mountains," and that sums up perfectly the setting of this small community, one of the few on the Oregon coast that could really be considered a village. The tiny Yachats River flows into the surf on the south edge of town, and to the east stand steep, forested mountains. The shoreline on which the town stands is rocky, with little coves here and there where you can find agates among the pebbles paving the beach. Tide pools offer hours of exploring, and, in winter, storm waves create a spectacular show. Uncrowded beaches, comfortable motels, and one of the coast's best restaurants add up to a great spot for a quiet getaway.

ESSENTIALS
GETTING THERE   From the north, take Ore. 34 west from Corvallis to Waldport and then head south on U.S. 101. From the south, take Ore. 126 west from Eugene to Florence and then head north on U.S. 101.

VISITOR INFORMATION   Contact the **Yachats Area Chamber of Commerce,** 241 U.S. 101 (P.O. Box 728), Yachats, OR 97498 (ⓒ **800/929-0477** or 541/ 547-3530; www.yachats.org).

YACHATS AREA ACTIVITIES & ATTRACTIONS
Looming over tiny Yachats is the impressive bulk of 800-foot-high Cape Perpetua, the highest spot on the Oregon coast. Because of the cape's rugged beauty and diversity of natural habitats, it has been designated the **Cape Perpetua Scenic Area** ⚲⚲⚲. The **Cape Perpetua Interpretive Center** (ⓒ **541/547-3289**) is on a steep road off U.S. 101 and houses displays on the natural history of the cape and the Native Americans who harvested its bountiful seafood for thousands of years. The visitor center is open daily from 9am to 5pm between Memorial Day and Labor Day (shorter hours spring through fall and closed in winter). Admission is $5 per vehicle. Within the scenic area are 18 miles of hiking trails, tide pools, ancient forests, scenic overlooks, and a campground. Guided hikes are offered (weather permitting) when the visitor center is open. If you're here on a clear day, be sure to drive to the top of the cape for one of the finest vistas on the coast. Waves and tides are a year-round source of fascination along these

rocky shores, and Cape Perpetua's tide pools are some of the best on the coast. There's good access to the tide pools at the pull-off at the north end of the scenic area. However, it is the more dramatic interactions of waves and rocks that attract most people to walk the short oceanside trail here: At the **Devil's Churn,** a spouting horn caused by waves crashing into a narrow fissure in the basalt shoreline sends geyserlike plumes of water skyward, and waves boil through a narrow opening in the rocks.

Right in Yachats, be sure to visit **Yachats State Park,** which is at the southern end of a .8-mile trail that leads north along a rocky stretch of coastline to **Smelt Sands State Recreation Site.** Along the route of the trail, there are little pocket beaches (where smelts spawn) and tide pools. At the north end of the trail, a wide, sandy beach stretches northward. Just across the bridge at the south end of town, you'll find the **Yachats Ocean State Park Wayside,** another good beach access.

Between April and October each year, **fishing** in Yachats takes an unusual twist. It's during these months that thousands of smelts, sardinelike fish, spawn in the waves that crash in the sandy coves just north of Yachats. The fish can be caught using a dip net, and so popular are the little fish that the town holds an annual **Smelt Fry** each year on the second Saturday in July.

Gray whales also come close to shore near Yachats. You can see them in the spring from Cape Perpetua, and throughout the summer several take up residence at the mouth of the Yachats River. South of Cape Perpetua, Neptune State Scenic Viewpoint at the mouth of Cummins Creek, and Strawberry Hill Wayside are other good places to spot whales, as well as sea lions, which can be seen lounging on the rocks offshore at Strawberry Hill.

A couple of historic buildings in the area are also worth a visit. Built in 1927, the **Little Log Church by the Sea,** 328 W. Third St. (© **541/547-3976**), is now a museum housing displays on local history. The museum is open Monday through Wednesday and Friday from noon to 3pm and Saturday and Sunday from 10am to 4pm.

The Yachats area has several crafts galleries, the most interesting of which is **Earthworks Gallery,** 2222 U.S. 101 N. (© **541/547-4300**), located north of town and focusing on glass and ceramic art.

WHERE TO STAY

In addition to the hotels listed below, plenty of rental homes are available in Yachats. Contact **Ocean Odyssey,** P.O. Box 491, Yachats, OR 97498 (© **800/800-1915** or 541/547-3637; www.ocean-odyssey.com), or **Yachats Village Rentals,** 230 Aqua Vista Loop (P.O. Box 44), Yachats, OR 97498 (© **888/288-5077** or 541/547-3501; www.97498.com). Rates range from around $100 to $200 per night.

Overleaf Lodge 🐦🐦 Overlooking the rocky shoreline at the north end of Yachats, this modern hotel offers some of the most luxurious and tastefully decorated rooms on the central coast. Built in a sort of modern interpretation of the traditional Victorian beach cottage, the lodge caters primarily to couples seeking a romantic escape. Guest rooms all have ocean views, and most have patios or balconies. For a truly memorable stay, book one of the Restless Waters rooms, which have whirlpool tubs overlooking the crashing waves below. If you don't want to spring for one of these rooms, you can still curl up in a sunny little window nook beside your balcony and watch the waves in relative comfort. Many rooms also have fireplaces. At press time, the hotel was in the process of adding new rooms and a spa.

280 Overleaf Lodge Lane (P.O. Box 291), Yachats, OR 97498. ☎ **800/338-0507** or 541/547-4880. Fax 541/547-4888. www.overleaflodge.com. 54 units. Late June to mid-Sept $150–$230 double, $260–$450 suite; mid-Sept to late June $105–$230 double, $240–$450 suite. Rates include continental breakfast. Children 6 and under stay free in parent's room. AE, DISC, MC, V. **Amenities:** Exercise room; full-service spa; Jacuzzi; sauna; business center; massage; guest laundry. *In room:* TV/DVD, dataport, fridge, coffeemaker, hair dryer, free local calls, Wi-Fi.

Shamrock Lodgettes ⊕ *(Finds* This collection of classic log cabins at the mouth of the Yachats River bewitched me and my wife the first time we saw it. Spacious lawns and old fir trees give the rustic cabins a relaxed old-fashioned appeal that just begs you to kick back and forget your cares. Each log cabin has a tile entry, hardwood floors, a kitchenette, a stone fireplace, and a big picture window that takes in a view of either the beach or the river. Other than that, they're pretty basic. The motel rooms are more up-to-date and have fireplaces and views. Some rooms have whirlpool tubs. The oceanfront rooms were all renovated in 2005.

105 U.S. 101 S. (P.O. Box 346), Yachats, OR 97498. ☎ **800/845-5028** or 541/547-3312. Fax 541/547-3843. www. shamrocklodgettes.com. 21 units (including 8 cabins). $69–$129 double; $99–$165 cabin. Children 6 and under stay free in parent's room. AE, MC, V. Pets accepted ($6). **Amenities:** Exercise room; Jacuzzi; sauna; massage. *In room:* TV, kitchen, fridge, coffeemaker, free local calls.

CAMPGROUNDS

Beachside State Recreation Site (☎ **541/563-3220**) is just north of Yachats on U.S. 101, but we don't particularly recommend it. To make reservations, contact **ReserveAmerica** (☎ **800/452-5687;** www.reserveamerica.com). For exploring the rugged Cape Perpetua area, the Forest Service's **Cape Perpetua Campground,** in a wooded setting set a little way back from the water, is your best option.

WHERE TO DINE

For tasty and creative sandwiches, such as albacore tuna with chipotle mayo on focaccia, stop in at **Grand Occasions Café,** 84 Beach St. (☎ **541/547-4409**), which also does good desserts and sells imported European meats and cheeses. For espresso, drop by **Toad Hall Coffee Gallery,** 237 W. Third St. (☎ **541/547-4044**), which is also an unusual little gift shop.

The Drift Inn ⊕ *(Finds* AMERICAN/NORTHWEST This unprepossessing place, right on U.S. 101 in the center of Yachats, may seem at first glance to be little more than a modern tavern (albeit a tavern with big windows, wooden booths, and polished wood floors), but looks can be deceiving. The Drift Inn actually has a split personality. Sure there's the standard beer-and-burgers menu, but at dinner, there are specials such as salmon topped with a sauté of hazelnuts, mushrooms, and blackberries.

124 U.S. 101 N. ☎ **541/547-4477.** www.the-drift-inn.com. Main courses $7–$19. MC, V. Sun–Thurs 8am–9pm; Fri–Sat 8am–9 or 9:30pm.

La Serre ⊕⊕ NORTHWEST For years, La Serre has served up the best food in the area, but, if you're like me, you'll be distracted by the dessert table before you even see a menu. Be sure to start your meal with an order of the clam puffs (a blend of clams, herbs, and cream cheese baked in puff pastry). The entree menu includes an excellent fisherman's stew, which is basically a cioppino with so much fish, shrimp, clams, crab, and oysters in it that you don't know where to start. The desserts, including tiramisu and berry cobbler, are as good as they look. There are inexpensive early-bird dinners until 6pm.

Second Ave. and Beach St. ☎ **541/547-3420.** Reservations highly recommended. Main courses $7.50–$27. AE, DC, MC, V. Mon and Wed–Thurs 5–8 or 9pm; Fri–Sun 4–9pm. Closed Jan.

SOUTH TO FLORENCE

More wide sandy beaches can be found south of Yachats at (in order from north to south) Stonefield Beach State Recreation Site, Muriel O. Ponsler Memorial Wayside, and Carl G. Washburne Memorial State Park (© **541/547-3416**). The latter offers 5 miles of beach, hiking trails, and a campground.

The next park to the south, **Heceta Head Lighthouse State Scenic Viewpoint,** offers the most breathtaking setting. Situated on a small sandy cove, the park has a stream flowing across the beach and several haystack rocks just offshore. As the name implies, the park is home to **Heceta Head Lighthouse,** the most photographed lighthouse on the Oregon coast. From mid-March to October daily between 11am and 3pm, volunteers lead guided tours of the lighthouse. Heceta (pronounced Huh-*see*-tuh) Head is a rugged headland that's named for Spanish explorer Capt. Bruno Heceta. The old lighthouse keeper's home is now a bed-and-breakfast (see below). There is a $3 day-use fee here.

At more than 300 feet long and 120 feet high, **Sea Lion Caves** *ൟൟ*, 91560 U.S. 101 N. (© **541/547-3111;** www.sealioncaves.com), 1 mile south of Heceta Head Lighthouse, is the largest sea cave in the United States. The cave was discovered in 1880, and since 1932 it has been one of the most popular stops along the Oregon coast. The cave and a nearby rock ledge are the only year-round mainland homes for Steller's sea lions, hundreds of which reside here throughout the year. This is the larger of the two species of sea lion that frequent this coast, and bulls can weigh almost a ton. The sea lions spend the day lounging and barking up a storm, and the bickering of the adults and antics of the pups are always entertaining. Although at any time of year you're likely to find quite a few of the sea lions here, it is during the fall and winter that the majority of the sea lions move into the cave. Today, a combination of stairs, pathways, and an elevator lead down from the bluff-top gift shop to a viewpoint in the cave wall. The best time to visit is late in the afternoon, when the sun shines directly into the cave and the crowds of people are smaller. Admission is $8 adults, $4.50 children 6 to 15. The caves are open daily from 9am and close 1 hour before darkness in the cave.

Another 6 miles south is the **Darlingtonia State Natural Site,** a small botanical preserve protecting a bog full of rare *Darlingtonia californica* plants, insectivorous pitcher plants also known as cobra lilies. You'll find this fascinating preserve on Mercer Lake Road.

WHERE TO STAY

Heceta Head Lightstation *ൟൟ*   Thanks to a spectacular setting on a forested headland, the Heceta Head Lighthouse is the most photographed lighthouse on the Oregon coast. And, although you can't spend the night in the lighthouse itself, you can stay in the former lighthouse keeper's home, a white-clapboard Victorian building high atop an oceanfront bluff and set behind a picket fence. The house is a National Historic Site and has been preserved much the way it might have been when it was active. Breakfasts are elaborate seven-course meals. Because this is one of the most popular B&Bs on the coast, you'll need to book your room 2 to 3 months in advance for a weekday stay and 5 to 6 months in advance for a weekend stay. Oh, and by the way, the inn is haunted.

92072 U.S. 101 S., Yachats, OR 97498. © 541/547-3696. www.hecetalighthouse.com. 6 units (4 with private bathroom). $133–$169 double with shared bathroom; $153–$251 double with private bathroom. Rates include full breakfast. DISC, MC, V. Children over 10 are welcome. *In room:* No phone, Wi-Fi.

Ocean Haven *ℛ* *Value* Rustic and cozy, the Ocean Haven is a great place to hole up with family or friends. Opt for either the North View or the South View room, and you'll find yourself with two walls of glass overlooking the ocean. When the weather's good, you're only a short walk from the beach and some of the best tide pools around; when it's stormy, watch the waves from your room. (Binoculars are provided.) The Shag's Nest cottage, located across the grass from the main lodge and perched on the edge of the bluff, is my favorite room here. Stay in the cottage and you can lie in bed gazing out to sea with a fire crackling in the fireplace. A minimum stay may apply, and there are a few nature-friendly house rules, but if you're looking for a good value, great views, and rooms that are a little bit unusual, this is the place. There's a shop here that sells organic foods. This place is very enviro-friendly (no Hummers allowed on premises).

94770 U.S. 101, Yachats, OR 97498. *✆* **541/547-3583**. www.oceanhaven.com. 5 units. $90–$100 double. AE, DISC, MC, V. **Amenities:** Concierge. *In room:* Kitchen, fridge, coffeemaker, no phone.

Sea Quest Bed and Breakfast *ℛℛ* Set on a low bluff above the beach, this sprawling contemporary inn is about as luxurious a place as you'll find on the central Oregon coast. Privacy and romance are high priorities here, and all rooms have private entrances, ocean views, and whirlpool tubs. The convivial great room on the second floor has expansive views. There's also a huge deck. Miles of beach stretch on either side of the inn.

95354 U.S. 101, Yachats, OR 97498. *✆* **800/341-4878** or 541/547-3782. www.seaq.com. 6 units. $160–$190 double; $350 suite. 2-night minimum on weekends; 3-night minimum on holidays. MC, V. *In room:* No phone.

CAMPGROUNDS

Just south of Cape Perpetua, there are a couple of campgrounds within Siuslaw National Forest. **Rock Creek Campground** (*✆* 541/547-3289; www.fs.fed.us/r6/ siuslaw) is tucked back in the woods along a pretty creek and is a good choice for tenters and anyone who dislikes crowds. **Carl G. Washburne Memorial State Park** (*✆* **800/551-6949** or 541/547-3416; www.oregonstateparks.org) is the area's state park option and is one of only a few coastal state parks that do not take reservations. Campsites are across the highway from a pretty beach just north of Heceta Head.

9 Florence & the Oregon Dunes National Recreation Area

50 miles S of Newport, 50 miles N of Coos Bay, 60 miles W of Eugene

Florence and the Oregon Dunes National Recreation Area, which stretches south of town for almost 50 miles, have long been popular summer vacation spots for Oregon families. The national recreation area is the longest unbroken, publicly owned stretch of coastline on the Oregon coast, and within its boundaries are 14,000 acres of dunes, some of which stand more than 500 feet tall.

Within this vast area of shifting sands—the largest area of sand dunes on the West Coast—there are numerous lakes both large and small, living forests, and skeletal forests of trees that were long ago "drowned" beneath drifting sands. Many area lakes are ringed with summer homes and campgrounds, and it is these lakes that are the primary destination of many vacationers. Consequently, water-skiing and fishing are among the most popular activities, followed by riding off-road vehicles (ORVs) through the sand dunes.

The Umpqua River divides the national recreation area roughly at its midway point, and on its banks you'll find the towns of Gardiner, Reedsport, and Winchester

Bay, each of which has a very distinct character. Gardiner was founded in 1841 when a Boston merchant's fur-trading ship wrecked near here. An important mill town in the 19th century, Gardiner has several stately Victorian homes. Reedsport is the largest of these three communities and is the site of the Umpqua Discovery Center, a museum focusing on the history and natural history of this region. The town of Winchester Bay is almost at the mouth of the Umpqua River and is known for its large fleet of charter-fishing boats.

Florence is one of the few towns on the Oregon coast with historic character. Set on the banks of the Siuslaw River, it is filled with restored wooden commercial buildings that house restaurants and interesting shops. The charm of the historic downtown is all the more appealing when compared to the unsightly sprawl of U.S. 101.

ESSENTIALS

GETTING THERE   Florence is on U.S. 101 at the junction with Ore. 126 from Eugene. Gardiner, Reedsport, and Winchester Bay are all on U.S. 101 at or near the junction with Ore. 38 from Elkton, which in turn is reached from I-5 by taking either Ore. 99 from Drain or Ore. 138 from Sutherlin.

VISITOR INFORMATION   For more information on the dunes, contact the **Oregon Dunes National Recreation Area,** 855 U.S. 101, Reedsport, OR 97467 (© **541/ 271-3611;** www.fs.fed.us/r6/siuslaw). From mid-May to mid-September, this visitor center is open in daily from 8am to 4:30pm; other months, it is closed on Saturday and Sunday.

For more information on Florence, contact the **Florence Area Chamber of Commerce,** 290 U.S. 101, Florence, OR 97439 (© **800/524-4864** or 541/997-3128; www. florencechamber.com).

There is a $5-per-car day-use fee within the recreation area.

THE OREGON DUNES NATIONAL RECREATION AREA

The first Oregon dunes were formed between 12 and 26 million years ago by the weathering of inland mountain ranges. Though the dunes are in constant flux, they reached their current size and shape about 7,000 years ago after the massive eruption of the Mount Mazama volcano, which emptied out the entire molten-rock contents of the Mount Mazama, and in the process created the caldera that would become Crater Lake.

Water currents and winds are factors responsible for the dunes. Currents move the sand particles north each winter and south each summer, while constant winds off the Pacific Ocean blow the sand eastward, piling it up into dunes that are slowly marching east. Over thousands of years, the dunes have swallowed up forests, leaving some groves of trees as remnant tree islands.

Freshwater trapped behind the dunes has formed numerous **freshwater lakes,** many of which are now ringed by campgrounds and vacation homes. These lakes are popular for fishing, swimming, and boating. The largest of the lakes lie outside the national recreation area and are, from north to south, Woahink Lake, Siltcoos Lake, Tahkenitch Lake, Clear Lake, Eel Lake, North Tenmile Lake, and Tenmile Lake. Smaller lakes that are within the recreation area include Cleawox Lake, Carter Lake, Beale Lake, and Horsfall Lake. Traditionally, these lakes have been in a constant state of flux; with the construction of homes around their shores, though, the lakes are now maintained at their current shape and size.

European beach grass is playing an even greater role in changing the natural dynamics of this region. Introduced to anchor sand dunes and prevent them from inundating roads and river channels, this plant has been much more effective than anyone ever imagined. Able to survive even when buried under several feet of sand, European beach grass has covered many acres of land and formed dunes in back of the beach. These dunes effectively block sand from blowing inland off the beach, and as winds blow sand off the dunes into wet, low-lying areas, vegetation takes hold, thus eliminating areas of former dunes. Aerial photos have shown that where once 80% of the dunes here were open sand, today only 20% are. It is predicted that within 50 years, these dunes will all have been completely covered with vegetation and will no longer be the barren, windswept expanses of sand seen today.

There are numerous options for exploring the dunes. **Jessie M. Honeyman Memorial State Park** 𝄞𝄞 (© 541/997-3641), 3 miles south of Florence, is a unique spot with a beautiful forest-bordered lake and towering sand dunes. The park offers camping, picnicking, hiking trails, and access to Cleawox and Woahink lakes. On Cleawox Lake, there is a swimming area and a boat-rental facility. The dunes adjacent to Cleawox Lake are used by off-road vehicles.

The easiest place to get an overview of the dunes is at the **Oregon Dunes Overlook,** 10 miles south of Florence. Here you'll find viewing platforms high atop a forested sand dune that overlooks a vast expanse of bare sand. Another easy place from which to view the dunes is the viewing platform on the Taylor Dunes Trail, which begins at the **Carter Lake Campground,** 7½ miles south of Florence. It is an easy ½-mile walk to the viewing platform.

There are several places to wander among these sand dunes. If you have time only for a quick walk, head to **Carter Lake Campground,** where you can continue on from the Taylor Dunes viewing platform. The beach is less than a mile beyond the viewing platform, and roughly half this distance is through dunes. From this same campground, you can hike the **Carter Dunes Trail.** The beach is 1½ miles away through dunes, forest, and meadows known as a *deflation plain.* A 3.5-mile loop trail leads from the **Oregon Dunes Overlook** (see above) out to the beach by way of Tahkenitch Creek, a meandering stream that flows through the dunes and out to the ocean. Another mile south of the Oregon Dunes Overlook, you'll find the **Tahkenitch Trail Head,** which accesses an 8-mile network of little-used trails that wander through dunes, forest, marshes, and meadows. However, for truly impressive dunes, the best route is the **John Dellenback Dunes Trail** 𝄞𝄞, which has its trail head a half mile south of **Eel Creek Campground** (10½ miles south of Reedsport). This 3-mile round-trip trail leads through an area of dunes 2 miles wide by 4 miles long. Don't get lost!

About 30% of the sand dunes are open to **off-road vehicles (ORVs),** and throngs of people flock to this area to roar up and down the dunes. If you'd like to do a little off-roading, you can rent a dune buggy from **Sandland Adventures,** 85366 U.S. 101 S. (© **541/997-8087;** www.sandland.com), 1 mile south of Florence (this company has a little amusement park as well); or **Sand Dunes Frontier,** 83960 U.S. 101 S. (© **541/997-3544;** www.sanddunesfrontier.com), 4 miles south of Florence. Both companies also offer guided tours of the dunes. The tours cost about $10 to $20 for adults and $5 for children. One-person dune buggies and ATVs rent for about $40 per hour. Down at the southern end of the recreation area, you can rent vehicles from **Spinreel Dune Buggy Rentals,** 67045 Spinreel Dr. (© **541/759-3313;** http://ride theoregondunes.com), located just off U.S. 101, about 9 miles south of Reedsport.

Fun Fact Iditarod in the Sand?

The area's most unusual annual event is the **Dune Musher's Mail Run** (www. oregondunemushers.com), which takes place each year in March and attracts dogsled teams from all over the United States and Canada. Teams race from Horsfall Beach near Coos Bay all the way to Florence, with miniteams of three or four dogs covering 55 miles in 2 days, and full-size teams of 5 to 12 dogs covering 72 miles in 2 days. For this race, dogsleds with fat tires (instead of skids) are used. Racers carry special commemorative envelopes that are canceled at both Horsfall Beach and Florence.

Ever heard of sand boarding? It's basically snowboarding in the sand, and at **Sand Master Park,** 87542 U.S. 101 (© **541/997-6006;** www.sandmasterpark.com), you (or your teenage kids) will find 40 acres of sculpted sand dunes designed to mimic a wintertime snowboard park (lots of jumps and rails). June through August, the park is open daily from 9am to 7pm; other months, it's open Thursday through Tuesday from 10am to 5pm. Sand boards rent for $16 to $25.

If you'd rather avoid the dune buggies and ORVs, stay away from the dunes between the South Jetty area (just south of Florence) and Siltcoos Lake; the area adjacent to Umpqua Lighthouse State Park just south of Winchester Bay; and the area from Spinreel Campground south to the Horsfall Dune & Beach Access Road, which is just north of the town of North Bend.

OTHER ACTIVITIES & ATTRACTIONS
IN THE FLORENCE AREA

Florence's **Old Town,** on the north bank of the Siuslaw River, is one of the most charming historic districts on the Oregon coast. The restored wood and brick buildings, many of which house interesting shops, galleries, and restaurants, capture the flavor of a 19th-century fishing village.

If you'd like to ride a horse along the beach, head north to **C&M Stables,** 90241 U.S. 101 N. (© **541/997-7540;** www.oregonhorsebackriding.com), which is located 8 miles north of Florence and offers rides either on the beach—and through the dunes—or into the coast range. A 2-hour ride on the beach will cost you $45 to $55.

If golf is your sport, try the 18-hole **Sandpines Golf Course,** 1201 35th St. (© **800/ 917-4653** or 541/997-1940; www.sandpines.com), which plays through dunes and pine forest and is one of Oregon's most popular courses. You'll pay $45 to $89 for 18 holes. This course was in the process of adding a new clubhouse at press time. Alternatively, try the 18-hole **Ocean Dunes Golf Links,** 3345 Munsel Lake Rd. (© **800/468-4833;** http://oceandunesgolf.com), which also plays through the dunes and charges $38 to $40 for 18 holes.

IN THE REEDSPORT AREA

In downtown Reedsport on the Umpqua River waterfront, you can visit the **Umpqua Discovery Center,** 409 Riverfront Way (© **541/271-4816;** www.umpquadiscovery center.com). This modern museum contains displays on the history and ecology of the area. The newest exhibit focuses on the natural history of the tidewater region. June through September, it's open daily from 9am to 5pm; other months, daily from 10am to 4pm. Admission is $8 for adults, $7 for seniors, and $4 for children 6 to 15. Outside the discovery center, you'll find an observation tower that is sometimes a good place to do a little bird-watching.

At the **Dean Creek Elk Viewing Area** ⋇, 1 mile east of town on Ore. 38, you can spot 120 or more elk grazing on 1,000 acres of meadows that have been set aside as a preserve. In summer, the elk tend to stay in the forest, where it's cooler.

In Winchester Bay, you can visit the historic **Umpqua River Lighthouse.** The original lighthouse was at the mouth of the Umpqua River and was the first lighthouse on the Oregon coast. It fell into the Umpqua River in 1861 and was replaced in 1894 by the current lighthouse. Adjacent to the lighthouse is the **Visitors Center & Museum,** 1020 Lighthouse Rd. (✆ 541/271-4631), which is housed in a former coast-guard station and contains historical exhibits and an information center. Here at the museum, you can arrange to join a tour of the lighthouse. Tours are offered daily between 10am and 4pm.

Across the street from the lighthouse is a **whale-viewing platform.** (The best viewing months are Nov–June.) Also nearby is the very pretty **Umpqua Lighthouse State Park** (✆ 541/271-4118), the site of the 500-foot-tall sand dunes that are the tallest in the United States. The park offers picnicking, hiking, and camping amid forests and sand dunes.

If you want to do some fishing on the Umpqua and need a guide to lead you to the best fishing holes, contact Todd Hannah at **The Oregon Angler** (✆ 800/428-8585; www.theoregonangler.com); rates are $150 for a day of fishing.

WHERE TO STAY
IN FLORENCE
Driftwood Shores Resort & Conference Center ⋇ (Kids)   Located several miles north of Florence's Old Town district, this is the only oceanfront lodging in the area. It's popular year-round, so book early. The rooms vary in size and amenities, but all have ocean views and balconies. Most also have kitchens, and the three-bedroom suites are as large as many vacation homes. The hotel's restaurant has ocean views from every table.

88416 First Ave., Florence, OR 97439. ✆ 800/422-5091 or 541/997-8263. Fax 541/997-5857. www.driftwoodshores. com. 136 units. $87–$248 double; $199–$299 suite. AE, DC, DISC, MC, V. **Amenities:** Restaurant (American); lounge; indoor pool; Jacuzzi; coin-op laundry. In room: TV, fridge, coffeemaker, hair dryer, iron, Wi-Fi.

The Edwin K Bed & Breakfast ⋇⋇   Located only 2 blocks from Old Town Florence, this 1914 Sears Craftsman home is one of the most luxurious B&Bs on the coast. The four upstairs rooms are the most spacious, and two overlook the Siuslaw River, which is just across the street and has a huge sand dune rising up on its far bank. One of these two front rooms has a claw-foot tub on a raised tile platform beside the bed; the other has a double whirlpool tub. Other rooms, although not as plush, are still comfortable. Breakfasts are lavish five-course affairs.

1155 Bay St. (P.O. Box 2687), Florence, OR 97439. ✆ 800/833-9465 or 541/997-8360. Fax 541/997-2423. www. edwink.com. 8 units. May–Oct $130–$150 double, $150–$170 apt/cottage; lower rates other months. Rates include full breakfast (except in apt/cottage). Children over 14 welcome in main house. DISC, MC, V. In room: No phone, fridge, hair dryer, Wi-Fi.

River House Inn ⋇   Overlooking the Siuslaw River drawbridge and sand dunes on the far side of the river, the River House is only 1 block from the heart of Florence's Old Town district. This modern motel offers comfortable and attractive rooms, most of which have views and balconies. The largest and most expensive have double whirlpool tubs. Riverfront rooms are worth requesting.

1202 Bay St., Florence, OR 97439. © 888/824-2750 or 541/997-3933. Fax 541/997-6263. www.riverhouseflorence. com. 40 units. Summer $89–$140 double; other months $79–$125 double. Children under 12 stay free in parent's room. AE, DISC, MC, V. **Amenities:** Coin-op laundry. *In room:* TV, coffeemaker, hair dryer, high-speed Internet access.

CAMPGROUNDS

North of Florence are the first of this region's many campgrounds, **Sutton** and **Alder Dune,** both of which are operated by the Forest Service. Just outside Florence at the Siuslaw River's north jetty is the relatively quiet **Harbor Vista County Park** (© 541/997-5987); with nice campsites and day-use areas, it's an alternative to crowded Honeyman State Park. South of Florence, you'll find more than a dozen Forest Service campgrounds and three state-park campgrounds within the Oregon Dunes National Recreation Area. With two lakes, swimming areas, canoe spots, sand dunes, and shady forests, **Jesse M. Honeyman Memorial State Park,** just a few miles south of Florence, is one of the most popular state parks in Oregon and stays full throughout the summer. Just south of here you'll find the Siltcoos Recreation Area, where **Lagoon Campground** and **Waxmyrtle Campground** are the best choices. **Carter Lake Campground,** on a popular swimming and boating lake, is another quiet choice in this area. The **Tahkenitch Campground,** however, is probably the best in the area. It's set in the forest on the edge of the dunes. South of Reedsport and Winchester Bay, you'll find **William M. Tugman State Park** (© 541/888-4902), at the south end of Eel Lake. **Eel Creek Campground,** adjacent to the Umpqua Dunes, is a quiet choice down at the southern end of the national recreation area. For reservations at the state park campgrounds, contact **ReserveAmerica** (© 800/452-5687; www.reserveamerica. com). Several of the national-forest campgrounds in the area accept reservations. Call the **National Recreation Reservation Service** (© 877/444-6777 or 518/885-3639; www.reserveusa.com).

WHERE TO DINE
IN FLORENCE

When you need a good cup of espresso, stop in at **Siuslaw River Coffee Roasters,** 1240 Bay St. (© 541/997-3443). If you're looking for some gourmet foods or wine, drop by **Grape Leaf,** 1269 Bay St. (© 541/997-1646), which also has a small wine bar and also serves light meals.

Bridgewater Seafood Restaurant ⚓ AMERICAN/SEAFOOD   Located in a restored building in Old Town, this eclectic eatery combines a Wild West storefront facade with a tropical interior complete with wicker furniture and potted plants. In the summer there's patio dining, and any time of year the lounge area is a cozy place to wait out the rain. The menu is long and includes everything from jambalaya and turkey enchiladas to pasta, burgers, and chowders.

1297 Bay St. © 541/997-9405. Reservations recommended. Main courses $8–$24. AE, DISC, MC, V. Mon–Fri 11am–8 or 9pm; Sat–Sun 8:30am–8 or 9pm.

International C-Food Market ⚓ SEAFOOD   Located on a dock on the old waterfront, this restaurant also happens to be a fish-processing facility, which means the seafood served here is as fresh as you'll find anywhere on the coast. The warehouse-like space has loads of windows providing views of the river, and the light at sunset can be gorgeous. The steamed Manila clams here are excellent, and the crab cakes are another good bet and, together with the steamed clams, make a great meal. Or, how about a seafood pizza or all-you-can-eat Dungeness crab?

1498 Bay St. ℭ **541/997-9646.** Reservations recommended. Main courses $9–$25. AE, DISC, MC, V. Daily 11am–8 or 9pm (open later in the summer).

Waterfront Depot ℛℛ (Finds NEW AMERICAN   This dark, cozy waterfront bar/restaurant is by far my favorite Florence restaurant. It's housed in the 1913 Mapleton railroad depot, which was moved here from farther up the Siuslaw River and is one of the many white historic buildings that line Bay Street. Inside, the restaurant is a well-balanced blend of hip bar and old-country-inn dining room. There are battered wooden floors and a beautiful little bar with underlit disks of art glass inset into the bar. The menu is on blackboards attached to the depot's old sliding doors, and though this menu is not very long, there's plenty of variety and the best values on the coast. Among the appetizers, the oyster stew is a phenomenal deal—a big bowl of full of fat, creamy oysters for under $5. Among the entrees, the grilled salmon is an equally good deal, as are the lamb shanks. For dessert, get a fat slice of cake.

1252 Bay St. ℭ **541/902-9100.** Reservations recommended. Main courses $6–$15. DISC, MC, V. Daily 4–10pm.

IN WINCHESTER BAY

If you're craving some smoked salmon or other fish, drop by **Sportsmen's Cannery & Smokehouse,** 182 Bayfront Loop, Winchester Bay (ℭ **541/271-3293**).

10 The Coos Bay Area

85 miles NW of Roseburg, 50 miles S of Florence, 24 miles N of Bandon

With a population of around 35,000, the Coos Bay area, consisting of the towns of Coos Bay, North Bend, and Charleston, is the largest urban center on the Oregon coast. Coos Bay and North Bend are the bay's commercial center and have merged into a single large town, while nearby Charleston maintains its distinct character as a small fishing port.

As the largest natural harbor between San Francisco and Puget Sound, Coos Bay has long been an important port. Logs, wood chips, and wood products are the main export. However, shipments of wood products have been down in recent years. In response to the economic downturn of the port, the bay area has been working hard to attract both more tourists and more industry. In downtown Coos Bay, there is an attractive waterfront boardwalk, complete with historical displays, and what was once a huge lumber mill is now the site of the equally large Mill Resort & Casino.

Even if it isn't the most beautiful town on the Oregon coast, Coos Bay has a lot of character and quite a few tourist amenities, including several good restaurants, moderately priced motels, and even a few B&Bs. But what makes Coos Bay a town not to be missed is its proximity to a trio of picturesque state parks.

ESSENTIALS

GETTING THERE   From the north, take Ore. 99 from just south of Cottage Grove. This road becomes Ore. 38. At Reedsport, head south on U.S. 101. From the south, take Ore. 42 from just south of Roseburg.

The North Bend Municipal Airport, 2348 Colorado St., is served by **Horizon Air** (ℭ **800/547-9308;** horizonair.com).

VISITOR INFORMATION   Contact the **Bay Area Chamber of Commerce & Visitor Center,** 50 E. Central Ave., Coos Bay, OR 97420 (© **800/824-8486** or 541/269-0215; www.oregonsbayareachamber.com).

GETTING AROUND   Car rentals are available in the Coos Bay area from **Hertz** (© **800/654-3131** or 503/249-8216; www.hertz.com) and **Enterprise Rent-a-Car** (© **800/736-8222** or 503/252-1500; www.enterprise.com).

A TRIO OF STATE PARKS & MORE

Southwest of Coos Bay you'll find three state parks and a county park that preserve some of the most breathtaking shoreline in the Northwest. The three parks are connected by an excellent trail that is perfect for a rewarding day hike.

Start your exploration of this beautiful stretch of coast by heading southwest on the Cape Arago Highway. In 12 miles you'll come to **Sunset Bay State Park** ✦ (© **800/551-6949** or 541/888-4902). This park has one of the few beaches in Oregon where the water actually gets warm enough for swimming (although folks from warm-water regions may not agree). Sunset Bay is almost completely surrounded by sandstone cliffs, and the entrance to the bay is quite narrow, which means the waters here stay fairly calm. Picnicking and camping are available, and there are lots of tide pools to explore.

Continuing on another 3 miles brings you to **Shore Acres State Park** ✦✦ (© **800/551-6949** or 541/888-4902), once the estate of local shipping tycoon Louis J. Simpson, who spent years developing his gardens. His ships would bring him unusual plants from all over the world, and eventually the gardens grew to include a formal English garden and a Japanese garden with a 100-foot lily pond. The gardens and his home, which long ago was torn down, were built atop sandstone cliffs overlooking the Pacific and a tiny cove. Rock walls rise up from the water and have been sculpted by the waves into unusual shapes. During winter storms, wave-watching is a popular pastime here. The water off the park is often a striking shade of blue, and **Simpson Beach,** in the little cove, just might be the prettiest beach in Oregon. A trail leads down to this beach. There is a $3 day-use fee here.

Cape Arago State Park ✦✦ (© **800/551-6949** or 541/888-4902) is the third of this trio of parks. Just offshore from the rugged cape lie the rocks and small islands of Simpson Reef, which provide sunbathing spots for hundreds of seals (including elephant seals) and sea lions. The barking of the sea lions can be heard from hundreds of yards away, and though you can't get very close, with a pair of binoculars you can see the seals and sea lions quite well. The best viewing point is at **Simpson Reef Viewpoint.** On either side of the cape are coves with quiet beaches, although the beaches are closed from March 1 to June 30 to protect young seal pups. Tide pools along these beaches offer hours of fascination during other months.

Also in the vicinity of these three state parks, you'll find **Bastendorff Beach County Park** (© **541/888-5353**), north of Sunset Bay at the mouth of Coos Bay, which offers a long, wide beach that's popular with surfers.

Four miles down Seven Devils Road from Charleston, you'll find the **South Slough National Estuarine Research Reserve** (© **541/888-5558;** www.southslough estuary.org). An interpretive center (daily 8:30am–4:30pm between Memorial Day and Labor Day; closed Sun other months) set high above the slough provides background on the importance of estuaries. South Slough is in the process of being restored after many years of damming, diking, and reclamation of marshlands by farmers. A hiking trail leads down to the marshes, and there is good canoeing and sea kayaking.

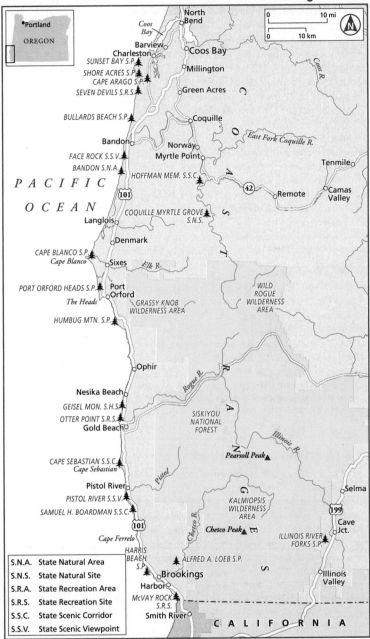

The Southern Oregon Coast

•Portland
OREGON

0   10 mi
0   10 km

N

Coos Bay
North Bend
Barview
Charleston
Coos Bay
SUNSET BAY S.P.
SHORE ACRES S.P.
CAPE ARAGO S.P.
SEVEN DEVILS S.R.S.
Millington

Green Acres

Coos R.

C

BULLARDS BEACH S.P.
Coquille

O

East Fork Coquille R.

Bandon
Norway
FACE ROCK S.S.V.
Myrtle Point
BANDON S.N.A.
HOFFMAN MEM. S.S.C.

A

Tenmile

42
Remote
Camas Valley

PACIFIC

S

101

OCEAN

COQUILLE MYRTLE GROVE
S.N.S.

Langlois

T

Denmark

CAPE BLANCO S.P.
Cape Blanco
Sixes

Elk R.

PORT ORFORD HEADS S.P.
Port Orford
The Heads

GRASSY KNOB WILDERNESS AREA

WILD ROGUE WILDERNESS AREA

HUMBUG MTN. S.P.

Ophir

Rogue R.

R

Nesika Beach
GEISEL MON. S.H.S.
OTTER POINT S.R.S.
Gold Beach

SISKIYOU NATIONAL FOREST

A

Illinois R.

Pearsoll Peak▲

CAPE SEBASTIAN S.S.C.
Cape Sebastian

N

Pistol

Pistol River
PISTOL RIVER S.S.V.
SAMUEL H. BOARDMAN S.S.C.

G

KALMIOPSIS WILDERNESS AREA

Selma

199
Cave Jct.

101

Chetco R.

Chetco Peak▲

E

ILLINOIS RIVER FORKS S.P.

Cape Ferrelo

HARRIS BEACH S.P.

ALFRED A. LOEB S.P.

S

Brookings
Harbor
McVAY ROCK S.R.S.
Smith River

Illinois Valley

CALIFORNIA

S.N.A.	State Natural Area
S.N.S.	State Natural Site
S.R.A.	State Recreation Area
S.R.S.	State Recreation Site
S.S.C.	State Scenic Corridor
S.S.V.	State Scenic Viewpoint

OTHER AREA ACTIVITIES & ATTRACTIONS

Charleston is the bay area's charter-fishing marina. If you'd like to do some sportfishing, contact **Bob's Sport Fishing** (© 800/628-9633 or 541/888-4241; www.bobs sportfishing.com) or **Betty Kay Charters** (© 800/752-6303 or 541/888-9021; www. bettykaycharters.com). Expect to pay around $65 for a 5-hour bottom-fishing trip and $165 for a 12-hour halibut-fishing trip.

In addition to all the outdoor recreational activities around the bay area, there are also a few museums. The **Coos Art Museum,** 235 Anderson Ave., Coos Bay (© **541/ 267-3901;** www.coosart.org), is a highly regarded little museum that hosts changing exhibits in a wide variety of styles and media. Runners will also be interested to know that up on the second floor of the museum, there is a small exhibit dedicated to long-distance runner Steve Prefontaine, who was from Coos Bay and who died in 1975. It's open Tuesday through Friday from 10am to 4pm and Saturday from 1 to 4pm; admission is $5 for adults and $2 for seniors and students.

Part of the renovation of the Coos Bay waterfront has been the construction of **The Mill Casino & Hotel,** 3201 Tremont Ave., North Bend (© **800/953-4800** or 541/756-8800; www.themillcasino.com). Here you can play slot machines, blackjack, poker, and bingo. There are several restaurants and a lounge.

WHERE TO STAY

Edgewater Inn ⭐ This is Coos Bay's only waterfront hotel, and though the water it faces is only a narrow stretch of the back bay, you can sometimes watch ships in the harbor. Guest rooms are large, and deluxe rooms are particularly well designed and spacious, with a breakfast bar and an extra-large TV. Other deluxe rooms have in-room spas. Most rooms also have balconies overlooking the water (and industrial areas).

275 E. Johnson Ave., Coos Bay, OR 97420. © **800/233-0423** or 541/267-0423. www.theedgewaterinn.com. 82 units. $83–$125 double. Rates include continental breakfast. AE, DC, DISC, MC, V. Pets accepted ($8 per day). **Amenities:** Indoor pool; exercise room; Jacuzzi; courtesy van; business center; dry cleaning. *In room:* A/C, TV/VCR, dataport, fridge, coffeemaker, hair dryer, iron, free local calls.

⌒ *Fun Fact* **Oregon Myrtlewood**

At Coos Bay you enter **myrtlewood** country. The myrtle tree grows only along a short section of coast in southern Oregon and northern California and is prized by woodworkers for its fine grain and durability. A very hard wood, it lends itself to all manner of platters, bowls, goblets, sculptures, and whatever. All along the south coast, you'll see myrtlewood factories and shops where you can see how the raw wood is turned into finished pieces. At the south end of the town of Coos Bay, watch for **The Oregon Connection,** 1125 S. First St. (© 800/255-5318 or 541/267-7804; www.oregonconnection.com), which is just off U.S. 101. This is one of the bigger myrtlewood factories. The **Real Oregon Gift,** 68794 Hauser Depot Rd. at U.S. 101 (© 877/755-2220 or 541/756-2220; www.realoregongift.com), 5 miles north of North Bend, is another large factory and showroom. Six miles south of Bandon on U.S. 101, watch for **Zumwalt's Myrtlewood Factory,** 47422 U.S. 101 (© 541/347-3654; www. zumwaltsmyrtlewood.com), which has a good selection and prices.

This Olde House 🍴 With its inlaid floors and crystal chandeliers, this 1893 mansion on a hill above downtown Coos Bay is the finest B&B in the area. Common areas capture the historical character of the home, while bedrooms are somewhat more modern, though with a historical flare. Although it is the most expensive, the huge master suite, which takes up the entire third floor of the inn, provides space, luxury, and decent views over the town. The least expensive room has its private bathroom across the hall. There's complimentary wine in the rooms and if you stay for 3 or more nights, the innkeeper will prepare you a complimentary gourmet dinner.

202 Alder Ave., Coos Bay, OR 97420. ⓒ 541/267-5224. www.bnbweb.com/thisoldehouse. 4 units. $97–$175 double. Rates include full breakfast. AE, MC, V. Young children not accepted. *In room:* TV, no phone.

CAMPGROUNDS

About 12 miles outside Coos Bay, you'll find **Sunset Bay State Park** (p. 216). To make a reservation, contact **ReserveAmerica** (ⓒ **800/452-5687;** www.reserveamerica. com). **Bastendorff Beach County Park** (ⓒ **541/888-5353**), north of Sunset Bay at the mouth of Coos Bay, is an alternative to the frequently full Sunset Bay State Park campground. This latter park does not take reservations.

WHERE TO DINE

Blue Heron Bistro 🍴 INTERNATIONAL   This odd little cafe in the heart of downtown Coos Bay is an eclectic international restaurant that specializes in seafood and both Italian and German fare. The Blue Heron also has one of the largest assortments of imported beers on the coast, and is the sort of place that's perfect for lunch, dinner, or just a quick bite to eat. Items range from German bratwurst to New Orleans–style oysters to pizzas and pastas.

100 Commercial Ave., Coos Bay. ⓒ 541/267-3933. www.blueheronbistro.com. Main courses $10–$19. AE, MC, V. Mon–Fri 11am–9pm; Sat–Sun 5–9pm.

Portside 🍴 *Kids* SEAFOOD   Charleston is home to Coos Bay's charter and commercial fishing fleets, so it's no surprise that it's also home to the area's best seafood restaurant. Check the daily fresh sheet to see what just came in on the boat. This place has been around for decades, and preparations tend toward traditional continental dishes, of which the house specialty is a bouillabaisse Marseillaise that's just swimming with shrimp, red snapper, lobster, crab legs, butter clams, prawns, and scallops. The restaurant overlooks the boat basin and is popular with families.

63383 Kingfisher Dr., Charleston. ⓒ 541/888-5544. www.portsidebythebay.com. Reservations recommended. Main courses $13–$39. AE, DC, MC, V. Daily 11:30am–10 or 11pm (9pm in winter).

11 Bandon

24 miles S of Coos Bay, 85 miles W of Roseburg, 54 miles north of Gold Beach

Once known primarily as the cranberry capital of Oregon (you can see the cranberry bogs south of town along U.S. 101), Bandon is now better known for its world-class Bandon Dunes Golf Resort. It's also set on one of the most spectacular pieces of coastline in the state. Just south of town, the beach is littered with boulders, monoliths, and haystack rocks that seem to have been strewn by some giant hand. Sunsets are stunning.

Just north of town the Coquille River empties into the Pacific, and at the river's mouth stands a picturesque lighthouse. The lighthouse is one of only a handful of Bandon buildings to survive a fire in 1936. Even though most buildings downtown date only from the 1930s, Bandon still has the quaint feel of a historic seaside village, and a waterfront boardwalk connects Bandon with the Coquille River. Be sure to take a stroll along the boardwalk while you're in town.

ESSENTIALS

GETTING THERE   From Roseburg, head west on Ore. 42 to Coquille, where you take Ore. 42S to Bandon, which is on U.S. 101.

VISITOR INFORMATION   For more information, contact the **Bandon Chamber of Commerce,** 300 Second St. (P.O. Box 1515), Bandon, OR 97411 (© 541/347-9616; www.bandon.com).

FESTIVALS   Bandon is the cranberry capital of Oregon, and each year in September the impending harvest is celebrated with the **Bandon Cranberry Festival.** Other festivals include the **Wine and Food Festival** held over Memorial Day weekend and the **Festival of Lights,** held each year during the Christmas season.

OUTDOOR ACTIVITIES

Head out of Bandon on Beach Loop Road, and you'll soon see why the rocks are a big draw. Wind and waves have sculpted monoliths along the shore into contorted spires and twisted shapes. The first good place to view the rocks and get down to the beach is at **Coquille Point,** at the end of 11th Street. Here you'll find a short, paved interpretive trail atop a bluff overlooking the beach, rock monoliths, and the river mouth. There's also a long staircase leading down to the beach. From here you can see Table Rock and the Sisters. From the **Face Rock Viewpoint** you can see the area's most famous rock, which resembles a face gazing skyward. Nearby stand rocks that resemble a dog, a cat, and kittens. A trail leads down to the beach from the viewpoint, so you can go out and explore some of the rocks that are left high and dry by low tide. South of the rocks, along a flat stretch of beach backed by dunes, there are several beach access areas, all of which are within **Bandon State Natural Area.**

Across the river from downtown Bandon, you'll find **Bullards Beach State Park** (© 541/347-2209). Within the park are beaches, a marsh overlook, hiking and horseback-riding trails, a picnic area, a campground, and a boat ramp. Fishing, crabbing, and clamming are all very popular. In the park you'll also find the 1896 **Coquille River Lighthouse.** This lighthouse is one of the only lighthouses to ever be hit by a ship—in 1903 an abandoned schooner plowed into the light. April through October, tours of the lighthouse are offered Tuesday through Sunday between 10am and 4pm.

At Bandon, as elsewhere on the Oregon coast, **gray whales** migrating between the Arctic and Baja California, Mexico, pass close to the shore and can often be spotted from land. The whales pass Bandon between December and February on their way south and between March and May on their way north. Gray days and early mornings before the wind picks up are the best times to spot whales. Coquille Point, at the end of 11th Street, and the bluffs along Beach Loop Road are the best vantage points.

More than 300 species of birds have been spotted in the Bandon vicinity, making this one of the best sites in Oregon for **bird-watching.** The **Oregon Islands National Wildlife Refuge,** which includes 1,400 rocks and islands off the state's coast, contains the famous monoliths of Bandon. Among the birds that nest on these rocks are rhinoceros auklets, storm petrels, gulls, and tufted puffins. The latter, with their large colorful beaks, are the most beloved of local birds, and their images show up on all manner of local souvenirs. The **Bandon Marsh National Wildlife Refuge,** at the mouth of the

Coquille River, is another good spot for bird-watching. In this area you can expect to see grebes, mergansers, buffleheads, plovers, and several species of raptors.

If you're interested in exploring the Coquille River, you can rent a sea kayak from **Adventure Kayak,** 315 First St. (© **541/347-3480;** www.adventurekayak.com), which also offers kayak tours during the summer months. Head upriver a little ways on a low tide and you'll likely see dozens of harbor seals resting on the beach. Boats rent for $25 to $40 for the first 2 hours, and tours are $35 to $65. If you'd rather ride a horse down the beach, contact **Bandon Beach Riding Stables,** 54629 Beach Loop Rd. (© **541/347-3423**), south of Face Rock. A 1-hour ride is $30.

The world-class **Bandon Dunes Golf Course,** 57744 Round Lake Dr. (© **888/ 345-6008** or 541/347-4380; www.bandondunesgolf.com), a classic Scottish-style links course, is Oregon's only oceanfront golf course and has made Bandon a major golfing destination. The course, notorious for its blustery winds, has been compared to Pebble Beach and St. Andrews. The summer greens fees are $185 for resort guests and $240 for nonguests ($95 for your second 18 holes). November to April, you can play here for $75 to $175. This is a walking course, and no golf carts are allowed; but caddies are available for an additional $50.

If that's out of your price range, there's always the **Bandon Face Rock Golf Course,** 3235 Beach Loop Dr. (© **541/347-3818**), which offers a scenic 9 holes not far from the famous Face Rock. Green fees are $15 for 9 holes.

OTHER AREA ACTIVITIES & ATTRACTIONS

The **West Coast Game Park** ⚘, 46914 U.S. 101 S. (© **541/347-3106;** www.game parksafari.com), 7 miles south of Bandon, bills itself as America's largest wild-animal petting park and is a must for families. Depending on what young animals they have at the time of your visit, you might be able to play with a leopard, tiger, or bear cub. The park is open daily from 9am to 7pm in summer, 9am to 5pm in spring and fall (call for hours in other months). Admission is $13 for adults, $12 for seniors, $8.50 for children 7 to 12, $5.50 for children 2 to 6.

Shopping is one of Bandon's main attractions, and in **Old Town Bandon,** just off U.S. 101, you'll find some interesting shops and galleries. A couple of galleries sell artworks by regional artists. One of the better ones is the **Bandon Glass Art Studio** at 240 U.S. 101 (© **541/347-4723;** www.dutchschulze.com), which is just across the highway from Old Town. Here you can watch glass direct from the furnace being made into the paperweights or fluted glass bowls the gallery sells.

At **Faber Farms,** 54982 Morrison Rd. (© **541/347-1166**), a working cranberry farm, you can see how cranberries are grown and sample a variety of cranberry products. If you visit in October, you'll be there for the harvest. To reach the farm, drive 1½ miles north of Florence, turn east on Morrison Road, and continue another mile.

WHERE TO STAY

Bandon Dunes Golf Resort ⚘⚘⚘   Although this is one of the most tasteful and luxurious accommodations on the Oregon coast, the emphasis is so entirely on the golf course that anyone not interested in the game will feel like an interloper. However, if golf is your game then you'll love this place. The lodge sits up on the dunes and looks out over the fairways to the Pacific. Accommodations are also available in a variety of rooms that are here called cottages, but which are not really cottages but rather multi-unit buildings arranged around a pretty little pond. These rooms don't have the golf-course views, but they are very comfortable.

57744 Round Lake Dr., Bandon, OR 97411. ☏ **888/345-6008** or 541/347-4380. www.bandondunesgolf.com. 147 units. $130–$320 double; $200–$1,500 suite. Children under 12 stay free in parent's room. AE, DC, DISC, MC, V. **Amenities:** 4 restaurants (Northwest, American); 2 lounges; 3 18-hole golf courses; exercise room; Jacuzzi; sauna; business center; room service; massage; babysitting; dry cleaning. *In room:* TV, coffeemaker, iron, free local calls.

Best Western Inn at Face Rock Resort 🏆🏆   Located about a mile south of Face Rock, this modern hotel is Bandon's original golf resort, and is adjacent to the 9-hole Bandon Face Rock Golf Course. Guest rooms here are the best on Beach Loop Drive, and there are plenty of recreational facilities. Although the hotel is across the street from the beach, many of the rooms have ocean views. The views from the hotel restaurant aren't nearly as good as at the nearby Lord Bennett's Restaurant. A short path leads down to the beach.

3225 Beach Loop Dr., Bandon, OR 97411. ☏ **800/638-3092** or 541/347-9441. Fax 541/347-2532. www.innatfacerock. com. 74 units. Mid-June to mid-Sept $142–$274 double; mid-Sept to mid-June $110–$234 double. Children under 17 stay free in parent's room. AE, DC, DISC, MC, V. Pets accepted ($15). **Amenities:** Restaurant (American); lounge; indoor pool; exercise room; Jacuzzi; sauna; concierge; coin-op laundry. *In room:* TV, dataport, coffeemaker, hair dryer, iron, free local calls.

Lighthouse Bed and Breakfast 🏆   Located on the road that leads to the mouth of the Coquille River, this riverfront B&B has a view of the historic Bandon Lighthouse, and, with its weathered cedar siding, large decks, and small sunroom, it's the quintessential Oregon beach house. Guest rooms range from a small room with the private bathroom across the hall to a spacious room with views of the ocean and lighthouse, a wood-burning stove, and a double whirlpool tub overlooking the river. Both the beach and Old Town Bandon are within a very short walk.

650 Jetty Rd. SW, Bandon, OR 97411. ☏ **541/347-9316.** www.lighthouselodging.com. 5 units. $135–$235 double; lower rates in winter. Rates include full breakfast. MC, V. Children over 12 accepted. *In room:* A/C, hair dryer, Wi-Fi.

Sunset Oceanfront Lodging 🏆 *Value*   Dozens of Bandon's famous monoliths rise from the sand and waves in front of this motel, making sunsets from the Sunset truly memorable. The rooms, however, with their the dated furnishings and paneled walls, aren't nearly as nice as the views. On the other hand, since there's everything here from economy motel rooms to condos, rustic cabins, and classic cottages, you should be able to find accommodations here to your liking. If you want something rustic and private, try to get one of the cottages. The adjacent Lord Bennett's Restaurant has *the* view in Bandon.

1865 Beach Loop Rd. (P.O. Box 373), Bandon, OR 97411. ☏ **800/842-2407** or 541/347-2453. www.sunsetmotel.com. 71 units. May 15–Oct 15 $52–$285 double; Oct 16–May 14 $40–$285 double. Children under 5 stay free in parent's room. AE, DISC, MC, V. Pets accepted ($10 per day). **Amenities:** Restaurant (seafood); lounge; indoor pool; Jacuzzi; concierge; business center; coin-op laundry; laundry service. *In room:* TV, dataport, coffeemaker, free local calls.

CAMPGROUNDS

Bullards Beach State Park (☏ **541/347-2209**), across the Coquille River from downtown Bandon, has 185 campsites and 13 yurts for rent. To make reservations, call **ReserveAmerica** (☏ **800/452-5687;** www.reserveamerica.com).

WHERE TO DINE

When it's time for espresso, stop in at **Rayjen Coffee Company,** 365 Second St. SE (☏ **541/347-1144**), in a cottage on the edge of Old Town. The **Bandon Baking Co. and Deli,** 160 Second St. (☏ **541/347-9440**) and **2 Loons Cafe,** 120 Second St. (☏ **541/347-3750**), are good places for pastries and sandwiches. For a quick meal of

Stormy Weather

"And the weather at the coast this weekend will be high winds and heavy rain, as another storm front moves in off the Pacific Ocean." This sort of forecast would keep most folks cozily at home, but in Oregon, where storm-watching has become a popular winter activity, it's the equivalent of "Surf's up!"

Throughout the winter, Oregon's rocky shores and haystack rocks feel the effects of storms that originate far to the north in cold polar waters. As these storms slam ashore, sometimes with winds topping 100 mph, their huge waves smash against the rocks with breathtaking force, sending spray flying. The perfect storm-watching days are those right after a big storm, when the waves are still big but the sky is clear. This is also the best time to go beachcombing—it's your best chance to find the rare handblown Japanese glass fishing floats that sometimes wash ashore on the Oregon coast.

Among the **best storm-watching spots** on the coast are the South Jetty at the mouth of the Columbia River in Fort Stevens State Park, Cannon Beach, Cape Meares, Depoe Bay, Cape Foulweather, Devil's Punchbowl on the Otter Crest Scenic Loop, Seal Rock, Cape Perpetua, Shore Acres State Park, Cape Arago State Park, Face Rock Viewpoint outside Bandon, and Cape Sebastian.

Some of the **best lodgings** for storm-watching are the Inn at Otter Crest north of Depoe Bay, the Channel House in Depoe Bay, the Overleaf Lodge Resort in Yachats, and the Sunset Motel in Bandon. The coast's **best restaurants** for storm-watching include the Pelican Pub & Brewery in Pacific City, Tidal Raves in Depoe Bay, and Lord Bennett's Restaurant in Bandon.

---

incredibly fresh fish and chips, you can't beat **Bandon Fish Market,** 249 First St. (*©* **541/347-4282**), which is right on the waterfront and has a few picnic tables.

Lord Bennett's Restaurant and Lounge *‹‹* AMERICAN   Lord Bennett's is the only restaurant in Bandon that overlooks this town's bizarre beachscape of contorted rock spires and sea stacks, and this alone makes it a must for a meal. The sunsets are unforgettable. Since sunsets come late in the day in the summer, you might want to eat a late lunch the day you plan to come here. We suggest starting dinner with some crab cakes before moving on to such main courses as oysters baked with spinach, bacon, and Pernod or lamb chops with a hazelnut crust. There's a decent wine list, and the desserts are both beautiful and delicious.

1695 Beach Loop Dr., next to the Sunset Motel. *©* **541/347-3663**. http://bandonbythesea.com/lord_ben.htm. Reservations recommended. Main courses $5–$11 lunch, $15–$26 dinner. AE, DISC, MC, V. Mon–Sat 11am–3pm and 5–9pm; Sun 11am–3pm and 5–9pm.

Wild Rose *‹‹* MEDITERRANEAN/ASIAN   This tiny cottage in downtown Bandon houses the most romantic little restaurant in town. The lace curtains and roses in the garden all say English country cottage, though the building itself looks more like an old Northwest fisherman's cabin. The menu here wanders all over the world, though it emphasizes Mediterranean and Asian flavors. However, highlights include a pistachio-crusted halibut and a Latin-style flank steak.

130 Chicago St. ⓒ **541/347-4428.** Reservations recommended. Main courses $16–$30. AE, DISC, MC, V. Wed–Mon 5–9pm (fall–spring closed Tues–Wed).

12 The Southern Oregon Coast

Port Orford: 27 miles S of Bandon; 79 miles N of Crescent City, CA; 95 miles W of Grants Pass. Gold Beach: 54 miles N of Crescent City, CA; 32 miles S of Port Orford. Brookings/Harbor: 26 miles N of Crescent City, CA; 35 miles S of Gold Beach

The 60-mile stretch of coast between Port Orford and the California state line is perhaps the most beautiful stretch of the entire Oregon coast, yet because of its distance from major metropolitan areas, it doesn't attract many visitors.

Port Orford, anchoring the northern end, is today little more than a wide spot in the road, yet it is the oldest town on the coast other than Astoria. Named by Captain George Vancouver on April 5, 1792, this natural harbor in the lee of Port Orford Heads became the first settlement right on the Oregon coast when, in 1851, settlers and soldiers together constructed Fort Orford. A fort was necessary because of hostilities with the area's native population. Eventually the settlers fled inland, crossing the Siskiyou Mountains.

Although the first settlers made camp here because there was something of a natural harbor, these days the area's fishing fleet is hauled out of the water nightly by a large crane. Working out of this tiny port is a small commercial fishing fleet.

Cape Blanco, located just north of Port Orford and discovered and named by Spanish explorer Martín de Aguilar in 1603, once made an even grander claim than Port Orford when it was heralded as the westernmost point of land in the lower 48. Today, that claim has been laid to rest by Cape Flattery, Washington, and Cape Blanco now only claims to be the westernmost point in Oregon.

In 19th-century California, gold prospectors had to struggle through rugged mountains in search of pay dirt, but here in Oregon they could just scoop it up off the beach. The black sands at the mouth of the Rogue River were high in gold, and it was this gold that gave Gold Beach its name. The white settlers attracted by the gold soon came in conflict with the local Rogue River (or TuTuNi) Indians. Violence erupted in 1856, but within the year the Rogue River Indian Wars had come to an end and the TuTuNis were moved to a reservation.

The TuTuNis had for centuries found the river to be a plentiful source of salmon, and when the gold played out, commercial fishermen moved in to take advantage of the large salmon runs. The efficiency of their nets and traps quickly decimated the local salmon population, and a hatchery was constructed to replenish the runs.

Brookings and Harbor compose the southernmost community on the Oregon coast. Because of the warm year-round temperatures, this region is known as the Oregon Banana Belt, and you'll see palm trees and other cold-sensitive plants thriving in gardens around town. Farms south of town grow nearly all of the Easter lilies sold in the United States. Other plants that thrive in this climate include coast redwoods, Oregon myrtles, and wild azaleas. Dividing the sister towns of Brookings and Harbor is the Chetco River, one of the purest and most beautiful rivers in the state.

ESSENTIALS

GETTING THERE There is no convenient way to get to this stretch of coast. Coming from the north, the nearest highway connection to I-5 is Ore. 42 from Roseburg to Bandon. Coming from the south, you must either follow U.S. 101 north through California or take U.S. 199 southwest from Grants Pass and then continue north on U.S. 101. There is also a narrow, winding road over the mountains to Gold Beach from Galice (near Grants Pass).

VISITOR INFORMATION   For more information on Port Orford, contact the **Port Orford & North Curry Chamber of Commerce,** Battle Rock Park, U.S. 101 S. (P.O. Box 637), Port Orford, OR 97465 (© **541/332-8055;** www.discover portorford.com). For information on the Gold Beach area, contact the **Gold Beach Promotion Committee,** 94080 Shirley Lane (P.O. Box 375), Gold Beach, OR 97444 (© **800/525-2334** or 541/247-7526; www.goldbeach.org), which, at press time, had plans to move its visitor center to South Beach Park at the south end of town, so be sure to call ahead. For more information on the Brookings area, contact the **Brookings-Harbor Chamber of Commerce,** 16330 Lower Harbor Rd., Brookings, OR 97415 (© **800/535-9469** or 541/469-3181; www.brookingsor.com).

THE PORT ORFORD AREA

Cape Blanco is now preserved as **Cape Blanco State Park** (© **541/332-6774**), where you'll find miles of beaches and hiking trails through windswept meadows, picnic areas, and a campground. This high headland is also the site of the **Cape Blanco Lighthouse,** which is the oldest continuously operating lighthouse in Oregon. Not far from the lighthouse is the **Hughes House Museum** (© **541/332-0248**), a restored Eastlake Victorian home that was built in 1898 and is furnished with period antiques. Both the lighthouse and the Hughes House are open to the public April through October from 10am to 4pm. Lighthouse admission is $2 for adults and $1 for children under 12.

For a good view of Port Orford and this entire section of coast, drive up to the **Port Orford Heads State Park,** which is located on the northern edge of town and has a short trail out to an overlook. The route to the wayside is well marked. Also here you can visit the **Port Orford Lifeboat Station** (© **541/332-0521;** www.portorford lifeboatstation.org), a small museum preserving the history of the coast guard on the southern Oregon coast. The museum is open April to October Thursday through Monday from 10am to 3:30pm; admission is free. Right in town, you can visit **Battle Rock Park** and learn the history of the rock refuge that rises out of Port Orford's beach. This is a good beach on which to walk, as is the beach at **Paradise Point State Recreation Site,** just north of town.

Right in town you'll find several art galleries. One of my favorites is the **Cook Gallery,** 705 Oregon St. (© **541/332-0045**), which features beautiful handcrafted wood furniture and sculptures, as well as prints and ceramics. North of town, check out the wood carvings at **A&T Myrtlewood,** 45683 U.S. 101, Sixes (© **541/348-2586;** www.aandtmyrtlewood.com). Right in town, you'll also find the **Antique Motorcycle & Auto Museum,** 1235 Oregon St. (© **541/332-0523;** http://antique motorcyclemuseum.com), a warehouselike private museum with motorcycles dating back to 1896. The museum is open Thursday through Monday from 10am to 5pm (Fri–Mon Oct 30–Mar 30). Admission is $5 for adults and $4 for children ages 6 to 17.

Six miles south of Port Orford, you'll find **Humbug Mountain State Park** (© **541/332-6774**), where Humbug Mountain rises 1,756 feet from the ocean. A pretty campground is tucked into the forest at the base of the mountain, and a trail leads to the summit.

About 12 miles south of Port Orford is a place the kids aren't going to let you pass by. The **Prehistoric Gardens,** 36848 U.S. 101 S. (© **541/332-4463**), is a lost world of life-size dinosaur replicas. Though they aren't as realistic as those in *Jurassic Park,* they'll make the kids squeal with delight. The gardens are open in the summer daily from 9am to between 7 and 9pm; other months, call for hours. Admission is $7 for adults, $6 for seniors and youths 11 to 17, $5 for children 3 to 10.

WHERE TO STAY

Castaway by the Sea ⚡ *Value*   Situated on a hill high above Port Orford harbor and commanding a sweeping panorama of the southern Oregon coast, this modest motel is far more comfortable than it appears from the outside. All the rooms take in the extraordinary view, and most have comfy little sunrooms from which to gaze off to sea. The rooms are quite large and well maintained, and some have kitchenettes. Out back there is a lawn with a few benches overlooking the harbor. The motel also rents out an adjacent historic house.

545 W. Fifth St. (P.O. Box 844), Port Orford, OR 97465. © 541/332-4502. Fax 541/332-9303. www.castawaybythesea. com. 13 units. $55–$85 double; $75–$135 suite. DISC, MC, V. Pets accepted ($5 per night). *In room:* TV, kitchen/kitchenette, fridge, coffeemaker.

Home by the Sea ⚡   Set high atop a bluff overlooking the beach and Battle Rock, this contemporary B&B has large guest rooms (and a downstairs living room) with some of the best views on the coast. The inn is a block off U.S. 101 and within walking distance of several restaurants and art galleries.

444 Jackson St. (P.O. Box 606), Port Orford, OR 97465. © 877/332-2855. www.homebythesea.com. 2 units. $105–$115 double. Rates include full breakfast. Children under 12 stay free in parent's room. MC, V. **Amenities:** Courtesy beach shuttle; guest laundry. *In room:* TV, fridge, hair dryer, iron, free local calls, Wi-Fi.

Wild Spring Guest Habitat ⚡⚡   With art classes, spiritual retreats, a meditative labyrinth, and enough tranquillity to restore the most frazzled soul, this south-coast woodland retreat is a blissful hideaway on the outskirts of Port Orford. Accommodations are in beautifully appointed cabins in the woods. With hardwood floors, living and dining areas, and slate-walled showers, these cabins are so comfortably and attractively furnished that you just might forget to go out and explore the beach. A central guest hall has a kitchen you can use, and on Saturday nights there's a hot-fudge sundae bar. The slate hot tub, with its ocean view, is reason enough to visit Port Orford and stay at this delightful little retreat.

92978 Cemetery Loop (P.O. Box R), Port Orford, OR 97465. © 866/333-WILD. Fax 775/542-1447. www. wildspring.com. 5 units. May–Oct $195–$245 double; Nov–Apr $175–$225. Rates include continental breakfast. Children 13 and older welcome. MC, V. Pets accepted ($25 per day). **Amenities:** Jacuzzi; bikes; massage. *In room:* TV/VCR, fridge, no phone, Wi-Fi.

CAMPGROUNDS

Cape Blanco State Park is the most popular camping spot in this area, and reservations aren't accepted for campsites. However, there are some basic cabins here that can be reserved through **ReserveAmerica** (© **800/452-5687**; www.reserveamerica.com).

WHERE TO DINE

If you need some good bread for your day's picnic, stop in at **Port Orford Bread-works,** 190 Sixth St. (© **541/332-4022**), which bakes a couple of different breads each day. The bakery also sells imported meats and cheeses and other gourmet food items and serves Italian food.

Paula's Bistro *✔ NORTHWEST*   This eclectic little eatery is an unexpected treat in an area not noted for its good restaurants. Although the menu changes almost daily, you can expect such dishes as roast quail stuffed with hazelnut-cherry rice, rib-eye steak with shiitake mushroom ravioli, or fresh albacore tuna with a Dijon mustard sauce.

236 U.S. 101. *✆* **541/332-9378.** Reservations recommended. Main courses $16–$19. AE, DISC, MC, V. Tues–Sat 5–9pm.

THE GOLD BEACH AREA

There is, of course, a beach at Gold Beach, though it's not really the area's main attraction. That distinction goes to the **Rogue River,** which empties into the Pacific here at the town of Gold Beach and is the most famous fishing and rafting river in the state. You can tour the river in powerful hydrojet boats, which have a very shallow draft and use water jets instead of propellers. These features allow these boats to cross rapids and riffles only a few inches deep. Along the way you may see deer, black bear, river otters, and bald eagles. A running narration covers the river's colorful history. Three different trips are available, ranging in length from 64 to 104 miles. Two companies operate these trips. **Rogue River Mail Boats** (*✆* **800/458-3511** or 541/247-7033; www.mailboat. com) leaves from a dock a quarter mile upriver from the north end of the Rogue River Bridge. **Jerry's Rogue Jets** (*✆* **800/451-3645** or 541/247-4571; www.roguejets.com) leaves from the Port of Gold Beach on the south side of the Rogue River Bridge. Fares range from $39 to $79 for adults and $16 to $37 for children.

Fighting salmon and steelhead are what have made the Rogue River famous, and if you'd like to hire a guide to take you to the best **fishing** holes, you have plenty of options. If you're looking to hire a guide, contact Steve and Eva Beyerlin of **Fish Oregon** (*✆* **800/348-4138** or 541/247-4138; www.fishoregon.com). A full day will cost around $150 to $225 per person. If you'd rather do your fishing offshore, contact **Five Star Charters,** Port of Gold Beach (*✆* **888/301-6840** or 541/247-0217; www.gold beachadventures.com), which offers charter fishing trips starting at $85 per person. Clamming and crabbing can also be quite productive around Gold Beach.

When you want to get out on the beach at Gold Beach, head north of town across the Rogue River to Nesika Beach. To reach the best stretch of this beach, take the North Nesika Beach turnoff and then continue north to the end of the road. Alternatively, continue a little farther north to Old Coast Road, where you'll find a steep trail down to the beach.

Jerry's Rogue River Museum (*✆* **541/247-4571;** www.roguejets.com), at the Port of Gold Beach and affiliated with Jerry's Jet Boat Tours, is the more modern and informative of the town's two museums. It focuses on the geology and cultural and natural history of the Rogue River. It's open daily in summer from 7:30am to 9pm and daily in the off season from about 8am to 6pm; admission is free. At the diminutive **Curry County Historical Museum,** 29419 Ellensburg Ave. (*✆* **541/247-6113;** www.curryhistory.com), you can learn more about the history of the area and see plenty of Native American and pioneer artifacts. The museum is open Tuesday through Saturday from 10am to 4pm. Admission is $2 for adults and 50¢ for children under 16. The museum is closed in January.

Golfers can play a round at the 9-hole **Cedar Bend Golf Course,** 34391 Squaw Valley Rd. (*✆* **541/247-6911**), 12 miles north of Gold Beach off U.S. 101. If you'd like to go horseback riding, contact **Hawk's Rest Ranch,** 94667 North Bank Pistol River Rd. (*✆* **541/247-6423;** www.siskiyouwest.com) in Pistol River, 10 miles south of Gold Beach. Expect to pay between $30 and $55 for a 90-minute ride.

Hikers have an abundance of options in the area. At the **Schrader Old-Growth Trail,** 10 miles up Jerry's Flat Road/South Bank Rogue Road near the Lobster Creek Campground, you can hike through an ancient forest of huge, majestic trees. In this same area, you'll also find the **Myrtle Tree Trail.** Along this short trail, you'll find the world's largest myrtle tree, which is 88 feet tall and 42 feet in circumference. For more information on hiking in the Gold Beach area, contact the **Siskiyou National Forest,** Gold Beach Ranger District, 29279 Ellensburg Ave., Gold Beach, OR 97444 (© **541/247-3600;** www.fs.fed.us/r6/siskiyou).

SOUTH TO BROOKINGS

Gold Beach itself is a wide sandy beach, but just a few miles to the south, the mountains once again march into the sea, creating what in my opinion is Oregon's single most spectacular section of coastline. Though it's only 30 miles from Gold Beach to **Brookings,** you can easily spend the whole day making the trip. Along the way are numerous viewpoints, picnic areas, hiking trails, and beaches.

The **Oregon Coast Trail,** which extends (in short sections) from California to Washington, has several segments both north and south of Gold Beach. The most spectacular sections of this trail are south of town at Cape Sebastian and in Samuel H. Boardman State Scenic Corridor.

The first place you'll come to as you drive south from Gold Beach is **Turtle Rock Wayside,** just south of town. Although this is little more than a roadside pull-off, it does have a nice view. The next place to stop is at **Cape Sebastian** ⊛⊛, which is 5 miles south of Gold Beach. This headland, which towers 700 feet above the ocean, is a good vantage point for whale-watching between December and March. A 2-mile trail leads from the parking area out to the end of the cape, and continues down to the beach at Hunter's Cove. This little-visited spot is one of the best places on the south coast for a hike.

Another 2 miles south on U.S. 101, you come to **Meyers Creek** ⊛⊛, which is at the **Pistol River State Scenic Viewpoint.** Here, scattered on the beach, you can get a closer look at some of the rugged monolithic rock formations that make this coastline so breathtaking. This is the most popular windsurfing and surfing beach on the south coast and is also a good clamming beach. About 2 miles farther south, you'll come to the sand dunes at the mouth of Pistol River.

South of Pistol River you enter the **Samuel H. Boardman State Scenic Corridor,** which has numerous viewpoints, **beaches** ⊛, picnic areas, and stretches of hiking trail. About 6 miles south of the Pistol River, you come to **Arch Rock Viewpoint** ⊛, a picnic area with a beautiful view of an offshore monolith that has been carved into an arch by the action of the waves. Two miles beyond this, you come to the **Natural Bridge Viewpoint.** These two arches were formed when a sea cave collapsed. In 2 more miles you cross the **Thomas Creek Bridge,** which at 345 feet high is the highest bridge in Oregon. In a little more than a mile, you come to **Whalehead Beach Viewpoint,** where a pyramidal rock just offshore bears a striking resemblance to a spy-hopping whale. There's a better view of Whalehead Rock a half mile south.

In another 1½ miles you'll come to **House Rock Viewpoint,** which offers sweeping vistas to the north and south. At **Cape Ferrelo Viewpoint** and **Lone Ranch Viewpoint** just to the south, you'll find a grassy headland. Just south of here, watch for the **Rainbow Rock Viewpoint,** which has a panorama of a stretch of beach strewn with large boulders. Go another 3 miles, to **Harris Beach State Park** (© **541/469-2021),** the last stop along this coast. Here you'll find picnicking and camping and a good view of **Goat Island,** which is the Oregon coast's largest island.

WHERE TO STAY

Ireland's Rustic Lodges ℛ *Finds* The name sums it all up—rustic cabins set amid shady grounds that are as green as Ireland (and beautifully landscaped, too). Though there are some modern motel rooms here, they just can't compare to the quaint old cabins, which have stone fireplaces, paneled walls, and unusual door handles made from twisted branches. Built in 1922, the cabins are indeed rustic and are not for those who need modern comforts. The mature gardens surrounding the cabins are beautiful any time of year, but particularly in late spring.

29346 Ellensburg Ave., Gold Beach, OR 97444. © 877/447-3526 or 541/247-7718. www.irelandsrusticlodges.com. 40 units. $90–$119 double; lower off-season rates. AE, DISC, MC, V. Pets accepted ($5–$10). *In room:* TV.

Jot's Resort ℛℛ *Kids* Stretching along the north bank of the Rogue River, Jot's has a definite fishing orientation and is very popular with families. The resort offers a wide variety of room sizes and rates, but every room has a view of the water and the Rogue River Bridge. The deluxe rooms are the most attractively furnished, while the condos are the most spacious (some have spiral staircases that lead up to loft sleeping areas). The dining room and lounge offer reasonably priced meals. Fishing guides and deep-sea charters can be arranged.

94360 Waterfront Loop (P.O. Box 1200), Gold Beach, OR 97444. © 800/367-5687 or 541/247-6676. Fax 541/247-6716. www.jotsresort.com. 140 units. Summer $120–$135 double, $155–$375 suite/condo; off-season rates $50–$60 double, $100–$250 suite/condo. AE, DISC, MC, V. Pets accepted ($10 per night). **Amenities:** Restaurant (American); lounge; indoor and outdoor pools; exercise room; Jacuzzi; sauna; fishing-boat rentals; activities desk; business center; babysitting; coin-op laundry. *In room:* TV, dataport, coffeemaker, hair dryer, iron.

Tu Tu Tun Lodge ℛℛℛ Tu Tu Tun Lodge, located 7 miles up the Rogue River from Gold Beach, is the most luxurious lodging on the south coast and has a national reputation for its sophisticated styling and its idyllic setting. The main lodge building incorporates enough rock and natural wood to give it a rustic feel without sacrificing any modern comforts, and the immense fireplace in the lounge is the center of activity. On warm days, the patio overlooking the river is a great spot for relaxing and sunning, and on cold nights logs crackle in a fire pit. The guest rooms are large and beautifully furnished with slate-topped tables and granite or tile counters. Each room has a private patio or balcony, and should you get an upstairs room, you'll have a high ceiling and an excellent river view. Some rooms also come with fireplaces or outdoor soaking tubs. The dining room overlooks the river and serves four-course fixed-price dinners ($46). Fishing guides and boat rentals can be arranged, and the lodge has its own dock.

96550 N. Bank Rogue Rd., Gold Beach, OR 97444. © 800/864-6357 or 541/247-6664. Fax 541/247-0672. www.tututun.com. 20 units. $165–$305 double, $260–$300 suite, $325–$425 house; lower rates in winter (dining room closed Nov–Apr). DISC, MC, V. May–Oct children 10 and older welcome; Nov–Apr all ages welcome. **Amenities:** Restaurant (Northwest); lounge; outdoor lap pool; 4-hole pitch-and-putt golf course; access to nearby health club; sea kayaks for guest use; lawn games; concierge; 24-hr. room service; massage; laundry service. *In room:* Dataport, fridge, hair dryer, iron, Wi-Fi.

CAMPGROUNDS

Up the Rogue River between Gold Beach and Agness, you'll find two campgrounds: **Lobster Creek** and **Quosatana.** A third, **Illahee** (for all three: © 541/247-3600; www.fs.fed.us/r6/Siskiyou), is another 6 miles past Agness, though not on the river.

WHERE TO DINE

The best meals in Gold Beach are served in the dining room at **Tu Tu Tun Lodge** (see review above). For delicious, filling breakfasts, head up the Rogue River a mile or so to **Indian Creek Café,** 94682 Jerry's Flat Rd. (© **541/247-0680**). If you want to take home some local seafood, head to the Port of Gold Beach and **Fisherman Direct Seafood** (© **541/247-9494**), which is in the Cannery Building. They sell canned and smoked salmon and albacore tuna.

Nor'wester Seafood ⚘ SEAFOOD/STEAK   Simply prepared fresh seafood and large portions are the mainstays of the menu at this dockside restaurant, which has long been a local favorite. Fish and chips are good, and the steak-and-seafood combinations are popular choices for big appetites; but we prefer such dishes as pasta and prawns with a tapenade sauce or salmon with a glaze made from sake, cayenne, ginger, and soy sauce. From the second-floor dining room, you can watch fishing boats on the Rogue River. The port is at the north end of town.

10 Harbor Way, Port of Gold Beach. © 541/247-2333. Reservations for 5 or more people only. Main courses $19–$50. AE, MC, V. Daily 5–9pm.

Riverview Restaurant ⚘ AMERICAN   At this restaurant just a mile or so up the Rogue River from Gold Beach, you can sit and watch fishermen battle huge salmon and unload their catch at the adjacent marina. You might also spot sea lions going after those very same salmon. So, what should you eat? How about salmon? Try it on a pizza with wild mushrooms. Alternatively, the fish tacos, which can be ordered two, three, or four at a time, are a good choice. The menu here is pretty simple—pastas, pizzas, burgers, salads, and a few basic entrees, but the view of the river is unsurpassed.

Jerry's Flat Rd. © 541/247-7321. Reservations recommended. Main courses $8–$26. AE, DC, DISC, MC, V. Daily 11:30am–9pm. Closed Oct–Dec.

THE BROOKINGS AREA

The Chetco River is known throughout Oregon as one of the best salmon and steelhead rivers in the state. It is also one of the prettiest rivers and offers opportunities for swimming, rafting, and canoeing. You can rent a sea kayak and paddle around near the mouth of the Chetco River; contact **Port Sport,** 16366 Lower Harbor Rd. (© **541/412-8880**), which rents kayaks ($10–$15 per hour) and also leads tours ($25–$50 per person).

For information on hiking in the area, which includes the high country of the Kalmiopsis Wilderness, contact the **Chetco Ranger District,** 539 Chetco Ave., Brookings, OR 97415 (© **541/412-6000;** www.fs.fed.us/r6/siskiyou).

If you want to head out to sea to do your fishing, contact **Tidewind Sportfishing** (© **541/469-0337;** www.tidewindsportfishing.com), which operates out of Harbor and offers both salmon- and bottom-fishing trips for $65 to $80 per person, as well as whale-watching excursions ($35 per person).

If golf is your game, don't pass up an opportunity to play the very scenic and challenging **Salmon Run Golf Course,** 99040 South Bank Chetco River Rd. (© **877/ 423-1234** or 541/469-4888; www.salmonrun.net), which charges $49 for 18 holes of golf. The clear waters of Jack Creek, which has spawning runs of salmon and steelhead, run through this course.

The area's botanical attractions are one of the most interesting reasons to pay a visit to the Brookings area. Not far from town, at **Alfred A. Loeb State Park** (© **541/ 469-2021**), which is 8 miles up the Chetco River from Brookings on North Bank Road, you can see old-growth myrtle trees (from which the ubiquitous myrtlewood souvenirs of the south coast are made). Myrtle *(Umbellularia californica)* grows naturally only along the southern Oregon and northern California coasts. The Brookings area is the northernmost range of the giant coast redwoods *(Sequoia sempervirens),* and just beyond Loeb State Park, you'll come to one of the largest stands of coast redwoods in Oregon. Here, the 1.3-mile **Redwood Nature Trail** loops past numerous big trees. This nature trail is connected to Loeb State Park via the .8-mile Riverview Trail. The region's wild azaleas, celebrated each year over Memorial Day weekend, come into bloom in May. The best place to see them is at **Azalea Park,** which is a couple of blocks east of U.S. 101 just before the bridge over the Chetco River at the south end of Brookings.

One of the more unusual places to visit in the area is the **Brandy Peak Distillery,** 18526 Tetley Rd. (℃ **541/469-0194;** www.brandypeak.com), which is located north of Brookings off U.S. 101. (Take Carpenterville Rd. for several miles up into the hills and then go right on Tetley Rd. and immediately right into the distillery.) This microdistillery produces varietal marc brandies (unaged brandies), as well as barrel-aged brandies, grappas, and pear brandy. All are produced in small wood-fired pot stills. The distillery is open for tours and tastings Tuesday through Saturday from 1 to 5pm between March and early January, and by appointment the rest of the year. If you want to be absolutely sure you'll find someone in, call before you come.

WHERE TO STAY

Best Western Beachfront Inn 🐾   Located on the edge of the marina in Brookings' sister town of Harbor (on the south side of the Chetco River), the Beachfront Inn is the only oceanfront accommodation in this area. Most rooms are fairly large and all have ocean views, balconies, microwaves, and refrigerators. The more expensive rooms also have whirlpool tubs with picture windows over them. There is an outdoor pool and a whirlpool.

16008 Boat Basin Rd., Harbor, OR 97415. ℃ **800/468-4081** or 541/469-7779. Fax 541/469-0283. 102 units. $99–$260 double. AE, DC, DISC, MC, V. Pets accepted ($10). **Amenities:** Outdoor pool; Jacuzzi. *In room:* TV, fridge, coffeemaker.

Chetco River Inn & Lavender Farm 🐾🐾 *finds*   Set on 35 very secluded acres on the banks of the Chetco River, this contemporary B&B caters to nature lovers and anglers and makes a great weekend retreat. However, in order to get away, you'll first have to find the lodge, which is 17 miles from town up North Bank Road (the last bit on gravel). The lodge makes use of alternative energy, yet is luxurious and filled with antiques. The Siskiyou National Forest surrounds the property, and hiking, swimming (there are lots of great swimming holes), and stargazing are popular pastimes. If you don't feel like leaving the woods, you can arrange to have meals at the lodge.

21202 High Prairie Rd., Brookings, OR 97415. ℃ **541/251-0087.** www.chetcoriverinn.com. 7 units (including 2 cottages). $135–$175 double. Rates include full breakfast. MC, V. **Amenities:** Guest laundry. *In room:* No phone.

South Coast Inn Bed & Breakfast 🐾🐾   This 1917 Craftsman bungalow was designed by the famous San Francisco architect Bernard Maybeck and is filled with the sort of beautiful architectural details that characterized the Arts and Crafts movement. The inn's most spacious guest room is dedicated to Maybeck. Two of the guest rooms have good views, and the cottage, across the garden from the main house, offers a more private setting. Guests have use of a large living room full of antiques (including an old grand piano), where a fire often crackles in the stone fireplace, although the weather never gets very cold.

516 Redwood St., Brookings, OR 97415. (C) **800/525-9273** or 541/469-5557. Fax 541/469-6615. www.southcoast inn.com. 6 units (including 1 cottage and 1 apt). $99–$159 double. Rates include full breakfast. AE, DISC, MC, V. Children over 12 welcome. **Amenities:** Sauna. *In room:* A/C, TV/VCR, hair dryer, Wi-Fi.

CAMPGROUNDS

The best base for exploring the scenic wonders of Samuel H. Boardman State Scenic Corridor is **Harris Beach State Park** ((C) **800/551-6949** or 541/469-2021; www. oregonstateparks.org), on the beach just north of Brookings. Up the North Bank Chetco River Road out of Brookings, you'll find **Alfred A. Loeb State Park** ((C) **800/ 551-6949** or 541/469-2021 for information, or 800/452-5687 for reservations; www. oregonstateparks.org), which is set amid redwood and myrtle trees along the banks of the beautiful Chetco River. A bit farther up the Chetco is the Forest Service's **Little Redwood Campground** ((C) **541/412-6000;** www.fs.fed.us/r6/siskiyou), which is the site of a very popular swimming hole.

WHERE TO DINE

If it's pizza you're craving, **Wild River Pizza Company,** 16279 U.S. 101 S., just south of Brookings ((C) **541/469-7454;** www.wildriverbrewing.com), turns out a crispy one, accompanied by their own microbrews. Locals swear by **The Hungry Clam,** at the Port of Brookings-Harbor ((C) **541/469-2526**), for fish and chips. For smoked salmon, head south of town to **The Great American Smokehouse,** 15657 U.S. 101 S. ((C) **541/469-6903;** www.smokehouse-salmon.com), which sells a wide variety of smoked and canned seafood and also has a sit-down restaurant.

8

The Columbia Gorge

The Columbia Gorge, which begins just a few miles east of Portland and stretches for nearly 70 miles along the shores of the Columbia River, is a dramatic landscape of mountains, cliffs, and waterfalls created by massive Ice Age floods. Flanked by national forests and snow-covered peaks on both the Oregon and Washington sides of the Columbia River, the Gorge is as breathtaking a landscape as you will find anywhere in the West, and the fascinating geology, dramatic vistas, and abundance of recreational opportunities make it a premier vacation destination almost any month of the year. Not only are there waterfalls, trails, and some of the world's best windsurfing, but there are also fascinating museums, resort hotels, hot springs, historic B&Bs, and even wineries. Between 1913 and 1922, a scenic highway (one of the first paved roads in the Northwest) was built through the Gorge, and, in 1986, much of the area was designated the Columbia Gorge National Scenic Area in an attempt to preserve the Gorge's spectacular and unique natural beauty.

The Columbia River is older than the hills. It's older than the mountains, too, which explains why this river flows not from the mountains but through them. The river was already flowing into the Pacific Ocean when the Cascade Range began rising millions of years ago. However, it was a series of recent events, geologically speaking, that gave the Columbia Gorge its very distinctive appearance. About 15,000 years ago, toward the end of the last Ice Age, huge dams of ice far upstream collapsed and sent floodwaters racing down the Columbia. As the floodwaters swept through the Columbia Gorge, they were as much as 1,200 feet high. Ice and rock carried by the floodwaters helped the river to scour out the sides of the once gently sloping valley, leaving behind the steep-walled gorge that we know today. The waterfalls that elicit so many oohs and aahs are the most dramatic evidence of these great floods.

The vast gorge that the Columbia River has formed as it slices through the mountains is effectively a giant bridge between the rain-soaked forests west of the Cascades and the desert-dry sagebrush scrublands of central Oregon. This change in climate is caused by moist air condensing into snow and rain as it passes over the crest of the Cascades. Most of the air's moisture falls on the western slopes, so the eastern slopes and the land stretching for hundreds of miles beyond lie in a rain shadow. Perhaps nowhere else on earth can you witness this rain-shadow effect so easily and in such a short distance. It's so pronounced that as you come around a bend on I-84 just east of Hood River, you can see dry grasslands to the east and dense forests of Douglas fir over your shoulder to the west. In between the two extremes lies a community of plants that's unique to the Columbia Gorge, and springtime here brings colorful displays of wildflowers.

In North America, the Columbia River is second only to the Mississippi in the volume of water it carries to the sea—but more than just water flows through the Columbia Gorge. As the only break over the entire length of the Cascade Range, the Gorge acts as a massive natural wind tunnel. During the summer, the sun bakes the lands east of the Cascades, causing the air to rise. Cool air from the west side then rushes up the river, whipping through Hood River with near gale force at times. These winds, blowing against the downriver flow of water, set up ideal conditions for windsurfing and kiteboarding on the Columbia. The reliability of the winds, and the waves they kick up, has turned Hood River into the Aspen of windsurfing.

For centuries the Columbia River has been an important route between the maritime Northwest and the dry interior.

Lewis and Clark canoed down the river in 1805, and pioneers followed the Oregon Trail to its shores at The Dalles. It was here at The Dalles that many pioneers transferred their wagons to boats for the dangerous journey downriver to Oregon City. The set of rapids known as The Dalles and the waterfalls of the Cascades were the two most dangerous sections of the Columbia Gorge, so towns arose at these two points to transport goods and people around the treacherous waters. Locks and a canal helped circumvent the two sections of white water, but now the rapids of the Columbia lie flooded beneath the waters behind the Bonneville and The Dalles dams. The ease of navigating the river today has dimmed the importance of the towns of Cascade Locks and The Dalles, both of which are steeped in the history of the Gorge.

1 The Columbia Gorge National Scenic Area ⟨★⟨★⟨★

Columbia Gorge: Begins 18 miles E of Portland

Stretching from the Sandy River in the west to the Deschutes River in the east, the Columbia Gorge National Scenic Area is one of the most breathtakingly dramatic places in the United States. Carved by floods of unimaginable power, this miles-wide canyon is flanked on the north by Mount Adams and on the south by Mount Hood, both of which rise more than 11,000 feet high. With its diaphanous waterfalls, basalt cliffs painted with colorful lichens, and dark forests of Douglas firs rising up from the banks of the Columbia River, the Gorge is a year-round recreational area where hiking trails lead to hidden waterfalls and mountain-top panoramas, mountain-bike trails meander through the forest, and windsurfers race across wind-whipped waters.

The Columbia Gorge National Scenic Area is also as controversial as it is beautiful. Over the years since this area received this federal designation, the fights over the use of private land within the Gorge have been constant. The pressure to develop this scenic marvel of the Northwest has been unrelenting, as landowners throughout the Gorge have fought against restrictions on development. To find out more about protecting the Gorge, contact the **Friends of the Columbia Gorge** (*©* **503/241-3762; www.gorgefriends.org**), which, each spring, offers numerous guided wildflower hikes.

ESSENTIALS

GETTING THERE   I-84 and the Historic Columbia River Highway both pass through the Gorge on the Oregon side of the Columbia.

VISITOR INFORMATION   Contact the **Columbia River Gorge National Scenic Area,** 902 Wasco Ave., Suite 200, Hood River, OR 97031 (*©* **541/308-1700;** www. fs.fed.us/r6/columbia). There's also a **Forest Service Visitor Center** (*©* **503/695-2372**) at Multnomah Falls Lodge (take the Historic Columbia River Hwy. or the

The Columbia Gorge

Multnomah Falls exit off I-84) and another in the lobby of **Skamania Lodge,** 1131 SW Skamania Lodge Dr. (© **509/427-2528**), in Stevenson, Washington.

LEARNING ABOUT THE GORGE & ITS HISTORY

Columbia Gorge Interpretive Center Museum 🎏🎏   Focusing on the Gorge's early Native American inhabitants and the development of the area by white settlers, this museum is your single best introduction to the Columbia Gorge. Exhibits contain historical photographs by Edward Curtis and others that illustrate the story of portage companies and paddle-wheelers that once operated along this stretch of the Columbia River. A 37-foot-high replica of a 19th-century fish wheel gives an understanding of how salmon runs have been threatened in the past and the present. Displays also frankly discuss other problems that the coming of civilization brought to this area. A slide program tells the history of the formation of the Gorge. When it's not cloudy, the center has an awesome view of the south side of the Gorge.

990 SW Rock Creek Dr., Stevenson. © **800/991-2338** or 509/427-8211. www.columbiagorge.org. Admission $6 adults, $5 seniors and students, $4 children 6–12, free for children 5 and under. Daily 10am–5pm. Closed Thanksgiving, Christmas, and New Year's Day.

A DRIVING TOUR

Though I-84 is the fastest road through the Columbia Gorge, it is not the most scenic route. The Gorge is well worth a full day's exploration and is best appreciated at a more leisurely pace on the **Historic Columbia River Highway** 🎏🎏, which begins 16 miles east of downtown Portland at the second Troutdale exit off I-84. Opened in 1915, this highway was a marvel of engineering at the time and, by providing access to automobiles, opened the Gorge to casual visits.

At the western end of the historic highway, you'll find **Lewis & Clark State Park,** which is near the mouth of the Sandy River. This park is popular with anglers and Portlanders looking to cool off in the Sandy River during the hot summer months. There is also a rock-climbing area within the park.

The first unforgettable view of the Gorge comes at the **Portland Women's Forum State Scenic Viewpoint,** which may also be your first encounter with the legendary Columbia Gorge winds. To learn more about the historic highway, and how it was built, stop at the recently restored **Vista House** (© **503/695-2230;** www.vistahouse. com), 733 feet above the river on **Crown Point.** Although there are displays of historical photos here at Vista House, most visitors can't concentrate on the exhibits, preferring to gaze at the some 30 miles of breathtaking views. Vista House is open daily from 9am to 6pm.

From Crown Point, the historic highway drops down into the Gorge and passes several picturesque **waterfalls.** The first of these is 249-foot **Latourell Falls** 🎏, a diaphanous wisp of a waterfall cascading over basalt cliffs stained lime-green by lichen. A 2.3-mile loop trail leads from this waterfall up to the smaller Upper Latourell Falls. East of these falls, you'll come to Shepherd's Dell Falls, Bridal Veil Falls, Mist Falls, and Wahkeena Falls, all of which are either right beside the road or a short walk away. If you're interested in a longer hike, there are trails linking several of the falls. However, for spectacular views, you can't beat the steep 4.4-mile round-trip hike to Angels Rest. The well-signposted trail head for this hike is on the historic highway near the community of Bridal Veil.

Multnomah Falls 🎏🎏🎏 is the largest and the most famous waterfall along this highway, and the state's most visited natural attraction. At 620 feet from the lip to the lower pool, it's the tallest waterfall in Oregon and the fourth tallest in the United States. An arched bridge stands directly in front of the falls part way up. This bridge is part of a steep paved trail that leads from the foot of the falls up to the top; from there, other trails lead off into the **Mount Hood National Forest.** The historic Multnomah Falls Lodge (see below) has a restaurant, snack bar, and gift shop, as well as a **National Forest Visitor Center** (© **503/695-2372**) with information on the geology, history, and natural history of the Gorge.

East of Multnomah Falls, the scenic highway passes by **Oneonta Gorge** 🎐🎐, a narrow rift in the cliffs. Through this tiny gorge flows a stream that serves as a watery pathway for anyone interested in exploring upstream to **Oneonta Falls.** Less than a half mile east of Oneonta Gorge, you'll come to **Horsetail Falls.** From these roadside falls, a trail leads uphill to Upper Horsetail Falls. The trail then passes behind the upper falls and continues another 2 miles to Triple Falls, passing above Oneonta Gorge along the way.

If you'd like to escape the crowds and see a little-visited waterfall, watch for Frontage Road on your right just before the historic highway merges with I-84. Drive east for 2 miles to a gravel parking area at the trailhead for **Elowah Falls** 🎐🎐. These 289-foot-tall falls are set in a beautiful natural amphitheater less than a mile from the road. Just be aware that this parking area is subject to car break-ins; don't leave any valuables in your vehicle.

Just after the two highways merge, you come to the exit for **Bonneville Lock and Dam** (© **541/374-8820**). The **Bradford Island Visitors Center** has exhibits on the history of this dam, which was built in 1927. One of the most important features of the dam is its fish ladder, which allows adult salmon to return upriver to spawn. Underwater windows let visitors see fish as they pass through the ladder. Visit the adjacent **Bonneville Fish Hatchery** (© **541/374-8393**) to see how trout, salmon, and sturgeon are raised before being released into the river. A **Sturgeon Viewing Center** 🎐🎐 allows you to marvel at several immense sturgeons through an underwater viewing window. At this same exit off I-84 (and at Eagle Creek), you'll find access to a section of the **Historic Columbia River Highway State Trail,** a paved multiuse trail that connects the town of Cascade Locks with Bonneville Dam. This trail incorporates abandoned sections of the Historic Columbia River Highway and is open to hikers and bikers. Near the western trailhead for this trail you'll also find the trail to **Wahclella Falls** 🎐, a little-visited yet very picturesque waterfall tucked back in a side canyon. The trail is less than a mile and relatively flat.

Beyond the dam is Eagle Creek, the single best spot in the Gorge for a hike. The **Eagle Creek Trail** 🎐🎐 leads past several waterfalls, and if you have time for only one hike in the Gorge, it should be this one. You'll also find a campground and picnic area here.

Not far beyond Eagle Creek is the **Bridge of the Gods,** which connects Oregon and Washington at the site where, according to a Native American legend, once stood a natural bridge used by the gods. Geologists now believe that the legend is based in fact; there is evidence that a massive rock slide may have once blocked the river at this point.

Just beyond the Bridge of the Gods is **Cascade Locks.** It was at this site that cascades once turned the otherwise placid Columbia River into a raging torrent that required boats to be portaged a short distance downriver. The Cascade Locks were built in 1896 and allowed steamships to pass unhindered. The locks made traveling between The Dalles and Portland much easier, but the completion of the Columbia River Scenic Highway, in 1915, made the trip even easier by land. With the construction of the Bonneville Lock and Dam, the cascades were flooded, and the locks became superfluous.

There are two small museums here at the locks. The **Cascade Locks Historical Museum,** Port Marina Park (© **541/374-8535**), which is housed in the old lock tender's house, includes displays of Native American artifacts and pioneer memorabilia, as well as the Northwest's first steam engine. The museum is open May through September, daily from noon to 5pm. Admission is by donation.

The **Port of Cascade Locks Visitors Center,** which has displays on river travel in the past, is also the ticket office for the **Sternwheeler *Columbia Gorge*** (© **800/ 643-1354** or 541/374-8427; www.sternwheeler.com), which makes regular trips on the river. These cruises provide a great perspective on the Gorge. Fares for the 2-hour scenic cruises are $20 for adults, $15 for seniors, and $10 for children; dinner, lunch, breakfast, and brunch cruises run $35 to $65 for adults and $20 to $45 for children. These cruises should not be missed on a visit to the Columbia Gorge.

Should you decide not to take the historic highway and stay on I-84, you may want to stop at **Rooster Rock State Park,** especially if it's a hot summer day. This park has a long sandy beach, and in a remote section of the park there's even a clothing-optional beach. From I-84 there's also easy access to Multnomah Falls, the main attraction of the Historic Columbia River Highway.

Another option is to cross to the Washington side of the Columbia River and take Wash. 14 east from Vancouver. This latter highway actually provides the most spectacular views of both the Columbia Gorge and Mount Hood. If you should decide to take this route, be sure to stop at **Beacon Rock State Park** (© **509/427-8265**), which has as its centerpiece an 800-foot-tall monolith that has a trail (mostly stairways and catwalks) leading to its summit. At one time there was talk of blasting the rock apart to build jetties at the mouth of the river. Luckily, another source of rock was used, and this amazing landmark continues to guard the Columbia. There is a $5 parking fee here. If you want to make better time, you can cross back to Oregon on the Bridge of the Gods. Continuing east on the Washington side of the river, you'll come to Stevenson, site of the above-mentioned Columbia Gorge Interpretive Center.

In the town of North Bonneville, a few miles west of Stevenson, you can swim in the mineral-water pool and soak in the hot tubs at **Bonneville Hot Springs Resort,** 1252 E. Cascade Dr. (© **866/459-1678** or 509/427-7767; www.bonnevilleresort. com), which charges $15 per day for the use of its pool and soaking tubs ($12 for seniors). Massages and other spa services are also available. East of Stevenson, in the town of Carson, you can also avail yourself of the therapeutic waters of the **Carson Hot Springs Resort** (© **800/607-3678**). This rustic "resort" has been in business since 1897 and has one building that looks every bit its age. However, it's just this old-fashioned appeal that keeps people coming back year after year. It's open daily from 8am to 7pm in summer and from 9am to 6pm other months, and charges $12 for a soak and post-soak wrap. An hour's massage is $55. At press time, Carson Hot Springs was in the process of adding a new hotel and has plans to build a new pool and treatment facility. Expect major changes when you visit.

WINDSURFING & OTHER ACTIVITIES

If you want to launch your sailboard along this stretch of the Gorge, try **Rooster Rock State Park,** near the west end of the Gorge, or **Viento State Park,** just west of Hood River. Both parks are right off I-84 and are well marked.

If you're interested in hiring a fishing guide, contact **Page's Northwest Guide Service** (© **866/760-3370** or 503/760-3373; www.fishingoregon.net), which will take you out for salmon, steelhead, walleye, and sturgeon on the Columbia or Willamette Rivers or on other area waters ($135–$150 per person, per day). **Reel Adventures** (© **877/544-REEL** or 503/622-5372; www.donsreeladventures.com) offers a similar fishing-guide service ($150 per person, per day).

WHERE TO STAY

Best Western Columbia River Inn 🐾   Located at the foot of the Bridge of the Gods and well situated for exploring the Gorge, this modern motel has splendid views from its riverview rooms. Many of the rooms also have small balconies, although nearby railroad tracks can make them a bit noisy. Luckily, rooms are well insulated against train noises. For a splurge, try a spa room.

735 Wanapa St., Cascade Locks, OR 97014. © **800/595-7108** or 541/374-8777. Fax 541/374-2279. www.bestwestern. com. 62 units. $69–$159 double. Rates include continental breakfast. Children under 12 stay free in parent's room. AE, DC, DISC, MC, V. Pets accepted ($10 fee). **Amenities:** Indoor pool; exercise room; Jacuzzi; coin-op laundry. *In room:* A/C, TV, dataport, fridge, coffeemaker, hair dryer, iron.

Bonneville Hot Springs Resort 🐾🐾   Although this hot springs resort doesn't have any views to speak of, it is still one of your best bets for a memorable stay in the Columbia Gorge. With lots of stone and wood detail work used in the construction, this hideaway in the woods has the feel of a modern mountain lodge, although the furnishings are more classically European in styling. The focal point of the lobby is a huge river-rock fireplace. There's an 80-foot-long mineral-water indoor pool, a full-service spa, and a big outdoor hot tub in a courtyard with an unusual stone wall down which water cascades. Guest rooms have balconies (ask for one overlooking the courtyard), beds with ornate wood headboards, and attractive bathrooms. Some of the rooms have their own mineral-water soaking tubs.

1252 E. Cascade Dr. (P.O. Box 356), North Bonneville, WA 98639. © **866/459-1678** or 509/427-7767. Fax 509/427-7733. www.bonnevilleresort.com. 78 units. $135–$265 double; $325–$399 suite. Children under 4 stay free in parent's room. AE, DC, DISC, MC, V. **Amenities:** Restaurant (Continental); lounge; indoor pool; exercise room; full-service spa; 3 Jacuzzis; room service; massage. *In room:* A/C, TV, dataport, fridge, coffeemaker, hair dryer, iron.

McMenamins Edgefield 🐾 *Finds*   Ideally situated for exploring the Columbia Gorge and Mount Hood, this flagship of the McMenamin microbrewery empire is the former Multnomah County poor farm. Today, the property includes not only tastefully decorated guest rooms with antique furnishings, but a brewery, a pub, a beer garden, a restaurant, a movie theater, a winery, a wine-tasting room, a distillery, a golf course, a cigar bar in an old shed, and extensive gardens. With so much in one spot, this makes a great base for exploring the area. The beautiful grounds give this inn the feel of a remote retreat, though you are still within 30 miles of Portland.

2126 SW Halsey St., Troutdale, OR 97060. © **800/669-8610** or 503/669-8610. Fax 503/492-7750. www.mcmenamins. com. 114 units (100 with shared bathroom). $50–$90 double with shared bathroom; $95–$115 double with private bathroom; $30 hostel bed per person. Children under 7 stay free in parent's room. AE, DC, DISC, MC, V. **Amenities:** 3 restaurants (Northwest, American); 6 lounges; 18-hole par-3 golf course; business center; massage. *In room:* No phone, Wi-Fi.

Skamania Lodge ✿✿✿   Boasting the most spectacular vistas of any hotel in the Gorge, Skamania Lodge is also the only golf resort around. However, it is also well situated whether you brought your sailboard, hiking boots, or mountain bike. The decor is classically rustic with lots of rock and natural wood, and throughout the hotel there are Northwest Indian artworks and artifacts on display. Huge windows in the lobby have superb views of the Gorge. Of course, the riverview guest rooms are more expensive than the forest-view rooms (which overlook more parking lot than forest), but these rooms are well worth the extra cost. There are also rooms with fireplaces.

1131 Skamania Lodge Way, Stevenson, WA 98648. ✆ **800/221-7117** or 509/427-7700. Fax 509/427-2547. www. skamania.com. 254 units. $119–$279 double; $229–$279 suite. Children under 17 stay free in parent's room. AE, DC, DISC, MC, V. **Amenities:** Restaurant (Northwest); lounge; indoor pool; 18-hole golf course; 2 tennis courts; exercise room; full-service spa; Jacuzzi; sauna; bike rentals; children's programs; activities desk; business center; room service; massage; babysitting; laundry service. *In room:* A/C, TV, dataport, minibar, coffeemaker, hair dryer, iron.

CAMPGROUNDS

Camping in the Gorge isn't quite the wonderful experience you might think. With an interstate highway and a very active railway line paralleling the river on the Oregon side and another railroad and a secondary highway on the Washington side, the Gorge tends to be quite noisy. However, there are a few camping options between Portland and Hood River, and these campgrounds do what they can to minimize the traffic noises. **Ainsworth State Park,** 3½ miles east of Multnomah Falls, has showers, and the RV sites are quite nice. At exit 41 off I-84, there is **Eagle Creek Campground,** the oldest campground in the National Forest system and popular for its access to the Eagle Creek Trail. At exit 51 off of I-84, there is **Wyeth Campground,** a U.S. Forest Service campground on the bank of Gordon Creek. Over on the Washington side of the Columbia River, there is also first-come, first-served camping at **Beacon Rock State Park,** which is located 7 miles west of the Bridge of the Gods. Because it is tucked back away from the highway and railroad tracks, this is just about the quietest campground in the Gorge.

WHERE TO DINE

The area's best place to eat is the dining room of the Skamania Lodge (see above).

Black Rabbit Restaurant ✿✿ NORTHWEST/REGIONAL AMERICAN   This casual-yet-upscale restaurant is located on the grounds of McMenamins Edgefield (reviewed above), and is the ideal place to stop for dinner on the way back to Portland after a day of exploring the Gorge. Start with the calamari (perhaps accompanied by a glass of Edgefield wine) and then move on to the seared ahi tuna with plum-miso glaze or pan-seared salmon fillet with fava-bean ragout and a slaw of red onions, fennel, and apples. If you aren't in the mood for a formal dinner, there is also a less expensive and less formal brewpub here.

McMenamins Edgefield, 2126 SW Halsey St., Troutdale. ✆ **503/669-8610.** Main courses $12–$26. AE, DISC, MC, V. Daily 7–10pm.

Multnomah Falls Lodge ✿ AMERICAN   Built in 1925 at the foot of Multnomah Falls, the historic Multnomah Falls Lodge may be the most touristy place to eat in the entire Gorge, but the setting is wonderful and the food isn't half bad. Breakfast, when the crowds haven't yet arrived, is one of the best times to eat here. Try the grilled salmon or trout and eggs. At dinner, stick with the prime rib or Yankee pot roast. For a peek at the falls, try to get a table in the conservatory room or, in summer, out on the patio.

Historic Columbia River Hwy. (or I-84, exit 31). ℂ 503/695-2376. Reservations recommended. Main courses $9–$15 lunch, $15–$20 dinner. AE, DISC, MC, V. Mon–Sat 8am–9pm; Sun 8am–2pm and 3–9pm.

Tad's Chicken 'n Dumplins ✸ *Finds* AMERICAN   Located on the banks of the Sandy River at the western end of the Historic Columbia River Highway, this rustic restaurant has been in business more than 50 years and, as its name implies, specializes in all-American chicken and dumplings. Sure, you can get a steak, pan-fried oysters, or salmon, but you'd be remiss if you passed up this opportunity to fill up on this restaurant's namesake dish. Try to get a seat on the enclosed back porch, which overlooks the river. If you're coming here after dark, just watch for the classic neon sign out front.

1325 E. Historic Columbia River Hwy., Troutdale. ℂ 503/666-5337. Reservations not accepted. Main courses $11–$30. AE, DISC, MC, V. Mon–Fri 5–10pm; Sat 4–10pm; Sun 2–10pm.

2 Hood River: The Windsurfing Capital of the Northwest

62 miles E of Portland, 20 miles W of The Dalles, 32 miles N of Government Camp

Each summer, hot air rising over the desert to the east of the Cascade Range sucks cool air up the Columbia River Gorge from the Pacific, and the winds howl through what is basically a natural wind tunnel. The winds are incessant and gusts can whip the river into a tumult of whitecaps. They used to curse these winds in Hood River. Not anymore.

Ever since the first person pulled into town with a sailboard, Hood River has taken to praying for wind. Hood River is now the windsurfing capital of America, which has given this former lumber town a new lease on life. People come from all over the world to ride the winds that howl up the Gorge. In early summer the boardheads roll into town in their "Gorge-mobiles," which are equivalent to surfers' woodies, and start listening to the wind reports. They flock to riverside parks on both the Oregon and Washington sides of the Columbia, unfurl their sails, zip up their wet suits, and launch themselves into the melee of hundreds of other like-minded souls shooting back and forth across a mile of windswept water. High waves whipped up by near-gale-force winds provide perfect launching pads for rocketing skyward. Aerial acrobatics such as flips and 360-degree turns are common sights. Now, even boardsailors have had to make way for the newest sport—kiteboarding. This sport replaces the sail with a kite, shortens the board, and enables even more radical maneuvers, and higher speeds, than windsurfing, and lots more time in the air instead of in the water. Even if you're not into this fast-paced sport, you'll get a vicarious thrill from watching the boardheads going for major airtime.

Windsurfing and kiteboarding may be the big event here in Hood River, but this is certainly not a one-trick town. Sometimes the winds just aren't accommodating and even boardheads can get bored sitting on shore waiting for conditions to improve. Hood River has become something of an outdoor sports mecca, with a rapidly developing reputation for excellent mountain biking, white-water kayaking and rafting, paragliding, rock climbing, hiking, skiing, and snowboarding. In other words, Hood River is full of active people.

Hood River does not exist on sports alone, however; and outside town, in the Hood River Valley, are apple and pear orchards, wineries, and vineyards. Hood River also claims a famous historic hotel and several good restaurants. Most of the town's old Victorian and craftsman houses have now been restored, giving Hood River a historic atmosphere to complement its lively windsurfing scene. All in all, this town makes a great base whether you're here for the sports, to explore the Gorge, or to visit nearby Mount Hood.

ESSENTIALS

GETTING THERE   Hood River is on I-84 at the junction with Ore. 35, which leads south to connect with U.S. 26 near the community of Government Camp.

Amtrak offers passenger-rail service to the town of Bingen, Washington, just across the Columbia River from Hood River. The station is at the foot of Walnut Street.

VISITOR INFORMATION   Contact the **Hood River County Chamber of Commerce,** 405 Portway Ave., Hood River, OR 97031 (© **800/366-3530** or 541/386-2000; www.hoodriver.org), near the river at exit 63 off I-84.

FESTIVALS   The Hood River Valley Blossom Festival is held in mid-April and celebrates the flowering of the valley's pear and apple trees. In mid-October the Hood River Valley Harvest Fest takes place at the Hood River Expo Center and the Autumn Fine Arts and Music Festival is held in Parkdale.

WINDSURFING & OTHER OUTDOOR ACTIVITIES ✹✹✹

If you're here to ride the wind or just want to watch, head to the Columbia Gorge Sailpark at Hood River Marina, the nearby Event Site, or The Hook, all of which are accessible via exit 63 off I-84. Across the river in Washington, try the fish hatchery (The Hatchery), west of the mouth of the White Salmon River, or Swell City, a park about 4 miles west of the bridge. If you're a windsurfer or kiteboarder, you'll find all kinds of windsurfing- and kiteboarding-related shops in downtown Hood River. Classes are available through **Hood River Water Play** (© **800/WND-SURF** or 541/386-WIND; www.hoodriverwaterplay.com) and **Gorge Wind Guide Service** (© **541/490-4401;** www.windguide.com).

When there isn't enough wind for sailing, there's still the option to go **rafting** on the White Salmon River. Companies offering raft trips on this river include **Zoller's Outdoor Odysseys** (© **800/366-2004** or 509/493-2641; www.zooraft.com), **Wet Planet Rafting** (© **800/306-1673;** www.wetplanetrafting.com), and **All Adventures Rafting** (© **877/641-RAFT** or 800/74-FLOAT; www.alladventures.net). Although the White Salmon can be rafted any time of year, the most popular season runs from April through September. A half-day trip will cost around $55 or $60 per person.

Mountain biking is also very popular, and Hood River bike shops can direct you to some fun area rides. Check at **Discover Bicycles,** 116 Oak St. (© **541/386-4820;** www.discoverbicycles.com), or **Mountain View Cycles,** 205 Oak St. (© **541/386-BIKE**), both of which rent bikes. Expect to pay between $5 and $12 per hour and between $25 and $55 per day.

If fly-fishing is your passion, drop by the **Gorge Fly Shop,** 201 Oak St. (© **541/386-6977;** www.gorgeflyshop.com), which can fill all your angling needs and point you to where the fish are biting; they also offer guided fly-fishing trips in the area.

Hikers have their choice of trails in Mount Hood National Forest (see "Mount Hood: Skiing, Hiking & Scenic Drives," in chapter 9), the Columbia Gorge (p. 254), or across the river (head up Wash. 141 to Mount Adams). At 12,276 feet in elevation, Mount Adams is the second-highest peak in Washington. For more information about hiking on Mount Adams, contact the **Gifford Pinchot National Forest,** Mount Adams Ranger District, 2455 Wash. 141, Trout Lake, WA 98650 (© **509/395-3400;** www.fs.fed.us/gpnf).

THE FRUIT LOOP (EXPLORING THE HOOD RIVER VALLEY)

Before windsurfing took center stage, the Hood River Valley was known as one of Oregon's top fruit-growing regions, and today the valley is still full of apple and pear orchards. From blossom time (Apr) to harvest season (Sept–Oct), the valley offers quiet country roads to explore. Along the way you'll find numerous farm stands, wineries, museums, and interesting shops that reflect the valley's rural heritage. Pick up a brochure called *Hood River County Fruit Loop Guide to Local Farm Stands* at the Hood River County Chamber of Commerce visitor center (see "Visitor Information," above).

Be sure to start your tour of the Hood River Valley by stopping at **Panorama Point,** off of Ore. 35 just south of town (follow the signs). This hilltop park provides a splendid view of the valley's orchards with Mount Hood looming in the distance.

In the fall, fruit stands pop up along the roads around the valley. **Rasmussen Fruit & Flower Farm,** 3020 Thomsen Rd. (© **800/548-2243** or 541/386-4622; www. rasmussenfarms.com), is one of the biggest and best farm stands in the valley and is off Ore. 35 about 6 miles south of Hood River. Also not to be missed is the nearby **Apple Valley Country Store,** 2363 Tucker Rd. (© **541/386-1971;** www.applevalley store.com), where you can stock up on seasonal and organic produce and other homemade specialties. The 3-pound fruit pies here are legendary. You'll find the store west of Rasmussen's on the opposite side of the valley. Also in the valley are numerous orchards and farms where you can pick your own fruit. Keep an eye out for U-PICK signs.

The Hood River Valley also grows quite a few acres of wine grapes. You can visit several wineries in the area and taste the local fruit of the vine. West of town, off Country Club Road (take Oak St./Cascade St. west from downtown), you'll find two wineries. **Cathedral Ridge Winery,** 4200 Post Canyon Dr. (© 800/516-8710 or 541/ 386-2882; www.cathedralridgewinery.com), produces a good Riesling as well as pinot gris, chardonnay, and a cabernet-merlot blend. **Hood River Vineyards,** 4693 Westwood Dr. (© 541/386-3772), makes excellent fruit wines and a variety of port-style dessert wines, including an excellent zinfandel port. Continuing south up the valley, turn left on Barrett Road and then right onto Tucker Road to reach **Pheasant Valley Vineyard & Winery,** 3890 Acree Dr. (© 866/357-WINE or 541/387-3040; www. pheasantvalleywinery.com), where you can sample the wines of both this winery and **Viento Wines** (© 503/434-9587; www.vientowines.com), which together are some of my favorite wines produced here in the Hood River Valley. There are usually some good values to be had here. Across the valley to the east, you'll find **Mt. Hood Winery,** 3189 Ore. 35 (© 541/386-8333; www.mthoodwinery.com), which has its tasting room in an old fruit stand and is only open from April through October. Across the Columbia River in Washington, near the town of Husum (take Wash. 141 north from White Salmon), you'll find **Wind River Cellars,** 196 Spring Creek Rd., Husum (© 509/493-2324; www.windrivercellars.com), with a wide range of reds and whites.

The little hamlet of Parkdale, at the south end of the Fruit Loop, is home to the fascinating little **Hutson Museum,** 4967 Baseline Rd. (© **541/352-6808**), which houses lapidary, archaeology, and anthropology collections, of which the rock collection and exhibits of Native American artifacts are a highlight. Museum days and hours vary with the seasons, so call ahead. Also in Parkdale you'll find the **Elliot Glacier Public House,** 4945 Baseline Rd. (© **541/352-1022**), a brewpub with a great view of Mount Hood from the picnic tables out back.

Any time between late March and late December, but especially during fruit-blossom time, the **Mount Hood Railroad** (℃ **800/872-4661** or 541/386-3556; www.mt hoodrr.com) offers a great way to see the Hood River Valley. The diesel locomotives operated by this scenic railroad company depart from the historic 1911 Hood River depot, pulling restored Pullman coaches on 4-hour excursions. The train winds its way up the valley to Parkdale, where you can get a snack at a cafe or visit the Hutson Museum. Fares are $23 for adults, $21 for seniors, and $15 for children 2 to 12. The schedule varies with the season (in July–Aug it's Tues–Sun), so call ahead to make a reservation. There are also regularly scheduled dinner, brunch, and other specialty excursions. Reservations are recommended.

OTHER ATTRACTIONS IN HOOD RIVER

Hood River County Historical Museum   Down by the river at Port Marina Park (take exit 63 off I-84), you'll find this small museum, with exhibits of Native American artifacts from this area. There are also displays on pioneer life, but many visitors find the museum's windsurfing exhibit most compelling.

300 E. Port Marina Dr. ℃ 541/386-6772. Admission by donation. Apr–Aug Mon–Sat 10am–4pm, Sun noon–4pm; Sept–Oct daily noon–4pm. Closed Nov–Mar.

International Museum of Carousel Art 🎠 *Kids*   Carousel fans won't want to miss this fun little museum. Although there isn't an actual working carousel on the premises, there are more than 150 carousel animals on display, which makes this the largest such collection in the country. The museum also houses a working 1917 Wurlitzer band organ and exhibits on various aspects of carousel history and art. The owners of the collection have assisted in the restoration of numerous historic carousels around the country.

304 Oak St. ℃ 541/387-4622. www.carouselmuseum.com. Admission $5 adults, $4 seniors and students, $2 children 2–10. Mon–Sat 11am–3pm; Sun noon–4pm.

SHOPPING

In downtown Hood River, drop in at the community-sponsored, not-for-profit **Columbia Art Gallery,** 101 Third St. (℃ **541/386-4512;** columbiaartgallery.org). If you're an avid cook, you'll want to stop in at **Annz Panz,** 315 Oak St. (℃ **541/387-2654**), a large and well-stocked cookware store with a cafe and espresso counter. The first Friday of each month, downtown galleries and shops are open from 5 to 8pm with local artists on hand to sell their work and demonstrate their skills. Between mid-May and mid-October, you can sample local produce at downtown **Hood River's Saturday Market** on Cascade Avenue between Fifth and Seventh streets from 9am to 3pm.

WHERE TO STAY

If you're looking for a bed-and-breakfast and those below are full, call **Roomfinder** (℃ **541/386-6767;** www.hoodriverroomfinder.com), a free service provided by the Hood River Bed & Breakfast Association.

Best Western Hood River Inn 🎠🎠   As the only area hotel located right on the water (there's a dock and private beach), the Best Western is popular with windsurfers. The convention hotel atmosphere (crowds of corporate types busily networking) is somewhat constraining, but if you like comfort and predictability, this is a good bet. The Riverside Grill serves dependable meals with a bit of Northwest imagination and a great view across the river.

1108 E. Marina Way, Hood River, OR 97031. (C) **800/828-7873** or 541/386-2200. Fax 541/386-8905. www.hood riverinn.com. 149 units. Mid-May to Sept $89–$159 double, $179–$229 suite; Oct to mid-May $89–$139 double, $159–$179 suite. AE, DC, DISC, MC, V. Pets accepted ($12). **Amenities:** Restaurant (international); lounge; outdoor pool; exercise room; Jacuzzi; business center; room service; coin-op laundry; dry cleaning. *In room:* A/C, TV, dataport, fridge, coffeemaker, hair dryer, iron.

Columbia Gorge Hotel ☆☆   Just west of Hood River off I-84, and in business since shortly after 1921, this little oasis of luxury offers a genteel atmosphere that was once enjoyed by Rudolph Valentino and Clark Gable. With its yellow-stucco walls and red-tile roofs, this hotel would be at home in Beverly Hills, and the hotel gardens could hold their own in Victoria, British Columbia. The hotel is perched more than 200 feet above the river on a steep cliff, and it is difficult to take your eyes off the view. At press time, the hotel was schedule to undergo extensive renovations, so by the time you plan to visit, this historic gem should once again be the finest hotel in the area. Be forewarned, though, that the rooms are rather cramped, as are the bathrooms. In addition to the hotel's famous breakfast, there is a complimentary champagne-and-caviar social hour each evening. On Sundays high tea is served.

4000 Westcliff Dr., Hood River, OR 97031. (C) **800/345-1921** or 541/386-5566. Fax 541/386-9141. www.columbia gorgehotel.com. 40 units. $199–$259 double; $279–$379 suite. Rates include multicourse breakfast. AE, DC, DISC, MC, V. Pets accepted ($25). **Amenities:** Restaurant (Northwest/Continental); lounge; concierge; business center; room service; massage and spa treatments. *In room:* A/C, TV, dataport, minibar, hair dryer, iron, free local calls, high-speed Internet access, Wi-Fi.

Hood River Hotel ☆   Built in 1913 and located in downtown Hood River, this hotel boasts a casual elegance and is an economical alternative to the pricey Columbia Gorge Hotel. Now don't expect much; this is sort of a historic hotel for young travelers. Canopy beds, ceiling fans, wood floors, and area rugs give the rooms a classic feel, but bathrooms in some rooms are little larger than closets. Most third-floor rooms have skylit bathrooms—my favorite. The riverview rooms are the most expensive, and there are suites with full kitchens as well. The hotel's casual dining room serves good Northwest meals. Light sleepers should be aware of the railroad tracks behind the hotel.

102 Oak Ave., Hood River, OR 97031. (C) **800/386-1859** or 541/386-1900. Fax 503/386-6090. www.hoodriverhotel.com. 41 units. $69–$119 double; $89–$169 suite. Rates include continental breakfast. AE, DC, DISC, MC, V. Pets accepted ($15 per day). **Amenities:** Restaurant (Northwest); lounge; exercise room; Jacuzzi; sauna; room service. *In room:* TV, Wi-Fi.

Inn at the Gorge ☆   Though this bed-and-breakfast is housed in a 1908 Victorian home, it's still a casual sort of place popular with windsurfing enthusiasts. Each of the three suites has a kitchenette. The sunny Garden Suite, with its claw-foot tub, is our favorite. There's also a storage area for windsurfing and skiing gear. The innkeepers can steer you to the best spots for your skill level. The inn also offers discounted lift tickets to Mount Hood Meadows ski area.

1113 Eugene St., Hood River, OR 97031. (C) **541/386-4429.** www.innatthegorge.com. 5 units. $89–$139 double. Rates include full breakfast. MC, V. *In room:* A/C, TV, fridge, Wi-Fi.

The Mosier House Bed & Breakfast ☆☆ *Finds*   This beautifully restored Victorian home is in the small town of Mosier, 5 miles east of Hood River, and the views of the Columbia Gorge from the inn's front porch are unforgettable. Inside, you'll find wood floors and period antiques, and although the four rooms with shared baths are all fairly small, they have the feel of an authentic vintage travelers' hotel. One of the shared bathrooms has a claw-foot tub, as does the room with the private bath. All in

all, this inn manages to capture a bygone era without being overly frilly or self-consciously romantic, and it makes an excellent base for exploring the eastern end of the Columbia Gorge.

704 Third Ave. (P.O. Box 476), Mosier, OR 97040. ℂ 541/478-3640. www.mosierhouse.com. 5 units (1 with private bathroom). $85–$100 double with shared bathroom; $125 double with private bathroom. Rates include full breakfast. Children under 10 stay free in parent's room. MC, V. *In room:* A/C, no phone, Wi-Fi.

Oak Street Hotel ✿ (Finds)   This little hotel is in a recently restored older home in downtown Hood River and shares space with a real-estate office. As sort of a cross between a B&B and a small inn, the Oak Street Hotel may not offer a lot of amenities but it does have loads of contemporary charm. Guest rooms are small but very attractively furnished. Room no. 5, with its views of the Columbia River, is my favorite. One of the best reasons to stay here is for the delicious baked goodies that are served at breakfast. Plus you'll be within a few blocks of several good restaurants.

610 Oak St., Hood River, OR 97031. ℂ 866/386-3845 or 541/386-3845. www.oakstreethotel.com. 9 units. $99–$149 double. Rates include continental breakfast. AE, DISC, MC, V. *In room:* A/C, Wi-Fi.

Vagabond Lodge ✿ (Kids)   If you've got a banker's tastes but a teller's vacation budget, you can take advantage of the Vagabond Lodge's proximity to the Columbia Gorge Hotel and enjoy the latter's gardens and restaurant without breaking the bank. Actually, the back rooms at the Vagabond are some of the best in Hood River simply for their views (some have balconies). In addition, this motel's grounds are also quite attractive. There are lots of big old oaks and evergreens, and natural rock outcroppings have been incorporated into the motel's landscaping. If you're in the mood for a splurge, ask for one of the suites. (Some have fireplaces; others whirlpool tubs.) A playground and lots of grass make this a good choice for families.

4070 Westcliff Dr., Hood River, OR 97031. ℂ 877/386-2992 or 541/386-2992. Fax 541/386-3317. www.vagabond lodge.com. 42 units. $49–$84 double; $78–$96 suite. Children under 11 stay free in parent's room. AE, DC, MC, V. Pets accepted ($5). *In room:* A/C, TV, fridge.

CAMPGROUNDS

Area campgrounds include **Toll Bridge Park,** on Ore. 35, 17 miles south of town, and **Tucker Park,** on Tucker Road (Ore. 281) just a few miles south of town. Both of these county parks are on the banks of the Hood River. Farther south, you'll find the **Sherwood Campground,** a national-forest campground also on the banks of the Hood River. (This campground is favored by mountain bikers.) Eight miles west of Hood River off I-84 is **Viento State Park,** which gets quite a bit of traffic noise both from the interstate and from the adjacent railroad tracks. Eleven miles east of town, you'll find **Memaloose State Park,** which has the same noise problems. These two state parks are popular with windsurfers.

WHERE TO DINE

For fresh-baked rustic breads and great sandwiches made with imported meats and cheeses, go to **Panzanella Bakery & Deli,** 102 Fifth St. (ℂ 541/386-2048). If you need some good picnic fare, stop in at **Hood River City Market,** 406 Oak Ave. (ℂ 541/386-9876), which has plenty of prepared foods as well as fixings for putting together your own meal. For creamy gelato and good espresso, stop in at **Doppio,** 310 Oak St. (ℂ 541/386-3000).

Brian's Pourhouse ✿✿ ECLECTIC   Located in an old house a few blocks up the hill from downtown Hood River, this restaurant is a casual, fun place with very creative food. In summer, the big deck is the place to eat, and any time of year, the stylish little bar area is a cozy place for a cocktail or a local microbrew. The menu is highly eclectic and ranges from fish tacos to seared ahi tuna seasoned with Moroccan spices. Sure, you can get a good porterhouse steak and mashed potatoes, but this is someplace to try some bold new flavors. Keep an eye out for the delicious *unagi* (eel) tempura sushi.

606 Oak St. ℂ 541/387-4344. www.brianspourhouse.com. Reservations recommended. Main courses $10–$22. AE, MC, V. Sun–Thurs 5–10pm; Fri–Sat 5–11pm.

Celilo Restaurant 𝒜𝒜 NORTHWEST   This new sister restaurant to the ever-popular Sixth Street Bistro is utterly hip in concept and is a big switch from the homey restaurants that have long been popular in Hood River. Think timber-town natural-wood decor meets modern urban-design aesthetic, and you'll have a good idea of what this place is like. The concept of fresh and local drives the kitchen here, so you can count on the menu sticking to whatever is in season—luckily, that can cover a lot of territory in this fertile region. Dishes with house-made pasta are always a good bet, and, in the fall, you might get your noodles sauced with fresh chanterelle mushrooms. Lots of fresh herbs flavor many of the dishes here.

16 Oak St. ℂ 541/386-5710. www.celilorestaurant.com. Reservations recommended. Main courses $15–$25. AE, MC, V. Thurs–Tues 5–9 or 10pm.

North Oak Brasserie 𝒜𝒜 ITALIAN   Located below street level, this dark, romantic place is one of the most formal, fine-dining restaurants in town and is under the same management as Stonehedge Gardens. The emphasis here is on traditional and creative Italian food and good wine. If you don't have to worry about your cholesterol, be sure to opt for the roasted garlic and brie soup. Keep an eye out for seasonal pasta dishes, including good ravioli dishes.

113 Third St. ℂ 541/387-2310. Reservations recommended. Main courses $7.50–$20. AE, DISC, MC, V. Tues–Thurs 11am–2pm and 5–9pm; Fri 11am–2pm and 5–10pm; Sat 5–10pm.

Sixth Street Bistro 𝒜𝒜 AMERICAN/INTERNATIONAL   Just a block off Oak Street toward the river, the Sixth Street Bistro has an intimate little dining room and patio on the lower floor and a lounge with a balcony on the second floor. Each has its own entrance, but they share a menu. There are numerous international touches, such as chicken satay, coconut red curry, and hummus, and also juicy burgers. You'll find seasonal specials and vegetarian dishes as well.

509 Cascade Ave. ℂ 541/386-5737. www.sixthstreetbistro.com. Reservations recommended. Main courses $7–$22. MC, V. Daily 11:30am–4pm and 5–10pm.

Stonehedge Gardens 𝒜𝒜 CONTINENTAL   Built as a summer vacation home in 1898, Stonehedge Gardens is in the woods west of downtown Hood River down a long gravel driveway off Cascade Drive. When you finally find the restaurant, you'll feel as though you've arrived at a remote Maine lodge. Inside the inn, there's a small lounge with a bar taken from an old tavern, and several dining rooms, all of which feel genuinely old-fashioned. Although the entree menu sticks to traditional continental dishes such as steak Diane, rack of lamb, and chicken cordon bleu, you'll find some more creative offerings such as grilled goat cheese with roasted garlic or seared ahi tuna. On a warm summer evening, the patio here is my favorite place in Hood River for dinner.

3405 Cascade Dr. ℂ 541/386-3940. Reservations recommended. Main courses $20–$25. AE, DISC, MC, V. Daily 5–9 or 10pm.

Wildflower Café ⚸ (Finds) INTERNATIONAL   If you're out this way viewing wild-flowers or exploring various sections of the Historic Columbia River Highway, this restaurant, a few miles east of Hood River in the small town of Mosier, is a great spot for breakfast, lunch, or dinner. The menu is eclectic and relies on fresh local ingredients as much as possible. Whether you're in the mood for pad Thai, macaroni and cheese, or chicken-fried steak, you'll find it here. The restaurant building was constructed using salvaged lumber, so it has a rustic, old-fashioned feel. Big windows look out to the Columbia River, and there's a big covered deck for warm days.

904 Second Ave. (at Main St.), Mosier. ℂ 541/478-0111. www.cafewildflower.com. Main courses $8–$15. AE, DISC, MC, V. Wed–Sun 8am–9pm.

HOOD RIVER AFTER DARK

Big Horse Brew Pub ⚸   Located in a vertiginous old house above downtown, this brewpub usually has a good selection of brews and food, and the views from the third floor can't be beat. 115 State St. ℂ 541/386-4411.

Full Sail Tasting Room & Pub   Full Sail brews some of the most consistently flavorful and well-rounded beers in the Northwest and has developed a loyal following. You have to walk right past the brewery to get to the pub, which is at the back of an old industrial building a block off Hood River's main drag. Big windows look out over the river. 506 Columbia St. ℂ 541/387-2247. www.fullsailbrewing.com.

EAST OF HOOD RIVER: WILDFLOWERS & VIEWS

East of Hood River, you'll find two more sections of the Historic Columbia River Highway (Ore. 30), one of which is open only to hikers and bikers. The other is open to automobiles. The former section, located between Hood River and Mosier and known as the **Historic Columbia River Highway State Trail** (ℂ 800/551-6949), was abandoned when I-84 was built and two tunnels on this section of the old highway were filled in. After the tunnels were re-excavated in order to open up this stretch as a 4.5-mile paved trail, a rock catchment had to be built along part of the route leading up to the tunnels from the west. Although the trail receives some traffic noise from I-84, it is a fascinating and easy hike or bike ride. To reach the western trailhead, head east out of downtown Hood River and continue east on Old Columbia River Drive. For the eastern trailhead, take exit 69 off I-84 and then take the first left. Starting from this latter trailhead makes for a much shorter hike. However, the main visitor center for the trail is at the western trailhead. There is a $3 fee to use the trail.

The second part of the old highway, beginning at exit 69 off I-84 and stretching from Mosier to The Dalles, climbs up onto the Rowena Plateau, where sweeping vistas take in the Columbia River, Mount Hood, and Mount Adams. Between March and May the wildflowers are some of the finest in the state. The best place to see them is at the Nature Conservancy's **Governor Tom McCall Preserve** (ℂ 503/230-1221). On spring weekends there are usually volunteers on hand guiding wildflower walks through the preserve.

3 The Dalles

128 miles W of Pendleton, 85 miles E of Portland, 133 miles N of Bend

The Dalles (rhymes with "the pals"), a French word meaning "flagstone," was the name given to this area by early-19th-century French trappers. These explorers may have been reminded of stepping stones or flagstone-lined gutters when they first gazed upon the flat basalt rocks that forced the Columbia River through a long stretch of rapids and cascades here. These rapids, which were a barrier to river navigation, formed a natural gateway to western Oregon.

For more than 10,000 years, Native Americans inhabited this site because of the ease with which salmon could be taken from the river as it flowed through the tumultuous rapids. The annual fishing season at nearby Celilo Falls was a meeting point for tribes from all over the West. Tribes would come to fish, trade, and stockpile supplies for the coming winter.

Although the Lewis and Clark expedition stopped here when they passed through the region in 1805 and 1806, white settlers, the first of whom came to The Dalles as missionaries in 1838, were latecomers to this area. However, by the 1840s, a steady flow of pioneers was passing through the region, which was effectively the end of the overland segment of the Oregon Trail. Pioneers who were headed for the mild climate and fertile soils of the Willamette Valley would load their wagons onto rafts at this point and float downriver to the mouth of the Willamette and then up that river to Oregon City.

By the 1850s, The Dalles was the site of an important military fort and had become a busy river port. Steamships shuttled from here to Cascade Locks on the run to Portland. However, the coming of the railroad in 1880, and later the flooding of the river's rapids, reduced the importance of The Dalles as a port town. Today, the city serves as the eastern gateway to the Columbia Gorge and, as such, is the site of the Columbia Gorge Discovery Center.

ESSENTIALS

GETTING THERE   The Dalles is on I-84 at the junction of U.S. 197, which leads south to Antelope, where it connects with U.S. 97.

Amtrak passenger trains stop across the Columbia River from The Dalles in Wishram, Washington. The station is at the west end of Railroad Avenue.

VISITOR INFORMATION   Contact **The Dalles Area Chamber of Commerce,** 404 W. Second St., The Dalles, OR 97058 (© **800/255-3385** or 541/296-2231; www.thedalleschamber.com).

LEARNING ABOUT THE GORGE

Columbia Gorge Discovery Center/Wasco County Historical Museum ⚑

These two museums, housed in one building on the outskirts of The Dalles, serve as the eastern gateway to the Columbia Gorge. In the museum building, constructed to resemble a Northwest Native American longhouse, you'll find exhibits on the geology and history of the Gorge. Among the most fascinating exhibits is a film of Native Americans fishing at Celilo Falls before the rising waters behind The Dalles Dam flooded the falls. On the surrounding museum grounds is a **Living History Park,** where on summer weekends interpreters discuss Native American traditions and pioneer experiences. There is also a short nature trail that leads past a small pond and links to a trail that stretches several miles to Lewis & Clark's Rock Fort campsite (see below).

5000 Discovery Dr. © **541/296-8600**. www.gorgediscovery.org. $6.50 adults, $5.50 seniors, $3 children 6–16. Daily 9am–5pm. Closed Thanksgiving, Christmas, and New Year's Day.

EXPLORING THE DALLES

Long before settlers arrived in The Dalles, Lewis and Clark's expedition stopped here. The site of their camp is called **Rock Fort** and it is one of their only documented campsites. The historic site is on First Street west of downtown, near the Port of The Dalles' industrial area northeast of Webber and Second streets.

Some of The Dalles's most important historic buildings can be seen at the **Fort Dalles Museum,** 500 W. 15th St. (*©* **541/296-4547**), at the corner of Garrison Street. Established in 1850, Fort Dalles was the only military post between Fort Laramie and Fort Vancouver. By 1867, the fort had become unnecessary, and after several buildings were destroyed in a fire, it was abandoned. Today, several of the original buildings, including a Carpenter-Gothic officers' home, are still standing. Though small, this is the oldest history museum in Oregon. Memorial Day through Labor Day, the museum is open daily from 10am to 5pm; call for hours in other months. Admission is $3, free for students.

Not far from the Fort Dalles Museum, at **Sorosis Park,** there's a good view of The Dalles, the Columbia River, and Mount Adams. To reach this park, drive 1 block west from the museum and turn left on Trevitt Street, which becomes Scenic Drive. Continue on this latter street to the park.

Within a decade of the establishment of Fort Dalles, this community became the county seat of what was the largest county ever created in the United States. Wasco County covered 130,000 square miles between the Rocky Mountains and the Cascade Range. The old **Wasco County Courthouse,** 410 W. Second St. (*©* **541/296-4798**), a two-story wooden structure built in 1859, has been preserved, and the inside looks much as it did when it was a functioning courthouse. June through August it's open Monday, Tuesday, Friday, and Saturday from 10am to 4pm; May and September, it's open from 11am to 3pm (closed other months). Admission is free.

The Dalles's other historic landmark is a much more impressive structure. **Old St. Peter's Landmark church** (*©* **541/296-5686**), at the corner of West Third and Lincoln streets, is no longer an active church, but its 176-foot-tall steeple is a local landmark. The church was built in the Gothic Revival style in 1897, and a 6-foot-tall rooster symbolizing The Dalles tops its spire. The church is open Tuesday through Friday from 11am to 3pm and Saturday and Sunday from 1 to 3pm.

If you're interested in learning more about the history and the historic buildings of The Dalles, pick up a copy of the historic walking tours brochure at the chamber of commerce. As you explore The Dalles, also keep an eye out for the city's many **historical murals.**

At the east of town rises **The Dalles Lock and Dam** (*©* **541/298-7650** or 541/296-1181), which provides both irrigation water and electricity. The dam, which was completed in 1957, stretches for 1½ miles from the Oregon shore to the Washington shore. One of the main reasons this dam was built was to flood the rapids that made this section of the Columbia River impossible to navigate. Among the numerous rapids flooded by the dam were Celilo Falls, which, for thousands of years before the dam, was the most important salmon-fishing area in the Northwest. Each year thousands of Native Americans would gather here to catch and smoked salmon, putting the dried fish away for the coming winter. The traditional method of catching the salmon was to use a spear or a net on the end of a long pole. Men would build precarious wooden platforms out over the river and catch the salmon as they tried to leap up the falls. You can still see traditional Native American fishing platforms near the Shilo Inn here in The Dalles. The dam's **visitor center** has displays on both the history of the river and the construction of the dam, and a small train takes visitors on free guided tours of the fish ladder and powerhouse. These tours are offered mid-May through late September Wednesday through Sunday from 9am to 5pm. To reach the visitor center, take exit 87 off I-84 and turn right on NE Frontage Road.

EAST OF THE DALLES

In addition to the two attractions listed here, you'll also find several wineries. **Maryhill Winery,** 9774 Wash. 14, Maryhill (© **877/627-9445;** www.maryhillwinery.com), has the best view of any winery in the Northwest and also produces some very good wines. **Cascade Cliffs Vineyard & Winery,** milepost 88.6, Wash. 14, Wishram (© **509/ 767-1100;** www.cascadecliffs.com), is set at the foot of 400-foot-tall basalt cliffs and produces one of the state's only Barberas. **Marshal's Winery,** 150 Oak Creek Rd., Dallesport (© **509/767-4633**), located 2 miles up a gravel road, is a tiny family-run winery that has produced some very quaffable cabernet sauvignons and merlots.

Columbia Hills State Park *Finds* Located between The Dalles Dam and Wishram on Wash. 14, Columbia Hills is the site of Horsethief Lake, a popular fishing area and campground. However, long before the area was designated a state park, this was a gathering ground for Native Americans. The park isn't far from the famous Celilo Falls, which were, before being inundated by the waters behind The Dalles Dam, the most prolific salmon-fishing spot in the Northwest. Native Americans created petroglyphs on rocks that are now protected within this park. The only way to see the park's petroglyphs is on ranger-led walks Friday and Saturday mornings at 10am. Reservations for these walks should be made at least 2 to 3 weeks in advance.

Wash. 14. © 509/767-1159. Admission $5 per car. Apr–Oct daily 6:30am–dusk. Closed Nov–Mar.

Maryhill Museum of Art/Stonehenge Monument *Finds* Between 1914 and 1926, eccentric entrepreneur Sam Hill built a grand mansion he called Maryhill. Though he never lived in the mansion, he did turn it into a museum that is today one of the state's finest. There is an acclaimed collection of sculptures and drawings by Auguste Rodin. An extensive collection of Native American artifacts includes the finest display of baskets in the state. Furniture, jewelry, and other items that once belonged to Hill's friend Queen Marie of Romania are also on display. The lush grounds surrounding the museum have sculptures, picnic tables, and plenty of shade trees, making A few miles east of Maryhill stands Hill's concrete reproduction of Stonehenge, which he had built as a memorial to local men who died in World War I.

35 Maryhill Museum Dr. (Wash. 14). © 509/773-3733. www.maryhillmuseum.org. Admission $7 adults, $6 seniors, $2 children 6–12. Mar 15–Nov 15 daily 9am–5pm. Closed Nov 16–Mar 14.

OUTDOOR ACTIVITIES

East of town 17 miles, you'll find the **Deschutes River State Recreation Area** (© **541/739-2322**), which is at the mouth of the Deschutes River and is the eastern boundary of the Columbia Gorge National Scenic Area. The park has several miles of hiking trails, and an old railway right of way that parallels the Deschutes River for 17 miles has been turned into a gravel mountain-biking and horseback-riding trail.

WHERE TO STAY

Although there are few hotels in The Dalles, you can stay in Hood River, which is only 20 miles away and has a better selection of accommodations plus lots of great restaurants.

CAMPGROUNDS

If you're want to pitch a tent or park an RV, try **Deschutes River State Recreation Area,** 17 miles east of The Dalles off I-84. For reservations, contact **ReserveAmerica**

(© **800/452-5687;** www.reserveamerica.com). On the Washington side of the Gorge, there is camping at **Columbia Hills State Park** (no reservations), near the community of Dallesport (take U.S. 197 north to Wash. 14 east).

WHERE TO DINE

Baldwin Saloon Historic Restaurant & Bar ☆ AMERICAN/CONTINENTAL
Built in 1876, the Baldwin Saloon has one of the few remaining cast-iron facades in town and is one of the only restaurants in The Dalles with much historic character. Brick walls, wooden booths, and a high ceiling add to the old-time feel, as do the collections of late-19th-century landscape paintings and large bar nudes. The menu is pretty straightforward and simple.

First and Court sts. © **541/296-5666.** www.baldwinsaloon.com. Reservations accepted only for parties of 6 or more. Main courses $8–$18. DISC, MC, V. Mon–Thurs 11am–9pm; Fri–Sat 11am–10pm.

9

The Cascades

From the schussing of January and the kayaking of April to the wildflowers of August and the splashes of fall foliage in October, Oregon's Cascade Range is a year-round recreational magnet. Stretching from the Columbia Gorge in the north to California in the south, the Cascades are a relatively young volcanic mountain range with picture-perfect, snowcapped volcanic peaks rising above lush green forests of evergreens. The Cascade's volcanic heritage sets this mountain range apart from others in the West, and throughout these mountains, signs of past volcanic activity are evident. Crater Lake, formed after a massive volcanic eruption, is the most dramatic evidence of the Cascades' fiery past. But you can also see evidence of volcanic activity in the cones of Mount Hood and Mount Jefferson, and in the lava fields of McKenzie Pass.

As spectacular as this volcanic geology is, however, it is not what draws most people to these mountains. The main attraction is the wide variety of outdoor sports activities available. Crystal-clear rivers, churned into white water as they cascade down from high in the mountains, provide numerous opportunities for rafting, kayaking, canoeing, and fishing. High mountain lakes hold hungry trout, and throughout the summer, lakeside campgrounds stay filled with anglers. The Pacific Crest Trail winds the entire length of the Cascades, but it is the many wilderness areas scattered throughout these mountains that are the biggest draw for day hikers and backpackers. Mountain bikers also find miles of national-forest trails to enjoy. In winter, skiers and snowboarders flock to more than half a dozen ski areas and countless miles of cross-country ski trails—and because winter lingers late in the high Cascades, the ski season here is one of the longest in the country. Skiing often begins in mid-November and continues on into April and even May and June at Mount Bachelor. In fact, on Mount Hood, high-elevation snowfields atop glacial ice allow a year-round ski season that attracts Olympic ski teams for summer training.

The Cascades also serve as a dividing line between the lush evergreen forests of western Oregon and the dry, high desert landscapes of eastern Oregon. On the western slopes, Douglas firs and western red cedars dominate, while on the east side, the cinnamon-barked ponderosa pine is most common. These trees were the lifeblood of the Oregon economy for much of the 20th century, but with few virgin forests left in the state, a litigious battle to protect the last old-growth forests has been raging here for decades. Today, visitors to the Cascades will be confronted at nearly every turn by the sight of clear-cuts scarring the mountainsides, yet it is still possible to find groves of ancient trees beneath which to hike and camp.

1 Mount Hood: Skiing, Hiking & Scenic Drives ★★★

60 miles E of Portland, 46 miles S of Hood River

At 11,235 feet, Mount Hood, a dormant volcano, is the tallest mountain in Oregon. Located fewer than 60 miles east of downtown Portland, it is also the busiest mountain in the state. Summer and winter, people flock here in search of cool mountain air filled with the scent of firs and pines. Campgrounds, hiking and mountain-biking trails, trout streams and lakes, downhill ski areas, and cross-country ski trails all provide ample opportunities for outdoor recreational activities on Mount Hood.

With five downhill areas and many miles of cross-country trails, the mountain is a ski bum's dream come true. One of the country's largest night-skiing areas is here, and at Timberline you can ski right through the summer. Because even those with a moderate amount of mountain-climbing experience can reach the summit fairly easily, Mount Hood is also the most climbed major peak in the United States.

One of the first settlers to visit Mount Hood was Samuel Barlow, who, in 1845, had traveled the Oregon Trail and was searching for an alternative to taking his wagon train down the treacherous waters of the Columbia River. Barlow blazed a trail across the south flank of Mount Hood, and the following year opened his trail as a toll road. The **Barlow Trail,** though difficult, was cheaper and safer than rafting down the river. The trail is now used for hiking and mountain biking.

During the Great Depression, the Works Progress Administration employed skilled craftsmen to build the rustic **Timberline Lodge** at the tree line on the mountain's south slope. Today, the lodge is a National Historic Landmark and is the main destination for visitors to the mountain. The lodge's views of Mount Hood's peak and of the Oregon Cascades to the south are superb and should not be missed.

Don't expect to have this mountain all to yourself, though. Because of its proximity to Portland, Mount Hood sees a lot of visitors throughout the year, and on snowy days the road back down the mountain from the ski areas can be bumper to bumper and backed up for hours. Also keep in mind that you'll need to have a Sno-Park permit in the winter (available at ski shops around the area) and a Northwest Forest Pass to park at trailheads in the summer (available at ranger stations, visitor centers, and a few outdoors-oriented shops).

ESSENTIALS

GETTING THERE   From Portland, Mount Hood is reached by taking I-84 east to exit 16 (Wood Village) and then following U.S. 26 east. From Hood River, take Ore. 35 south. These two highways meet just east of the town of Government Camp, which is the main tourist town on the mountain. The Lolo Pass Road is a gravel road that skirts the north and west sides of the mountain connecting these two highways.

VISITOR INFORMATION   For more information on Mount Hood, contact the **Mount Hood Information Center,** 65000 E. U.S. 26, Welches, OR 97067 (© **888/622-4822** or 503/622-4822; www.mthood.org), or the **Mount Hood Ranger District,** 6780 Ore. 35 S., Parkdale, OR 97041 (© **541/352-6002;** www.fs.fed.us/r6/mthood).

SUMMER ON THE MOUNTAIN

In snow-free months, most visitors are heading to historic **Timberline Lodge** (see "Where to Stay," below). Besides having a fabulous view of Mount Hood, the lodge is surrounded by meadows that burst into bloom in July and August. Here you can

The Cascades

access the 41-mile-long **Timberline Trail,** which circles the mountain. If you just have time for a short hike, head west from the lodge on this trail rather than east. The route east passes through dusty ash fields and then drops down into the hot, barren White River Valley. You'll find snow here year-round, and there's even summer skiing at the **Timberline Ski Area.** The lift-accessed ski slopes are high above the lodge on the Palmer Glacier and are open only in the morning. In summer, you can ride the lift even if you aren't skiing.

In summer, you can also ride the lift at **Mt. Hood Skibowl Action Park,** U.S. 26, Government Camp (© **503/222-2695;** www.skibowl.com), where there are mountain-biking trails, hiking trails, an alpine slide (sort of a summertime bobsled run), and numerous other rides and activities.

One of the most popular and most enjoyable hikes on Mount Hood is the trail to **Mirror Lake** ⍟, which, as its name implies, reflects the summit of Mount Hood in its mirrorlike waters. The trail is fairly easy and is good for families with young children. If you want to add a bit more challenge, you can continue to the summit of Tom, Dick & Harry Mountain, the backside of which in winter serves as the Mt. Hood Skibowl. The view from the summit is superb, and in late summer there are huckleberries along the trail. You'll find the trailhead right on U.S. 26 just before you reach Government Camp.

The east side of the mountain, accessed by Ore. 35 from Hood River, is much drier and less visited than the south side. Here on the east side, you'll find good hiking trails in the vicinity of **Mount Hood Meadows,** where the wildflower displays in late July and August are some of the best on the mountain. The loop trail past Umbrella and Sahalie falls is particularly enjoyable. Also on this side of the mountain, you'll find the highest segment of the Timberline Trail. This section of trail climbs up **Cooper Spur** ridge from historic Cloud Cap Inn (no longer open to the public). The close-up views of the mountain and the distant views of eastern Oregon's dry landscape make this one of my favorite hiking destinations on Mount Hood. To reach the trailhead, follow signs off Ore. 35 for Cooper Spur and Cloud Cap. On the east side of Ore. 35, off Forest Service Road 44, you'll also find the best **mountain-biking trails** in the area. Among these are the Surveyor's Ridge Trail and the Dog Mountain Trail.

If you're interested in a little adventure and an alternative route from the west side of the mountain to the Hood River area, try exploring the gravel **Lolo Pass Road,** which is usually in good enough condition for standard passenger cars. Be sure to have a Forest Service map (available from the **Mount Hood Information Center,** 65000 E. U.S. 26 [P.O. Box 1120], Welches, OR 97067; © **888/622-4822** or 503/622-4822), since roads out here are not well marked and it's easy to get lost. Branching off from the Lolo Pass Road are several smaller roads that lead to some of the best hiking trails on Mount Hood. Also off the Lolo Pass Road, you'll find **Lost Lake,** one of the most beautiful (and most photographed) lakes in the Oregon Cascades. When the water is still, the view of the mountain and its reflection in the lake is positively sublime. Here you'll find campgrounds, cabins, picnic areas, good fishing, and hiking trails that lead both around the lake and up a nearby butte.

Down at the base of the mountain, just west of the community of Welches, you can learn about the forests, rivers, and fish of the Northwest at the Bureau of Land Management's **Wildwood Recreation Site** (© **503/622-3696**). Within this 550-acre park there are 2.5 miles of trails, including a boardwalk that crosses a wetland area. The highlight of the trail is an underwater fish-viewing window on the Cascade

Streamwatch Trail. There's also a playground here, which makes this a good stop for families with small children. Fishing and swimming in the Salmon River are also popular activities here. There's also access to the steep and strenuous Boulder Ridge Trail and the much easier Old Salmon River Trail. There's a day-use fee of $3 here.

It's also possible to do some paddling while you're in the area. **Clackamas River Adventures** (© **800/909-RAFT**; www.clackamasriver.com), operates white-water rafting trips on the Clackamas River, which has its source on the flanks of Mount Hood. The 1-day trips cost $60 to $75 per person for adults and $50 to $60 for children ages 6 to 16. Shorter trips are also offered. **River Drifter** (© **800/972-0430**; www.riverdrifters.net) offers similar Clackamas River trips, but does runs down the Sandy River, which is more convenient if you're short on time. Sandy River trips, which are only offered in the spring and fall, cost $85 per person. For a tamer paddle experience, rent a kayak from **Wy'East Kayak Rentals** (© **503/622-6895**; www.wyeastkayak.com), and head out on an area lake. Rental prices start at $20 per hour, and kayaks can be delivered to four area lakes.

If you're interested in a more strenuous mountain experience, the Mount Hood area offers plenty of mountain- and rock-climbing opportunities. **Timberline Mountain Guides,** P.O. Box 1167, Bend, OR 97709 (© **541/312-9242**; www.timberlinemtguides.com), leads summit climbs on Mount Hood. They also offer snow-, ice-, and rock-climbing courses. A 2-day Mount Hood mountaineering course with summit climb costs $390.

WINTER ON THE MOUNTAIN

Although snowpacks that can be slow to reach skiable depths and frequent mid-winter rains make the ski season on Mount Hood unpredictable, in an ordinary year the regular ski season runs from around Thanksgiving right through March or April. Add to this the summer skiing on the Palmer Glacier at Timberline Ski Area, and you have the longest ski season in the United States. There are five ski areas on Mount Hood, though two of these are tiny operations that attract primarily beginners and families looking for an economical way to all go schussing together. For cross-country skiers, there are many miles of marked ski trails, some of which are groomed.

The single most important thing to know about skiing anywhere in Oregon is that you'll have to have a **Sno-Park permit.** These permits, which sell for $3 a day or $15 for the season, allow you to park in plowed parking areas on the mountain. You can get permits at ski shops in Sandy and Hood River and at a few convenience stores. Expect to pay a service fee wherever you buy your pass.

Mt. Hood Skibowl (© **503/272-3206**; 800/754-2695 or 503/222-2695 for snow report; www.skibowl.com), located in Government Camp on U.S. 26, the closest ski area to Portland, offers 1,500 vertical feet of skiing and has more expert slopes than any other ski area on the mountain. Skibowl is also one of the largest lighted ski areas in the country. Adult lift-ticket prices range from $30 to $36 for an all-day pass. Call for hours of operation.

Timberline Ski Area (© **503/222-2211**; www.timberlinelodge.com) is the highest ski area on Mount Hood and has one slope that is open throughout the summer. This is the site of the historic **Timberline Lodge.** Adult lift-ticket prices range from $20 for night skiing to $46 for an all-day pass. Call for hours of operation.

Mount Hood Meadows ★★ (© **800/SKI-HOOD**; 503/227-7669 for snow report; www.skihood.com), 12 miles northeast of Government Camp on Ore. 35, is the largest ski resort on Mount Hood, with more than 2,000 skiable acres, 2,777 vertical feet, five high-speed quad lifts, and a wide variety of terrain. This is the closest Mount Hood comes to having a destination ski resort, and consequently, it is here that you'll find the most out-of-state skiers. Lift-ticket prices range from $22 for night skiing to $52 for a peak-season all-day pass. Call for hours of operation.

If you're interested in **cross-country skiing,** there are plenty of trails. For views, head to the **White River Sno-Park,** east of Government Camp. The trails at **Glacier View Sno-Park,** across U.S. 26 from Mount Hood Skibowl, are good for beginner and intermediate skiers. The mountain's best-groomed trails are at the **Mount Hood Meadows Nordic Center** ($10 trail pass) on Ore. 35 and at **Teacup Lake** ($5 donation requested), which is across the highway from the turnoff for Mount Hood Meadows. Teacup Lake is maintained by a local ski club (www.teacupnordic.org) and has the best system of groomed trails on the mountain. In the town of Sandy and at Government Camp are numerous ski shops that rent cross-country skis.

If skiing isn't your thing, but you still like snow, how about going for a ride on a dog sled? **Mt. Hood Sled Dog Tours** (✆ 503/622-MUSH) will take two of you out mushing through the snow for $175.

EN ROUTE TO THE MOUNTAIN

If you like sweet wines, watch for the **Wasson Brothers wine tasting room,** 17020 Ruben Lane at U.S. 26 (✆ 503/668-3124; www.wassonbrotherswinery.com), as you drive through Sandy. This winery produces a wide range of fruit wines, and also does quite a few dry varietals. The tasting room is open daily from 9am to 5pm. Also, if you or anyone in your car has a sweet tooth, keep an eye out for the **Oregon Candy Farm,** 48620 SE U.S. 26, Sandy (✆ 503/668-5066), which is 5½ miles east of Sandy and has huge assortment of homemade candies. The Candy Farm is open Monday through Friday from 9am to 5pm and Saturday and Sunday from noon to 5pm.

WHERE TO STAY
ON THE MOUNTAIN

Collins Lake Resort 🞨🞨   This new townhouse-condominium resort development in the heart of Government Camp is the biggest thing to hit Mount Hood since Timberline Lodge was built. Affiliated with Mt. Hood Skibowl, which is just across the highway from the resort, Collins Lake offers by far the most luxurious and spacious accommodations on the mountain. These are condos, so interior decor is up to owners, but don't worry too much. These three-story, two- and three-bedroom townhouses are beautiful, with hardwood floors and gorgeous kitchens with granite counters. Be sure to ask about free midweek skiing at Skibowl if you stay here on a weeknight in winter.

88149 E. Creek Ridge Rd. (P.O. Box 250), Government Camp, OR 97028. ✆ 800/234-6288. www.stayandplay hood.com. 78 units. $169–$249 double. Children under 13 stay free in parent's room. AE, DISC, MC, V. **Amenities:** 2 outdoor pools; Jacuzzi; sauna; ski shuttle. *In room:* A/C, TV, dataport, kitchen, fridge, coffeemaker, hair dryer.

Falcon's Crest Inn 🞨   This sprawling chalet-style lodge tucked into the trees on the edge of Government Camp is your best bet on Mount Hood for a B&B within walking distance of the ski slopes. Both suites, one of which is done up in a Mexican theme, have whirlpool tubs (one outside on a deck), and though a bit incongruous in this mountain setting, the Safari Room, with its deck and view of the ski slopes, is a great choice. The inn also serves elegant six-course dinners for $40 (Cornish game hen, poached salmon, beef Wellington) by reservation.

87287 Government Camp Loop Hwy. (P.O. Box 185), Government Camp, OR 97028. ✆ 800/624-7384 or 503/272-3403. Fax 503/272-3454. www.falconscrest.com. 5 units. $95–$125 double; $169–$179 suite. Rates include full breakfast. AE, DC, DISC, MC, V. **Amenities:** Restaurant (Continental); massage.

Mt. Hood Inn ✦   Located at the west end of Government Camp right on the highway, this modern budget hotel doesn't have a lot of character, but the adjacent Mt. Hood Brew Pub makes this a great place to stay if you enjoy craft beers. Pine furnishings give the guest rooms here a contemporary rustic feel. The king spa rooms, with two-person whirlpool tubs beside the king-size beds, are definitely the best rooms, but they're somewhat overpriced. Other rooms have refrigerators and microwaves.

87407 E. Government Camp Loop, Government Camp, OR 97028. ✆ 800/443-7777 or 503/272-3205. Fax 503/272-3307. www.mthoodinn.com. 55 units. Summer and winter $149–$169 double; spring and fall $99–$109 double. Rates include continental breakfast. Children 12 and under stay free in parent's room. AE, DC, DISC, MC, V. Pets accepted ($10). **Amenities:** Jacuzzi; coin-op laundry. *In room:* TV, fridge, coffeemaker.

Timberline Lodge ✦✦   Constructed during the Great Depression of the 1930s as a WPA project, this classic alpine ski lodge overflows with craftsmanship. The grand stone fireplace, huge exposed beams, and wide-plank floors of the lobby impress every first-time visitor. Woodcarvings, imaginative wrought-iron fixtures, hand-hooked rugs, and handmade furniture complete the rustic picture. Unfortunately, guest rooms, which vary considerably in size, are not as impressive as the public areas of the lodge. The smallest rooms lack private bathrooms, and windows in most rooms fail to take advantage of the phenomenal views that could be had here. However, you can always visit the Ram's Head lounge for a better view of Mount Hood.

Timberline, OR 97028. ✆ 800/547-1406 or 503/622-7979. Fax 503/622-0710. www.timberlinelodge.com. 70 units (10 without bathroom). $85–$95 double with shared bathroom; $135–$250 double with private bathroom. Children 12 and under stay free in parent's room. AE, DC, DISC, MC, V. **Amenities:** 2 restaurants (Northwest, American); 2 lounges; small outdoor pool; Jacuzzi; sauna; children's ski programs; coin-op laundry. *In room:* Dataport, hair dryer, iron, Wi-Fi.

AT THE BASE OF THE MOUNTAIN
The Resort at the Mountain ✦✦   This golf resort is set in a large clearing in the dense woods at the base of Mount Hood. It's a bit of a drive to Timberline or Government Camp and the area's hiking trails and ski areas, but if a round of golf in a gorgeous setting sounds tempting, this is one of your best choices in the Mount Hood area. Beautifully landscaped grounds incorporating concepts from Japanese garden design hide the resort's many low-rise buildings and make this a tranquil woodsy retreat. The guest rooms are large and have either a balcony or a patio. The main lodge has a formal dining room, while a more casual dining room overlooks the golf course. In addition to the amenities listed below, there are horseshoe pits, croquet and lawn bowling courts, volleyball and badminton courts, nature trails, and a pro shop.

68010 E. Fairway Ave., Welches, OR 97067. ✆ 800/669-7666 or 503/622-3101. www.theresort.com. 160 units. May–Oct $139–$199 double, $219–$289 suite; Nov–Apr $99–$139 double, $159–$199 suite. Children under 18 stay free in parent's room. AE, DC, DISC, MC, V. **Amenities:** 2 restaurants (Northwest, American); 2 lounges; outdoor pool; 27-hole golf course; 4 tennis courts; exercise room; spa; Jacuzzi; bike rentals; business center; room service; massage; coin-op laundry; dry cleaning. *In room:* TV/VCR, dataport, coffeemaker, hair dryer, iron, high-speed Internet access.

NORTHEAST OF THE MOUNTAIN
Cooper Spur Mountain Resort ✦ *Value*   If you want to get away from it all, try this surprisingly remote lodge in the off season. (During ski season it can be difficult to get a reservation.) The inn consists of a main building and a handful of modern log

cabins. These latter accommodations should be your first choice here. The cabins have two bedrooms and a loft area reached by a spiral staircase. There are also rooms with full kitchens. The inn's restaurant serves decent, reasonably priced steaks. At the end of the day you can soak yourself in one of the inn's whirlpool spas.

10755 Cooper Spur Rd., Mount Hood, OR 97041. 🕐 541/352-6692. www.cooperspur.com. 16 units. $99–$109 double; $159–$269 cabin or suite; $375–$399 log house. AE, DISC, MC, V. **Amenities:** Restaurant (American); tennis court; spa; Jacuzzi; massage. *In room:* TV.

WHERE TO DINE
ON THE MOUNTAIN
Cascade Dining Room ✿✿ NORTHWEST   It may seem a bit casual from the lobby and there are no stunning views of Mount Hood even though it's right outside the window, but the Cascade Dining Room is by far the best restaurant on Mount Hood. The menu changes regularly, but might include pinot noir–glazed chicken, apple-cider–braised pork loin, or beef tenderloin with wild mushrooms. There are also always several interesting vegetarian offerings. There's a good wine selection, and desserts showcase a variety of local seasonal ingredients such as raspberries, pears, and apples. Although the food here is good and the wine list is superb, the service rarely rises to the occasion.

In Timberline Lodge, Timberline. 🕐 503/622-0700. Reservations highly recommended. Main courses $13–$15 lunch, $17–$38 dinner; 4-course prix-fixe dinner $29. AE, DC, DISC, MC, V. Summer daily 7:30–10am, noon–2pm, and 6–8 or 9pm.

Mt. Hood Brew Pub ✿ PUB FOOD   This brewpub on the edge of Government Camp offers good microbrews and pub food (sandwiches, salads, pasta, pizzas), as well as comfort food such as meatloaf. There are also some good seafood dishes, including fish tacos and a daily seafood special. There are at least six beers on tap (including cask-conditioned ales and a couple of daily choices on the nitro taps), and a large selection of Northwest wines.

87304 E. Government Camp Loop. 🕐 503/622-0724. www.mthoodbrewing.com. Main courses $8.50–$15. AE, DC, DISC, MC, V. Sun–Thurs noon–9pm; Fri–Sat noon–10pm.

AT THE BASE OF THE MOUNTAIN
Calamity Jane's ✿ *Finds* BURGERS   What, you ask, is a $13 hamburger? Well, at Calamity Jane's, it's a 1-pound pastrami-and-mushroom burger. If you think that's outrageous, wait until you see the other burgers listed on the menu. There's the peanut-butter burger, the George Washington burger (with sour cream and sweet pie cherries), the hot-fudge-and-marshmallow burger—even an unbelievably priced inflation burger. Not all the burgers at this entertaining and rustic eatery are calculated to turn your stomach—some are just plain delicious. There are even pizza burgers. This place is just east of Sandy on U.S. 26.

42015 U.S. 26, Sandy. 🕐 503/668-7817. Burgers $5.75–$13. AE, DISC, MC, V. Sun–Thurs 11am–9pm; Fri–Sat 11am–10pm.

The Rendezvous Grill ✿✿ MEDITERRANEAN   Located right on U.S. 26 in Welches, this casual, upscale restaurant is a great choice for dinner on your way back to Portland. Although the emphasis is on the Mediterranean, other flavors also show up. Don't miss the rigatoni with alder-smoked chicken with toasted hazelnuts and dried cranberries. The Shanghai shrimp with Chinese candied walnuts, and the ever-popular Dungeness crab and bay shrimp cakes, which are available both at lunch and dinner, are also good bets.

67149 E. U.S. 26, Welches. 🕐 503/622-6837. www.rendezvousgrill.net. Reservations recommended. Main courses lunch $8–$12, dinner $17–$25. AE, DISC, MC, V. Wed–Sun 11:30am–2:30pm and 5–9pm (open daily in summer).

2 The Santiam Pass, McKenzie Pass & McKenzie River

Santiam Pass: 82 miles SE of Salem, 40 miles NW of Bend; McKenzie Pass: 77 miles NE of Eugene, 36 miles NW of Bend

As the nearest mountain recreational areas to both Salem and Eugene, the Santiam Pass, McKenzie Pass, and McKenzie River routes are some of the most popular in the state. Ore. 22, which leads over Santiam Pass, is also one of the busiest routes to the Sisters and Bend areas in central Oregon. Along these highways are some of the state's best white-water-rafting and fishing rivers, some of the most popular and most beautiful backpacking areas, and good downhill and cross-country skiing. In the summer, the Detroit Lake recreation area is the main attraction along Ore. 22 and is a favorite of water-skiers and lake anglers. In winter, it's downhill and cross-country skiing at Santiam Pass that brings people up this way.

Ore. 126, on the other hand, follows the scenic McKenzie River and is favored by white-water rafters and drift-boat anglers fishing for salmon and steelhead. Several state parks provide access to the river. During the summer, Ore. 126 connects to Ore. 242, a narrow road that climbs up and over McKenzie Pass, the most breathtaking pass in the Oregon Cascades.

ESSENTIALS

GETTING THERE   Santiam Pass is a year-round pass and is reached by Ore. 22 from Salem, U.S. 20 from Albany, and Ore. 126 from Eugene. McKenzie Pass is on Ore. 242 and lies to the south of Santiam Pass. It can be reached by all the same roads that lead to Santiam Pass, but it is closed during in winter.

VISITOR INFORMATION   For more information on outdoor recreation in this area, contact the **Detroit Ranger Station,** HC73, Box 320, Mill City, OR 97360 (© **503/854-3366**); or the **McKenzie Ranger Station,** 57600 McKenzie Hwy., McKenzie Bridge, OR 97413 (© **541/822-3381**). Also check the website of the Willamette National Forest (www.fs.fed.us/r6/willamette). For more general information, contact the **McKenzie River Chamber of Commerce,** 44643 McKenzie Hwy., Leaburg, OR 97489 (© **541/896-3330;** members.aol.com/mcrvcofc/chamber.htm), which operates a visitor center at the old Leaburg fish hatchery on Leaburg Lake east of Springfield on the McKenzie Highway.

ALONG THE SANTIAM PASS HIGHWAY

Detroit Lake is the summertime center of activity on this route—fishing and water-skiing are the most popular activities. North of the lake, you'll find the **Breitenbush Hot Springs Retreat and Conference Center** (© **503/854-3321** or 503/854-3320; www.breitenbush.com), a New Age community/retreat center that allows day use of its hot springs by advance reservation. The fee is between $12 and $25 per person, and vegetarian meals ($10) are available. Breitenbush offers massage, yoga, meditation classes, and a wide range of other programs focusing on holistic health and spiritual growth.

At Santiam Pass, you'll find the **Hoodoo Ski Area** (© **541/822-3337** for snow report, or 541/822-3799; www.hoodoo.com), which is the best little ski area in Oregon. The ski area has five chair lifts and more than 30 runs for all levels of experience. Lift tickets are $32 to $39 for adults and $24 to $28 for children. Night skiing is available. Here you'll also find an awesome tubing run for the kids and the **Hoodoo Nordic Center,** which has almost 10 miles of groomed cross-country ski trails and charges $10 to $12 for a trail pass. Also in the Santiam Pass area, you'll find several

Sno-Parks. The Maxwell, Big Springs, and Lava Lake East Sno-Parks access the best trails in the area. In recent years, however, these trails have become very popular with snowshoers. Consequently, you might want to leave the skinny skis at home and bring snowshoes instead.

UP THE MCKENZIE RIVER

The McKenzie River is one of Oregon's most popular white-water-rafting rivers, and the cold blue waters challenge a wide range of experience levels. **Oregon Whitewater Adventures** (© 800/820-RAFT or 541/746-5422; www.oregonwhitewater.com) and **A Helfrich's McKenzie River Rafting and Fishing Trips** (© 800/328-7688 or 541/726-5039; www.raft2fish.com) both offer half- and full-day trips. Expect to pay $50 to $55 for a half-day of rafting and $70 to $75 for a full day. For a tamer white-water experience, try the pontoon platform boats of **Helfrich River Outfitters** (© 800/507-9899 or 541/741-1905; www.helfrichoutfitter.com).

If you're interested in seeing this area by bike, contact **Oregon Adventures** (© 541/968-5397; www.oregon-adventures.com), which offers a variety of bike rides, both road and trail, for $35 to $55 for a half-day ride and $85 for a full-day mountain-bike ride. This company can also arrange rafting trips, guided hikes, and even skydiving.

The McKenzie River town of Blue River is home to one of the best golf courses in Oregon. **Tokatee Golf Club,** 54947 McKenzie Hwy., McKenzie Bridge (© 888/865-2833 or 541/822-3220; www.tokatee.com), gets consistently high ratings and has a spectacular setting with views of snowcapped Cascade Peaks and lush forests. The greens fee is $40 ($30 for electric cart) for 18 holes.

Off Ore. 126, between the towns of Blue River and McKenzie Bridge, you'll find the turnoff for the **Aufderheide National Scenic Byway** (Forest Service Rd. 19). This road meanders for 54 miles through the foothills of the Cascades, first following the South Fork McKenzie River (and Cougar Reservoir) and then following the North Fork of the Middle Fork Willamette River, which offers excellent fly-fishing and numerous swimming holes. Along the route, you'll find several hiking trails, and, at the south end of Cougar Reservoir, a trail that leads to the very popular **Terwilliger Hot Springs.** The southernmost stretch of Forest Service Road 19 is the most scenic portion and passes through a deep, narrow gorge formed by the North Fork of the Middle Fork Willamette River. At the southern end of the scenic byway is the community of Westfir, which is the site of the longest covered bridge in Oregon.

Between the turnoff for McKenzie Pass and the junction of Ore. 126 and U.S. 20, you'll find some of the Cascades' most enchanting water features. Southernmost of these is **Belknap Resort and Hot Springs** (© 541/822-3512), where, for $4.50 an hour or $8.50 a day, you can soak in a hot mineral swimming pool. Just north of Trail Bridge Reservoir, on a side road off the highway, a 4-mile round-trip hike on a section of the McKenzie River Trail leads to the startlingly blue waters of the **Tamolitch Pool** 🐾🐾. This pool is formed by the McKenzie River welling up out of the ground after flowing underground for 3 miles. Five miles south of the junction with Ore. 20, you'll come to two picturesque waterfalls, **Sahalie Falls** and **Koosah Falls.** Across the highway from these falls is **Clear Lake,** the source of the McKenzie River. This spring-fed lake truly lives up to its name, and a rustic lakeside resort rents rowboats so you can get out on the water and see for yourself. Be sure to hike the trail on the east side of the lake; it leads to the turquoise waters of **Great Springs,** which is connected to the lake by a 100-yard stream.

One of the most breathtaking sections of road in the state begins just east of **Belknap Hot Springs.** Ore. 242, which is open only in the summer, is a narrow, winding road that climbs up through forests and lava fields to **McKenzie Pass** 👣👣, from which there's a sweeping panorama of the Cascades and some of the youngest lava fields in Oregon. An observation building made of lava rock provides sighting tubes so that you can identify all the visible peaks, and a couple of trails will lead you out into this otherworldly landscape. In autumn, this road has some of the best fall color in the state. On the west side of the pass, the short **Proxy Falls** trail leads through old lava flows to a waterfall that in late summer has no outlet stream. The water simply disappears into the porous lava.

WHERE TO STAY

Belknap Lodge & Hot Springs 👣 *(Finds)*   Set on the banks of the McKenzie River, this lodge is one of the most enjoyable mountain retreats in the state. Extensive lawns and perennial gardens have been planted, turning this clearing in the forest into a burst of color in the summer. Guest rooms vary in size, but all have comfortable modern furnishings. Some also have whirlpool tubs or decks overlooking the roaring river. The cabins are more rustic than the lodge rooms. Water from the hot springs, which are on the far side of the river and reached by a footbridge, is pumped into two small pools. The lodge also has sites for tents and RVs ($19–$20).

59296 N. Belknap Springs Rd. (P.O. Box 2001), McKenzie Bridge, OR 97413. © **541/822-3512.** Fax 541/822-3327. www.belknaphotsprings.com. 18 units. $85–$110 double; $80–$400 cabin; $145–$185 suite. Rates for lodge include continental breakfast. AE, DISC, MC, V. **Amenities:** 2 hot springs–fed outdoor pools; massage. *In room:* No phone.

Holiday Farm Resort 👣 *(Finds)*   This beautifully situated getaway is a collection of renovated white cottages perched on the edge of the McKenzie River, and the setting under the big trees is as idyllic as you'll find in Oregon. Grab a book and a seat on your private riverside deck and you may never give a thought to pulling on your hiking boots. Holiday Farm started out as a stagecoach stop and has been around long enough to have hosted U.S. President Herbert Hoover. A formal dining room (closed in winter) and a more casual lounge serve meals. Guests have 800 feet of riverfront to enjoy and two private lakes for fishing and swimming.

54455 McKenzie River Dr., Blue River, OR 97413. © **800/823-3715** or 541/822-3715. www.holidayfarmresort.com. 15 units. Apr–Oct $150–$225 cottage for 2 people; Nov–Mar $112–$180 cottage for 2 people. AE, MC, V. **Amenities:** Restaurant (international); lounge. *In room:* Kitchen, no phone.

Log Cabin Inn 👣   Situated on 6½ acres in the community of McKenzie Bridge, this log lodge was built in 1906 after the original 1886 lodge (a stagecoach stop) burned to the ground. Today, you can stay in rustic cabins, all but one of which have their own fireplaces. The one cabin without a fireplace does, however, have a kitchen, which the others do not. Although the one duplex log cabin has cramped rooms, it has a lot of woodsy character. There are also large teepees that sleep up to six people for anyone interested in camping. The lodge's restaurant (p. 264) is renowned for its high-quality meals, which include such game as elk, venison, and buffalo. Be sure to check the old guest registers for the signatures of Herbert Hoover, Clark Gable, and the Duke of Windsor.

56483 McKenzie Hwy., McKenzie Bridge, OR 97413. © **800/355-3432** or 541/822-3432. Fax 541/822-6173. www.logcabininn.com. 8 cabins. $65–$135 cabin for 2–4 people. 2-night minimum stay on weekends Apr–Oct. DISC, MC, V. **Amenities:** Restaurant (American); lounge. *In room:* Coffeemaker.

CAMPGROUNDS

There are several campgrounds along the McKenzie River on Ore. 126. Of these, the **Delta Campground,** set under huge old-growth trees between Blue River and McKenzie Bridge, is one of the finest. If you are up this way to hike, mountain bike, or do some flat-water canoeing, there is no better choice than Clear Lake's **Coldwater Cove Campground** (© 877/444-6777; www.reserveusa.com) on Ore. 126 just south of Santiam Pass junction. South of here on Ore. 126, the **Trail Bridge Campground** makes a good alternative to Coldwater Cove. Along the popular McKenzie Pass Highway (Ore. 242), you'll find **Scott Lake Campground, Alder Springs Campground,** and **Lava Camp Lake Campground.**

Along the Aufderheide National Scenic Byway, you'll find several campgrounds. **Cougar Crossing,** toward the north end of the scenic byway, is the closest campground to Terwilliger Hot Springs. South of here you'll find **Frissell Crossing, Homestead,** and **French Pete,** all of which are on the banks of the South Fork of the McKenzie River. Toward the south end of this road is **Kiahanie Campground,** which is on the North Fork of the Middle Fork of the Willamette River and is popular with fly anglers.

WHERE TO DINE

For burgers, try the **Vida Cafe,** 45641 McKenzie Hwy. (© **541/896-3289**), near milepost 26, or, at milepost 38, the **Finn Rock Grill,** 50660 McKenzie Hwy. (© **541/822-6080**), which has a deck beside the river.

Log Cabin Inn ⭐ AMERICAN   If you've been searching for the quintessential Cascades dining experience, this is it. This log-cabin restaurant has been in business since 1906, and serves mountain classics such as pan-fried trout and charbroiled venison medallions. You should be sure to start with the delicious beer-cheese soup and finish with the marionberry cobbler. In the warmer months, the big veranda, surrounded by colorful flower gardens, is the place to eat. For only $13, Sunday brunch here is a great deal, and at lunch other days of the week, keep an eye out for wild-game stew.

56483 McKenzie Hwy., McKenzie Bridge. © 541/822-3432. Main courses $9–$15 lunch, $18–$25 dinner. DISC, MC, V. Mon–Fri 11:30am–9pm, Sat–Sun 9:30am–9pm; reduced hours in winter.

3 The Willamette Pass Route

Oakridge: 41 miles SE of Eugene; Willamette Pass: 68 miles SE of Eugene

Ore. 58, which connects Eugene with U.S. 97 north of Crater Lake, is the state's fastest and straightest route over the Cascades. This is not to imply, however, that there isn't anything along this highway worth slowing down for. Flanked by two wilderness areas, Waldo Lake and Diamond Peak, and three major lakes, Waldo, Odell, and Crescent, Ore. 58 provides access to a wide range of recreational activities, chief among which are mountain biking, fishing, and boating in summer and both downhill and cross-country skiing in winter.

The sister towns of Oakridge and Westfir are the only real towns on this entire route and are the only places where you'll find much in the way of services. Westfir is also the southern terminus of the Aufderheide National Scenic Byway, which winds through the Cascade foothills to just outside the town of McKenzie Bridge on Ore. 126. For information on this scenic drive, see above.

ESSENTIALS

GETTING THERE   Ore. 58 begins just south of Eugene off I-5 and stretches for 92 miles to U.S. 97.

VISITOR INFORMATION   For more information on recreational activities in this area, contact the **Middle Fork Ranger Station,** 46375 Ore. 58, Westfir, OR 97492 (© **541/782-2283;** www.fs.fed.us/r6/willamette). Another source of information is the **Oakridge-Westfir Area Chamber of Commerce,** P.O. Box 217 Oakridge, OR 97463 (www.oakridgechamber.com).

WHAT TO SEE & DO: HOT SPRINGS TO SNOW SKIING

In the Willamette National Forest outside the logging town of Oakridge are miles and miles of great **mountain-biking trails** that have turned the Oakridge area into one of Oregon's top mountain-biking regions. Stop by the ranger station in Westfir to get maps and information on riding these trails. One of the most scenic rides is the 22-mile trail around Waldo Lake. You'll also find trails at Willamette Pass Ski Area, where, in summer, the cross-country ski trails are great for biking. This ski area also operates a summertime sightseeing gondola that will also carry your bike up to the top of the mountain for you. An all-day pass costs $12 for adults, $8 for youths, and $1 for children under 5.

If you're keen to soak in some natural hot springs, you'll find some right beside Ore. 58 about 10 miles east of Oakridge. **McCredie Hot Springs** are neither the hottest nor the most picturesque springs in the state, and with traffic noise and crowds, they aren't the most pleasant either. But if you want a quick soak without having to go wandering down gravel roads, they do the trick.

Just before reaching Willamette Pass, you'll see signs for **Salt Creek Falls,** which are well worth a stroll down the short trail to the falls overlook. At 286 feet high, these are the second-highest falls in the state. Longer hiking trails also lead out from the falls parking area.

Also just before Willamette Pass is the turnoff for Forest Service Road 5897, which leads 10 miles north to **Waldo Lake,** one of the purest lakes in the world. The lake, which is just over a mile high, covers 10 square miles and is 420 feet deep. When the waters are still, it is possible to see more than 100 feet down into the lake. Because this is such a large lake, and because there are reliable afternoon winds, it is popular for sailboating and windsurfing. Powerboaters, canoeists, and sea kayakers also frequent the lake. There are several campgrounds along the east shore of the lake, while the west shore abuts the Waldo Lake Wilderness Area. The 22-mile loop trail around the lake is popular with mountain bikers and backpackers, but shorter day hikes, particularly at the south end, are rewarding. The mosquitoes here are some of the worst in the state, so before planning a trip up here, be sure to get a bug report from the Middle Fork Ranger Station.

Just over Willamette Pass lie two more large lakes. **Odell Lake** is best known by anglers who come to troll for kokanee salmon and Mackinaw trout. However, it's also a good windsurfing lake. Although the waters never exactly get warm, **Crescent Lake** is the area's best for swimming, notably at Symax Beach, on the lake's northeast corner.

At **Willamette Pass Ski Area** (© **541/345-SNOW;** www.willamettepass.com), 69 miles southeast of Eugene on Ore. 58, you'll find 29 downhill runs and 12 miles of groomed cross-country trails. The ski area is open daily from around Thanksgiving to mid-April. Night skiing is available on Friday and Saturday nights from late December to March. Adult lift tickets are $36 per day.

WHERE TO STAY

Westfir Lodge ☞   Set at the southern end of the Aufderheide National Scenic Byway, this inn makes an excellent base for exploring both the McKenzie River to the north and the Willamette Pass area to the east. The inn is housed in what was once the company headquarters for a long-gone lumber mill and has a very Victorian feel inside and beautiful flower gardens outside. Directly across the street is the longest covered bridge in Oregon. Although all the rooms have private bathrooms, only four of these are actually in the room itself; others are across the hall from the guest room. An eclectic assemblage of antiques and artifacts from the innkeepers' world travels fills the guest rooms and many public rooms.

48365 First St., Westfir, OR 97492. ☏ 541/782-3103. www.westfirlodge.com. 8 units. $60–$90 double. Rates include full breakfast. No credit cards. *In room:* A/C.

CAMPGROUNDS

On Waldo Lake, the **North Waldo Campground,** with its swimming area and boat launch, should be your first choice. Second choice on the lake should be **Islet Campground** or, at the south end of the lake, **Shadow Bay Campground.** If you have a boat, you can camp at primitive campsites along the west shore of the lake. **Gold Lake Campground,** just west of Willamette Pass on Forest Service Road 500, is a quiet spot on a pretty fly-fishing-only lake that allows no motorboats. Just over Willamette Pass, there are several campgrounds on Odell Lake. **Odell Creek Campground** at the east end of the lake is the quietest campground on this lake.

WHERE TO DINE

Most people heading up this way plan to be self-sufficient when mealtime rolls around, whether they're camping or staying in a cabin. If you don't happen to have a full ice chest, you'll find a few basic restaurants in Oakridge. Although none are particularly memorable, they're the only places to get a meal other than in the dining room of the Odell Lake Lodge or at the Willamette Pass Ski Area.

4 The North Umpqua–Upper Rogue River Scenic Byway

Diamond Lake: 76 miles E of Roseburg, 80 miles NE of Medford

Ore. 138, which heads east out of Roseburg and leads to Diamond Lake and the north entrance to Crater Lake National Park, is one of the state's most scenic highways. Along much of its length, the highway follows the North Umpqua River, which is famed among fly anglers for its fighting steelhead and salmon. As far as I'm concerned, this deep aquamarine stream is the most beautiful river in Oregon and is well worth a visit even if you don't know a wooly bugger from a muddler minnow (that's fly talk, for the uninitiated). Between Idleyld Park and Toketee Reservoir, you'll find numerous picnic areas, boat launches, swimming holes, and campgrounds.

As Ore. 138 approaches the crest of the Cascades, it skirts the shores of Diamond Lake, which is a major recreational destination (though it's certainly not as beautiful as nearby Crater Lake). Almost a mile in elevation, Diamond Lake is set at the foot of jagged Mount Thielsen, a spire-topped pinnacle known as the "lightning rod of the Cascades." The lake offers swimming, boating, fishing, camping, hiking, biking, and, in winter, snowmobiling and cross-country skiing. Just beyond Diamond Lake is the north entrance to Crater Lake National Park.

The 24-mile-long Ore. 230 connects the Diamond Lake area with the valley of the upper Rogue River at the community of Union Creek. Although this stretch of the Rogue is not as dramatic as the North Umpqua or the lower Rogue River, it has its charms, including a natural bridge, a narrow gorge, and some grand old trees.

ESSENTIALS

GETTING THERE   The North Umpqua River is paralleled by Ore. 138, which connects Roseburg, on I-5, with U.S. 97, which parallels the Cascades on the east side of the mountains. This highway leads to the north entrance of Crater Lake National Park.

VISITOR INFORMATION   For information on recreational activities in this area, contact the **North Umpqua Ranger District,** 18782 N. Umpqua Hwy., Glide, OR 97443 (© 541/496-3532); or the **Diamond Lake Ranger District,** 2020 Toketee RS Rd., Idleyld Park, OR 97447 (© 541/498-2531). Also check the websites of the **Rogue River-Siskiyou National Forest** (www.fs.fed.us/r6/rogue) and the **Umpqua National Forest** (www.fs.fed.us/r6/umpqua).

WHAT TO SEE & DO: FLY-FISHING, RAFTING & A WATERFALL

Oregon abounds in waterfalls and white-water rivers, but in the town of Glide, 12 miles east of Roseburg, you'll find the only place in the state where rivers collide. At the interesting **Colliding Rivers Viewpoint,** the North Umpqua River, rushing in from the north, slams into the white water of the Little River, which flows from the south, and the two rivers create a churning stew. However, this phenomenon is really only impressive during times of winter rains or during spring snowmelt season.

The most celebrated portion of the North Umpqua is the 31-mile stretch from Deadline Falls, in Swiftwater Park, to Soda Springs Dam. This stretch of river is open to fly-fishing only. Between June and October, you can often see salmon and steelhead leaping up Deadline Falls, which has a designated salmon-viewing area down a short trail on the south bank of the river. For fly-fishing needs and advice, stop in at the **Blue Heron Fly Shop,** 109 Hargis Lane, Idleyld Park (© 541/496-0448), which is just off Ore. 138, or **Steamboat Inn,** 42705 North Umpqua Hwy. (© 541/498-2230), in Steamboat. If you want to hire a guide to take you out fishing on the North Umpqua River, try **Jerry Q. Phelps** (© 541/672-8324; www.jerryphelpsguideservice. com). Expect to pay around $350 per day.

If you'd rather just paddle the river in a kayak or raft, contact **North Umpqua Outfitters** (© 888/789-7152 or 541/673-4599; www.nuorafting.com), which charges $105 to $115 for its rafting trips.

At the turnoff for Toketee Reservoir, you'll find the trail head for the .5-mile hike to **Toketee Falls** ✦. This double cascade plummets 120 feet over a wall of columnar basalt and is one of the most picturesque waterfalls in the state. The viewing area is on a deck perched out on the edge of a cliff. Also in this same area, past the Toketee Lake Campground, you'll find **Umpqua Hot Springs,** which are down a short trail. These natural hot springs perch high above the North Umpqua River, on a hillside covered with mineral deposits. For longer hikes, consider the many segments of the 79-mile **North Umpqua Trail,** which parallels the river from just east of Glide all the way to the Pacific Crest Trail. The lower segments of this trail are also popular mountain-biking routes.

At **Diamond Lake,** just a few miles north of Crater Lake National Park, you'll find one of the most popular mountain recreation spots in the state. In summer, the popular and somewhat run-down **Diamond Lake Resort** is the center of area activities.

Here you can rent boats, swim at a small beach, and access the 10.5-mile paved hiking/biking trail that circles Diamond Lake.

Near the community of Union Creek, west of Crater Lake National Park on Ore. 62, are the Rogue River Gorge and a small natural bridge formed by a lava tube. The gorge, though only a few feet wide in places, is quite dramatic and has an easy trail running alongside.

In winter, Diamond Lake Resort serves as the region's main snowmobiling destination, but it's also a decent area for cross-country skiers, who will find rentals and groomed trails at Diamond Lake Resort. There are also many more miles of marked, but not groomed, cross-country ski trails in the area; the more interesting trails are found at the south end of the lake. Snowmobile rentals and tours are also available. You can also do some downhill skiing on untracked nearby slopes through the Diamond Lake Resort's **Cat Ski Mt. Bailey** (www.catskimtbailey.com), which charges $250 for a day of skiing and also offers multiday packages. For more information on these activities, contact **Diamond Lake Resort** (© 800/733-7593; www.diamondlake.net).

WHERE TO STAY & DINE

Prospect Historical Hotel ☆ *(Finds)*   This combination historic hotel and adjoining modern motel is in the tiny hamlet of Prospect, 30 miles from Crater Lake's Rim Village. The hotel, built in the 1880s, is a big white building with a wraparound porch, and although the small rooms have few furnishings, their country styling lends them a bit of charm. If you stay in one of these rooms, you'll get air-conditioning and a full breakfast. The motel rooms are much larger and have TVs, telephones, and coffeemakers; some also have kitchenettes. The elegant dining room, which is open May through October, serves good food.

391 Mill Creek Dr. (P.O. Box 50), Prospect, OR 97536. © 800/944-6490 or 541/560-3664. Fax 541/560-3825. www.prospecthotel.com. 24 units. $55–$95 double; $130–$150 suite. DC, DISC, MC, V. Pets accepted. **Amenities:** Restaurant (American). *In hotel room:* A/C. *In motel room:* A/C, TV, fridge, coffeemaker.

Steamboat Inn ☆☆   Located roughly midway between Roseburg and Crater Lake, this inn on the banks of the North Umpqua River is by far the finest lodging on the river. Although the lodge appeals primarily to anglers, the beautiful gardens, luxurious guest rooms, and gourmet meals also attract a fair number of people looking for a quiet getaway in the forest and a base for hiking and biking. If you aren't springing for one of the suites, which have their own soaking tubs overlooking the river, your best bets will be the streamside rooms, misleadingly referred to as cabins. These have gas fireplaces and open onto a long deck that overlooks the river. The hideaway cottages are more spacious but don't have river views and are half a mile from the lodge (and the cozy dining room). Dinners ($45) are multicourse affairs and are open to the public by reservation. There's a fly-fishing shop on the premises. Some units here have telephones and some have air-conditioning.

42705 N. Umpqua Hwy., Steamboat, OR 97447-9703. © 800/840-8825 or 541/498-2230. Fax 541/498-2411. www.thesteamboatinn.com. 20 units (including 5 cottages and 5 houses). $155 cabin; $195–$200 cottages and houses; $275 suites. Children under 4 stay free in parent's room. MC, V. Closed Jan–Feb. **Amenities:** Restaurant (Northwest); bike rentals; massage (seasonal). *In room:* Coffeemaker, hair dryer.

CAMPGROUNDS

Along the North Umpqua River, between Idleyld Park and Diamond Lake, you'll find the Bureau of Land Management's **Susan Creek Campground,** the most upscale public campground along the North Umpqua. (It even has hot showers.) The large **Horseshoe**

Bend Campground, near Steamboat, is popular with rafters and kayakers on weekends and has well-separated campsites, big views of surrounding cliffs, and access to the North Umpqua Trail. **Toketee Lake Campground,** at Toketee Reservoir, is situated back from the lake, but there are a few sites on the river.

Diamond Lake has three U.S. Forest Service campgrounds—Diamond Lake, Broken Arrow, and Thielsen View—with a total of 450 campsites. Here you'll also find the **Diamond Lake RV Park,** 3500 Diamond Lake Loop (© **541/793-3318;** www.diamondlakervpark.com).

Southwest of the Crater Lake National Park, on Ore. 62, you'll find **Farewell Bend Campground,** which is set amid big trees on the Rogue River. The next campgrounds are **Union Creek** and **Natural Bridge,** both of which are also along the Rogue River. North of Ore. 62, on Ore. 230, you'll find the **Hamaker Campground,** on a pretty bend in the Rogue River with big trees and meadows across the river.

5 Crater Lake National Park ★★★

71 miles NE of Medford, 83 miles E of Roseburg, 60 miles N of Klamath Falls

Nothing in the forests of the southern Oregon Cascades prepares you for Crater Lake. There are no preliminaries, no teasing glimpses through the trees. You drive through a rather unremarkable mountain forest, wondering why this place was ever made into a national park, and then, with little warning and no fanfare, you arrive at the edge of a cliff and gaze down 1,000 feet to a circular bowl of water a mesmerizing shade of sapphire blue. The view takes your breath away (or is it the elevation?), and you quickly understand why this lake became a national park way back in 1902.

At 1,932 feet deep, Crater Lake is the deepest lake in the United States (and the seventh deepest in the world). The crater (or, more accurately, the caldera) that holds the serene lake was born in an explosive volcanic eruption 7,700 years ago. When the volcano, now known as Mount Mazama, erupted, its summit (thought to have been around 12,000 ft. high) collapsed, leaving a crater 4,000 feet deep. Thousands of years of rain and melting snow turned the empty heart of this volcano into today's cold, clear lake, which today is surrounded by crater walls that in places are nearly 2,000 feet tall. Toward one end of the lake, the cone of Wizard Island rises from the lake. This island is the tip of a new volcanic peak that has been building slowly since Mount Mazama's last eruption.

ESSENTIALS

GETTING THERE   If you're coming from the south on I-5, take exit 62 in Medford and follow Ore. 62 for 75 miles. If you're coming from the north, take exit 124 in Roseburg and follow Ore. 138. From Klamath Falls, take U.S. 97 north to Ore. 62. In winter, only the south entrance is open. Due to deep snowpack, the north entrance usually doesn't open until some time in late July.

VISITOR INFORMATION   For more information, contact **Crater Lake National Park,** P.O. Box 7, Crater Lake, OR 97604 (© **541/594-3100;** www.nps.gov/crla).

ADMISSION   Park admission is $10 per vehicle.

SEEING THE HIGHLIGHTS

After your first breathtaking view of the lake, you may want to stop by one of the park's two visitor centers. The **Steel Information Center** is between the south park entrance and the Rim Village, which is where you'll find the smaller and less thorough

Rim Village Visitor Center. A dining room/gift shop and the parking area at Rim Village have been undergoing renovations that should be done by the time you visit the park. Though the park is open year-round, in winter, when deep snows blanket the region, only the road to Rim Village is kept clear. During the summer (roughly beginning in late June), the **Rim Drive** ✿✿ provides many viewing points along its 39-mile length.

Narrated boat trips ✿✿ around the lake are the park's most popular activity. These tours last 2 hours and begin at Cleetwood Cove, at the bottom of a very steep 1-mile trail that descends 700 feet from the rim to the lakeshore. Before deciding to take a boat tour, be sure you're in good enough physical condition to make the steep climb back up to the rim. Bring warm clothes because it can be quite a bit cooler on the lake than it is on the rim. A naturalist on each boat provides a narrative on the ecology and history of the lake, and all tours include a stop on Wizard Island. Tours are offered from July to mid-September and cost $24 for adults and $14 for children ages 3 to 11.

Of the many miles of **hiking trails** within the park, the mile-long Cleetwood Trail is the only trail that leads down to the lakeshore, and it's a steep and tiring hike back up from the lake. The trail to the top of Mount Scott, although it's a rigorous 2.5 miles, is the park's most rewarding hike. Shorter trails with good views include the 0.8-mile trail to the top of the Watchman, which overlooks Wizard Island, and the 1.7-mile trail up Garfield Peak. The short Castle Crest Wildflower Trail is best hiked in late July or early August. Backpackers can hike the length of the park on the Pacific Crest Trail (PCT) or head out on a few other trails that lead into more remote, though less scenic, corners of the park.

Other summertime park activities include children's programs, campfire ranger talks, history lectures, and guided walks. To find out about these, check in *Reflections,* a free park newspaper given to all visitors when they enter the park.

In winter, **cross-country skiing** is popular on the park's snow-covered Rim Drive and in the backcountry. At Rim Village, you'll find several miles of well-marked ski trails, affording some of the best views in the state, weather permitting. Skiers in good condition can usually make the entire circuit of the lake in 2 days but must be prepared to camp in the snow. Spring, when the weather is warmer and there are fewer severe storms, is actually the best time to ski around the lake.

WHERE TO STAY & DINE

Crater Lake Lodge ✿✿   Perched on the edge of the rim overlooking Crater Lake, this lodge is the finest national-park lodge in the Northwest. The views are breathtaking, and the amenities are modern without sacrificing the rustic atmosphere (a stone fireplace and ponderosa-pine-bark walls in the lobby). Slightly more than half of the guest rooms overlook the lake, and although most rooms have modern bathrooms, eight have claw-foot bathtubs. The very best accommodations are the corner rooms on the lake side of the lodge. The lodge's dining room provides a view of both Crater Lake and the Klamath River basin. Reservations are hard to come by. Plan as far in advance as possible.

Mailing address: 1211 Ave. C, White City, OR 97503. ☎ **541/830-8700.** Fax 541/830-8514. www.craterlake lodges.com. 71 units. $123–$170 double; $238 suite. Children under 12 stay free in parent's room. AE, DC, DISC, MC, V. Closed mid-Oct to mid-May. **Amenities:** Restaurant (Northwest); lounge. *In room:* No phone.

Mazama Village Motor Inn ✿   Though the Mazama Village Motor Inn isn't on the rim of the crater, it's just a short drive away and should be your second choice of lodgings on a Crater Lake vacation. The modern motel-style guest rooms are housed in 10 steep-roofed buildings that look much like traditional mountain cabins. A laundry, gas station, and general store make Mazama Village a busy spot in the summer.

Mailing address: 1211 Ave. C, White City, OR 97503. ℂ 541/830-8700. Fax 541/830-8514. www.craterlakelodges. com. 40 units. $110 double. Children under 12 stay free in parent's room. AE, DC, DISC, MC, V. Closed mid-Oct to mid-May. *In room:* Coffeemaker, no phone.

CAMPGROUNDS

Tent camping and RV spaces are available on the south side of the park at the **Mazama Campground,** where there are more than 200 sites ($18–$20 per night). This campground is open mid-June through early October. There are also 16 tent sites available at **Lost Creek Campground** ($10 per night) on the park's east side. This campground is open mid-July through mid-September. Reservations are not accepted at either campground. For information on campgrounds outside the park, see "Campgrounds" in "The North Umpqua–Upper Rogue River Scenic Byway" section above.

6 The Klamath Falls Area: Bird-Watching & Native American Artifacts

65 miles E of Ashland, 60 miles S of Crater Lake

Unless you are an avid bird-watcher or are looking for a cheap place to stay close to Crater Lake National Park, you won't find too much to attract you to the Klamath Falls area. However, this region, a wide, windswept expanse of lakes, high desert, and mountain forests just north of the California line, has a history of human presence that stretches back more than 14,000 years. The large lakes in this dry region have long attracted a wide variety of wildlife (especially waterfowl), which once provided a food source for the area's Native American population. The prehistoric residents of the region lived on the banks of the Klamath Basin's lakes and harvested fish, birds, and various marsh plants. Today, two local museums exhibit extensive collections of Native American artifacts that have been found in this area.

Upper Klamath Lake and adjacent Agency Lake have shrunk considerably over the years as shallow, marshy areas have been drained to create pastures and farmland. Today, however, as the lake's native fish populations have become threatened and migratory bird populations in the region have plummeted, there is a growing movement to restore some of the region's drained marshes to more natural conditions. Although large portions of the area are now designated as national wildlife areas that offer some of the best bird-watching in the Northwest, farming and ranching are still considered the primary use of these wildlife lands. Conflicts between local farmers and environmentalists over how best to manage this region's limited water supply often occur during the summer dry season.

The region's shallow lakes warm quickly in the hot summers here, and, partly because of the excess nutrients in the waters from agricultural runoff, they support large blooms of blue-green algae. Although the algae blooms deprive the lake's fish of oxygen, they provide the area with its most unusual agricultural activity. The harvesting and marketing of Upper Klamath Lake's blue-green algae as a dietary supplement has become big business throughout the country as people have claimed all manner of health benefits from this chlorophyll-rich dried algae.

ESSENTIALS

GETTING THERE   Klamath Falls is on U.S. 97, which leads north to Bend and south to I-5 near Mount Shasta in California. The city is also connected to Ashland by the winding Ore. 66 and to Medford by Ore. 140, which continues east to Lakeview in eastern Oregon. The **Klamath Falls Airport,** 6775 Arnold Ave. (© **541/883-5372;** www.klamathfallsairport.com), is served by Horizon Air from Portland. Amtrak's *Coast Starlight* trains stop here en route between San Francisco and Portland.

VISITOR INFORMATION   For more information on the region, contact the **Great Basin Visitor Association,** 507 Main St., Klamath Falls, OR 97601 (© **800/ 445-6728** or 541/882-1501; www.klamathcounty.net).

GETTING AROUND   Rental cars are available at Klamath Falls Airport from Budget, Enterprise, and Hertz.

DELVING INTO LOCAL HISTORY

In addition to the two museums listed here, you might want to drive by the historic **Ross Ragland Theater & Cultural Center,** 218 N. Seventh St. (© **541/884-0651;** www.rrtheater.org), an impressive Art Deco theater in downtown Klamath Falls. The theater stages a wide variety of performances throughout the year.

Favell Museum of Western Art and Indian Artifacts ★★ *(Finds)*   Anyone with an interest in Native American artifacts or Western art will be fascinated by a visit to this unusual museum, considered one of the best Western museums in the country. On display are thousands of arrowheads (including one made from fire opal), obsidian knives, spear points, stone tools of every description, baskets, pottery, and even ancient shoes and pieces of matting and fabric. Though the main focus is on the Native Americans of the Klamath Basin and Columbia River, there are artifacts from Alaska, Canada, other regions of the United States, and Mexico. Few museums anywhere in the country have such an extensive collection on display, and the cases of artifacts can be overwhelming, so take your time. There's also an extensive collection of Western art by more than 300 artists, including members of the famous Cowboy Artists of America Association. You also find the world's largest publicly displayed miniature gun collection here.

125 W. Main St. © **541/882-9996.** www.favellmuseum.org. Admission $6 adults, $5 seniors, $3 children 6–16. Mon–Sat 9:30am–5:30pm.

Klamath County Museum ★   More Native American artifacts, this time exclusively from the Klamath Lakes area, are on display in this museum, while a history of the Modoc Indian Wars chronicles the most expensive campaign of the American West. Also of particular interest are the early-20th-century photos by local photographer Maud Baldwin. In addition, there's an extensive collection of stuffed birds.

1451 Main St. © **541/883-4208.** Admission $3 adults, $2 seniors and students, $1 children 5–12. Tues–Sat 9am–5pm.

BIRD-WATCHING & OTHER OUTDOOR ACTIVITIES

In this dry region between the Cascades and the Rocky Mountains, there are few large bodies of water, so the lakes and marshes of the Klamath Basin are a magnet for birds. White pelicans, great blue herons, sandhill cranes, egrets, geese, ducks, grebes, bitterns, and osprey can all be seen in the area at different times of year. However, the main attraction for many human visitors is the annual winter gathering of bald eagles. In the winter the region is home to as many as 500 bald eagles, making this the largest concentration of bald eagles in the Lower 48. Each winter morning, starting about 30 minutes before sunrise, as many as 100 eagles can be seen heading out to the marshes from their roosting areas in the **Bear Valley National Wildlife Refuge** near the town of Worden, 11 miles south of Klamath Falls. To find the eagle-viewing area, drive south out of Klamath Falls on U.S. 97 through the community of Worden and almost to the California state line. Turn west onto the Keno-Worden Road, and, just after the railroad tracks, turn left onto a dirt road. Follow this road for a half mile or so and pull off on the shoulder. Now start scanning the skies for eagles heading east to the marshlands. For more information on bird-watching in the area, contact the **Klamath Basin National Wildlife Refuges,** 4009 Hill Rd., Tulelake, CA 96134 (© **530/667-2231;** http://klamathbasinrefuges.fws.gov).

The easiest way to get out on the waters of Klamath Lake is on an excursion aboard the *Klamath Belle* (© 541/883-4622; www.klamathbelle.com), a replica paddle wheeler. There are sunset cruises ($7.95), family "Ice Cream Social" cruises ($13 adults, $4.50 children 4–10), and dinner and brunch cruises ($30–$40 adults, $25–$38 seniors, $13–$19 children 4–12). Cruises operate early spring to late fall.

If, on the other hand, you want to get out and paddle yourself around one of the local lakes, check out the **Upper Klamath Canoe Trail,** which begins near the junction of Ore. 140 and West Side Road northwest of Klamath Falls. The canoe trail wanders through marshlands on the edge of Upper Klamath Lake. For more information, contact the **Fremont-Winema National Forests,** Klamath Ranger District, 1936 California Ave., Klamath Falls, OR 97601 (© **541/885-3400;** www.fs.fed.us/r6/frewin). Canoes and kayaks can be rented at the adjacent **Rocky Point Resort,** 28121 Rocky Point Rd. (© **541/356-2287**), for $25 for half a day or $30 for a full day.

About 35 miles northwest of Klamath Falls on Ore. 140, you'll find the region's main mountain recreation area. Here, in the vicinity of **Lake of the Woods** and **Fish Lake,** you'll find the fun High Lakes mountain-bike trail, which leads through a rugged lava field. Also in the area is the hiking trail to the summit of Mount McLoughlin. In winter, this same area has cross-country ski trails. There are rustic cabin resorts and campgrounds on both Lake of the Woods and Fish Lake.

WHERE TO STAY

Lake of the Woods 🌾 *Kids*   Lake of the Woods is one of the prettiest lakes in southern Oregon, and is a great spot for families. The log cabins, with their red doors and green trim, look as though they belong in a national park, and the Saturday night barbecues, vintage outdoor movie nights, and wildlife shows put on by local wildlife-protection organizations give this place the feel of an old-fashioned summer camp for the whole family. Most cabins, although rustic, have full kitchens or kitchenettes, as well as an old-time mountain-cabin decor. You can rent motorboats and canoes for exploring the lake and mountain bikes for exploring the area trails (one of which leads through an ancient lava flow). Or, just spend your time swimming in the lake.

950 Harriman Rte., Klamath Falls, OR 97601-8518. © **866/201-4194** or 541/949-8300. www.lakeofthewoodsresort.com. 26 units. Memorial Day weekend to Sept $89–$179 cabin for 2 people; mid-Dec to late Feb $69–$175 cabin for 2 people. 2-night minimum. AE, DISC, MC, V. Closed Oct–Nov and Mar to Memorial Day weekend. Pets accepted. **Amenities:** Restaurant (American); lounge; watersports rentals; cross-country ski and snowshoe rentals. *In room:* No phone.

Rocky Point Resort 🌾 *Finds*   This rustic fishing resort on the west shore of Upper Klamath Lake is the sort of place that conjures up childhood memories of summer vacations by the lake. Neither the rooms nor the cabins are anything special, but the setting is bewitching. Shaded by huge old ponderosa pine trees and partly built atop the rocks for which this point is named, the resort has a great view across the waters and marshes of the Upper Klamath National Wildlife Refuge. Green lawns set with Adirondack chairs go right down to the water, where there is a small boat-rental dock. The rustic restaurant and lounge boast the best views on the property. The Upper Klamath Lake canoe trails originate here, and the bird-watching is excellent, but fishing is still the most popular pastime. The resort also has tent and RV sites.

28121 Rocky Point Rd., Klamath Falls, OR 97601. © 541/356-2287. Fax 541/356-2222. www.rockypointoregon.com. 9 units. $70 double; $99–$139 cabin. AE, DISC, MC, V. Closed Nov–Apr. Pets accepted in cabins ($5 per night). **Amenities:** Restaurant (American); lounge; watersports rentals; coin-op laundry. *In room:* Coffeemaker, no phone.

Running Y Ranch Resort ⭐⭐ *Kids*   With an Arnold Palmer–designed golf course and lots of houses for sale, this remote resort is obviously aiming primarily to tempt golfers into buying second homes. However, with horseback riding, canoe rentals, bike trails, a game room, a winter ice-skating rink, and other kid-oriented activities, it's obvious that golfers should bring the family. The Running Y is located northwest of Klamath Falls off Ore. 140 close to the shore of Upper Klamath Lake and is set amid ponderosa pines. Although remote, it is almost as luxurious as any of the central Oregon resorts in the Bend and Sisters areas. The hotel has a mountain-lodge feel that seems appropriate to a national park, and guest rooms, though not nearly as luxurious as in Sunriver near Bend, have a bit of Western feel in their furnishings. Some rooms also have balconies. Dining options here are limited to a restaurant at the golf course and a snack bar across the parking lot from the hotel.

5500 Running Y Rd., Klamath Falls, OR 97601. © 888/850-0275 or 541/850/5500. Fax 541/850-5593. www.runningy. com. 83 units. May 16–Sept 15 $159–$179 double, $224–$299 suite or town house; Sept 16–May 15 $119–$139 double, $199–$299 suite or town house. AE, DC, DISC, MC, V. Pets accepted ($25). **Amenities:** 2 restaurants (Northwest, American); lounge; indoor pool; 2 tennis courts; health club; full-service spa; Jacuzzi; sauna; watersports rentals; bike rentals; horseback riding; children's programs; concierge; massage. *In room:* A/C, TV/VCR, dataport, coffeemaker, hair dryer, iron.

CAMPGROUNDS

Along Ore. 140 between Klamath Falls and Medford are several national forest campgrounds. On Fish Lake, **Fish Lake Campground** and **Doe Point Campground** are in nice locations, but they both get a lot of traffic noise. Just west of Fish Lake on Forest Service Road 37, the **North Fork Campground** provides a quieter setting on a trout stream and a scenic mountain-bike trail. **Sunset Campground** and **Aspen Point Campground** on Lake of the Woods are popular in summer with the boating, fishing, and water-skiing crowd. The latter campground is near Great Meadow Recreation Area, has a swimming beach, and is right on the High Lakes mountain-bike trail.

WHERE TO DINE

For dinner with the best view in the area, make a reservation at the **Rocky Point Resort** (see above), which is 30 minutes outside Klamath Falls and is open Wednesday through Sunday in summer and on weekends in spring and fall.

10

Southern Oregon

Stretching from the California state line in the south to a little way north of Roseburg, southern Oregon is a mountainous region that has far more in common with Northern California than it has with the rest of Oregon. The landscape is much drier than in northwestern Oregon, and dominating the region are the Siskiyou Mountains, a jumble of rugged peaks and rare plants that link the Cascades and the Coast Range.

It was gold that first brought European settlers to this area, and it was timber that kept them here. The gold is all played out now, but the legacy of the gold-rush days, when stagecoaches traveled the rough road between Sacramento and Portland, can be seen in picturesque towns such as Jacksonville and Oakland.

Although southern Oregon is a long drive from the nearest metropolitan areas, it is relatively easy to plan a multiday trip from San Francisco or Portland. From Ashland, the southernmost city in the region, it's roughly a 6-hour trip to either Portland or San Francisco.

Ashland is the region's most popular destination and is renowned for its **Oregon Shakespeare Festival,** which attracts tens of thousands of theatergoers annually. The festival, which now stretches through most of the year, has turned what was once a sleepy mill town into a facsimile of Tudor England. Not to be outdone, the **Britt Festivals** in the nearby historic town of **Jacksonville** offer performances by internationally recognized musicians and dance companies throughout the summer.

However, it isn't just the Bard that attracts visitors to this region. The rugged beauty of the Siskiyous and the wild waters of the Rogue and Umpqua rivers are a big draws as well. Crater Lake National Park hides within its boundaries a sapphire jewel formed by the massive eruption of Mount Mazama less than 7,000 years ago. In this same area rise two of the most fabled fly-fishing rivers in the country. Ever since Zane Grey wrote of the fighting steelhead and salmon of the Rogue and Umpqua rivers, fly-fishers have been casting their lines in hopes of hooking a few of these wily denizens of the Cascade Range's cold waters. (For information on Crater Lake and the North Umpqua River, see chapter 9.)

1 Ashland & the Oregon Shakespeare Festival

285 miles S of Portland, 50 miles W of Klamath Falls, 350 miles N of San Francisco

With classy cocktail bars and upscale restaurants, live jazz in the clubs and cafes, lots of art galleries, and day spas that take advantage of Ashland's famed Lithia Springs mineral waters, Ashland has become the most cosmopolitan community between San Francisco and Portland. Sure, this is still a small town 5 to 6 hours by car from either of these cities, but more than half a century of staging Shakespeare plays has turned it into Oregon's preeminent arts community, which in turn has attracted the city's diverse population. Because this is one of the best little arts towns in America, come prepared to fall in love.

Ashland's rise to stardom began on a midsummer's night back in 1935. In a small Ashland theater built as part of the Chautauqua movement, Angus Bowmer, an English professor at Southern Oregon University, staged a performance of Shakespeare's *As You Like It.* Despite the hard times that the Great Depression had brought to this quiet mill town in the rugged Siskiyou Mountains, the show was a success. The Depression had, however, dashed any hopes local businessman Jesse Winburne had of turning Ashland into a mineral-springs resort. However, before the Depression struck, Winburne had managed to construct beautiful **Lithia Park.** Luckily, the fruits of each man's labor remain, and today their legacies have turned the town into one of Oregon's most popular destinations.

Today, the **Oregon Shakespeare Festival,** born of Bowmer's admiration for the Bard, has become a world-class repertory festival that stretches across 9 months, and although Ashland never became a mineral-springs resort, Lithia Park, through which still flow the clear waters of Winburne's dreams, has become the town's centerpiece. Around town you'll find great shopping, and nearby there are several wineries. Head farther afield, and you can hike and bike in the mountains and forests that surround Ashland. In other words, there's plenty to do when the curtains go down and the stages are dark.

ESSENTIALS

GETTING THERE   Ashland is located on I-5. From the east, Ore. 66 connects Ashland with Klamath Falls.

The nearest airport is the **Rogue Valley International–Medford Airport** in Medford, which is served by America West, Horizon Airlines, and Skywest Airlines (United Express and Delta Connection). A taxi from the airport to Ashland will cost around $20. Call **Yellow Cab** (© 541/482-3065).

VISITOR INFORMATION   Contact the **Ashland Chamber of Commerce,** 110 E. Main St. (P.O. Box 1360), Ashland, OR 97520 (© 541/482-3486; www.ashland chamber.com). You can also contact the **Southern Oregon Visitors Association,** P.O. Box 1645, Medford, OR 97501 (© 541/552-0520; www.sova.org).

GETTING AROUND   If you need a taxi, call **Yellow Cab** (© 541/482-3065). Car-rental companies with offices at the Rogue Valley International Airport are Avis, Budget, Hertz, and National. **Rogue Valley Transportation District** (© 541/779-2877; www.rvtd.org) provides public bus service in the Ashland area.

FESTIVALS   The month-long Yuletide **Holiday Festival of Light** held each year in December is Ashland's other big annual festival.

THE OREGON SHAKESPEARE FESTIVAL

The raison d'être of Ashland, the Oregon Shakespeare Festival is an internationally acclaimed theater festival with a season that runs from February to October. The season typically includes three or four works by Shakespeare plus eight other classic or contemporary plays. These plays are performed in repertory, with as many as four staged on any given day.

The festival complex, often referred to as "the bricks" because of its brick courtyard, is in the center of town and contains three theaters. The visually impressive outdoor **Elizabethan Theatre,** modeled after England's 17th-century Fortune Theatre, is used only in the summer and early fall. The **Angus Bowmer Theatre** is the festival's largest indoor theater. The festival's newest theater, known simply as the **New Theatre,** is a small state-of-the-art venue used primarily for contemporary and experimental plays.

In addition to the plays, there are **backstage tours** (tickets are $11 for adults and $8.25 for children). Throughout the festival season there are also talks and special performances. The opening of the Elizabethan Theatre is celebrated each June in Lithia Park with the elaborate Feast of Will.

For more information and upcoming schedules, contact the **Oregon Shakespeare Festival,** 15 S. Pioneer St., Ashland, OR 97520 (℗ **541/482-4331;** www.osfashland. org). Ticket prices range from $29 to $72; children's and preview tickets are less expensive. In spring and fall, all ticket prices are discounted 20% to 25%.

EXPLORING ASHLAND & ITS SURROUNDINGS

The **Schneider Museum of Art,** 1250 Siskiyou Blvd. (℗ **541/552-6245;** www.sou. edu/sma), on the campus of the Southern Oregon University, mounts art exhibits of a quality you'd expect in a museum in a major city. The museum is open Tuesday through Saturday from 10am to 4pm (until 7pm on first Fri of each month). Admission is by $3 suggested donation.

Ashland's first claim to fame was its healing mineral waters, and today you can still relax and be pampered at one of the city's day spas. **The Phoenix,** 2425 Siskiyou Blvd.

(ⓒ **541/488-1281;** www.thephoenixspa.com) and **The Blue Giraffe,** 51 Water St. (ⓒ **541/488-3335;** www.bluegiraffespa.com), both offer various body treatments, skin care, and massages. In addition, **Waterstone Mineral Springs Spa,** 2165 W. Jackson Rd. (ⓒ **541/488-0325;** www.waterstonespa.com), which is located at Lithia Springs Resort, not only offers a wide range of spa treatments, but also utilizes some of Ashland's natural mineral springs.

If you happen to have the kids along, you may want to schedule time for a visit to the **Science Works Hands-On Museum,** 1500 E. Main St. (ⓒ **541/482-6767;** www. scienceworksmuseum.org), which is filled with fun interactive science exhibits. The museum is open Wednesday through Saturday from 10am to 4pm and Sunday from noon to 4pm. Admission is $7.50 for adults and $5 for seniors and children ages 2 to 12.

WINE TOURING

Ashland Vineyards This winery produces its wine from fruit grown on the surrounding vineyards, which are planted with a wide variety of grapes, including varietals grown both in the Bordeaux region and in parts of Italy. Best for white wines such as chardonnay and sauvignon blanc.

2775 E. Main St. ⓒ **541/488-0088.** www.winenet.com. Tues–Sun 11am–5pm. From I-5, take exit 14, drive east and follow signs.

EdenVale Wines ⚡ This winery, beside a historic mansion on the outskirts of Medford, is best known for its Griffin Creek label, but the EdenVale Winery label is now the main label here. In the tasting room, you can also sample wines from other small wineries in southern Oregon. Between mid-June and mid-September, there's live jazz in the gardens here on Thursday evenings.

2310 Voorhies Rd., Medford. ⓒ **541/512-2955.** www.edenvalleyorchards.com. Summer Mon–Sat 10am–6pm, Sun noon–4pm; other months Tues–Sat 10am–5pm, Sun noon–4pm. From Ore. 99 north of Phoenix, turn west on S. Stage Rd. and left again on Voorhies Rd.

Paschal ⚡ This winery, associated with Joe Dobbes (one of Oregon's top winemakers), produces a wide variety of wines. The red wines, including cabernet sauvignon, Syrah, and merlot, tend to have a lot of tannins. The white wines are usually more accessible and drinkable. The chardonnay here is only lightly oaked, which lets the fruit show through.

1122 Suncrest Rd., Talent. ⓒ **800/446-6050** or 541/535-7957. www.paschalwinery.com. Summer daily 11am–6pm; other months Tues–Sun 11am–5pm. From Ore. 99 north of Ashland, take W. Valley View Rd. and turn left onto Suncrest Rd.

Rising Sun Farms Although this little tasting room is first and foremost the retail outlet for a local company that produces a wide variety of gourmet foods, the owners also produce some good wines. Stop in for some pinot noir and take home some fruit-flavored balsamic sauce, a marionberry cheese torta, or caramelized onion cheese dip. The shop also sells a number of other regional wines.

5126 S. Pacific Hwy., Phoenix. ⓒ **800/888-0795** or 541/535-8331, ext. 201. www.risingsunfarms.com. Daily 10am–5pm.

RoxyAnn Winery Although this winery is actually on the east side of Medford, it is close enough to Ashland to make it an appropriate stop on an afternoon's wine tasting in the area. RoxyAnn started out as the Hillcrest Orchard, which has been producing fruit for 100 years. A wide variety of wines are produced here under several different labels.

3285 Hillcrest Rd., Medford. ⓒ **541/776-2315.** www.roxyann.com. Daily 11am–6pm. From exit 27 off I-5, drive east on Barnett Rd., turn left on Phoenix Rd., and right on Hillcrest Rd.

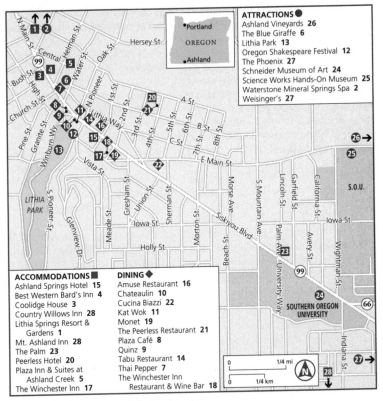

ATTRACTIONS ●
Ashland Vineyards **26**
The Blue Giraffe **6**
Lithia Park **13**
Oregon Shakespeare Festival **12**
The Phoenix **27**
Schneider Museum of Art **24**
Science Works Hands-On Museum **25**
Waterstone Mineral Springs Spa **2**
Weisinger's **27**

ACCOMMODATIONS ■
Ashland Springs Hotel **15**
Best Western Bard's Inn **4**
Coolidge House **3**
Country Willows Inn **28**
Lithia Springs Resort & Gardens **1**
Mt. Ashland Inn **28**
The Palm **23**
Peerless Hotel **20**
Plaza Inn & Suites at Ashland Creek **5**
The Winchester Inn **17**

DINING ◆
Amuse Restaurant **16**
Chateaulin **10**
Cucina Biazzi **22**
Kat Wok **11**
Monet **19**
The Peerless Restaurant **21**
Plaza Café **8**
Quinz **9**
Tabu Restaurant **14**
Thai Pepper **7**
The Winchester Inn Restaurant & Wine Bar **18**

Weisinger's ☞ Just south of town, this family-owned winery has a great view over the hills and valleys. Dry whites are a strong point, though if you like wines with a lot of tannin, you may like Weisinger's merlot and Petite Pompadour, a Bordeaux-style blend of cabernet Franc, merlot, Malbec, and cabernet sauvignon.

3150 Siskiyou Blvd. ☎ **800/551-9463** or 541/488-5989. www.weisingers.com. May–Sept daily 11am–5pm; Oct–Apr Wed–Sun 11am–5pm. Take Ore. 99 (Siskiyou Blvd.) south from downtown Ashland.

ENJOYING THE GREAT OUTDOORS

No visit to Ashland is complete without taking a long, leisurely stroll through beautiful **Lithia Park.** This 100-acre park follows the banks of Ashland Creek starting at the plaza. Shade trees, lawns, flowers, ponds, fountains, and, of course, the babbling brook are reminiscent of an English garden.

Summertime thrill seekers shouldn't pass up the chance to do some **white-water rafting** ☞ on the Rogue or Klamath River while in southern Oregon. Several companies offer trips between April and October. Try **Noah's River Adventures,** 53 N. Main St. (☎ **800/858-2811** or 541/488-2811; www.noahsrafting.com), or **The Adventure Center,** 40 N. Main St. (☎ **800/444-2819** or 541/488-2819; www.raftingtours.com), both of which have trips lasting from half a day to 5 days. Prices range from $59 to $79 for a half-day trip to between $109 to $149 for a full day, depending on the length and type of the trip. The former company also offers salmon- and steelhead-fishing trips, and the latter offers fishing trips as well as downhill bike rides ($69) from the top of Mount Ashland.

Bikes ($10 per hr. or $35 per day) can be rented at **Bear Creek Bicycles,** 1988 Ore. 99N (© **541/488-4270**), which is just around the corner from the Bear Creek path. This paved path is a great, easy route to ride.

If you'd rather go horseback riding before the play, get in touch with **City Slickers Trail Rides** (© **541/951-4611;** www.oregontrailrides.com), which charges $40 for a 1-hour ride and $70 for a 2-hour ride.

Miles of **hiking trails,** including the Pacific Crest Trail, can be found up on Mount Ashland in the Rogue River-Siskiyou National Forest. Another stretch of the Pacific Crest Trail lies within the **Cascade-Siskiyou National Monument,** which is located south and east of Ashland. This monument was created to preserve an area of outstanding botanical diversity, but is limited in its recreational opportunities. For more information, contact the Medford office of the **Bureau of Land Management,** 3040 Biddle Rd., Medford (© **541/618-2200**).

In the winter, there's good downhill and cross-country **skiing** at **Mt. Ashland Ski & Snowboard Resort,** 15 miles south of Ashland (© **541/482-2897** for information or **541/482-2754** for snow report; www.mtashland.com). All-day lift tickets for adults are $39. You can rent cross-country skis and pick up ski-trail maps at **Ashland Outdoor Store,** 37 Third St. (© **541/488-1202;** www.outdoorstore.com).

SHOPPING

Ashland has the best shopping in southern Oregon. Interesting and unusual shops line East Main Street, so when the curtains are down on the stages, check the windows of downtown.

Art galleries abound in Ashland, and on the first Friday of the month, many are open late. My all-around favorite place to check out works by local artists is at **Ashland Art Works,** 291 Oak St. (© **541/488-4735;** www.ashlandartworks.com), an artists' cooperative of four separate galleries all housed in a collection of cottages on the banks of Ashland Creek. For contemporary art, check out the **Hanson Howard Gallery,** 82 N. Main St. (© **541/488-2562;** www.hhgallery.com). Right on the plaza, be sure to check out the **Ashland Hardwood Gallery,** 17 N. Main St. (© **541/488-6200;** www.hardwoodgallery.com), which is filled with fascinating works of art in wood. **Davis & Cline,** 525 A St., Ste. 1 (© **541/482-2069;** www.davisandcline.com), which is located in the historic Railroad District about 8 blocks from the plaza, is another of our favorite contemporary art galleries here in town. This gallery even sells Dale Chihuly art glass. And for wearable art, stop by **The Web-sters,** 11 N. Main St. (© **541/482-9801;** www.yarnatwebsters.com), a knitting and weaving store carrying beautiful sweaters, woven jackets, and accessories. Between the first weekend in May and the last weekend in October, be sure to stop by the **Lithia Artisan's Market of Ashland** (© **541/858-7187;** www.lithiaartisansmarket.com) on Calle Guanajuato. The location is on the banks of Ashland Creek behind the stores on the north side of the plaza. Market hours are Saturday from 10am to 6pm and Sunday from 11am to 5pm. For a well-rounded selection of wines and other gourmet treats, you can't beat the **Chateaulin Wine Shoppe,** 52 E. Main St. (© **541/488-9463**), which is located next door to Chateaulin restaurant.

WHERE TO STAY

It seems Shakespeare and B&Bs go hand in hand. At last count, there were more than 30 bed-and-breakfasts in town. If your reason for coming to Ashland is to attend the Shakespeare Festival and you plan to stay at a B&B, you'll find it most convenient to choose an inn within walking distance of the theaters. By doing so, you'll also be within walking distance of the town's best restaurants and shopping and won't have to deal with finding a parking space before the show. For a comprehensive list of Ashland inns, contact **Ashland's Bed & Breakfast Network** (© **800/944-0329;** www. abbnet.com).

IN TOWN
Expensive
Ashland Springs Hotel ★★ *Finds*   First opened in 1925, this nine-story historic hotel is one of the finest hotels between Portland and San Francisco. In the light-filled lobby there are cases full of Victorian-era natural-history displays, and, on the mezzanine overlooking the lobby, tea is served on the weekends. Guest rooms are luxuriously appointed and beds sport crisp white linens, feather pillows, and down comforters. Although all the rooms have large windows, the corner rooms are worth requesting, as are rooms facing east over the city and the valley. Be sure to notice the fascinating collection of pressed plants that is on display behind the reception desk, in the elevator, and in guest rooms.

212 E. Main St., Ashland, OR 97520. © 888/795-4545 or 541/488-1700. Fax 541/488-1701. www.ashlandsprings hotel.com. 70 units. Mid-May to early Oct $139–$209 double; early Oct to mid-May $89–$164 double. Rates include continental breakfast. Children under 12 stay free in parent's room. AE, DC, DISC, MC, V. Pets accepted ($30 per night). **Amenities:** Restaurant (American); lounge; affiliated adjacent full-service spa; concierge; laundry service. *In room:* A/C, TV, dataport, fridge, hair dryer, iron, free local calls, high-speed Internet access.

Best Western Bard's Inn ★   If you prefer motels to B&Bs and want to be within walking distance of downtown, the Bard's Inn should be your first choice in Ashland. This motel's best feature is that it's only 2 blocks from the festival theaters. The rooms are large and comfortable, and those in the annex have patios or balconies, though they get a bit of traffic noise. The older rooms have all been refurbished.

132 N. Main St., Ashland, OR 97520. © 800/533-9627 or 541/482-0049. Fax 503/488-3259. www.bestwestern. com. 91 units. Mid-May to mid-Oct $129–$184 double; mid-Oct to mid-May $80–$144 double. Rates include continental breakfast. AE, DC, DISC, MC, V. Pets accepted. **Amenities:** Small outdoor pool; Jacuzzi. *In room:* A/C, TV, fridge, coffeemaker, hair dryer, iron.

Coolidge House ★★   Located right on busy North Main Street only 3 blocks from the theaters, this 1875 Victorian sits high above the street on a hill with commanding views across the valley. Although this is one of the oldest homes in Ashland, inside you'll find not only interesting antiques but also some decidedly modern amenities. Guest suites have sitting rooms and large luxurious bathrooms, most of which come with either a whirlpool tub or a claw-foot tub. The Parlor Suite, with its draped window seat, is the inn's most romantic room. However, if views and space are what you seek, opt for the Sun Suite or the Grape Arbor. There is a pleasant patio in the back garden.

137 N. Main St., Ashland, OR 97520. © 800/655-5522 or 541/482-4721. www.coolidgehouse.com. 6 units. June–Oct $145–$195 double; Nov–Mar $95–$130 double; Apr–May $120–$160. Rates include full breakfast. 2-night minimum on weekends Apr–Oct. Children over 12 are welcome. MC, V. **Amenities:** Access to nearby health club (June–Sept). *In room:* A/C, no phone.

Country Willows Inn 🐾🐾   Located just outside town and surrounded by 5 acres of rolling hills and pastures, the Country Willows B&B offers the tranquillity of a farm only minutes from Ashland's theaters and excellent restaurants. If you're looking for a very special room, consider the Sunrise Suite, which is in a renovated barn behind the main house: it has pine paneling, a high ceiling, a king-size bed, a gas fireplace, and, best of all, an old-fashioned tub for two with its very own picture window and skylight. Rooms in the restored farmhouse are smaller, but some offer excellent views across the valley. Ducks, geese, and goats call the farm home, and there's a 2-mile hiking trail that starts at the back door. You'll also find a pool and whirlpool on the grounds.

1313 Clay St., Ashland, OR 97520. ℂ 800/WILLOWS or 541/488-1590. Fax 541/488-1611. www.countrywillows inn.com. 9 units. Mar–Oct $115–$165 double, $185–$245 suite; Nov–Feb $92–$132 double, $148–$196 suite. Rates include full breakfast. AE, DISC, MC, V. Children over 12 are welcome. **Amenities:** Outdoor pool; access to nearby health club; Jacuzzi; bikes; concierge. *In room:* A/C, dataport, hair dryer, iron.

Lithia Springs Resort & Gardens 🐾   With its white fences and collection of cottages surrounded by colorful perennial gardens and wide lawns, this little resort on the edge of town has the feel of an English country estate. However, the hillsides that rise up from the edge of the property are purely southern Oregon. Guest accommodations include large suites with double whirlpool tubs, cottages, and even a converted water tower. Fans of mineral springs will definitely want to stay here; the water that flows from the taps here is super-soft mineral water that smells awful but feels great on your skin. The resort's little Waterstone Mineral Springs Spa takes advantage of these natural spring waters for its many spa treatments.

2165 W. Jackson Rd., Ashland, OR 97520. ℂ 800/482-7128. www.ashlandinn.com. 23 units. $129 double; $159– $249 suite; $179 cottage. Rates include full breakfast and afternoon wine and snacks. AE, DISC, MC, V. 2- to 3-night minimum. **Amenities:** Full-service spa; concierge; massage. *In room:* A/C, TV, coffeemaker, hair dryer, iron, no phone, Wi-Fi.

Mt. Ashland Inn 🐾🐾   Located on 160 acres on the side of Mount Ashland, this massive log home commands distant panoramas from its forest setting, and though the inn is only 20 minutes from downtown Ashland, you're in a different world up here. The Pacific Crest Trail, which stretches from Canada to Mexico, passes through the front yard, and just a few miles up the road is the Mt. Ashland Ski Area. Whether you're in the area for an active vacation or a few nights of theater, this lodge makes a very special base of operations. The decor is straight out of an Eddie Bauer catalog, and every room has a Jacuzzi and a gas fireplace. One guest bathroom even has a stone wall with a built-in waterfall. The Sky Lakes Wilderness Suite has views of Mount Shasta and is the best room in the house. In the winter, the inn has complimentary cross-country skis, snowshoes, and sleds for the use of the guests.

550 Mt. Ashland Rd., Ashland, OR 97520. ℂ 800/830-8707 or 541/482-8707. www.mtashlandinn.com. 5 units. $160–$200 suite. Rates include full breakfast. 2-night minimum on weekends. DISC, MC, V. Children 10 and older are welcome. **Amenities:** Jacuzzi; sauna; cross-country skis and snowshoes; massage. *In room:* Fridge, hair dryer, iron, free local calls, Wi-Fi.

Peerless Hotel 🐾🐾   Located in the historic Railroad District 7 blocks from the festival theaters, this restored 1900 brick boarding house is one of Ashland's most interesting lodgings. With the feel of a small historic hotel rather than a B&B, the Peerless is filled with antiques and an eclectic array of individually decorated guest rooms. Of these, the West Indies Suite, with its balcony, double whirlpool tub, and view of Ashland, is by far the most luxurious. However, all other rooms feature lush fabrics, unusual murals, stenciling, and tile work that add up to unexpected luxury. Most rooms have either a whirlpool tub or a claw-foot tub. (One even has two side-by-side claw-foot tubs.) The hotel's restaurant (p. 285) is one of the finest in Ashland.

243 Fourth St., Ashland, OR 97520. © 800/460-8758 or 541/488-1082. www.peerlesshotel.com. 6 units. Early June to early Nov $143–$195 double, $225–$242 suite; early Nov to mid-Feb $74–$105 double, $142–$163 suite; mid-Feb to early June $104–$143 double, $176–$198 suite. Rates include full breakfast (continental breakfast in winter). AE, DC, DISC, MC, V. Children over 14 welcome. **Amenities:** Restaurant (Northwest); lounge; access to nearby health club; room service. *In room:* A/C, TV, fridge, iron, free local calls.

Plaza Inn & Suites at Ashland Creek 🎭🎭 A bold and colorful decor imbues this luxurious new hotel with a distinctly theatrical character, making this one of the most enjoyable lodgings in Ashland. In the guest rooms, the triple-sheeted beds have bedspreads printed with excerpts from Shakespeare's poems, and carpets have a bold black-and-blue diamond pattern. It all inspires you to make a grand entrance. To inspire pleasant midsummer nights' dreams (or any other night, for that matter), there's even a pillow menu from which to choose just the right pillow. In summer, you can breakfast on the patio beside a small pond. There's a complimentary evening reception featuring local wines, and after a show, you can make yourself a peanut-butter-and-jelly sandwich. The Plaza Suites are only 2 blocks from the plaza itself, and there's a day spa right next door.

98 Central Ave., Ashland, OR 97520. © 888/488-0358 or 541/488-8900. Fax 541/488-8906. www.plazainnashland. com. 91 units. Mid-June to mid-Oct $139–$179 double, $199–$249 suite; mid-Oct to Mar $69–$89 double, $99–$119 suite; Apr to mid-June $89–$109 double, $119–$139 suite. Rates include continental breakfast. AE, DC, DISC, MC, V. Pets accepted ($25). **Amenities:** Exercise room; Jacuzzi; concierge; coin-op laundry; laundry service; dry cleaning. *In room:* A/C, TV, dataport, fridge, coffeemaker, hair dryer, iron.

The Winchester Inn 🎭🎭 With its massive old shade trees, English tea gardens, and elegant, international restaurant (p. 285), the Winchester is Ashland's premier historic inn. Though it styles itself as a country inn, it's actually right in town within a few blocks of the theaters. The rooms are very comfortably furnished with antiques and modern bath fixtures, including sinks built into old bureaus in some rooms. I prefer the upstairs rooms, which get quite a bit more light than those on the ground floor. There are also rooms in the building next door. If you want a bit more space, stay in one of the six suites, two of which are in the old carriage house. The suites also come with TVs and VCRs. Throughout the year, special events are held here, including murder-mystery weekends and Christmas Dickens feasts.

35 S. Second St., Ashland, OR 97520. © 800/972-4991 or 541/488-1113. Fax 541/488-4604. www.winchesterinn. com. 19 units. $129–$168 double; $175–$239 suite. Rates include full breakfast. Children under 8 stay free in parent's room. AE, DISC, MC, V. **Amenities:** Restaurant (international); lounge; access to nearby health club; dry cleaning. *In room:* A/C, dataport, hair dryer, iron, free local calls, high-speed Internet access, Wi-Fi.

Moderate
The Palm 🎭 *Value* Although it's located about a mile from the theaters of the Shakespeare Festival, this older but upgraded motor court is an excellent value. The collection of little Cape Cod cottages is surrounded by colorful perennial gardens, and there's even a tiny swimming pool on the grounds. All the old cottages have been completely redone and have a classic cottage feel. Some rooms have kitchens.

1065 Siskiyou Blvd., Ashland, OR 97520. © 877/482-2635 or 541/482-2636. www.palmcottages.com. 13 units. Summer $85–$125 double; fall and spring $59–$95 double; winter $49–$89 double. MC, V. **Amenities:** Outdoor pool. *In room:* A/C, TV, dataport, Wi-Fi.

WHERE TO DINE

If you're headed to the theater after dinner, let your waitstaff know. They will usually do whatever they can to make sure you aren't late! For a light post-theater meal, try Chateaulin (see below).

EXPENSIVE

Amuse Restaurant ⟪⟫ NORTHWEST/FRENCH   Ashland may be a long way from Seattle or Portland, but that doesn't mean you can't have a thoroughly urban dining experience. Amuse is by far the most contemporary restaurant in town and is thoroughly stylish. The food here comes to your table looking almost too good to eat. The menu changes regularly, but you might start with an earthy mushroom bisque or some foie gras. From there, it might be seared Columbia River sturgeon or duck breast with lentils and mission figs. In summer, request a table on the patio.

15 N. First St. ⟪⟫ 541/488-9000. www.amuserestaurant.com. Reservations recommended. Main courses $19–$29. AE, DC, DISC, MC, V. Wed–Sun 5:30–9pm.

Chateaulin ⟪⟫ FRENCH   Located just around the corner from the festival theaters, this has long been one of the finest restaurants in town. Exposed brick walls and old champagne bottles give Chateaulin a casually elegant appearance that's accented by Art Nouveau touches and dark-wood furnishings. The menu is almost as traditional as the decor; you can start your meal with escargots or house pâté and then move on to rack of lamb. A separate bar menu (items are $7–$10) caters to smaller or après-theater appetites. The restaurant's award-winning wine list features French wines, as well as lots of hard-to-find wines from Oregon, Washington, and California. For visitors on a budget, there is a more affordable and contemporary prix-fixe menu ($33) that changes weekly. There's also an attached wine and gourmet-foods store for classy picnic fare.

50 E. Main St. ⟪⟫ 541/482-2264. www.chateaulin.com. Reservations recommended. Main courses $21–$37. AE, DC, DISC, MC, V. June–Oct Mon 5:30–9:30pm, Tues–Sun 5–9:30pm; Nov–May Wed–Sun 5:30–9pm.

Cucina Biazzi ⟪⟫ TUSCAN   Housed in a little bungalow on the edge of downtown, this cozy little Italian cottage is the perfect spot for a romantic pretheater dinner. If it's warm out, try for a table on the patio in the shade of the wisteria and grape vines. The menu here changes with the seasons, but you might find that the antipasto course is a salad of Tuscan white beans, mushrooms, marinated artichokes, asiago cheese, and other tempting ingredients. For your pasta course, be sure to order the delicious angel-hair pasta with spinach, garlic, and lemon; it's long been a favorite here. Main-course options might include pork loin encrusted with rosemary and garlic or fragrant grilled prawns that have been marinated in Italian seasonings. For a

---

⟪Tips⟫ Food, Glorious Food!

As you meander around southern Oregon, keep your eyes out for local gourmet foods. Some of my favorites include the chocolate bars produced by Ashland's **Dagoba Organic Chocolate**, the cocoa-covered cracked cocoa beans produced by **Lillie Belle Farms** in Jacksonville, the savory and sweet tortas made by **Rising Sun Farms** in Phoenix, and the buffalo sausage and jerky made by **Full Circle Bison Ranch** in Williams.

switch on the American norm, the salad course comes last here (but before dessert—save room). Service is generally excellent.

568 E. Main St. ✆ **541/488-3739**. Reservations recommended in summer. 4-course prix-fixe dinner $25–$33. MC, V. Daily 5:30–8:30pm; hours may be shorter in winter.

Monet *✿✿* FRENCH   For fine French cuisine with an emphasis on lighter, more contemporary preparations, it's hard to beat Monet. Owned and operated by chef Pierre Verger, Monet has been in business for more than a decade, a testament to the popularity and quality of the restaurant's Gallic cuisine. Be sure to start with the smoked salmon wrapped around avocado mousse and served with a lemon-lime vinaigrette. From there, you've got plenty of good choices, including a filet mignon with the chef's sauce of the day. For lighter appetites, there are always several interesting salads and an excellent French onion soup. Though the big white house looks rather plain from the outside, inside you'll find a somewhat formal and impeccably set dining room. On warm days, you may want to dine in the garden surrounded by many of the same flowers that grow in Monet's famous garden in France.

36 S. Second St. ✆ **541/482-1339**. www.mind.net/monet. Reservations recommended. Main courses $17–$30. MC, V. Tues–Sun 5:30–8:30pm. Closed Jan.

The Peerless Restaurant *✿✿* NORTHWEST   With its theatrical warehouse-tropical decor, this upscale restaurant a few blocks from the plaza seems decidedly out of place in the southern Oregon hills, but good food is good food no matter where it's served. And the cuisine served here is some of the best in Oregon. Flavor combinations are often complex and can seem at first to be a bit contrived (halibut and buffalo with white beans and gorgonzola), but one bite will convince you that chef Patrick O'Toole knows what he's doing. Because The Peerless is out of Ashland's restaurant mainstream, it tends to work just a little bit harder to satisfy its customers, so although prices are high, dinners here are the best in Ashland. In summer, there's a garden patio for summertime alfresco dining.

265 Fourth St. ✆ **541/488-6067**. www.peerlessrestaurant.com. Reservations recommended. Main courses $20–$35. AE, DISC, MC, V. Tues–Sat 5:30–9pm.

The Winchester Inn Restaurant & Wine Bar *✿✿* INTERNATIONAL   Located on the ground floor of Ashland's premier inn, this restaurant and wine bar melds a historic Victorian setting with an eclectic international menu that visits such far-flung culinary destinations as China, Mexico, Greece, and the Mediterranean. Starters here tend toward such delectable preparations as seared scallops with roasted poblano-chile relish or baked brie in a peppernut crust served with apple-pear chutney. Teng dah beef, the inn's signature French-Vietnamese dish, is an unusual treatment of filet mignon, marinated in soy sauce and flavored with lemon zest, garlic, black pepper, and anise. Sunday brunch is the perfect way to finish a weekend of theater before heading home. The dining rooms overlook the inn's English gardens, and in summer there is dining on the porch and deck as well. During the Christmas season, there are special Dickens feasts here.

35 S. Second St. ✆ **541/488-1113**. www.winchesterinn.com. Reservations highly recommended. Main courses $15–$23; prix-fixe dinner $20–$45; Sun brunch $8.50–$15. AE, DISC, MC, V. Summer Mon–Sat 5:30–8:30pm; Sun 9:30am–12:30pm (brunch) and 5:30–8:30pm. Closed Jan.

MODERATE

Kat Wok *✿* PACIFIC RIM   With the sort of clever ambience you'd find in a hip restaurant in Portland or Seattle, Kat Wok is a prime example of Ashland's cosmopolitan atmosphere. If you happen to enter from "the bricks," you'll think you've stumbled onto a theater's backstage. Each table is dramatically lit, and there are tables on a catwalklike mezzanine (hence the name). Kat Wok is popular with people of all ages who come here for light Asian-style cuisine, such as an Asian pear salad with roasted chicken, sesame-crusted pork medallions, or Szechwan green beans. Later in the evening, Kat Wok becomes a nightclub with live music.

62 E. Main St. ℂ 541/482-0787. www.katwok.com. Reservations recommended. Main courses $13–$20. AE, MC, V. Mon–Tues 5–9pm; Wed–Sun 11:30am–2:30pm and 5–9pm.

Plaza Café ⓐ *Value* REGIONAL AMERICAN   Located on the plaza in downtown Ashland, this cafe has an upscale urban atmosphere with a high ceiling and art on the brick walls. It's practically next door to Quinz (see below) and is much less formal than its neighbor. I enjoy the blackened salmon with raspberry sauce and the Tuscan herb-marinated chicken. Salads are generous and fresh and feature local organic produce. Prices here (including those for wine) are quite reasonable. There's also creekside seating out in back of the restaurant. Brunch is served on Sunday.

47 N. Main St. ℂ 541/488-2233. Reservations recommended. Main courses $8–$23. DISC, MC, V. Mon 11am–8pm; Tues–Thurs 11am–3:30pm; Fri 11am–9pm; Sat 9am–9pm; Sun 9am–8pm.

Tabu Restaurant ⓐⓐ NUEVO LATINO   If it's a trend in San Francisco or Seattle, you can bet it will show up in Ashland *mas rapido*. At least that's certainly the case with Nuevo Latino food, which has been something of a south-of-the-border revolution in the Northwest in the past few years. Casual and not too expensive, Tabu may seem like the absolute antithesis of a pretheater restaurant, but there's only so much French food you can eat. The fish tacos, which come three to a plate, each with its own distinctive sauce, are my favorite dish here. For a side dish, try the unusual white beans in *mole verde* (green sauce).

16 N. Pioneer St. ℂ 541/482-3900. www.taburestaurant.com. Main courses $10–$22. AE, MC, V. Sun–Mon 5–8 or 9pm; Tues–Sat 5–9pm.

INEXPENSIVE

For great breakfasts, head to the **Ashland Bakery Café,** 38 E. Main St. (ℂ **541/482-2117;** www.ashlandbakery.com), for polenta pancakes or a smoked-salmon scramble. If you're late for the theater or forgot to make dinner reservations, you can still get a slice or two of organic pizza at **Cozmic Pizza,** 143 A St. (ℂ **541/482-0844**), in the A Street Marketplace in the Railroad District. If you're in need of a latte and a muffin, head to **The Beanery,** 1602 Ashland St. (ℂ **541/488-0700**), which, though a bit removed from downtown, is the locals' favorite coffeehouse. If you want to sip a latte with some left-leaning SOU students, stop by **Evo's Java House,** 376 E. Main St. (ℂ **541/482-2261**), where they even have vegan donuts. If it's a hot day and nothing will do but some ice cream, chill out at the **Lithia Fountain & Grill,** Second and Main streets (ℂ **541/488-0179**), an old-fashioned soda fountain that dates back to 1909.

Quinz ⓐⓐ MEDITERRANEAN   With its colorful decor, convenient location on the plaza, and prompt service, Quinz is a good place to stop for reasonably priced Mediterranean-influenced food. The menu is fairly long and includes plenty of options for light eaters as well as the famished. You can get anything from Italian sausage risotto to maple barbecue–glazed pork chop. Don't-miss dishes include the Moroccan lamb meatballs in cumin-coriander tomato sauce and the souvlaki.

29 N. Main St. ℂ 541/488-5937. Reservations recommended. Small plates $5–$9; large plates $11–$16. DISC, MC, V. Mon–Sat 11:30am–2pm and 5–9pm; Sun 5–9pm.

Thai Pepper ⍟ THAI   If menu prices around Ashland have left you wondering how you're going be able to afford dinner *and* a show, search out this elegant little Thai restaurant. Thai Pepper has long been a local favorite for its spicy, fragrant food, and its great location on the banks of Ashland Creek. I like to start with the lime-beef salad with mango chutney, but the rather untraditional tiger rolls, made with cream cheese and crab, are a perennial favorite here. The menu includes lots of vegetarian dishes. You'll find the restaurant down a flight of stairs from the street. In summer, try to get a seat on the deck.

84 N. Main St. ℂ 541/482-8058. Reservations recommended. Main courses $12–$16. AE, DC, DISC, MC, V. Mon–Sat 11:30am–2pm and 5:30–9pm; Sun 11:30am–2pm and 5:30–8:30pm.

ASHLAND AFTER DARK

The Oregon Shakespeare Festival may be the main draw, but Ashland is overflowing with talent. From experimental theater to Broadway musicals, the town sees an amazing range of theater productions. To find out what's going on while you're in town, pick up a free copy of *Sneak Preview*. If you've had enough Shakespeare or happen to be in town when the Oregon Shakespeare Festival is not staging performances, check out the performance calendars of the **Oregon Cabaret Theatre,** First and Hargadine streets (ℂ 541/488-2902; www.oregoncabaret.com), a professional dinner theater; **Oregon Stage Works,** 185 A St. (ℂ 541/488-2334; www.oregonstageworks. org), a small theater staging everything from classics to world premiers; the town of Talent's little **Camelot Theatre Company,** Talent Avenue and Main Street (ℂ 541/ 535-5250; www.camelottheatre.org), which specializes in making live theater affordable; or the **Department of Theatre Arts at Southern Oregon University,** 1250 Siskiyou Blvd. (ℂ 541/552-6348; www.sou.edu/thtr), which stages well-regarded student productions. The university also has its **One World Performing Arts series** (ℂ 541/552-6461; www.oneworldseries.org), which brings in touring musical acts and other performers.

If you're just looking for someplace to heft a pint of local microbrew, stop by **Standing Stone Brewing,** 101 Oak St. (ℂ 541/482-2448; www.standingstonebrewing.com). Or, to keep with the merrie olde England theme of Ashland, head to **The Black Sheep,** 51 N. Main St. (ℂ 541/482-6414; www.theblacksheep.com), an English pub on the plaza. Thursday through Saturday nights, you can do a little salsa dancing at the Nuevo Latino restaurant **Tabu,** 16 N. Pioneer St. (ℂ 541/482-3900).

2 Jacksonville & Medford: After the Gold Rush

16 miles N of Ashland, 24 miles E of Grants Pass

Jacksonville is a snapshot from southern Oregon's past. After the Great Depression it became a forgotten backwater, and more than 80 buildings from its glory years as a gold-mining boom town in the mid-1800s were left untouched. The entire town has been restored to much the way it looked in the late 19th century, thanks in large part to the photos of pioneer photographer Peter Britt, who moved to Jacksonville in 1852 and operated the first photographic studio west of the Rockies. His photos of 19th-century Jacksonville have provided preservationists with invaluable 150-year-old glimpses of many of the town's historic buildings. Where Britt's home once stood, visitors now attend the performances of the **Britt Festivals,** another southern Oregon cultural binge that rivals the Oregon Shakespeare Festival in its ability to stage first-rate entertainment.

Though thousands of eager gold-seekers were lured into California's Sierra Nevada by the **gold rush** of 1849, few struck it rich. Many of those who were smitten with gold fever and were unwilling to give up the search for the mother lode headed out across the West in search of golder pastures. At least two prospectors hit pay dirt in the Siskiyou Mountains of southern Oregon in 1851, at a spot that would soon be known as Rich Gulch. Within a year Rich Gulch had become the site of booming Jacksonville, and within another year the town had become the county seat and commercial heart of southern Oregon. Over the next half century, Jacksonville developed into a wealthy town with brick commercial buildings and elegant Victorian homes. However, in the 1880s, the railroad running between Portland and San Francisco bypassed Jacksonville in favor of an easier route 5 miles to the east. It was at this spot that the trading town of **Medford** began to develop.

Despite a short rail line into Jacksonville, over the years more and more business migrated to the main railway in Medford. Jacksonville's fortunes began to decline, and by the time of the Depression, residents were reduced to digging up the streets of town for the gold that lay there. In 1927, the county seat was moved to Medford, and Jacksonville was left with its faded grandeur and memories of better times.

Off the beaten path, forgotten by developers and modernization, Jacksonville inadvertently preserved its past in its buildings. In 1966, the entire town was listed on the National Register of Historic Places, and Jacksonville, with the aid of Britt's photos, underwent a renaissance that has left it a historical showcase. Together the Britt Festivals and Jacksonville's history combine to make this one of the most fascinating towns anywhere in the Northwest.

ESSENTIALS

GETTING THERE Medford is right on I-5, 30 miles north of the California state line, and Jacksonville is 5 miles west on Ore. 238.

America West Airlines, Horizon Air, and SkyWest (United Express and Delta Connection) serve **Rogue Valley International–Medford Airport,** at 3650 Biddle Rd., Medford.

VISITOR INFORMATION Contact the **Jacksonville Chamber of Commerce,** 185 N. Oregon St. (P.O. Box 33), Jacksonville, OR 97530 (© **541/899-8118;** www.jacksonvilleoregon.org), or the **Medford Visitor & Convention Bureau,** 101 E. Eighth St., Medford, OR 97501 (© **800/469-6307** or 541/779-4847; www.visit medford.org).

THE BRITT FESTIVALS & OTHER AREA PERFORMANCES

Each summer between early June and mid-September, people gather several nights a week for folk, pop, country, jazz, and classical music concerts; theater; and modern dance performances. The Britt Festivals are a celebration of music and the performing arts featuring internationally renowned performers. The setting for most of the performances is an amphitheater on the grounds of Britt's estate. Located only a block from historic California Street, the ponderosa pine–shaded amphitheater provides not only a great setting for the performances but a view that takes in distant hills and the valley far below. When planning to attend a show, be sure that it will be held here on the festival grounds; some concerts are now held at the Lithia Motors Amphitheater in nearby Central Point. This latter amphitheater lacks the character of the original Britt Pavilion amphitheater.

Both reserved and general-admission tickets are available for most shows. If you opt for a general-admission ticket, arrive early to claim a prime spot on the lawns behind the reserved seats—and be sure to bring a picnic. For information, contact the festival at 216 W. Main St., Medford (© 800/882-7488 or 541/773-6077; www.britt fest.org). Tickets range from $1 to $85.

Not wanting to lose out to its better-known neighbors, Medford has a renovated old downtown theater now known as the **Craterian Ginger Rogers Theater,** 23 S. Central Ave. (© 541/779-3000; www.craterian.org), in honor of the famous dancer who lived in the area after her retirement. The theater stages everything from performances by the Rogue Opera (© 541/608-6400; http://rogueopera.com) to touring Broadway shows and classical music performances.

When the Britt Festivals have closed up shop for the year, you can still catch Dixieland jazz at the annual **Medford Jazz Jubilee** (© 800/599-0039 or 541/770-6972; www.medfordjazz.org), which is held in mid-October.

MUSEUMS & HISTORIC HOMES

With more than 80 buildings listed on the National Register of Historic Places, Jacksonville boasts that it's the most completely preserved historic town in the nation. Whether or not this claim is true, there are certainly enough restored old buildings to make the town a genuine step back in time. Along California Street you'll find restored brick commercial buildings that now house dozens of interesting shops, art galleries, and boutiques. On the side streets you'll see the town's many Victorian homes.

Beekman House   At the 1876 Beekman House, history comes alive as actors in period costume portray the family of an early Jacksonville banker. The 19th-century Beekman Bank, 101 W. California St., also has historical displays in a window facing the street.

470 E. California St. © 541/773-6536. Admission $3 adults, $2 seniors and children 6–12. Memorial Day to Labor Day Wed–Sun noon–5pm.

Butte Creek Mill   In nearby Eagle Point, you can visit Oregon's only operating water-powered flour mill. The Butte Creek Mill was built in 1873, and its millstones are still grinding out flour. After looking around at the workings of the mill, you can stop in at the mill store and buy a bag of flour or cornmeal. Also on this same block is the **Eagle Point Museum** (© 541/826-4166), in case you want to learn more about local history. During the summer, it's open Sunday through Friday from noon to 4pm and Saturday from 10am to 4pm; in the fall and winter, it's closed on Sunday and Monday. The Antelope covered bridge is also here in Eagle Point.

402 N. Royal Ave., Eagle Point. © 541/826-3531. www.buttecreekmill.com. Free admission. Mon–Thurs 9am–6pm; Fri–Sat 9am–5pm; Sun 11am–5pm.

Jacksonville Museum of Southern Oregon History   In order to get some background on Jacksonville, make this museum your first stop in town. Housed in the 1883 county courthouse, the museum has displays on the history of Jacksonville, including 19th-century photos by Peter Britt. The price of admission also includes the adjacent Children's Museum, housed in the former jail.

206 N. Fifth St. © 541/773-6536. Admission $3 adults, $2 seniors and children 6–12. Wed–Sun 10am–5pm.

MORE TO SEE & DO

Pears and roses both grow well in the Jacksonville and Medford area, and these crops have given rise to two of the country's best-known mail-order businesses. **Harry and**

David's Country Village, 1314 Center Dr. (© 877/322-8000 or 541/864-2278; www.harryanddavid.com), is the retail outlet of a fruit company specializing in mail-order gift baskets. You'll find the store just 1 mile south of Medford at exit 27 off I-5. You can tour the Harry and David's packinghouse and then wander through the store in search of bargains. The store is open Monday through Saturday from 9am to 8pm and on Sunday from 10am to 6pm. Associated with this store is the **Jackson and Perkins rose test garden** and mail-order rose nursery. Not far away, in the town of Central Point, you can see how cheese is made at the **Rogue Creamery,** 311 N. Front St. (© 866/665-1155 or 541/665-1155; www.roguecreamery.com), which is known for its blue cheeses, including the delicious Oregonzola. The creamery is open Monday through Saturday from 9am to 5pm and Sunday from noon to 5pm. Both Harry and David's and the Rogue Creamery are part of the **Southern Oregon Wine and Farm Tour** (www.oregonwineandfarmtour.com).

There are lots of great stores in Jacksonville, and one of our favorites is the **GeBzz Gallery,** 150 S. Oregon St. (© 541/899-7535; www.artgalleryoffinecraft.com), which carries a diverse selection of contemporary art works.

OUTDOOR ACTIVITIES

Rafting and **fishing** on the numerous fast-flowing, clear-water rivers of southern Oregon are two of the most popular sports in this region, and Medford makes a good base for doing a bit of either, or both. **Arrowhead River Adventures** (© 800/227-7741 or 541/830-3388; www.arrowheadadventures.com), **River Trips Unlimited** (© 800/460-3865 or 541/779-3798; www.roguefishing.com), and **Rogue Excursions** (© 800/797-4293 or 541/549-8005; www.fishandraft.com) all offer both rafting and fishing trips. A day of rafting will cost $85 to $120, and fishing trips cost about $150 per person per day (with a minimum of two people).

If you're here in the spring, you can catch the colorful **wildflower displays** at Table Rocks. These mesas are just a few miles northeast of Medford, and because of their great age and unique structure, they create a variety of habitats that allow the area to support an unusual diversity of plants. For more information, contact the **Bureau of Land Management,** Medford District Office, 3040 Biddle Rd., Medford, OR 97504 (© 541/618-2200).

Information on **hiking** and **backpacking** is available from the **Rogue River-Siskiyou National Forest,** 333 W. Eighth St. (P.O. Box 520), Medford, OR 97501 (© 541/858-2200; www.fs.fed.us/r6/rogue).

WINE TOURING

The Applegate Valley has recently become one of the best places in southern Oregon to spend a day wine touring. There are more than half a dozen wineries in the area that you can now visit on a regular basis. For more information on area wineries, contact **Applegate Valley Wineries Information** (© 541/846-9900; www.applegatewinetrail.com).

Wine connoisseurs also won't want to miss perusing the wine racks at the **Jacksonville Inn Wine Shop,** 175 E. California St., Jacksonville (© 541/899-1900), where you might find a bottle of 1811 Tokay Essencia for $5,500 or a bottle of Chateau Lafite-Rothschild for $1,500. Oregon wines (and beef jerky) can also be tasted at the **Gary R. West Tasting Room,** 690 N. Fifth St., Jacksonville (© 541/899-1829; www.garywest.com).

Bridgeview Applegate Tasting Room   Bridgeview has its main facility near Cave Junction, but this tasting room is a bit more convenient if you are staying in Ashland or

Jacksonville and are out for a day of wine tasting. Bridgeview is best known for its inexpensive white wines, at least two of which come in distinctive blue bottles.

16995 N. Applegate Rd., Grants Pass. ℂ 541/846-1039. www.bridgeviewwine.com. Daily 11am–5pm. From Jacksonville, drive west on Ore. 238 and turn right onto N. Applegate Rd.

Devitt Winery & Vineyards 🏵🏵 *(Finds)*   This tiny family-run winery is the retirement occupation of James Devitt and his wife, Susan. Devitt had a winery in the Napa Valley area more than 20 years ago, and has now brought to his Applegate Valley operation the winemaking skills he developed years ago. Look for good cabernet sauvignon and cabernet Franc in the $25 to $30 range. Also plenty of less expensive wines.

11412 Ore. 238, Jacksonville. ℂ 541/899-7511. www.devittwinery.com. Daily 11am–5pm. From Jacksonville, drive west on Ore. 238.

Troon Vineyard   This winery has the prettiest facility in the Applegate Valley, with a Mediterranean look to the winery and tasting room. However, Troon's wines seem to be made for people who don't normally drink wine. The winery made its name with its unusual Druid's Fluid sweet red wine (zinfandel, Syrah, cabernet sauvignon blend) that has up to 3% residual sugar. You might encounter several rose or blush wines.

1475 Kubli Rd., Grants Pass. ℂ 541/846-9900. www.troonvineyard.com. Daily 11am–6pm. Closed Jan. From Jacksonville, take Ore. 238 west to N. Applegate Rd.

Valley View Vineyard   This is the oldest winery in the area and is the first you'll come to as you head out into the Applegate Valley from Jacksonville. Valley View is known for its big red wines but also produces good dry whites. They have a second tasting room right in Jacksonville at Jacksonville Mercantile, 120 E. California St., Jacksonville (ℂ **541/899-1047**).

1000 Upper Applegate Rd., Ruch. ℂ **800/781-WINE** or 541/899-8468. www.valleyviewwinery.com. Daily 11am–5pm. From Jacksonville, drive west on Ore. 238 to Ruch, and turn left onto Upper Applegate Rd.

Wooldridge Creek Vineyard & Wines 🏵   Of all the wineries in the area, this one feels both substantial and of the region. Think modern yet rustic. The tasting room, with its fireplace and comfy chairs, begs you to stop here for the rest of the afternoon. The winery's premium Warrick label wines, including a white blend of chardonnay and Viognier, are some of the best wines made in this valley.

818 Slagle Creek Rd., Grants Pass. ℂ 541/846-6364. www.wcwinery.com. Daily 11am–5pm. From Jacksonville, drive west on Ore. 238, turn right onto N. Applegate Rd., and right again onto Slagle Creek Rd.

WHERE TO STAY
IN JACKSONVILLE
Historic Orth House 🏵🏵   This 1880 Italianate brick house stands behind majestic old shade trees 1 block from busy California Street. The picket fence and inviting front porch bring back small-town America and slower times. Inside, the glowing woodwork, pressed-tin ceilings, and antique furnishings conjure up the 19th century. Don't miss the inn's extensive collection of teddy bears and antique toys. One of our favorite rooms is romantic Josie's Room with its in-room claw-foot tub. Keep an eye out for deer in the yard.

105 W. Main St. (P.O. Box 1437), Jacksonville, OR 97530. ℂ **800/700-7301** or 541/899-8665. www.orthbnb.com. 3 units. May–Oct $135–$150 double, $175 suite; Nov–Apr $110–$135 double, $140 suite. Rates include full breakfast. MC, V. *In room:* A/C, free local calls, Wi-Fi.

Jacksonville Inn ⟨⟩ ⟨⟩   Located in the heart of the town's historic business district in a two-story brick building, the Jacksonville Inn is best known for its gourmet restaurant (p. 293). Upstairs, however, there are eight antiques-filled rooms that offer traditional elegance mixed with modern amenities. Rooms are elegantly furnished and several have exposed brick walls that conjure up the inn's past. (Part of the inn was built in 1861.) Room 1, with its queen-size canopy bed and whirlpool tub for two, is the most popular. If you're looking for more privacy and greater luxury, consider the cottages, which are a couple of blocks away and have whirlpool tubs, steam showers, and entertainment centers.

175 E. California St. (P.O. Box 359), Jacksonville, OR 97530. ⟨⟩ 800/321-9344 or 541/899-1900. Fax 541/899-1373. www.jacksonvilleinn.com. 12 units (including 4 cottages). $145–$189 double; $250–$395 cottage. Rates include full breakfast. AE, DISC, MC, V. **Amenities:** Restaurant (Northwest/Continental); lounge. *In room:* A/C, TV, fridge, hair dryer, iron, Wi-Fi.

McCully Country House Inn ⟨⟩ ⟨⟩   Built in 1861, the McCully House is one of the oldest buildings in Oregon being used as an inn, and with its classic, symmetrical lines and simple pre-Victorian styling, it looks as if it could easily be an 18th-century New England inn. If you like being steeped in local history, this is Jacksonville's best choice. In the McCully Room, you'll even find the original black-walnut master bedroom furnishings. Surrounding the inn, and enclosed by a white picket fence, is a formal rose garden with an amazing variety of roses. The inn houses one of Jacksonville's finest restaurants (p. 294), and the downstairs parlors now serve as dining rooms. However, in summer, most people prefer to eat outside in the garden.

240 E. California St. (P.O. Box 13), Jacksonville, OR 97530. ⟨⟩ 800/367-1942 or 541/899-1942. www.mccullycountry houseinn.com. 3 units. $135 double. Rates include continental breakfast. AE, MC, V. **Amenities:** Restaurant (New American). *In room:* A/C, no phone.

The Stage Lodge ⟨⟩   Jacksonville has several bed-and-breakfast inns, but it's short on moderately priced motels. Filling the bill in the latter category is this motel designed to resemble a 19th-century stage stop, with gables, clapboard siding, and turned-wood railings along two floors of verandas. These details allow the lodge to fit right in with all the original buildings in town. The rooms are spacious and comfortable and have a few nice touches such as ceiling fans, TV armoires, and country decor.

830 N. Fifth St. (P.O. Box 1316), Jacksonville, OR 97530. ⟨⟩ 800/253-8254 or 541/899-3953. www.stagelodge.com. 27 units. $88–$98 double; $175 suite. AE, DC, DISC, MC, V. Pets accepted ($10 per day). *In room:* A/C, TV.

IN MEDFORD

In addition to the B&B listed below, you'll find dozens of inexpensive chain motels clustered along I-5.

Under the Greenwood Tree ⟨⟩ ⟨⟩   Located just west of Medford and taking its name from the 300-year-old oaks that shade the front yard, this B&B offers a step back in time to the days of iced tea on the veranda, croquet on the lawn, and stolen kisses behind the barn. Romance is the name of the game here, with beds piled with plump pillows and lace curtains swaying in the summer breezes. The guest rooms are furnished with antiques, and two have separate sitting rooms. Throughout the house you'll find antique quilts and Tibetan carpets, which give the inn a touch of country class, and in summer, fresh-cut flower arrangements fill the house. Out back there is a huge deck that overlooks the inn's 10 acres of land and its gazebo, garden, and barns.

3045 Bellinger Lane, Medford, OR 97501. ⟨⟩ 541/776-0000. www.greenwoodtree.com. 4 units. $120–$140 double. Rates include full breakfast. AE, DC, DISC, MC, V. **Amenities:** Bikes; massage. *In room:* A/C, dataport, hair dryer, free local calls.

IN THE APPLEGATE VALLEY

Applegate Lodge ✸✸ *Finds*   Situated on the bank of the Applegate River 16 miles outside Jacksonville, this lodge boasts one of the prettiest settings in southern Oregon and is a masterpiece of woodworking, with burnished woods (including rare fiddle-back redwood paneling) and unique wooden details throughout. The high-ceilinged great room with a river-rock fireplace features a wall of glass looking out on the river, and across the length of the lodge is a deck where you can sit and listen to the river. The guest rooms are all very large, and several of them have loft sleeping areas. Lots of peeled log furniture gives the inn a solidly western feel. Right next door is the Applegate River Ranch House (p. 294). The river here is great for swimming.

15100 Ore. 238 (P.O. Box 3282), Applegate, OR 97530. © 541/846-6690. www.applegateriverlodge.com. 7 units. $140–$155 double; lower rates in winter. Rates include continental breakfast. DISC, MC, V. Pets accepted. **Amenities:** Restaurant (steak/seafood); lounge; massage. *In room:* A/C.

WHERE TO DINE
IN JACKSONVILLE

In addition to the establishments mentioned below, **Good Bean Coffee,** 165 S. Oregon St. (© **541/899-8740**), is *the* place for a cup of espresso. **MacLevin's Whole Foods Saloon,** 150 W. California St. (© **541/899-1251**), will pack up a deli-style picnic for a Britt performance (or any other occasion).

Bella Union Restaurant & Saloon ✸ ITALIAN/AMERICAN   For casual dining or someplace to just toss back a cold beer or sip an Italian soda, the Bella Union is Jacksonville's top choice. The lounge evokes the days when the Bella Union was one of Jacksonville's busiest saloons, and in the back of the building is a garden patio. However, it's the main dining room up front that's most popular. Old wood floors, storefront windows, and exposed brick walls conjure up images of gold miners out on the town. Meals range from pizzas and pastas to a delicious chicken marinated in Gorgonzola and walnut pesto.

170 W. California St. © **541/899-1770.** www.bellau.com. At dinner, call ahead to be placed on wait list. Main courses $8–$23. AE, DISC, MC, V. Mon–Sat 11:30am–10pm; Sun 10am–2pm and 4–10pm.

Gogi's Restaurant ✸✸ REGIONAL AMERICAN   With an ambience somewhere between the casual atmosphere of Bella Union and the formality of the Jacksonville Inn Dinner House, this restaurant is a gleaming and comfortable little bistro. The small plates, such as crispy calamari with wasabi aioli or warm mozzarella with basil, marinated tomatoes, and olive oil, make good choices for sharing around the table. Other tasty standouts include grilled duck breast with wild rice and dried-cranberry reduction, and rack of lamb in an almond-honey crust with a red-wine reduction sauce. Gogi's also packs box lunches for people attending Britt Festivals events.

235 W. Main St. © 541/899-8699. Reservations recommended. Main courses $19–$23. DISC, MC, V. Wed–Sun 5–9pm.

Jacksonville Inn Dinner House ✸✸ *Value* CONTINENTAL/MEDITERRANEAN   Old-world atmosphere, either in the cozy and cellarlike downstairs or in the airier upstairs dining room, sets the mood for reliable continental fare. Together the cuisine and the decor attract well-heeled families and retirees that favor well-prepared, though familiar, dishes such as lamb chops, veal scaloppini, or prime rib. The bistro menu is lighter and leans toward Mediterranean influences, with such dishes as goat-cheese ravioli and roasted garlic pasta. Pears are a mainstay of the local economy and show up frequently in both entrees and desserts. The inn's wine shop gives diners access to a cellar boasting more than 2,000 wines. In summer, ask for a table on the patio.

175 E. California St. ✆ **541/899-1900.** www.jacksonvilleinn.com. Reservations recommended. Main courses lunch $9–$15, dinner $14–$32. AE, DISC, MC, V. Mon 7:30–10:30am and 5–9 or 10pm; Tues–Sat 7:30–10:30am, 11:30am–2pm, and 5–9 or 10pm; Sun 7:30am–2pm and 5–9pm. Bistro menu served daily 4pm–closing.

McCully House Inn 🦒🦒 NEW AMERICAN   The McCully House is one of the oldest homes in Jacksonville, and though the dining rooms have plenty of historic atmosphere, the beautiful gardens are the place to dine on a summer evening. The menu includes lots contemporary interpretations of classic comfort foods, including a tasty buffalo meatloaf stuffed with smoked mozzarella cheese and a flank steak marinated in gin martini. The wine list includes reasonably priced Oregon and Washington wines.

240 E. California St. ✆ **541/899-1942.** www.mccullyhouseinn.com. Main courses $17–$29. AE, MC, V. Tues–Sat 5–9pm.

IN THE APPLEGATE VALLEY

Applegate River Ranch House 🦒 *Finds* STEAK/SEAFOOD   With a deck overlooking the beautiful Applegate River, the location here just can't be beat. We like to enjoy the view with a plate of succulent oak-wood-broiled mushrooms and a glass of chardonnay followed by the "angels on horseback" (large prawns wrapped in bacon and then broiled with mushrooms, apples, and water chestnuts). From the chicken to various cuts of beef, anything broiled over the local red-oak wood is delicious. For dessert, top it all off with a piece of the "hula" pie, which is made with macadamia nuts and ice cream. On Wednesday nights there is live music.

15100 Ore. 238, Applegate. ✆ **541/846-6690.** www.applegateriverlodge.com. Reservations recommended in summer and on weekends. Main courses $11–$23. DISC, MC, V. Wed–Sun 5–9pm.

3 Grants Pass & the Rogue River Valley

63 miles S of Roseburg, 40 miles NW of Ashland, 82 miles NE of Crescent City

"It's the climate," proclaims a sign at the entrance to Grants Pass, and with weather almost as reliably pleasant as California's, the town has become a popular base for outdoor activities of all kinds. The Rogue River runs through the center of town, so it's not surprising that most local recreational activities revolve around the waters of this famous river. Grants Pass is located at the junction of I-5 and U.S. 199 and is the last large town in Oregon if you're heading over to the redwoods, which are about 90 miles southwest on the northern California coast. About the same distance to the northeast, you'll find Crater Lake National Park, so Grants Pass makes a good base if you're trying to see a lot of this region in a short time.

The city is slowly reviving its few blocks of historic commercial buildings, and it's worth wandering down SW G Street to see what's new along the historic blocks.

ESSENTIALS

GETTING THERE   Grants Pass is at the junction of I-5 and U.S. 199. The **Rogue Valley International–Medford Airport,** 3650 Biddle Rd. (✆ **541/776-7222**), Medford, is served by America West Airlines, Horizon Air, and SkyWest (United Express and Delta Connection).

VISITOR INFORMATION   Contact the **Grants Pass Visitors & Convention Bureau,** 1995 NW Vine St., Grants Pass, OR 97526 (✆ **800/547-5927** or 541/476-7717; www.visitgrantspass.org).

FESTIVALS   **Boatnik,** held Memorial Day weekend, is Grants Pass's biggest annual festival and includes jet-boat and hydroplane races on the Rogue River, as well as lots of festivities at Riverside Park.

OUTDOOR ACTIVITIES

Grants Pass is midway between the source of the Rogue River and the river's mouth, and is an ideal base for river-oriented activities. The Rogue, first made famous by Western novelist and avid fly-fisherman Zane Grey, is now preserved for much of its length as a National Wild and Scenic River. Originating in Crater Lake National Park, the river twists and tumbles through narrow gorges and steep mountains as it winds its way to the coast at Gold Beach. The most famous section of the river is 250-foot-deep **Hellgate Canyon,** where the river narrows and rushes through a cleft in the rock. The canyon can be seen from an overlook on Merlin-Galice Road, which begins at exit 61 off I-5. From I-5, it's about 10 miles to the canyon overlook.

Several area companies offer **river trips** of varying length and in a variety of watercraft. You can spend the afternoon paddling the Rogue in an inflatable kayak or several days rafting the river with stops each night at riverside lodges. If you have only enough time for a short trip on the river, I'd recommend a jet-boat trip down to Hellgate Canyon, which, as mentioned above, is the most scenic spot on this section of the river. **Hellgate Jetboat Excursions,** 966 SW Sixth St., Grants Pass (© **800/648-4874** or 541/479-7204; www.hellgate.com), operates five different jet-boat trips (three of which include a meal at a riverside ranch). Adult ticket prices range from $30 to $55.

Local **white-water-rafting** companies offer half-day, full-day, and multiday trips, with the latter stopping either at rustic river lodges or at campsites along the riverbanks. Area rafting companies include **Rogue Wilderness** (© **800/336-1647** or 541/479-9554; www.wildrogue.com); **Galice Resort,** 11744 Galice Rd., Merlin (© **541/476-3818;** www.galice.com); **Orange Torpedo Trips,** 209 Merlin Rd., Merlin (© **800/635-2925** or 541/479-5061; www.orangetorpedo.com); and **Rogue River Raft Trips,** Morrison's Lodge, 8500 Galice Rd., Merlin (© **800/826-1963** or 541/476-3825; www.rogueriverraft.com). Expect to pay around $50 to $55 for a half-day and $70 to $75 for a full day. Three-day lodge or camping trips are in the $580 to $680 range.

At several places near Merlin, you can rent rafts and kayaks of different types and paddle yourself downriver. Try **White Water Cowboys,** 209 Merlin-Galice Rd., Merlin (© **541/479-0132**); **Galice Resort Store,** 11744 Galice Rd., Merlin (© **541/476-3818;** www.galice.com); or **Ferron's Fun Trips** (© **800/404-2201** or 541/474-2201; www.roguefuntrips.com). Rental rates range from $25 to $40 for inflatable kayaks and from $60 to $70 for rafts.

If **fishing** is your passion, the steelhead and salmon of the Rogue River probably already haunt your dreams. To make those dreams a reality, you'll want to hire a guide to take you where the fish are sure to bite. Good local guide services include Rogue Wilderness (mentioned above), and **Rogue Excursions** (© **800/797-4293** or 541/549-8005; www.fishandraft.com), which charges $350 per boat with two clients.

OTHER THINGS TO SEE & DO

Though most people visiting Grants Pass are here to enjoy the mountains and rivers surrounding the town, history buffs can pick up a free map of the town's historic buildings at the Tourist Information Center. Two small art museums—the **Grants Pass Museum of Art,** 229 SW G St. (© **541/479-3290;** www.gpmuseum.com), and Rogue Community College's **Wiseman Gallery,** 3345 Redwood Hwy. (© **541/956-7339;** www.roguecc.edu/galleries/wiseman.asp)—offer changing exhibits of classical and contemporary art by local and national artists. Rogue Community College also operates the **Fire House Gallery,** Fourth and H streets (© **541/956-7489**), in downtown Grants Pass. On the first Friday of each month, art galleries and other stores in downtown stay open late. During this roving gallery party, there's always live entertainment of some sort.

Wildlife Images Rehabilitation and Education Center ⚘, 11845 Lower River Rd. (© **541/476-0222;** www.wildlifeimages.org), is dedicated to nurturing injured birds of prey and other wild animals back to health and then releasing them back into the wild, if possible. The center is 14 miles south of Grants Pass and is open for tours daily by reservation only. Admission is by donation. One of the best things about this place is that you can get closer to the animals than you can at a zoo.

Riverside Park, in the center of town, is a popular place to play, especially in the warmer months when people come to cool off in the river.

About midway between Medford and Grants Pass and about 6 miles off I-5 (take exit 40), you'll find one of Oregon's most curious attractions: the **Oregon Vortex,** 4303 Sardine Creek Rd., Gold Hill (© **541/855-1543;** www.oregonvortex.com). Straight out of *Ripley's Believe It or Not,* this classic tourist trap is guaranteed to have the kids, and many adults, oohing and aahing in bug-eyed amazement at the numerous strange phenomena that defy the laws of physics. People grow taller as they recede. You, and the trees surrounding the House of Mystery, lean toward magnetic north rather than stand upright. Seeing is believing—or is it? It's open March through May and September through October, daily from 9am to 4:15pm; June through August, daily from 9am to 5:15pm (closed Nov–Feb). Admission is $8.50 for adults, $7.50 for seniors, $6.50 for children 6 to 11.

Also in Gold Hill, you'll find the large **Del Rio Vineyards,** 52 N. River Rd. (© **541/855-2062;** www.delriovineyards.com), which is just off I-5 at exit 43. This winery makes its own wine and the vineyard provides grapes to many of Oregon's best wineries (in the tasting room here, you can sample wines made by some of these wineries). The tasting room is open daily 11am to 5pm. You can also taste local wines in downtown Grants Pass at the **Oregon Outpost,** 137 G St. (© **541/474-2918**), which also sells a wide variety of gourmet foods from Oregon.

Fourteen miles north of Grants Pass in Sunny Valley, you'll find the **Applegate Trail Interpretive Center,** 500 Sunny Valley Loop, Sunny Valley (© **888/411-1846** or 541/472-8545; www.rogueweb.com/interpretive). This small museum documents the little-known Applegate Trail, which was an alternative to the Oregon Trail. To find the museum, take exit 71 off I-5 and go 2 blocks east. Between mid-March and mid-November, the museum is open daily from 10am to 5pm; other months, it is closed Monday through Wednesday. Admission is $5.95 for adults, $4.95 for seniors and children 13 to 18.

WHERE TO STAY
IN TOWN

The Lodge at Riverside ⚘⚘   You'll likely do a double take when you see the log-cabin lodge fronting this recently renovated and upgraded riverside hotel. Although the original building is built of cinder blocks, it is now painted brown with green trim and looks as if it belongs in a national park. The log-walled lobby is decorated with mounted trophy animals, including a black bear and an elk head. Guest rooms are large and quite plush, with a sort of modern cabin decor. There are overstuffed wicker easy chairs, plus more wicker chairs on the balconies. All the rooms have river views, and if you can ignore the traffic noise from the adjacent bridge, you can almost imagine you're out in the wilderness.

955 SE Seventh St., Grants Pass, OR 97526. (C) **877/955-0600** or 541/955-0600. Fax 541/955-0611. www.thelodge atriverside.com. 33 units. $125–$175 double; $325 suite. AE, DC, DISC, MC, V. **Amenities:** Outdoor pool; Jacuzzi. *In room:* A/C, TV/DVD, dataport, coffeemaker, hair dryer, iron, Wi-Fi.

Riverside Inn & Conference Center 🏵🏵

Located in downtown Grants Pass, the Riverside Inn is right on the bank of the Rogue River. A weathered wood exterior and cedar-shingle roof give the two-story inn a bit of Northwest flavor, though the setting between two busy bridges is not exactly idyllic. Luckily, a park across the river means the views from most rooms are quite pleasant. The inn sprawls over 2 blocks, and most rooms have been upgraded in recent years. Our favorites are the fireplace rooms in the west section and the whirlpool riverview suites. Though the riverview rooms are a bit more expensive than nonview rooms, they're certainly worth the price. Avoid the rooms near the road, which can be quite noisy. The inn's restaurant and lounge offer a great view of the river. Jet-boat tours to Hellgate Canyon leave from the resort.

971 SE Sixth St., Grants Pass, OR 97526. (C) **800/334-4567** or 541/476-6873. www.riverside-inn.com. 127 units. $99–$199 double, $275 suite; lower rates Nov–Mar. AE, DC, DISC, MC, V. Pets accepted ($10). **Amenities:** Restaurant (American); lounge; outdoor pool; access to nearby health club; day spa; Jacuzzi; massage; dry cleaning. *In room:* A/C, TV, dataport, coffeemaker, free local calls.

OUTSIDE OF TOWN

Morrison's Rogue River Lodge 🏵🏵

If you're in the area to do a bit of fishing or rafting, we can think of no better place to stay than at Morrison's. Perched on the banks of the Rogue, this fishing lodge epitomizes the Rogue River experience. The main lodge is a massive log building that's rustic yet comfortable, with a wall of glass that looks across wide lawns to the river. Although there are B&B–style accommodations in the main lodge, the cabins seem more appropriate in this setting. The spacious cabins stand beneath grand old trees, and all have good views of the river. Fireplaces will keep you warm and cozy in the cooler months. The dining room serves surprisingly creative four-course dinners ($25–$36). Fishing and rafting trips are the specialty here, but, in addition to amenities listed below, there is also a private beach.

8500 Galice Rd., Merlin, OR 97532. (C) **800/826-1963** or 541/476-3825. Fax 541/476-4953. www.morrisonslodge. com. 13 units. $230–$390 double. Rates include 2–3 meals per day. Children under 3 stay free in parent's room. AE, DISC, MC, V. Closed mid-Nov to Apr. **Amenities:** Restaurant (Northwest); lounge; outdoor pool; putting green; 2 tennis courts; concierge; room service (breakfast only); coin-op laundry. *In room:* A/C, TV/VCR/DVD, dataport, fridge, coffeemaker, hair dryer, free local calls, high-speed Internet access.

Pine Meadow Inn–A Garden Retreat 🏵🏵

Situated between a meadow and a pine forest on 9 acres of land near the Rogue River, this modern farmhouse B&B is secluded, yet close to town. The tranquil setting, with a hot tub and koi pond in the backyard, makes it easy to slow down and relax. The upstairs guest rooms are all furnished with antiques. Breakfasts often feature fresh organic produce from the inn's own gardens. The inn is located close to the wild and scenic stretch of the Rogue River and makes a good base if you are planning on doing some rafting or fishing.

1000 Crow Rd., Merlin, OR 97532. (C) **800/554-0806** or 541/471-6277. www.pinemeadowinn.com. 4 units. Feb–Oct $95–$130 double. Rates include full breakfast. Children over 12 welcome. AE, MC, V. Closed late Oct to Feb 1. **Amenities:** Jacuzzi. *In room:* A/C, hair dryer, iron, free local calls.

Weasku Inn 🏵🏵 *Finds*

Set on the bank of the Rogue River, this log lodge built in 1924 was once *the* area fishing lodge. That was back in the days when Clark Gable, Carole Lombard, Walt Disney, Zane Grey, Bing Crosby, and Herbert Hoover used to stay here. Today, the renovated lodge is once again the sort of place where such luminaries would feel comfortable. Guest rooms, on the second floor of the old log lodge, are spacious and modern and have interesting details such as bent-willow furnishings. The riverside cabins are in a modern lodge style with whirlpool tubs, fireplaces, and private decks. Set beneath towering trees a few miles out of Grants Pass, this inn is one of the most memorable lodgings in the state, the quintessential mountain/fishing lodge.

5560 Rogue River Hwy., Grants Pass, OR 97527. ✆ 800/493-2758 or 541/471-8000. www.weaskuinn.com. 17 units. $185–$190 double; $205–$325 suite/cabin. Rates include continental breakfast. AE, DC, DISC, MC, V. *In room:* A/C, TV, dataport, fridge, coffeemaker, hair dryer, iron.

Wolf Creek Inn 🕊 *Finds*   Originally opened in 1883 on the old stagecoach road between Sacramento and Portland, the Wolf Creek Inn is a two-story clapboard building with wide front verandas along both floors. Today the inn, which is 25 miles north of Grants Pass and just off I-5, is the oldest hotel in Oregon and is owned and managed by the Oregon State Parks and Recreation Division. The interior is furnished in period antiques dating from the 1870s to the 1930s. On a winter's night there's no cozier spot than by the fireplace in the downstairs "ladies parlor." The guest rooms are small and comfortably furnished, much as they might have been in the early 1900s. Meals are available in the inn's dining room. All in all, this inn has a genuinely timeless feel. Nearby are hiking trails and a small ghost town.

100 Front St. (P.O. Box 6), Wolf Creek, OR 97497. ✆ 541/866-2474. Fax 541/866-2692. www.thewolfcreekinn.com. 9 units. $80–$107 double; lower rates in winter. Rates include full breakfast. MC, V. **Amenities:** Restaurant (American). *In room:* No phone.

CAMPGROUNDS

Along the Rogue River east of Grants Pass, you'll find the very busy **Valley of the Rogue State Park** (✆ **541/582-1118**) just off I-5 near the town of Rogue River. West of Grants Pass, there are several county-operated campgrounds, of which **Indian Mary Park,** near Galice on Merlin-Galice Road in the Hellgate Canyon area, is the nicest. Near Indian Mary Park, you'll also find **Almeda Park,** which is close to the Grave Creek trail head of the Rogue River Trail.

WHERE TO DINE

For tasty sandwiches and panini, don't miss **Trattoria Rosso's,** 225 SE Sixth St. (✆ **541/476-8708**), in downtown Grants Pass. If all you need is a pizza and a microbrew, try **Wild River Brewing & Pizza Co.,** 595 NE E St. (✆ **541/471-7487;** www. wildriverbrewing.com). Alternatively, check out the same company's **Wild River Pub,** 533 NE E St. (✆ **541/474-4456**). For espresso drinks and light meals, visit the **Bluestone Bakery,** 412 NW Sixth St. (✆ **541/471-1922**). **The Cake Shop,** 215 Galice Rd., Merlin (✆ **541/479-0188**), is open only Friday through Sunday; but if you happen to be there during that time, it's worth a stop for the Wisconsin cheese rolls. **Morrison's Rogue River Lodge,** 8500 Galice Rd., Merlin (✆ **800/826-1963**), serves the best meals on the river. For nonguests, dinners are $26 to $35. Reservations are required. See "Outside of Town," above, for details.

The Laughing Clam 🕊 SEAFOOD/PUB FARE   Located in a historic building in the historic G Street neighborhood, this pub is furnished in "shabby chic" and sports a bar that came around Cape Horn by ship a long time ago. They serve up tasty salads, sandwiches, and pastas, and there are also plenty of meatless and seafood selections to accompany a microbrew or glass of Oregon wine. I like the scallops in pesto, and, at lunch, the cosmic Cajun sandwich, which is made with a big slab of blackened catfish.

121 SW G St. ✆ 541/479-1110. Main courses $6.50–$16. MC, V. Mon–Thurs 11am–9pm; Fri–Sat 11am–10pm; Sun noon–8pm.

River's Edge ⚓ INTERNATIONAL   If you're eager to soak up as much Rogue River atmosphere as you can while you're in Grants Pass, be sure to have a meal at this elegant restaurant on the banks of the river. Three levels of decks outside provide plenty of seating in pleasant weather, and even if you have to eat inside, there are big windows that let you gaze out at the water. The menu is pretty eclectic and includes everything from fish tacos to Asian chicken salad to king crab and lamb chops. Come for lunch and you'll get good views of the river and will save considerably on your bill.

1936 Rogue River Hwy. ✆ 541/479-3938. Reservations recommended. Main courses $6–$12 lunch, $10–$30 dinner. AE, MC, V. Mon–Thurs 11am–3:30pm and 4–9pm; Fri–Sat 11am–3:30pm and 4–10pm; Sun 10am–3:30pm and 4–9pm.

Summer Jo's Farm, Garden & Restaurant ⚓⚓ *Finds* STEAK/SEAFOOD Located out in the country on an organic farm growing flowers, herbs, and vegetables, this casual restaurant provides a glimpse of the good life, Grants Pass style. If you like gardens, you'll especially enjoy a meal here in high summer when the gardens are bursting with life and color. The cafe also uses organically grown herbs and produce from the surrounding farm. With the exception of the creative vegetarian cuisine, dishes tend toward the traditional. Brunch is served inside or outside on the lawn.

2315 Upper River Rd. Loop. ✆ **541/476-6882**. www.summerjo.com. Reservations recommended. Main courses $11–$15 brunch, $15–$29 dinner. AE, MC, V. Wed–Sat 9:30am–2pm and 5–8:30pm; Sun 9:30am–2pm. Closed Jan. Drive west on G St. and look for the sign; it's 1½ miles from downtown Grants Pass.

4 Oregon Caves National Monument & the Illinois Valley

Cave Junction: 30 miles SW of Grants Pass, 56 miles NE of Crescent City

For many people, U.S. 199 is simply the road to the redwoods from southern Oregon. However, this remote stretch of highway passes through the Illinois Valley and skirts the Siskiyou Mountains, two areas that offer quite a few recreational activities. The Illinois River, which flows into the Rogue River, is an even wilder river than the Rogue, and experienced paddlers looking for real white-water adventures often run its Class V waters. Because the Siskiyou Mountains are among the oldest in Oregon, they support a unique plant community. These mountains are also known for their rugged, rocky peaks, which, though not very high, can be very impressive.

In 2002, a huge forest fire ravaged much of the forest in this area. However, in some areas, the fire only cleared out the underbrush and left the mature trees undamaged. If you are planning on doing hiking around here, be sure to check the status of the area in which you plan to hike.

ESSENTIALS

GETTING THERE   Cave Junction is on U.S. 199 between Grants Pass and the California state line. Oregon Caves National Monument is 20 miles outside Cave Junction on Ore. 46.

VISITOR INFORMATION   For more information on this area, contact the **Illinois River Valley Visitor Center,** 201 Caves Hwy., Cave Junction, OR 97523 (✆ **541/592-4076**).

EXPLORING THE CAVES

Great Cats World Park   With tigers, leopards, cougars, and other exotic wild cats, this 10-acre wildlife park is the newest such establishment to open here in southern Oregon. Interactive programs allow visitors to watch as big cats demonstrate their hunting skills. In addition to the big cats, there are many other wild animals here, from a red-tailed boa to tarantulas.

27919 Redwood Hwy., Cave Junction. © 541/592-2957. www.greatcatsworldpark.com. Admission $10 adults, $8 seniors, $7 children ages 4–12. Mar–Oct daily 10am–6pm; Feb and Nov Sat–Sun 11am–6pm. Located 1¼ miles south of Cave Junction on U.S. 199.

Oregon Caves National Monument 🐾   High in the rugged Siskiyou Mountains, a clear mountain stream cascades through a narrow canyon, and here stands one of southern Oregon's oldest attractions. Known as the marble halls of Oregon and first discovered in 1874, the caves, which stretch for 3 miles under the mountain, were formed by water seeping through marble bedrock. The slight acidity of the water dissolves the marble, which is later redeposited as beautiful stalactites, stalagmites, draperies, soda straws, columns, and flowstone. Guided tours of the caves take about 1½ hours, and up above ground there are several miles of hiking trails that start near the cave entrance. Bear in mind that children under 42 inches tall are not allowed on tours, but there are sometimes special tours for small children; call for information. To reach the monument, take Ore. 46 out of Cave Junction and follow the signs.

19000 Caves Hwy. © 541/592-2100. www.nps.gov/orca. Admission $8 adults, $5.50 children under 17. Cave tours mid-Mar to late May and mid-Oct to late Nov daily 10am–4pm; late May to mid-June and Labor Day to mid-Oct daily 9am–5pm; mid-June to early Sept daily 9am–6pm. Closed late Nov to mid-Mar.

OTHER THINGS TO SEE & DO IN THE ILLINOIS VALLEY

The Illinois River, when it isn't raging through rock-choked canyons, creates some of the best **swimming holes** in the state. Try the waters at Illinois River Forks State Park, just outside Cave Junction, or ask at the **Illinois Valley Ranger District,** 26568 Redwood Hwy., Cave Junction, OR 97523 (© **541/592-4000;** www.fs.fed.us/r6/siskiyou), for directions to other good swimming holes in the area. At this ranger station, you can also pick up information and directions for **hiking trails** in the Siskiyous, where the 180,000-acre Kalmiopsis Wilderness is a destination for backpackers. Unfortunately, this wilderness was the site of the huge Biscuit Fire in 2002. This massive blaze burned the entire wilderness and other adjacent forests. Because some areas survived the fire better than others, it is important to check with the ranger station about conditions of trails before heading out hiking.

To learn more about the history of the region, drop by the **Kerbyville Museum,** 24195 Redwood Hwy., Kerby (© **541/592-5252**). The museum is usually open Monday through Friday from 10am to 3pm, and admission is $5 for adults and $4 for seniors.

WINE TOURING

The Cave Junction area is one of the warmest regions of Oregon and consequently produces some of the best cabernet sauvignons and merlots in the state. This is about as far south as you can get and still claim to be producing Oregon wines—just a few more miles and you're in California (though it's still a long way to Napa Valley).

Bear Creek Winery   This winery is affiliated with the nearby Bridgeview Winery and is home to one of the oldest vineyards in Oregon. The winery produces a wide range of reds and whites and can sometimes have some very good deals.

6220 Caves Hwy., Cave Junction. © 541/592-3977. www.sv-wine.com. Memorial Day to Labor Day daily noon–5pm. From Cave Junction, drive east on Ore. 46 to just past the 2nd turnoff for Holland Loop Rd.

Bridgeview ✛ Best known for its distinctive blue bottles, Bridgeview is one of the largest wineries in the state and produces primarily inexpensive white wines. This place is not for wine snobs, but for those who enjoy a pleasant glass of wine with dinner. The tasting room boasts an idyllic setting beside a large pond that is stocked with trout. (Don't forget to feed them.) Whites are usually under $10, while most reds tend to be around $20.

4210 Holland Loop Rd. ✆ 877/273-4843 or 541/592-4688. www.bridgeviewwine.com. Daily 11am–5pm. From Cave Junction, go east on Ore. 46 and turn right on Holland Loop Rd.

Foris ✛ Full-bodied and complex red wines are the hallmark of Foris Vineyards Winery. The pinot noir, and cabernet sauvignon/merlot/cabernet Franc blend can be outstanding. They also do very good chardonnay, a popular and inexpensive pinot gris, and even a port. Lots of good values here.

654 Kendall Rd., Cave Junction. ✆ 800/843-6747. www.foriswine.com. Daily 11am–5pm. Closed major holidays.

WHERE TO STAY

Chateau at the Oregon Caves ✛
A narrow road winds for 20 miles south from Cave Junction into the Rogue River–Siskiyou National Forest, climbing through deep forests before finally coming to an end in a narrow, steep-walled canyon. At the very head of this canyon stands the Oregon Caves Chateau, a rustic six-story lodge built in 1934. The lodge has thick bark siding, and inside the lobby there are two marble fireplaces and huge fir beams supporting the ceiling. Because the lodge is in a wooded canyon, there are no sweeping vistas. Guest rooms aren't nearly as grand as the lobby, but do have the original Monterey-style furnishings and a rustic mountain-lodge character. A 1930s-style soda fountain (an absolute classic) serves burgers, shakes, and other simple meals, while in the main dining room steak and seafood dinners are available.

P.O. Box 1824, Cave Junction, OR 97523. ✆ 541/592-3400. www.oregoncavesoutfitters.com. 23 units. $80–$105 double; $125–$135 suite. MC, V. Closed late Oct to early May. **Amenities:** 2 restaurants (steak/seafood, American). *In room:* No phone.

Out 'n' About Treehouse Treesort ✛ *Finds*
This is by far the most unusual accommodation in southern Oregon: a complex of treehouses. Choices include a Tree Room Schoolhouse, the Swiss Family Complex (complete with swinging bridge to the kids' room), the Peacock Perch, the Cabintree (actually a landlocked cabin), a saloon-style treehouse, and a "Cavaltree" fort (big hit with kids). The Tree Room Schoolhouse has a bathroom and the Treezebo and Forestree have a toilet and sink. Despite the address, Out 'n' About is actually located in the community of Takilma.

300 Page Creek Rd., Cave Junction, OR 97523. ✆ 541/592-2208. www.treehouses.com. 11 units. $110–$200 double. 2- to 3-night minimum. Rates include full breakfast. AE, DISC, MC, V. **Amenities:** Outdoor pool; horseback riding. *In room:* No phone.

CAMPGROUNDS

Although there are no campgrounds in Oregon Caves National Monument, there are a couple of national-forest campgrounds nearby. On the road to the national monument, you'll find **Grayback Campground** and **Cave Creek Campground,** both of which are in forest settings on creek banks.

WHERE TO DINE

Wild River Brewing & Pizza Company ✛ *Finds* PIZZA/DELI
If you're a fan of microbrewery ales, a pleasant surprise awaits you in the crossroads community of Cave

Junction. This very casual combination pizza parlor and deli also happens to be a respectable little brewery specializing in British ales. The rich and flavorful ales go great with the pizzas. For fans of the unusual, there's a pizza with smoked sausage and sauerkraut and another with avocado and sprouts.

249 N. Redwood Hwy. © **541/592-3556.** www.wildriverbrewing.com. Sandwiches $3.50–$5.50; pizzas $4–$20. DISC, MC, V. Mon–Thurs 11:30am–9:30 or 10pm; Fri 11:30am–10pm; Sat noon–10pm; Sun noon–9:30pm.

5 The Roseburg Area: Lions & Tigers & Wineries

68 miles N of Grants Pass, 68 miles S of Eugene, 83 miles W of Crater Lake National Park

Although primarily a logging mill town, Roseburg is set at the mouth of the North Umpqua River and, consequently, is well situated for exploring one of the prettiest valleys in Oregon. The surrounding countryside bears a striking resemblance to parts of northern California, so it should come as no surprise that there are a half dozen wineries in the area. The hills south of town also look a bit like an Africa savanna, which may be why the Wildlife Safari park is located here. Today this drive-through wildlife park is one of the biggest attractions in southern Oregon. In downtown Roseburg, you'll find numerous old Victorian homes, and a drive through these old neighborhoods will be interesting for fans of late-19th-century architecture.

ESSENTIALS

GETTING THERE   Roseburg is right on I-5 at the junction with Ore. 138, which leads east up the North Umpqua River to Crater Lake National Park.

VISITOR INFORMATION   For more information on this area, contact the **Roseburg Visitors & Convention Bureau,** 410 SE Spruce St. (P.O. Box 1262), Roseburg, OR 97470 (© **800/444-9584** or 541/672-9731; www.visitroseburg.com).

WHAT TO SEE & DO: LOCAL HISTORY & A WILDLIFE PARK

Douglas County Museum of History & Natural History ⊛   South of town at the Douglas County Fairgrounds, you'll find this surprisingly well-designed museum. It is housed in an unusual, large building that resembles an old mining structure or mill. Inside are displays on the history and natural history of the region. Pioneer farming and mining displays interpret the settlement of the region, but it's the very large elk that really grabs people's attention. Interesting traveling exhibits often show up here, so it's worth checking to see what is scheduled.

123 Museum Dr. (exit 123 off I-5). © **541/957-7007.** www.co.douglas.or.us/museum. $3.50 adults, $1 children 4–17. Mon–Fri 9am–5pm; Sat 10am–5pm; Sun noon–5pm. Closed Thanksgiving, Christmas, New Year's Day, and Easter.

Wildlife Safari ⊛⊛ (Kids)   This 600-acre drive-through nature park is home to wild animals from around the world. You'll come face-to-face with curious bears, grazing gazelles and zebras, ostriches, and even lumbering elephants and rhinos. You can also visit the educational center or attend an animal show. Convertibles are not allowed in the lion, cheetah, or bear enclosures.

Off Ore. 42, just outside Winston (south of Roseburg). © **541/679-6761.** www.wildlifesafari.org. Admission summer $18 adults, $15 seniors, $12 children 4–12, free for children under 4; other months admission discounted $3. Spring–fall daily 9am–5pm; winter daily 10am–4pm. Closed Christmas.

THE NEARBY HISTORIC TOWN OF OAKLAND

About 15 miles north of Roseburg is the historic town of Oakland, which is listed on the National Register of Historic Places. The town was founded in the 1850s, and most of the buildings date from the 1890s. Soaking up the atmosphere on a stroll through town is a pleasant way to spend a morning or an afternoon. You can pick up a self-guided walking-tour map at the **Oakland Museum**, 130 Locust St. (© **541/ 459-4531**), which is housed in an 1893 brick building and contains collections of historic photos, old farm tools, household furnishings, and clothing from Oakland's past. Admission is by suggested $2 donation, and the museum is open daily from 12:30 to 3:30pm.

WINE TOURING

The Roseburg area is home to more than half a dozen wineries, all of which are located within a few miles of I-5.

Abacela Winery 𝕬𝕬 This winery produces some of the best red wines in Oregon and has become so popular in the past few years that they have begun releasing their wines when they are still quite young. Tempranillo is the specialty, but they also do an excellent Syrah, and their Dolcetto always sells out quickly. Don't miss this one.

12500 Lookingglass Rd., Roseburg. © 541/679-6642. www.abacela.com. Daily 11am–5pm. Take exit 119 off I-5, drive west 2 miles, turn right on Lookingglass Rd., and continue 2 miles.

Champagne Creek Cellars The tasting room at this winery is housed in a beautifully weathered old barn set in a grove of shady oak trees, and although the winery produces some decent inexpensive white wines, you'll have to spend $20 or more to get a good red wine here.

340 Busenbark Lane, Roseburg. © 800/WINE-4-US or 541/673-7901. www.champagnecreek.com. Daily 11am– 6pm. From Roseburg, go west on Garden Valley Rd., and turn left on Melrose Rd.

Girardet Wine Cellars & Vineyard 𝕬 Although this winery is unique in Oregon for producing such obscure wines as Baco Noir and Seyval Blanc, Girardet is best known for its big, bold red wines, which include the unusual Marechal Foch.

895 Reston Rd., Roseburg. © 541/679-7252. www.girardetwine.com. Daily 11am–5pm. Closed major holidays. Take Ore. 42 (exit 119) west from I-5 south of Roseburg, go 9 miles, and turn right on Reston Rd. (before Tenmile).

Henry Estate Winery This winery on the bank of the Umpqua River produces a wide range of wines, which are generally not very remarkable. However, they do on occasion produce decent pinot noir. Grapes are grown on a special trellising system known as a Scott Henry trellis, named for the winery's founder and now used all over the world.

687 Hubbard Creek Rd., Umpqua. © 800/782-2686 or 541/459-5120. www.henryestate.com. Daily 11am–5pm. Closed major holidays. From exit 136 off I-5 at Sutherlin, go west on through Umpqua and cross the Umpqua River.

Hillcrest Vineyard 𝕬𝕬 This winery is worth seeking out if for no other reason than that it's Oregon's oldest continuously operating winery producing wines from vinifera (European) grapes. Vineyards here were first planted in 1961. The current owners of the winery, Dyson and Susan DeMara, are producing the best wines in southern Oregon and are slowly going through the old wines that were on hand when they bought the winery.

240 Vineyard Lane. © 541/673-3709. Daily 11am–5pm. From Roseburg, go west on Garden Valley Rd., and turn left on Melrose Rd., right on Doerner Rd., right onto Elgarose Rd., and left onto Vineyard Lane.

MarshAnne Landing Winery Located outside the historic town of Oakland on the site of a former stagecoach stop, this winery specializes in Bordeaux and Rhone varietals. Despite the flying saucers on the labels, the winery's name is a reference to owners Gregory Marsh and Frances Anne Cramer.

381 Hogan Rd., Oakland. ℭ **541/459-8497.** www.marshannelanding.com. Memorial Day weekend to Labor Day weekend Sat–Sun 11am–5pm; other times by appointment. Take exit 142 (Metz Hill) off I-5, drive east on Goodrich Hwy. to a right onto Hogan Rd.

Melrose Vineyards   With its tasting room in a converted 100-year-old barn, this vineyard has for many years sold grapes to other Oregon wineries. Today they're busy producing decent wines from their own grapes. Prices are reasonable for most of their wines. Their merlot can be quite good.

885 Melqua Rd., Roseburg. ℭ **541/672-6080.** www.melrosevineyards.com. Apr–Dec daily 11am–5pm; Jan–Mar by appointment. From Roseburg, go west on Garden Valley Rd., turn left on Melrose Rd., continue almost to the community of Melrose, and turn right on Melqua Rd.

Palotai Vineyard and Winery   Here at this little family-run winery you can sample the wines of Hungarian-born Gabor Palotai, who learned winemaking in the Old World. There's a wide range of wines available here, including Palotai's version of Hungary's popular "Bull's Blood" red wine.

272 Capital Lane, Roseburg. ℭ **541/464-8127.** Apr–Dec Fri–Sun 11am–5pm. From Roseburg, go west several miles on Garden Valley Rd., and turn left on Old Garden Valley Rd.

Spangler Vineyards   This small winery, formerly La Garza Cellars, just off I-5 is very convenient if you just want to make a quick foray into the world of Oregon wines. They specialize in cabernet sauvignon but also do a dry Riesling. The reserve cabernets (around $25) can be excellent, and they are among the best you'll find from the state.

491 Winery Lane, Roseburg. ℭ **541/679-9654.** www.spanglervineyards.com. May–Oct Tues–Sun 11am–5pm; Nov–Apr Thurs–Sun 11am–5pm. 5 miles south of Roseburg, take exit 119 off I-5 and go west a half mile.

WHERE TO STAY
IN ROSEBURG

Holiday Inn Express ☏   Although located just off I-5, this modern economy hotel also happens to sit on the banks of the Umpqua River, and every room has a balcony and a view of the river. The Jacuzzi is set in a gazebo amid green lawns between the hotel building and the river. Downtown Roseburg and a couple of good restaurants are a short walk away.

375 W. Harvard Blvd., Roseburg, OR 97470. ℭ **800/898-7666** or 541/673-7517. Fax 541/673-8331. www.hi express.com. 100 units. $85–$139 double. Rates include continental breakfast. AE, DC, DISC, MC, V. Pets accepted ($5 fee). **Amenities:** Indoor pool; exercise room; Jacuzzi; business center; guest laundry. *In room:* A/C, TV, dataport, coffeemaker, hair dryer, iron, Wi-Fi.

WHERE TO DINE
IN ROSEBURG

Dino's Ristorante Italiano ☏ ITALIAN   Ask anyone in Roseburg where to get the best meal in town, and they'll invariably send you to Dino's, a little Italian restaurant in downtown Roseburg. Dino, the restaurant's owner and ultimate Italian host, is not only the area's most respected restaurateur but also a winemaker, producing decent wines at his own winery (which is not open to the public). This is a good place for a romantic dinner or simply to satisfy your Italian-food cravings with the likes of portobello-and-ricotta ravioli or lasagna Bolognese.

404 SE Jackson St. ℭ **541/673-0848.** Main courses $12–$18. AE, DISC, MC, V. Mon–Sat 5–9pm.

McMenamins Roseburg Station Pub & Brewery ⚘ PUB Another jewel in the McMenamins brewpub crown, the Roseburg Station Pub is a good example of how McMenamins breathes new life into historic buildings. This restored train station celebrates Roseburg's rail culture and is a casual place for dinner and a microbrew. An eclectic collection of chandeliers decorates the 16-foot ceiling, and street signs from around the world punctuate the room. A straightforward menu features burgers, sandwiches, and a handful of more creative entrees. Be sure to accompany your meal with one of the craft ales for which the McMenamins pubs are famous.

700 Sheridan St. ✆ 541/672-1934. www.mcmenamins.com. Main courses $5.25–$15. AE, DISC, MC, V. Mon–Thurs 11am–11pm; Fri–Sat 11am–midnight; Sun noon–10pm.

IN OAKLAND

Tolly's ⚘ *Kids* SODA FOUNTAIN/REGIONAL AMERICAN Since 1964, folks from all over the region have been stopping at Tolly's in downtown Oakland to have dinner or sometimes just a root-beer float or sundae. Housed in a storefront on Locust Street, Tolly's is both an elegant restaurant and an old-fashioned soda fountain. You can hop onto a stool at the counter and sip a cold malted milk shake in a tall glass, or linger over a dinner of steak or perfectly prepared salmon. Check out the case for deliciously decadent desserts.

115 Locust St., Oakland. ✆ 541/459-3796. www.tollysrestaurant.com. Reservations recommended for dinner. Main courses lunch $8–$14, dinner $18–$28. AE, DC, MC, V. Mon–Tues 10am–2:30pm; Wed–Sat 8:30am–9pm; Sun 8:30am–5pm.

NORTH OF ROSEBURG: A SERIOUS ICE-CREAM STOP

Consider yourself very lucky if you happen to be driving north from Roseburg on I-5 on a hot summer day. Respite from the heat lies just off the interstate at the Rice Hill exit ramp, at legendary **K&R Drive Inn** (✆ **541/849-2570**), where every scoop of ice cream you order is actually a double scoop! Remember this before you order two scoops of Rocky Road. The K&R is open daily from 10am to 9pm in summer, daily from 10:30am to 8pm in winter.

11

Central Oregon

On the west side of the Cascade Range, rain is as certain as death and taxes. But cross the dividing line formed by the mountains and you leave the deluge behind and enter the region known as central Oregon. The term "central Oregon" is a bit of a misnomer. It does not so much refer to a geographical area as to a recreational region, and it doesn't actually lie in the central part of the state. It does, however, bask under blue skies nearly 300 days of the year—in fact, central Oregon gets so little rain that parts of the region are considered high desert. Such a natural attraction is a constant enticement for Oregonians living west of the Cascades. In summer, people head to central Oregon for golfing, hiking, fishing, rafting, and camping, and in winter they descend on the ski slopes of Mount Bachelor, Oregon's best ski resort.

All this popularity is due to the Cascade Range, which causes a climatological rain-shadow effect that creates a distinct and visible dividing line between the wet west side and the dry east side. Ponderosa pines, rather than Douglas firs and western red cedars, dominate the eastern foothill forests of this region. Farther east, where there is even less annual rainfall, juniper and sagebrush country takes over. It is this classically Western environment that has in part led to the adoption of a Wild West theme in the town of Sisters, which has covered wooden sidewalks and false-fronted buildings (albeit in modern pastel colors).

On closer inspection, however, it becomes evident that it is more than just a lack of rainfall that sets this region apart. Central Oregon's unique volcanic geography provides the scenic backdrop to the region's many recreational activities. Obsidian flows, lava caves, cinder cones, pumice deserts—these are the sorts of features that make the central Oregon landscape unique.

Despite the region's volcanic legacy, the greens and fairways of the region's many golf courses are what come to mind when many people think of central Oregon. The abundant sunshine here has made this area home to most of the state's golf resorts. Between Kah-Nee-Ta in the north and Sunriver in the south, there are half a dozen major golf resorts and dozens of golf courses.

Despite the dryness of the landscape here, water is one of the region's primary recreational draws. The Deschutes River is the state's most popular rafting river, and is fabled among fly anglers for its steelhead runs and its wild red-side rainbow trout. West of Bend, a scenic highway loops past a dozen or so lakes, each with its own unique character and appeal. Closer to Bend, the Deschutes River cascades over ancient lava flows, forming impressive waterfalls that are favorite destinations of area hikers.

However, for solitude and scenic grandeur, most hikers and backpackers head out from Sisters and Bend into the Three Sisters Wilderness, which encompasses its snow-clad namesake peaks. Outside the wilderness, there are also many miles of mountain-biking trails that have made the Bend and Sisters areas

Central Oregon & North Central Oregon

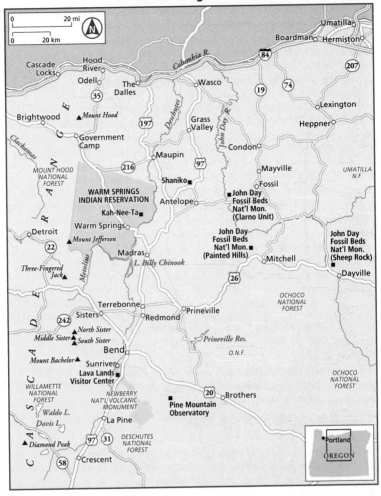

the best mountain-biking destination in the state.

Although the open slopes of Mount Bachelor ski area attract the most visitors in the winter, the area also has many miles of cross-country ski trails, including the state's finest Nordic center (at Mount Bachelor, of course). Snowmobiling is also very popular.

1 North Central Oregon & the Lower Deschutes River

Maupin: 95 miles N of Bend, 100 miles E of Portland, 40 miles S of The Dalles

Dominated by two rivers—the Deschutes and the John Day—north central Oregon is the driest, most desertlike part of this region. It is also the closest sunny-side destination for rain-soaked Portlanders, which has long made it a popular spot for weekend getaways.

Hot springs, canyon lands, and some of the best rafting and fishing in the state are the main draws in this part of central Oregon. For many visitors, the high-desert landscape is a fascinating change from the lushness of the west side of the Cascades. For others it is just too bleak and barren. But there is no denying that the Deschutes River is one of the busiest rivers in the state. Rafters and anglers descend en masse throughout the year—especially in summer—to challenge the rapids and the red-side trout under sunny skies.

Even if the Deschutes is not your primary destination, this region has several unusual attractions that make it worthwhile for a weekend's exploration. First and foremost of these is the Kah-Nee-Ta Resort, which, with its warm-spring swimming pool and its proximity to Portland, is a powerful enticement after several months of gray skies and constant drizzle west of the Cascades.

Not far from the resort, in the town of Warm Springs, is a fascinating modern museum dedicated to the cultures of Northwest Native Americans. A forgotten page of pioneer days can be found at nearby Shaniko, a ghost town that once made it big as a wool-shipping town. Much older history, up to 40 million years of it, is laid bare in the three units of the John Day Fossil Beds National Monument. If the stark hills of the national monument don't give you enough sense of being in the desert, be sure to visit The Cove Palisades State Park, where three steep-walled canyons have been flooded by the waters of Lake Billy Chinook.

ESSENTIALS

GETTING THERE   Maupin, which is the staging site for most rafting and fishing trips on the lower Deschutes River, is at the junction of U.S. 197, the main route from The Dalles south to Bend, and Ore. 216, which connects to U.S. 26 east of Mount Hood.

VISITOR INFORMATION   For more information on this area, contact the **Greater Maupin Area Chamber of Commerce,** P.O. Box 220, Maupin, OR 97037 (© **541/395-2599;** www.maupinoregon.com).

RAFTING, FISHING & OTHER AQUATIC ACTIVITIES

Flowing through a dry sagebrush canyon lined with basalt cliffs, the lower Deschutes River, from the U.S. 26 bridge outside Warm Springs down to the Columbia River, is one of the most popular stretches of white water in Oregon. This section of the river provides lots of Class III rapids, and 1-day **rafting trips** here are very popular. However, at almost 100 miles in length, the lower Deschutes also provides several options for multiday rafting trips.

Popular 1-day splash-and-giggle trips, which are offered by dozens of rafting companies, usually start just upstream from Maupin and end just above the impressive Sherar's Falls. Some companies also offer 2- and 3-day trips. Rafting companies operating on the lower Deschutes River include **All Star Rafting** (© **800/909-7238;** www.asrk.com), which also rents rafts and offers kayaking lessons; **Imperial River Company** (© **800/395-3903** or 541/395-2404; www.deschutesriver.com), which operates a bed-and-breakfast inn for rafters in Maupin; and **Rapid River Rafters** (© **800/962-3327** or 541/382-1514; www.rapidriverrafters.com). Expect to pay around $65 to $90 for a day trip up to around $335 to $350 for a 3-day trip.

If you're just passing through the region but would like to catch a glimpse of some of the lower Deschutes River's more dramatic sections, you can visit **Sherar's Falls,** which are at the Sherar Bridge on Ore. 216, between Tygh Valley and Grass Valley. Native Americans can sometimes be seen dip-netting salmon from the waters of these falls, which can also be reached by following the river road north from Maupin for 8 miles. Just west of Sherar Bridge, you'll also find **White River Falls State Park,** where there are more waterfalls.

The stretch of the Deschutes River from Pelton Dam to the Columbia River is one of Oregon's most legendary stretches of **fishing** water and is managed primarily for wild steelhead and the famed red-side rainbow trout. Together these two types of fish provide fly anglers with nearly year-round action. From the mouth of the river upstream to several miles above Maupin, there are several good access points. Fly-fishing supplies and equipment rentals are available in Maupin at the **Deschutes Canyon Fly Shop,** 599 S. U.S. 197, Maupin (© **541/395-2565;** www.flyfishingdeschutes.com).

Twelve miles south of Madras, you'll find one of the most unlikely settings in the state. **Lake Billy Chinook,** an artificial lake created by the construction of Round Butte Dam in 1964, fills the canyons of the Metolius, Crooked, and Deschutes rivers, and seems lifted straight out of the canyon lands of Arizona or Utah. Here, nearly vertical basalt cliffs rise several hundred feet above the lake waters, and sagebrush and junipers cling to the rocky hillsides. The lake is most popular with water-skiers and anglers who come to fish for kokanee (landlocked sockeye salmon) and bull trout (also known as dolly vardens). **The Cove Palisades State Park** (© **541/546-3412**), which is on the south shore, offers easy 3-hour sea-kayak tours of the lake. These tours are offered throughout the summer. Tours cost $10 for adults and $7 for children under 14; reservations are recommended. At the state park, you'll also find boat ramps, a marina, campgrounds, picnic areas, and swimming beaches. There are even houseboats for rent (see below), and at the marina you'll find a restaurant atop a hill overlooking the lake. The park day-use fee is $3.

A NATIVE AMERICAN HERITAGE MUSEUM

The Museum at Warm Springs 🏚🏚 (Finds) For thousands of years the Warm Springs, Wasco, and Paiute tribes have inhabited this region and adapted to its environment. At this fascinating, don't-miss museum, you'll learn the history of these peoples. Designed to resemble a traditional encampment and accented by architectural details drawn from the cultures of the three tribes, the museum houses the tribes' outstanding collection of regional Native American artifacts. To better display these artifacts, various styles of traditional houses have been reconstructed at the museum and serve as backdrops for displays on everything from basketry and beadwork to fishing and root gathering. Temporary exhibits, including exhibitions of Native American artwork, fill out the main collection and focus on specific topics.

2189 U.S. 26, Warm Springs. © 541/553-3331. www.warmsprings.biz/museum. Admission $6 adults, $5 seniors, $4.50 students, $3 children 5–12. Daily 9am–5pm (closed Mon–Tues in winter). Closed Thanksgiving, Christmas, and New Year's Day.

A GHOST TOWN & A FOSSIL EXCURSION

Between 1900 and 1911, **Shaniko** was the largest wool-shipping center in the country, and it claims to have been the site of the last range war between cattle ranchers and sheepherders. However, when the railroad line from the Columbia River down to Bend bypassed Shaniko, the town fell on hard times. Eventually, when a flood washed out the railroad spur into town, Shaniko nearly ceased to exist. Today the false-fronted buildings and wooden sidewalks make this Oregon's favorite and liveliest ghost town.

Antiques shops, a wedding chapel, and a historic hotel make for a fun excursion or overnight getaway.

The **John Day Fossil Beds National Monument,** 32651 Ore. 19, Kimberly, OR 97848 (© **541/987-2333;** www.nps.gov/joda), consisting of three individual units separated by as much as 85 miles, preserves a 40-million-year fossil record indicating that this region was once a tropical or subtropical forest. From tiny seeds to extinct relatives of rhinoceroses and elephants, an amazing array of plants and animals has been preserved in one of the world's most extensive and unbroken fossil records.

To see fossil leaves, twigs, branches, and nuts in their natural state, visit the **Clarno Unit** (© 541/763-2203), 23 miles southeast of Shaniko and U.S. 97. Here, ancient mudflows inundated a forest, and today these ancient mudflows appear as eroding cliffs, at the base of which a quarter-mile trail leads past numerous fossils. Although you can't collect fossils in the national monument, you can dig them up behind the Wheeler High School in the small town of **Fossil,** 20 miles east of the Clarno Unit. From the Clarno Unit, it is an 85-mile drive on Ore. 218 and Ore. 19 to the national monument's **Sheep Rock Unit,** which is the site of the monument's **Thomas Condon Paleontology Center** and the **James Cant Ranch** visitor center and ranch museum. Here you can get a close-up look at numerous fossils and sometimes watch a paleontologist at work. The visitor center is open daily in summer from 8:30am to 5pm; spring and fall, it's open daily from 8:30am to 4:30pm (closed holidays Thanksgiving to Feb). The James Cant Ranch is open Monday through Thursday from 8:30am to 4:30pm. Just north of the visitor center you'll pass **Blue Basin,** where there's an interpretive trail.

From the Sheep Rock Unit, the monument's **Painted Hills Unit** (© 541/462-3961), along the John Day River near Mitchell, is another 30 miles west on U.S. 26. You won't see any fossils here, but you will see strikingly colored rounded hills that are favorites of photographers. The weathering of volcanic ash under different climatic conditions created the bands of color on these hills.

WHERE TO STAY & DINE

In addition to the resort and the historic hotel listed below, you'll find three modern log cabins for rent on the shore of Lake Billy Chinook at **The Cove Palisades State Park.** These cabins rent for $70 per night for up to five people ($48 Oct–Apr) and are right beside the water. For reservations, contact **ReserveAmerica** (© **800/452-5687;** www.reserveamerica.com). Houseboats are also available for rent at Lake Billy Chinook. Contact **Cove Palisades Marina** (© 541/546-3521; www.covepalisadesmarina. com), for $2,195 to $6,995 per week in summer (lower rates in spring and fall), or **Lake Billy Chinook Houseboats,** P.O. Box 1921, Redmond, OR 97756 (© **866/ 546-2939** or 541/504-5951; www.lakebillychinook.com), for $1,650 to $2,575 per week.

Hotel Condon 🏵 Although the town of Condon is way off the beaten path, it is fairly convenient if you have spent the day visiting different units of the John Day Fossil Beds National Monument. This restored historic hotel in downtown Condon has a classic small-town feel, but guest rooms have modern furnishings and good beds. Within the hotel, you'll find one of Condon's best restaurants and a lounge designed to resemble a saloon.

202 S. Main St., Condon, OR 97823. © **800/201-6706** or 541/384-4624. www.hotelcondon.com. 18 units. Apr 15–Dec 31 $70–$90 double, $95–$105 suite; Jan 1–Apr 14 $55–$75 double, $75–$85 suite. Rates include continental breakfast. Children 6 and under stay free in parent's room. AE, DISC, MC, V. Pets accepted. **Amenities:** Restaurant (American); lounge; concierge; business center; room service. *In room:* A/C, TV, hair dryer, iron, high-speed Internet access.

Tips Travelers' Tip

For reservations at Forest Service campgrounds, contact the **National Recreation Reservation Service** (© **877/444-6777**; www.reserveusa.com).

Imperial River Company   Popular primarily with people heading out rafting on the Deschutes River, this lodge may not be your classic B&B, but it is the most comfortable place for many miles around. Guest rooms, all of which have private entrances, sport Oregon themes and have handmade quilts on the beds. The riverview rooms are the best and have whirlpool tubs. Dinner is available, and meals feature local beef and lamb. Imperial River Company also offers a wide variety of rafting trips.

304 Bakeoven Rd., Maupin, OR 97037. © 800/395-3903 or 541/395-2404. Fax 541/395-2494. www.deschutes river.com. 25 units. Apr–Thanksgiving $75–$110 double, $150 suite; Thanksgiving–Mar $50–$70 double, $125 suite. Rates include full breakfast (except in winter). Children under 6 stay free in parent's room. AE, DISC, MC, V. Pets accepted ($10). **Amenities:** Restaurant (American/Northwest); lounge. *In room:* A/C.

Kah-Nee-Ta High Desert Resort & Casino ★★ (Kids   Located 120 miles from Portland and set in a remote high-desert canyon, Kah-Nee-Ta Resort, operated by the Confederated Tribes of the Warm Springs Reservation, is the closest sunny-side resort to rain-soaked Portland. The main attraction here is the resort's huge warm-springs-fed main swimming pool (fed by the spring for which the Warm Springs Reservation is named). Because Kah-Nee-Ta offers a wide range of activities and accommodations, it is particularly popular with families, who tend to stay in the resort's large and modern mountain-lodge-style "Village" rooms, which are located beside the main pool. Couples tend to opt for rooms in the main lodge, which is set high on a hillside adjacent to the resort's casino. Rooms here are quite a bit nicer than at resorts in the Sisters area. Down by the main pool, you'll also find teepees and RV sites. The main dining room has a great view and serves creative Northwest dishes. Salmon bakes and Native American dance performances are all part of a stay here.

P.O. Box 1240, Warm Springs, OR 97761. © 800/554-4786 or 541/553-1112. www.kahneeta.com. 169 units (plus 20 teepees). $89–$166 double; $182–$306 suite or cottage; $73 teepee (for 3 people). Children under 14 stay free in parent's room. AE, DC, DISC, MC, V. **Amenities:** 2 restaurants (American/Northwest, American); lounge; casino; 2 outdoor pools; 18-hole golf course and miniature golf; 2 tennis courts; 2 exercise rooms; full-service spa; 3 Jacuzzis; sauna; kayak rentals and white-water-rafting trips; bike rentals; horseback riding; children's programs; game room; courtesy resort shuttle; massage; coin-op laundry. *In room:* A/C, TV, coffeemaker, hair dryer, iron.

CAMPGROUNDS

Downriver from Sherar's Falls, there are many undeveloped campsites along the Deschutes River. At Lake Billy Chinook, west of U.S. 97 between Madras and Redmond, there are several campgrounds. The most developed are the two at **The Cove Palisades State Park.** Reservations can be made through **ReserveAmerica** (© **800/452-5687;** www.reserveamerica.com). Farther west, up the Metolius arm of the reservoir on F.S. Road 64, you'll find the Forest Service's primitive **Perry South Campground.** A little bit farther west is the **Monty Campground,** which is the lowermost campground on the Metolius River's free-flowing waters.

2 The Sisters Area

108 miles SE of Salem, 92 miles NE of Eugene, 21 miles NW of Bend

Lying at the eastern foot of the Cascades, the small town of Sisters takes its name from the nearby Three Sisters mountains, which loom majestically over the town. Ponderosa pine forests, aspen groves, and wide meadows and pastures surround Sisters, giving it a classic Western setting that the town has taken to heart. Today, Sisters is designed to resemble an old cow town; modern buildings sport false fronts and covered sidewalks. However the predominantly pastel color schemes are more 1990s than 1890s.

Once just someplace to stop for gas on the way to Bend, Sisters is now a destination in itself. A few miles outside of town is the Black Butte Resort, one of the state's finest golf resorts, and also nearby is the tiny community of Camp Sherman, which has been a vacation destination for nearly a century. Sisters is also Oregon's llama capital, with numerous large llama ranches around the area.

ESSENTIALS

GETTING THERE   Sisters is at the junction of U.S. 20 (which connects I-5 near Corvallis with Bend), Ore. 126 (which links Redmond with Eugene), and Ore. 242 (the McKenzie Pass scenic highway). From the Portland area, take Ore. 22 east from Salem. Horizon and SkyWest Airlines (United Express and Delta Connection) serve **Roberts Field** (© 541/548-0646, ext. 3499; www.flyrdm.com), the Redmond airport, 20 miles east of Sisters.

VISITOR INFORMATION   Contact the **Sisters Area Chamber of Commerce,** 164 N. Elm St. (P.O. Box 430), Sisters, OR 97759 (© 541/549-0251; www.sisters chamber.com).

FESTIVALS   During the annual **Sisters Outdoor Quilt Show** on the second Saturday in July, buildings all over town are hung with quilts. The **Sisters Rodeo,** held the second weekend of June, also attracts large crowds. In early September, a mighty wind blows into town during the **Sisters Folk Festival** (© 541/549-4979; www.sistersfolk festival.com). In late September or early October, sisters get together for a weekend in Sisters during the **Sisters in Sisters Celebration** (© 541/549-0251; www.sistersin sisters.com).

ENJOYING THE OUTDOORS

Although shopping may be the number-one recreational activity right in Sisters, the surrounding lands are the town's real main attraction. Any month of the year, you'll find an amazing variety of possible activities within a few miles of town. Northwest of Sisters, in the community of Camp Sherman, is one of the area's most unusual outdoor attractions—the springs that form the **headwaters of the Metolius River.** Cold, crystal-clear waters bubble up out of the ground and, within only a few hundred yards, produce a full-blown river. Follow signs from the Camp Sherman turnoff from U.S. 20.

FLY-FISHING   If you need some fly-fishing supplies or want to hire a guide to take you out on the local waters, try **The Fly Fisher's Place,** 151 W. Main Ave., Sisters (© 541/549-3474; www.flyfishersplace.com). The folks here can guide you to the best **fly-fishing** spots on the Metolius, Deschutes, McKenzie, and Crooked rivers.

GOLFING   At **Black Butte Ranch** (© 800/399-2322 or 541/595-1500; www.black butteranch.com), west of Sisters, you'll find two courses surrounded by ponderosa

You may want to consider how you'll respond to hearing:

"We thought you were coming home yesterday."

ACTUALLY, YOU SHOULD JUST PLAN ON STAYING AN EXTRA DAY.
Whether you've been here before, or this is your first visit, we'll make you happy that you did. As the official 'brainiacs' of Bend, we know what to do, where to go, what to see, where to sleep and also what you can tell your boss if you happen to arrive back to work a day late. Our new website and downtown Visitor Center offer all the information you need to enjoy every culture-history-nature-adventure-fun-filled-day you spend here in beautiful BEND, OREGON. Yes, even that extra day.

BEND, OREGON
VISITOR
BEND
& CONVENTION BUREAU

FOR A VISITOR'S GUIDE, PLEASE CALL 877.245.8484 OR GO TO VISITBEND.COM
OUR DOWNTOWN VISITOR CENTER LOCATION: 917 NW HARRIMAN, BEND, OREGON 97701

pines and aspens (greens fees $42–$65). At **Eagle Crest,** 1522 Cline Falls Rd., Redmond (© **877/818-0286** or 541/923-4653; www.eagle-crest.com), east of Sisters, you get a more desertlike experience with junipers and sagebrush surrounding the fairways (greens fees $35–$60). There are great views at both resorts. However, the best golf value in the area is the **Crooked River Ranch Golf Course,** 5010 Clubhouse Rd., Crooked River Ranch (© **800/833-3197** or 541/923-6343; www.crookedriver ranch.com), which is northwest of Redmond off U.S. 97 and plays through and alongside a spectacular canyon (greens fees $35–$40 in summer).

HIKING West and south of Sisters, several excellent scenic trails lend themselves to both day hikes and overnight trips. Many of these trails lead into the Mount Washington, Mount Jefferson, and Three Sisters wilderness areas. Near Camp Sherman, you can hike to the summit of Black Butte for 360-degree views or hike along the spring-fed Metolius River. Farther west off U.S. 20, you'll find trails leading up to the base of craggy Three Fingered Jack. South of town there are trail heads leading into the Three Sisters Wilderness. (The Chambers Lakes area is particularly scenic.) The hike up Tam McArthur Rim is another good one if you're looking for spectacular views. Stop by the **Sisters Ranger Station,** Pine Street and U.S. 20 (© **541/549-7700;** www.fs.fed.us/r6/centraloregon), at the west end of town, for information and trail maps.

To the east of Sisters outside the town of Terrebonne, there are several miles of very scenic hiking trails within **Smith Rock State Park** (© **800/551-6949** or 541/548-7501; www.oregonstateparks.org). The park's 400-foot crags and the meandering Crooked River provide the backdrops for hikes through high desert scrublands. Hiking trails lead through the canyon and up to the top of the rocks. The view of the Cascades framed by Smith Rock is superb. There is a $3 day-use fee here.

HORSEBACK RIDING If Sisters has put you in a cowboy state of mind, you can saddle up a palomino and go for a ride at **Black Butte Stables** (© **541/595-2061;** www.oregoncowboy.com), which has stables at Black Butte Ranch west of Sisters. These stables offer a variety of rides, with an hour ride costing $35.

MOUNTAIN BIKING Sisters makes an excellent base for mountain bikers, who will find dozens of miles of trails of all skill levels within a few miles of town. In fact, one easy ride, the Sisters Bike Trail, starts only a few blocks south of downtown's many shops at the Village Green Park on Elm Street. Other fun rides include the Butte Loops Trail around Black Butte and the strenuous Green Ridge Trail. Stop by the **Sisters Ranger Station,** Pine Street and U.S. 20 (© **541/549-7700**), at the west end of town for information and trail maps. You can rent bikes in town at **Eurosports,** 182 E. Hood Ave. (© **541/549-2471**), for $18 to $30 per day.

ROCK CLIMBING Located east of Terrebonne, **Smith Rock State Park** is one of central Oregon's many geological wonders. Jagged rock formations tower above the Crooked River here and attract rock climbers from around the world. A couple of shops in the area cater primarily to climbers. If you want to learn how to climb, contact **First Ascent Climbing Services** (© **800/325-5462** or 541/548-5137; www.go climbing.com), which offers classes ($250 for an all-day private class).

OTHER AREA ATTRACTIONS

Rail-travel enthusiasts might consider an excursion on the **Crooked River Railroad Company Dinner Train,** U.S. 97 at O'Neil Road, Redmond (© **541/548-8630;**

www.crookedriverrailroad.com). The 38-mile, approximately 3-hour rail excursion travels from Redmond to Prineville and back. Restored dining cars are the setting for dinners or brunches that may feature train-robbery or murder-mystery themes. Fares are $65 to $78 for adults and $39 for children 4 through 12. Reservations are required.

Fans of folk art should be sure to stop by the **Petersen Rock Gardens & Museum,** 7930 SW 77th St., Redmond (© **541/382-5574**), 9 miles north of Bend just off U.S. 97. This 4-acre folk-art creation consists of buildings, miniature bridges, terraces, and tiny towers all constructed from rocks. The gardens, built between 1935 and 1952 by a Danish immigrant farmer, are open daily from 9am to dusk. A museum here is open daily from 9am to 5:30pm in summer and from 9am to 4:30pm in winter. Admission is $3 for adults, $1.50 for children 12 to 16, and 50¢ for children 6 to 11.

WHERE TO STAY

Black Butte Ranch ✶✶✶ (Kids)
Located 8 miles west of Sisters, the Black Butte Ranch resort community has the most breathtaking mountain views of any Central Oregon resort and is set amid aspen-ringed meadows. Add a pair of golf courses, 18 miles of paved biking/jogging paths, and lots of recreational activities and you have a great family vacation resort. The biggest drawback is that, because this is a condominium development, rooms and vacation homes here are very hit and miss. The accommodations are set amid open lawns between the forest and the meadows, and most have fireplaces and kitchens. In the majority of rooms, large decks and sliding glass doors let you enjoy the views. In the resort's main dining room, which serves good steaks, large windows provide nearly every table with a view of the mountains or adjacent lake. In winter, you're a long way from Mount Bachelor's ski slopes, though the slopes at Hoodoo Ski Area are nearby.

P.O. Box 8000, Black Butte Ranch, OR 97759. © **800/452-7455** or 541/595-6211. www.blackbutteranch.com. 124 units. May–Oct $110–$235 condo, $200–$250 cabin, $175–$390 home; Nov–Apr $85–$190 condo, $150–$200 cabin, $150–$295 home (2- to 6-night minimums July–Aug). AE, DC, DISC, MC, V. **Amenities:** 2 restaurants (American); lounge; 4 outdoor pools; 2 18-hole golf courses; 23 tennis courts; exercise room; Jacuzzi; watersports rentals; bike rentals; horseback riding; children's programs; game room; massage. *In room:* TV, dataport, coffeemaker.

Conklin's Guest House ✶✶
Surrounded by meadows and with an unobstructed view of the mountains, Conklin's B&B is an excellent choice for anyone who has become enamored of Sisters' Western charm. The inn's country decor fits right in with the town, and a duck pond and a trout pond provide a bit of a farm feel. There's even a swimming pool. Our favorite room has a big claw-foot tub surrounded by windows that look out to the Cascades. This room also has its own little balcony. Breakfast is served in a tile-floored sunroom.

69013 Camp Polk Rd., Sisters, OR 97759. © **800/549-4262** or 541/549-0123. Fax 541/549-4481. www.conklins guesthouse.com. 5 units. June–Dec $90–$150 double; Jan–May $70–$130 double. Rates include full breakfast. Children 12 and older accepted. No credit cards. **Amenities:** Outdoor pool; massage; guest laundry. *In room:* No phone.

Grand Palace Hotel ✶ (Finds)
Located right in downtown Sisters in a false-fronted building that is one of the oldest buildings in town, this second-floor inn is run by a family that started out with an antique shop on the ground floor of this same building. In fact, the rooms are filled with antique furniture, and if you see something you like, you can buy it. Rooms vary in size and most are suites with tiny bedrooms. However, these rooms have so much character and are decorated with such a fun Western style, that it's easy to overlook the cramped quarters in some rooms.

101 E. Cascade Ave. (P.O. Box 2204), Sisters, OR 97759. © **541/549-2211** or 541/771-7731. Fax 541/549-2262. www.grandpalacehotelsisters.com. 5 units. Summer $89–$189 double; other months $49–$139 double. 2-night minimum on weekends. Children under 2 stay free in parent's room. MC, V. *In room:* kitchen, no phone.

The Lodge at Suttle Lake ✿   Set on the shores of Suttle Lake, just east of Santiam Pass, this newly opened mountain lodge sports a classic Adirondack lodge decor. Throw in an ornately carved front door and some very detailed chainsaw art in the lodge lobby, and you have the quintessential Cascadian mountain lodge. In the main lodge, the large lakeview rooms are the ones to ask for, or, for even more space, go for a cabin with a loft sleeping area and complete kitchen. While some of the cabins go a bit overboard with the cutesy cabin decor, these are still immensely comfortable accommodations, the best you'll find at any lakeside setting in the state. Multicourse fixed-price dinners ($35) are served on weekends.

13300 U.S. 20, Sisters, OR 97759. © **541/595-2628.** Fax 541/595-2267. www.thelodgeatsuttlelake.com. 24 units. $135–$240 double; $135–$425 cabin. 2-night minimum in summer; 3- to 4-night minimum on holidays. AE, DISC, MC, V. **Amenities:** Restaurant (American); lounge; boat rentals; bike rentals. *In room:* TV, high-speed Internet access.

Metolius River Resort ✿✿ *Finds*   Despite the name, this hardly ranks as a resort. However, it's perfect for those seeking peace and quiet or a romantic getaway. Set on the banks of the crystal-clear, spring-fed Metolius River 14 miles west of Sisters, the contemporary cedar-shingled two-story cabins are exceptional, offering modern amenities and styling with a bit of a rustic feel. Peeled-log beds, wood paneling, river-stone fireplaces, and green roofs give the cabins a quintessentially Western appeal. Although the Metolius River is legendary as the most difficult trout-fishing stream in Oregon, the cabins here are particularly popular with trout anglers. Not far away, you'll find the springs of the Metolius, where the river comes welling up out of the ground.

25551 SW F.S. Rd. 1419, Camp Sherman, OR 97730. © **800/81-TROUT.** www.metoliusriverresort.com. 11 cabins. $180–$195 double. 2- to 3-night minimum. Children under 2 stay free in parent's room. MC, V. **Amenities:** Restaurant (Northwest). *In room:* TV/VCR, dataport, kitchen, fridge, coffeemaker, hair dryer, free local calls.

CAMPGROUNDS

About a dozen Forest Service campgrounds are strung out along F.S. Road 14 north of Camp Sherman. All of these campgrounds are on the banks of the river and are most popular with anglers. The **Camp Sherman Campground** is only a half mile north of Camp Sherman. South of Sisters, at the end of F.S. Road 16, there are three campgrounds at or near Three Creek Lake. All of these campgrounds are reserved on a first-come, first-served basis.

WHERE TO DINE

No visit to Sisters is complete without a stop at the **Sisters Bakery,** 251 E. Cascade St. (© **541/549-0361**), for marionberry pastries and bear claws. For meals with a view of the mountain, you can't beat the **Restaurant at Black Butte Ranch** (see "Where to Stay," above).

Bronco Billy's Ranch Grill and Saloon ✿ STEAK/SEAFOOD/MEXICAN Located in the old Hotel Sisters building (no longer a hotel), Bronco Billy's serves up good old-fashioned Wild West grub in the form of belt-loosening platters of barbecued ribs, steaks, and green-chile burgers. Step through the swinging saloon doors leading from the dining room to the bar and you'll find genuine Western decor, including various trophy animal heads on the walls.

190 E. Cascade St. ℂ **541/549-7427.** www.broncobillysranchgrill.com. Reservations recommended. Main courses $9–$20. MC, V. Daily 11:30am–9 or 9:30pm (winter Mon–Thurs 5–9 or 9:30pm, Fri–Sun 11:30am–9 or 9:30pm).

Kokanee Café *(Finds)* NORTHWEST   This out-of-the-way place, located about 14 miles west of Sisters adjacent to the Metolius River Resort in Camp Sherman, is one of the best restaurants in the region. The interior of the log building is contemporary rustic with an open-beamed ceiling and a wrought-iron chandelier, and out back there's a deck under the ponderosa pines. The menu is short and almost always includes some sort of fresh rainbow trout entree, as well as such interesting dishes as buffalo short ribs with zinfandel–ancho chile demi-glace. There are also daily specials—often seafood prepared in whatever style is currently the rage. Lots of reasonably priced wines are available by the bottle or glass, with the emphasis on Oregon wines.

25545 SW F.S. Rd. 1419, Camp Sherman. ℂ **541/595-6420.** Reservations highly recommended. Main courses $22–$30. MC, V. Late Apr–May and Oct Thurs–Sun 5–9pm; June–Sept daily 5–9pm; closed late Oct to late Apr.

3 Bend & Sunriver: Skiing, Hiking, Fishing, Mountain Scenery & More

160 miles SE of Portland, 241 miles SW of Pendleton

Situated on the banks of the Deschutes River, Bend is the largest city east of the Oregon Cascades, and the surrounding area has more resorts than any other region in the state. To understand why a small town on the edge of a vast high desert could attract so many vacationers, just look to the sky. It's blue. And the sun is shining. For the webfoots who spend months under gray skies west of the Cascades, that's a powerful attractant.

However, Bend doesn't end with sunny skies. It is also home to Mount Bachelor, the biggest and best ski area in the Northwest. Several other mountains—the Three Sisters and Broken Top among them—provide a breathtaking backdrop for the city, and their pine-covered slopes, many lakes, and trout streams attract hikers, mountain bikers, and anglers. A lively downtown filled with interesting shops, excellent restaurants, and attractive Drake Park (which is named for the city's founder, A. M. Drake, and not for the ducks that are the park's major attraction) complements the outdoor offerings of the area.

ESSENTIALS
GETTING THERE   Bend is at the junction of U.S. 97, which runs north and south, and U.S. 20, which runs east to west across the state. From the Portland area, the most direct route is by way of U.S. 26 to Madras and then south on U.S. 97.

Horizon and SkyWest Airlines (United Express and Delta Connection) serve **Roberts Field/Redmond Municipal Airport,** 2522 SE Jesse Butler Circle, (ℂ **541/ 548-0646,** ext. 3499), 16 miles north of Bend. **CAC Transportation** (ℂ **800/847-0157** or 541/389-7469) operates the Central Oregon Breeze shuttle between Portland and Bend, with a stop at the Redmond Airport. Round-trip tickets are $81 for adults, $72 for seniors and students. There are also taxis operating from the Redmond Airport.

VISITOR INFORMATION   Contact the **Bend Visitor & Convention Bureau,** 917 Harriman St., Suite 101, Bend, OR 97701 (ℂ **800/949-6086** or 541/382-8048; www.visitbend.org). You can also contact the **Central Oregon Visitor Association,** 572 SW Bluff Dr., Suite C, Bend, OR 97702 (ℂ **800/800-8334** or 541/389-8799; www.visitcentraloregon.com).

Bend

ATTRACTIONS ●
High Desert Museum **8**
Mirror Pond Gallery **13**
Old Mill District **3**
Sunbird Gallery **12**

ACCOMMODATIONS ■
Entrada Lodge **7**
McMenamins Old St. Francis
   School Hotel **9**
Mount Bachelor Village Resort **6**
Pine Ridge Inn **5**
The Riverhouse **1**

DINING ◆
Bellatazza **11**
Chocolate et Gâteaux **10**
Cork **15**
Deschutes Brewery &
   Public House **16**
Di Lusso Baking **2**
Pine Tavern Restaurant **14**
Zydeco Kitchen & Cocktails **4**

GETTING AROUND   Car rentals are available from **Avis, Budget, Enterprise,** and **Hertz.** If you need a taxi, call **Owl Taxi Service** (© 541/382-1584).

FESTIVALS   The **Sunriver Music Festival** (© 541/593-9310; www.sunrivermusic. org) is a big classical-music binge that takes place in mid-August. When this festival finishes up, the **Cascade Festival of Music** (© 888/545-7435 or 541/383-2202; www.cascademusic.org), held the last week in August and the first week in September in Drake Park, picks up the baton.

EXPLORING THE BEND AREA

If you'd like to have a guide show you around the area, contact **Wanderlust Tours** (© 800/962-2862 or 541/389-8359; www.wanderlusttours.com), which offers summer canoe trips and winter snowshoe trips to many of the region's natural attractions. Rates range from $40 to $65.

The High Desert Museum 🐾🐾🐾 (Kids)   Bend lies on the westernmost edge of the Great Basin, a region that stretches from the Cascade Range to the Rocky Mountains and is often called the high desert. Through the use of historical exhibits, live animal displays, and reconstructions of pioneer buildings, this combination museum and zoo, one of the finest in the Northwest, brings the cultural and natural history of the region into focus. In the main building is a walk-through timeline of Western history, as well as a fascinating exhibit on the region's Plateau Indians. The natural history of the region comes alive in the Desertarium, where live animals of the region can be observed in a very natural setting. Outside, frolicking river otters and slow-moving porcupines are the star attractions, but the birds of prey center is just as interesting. A pioneer homestead and a forestry exhibit with a steam-driven sawmill round out the outdoor exhibits. Informative talks are scheduled throughout the day. The museum's cafe is a good place for lunch.

59800 S. U.S. 97. ⓒ 541/382-4754. www.highdesertmuseum.org. Admission $12 adults, $11 seniors, $7 children 5–12. Daily 9am–5pm. Closed Thanksgiving, Christmas, and New Year's Day. Take U.S. 97 3½ miles south of Bend.

EXPLORING CENTRAL OREGON'S VOLCANIC LANDSCAPE

From snow-covered peaks to lava caves, past volcanic activity and geologic history are visible everywhere around Bend. For a sweeping panoramic view of the Cascade Range, head up to the top of **Pilot Butte** at the east end of Greenwood Avenue. From the top of this cinder cone, you can see all of the Cascades' major peaks—from Mount Hood to Mount Bachelor—every one of which is volcanic in origin.

To the south of Bend lies a region of relatively recent volcanic activity that has been preserved as the **Newberry National Volcanic Monument** (ⓒ 541/593-2421; www. fs.fed.us/r6/centraloregon/newberrynvm/index.shtml). The best place to start an exploration of the national monument is at the **Lava Lands Visitor Center,** 58201 S. U.S. 97, 13 miles south of Bend and open from late April through mid-October. Here you can learn about the titanic forces that sculpted this region. An interpretive trail outside the center wanders through a lava flow at the base of 500-foot-tall **Lava Butte** ⓡ, an ominous black cinder cone, and a road leads to the top. From the summit of the cinder cone you have an outstanding view of the Cascades. A $5 Northwest Forest Pass is necessary to visit the Lava Lands Visitor Center. If you don't already have one, you can purchase

---

Moments Seeing Stars

Central Oregon's clear skies not only provide the region with abundant sunshine but also allow the stars to shine brightly at night. At two area observatories you can get a closer look at those stars. At the small **Pine Mountain Observatory** (ⓒ 541/382-8331; http://pmo-sun.uoregon.edu), 26 miles southeast of Bend off U.S. 20, you can gaze at the stars and planets through 15- to 32-inch telescopes. Admission is a $3 suggested donation, and the observatory is open from late May through late September on Friday and Saturday nights with programs starting between 8pm and 9pm, depending on the month.

In the resort community of Sunriver, south of Bend, the **Sunriver Nature Center & Observatory** (ⓒ 541/598-4406; www.sunrivernaturecenter.org) has star-gazing programs, with days and hours varying with the seasons. The observatory can be found by following the Nature Center signs through Sunriver. Admission is $6 for adults and $4 for children. There are also daytime solar viewing programs here.

one here. As you leave the parking lot of the Lava Land
(F.S. Rd. 9702) to the right leads to the trail head for th
which are an easy .8-mile walk from the trail head. Be
if you visit the falls during the summer.

A mile to the south, you'll find **Lava River C**
formed by lava flows. The cave is more than a m
explore. A $5 Northwest Forest Pass is necessary
The cave is open mid-May through Labor Day
rentals after 4pm). Be sure to bring warm clothes! Whe.
scape, it often inundated pine forests, leaving in its wake only ...
Lava Cast Forest, 9 miles down a very rough road off U.S. 97 south
Cave, a paved trail leads past such molds. Continuing farther south on U.S. 9,
bring you to the turnoff for the **Newberry Caldera** area, the centerpiece of the monument. Covering 500 square miles, the caldera contains Paulina and East Lakes and
numerous volcanic features, including an astounding flow of obsidian. There are
rental cabins and campgrounds within the national monument, and 150 miles of hiking trails.

HITTING THE SLOPES & OTHER WINTER SPORTS

If downhill skiing is your passion, you probably already know about the fabulous skiing conditions and myriad runs of **Mount Bachelor** ✦✦✦ (© **800/829-2442,** 541/
382-2442, or, for snow reports, 541/382-7888; www.mtbachelor.com), 22 miles west
of Bend on the Cascades Lakes Highway. With a 3,365-foot vertical drop, 70 runs, 10
lifts, 6 day-lodges, and 4 terrain parks, it's no wonder this place is so popular. All-day
lift tickets are $49 to $52 for adults, $42 to $45 for teenagers 13 to 18, $30 to $32 for
children 6 to 12, and free for children 5 and under. There's also a tubing park for families, and for snowboarders, a half pipe with 18-foot walls. The ski area's **Super Shuttle** ($5 each way) operates to and from Bend and leaves from the west side of town at
the corner of Colorado Avenue and Simpson Street, where there's a large parking lot.

Cross-country skiers will also find plenty of trails to choose from. Just be sure to
stop by a ski shop and buy a **Sno-Park** permit before heading up to the cross-country
trails, the best of which are along the Cascades Lakes Highway leading to Mount
Bachelor ski area. At the ski area itself, there are 35 miles of groomed trails. Passes to
use these trails are $13 to $14 for adults and $6 to $7 for children 6 to 12 years old.
Ski shops abound in Bend, and nearly all of them rent both downhill and cross-country equipment. If you're heading to Mount Bachelor, you can rent equipment there,
or try the **Powder House,** 311 SW Century Dr. (© **541/389-6234**), on the way out
of Bend heading toward Mount Bachelor.

If you've had enough skiing, how about a **dogsled ride?** At **Mount Bachelor**
(© **541/382-1709**), you can participate in 1½-hour programs that include a dogsled
ride and an orientation session on the care of sled dogs. Rates are $75 for adults, $30
for children under 80 pounds. All-day trips to Elk Lake ($375) are also available.

Easy 1-hour **snowshoe walks** are led by ranger-naturalists on weekends and holidays starting from the **West Village Ski & Sport Building** at Mount Bachelor. For
more information, call © **541/383-4771.**

SUMMER ACTIVITIES

If you want to do some mountain hiking without all that uphill slogging, head to
Mount Bachelor (© **800/829-2442** or 541/382-2442; www.mtbachelor.com), where,

...arly September, a chair lift operates to the 9,065-foot summit. The
...ults, $11 for seniors, and $8 for children ages 6 to 12. From here you
... the chair or hike down.

If fishing is your passion, you've come to the right place. The Deschutes
...s right through downtown Bend, and good trout waters can be found both
...m and downstream from town. The lakes of the Cascade Lakes Highway west
...d are, however, the most popular fishing destinations in the area. Of these, Hos-
... Lake (a catch-and-release fly-fishing-only lake), and Crane Prairie and Wickiup
...servoirs, which are known for their trophy trout, are among the most fabled area
fishing spots. If you're not familiar with these rivers and lakes, you may want to hire
a guide to show you where to hook a big one. Try contacting **Garrison's Fishing
Guide Service** (© **541/593-8394;** www.garrisonguide.com). Expect to pay around
$175 for a day of fishing. Fly-fishing supplies are available at **The Fly Box,** 1255 NE
Third St. (© **541/388-3330**), and in Sunriver at **Sunriver Fly Shop,** 56805 Venture
Lane (© **541/593-8814;** www.sunriverflyshop.com).

GOLF For many of central Oregon's visitors, Bend's abundance of sunshine means
only one thing—plenty of rounds of golf at the area's many golf courses. Of the resort
courses in the area, the three courses at **Sunriver** (© **800/962-1769** or 541/593-
1000; www.sunriver-resort.com)—Meadows, Woodlands, and Crosswater (open to
hotel guests and members only)—are the most highly regarded. Expect to pay anywhere from $50 to $175, depending on which course you play and when.

Right in Bend, you'll find more reasonable prices at the Riverhouse Resort's **River's
Edge Golf Course,** 3075 N. Business U.S. 97 (© **541/389-2828;** www.riverhouse.
com), where 18 holes will cost you $29 to $73 in the summer. The recently renovated
and upgraded **Widgi Creek Golf Club,** 18707 Century Dr. (© **541/382-4449;**
www.widgi.com), is another of the area's highly regarded semiprivate clubs. Greens
fees range from $30 to $90, depending on the season.

HIKING Hiking is one of the most popular summer activities here, but keep in
mind that high-country trails may be closed by snow until late June or early July.

My favorite trail in the Bend area is the **Deschutes River Trail** ☆☆, which parallels the Deschutes for nearly 9 miles. Any stretch of this trail is beautiful. To reach the
trail, drive the Cascades Lakes Highway 6 miles west from Bend, turn left at a sign for
the Meadow Picnic Area, and continue 1⅓ miles to the trail head at the picnic area.
Another enjoyable, though strenuous, hike is to the summit of **Pilot Butte,** a cinder
cone within the Bend city limits. To find the trail head, drive east from downtown on
Greenwood Avenue and watch for signs. For a few more recommended hikes, see "A
Scenic Drive Along the Cascade Lakes Highway," below.

The **Three Sisters Wilderness,** which begins just over 20 miles from Bend and Sisters, offers secluded hiking among rugged volcanic peaks. Permits are required for
overnight trips in the wilderness area and are available at trail heads. Currently, you'll
also need a Northwest Forest Pass (available at the Bend and Sisters ranger stations) to
park at area trail heads. Contact the **Bend/Fort Rock Ranger Station,** 1230 NE
Third St., Suite A-262, Bend (© **541/383-4000;** www.fs.fed.us/r6/centraloregon), or
the **Sisters Ranger Station,** Pine Street and U.S. 20 (© **541/549-7700;** www.fs.fed.
us/r6/centraloregon) in Sisters for trail maps and other information.

HORSEBACK RIDING   Down in Sunriver, you can get saddled up and ride the meadows and ponderosa pine forests at **Sunriver Stables** (© **541/593-6995**), which offers a variety of rides, with an hour's ride costing $30. Be sure to call for a reservation.

MOUNTAIN BIKING 🎇   Mountain biking is one of the most popular activities in central Oregon, partly because when the snow melts, the cross-country ski trails become mountain-bike trails. Contact the **Bend/Fort Rock Ranger Station,** 1230 NE Third St., Suite A-262 (© **541/383-4000;** www.fs.fed.us/r6/centraloregon), to find out about trails open to mountain bikes. The most scenic trail open to bikes is the Deschutes River Trail mentioned above. Mountain bikes (and touring bikes) can be rented from **Hutch's Bicycles,** 725 NW Columbia St. (© **541/382-9253;** www. hutchsbicycles.com), which charges $25 to $45 per day for mountain bikes.

High Cascade Descent (© 800/296-0562 or 541/389-0562; www.paulinaplunge. com) offers guided mountain-bike rides in Newberry National Volcanic Monument. The Paulina Plunge is an easy downhill ride that includes stops at waterfalls and a natural water slide and costs $55 to $60. These tours are outrageously fun, and should not be missed if you're at all athletic. Both mountain-bike and road-bike tours are offered by **Cog Wild Bicycle Tours,** 130 SW Century Dr. (© **800/818-1902** or 541/ 385-7002; www.cogwild.com). Tours vary in length and degree of difficulty, so there's something for every level of rider and a wide range of prices. Cog Wild also offers a combination mountain-biking-and-white-water-rafting trip on the McKenzie River for $155 to $170 per person with bike rental.

KAYAKING & WHITE-WATER RAFTING   The Deschutes River, which passes through Bend, is the most popular river in Oregon for white-water rafting, although the best sections of river are 100 miles north of here (see the earlier "North Central Oregon & the Lower Deschutes River" section for details). However, numerous local companies offer trips both on the lower section of the Deschutes and on the stretch of the upper Deschutes between Sunriver and Bend. This latter stretch of the river is known as the Big Eddy run, and though it is short and really has only one major rapid, it offers a quick introduction to rafting. **Sun Country Tours** (© **800/770-2161** or 541/382-6277; www.suncountrytours.com) does both the Big Eddy run ($42) and the lower Deschutes ($100). **Rapid River Rafters,** 1151 SE Centennial Court #5 (© **800/962-3327** or 541/382-1514; www.rapidriverrafters.com), also offers full-day trips on the lower Deschutes ($80–$90).

For a much mellower experience, book a kayak tour with **Alder Creek Kayak & Canoe** (© **541/317-9407;** www.aldercreekbend.com), which leads tours on the gentle waters of the upper Deschutes River ($95). This company also rents canoes and kayaks, with rates starting at $20 for 2 hours, so, if you have a car you can put a boat on top of, you can head out to one of the lakes on the Cascade Lakes Highway. Sparks Lake and Hosmer Lake are my two favorite paddling spots.

A SCENIC DRIVE ALONG THE CASCADE LAKES HIGHWAY 🎇

During the summer, the **Cascade Lakes Highway** is the most popular excursion out of Bend. This National Scenic Byway is an 87-mile loop that packs in some of the finest scenery in the Oregon Cascades. Along the way are a dozen lakes and frequent views of the jagged Three Sisters peaks and the rounded Mount Bachelor. The lakes provide ample opportunities for boating, fishing, swimming, and picnicking. At the **Bend Visitor & Convention Bureau,** 917 Harriman St., Suite 101 (© **800/949-6086** or 541/382-8048), you can pick up a guide to the Cascade Lakes National

Scenic Byway. Keep in mind that from mid-November to late May, this road is closed west of Mount Bachelor due to snow.

The first area of interest along the highway is **Dutchman Flat,** just west of Mount Bachelor. A thick layer of pumice produces desertlike conditions that support only a few species of hardy plants. A little farther and you come to **Todd Lake,** a pretty little lake a bit off the highway; it's reached by a short trail. Swimming, picnicking, and camping are all popular here.

Sparks Lake, the next lake along this route, is shallow and marshy and has lava fields at its southern end. An easy trail with frequent glimpses of the lake meanders through these forested lava fields. To find this trail, drive to the end of the Sparks Lake access road. The lake is a popular canoeing spot, though you'll need to bring your own boat. At the north end of the lake, closer to the highway, you'll also find the trail head for a popular mountain-biking trail that heads south to Lava Lake. Across the highway from the marshes, at the north end of the lake, is the **trail head for Green Lakes,** a series of small lakes that are in the Three Sisters Wilderness at the foot of Broken Top Mountain. This is one of the most popular backpacking routes in the region and offers spectacular scenery. The hike to Green Lakes can also be done as a day hike. West of the Green Lakes trail head is an area known as **Devils Garden,** where several springs surface on the edge of a lava flow. On a boulder here you can still see a few **Native American pictographs.**

With its wide-open waters and reliable winds, **Elk Lake** is popular for sailing and windsurfing. There are cabins, a lodge, and campsites around the lake. **Hosmer and Lava Lakes** are both known as good fishing lakes, while spring-fed **Little Lava Lake** is the source of the Deschutes River. **Cultus Lake,** with its sandy beaches, is a popular swimming lake. At the **Crane Prairie Reservoir** you can observe osprey between May and October. The **Twin Lakes** are examples of volcanic maars (craters) that have been filled by springs. These lakes have no inlets or outlets.

IN-TOWN EXPLORING

Downtown Bend is full of great shops, women's clothing boutiques, and art galleries, and it's easy to spend an afternoon shopping here. Be sure to check out the contemporary Native American art work at **Sunbird Gallery,** 916 NW Wall St. (© **541/389-9196;** www.sunbirdartgallery.com), and the works by regional artists at **Mirror Pond Gallery,** 875 NW Brooks St. (© **541/317-9324;** www.centraloregonarts.com). On the first Friday of each month, Bend galleries stay open from 5 to 9pm for a gallery walk. Also be sure to check out the shops in the **Old Mill District** (www.theoldmill.com), a redeveloped area of town that once housed several lumber mills. Today the old mill buildings have been converted into shopping arcades, and new buildings with the look of old mill buildings have been added. You'll find the Old Mill District south of downtown.

WHERE TO STAY
EXPENSIVE

Pine Ridge Inn 🏚🏚 This small luxury inn on the outskirts of town provides alternative accommodations for anyone who wants first-class surroundings but doesn't need all the facilities (and crowds) of the area's family-oriented resorts. This is an ideal choice for romantic vacations and honeymoons, but it is also a favorite of business travelers who need to be close to town. The inn is set on a bluff high above the Deschutes River, though you'll pay extra for a river view. Whether you get a regular

room or a suite, you'll have tons of space that includes featu
rooms and fireplaces. Lots of antiques and artworks by regi
tive style. Although the inn doesn't have a restaurant, there
noon wine-and-cheese tasting.

1200 SW Century Dr., Bend, OR 97702. ⓒ 800/600-4095 or 541/389-6137. Fax
com. 20 units. $130–$185 double; $190–$325 suite. Rates include full breakfast
Access to nearby health club; concierge; massage; dry cleaning. In room: A/C, TV/
hair dryer, iron.

MODERATE

McMenamins Old St. Francis School Hotel ⓡ (Finds) Attention, lapsed Catholics
(and anyone else who ever attended a parochial school): You can finally sleep in class
without getting your knuckles smacked by a ruler. McMenamins, the Portland-based
brewpub empire, has converted this former Catholic school into the coolest hotel in
central Oregon. While guest rooms are fairly basic, they do have wood paneling and
feel like cabins. There are also four cute cottages available. What makes this place
really special, though, are all the great little bars and garden spaces scattered around
the property. There's a pub, of course, plus a cigar bar in an old shed, a billiards room,
and a nightclub that features live music. There's also a very comfy movie theater that
serves food and beer. After a long day of hiking or skiing, you can soak your muscles
in the giant hot tub, which is designed to resemble a classic Turkish bath.

700 NW Bond St., Bend, OR 97701. ⓒ 877/661-4228 or 541/382-5174. Fax 541/330-8561. www.mcmenamins.com.
23 units. $94–$125 double; $150–$300 cottage; $30 hostel bed. Children 6 and under stay free in parent's room. AE,
DC, DISC, MC, V. Amenities: Restaurant (American); 4 lounges; hot soaking pool; movie theater. In room: TV, dataport, coffeemaker, hair dryer, iron, Wi-Fi.

Mount Bachelor Village Resort ⓡ Set along the top of a narrow ridge overlook-
ing the Deschutes River, this neatly manicured resort on the road to Mount Bachelor
is a somewhat more relaxed version of the family ski-and-summer resorts so common
in central Oregon. The resort is close enough to town to make going out for dinner
convenient but deep enough in the pine forests to feel away from it all. Keep in mind
that this is a condominium resort; most of the accommodations have separate bedrooms, and many have fireplaces and kitchens. For the best views, request a River
Ridge condo, right on the edge of the bluff. These rooms are quite simply some of the
nicest places to stay in the area, with private outdoor hot tubs on the view decks and
whirlpool tubs in the bathrooms. A 2-mile nature trail surrounding the property leads
down to the banks of the Deschutes River.

19717 Mount Bachelor Dr., Bend, OR 97702. ⓒ 800/583-4923 or 541/389-5900. Fax 541/388-7401. www.mtbachelor
village.com. 120 units. $110–$159 double; $135–$395 suite/condo. 2-night minimum stay. AE, DC, DISC, MC, V.
Amenities: Restaurant (Northwest/American); lounge; outdoor pool; 6 tennis courts; access to nearby health club; 2
Jacuzzis; seasonal children's programs; concierge; business center. In room: A/C, TV/VCR, dataport, kitchen, fridge, coffeemaker, hair dryer, iron, free local calls, high-speed Internet access.

INEXPENSIVE

Entrada Lodge ⓡ (Value) Located a few miles west of Bend on the road to Mount
Bachelor ski area, this motel is in a tranquil setting shaded by tall pine trees. Stay here
and you'll be just a little bit closer to Mount Bachelor in winter and the region's many
lakes and hiking and mountain-biking trails in summer. Although you'll have to drive
back into town or to a nearby resort for meals, it's worth that small inconvenience to
get such a pleasant setting at economical rates. The Deschutes National Forest borders

nd a trail leads from the parking lot to the popular Deschutes River
is only a mile away.

.ry Dr., Bend, OR 97702. © **541/382-4080**. 79 units. $69–$89 double; $129 suite. Rates include conti-
.reakfast. AE, DC, DISC, MC, V. Pets accepted ($5 per day). **Amenities:** Outdoor pool; Jacuzzi; coin-op laun-
.n room: A/C, TV, dataport, coffeemaker, hair dryer, iron.

The Riverhouse ★★ *(Value*   Located at the north end of town on the banks of a nar-
row stretch of the Deschutes River, the Riverhouse is one of the best hotel deals in the
state; and with its golf course and other resort facilities, it's an economical choice for
anyone who wants resort amenities without the high prices. Try to get a ground-floor
room; these allow you to step off your patio and almost jump right into the
Deschutes. However, the rooms on the upper floor have a better view of this rocky
stretch of river. The hotel's main dining room also has a view of the river, and there's
a poolside cafe and a lounge that features a variety of live entertainment. Without a
doubt, this is the best deal in Bend. Book early.

3075 N. U.S. 97, Bend, OR 97701. © **800/547-3928**, 866/453-4480, or 541/389-3111. www.riverhouse.com. 220
units. $82–$140 double; $123–$245 suite. Rates include continental breakfast. AE, DC, DISC, MC, V. Pets accepted.
Amenities: 2 restaurants (steak, American); lounge; 2 pools (1 indoor, 1 outdoor); 18-hole golf course; tennis courts;
exercise room; Jacuzzi; saunas; business center; room service; coin-op laundry. *In room:* A/C, TV, dataport, refrigera-
tor, coffeemaker, hair dryer, iron, free local calls.

Seventh Mountain Resort ★★ *(Kids*   Offering the closest accommodations to
Mount Bachelor, this sprawling resort is especially popular with skiers. But summer is
still the high season here, and during the warm months, families descend on the property to take advantage of the seemingly endless array of recreational activities. The
guest rooms, which come in a wide range of sizes (some with balconies and/or
kitchens), are done in a country decor and many have been recently redone. My
favorites are the rooms perched on the edge of the wooded Deschutes River canyon.
Golfers should note that Widgi Creek Golf Course is adjacent to the resort. In addition to the amenities listed below, the resort also has a roller-skating/ice-skating rink,
hiking/jogging trails, a miniature golf course, playgrounds and playing fields, and volleyball and basketball courts. All in all, this is the best place to stay in the immediate
Bend vicinity.

18575 SW Century Dr., Bend, OR 97702. © **800/452-6810** or 541/382-8711. Fax 541/382-3517. www.seventh
mountain.com. 240 units. $89–$139 double; $129–$139 suite or condo. AE, DC, DISC, MC, V. **Amenities:** 2 restaurants (American); lounge; 2 outdoor pools; 4 tennis courts; exercise room; access to nearby health club; 3 Jacuzzis;
sauna; bike rentals; horseback riding; children's programs; concierge; business center; massage; babysitting; coin-op
laundry; laundry service. *In room:* A/C, TV/VCR, fridge, coffeemaker, hair dryer, iron, free local calls, high-speed Internet access, Wi-Fi.

IN SUNRIVER

The resort community of Sunriver is Oregon's most popular summer destination
resort and has hundreds of condos, cabins, and vacation homes at a wide range of
prices. **Sunset Realty** (© **800/541-1756** or 541/593-5018; www.sr-sunset.com) is
one of the area's biggest rental companies.

Sunriver Lodge & Resort ★★★ *(Kids*   This sprawling resort is less a hotel than a
town unto itself, and with a wealth of activities available for active vacationers, it is the
first choice of many families vacationing in central Oregon. Most of the lodge accommodations overlook both the golf course and the mountains. My favorite rooms are
the loft suites, which have stone fireplaces, high ceilings, and rustic log furniture;

although the rooms in the River Lodge building are the most luxurious. Pine trees shade the grounds, and 33 miles of paved bicycle paths connect the resort with the surrounding community. However, no matter how impressive the other facilities are, it is the three golf courses that attract the most business. The resort's main dining room features creative Northwest cuisine and has superb views of the mountains. An adjacent lounge offers a cozy fireplace.

1 Center Dr. (P.O. Box 3609), Sunriver, OR 97707. © **800/801-8765** or 541/593-1000. Fax 541/593-5458. www. sunriver-resort.com. 530 units. $124–$349 double; $169–$339 suite. AE, DC, DISC, MC, V. **Amenities:** 5 restaurants (Northwest, American); 2 lounges; 2 outdoor pools, 1 indoor pool; 3 18-hole golf courses, 9-hole putting course; 35 tennis courts (3 indoor courts); full-service spa; Jacuzzi; sauna; canoe and kayak rentals; bike rentals; children's programs, concierge; complimentary resort shuttle; room service; massage; guest laundry. In room: A/C, TV, dataport, coffeemaker, hair dryer, iron.

CAMPGROUNDS

The closest campground to Bend is **Tumalo State Park,** 5 miles northwest of Bend off U.S. 20. The biggest campground in the area is **La Pine State Park,** which is accessible from U.S. 97 between Sunriver and La Pine. Reservations can be made at these parks through Reserve America (© **800/452-5687;** www.reserveamerica.com).

Of the many campgrounds along the Cascade Lakes Highway, the walk-in **Todd Lake Campground,** 25 miles west of Bend, is my favorite because it is enough of a walk from the parking lot to keep things pretty quiet. **Devil's Lake Campground,** also a walk-in campground, is another favorite of mine. Farther south, there are lots of campgrounds on the many lakes along this road. Two of my favorites are the **Mallard Marsh** and **South** campgrounds, both of which are on beautiful Hosmer Lake. The campgrounds at **Lava Lake** and **Little Lava Lake** are also fairly quiet, and the view from Lava Lake is the finest at any campground on this stretch of road.

WHERE TO DINE
IN BEND

Coffee addicts will want to drop by **Bellatazza,** 869 NW Wall St. (© **541/318-0606**) for good espresso. For good rustic bread and sandwiches, drop by **Di Lusso Baking,** 1135 NW Galveston St. (© **541/383-8155;** www.dilusso.com). For pastries and imported Belgian chocolates, don't miss **Chocolate et Gâteaux,** 141 NW Minnesota St. (© **541/318-8457**), in downtown Bend. If it happens to be summer and you're craving a meal with an unforgettable view, head to **Mount Bachelor** (© **541/382-2442**) and take the chair lift up to the Pine Marten Lodge, where you can have lunch, dinner, or just drinks.

Expensive

Cork *&&* ECLECTIC   Small and romantic, this place is evenly split between its dining room and its wine bar, so whether you're looking to have a romantic dinner or just a glass of wine, this is Bend's top spot for couples. The menu shows a lot of Asian influences but is more fusion than anything else, so expect highly imaginative combinations of flavors and ingredients. You might get something as simple as a pumpkin seed–crusted rack of pork with delicious, spicy macaroni and cheese or something as unusual as the hoisin duck salad, which is served on a wafer of fried soba noodles. Needless to say, there are lots of great wines available by the glass.

150 NW Oregon Ave. © **541/382-6881.** Reservations recommended. Main courses $22–$27. MC, V. Tues–Sat 5:30–9 or 9:30pm (wine bar opens at 5pm).

Moderate

Pine Tavern Restaurant ⚔ AMERICAN/NORTHWEST   Opened in 1936, the Pine Tavern Restaurant has been a local favorite for generations, and neither the decor nor the view has changed much over the years. Knotty pine and cozy booths give the restaurant an old-fashioned feel, while a 250-year-old ponderosa pine growing up through the center of one dining room provides a bit of grandeur. The menu is designed to appeal to a wide range of tastes and includes such comfort foods as meat loaf and baby back ribs, but the prime rib and the sourdough scones with honey butter are what this place is best known for. Try to get a table in the back room, which overlooks Mirror Pond.

967 NW Brooks St. ⓒ 541/382-5581. www.pinetavern.com. Reservations recommended. Main courses $5–$13 lunch, $14–$28 dinner. AE, DISC, MC, V. Mon–Sat 11:30am–2:30pm and 5:30–9:30pm; Sun 5:30–9:30pm.

Zydeco Kitchen & Cocktails ⚔⚔ NEW AMERICAN   Wedged between a Burger King and a Porsche dealer, this rather nondescript restaurant on Bend's busy Third Street is currently my favorite restaurant in town. With creative food and good service, this restaurant is a far more enjoyable place for dinner than some of the much publicized downtown restaurants. Despite the name, this is not specifically a Cajun or New Orleans restaurant, although you can start your meal with wonderful shrimp and grits cakes. After that, I always go for the grilled trout with Dungeness crab and spicy Zydeco sauce. Be sure to start your meal with a blueberry martini and finish up with the almond wet cake, which is like the classic Latin American dessert *tres leches* cake. If you've got a dog at home, Zydeco will send you home with a complimentary house-baked dog biscuit.

1085 SE Third St. ⓒ 541/312-2899. www.zydecokitchen.com. Reservations recommended. Main courses $9–$22. MC, V. Tues–Sat 4:30–9 or 9:30pm.

Inexpensive

Deschutes Brewery & Public House ⚔⚔ *Value* REGIONAL AMERICAN   For good handcrafted ales (I'm partial to the Mirror Pond Pale Ale and the Obsidian Stout) and a range of pub food more creative and tastier than you'd expect, this bustling pub is the place. The buffalo wings are some of the best we've ever had and are available in three different renditions. Not only do the cooks do an exemplary job on the normal pub menu, but they also prepare more complex daily specials, and there are daily sausage specials as well. Mustard, pastrami, root beer, and ginger ale are all made in-house. Bring the family—even the ones who don't drink beer.

1044 NW Bond St. ⓒ 541/382-9242. www.deschutesbrewery.com. Main courses $7–$11. AE, DISC, MC, V. Mon–Thurs 11am–11pm; Fri–Sat 11am–midnight; Sun 11am–10pm.

IN SUNRIVER

For the best views and food in Sunriver, make a reservation at the **Meadows at the Lodge** restaurant at Sunriver Lodge (p. 324).

Trout House Restaurant ⚔ *Value* NORTHWEST/AMERICAN   One of the best things about this little restaurant is that it's right on the Deschutes River and is a great place for a waterfront breakfast, lunch, or dinner. It's a popular spot with visitors, so be sure to make reservations during the summer. Seafood predominates, with trout available at all three meals. Razor clams (in season), pan-fried oysters, and blackened salmon with a tequila, lime, and sour-cream sauce can assuage a hunger earned by canoeing on the river or playing an exhausting round of golf.

Next to the Marina in Sunriver. *©* **541/593-8880.** Reservations recommended. Main courses $8–$14 lunch, $14–$26 dinner. DISC, MC, V. Apr–Oct daily 8am–9pm; Nov–Mar Thurs–Mon 8am–9pm.

BEND AFTER DARK

For good handcrafted ales and pub food, the **Bend Brewing Co.,** 1019 Brooks St. (*©* 541/383-1599; www.bendbrewingco.com), is a good alternative to the Deschutes Brewery Public House (see above). If you're on your way back from Mount Bachelor and are dying for a beer, stop in at **The Lodge at Cascade Lakes Brewing Co.,** 1441 SW Chandler Ave. (*©* 541/388-4998). In downtown Bend, you'll also find **McMenamin's Old St. Francis School Hotel,** 700 NW Bond St. (*©* 541/330-8563; www. mcmenamins.com; p. 323), which is home to a pub, several small bars, and a movie theater where you can get McMenamins beers. At **Bendistillery,** 850 Brooks St. (*©* 541/388-6868; www.bendistillery.com), you can get a martini made with this micro-distillery's own gin or vodka. The gin is made with local juniper berries, and there is a delicious hazelnut-espresso vodka. Hip and retro, the **Astro Lounge,** 147 NW Minnesota Ave. (*©* 541/388-0116), is Bend's most popular singles bar. For good wines by the glass, head to **Vino Mercato,** 916 NW Wall St. (*©* 541/385-6979; www.vinomercato.com) or **Cork** (p. 325).

The **Les Schwab Amphitheater,** 520 SW Powerhouse Dr. (*©* **541/322-9383;** www.bendconcerts.com), in the Old Mill District, books all kinds of great music each summer. The band shell and big, grassy field have seen the likes of Bob Dylan, James Brown, and Lyle Lovett.

Eastern Oregon

So different is eastern Oregon from the wet west side of the Cascades that it is often difficult to remember that it is still the same state. Indeed, the dry eastern ranch lands, deserts, canyons, and mountain ranges of this region have more in common with the landscapes of neighboring Idaho and Nevada. Yet, Oregon it is, and though it is remote, the fascinating geography makes it an interesting region to explore when you've had enough of the verdant landscapes west of the Cascades.

With huge cattle ranches sprawling across the countryside (cattle greatly outnumber people in these parts) and the **Pendleton Round-Up** attracting cowboys and cowgirls from around the country, this region is Oregon's Wild West. This part of the state is also steeped in the history of the Oregon Trail, and although it was to the Willamette Valley that most wagon trains were heading, it is here that signs of their passing 150 years ago still abound. All across this region, **wagon ruts** left by those stalwart overlanders can still be seen, and the history of the Oregon Trail immigrants is chronicled at several regional museums. Although the first pioneers never thought to stop and put down roots in this region, when gold was discovered in the Blue Mountains in the

1860s, fortune seekers flocked to the area. Boom towns flourished and as quickly disappeared, leaving the land to the cattle ranchers and wheat farmers who still call this area home.

Today, however, the region also attracts a handful of outdoors enthusiasts. They come to hike and horseback ride in the Eagle Cap Wilderness of the Wallowa Mountains, to bird-watch in the Malheur National Wildlife Refuge, to ski in the Blue Mountains, to explore the deepest canyon in the United States, and to raft and fish the Snake, Owyhee, and Grande Ronde rivers. On the north side of the Wallowa Mountains, the small town of Joseph has become a center for Western art, with several bronze foundries casting sculptures that are sold all over the country.

Because this region is so far from the state's population centers, it is little visited by west-siders, who rarely venture farther east than the resorts of central Oregon. Eastern Oregon is also so vast, and the road distances so great, that it does not lend itself to quick weekend trips. At the very least, it takes a 3-day weekend to get out to Joseph and the Wallowa Mountains or the Malheur National Wildlife Refuge. Should you travel to this part of the state, leave yourself plenty of time for getting from point A to point B.

1 Pendleton

125 miles E of The Dalles, 52 miles NW of La Grande, 40 miles S of Walla Walla, Washington

If not for its famous woolen mills, few people outside the region would be familiar with the Pendleton name. But because the blankets and clothing long manufactured by the **Pendleton Woolen Mills** (here and at other mills around the region) have

Eastern Oregon

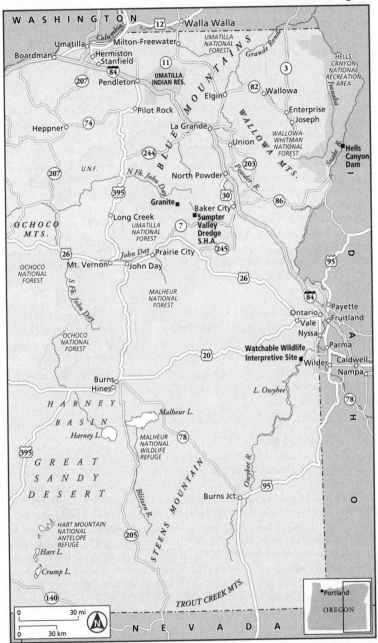

WASHINGTON

Walla Walla

12

Umatilla

Milton-Freewater

Columbia

UMATILLA
NATIONAL
FOREST

Grande Ronde

HELLS
CANYON
NATIONAL
RECREATION
AREA

Boardman

Hermiston
Stanfield

84

11

UMATILLA
INDIAN RES.

3

207

Pendleton

Elgin

82

Wallowa

Pilot Rock

La Grande

Enterprise
Joseph

Heppner

74

WALLOWA

WALLOWA-
WHITMAN
NATIONAL
FOREST

Union

207

244

U.N.F.

N Fk. John Day

BLUE MOUNTAINS

MTS.

Powder R.

203

Snake R.

Hells
Canyon
Dam

North Powder

395

Granite

30

86

OCHOCO
MTS.

Long Creek

UMATILLA
NATIONAL
FOREST

Baker City

Sumpter
Valley
Dredge
S.H.A.

7

245

John Day

Prairie City

OCHOCO
NATIONAL
FOREST

26

Mt. Vernon

John Day

95

S Fk. John Day

MALHEUR
NATIONAL
FOREST

26

84

Payette

OCHOCO
NATIONAL
FOREST

Ontario

Fruitland

20

Vale

Nyssa

Parma

Watchable Wildlife
Interpretive Site

Wilder

Caldwell

Burns

Hines

L. Owyhee

Nampa

HARNEY   BASIN

Malheur L.

78

Harney L.

395

MALHEUR
NATIONAL
WILDLIFE
REFUGE

78

GREAT
SANDY
DESERT

Blitzen R.

STEENS MOUNTAIN

Owyhee R.

95

Burns Jct.

HART MOUNTAIN
NATIONAL
ANTELOPE
REFUGE

205

Hart L.

Crump L.

140

0   30 mi

N

0   30 km

TROUT CREEK MTS.

NEVADA

Portland

OREGON

329

gained such a reputation, the name has become as much a part of the West as Winchester, Colt, and Wells Fargo. Today, Pendleton blankets and clothing are as popular as ever, and the town's mill is one of its biggest attractions.

But what brings even more visitors to town than the mill is a single annual event—the **Pendleton Round-Up.** Located at the western foot of the Blue Mountains in northeastern Oregon, Pendleton prides itself on being a real Western town; and as the site of one of the largest and oldest rodeos in the West, it has a legitimate claim. Each year in mid-September, the round-up fills the town with cowboys and cowgirls, both real and urban. For the rest of the year, Pendleton sinks back into its quiet small-town character and begins preparing for the next round-up.

Once the homeland of the Cayuse, Umatilla, Walla Walla, and Nez Perce Indians, the Pendleton area began attracting settlers in the 1840s, as pioneers who had traveled the Oregon Trail started farming along the Umatilla River. In the 1850s, gold strikes created boomtowns in the nearby mountains, and Pendleton gained greater regional significance. Sheep ranching and wheat farming later became the mainstays of the local economy, and by the turn of the century, Pendleton was a rowdy town boasting dozens of saloons and legal bordellos. Today Pendleton is a much quieter place, one that few people notice as they rush by on the interstate. But those who do pull off find a quiet town whose downtown historic district is filled with attractive brick buildings and some stately old Victorian homes.

ESSENTIALS

GETTING THERE   I-84 runs east to west through Pendleton. From the south take U.S. 395; from the north, Ore. 11, which leads to Walla Walla, Washington. **Horizon Airlines** (© 800/547-9308; www.horizonair.com) has service to the **Eastern Oregon Regional Airport,** which is located about 4 miles west of downtown Pendleton.

VISITOR INFORMATION   Contact the **Pendleton Chamber of Commerce,** 501 S. Main St., Pendleton, OR 97801 (© 800/547-8911 or 541/276-7411; www.pendleton-oregon.org).

GETTING AROUND   **Hertz** rents cars at the Eastern Oregon Regional Airport.

THE PENDLETON ROUND-UP

The Pendleton Round-Up and Happy Canyon Pageant, held the second week of September each year, is one of the biggest rodeos in the country and has been held since 1910. In addition to daily rodeo events, there's a nightly pageant that presents a history of Native American and pioneer relations in the area. After the pageant, there's live country-and-western music in the **Happy Canyon Dance Hall.** A country-music concert and a parade round out the events. **The Hall of Fame,** 1205 SW Court Ave. (under the south grandstand), holds a collection of cowboy and Indian memorabilia. The city is packed to overflowing during round-up week, so if you plan to attend, reserve early. Tickets sell for $11 to $18, and some types of tickets sell out a year in advance. For more information, contact the **Pendleton Round-Up Association,** P.O. Box 609, Pendleton, OR 97801 (© **800/45-RODEO** or 541/276-2553; www.pendletonroundup.com).

EXPLORING PENDLETON

If you happen to be in town any other week of the year, there are still a few things worth doing. This is the hometown of **Pendleton Woolen Mills,** 1307 SE Court

Place (© **800/568-3156** or 541/276-6911), the famed manufacturer of Native American–inspired blankets and classic wool sportswear. At the mill here in Pendleton, the raw wool is turned into yarn and then woven into fabric before being shipped off to other factories to be made into clothing. Tours are offered Monday through Friday at 9 and 11am, and 1:30 and 3pm. Also at the mill is a salesroom that's open Monday through Saturday from 8am to 6pm and Sunday from 9am to 5pm.

At one time there were supposedly 10 miles of underground passages and rooms beneath the streets of Pendleton, where gamblers, drinkers, and Chinese laborers rubbed shoulders. Over the years, these spaces were home to speakeasies and saloons, opium dens, and the living quarters of Chinese laborers who were forbidden to be above ground after dark. On walking tours operated by **Pendleton Underground Tours,** 37 SW Emigrant Ave. (© **800/226-6398;** www.pendletonundergroundtours. com), you can learn all about old Pendleton's shady underside. After exploring the underground, you'll visit a former bordello, whose rooms have been decorated much the way they once might have looked. Between March and October, tours are offered Monday through Saturday from 9:30am to 3pm; call for a schedule in other months. Tickets are $10. Reservations are strongly recommended.

At the **Heritage Station/Umatilla County Historical Society Museum,** 108 SW Frazer Ave. (© **541/276-0012;** www.umatillahistory.org), you can learn about the region's more respectable history. The museum is partly housed in the city's 1909 railway depot and contains changing exhibits that focus on regional history, including the Oregon Trail, Pendleton Woolen Mills, and Native American culture. This little museum is well worth a visit, and is open Tuesday through Saturday from 10am to 4pm; admission is $4 for adults and $2 for children.

At the **Pendleton Center for the Arts,** 214 N. Main St. (© **541/278-9201;** www. pendletonarts.org), in a renovated Carnegie Library, there are regularly scheduled art exhibits.

If you're looking for glimpses of the **Oregon Trail,** head 20 miles west of Pendleton to the town of Echo, where you can see wagon ruts left by early pioneers. There's an interpretive exhibit in town at Fort Henrietta Park on Main Street; and a mile of ruts can also be seen about 5½ miles west of town north of Ore. 320.

EAST OF TOWN: NATIVE AMERICAN HISTORY & A CASINO

East of Pendleton, at exit 216 off I-84, you'll find a complex of attractions operated by the Confederated Tribes of the Umatilla Indian Reservation. Included here is the **Wildhorse Casino Resort,** 72777 Ore. 31 (© **800/654-WILD;** www.wildhorse resort.com), a golf course, a motel, an RV park, and the following museum.

Tamástslikt Cultural Institute 𝒜𝒜   This modern museum focuses on the impact the Oregon Trail had on the Native Americans of this region. The exhibits incorporate artifacts, life-size dioramas, and audio and video presentations that document the effect pioneer settlement had on the indigenous Cayuse, Walla Walla, and Umatilla Indians who were living in the region when the first settlers arrived. Exhibits are well done and quite interesting. Worth a stop.

72789 Ore. 331. © 541/966-9748. www.tamastslikt.com. Admission $6 adults; $4 seniors, students, and children; and free for children under 5. Daily 9am–5pm. Closed Thanksgiving, Christmas, and New Year's Day.

WHERE TO STAY
Bar M Ranch at Bingham Hot Springs 𝒜   This historic 3,000-acre dude ranch is about 30 miles northeast of Pendleton in the Blue Mountains. Originally built in

1864, the ranch's buildings were once part of a stagecoach stop. Today the old log building is a rustic lodge for guests. There are also a couple of cabins and the old homestead building. As the name implies, there are hot springs here, which can feel mighty welcome at the end of a long day in the saddle. With its hot-springs-fed swimming pool, horseback riding, petting zoo, recreation barn, and game room, this is the ultimate eastern Oregon family-vacation spot.

58840 Bar M Lane, Adams, OR 97810. © 888/824-3381 or 541/566-3381. www.barmranch.com. 15 units. Mid-May to mid-Sept $358–$458 double, $416–$498 cabin or house; mid-Sept to mid-May $168–$182 double, $182–$210 cabin or house. Lower rates for children under 17. 3-night minimum mid-June to mid-Aug. Rates include all meals, horseback riding twice per day (horseback riding not included in off season). MC, V. **Amenities:** Dining room (American); swimming pool; hot tub; horseback riding; bikes; game room. *In room:* No phone.

The Parker House Bed and Breakfast 🖈🖈   Built in 1917, this Italianate villa is only 2 blocks from downtown Pendleton and is surrounded by colorful perennial gardens. As befits the villalike surroundings, a formal atmosphere reigns. The Gwendolyn Room, with its fireplace and semiprivate balcony, is the best room in the house; and in the Mandarin Room, you'll find the original Chinese wallpaper and Asian styling. In all the guest rooms are plenty of antiques. Guest rooms share a bathroom, but what a bathroom it is, with the original multiple-head shower and lots of big old porcelain fixtures.

311 N. Main St., Pendleton, OR 97801. © 800/700-8581 or 541/276-8581. www.parkerhousebnb.com. 6 units (all with shared bathroom). $85–$145 double. Rates include full breakfast. AE, MC, V. *In room:* A/C, no phone.

Wildhorse Casino Resort 🖈   Whether or not you're interested in gambling, the Wildhorse Casino Resort is a good place to stay in the area. Not only are the rooms modern and comfortable, but there are also plenty of recreational amenities, including the casino with its casual restaurant. The Tamástslikt Cultural Institute (p. 331) is also nearby. The hotel is 4 miles east of Pendleton and has nice views of the nearby foothills of the Blue Mountains.

72777 Ore. 331, Pendleton, OR 97801. © 800/654-9453 or 541/278-2274. www.wildhorseresort.com. 100 units. $65–$85 double; $109–$119 suite. Rates include continental breakfast. AE, DISC, MC, V. **Amenities:** 4 restaurants (American); indoor and outdoor pools; 18-hole golf course; Jacuzzi; sauna; room service; babysitting; coin-op laundry; laundry service. *In room:* A/C, TV, coffeemaker, hair dryer, iron, free local calls.

Working Girls Hotel 🖈 *Finds*   Pendleton likes to play up its Wild West heritage, and there was a time when brothels were legal here. The historic building that now houses the Working Girls Hotel was just such an establishment, and although female companionship doesn't come with the rooms anymore, you will get comfortable accommodations. The rooms all have private bathrooms, but only one of these is actually in the room; all others have their bathrooms directly across the hall. The hotel is operated in conjunction with Pendleton Underground Tours.

17 SW Emigrant Ave., Pendleton, OR 97801. © 800/226-6398 or 541/276-0730. 5 units. $60–$75 double. MC, V. No children permitted. *In room:* A/C, no phone.

WHERE TO DINE

If you're looking for someplace to get a sandwich or a bowl of soup, drop by **The Great Pacific Wine and Coffee Company,** 403 S. Main St. (© **541/276-1350**). Cookies, muffins, truffles, and other sweets round out the menu. For good espresso, drop by **Dark Canyon Coffee Roasters,** 428 S. Main St. (© **541/276-2242**).

Raphael's Restaurant ✦✦ NORTHWEST This restaurant has long been Pendleton's best fine-dining establishment and should be your top choice for dinner while you're in town. Housed in a 1904 Queen Anne–style home, the restaurant is known for its Indian-style salmon (made with huckleberry purée), hickory-smoked prime rib, barbecued elk chops, and a variety of fettuccines.

233 SE Fourth St. ⓒ 888/944-CHEF or 541/276-8500. www.raphaelsrestaurant.com. Reservations recommended. Main dishes $17–$34. AE, DISC, MC, V. June 1–Sept 15 Tues–Sat 5–9pm; Sept 16–May 31 Tues–Thurs 5–8pm, Fri–Sat 5–9pm.

2 La Grande, Baker City & the Blue Mountains

La Grande: 260 miles E of Portland, 52 miles SE of Pendleton; Baker City: 41 miles SE of La Grande, 75 miles NW of Ontario

Though pioneers traveling the Oregon Trail in the 1840s found good resting places in the Powder River and Grande Ronde valleys, where Baker City and La Grande now stand, few stayed to put down roots in this remote region. It would not be until the 1860s that pioneers actually looked on these valleys as a place to live and make a living. However, even those first pioneers who just passed through left signs of their passage that persist to this day. **Wagon ruts** of the Oregon Trail can still be seen in this region, and outside of Baker City stands the most interesting and evocative of the state's museums dedicated to the Oregon Trail experience.

By 1861, however, the Blue Mountains, which had been a major impediment to wagon trains, were crawling with people—gold prospectors, not farmers. A gold strike in these mountains started a small gold rush that year, and soon prospectors were flocking to the area. The gold didn't last long—when mining was no longer financially feasible, the miners left the region. In their wake, they left several ghost towns, but the prosperity of those boom times also gave the region's larger towns an enduring legacy of stately homes and opulent commercial buildings, many built of stone that was quarried in the region. Today, the historic commercial buildings of Baker City, the ornate Victorian homes of Union, and the Elgin Opera House are reminders of past prosperity. Although the gold has played out, signs of those raucous days, from gold nuggets to ghost towns, are now among the region's chief attractions.

One of the most arduous and dangerous sections of the Oregon Trail—the crossing of the Blue Mountains—lies just west of present-day La Grande. These mountains are no longer the formidable obstacles they once were, but they are still among the least visited in Oregon. The Blues, as they are known locally, offer a wide variety of recreational activities, including skiing, soaking in hot springs, hiking, mountain biking, fishing, and camping. With their numerous hotels and restaurants, both La Grande and Baker City make good bases for exploring this relatively undiscovered region.

ESSENTIALS

GETTING THERE Both La Grande and Baker City are on I-84. La Grande is at the junction of Ore. 82, which heads northeast to Joseph and Wallowa Lake. Baker City is at the junction of Ore. 7, which runs southwest to John Day, and Ore. 86, which runs east to the Hells Canyon National Recreation Area.

VISITOR INFORMATION Contact the **Baker County Visitors and Convention Bureau,** 490 Campbell St., Baker City, OR 97814 (ⓒ **800/523-1235** or 541/523-3356; www.visitbaker.com), or **Union County Tourism,** 102 Elm St., La Grande, OR 97850 (ⓒ **800/848-9969** or 541/963-8588; www.visitlagrande.com).

OREGON TRAIL SITES

Oregon Trail history is on view west of La Grande, in downtown Baker City, and just north of Baker City. At the **Oregon Trail Interpretive Park at Blue Mountain Crossing** (℃ 541/963-7186), at exit 248 off I-84, you'll find a .5-mile trail that leads past wagon ruts in the forest. Informational panels explain the difficulties pioneers encountered crossing these rugged mountains. On most weekends between Memorial Day and Labor Day, there are living history programs as well.

National Historic Oregon Trail Interpretive Center 👁👁   Atop sagebrush-covered Flagstaff Hill, just north of Baker City, stands a monument to the largest overland migration in North American history. Between 1842 and 1860, an estimated 300,000 people loaded all their worldly belongings onto wagons and set out to cross the continent to the promised land of western Oregon. Their route took them through rugged landscapes, and many perished along the way. This museum commemorates the journeys of these hardy souls, who endured drought, dysentery, and starvation in the hopes of a better life. Through the use of diary quotes, a life-size wagon-train scene, artifacts, and interactive exhibits, the center takes visitors through every aspect of life on the trail. Outside, a trail leads to ruts left by the wagons on their journey west.

22267 Ore. 86, Baker City. ℃ 541/523-1843. oregontrail.blm.gov. $5 adults, $3.50 seniors, free for children under 16. Apr–Oct daily 9am–6pm; Nov–Mar daily 9am–4pm. Closed Thanksgiving, Christmas, and New Year's Day.

Oregon Trail Regional Museum 👁   In a large building that once housed Baker City's public swimming pool, this museum is filled with pioneer memorabilia, including a large collection of stagecoaches and an extensive mineral collection.

2480 Grove St., Baker City. ℃ 541/523-9308. Admission $5 adults, $4.50 seniors. Late Mar–Oct daily 9am–5pm.

EXPLORING BAKER CITY

At the Baker City Visitors and Convention Bureau, you can pick up a brochure that outlines a **walking tour** of the town's most important historic buildings, including the restored **Geiser Grand Hotel,** which, when it first opened, was one of the finest hotels in the west. (See "Where to Stay," below, for details.)

If you'd like to take a look inside one of Baker City's restored old homes, drop by the **Adler House Museum,** 2305 Main St. (℃ 541/523-9308), a stately Victorian structure. Everything on the second floor, from the wallpaper to the furniture, is original, dating to the 1890s. The first floor has been refurbished and decorated to look the way it might have more than 100 years ago. The museum is open from May through September, Friday through Monday from 10am to 2pm. Admission is $5 per adult.

Baker City's fortunes were made by gold mines in the Blue Mountains, and if you'd like to see some samples from those golden years, stop in at the **U.S. Bank** on Main

---

⟨Tips⟩ An Almost Grand Old Opera House

In the town of **Elgin,** 18 miles north of La Grande on Ore. 82, you can take in a play or concert at the restored **Elgin Opera House,** 104 N. Eighth St. (℃ 541/437-2014), which was built in 1912. The opera house is also home to a small historical museum that's open Tuesday through Saturday from 10am to 4pm between mid-May and mid-October.

Street in Baker City. The gold collection here includes a nugget that weighs in at 80.4 ounces.

OUTDOOR ACTIVITIES
SPRING THROUGH FALL

If you're interested in **bird-watching,** head out to the **Ladd Marsh Wildlife Area,** 59116 Pierce Rd. (© 541/963-4954; www.dfw.state.or.us), 5 miles south of La Grande off I-84 at the Foothill Road exit (exit 268). March through May, the refuge has lots of waterfowl, and in summer, the wetland is home to sandhill cranes, geese, ducks, avocets, black-necked stilts, and numerous raptors. Also keep an eye out for elk. The best way to visit this area is by walking the 1.3-mile nature trail east of I-84 near exit 268.

The **hot springs** of this region have been attracting people since long before the first white settlers arrived, and you can still soak your sore muscles in thermal waters at **Lehman Hot Springs** (© 541/427-3015; www.lehmanhotsprings.com), which is in a remote forested setting near Ukiah, 38 miles west of La Grande on Ore. 244. Here you'll find a large hot swimming pool, perfect for an afternoon of lounging around. There are also two smaller and hotter soaking pools, as well as an unheated swimming pool. Also on the premises are campsites and some rustic accommodations, and nearby there are hiking, mountain-biking, cross-country-ski, and snowmobiling trails. In summer, the springs are open Wednesday through Friday from 10am to 8pm and Saturday and Sunday from 9am to 8pm. (Call for hours the rest of the year.) Admission is $7.

In summer, there are plenty of nearby trails for hiking or mountain biking. My favorite trails are those that radiate out from Anthony Lake, high in the Elkhorn Mountains 45 minutes from Baker City. These trails start at an elevation of over 7,000 feet and meander through open forests with views of craggy granite peaks. The 8-mile loop hike from Anthony Lake up the Elkhorn Crest Trail to Dutch Flat Saddle and back to Anthony Lake via Crawfish Basin Trail makes good day hike. By the way, the campground at Anthony Lake might just be my favorite campground in the state. Contact the **Wallowa-Whitman National Forest,** La Grande Ranger District, 3502 Ore. 30, La Grande, OR 97850 (© 541/963-7186), or **Baker Ranger District,** 3165 10th St., Baker City, OR 97814 (© 541/523-4476), for more information. On the Internet, visit www.fs.fed.us/r6/w-w.

If you happen to have your golf clubs with you, play a round at Union's **Buffalo Peak Golf Course,** 1224 E. Fulton St. (© 866/202-5950 or 541/562-5527; www. buffalopeakgolf.com), a scenic and challenging 18-hole course on the outskirts of Union. Greens fees run $25 to $29 for 18 holes.

WINTER SPORTS & ACTIVITIES

With the highest base elevation and the most powderlike snow in the state, **Ski Anthony Lakes** (© 541/856-3277; www.anthonylakes.com), 45 minutes west of Baker City, is a good little ski area—small, but with a nice variety of terrain. Daily lift tickets are $32. You'll also find good groomed cross-country ski trails here, and the area is very popular with snowmobilers.

Winter is also the best time of year to see some of the region's Rocky Mountain elk. Each year December through February, the Oregon Department of Fish & Wildlife feeds a large herd of elk at the **Elkhorn Wildlife Area,** 61846 Powder River Lane (© 541/898-2826), in North Powder, about halfway between La Grande and Baker

City. You can usually see between 150 and 200 elk. During the Christmas holidays, **T and T Tours** (© **541/856-3356;** www.tnthorsemanship.com) takes visitors out to the feeding area by horse-drawn wagon. Tours last about a half-hour and cost $6 for adults and $4 for children. To reach Elkhorn, take exit 285 off I-84 and follow the WILDLIFE VIEWING signs.

THE ELKHORN MOUNTAIN SCENIC LOOP

Rising up on the outskirts of Baker City is the Elkhorn Range of the Blue Mountains. A paved loop road winding up and around the south side of these mountains features scenic vistas, access to the outdoors throughout the year, and even a couple of sparsely inhabited ghost towns. Start this loop by heading south out of Baker City on Ore. 245 and then take Ore. 7 west to **Sumpter,** 30 miles from Baker City.

As you approach Sumpter, you'll notice that the valley floor is covered with large piles of rocks. These are the tailings (the refuse left after the mining operations have worked over the land), from the Sumpter Dredge, preserved as the **Sumpter Valley Dredge State Heritage Area** (© **541/894-2486**), which has been undergoing restoration. Between 1935 and 1954, the ominous-looking dredge laid waste to the valley floor as it sat in its own little pond sifting through old streambed gravel for gold. Although you can stop and view the dredge any time of year, between May and October it is possible to board the strange machine (open daily 7am–5pm), which now has a few interpretive exhibits on board. Admission is by donation.

In its wake, the dredge left 6 miles of tailings that formed hummocks of rock and gouged-out areas that have now become small ponds. Although such a mining-scarred landscape isn't usually scenic, the Sumpter Valley is surprisingly alive with birds attracted to the ponds.

A favorite way of visiting the Sumpter Dredge is aboard the **Sumpter Valley Railroad** (© **866/894-2268** or 541/894-2268; www.svry.com), which operates a classic steam train on a 5-mile run from west of Phillips Reservoir to the Sumpter Valley Dredge. This railway first began operation in 1890 and was known as the stump dodger. Excursions are operated on Saturdays, Sundays, and holidays from Memorial Day weekend through September; round-trip fares are $13 for adults, $12 for seniors, and $8 for children 6 to 16.

Gold kept Sumpter alive for many decades, and a bit of gold-mining history is still on display in this rustic mountain town, which, though it has a few too many people to be called a ghost town, is hardly the town it once was. In the boom days of the late 19th and early 20th century, Sumpter boasted several brick buildings, hotels, saloons, and a main street crowded with large buildings. However, when a fire destroyed the town in 1917, it was never rebuilt. Today, only one brick building and a few original wooden structures remain. At **The Gold Post Grocery & Mercantile/Museum** (© **541/894-2362**), you can see old photos of Sumpter as well as various artifacts from the town's gold-mining heyday.

Continuing west on a winding county road for 14 miles will bring you to **Granite** ⚘, another ghost town with a few flesh-and-blood residents. The weather-beaten old buildings on a grassy hillside are the epitome of a Western ghost town, and most buildings are marked. You'll see the old school, general store, saloon, bordello, and other important town buildings.

Beyond Granite, the road winds down to the North Fork of the John Day River and then heads back across the mountains by way of the Anthony Lakes area.

Although Anthony Lakes is best known for its small ski area, in summer there are hiking trails (see above) and fishing in the area's small lakes. The vistas in this area are the best on this entire loop drive, with rugged, rocky peaks rising above the forest. Also in this same area, you'll catch glimpses of the irrigated pastures of the Powder River Valley far below.

Coming down onto the valley floor, you reach the tiny farming community of Haines, which is the site of the **Eastern Oregon Museum,** Third Street (© **541/856-3233**), a small museum cluttered with all manner of artifacts of regional historic significance. It's open May 15 to September 15 Thursday through Monday from 9:30am to 4:30pm; admission is by donation. Here in Haines you'll also find the Haines Steakhouse (see below), a favorite of area residents.

WHERE TO STAY
IN LA GRANDE
Stange Manor Bed & Breakfast ⋆   This Georgian colonial mansion, built in the 1920s, looks a bit like the White House and is the best place to stay in La Grande. It's filled with beautiful woodwork and comfortable guest rooms, a couple of which have the original bathroom fixtures. The best deal here is the three-room suite, which has a fireplace and a sun porch that has been converted into a sleeping room. Breakfasts are elegant affairs served in the formal dining room.

1612 Walnut St., La Grande, OR 97850. © **888/286-9463** or 541/963-2400. www.stangemanor.com. 4 units. $98–$105 double; $115 suite. Rates include full breakfast. MC, V. Children over 11 are welcome. *In room:* TV, dataport, hair dryer, iron.

IN UNION
The Union Hotel ⋆ *Value*   Although Union today is a sleepy town, it was once the county seat and a booming little place. This grand little hotel first opened its doors in 1921, and now, after a extensive renovation, has become one of eastern Oregon's more interesting historic hotels. Surrounded by lawns and shade trees, the three-story brick hotel goes a long way toward conjuring up Union's lively past. The lobby, with its white-tile floor, could be straight out of a movie set, while the upstairs guest rooms are decorated in various themes. To make the most of a visit here, try to stay in the room with the whirlpool tub. Although Union is 14 miles from La Grande, the location is still fairly convenient for exploring this region.

326 N. Main St. (P.O. Box 569), Union, OR 97883. © **888/441-8928** or 541/562-6135. www.theunionhotel.com. 16 units. $39–$119 double. Children welcome, though over 8 years old preferred. AE, DISC, MC, V. *In room:* no phone.

IN BAKER CITY
Geiser Grand Hotel ⋆⋆ *Finds*   Built in 1889 at the height of the region's gold rush, the Geiser Grand is by far the grandest hotel in eastern Oregon. With its corner turret and clock tower, the hotel is a classic 19th-century Western luxury hotel. In the center of the hotel is the Geiser Grill dining room, above which is suspended the largest stained-glass ceiling in the Northwest. Throughout the hotel, including in all the guest rooms, ornate crystal chandeliers add a crowning touch. Guest rooms also feature 10-foot windows, most of which look out to the Blue Mountains. The two cupola suites are the most luxurious and evocative of the past. These two suites also have whirlpool tubs. Meals are served both in the formal Geiser Grill and in the much more relaxed 1889 saloon. No trip to eastern Oregon is complete without a stay at this grande dame of the old West.

1996 Main St., Baker City, OR 97814. © 888/434-7374 or 541/523-1889. Fax 541/523-1800. www.geisergrand. com. 30 units. $79–$109 double; $129–$199 suite. Children under 12 stay free in parent's room. AE, DISC, MC, V. Pets accepted ($15 per night). **Amenities:** Restaurant (American); lounge; access to nearby health club; 24-hour room service; massage; dry cleaning. *In room:* A/C, TV/VCR, dataport, hair dryer, iron, free local calls, high-speed Internet access, Wi-Fi.

CAMPGROUNDS

You'll find several national forest campgrounds along the Elkhorn National Scenic Byway, including **Union Creek Campground** (© 541/523-4476; www.fs.fed.us/r6/w-w; reservations not taken), which is on the shore of Phillips Reservoir southeast of Baker City. Others can be found near Anthony Lakes.

WHERE TO DINE

IN LA GRANDE

For good pastries and fresh-baked bread, stop in at **Kneads,** 1113 Adams Ave. (© 541/963-5413).

Foley Station ⭐ AMERICAN/NORTHWEST Although the focus at Foley Station has always been on breakfasts and lunches, the restaurant is also open for dinner, and the menu is far more contemporary and creative than at any other restaurant in town. Expect an eclectic mélange of flavors, including the likes of mango melba waffles at breakfast and almond-crusted chicken with bay shrimp and tomato-basil beurre blanc.

1114 Adams Ave. © 541/963-7473. www.foleystation.com. Reservations recommended for dinner. Main dishes $6.25–$16 lunch, $7–$29 dinner. MC, V. Wed–Sun 7am–10pm.

Ten Depot Street ⭐ *Value* STEAK/SEAFOOD Housed in a historic brick commercial building, this restaurant has a classic 19th-century feel, complete with a saloon on one side. Although the steaks and prime rib are what most people order, the salads are large and flavorful, and there are even some vegetarian dishes. The $7.50 blue-plate specials on weeknights are a particularly good value, and there are also other inexpensive nightly specials. Also keep an eye out for dishes prepared with emu. There's live music (usually rock) in the bar on the weekends.

10 Depot St. © 541/963-8766. Reservations recommended. Main courses $7.50–$33. AE, MC, V. Mon–Sat 5–10pm.

IN THE BAKER CITY AREA

For pub food and microbrews, there's **Barley Brown's Brew Pub,** 2190 Main St. (© 541/523-4266). For espresso, try **Mad Matilda's Coffee House,** 1917 Main St. (© 541/523-4588).

Baker City Café/Pizza a Fetta ⭐ SANDWICHES/PIZZA Locals flock to this casual, down-home spot not only for its good pizzas and but also for its fun country-clutter sort of decor. If you're not in the mood for pizza, there are sandwiches, soups, and a daily pasta dish.

1840 Main St. © 541/523-6099. Sandwiches $6–$8; pizzas $15–$27. MC, V. Mon–Fri 8am–3pm, Sat 11am–2pm.

The Grill ⭐ AMERICAN Located in the central court of the historic Geiser Grand Hotel, this restaurant, with its stained-glass ceiling, conjures a gold rush–era elegance. Mesquite-smoked prime rib and the wide variety of steaks are always good bets, but this restaurant is also committed to serving excellent fresh seafood dishes, including line-caught wild salmon. There are also plenty of pasta dishes. Before or after dinner, you'll need to spend a little time in the 1889 saloon just to complete your historical evening. At lunch you can order a buffalo burger.

Chinese History in Eastern Oregon

In the town of John Day, the fascinating little **Kam Wah Chung & Co. Museum** ♠♠ (© 541/575-2800), on Northwest Canton Street adjacent to City Park, is well worth a visit. It preserves the home and shop of a Chinese doctor who, for much of the first half of the 20th century, administered to his fellow countrymen laboring here. The building looks much as it might have at the time of the doctor's death and contains an office, a pharmacy, a general store, and living quarters. It's open May through October only, Monday through Saturday from 9am to noon and 1 to 5pm, and on Sunday from 1 to 5pm. Admission is free.

You'll find more Chinese history in Baker City, where an old Chinese cemetery can be seen on Allen Street, just east of exit 304 off of I-84. This cemetery has a modern Chinese pavilion that was built in Souzhou, China, designed by the same company that built the Portland Classical Chinese Garden. The Pendleton Underground tour in Pendleton (p. 331) also focuses on the region's Chinese history.

Geiser Grand Hotel, 1996 Main St. © 541/523-1889. www.geisergrand.com. Reservations recommended. Main courses $11–$19. AE, DISC, MC, V. Daily 8am–9pm.

Haines Steakhouse ♠ STEAK   Thick, juicy steaks are the specialty of the house here, but it's the decor as much as the food that attracts people. Log walls and booths, a chuck-wagon salad bar, mounted buffalo and elk heads, a totem pole, and an old buggy keep diners amused as they eat. This is a longtime favorite in the area.

910 Front St., Haines. © 541/856-3639. www.hainessteakhouse.com. Reservations recommended. Main courses $7.50–$27. AE, DISC, MC, V. Mon and Wed–Fri 5–10pm; Sat 4–10pm; Sun 1–9pm.

3 Joseph, Enterprise & the Wallowa Mountains

Joseph: 355 miles E of Portland, 80 miles E of La Grande, 125 miles N of Baker City

The Wallowa Mountains, which stand just south of the town of Joseph, are a glacier-carved range of rugged beauty that has been called both the Alps of Oregon and the Little Switzerland of America. Though the range is small enough in area to drive around in a day, it is big on scenery and contains the largest designated wilderness area in the state: the **Eagle Cap Wilderness.**

In the northeast corner of the mountains lies Wallowa Lake, which was formed when glacial moraines blocked a valley that had been carved by the glaciers. With blue waters reflecting the rocky peaks, the lake has long attracted visitors. In the fall, the lake also attracts bald eagles that come to feed on spawning kokanee salmon, which turn a bright red in the spawning season.

The town of Joseph, just north of Wallowa Lake, is a center for the casting of Western-themed **bronze sculptures,** and there are several art galleries and foundries in the area. With its natural beauty, recreational opportunities, and artistic bent, this corner of the state today has more to offer than any other area in eastern Oregon.

ESSENTIALS

GETTING THERE   Ore. 82 connects Joseph to La Grande in the west, and Ore. 3 heads north from nearby Enterprise to Lewiston, Idaho, by way of Wash. 129.

VISITOR INFORMATION   For more information, contact the **Wallowa County Chamber of Commerce,** 115 Tejaka Lane (P.O. Box 427), Enterprise, OR 97828 (© **800/585-4121** or 541/426-4622; www.wallowacountychamber.com).

FESTIVALS   Check out the rowdy **Chief Joseph Days Rodeo** (www.chiefjoseph days.com), over the last full weekend in July. In mid-July, the Nez Perce hold their annual **TamKaLiks Celebration** (www.wallowanezperce.org) and pow wow in the nearby town of Wallowa. The **Alpenfest,** on the third weekend after Labor Day, is the other big annual event in the area.

EXPLORING JOSEPH

Though the lake and mountains are the main attractions of this area, the presence of several bronze foundries in Joseph and Enterprise has turned the area into something of a Western art community. Along Main Street in Joseph, you'll find several galleries that specialize in bronze statues and Western art. You'll also find more than half a dozen life-size bronze wildlife and Western art sculptures in sidewalk gardens along Main Street.

Valley Bronze of Oregon has a gallery at 18 S. Main St. (© **541/432-7445;** www. valleybronze.com), and is one of the largest bronze foundries in the country. Tours of the foundry ($15 per person) are offered Monday through Thursday at 4pm and Friday through Sunday at 1pm. **Parks Bronze,** 331 Golf Course Rd., Enterprise (© **541/426-4595**), offers foundry tours Monday through Friday. A 24-hour notice is requested.

At the **Wallowa County Museum,** 110 S. Main St. (© **541/432-6095;** www.co. wallowa.or.us/museum), you can see pioneer artifacts, displays on the Nez Perce Indians, and other items donated to the museum by local families. This old-fashioned community museum is housed in a former bank building and is open daily from 10am to 5pm between Memorial Day and the third weekend in September.

On Saturdays between mid-July and the end of October, you can go for a train ride on the **Eagle Cap Excursion Train** (© **800/323-7330** or 541/963-9000; www.eagle captrain.com) Trains run between Wallowa and Joseph and fares range from $60 to $90 for adults.

OUTDOOR ACTIVITIES

Down at the south end of Wallowa Lake, you'll find **Wallowa Lake State Park** (© **541/432-4185**), where there is a swimming beach, picnic area, and campground. Adjacent to the park is the **Wallowa Lake Marina** (© **541/432-9115**), where you can rent canoes, rowboats, paddleboats, and motorboats (May–Sept). This end of the lake has an old-fashioned mountain resort feel, with pony and kiddy rides, go-cart tracks, miniature golf courses, and the like. It is also the trail head for several trails into the Eagle Cap Wilderness. The park is home to numerous large deer, which have become accustomed to begging for handouts from campers. Although the deer are entertaining, they are still wild animals and can be dangerous.

For a different perspective on the lake, ride the **Wallowa Lake Tramway,** 59919 Wallowa Lake Hwy. (© **541/432-5331;** www.wallowalaketramway.com) to the top of 8,200-foot Mount Howard. This is the steepest tramway in America and provides

"I Will Fight No More Forever"

The Wallowa Mountains and Hells Canyon areas were once the homeland of the **Nez Perce people.** Sometime in the early 1700s, the Nez Perce acquired horses that were descended from Spanish stock and that had been traded northward from the American Southwest. The Nez Perce land, which encompassed rolling hills covered with lush grasses, proved to be ideal for raising horses, and the tribe began selectively breeding horses, emphasizing traits of speed and endurance. Their horses eventually became far superior to those used by other tribes and came to be known as **Appaloosas.** Eventually, the hills in southeast Washington where these horses were first bred came to be known as the **Palouse Hills.**

The Nez Perce had befriended explorers Lewis and Clark in 1805 and remained friendly to white settlers when other Indian tribes were waging wars. This neutrality was "rewarded," however, with treaties that twice cut the size of their reservation in half. When one band refused to sign a new treaty and relinquish its land, the stage was set for one of the great tragedies of Northwest history.

En route to a reservation in Idaho, several Nez Perce men ignored orders from the tribal elders and attacked and killed four white settlers to exact revenge for the earlier murder by whites of the father of one of these Nez Perce men. This attack brought on the ire of settlers, and the cavalry was called in to hunt down the Nez Perce. Tribal elders decided to flee to Canada, and, led by Chief Joseph (also known as Young Joseph), 700 Nez Perce, including 400 women and children, began a 2,000-mile march across Idaho and Montana on a retreat that lasted 4 months.

Along the way, several skirmishes were fought, and the cavalry finally succeeded in defeating the Nez Perce only 40 miles from Canada. At their surrender, Chief Joseph spoke the words for which he has long been remembered: "Hear me my Chiefs, I am tired; my heart is sick and sad. From where the sun now stands, I will fight no more, forever."

The town of Joseph is named after Chief Joseph, and on the outskirts of town, you'll find the grave of his father, Old Joseph. Young Joseph is buried on the Colville Indian Reservation in central Washington. Right in town, you can view historic photos and read quotes from Chief Joseph at the **Nez Perce Wallowa Homeland Photography Exhibit,** Main Street (© **541/886-3101**). Not far from Joseph, in Spalding, Idaho (near Lewiston), you can learn more about the Nez Perce at **Nez Perce National Historical Park.**

---

great views both from the gondolas and from the summit of Mount Howard. The views take in Wallowa Lake and the surrounding jagged peaks. The tramway operates May through September (call for winter hours), daily from 10am to 4pm (in July through Labor Day until 5pm); the fare is $19 for adults and $16 for students 13 to 17, and $12 for children 4 to 12. Food is available at the **Summit Grill & Alpine Patio.**

Because most hikes on the north side of the Wallowas start out in valleys and can take up to a dozen miles or so to reach the alpine meadows of the higher elevations, there aren't a lot of great day hikes here. The **backpacking,** however, is excellent. If you're looking for **day hikes,** try taking the tramway to the top of Mount Howard, where there are about 2 miles of easy walking trails with great views. If you'd like to head into the **Eagle Cap Wilderness** to the popular **Lake Basin** or anywhere else in the Wallowas, you'll find the trail head less than a mile past the south end of the lake. For more information on hiking in the Wallowas, contact the **Wallowa Valley Ranger District,** 88401 Ore. 82, Enterprise, OR 97828 (© **541/426-4978;** www.fs.fed.us/ r6/w-w). This ranger station also serves as the Wallowa Mountains Visitor Center and has interesting displays on the flora and fauna of the region.

Horse packing into the Wallowas is a popular activity, and rides of a day or longer can be arranged through **Eagle Cap Wilderness Pack Station,** 59761 Wallowa Lake Hwy., Joseph, OR 97846 (© **800/681-6222** or 541/432-4145; www.eaglecapwilderness packstation.com), which offers trips into the Eagle Cap Wilderness during the summer. These stables also offer hourly, half-day, and full-day rides. **Millar Pack Station,** 69498 Sherrod Rd., Wallowa, OR 97885 (© **541/886-4035;** www.millarpackstation.com), offers similar overnight pack trips. Expect to pay $175 to $225 per person per day for a guided trip.

This region also offers some of the best **trout fishing** in Oregon, and if you're look-ing for a guide to take you to the best holes, contact **Eagle Cap Fishing Guides,** P.O. Box 865, Joseph, OR 97846 (© **800/940-3688;** www.eaglecapfishing.com), or the **Joseph Fly Shoppe,** 203 N. Main St., Joseph, OR 97846 (© **541/432-4343;** www. josephflyshop.com). Expect to pay anywhere from $340 to $395 for a day of fishing for one or two people.

In winter, the Wallowas are popular with cross-country and backcountry skiers. Check at the ranger station in Enterprise for directions to trails. You'll also find a small downhill ski area and groomed cross-country trails at **Ferguson Ridge,** which is 9 miles southeast of Joseph on Tucker Down Road.

Wing Ridge Ski Tours, P.O. Box 714, Joseph, OR 97846 (© **800/646-9050;** www.wingski.com), leads experienced skiers on hut-to-hut ski tours for $415 for a 5-day trip. The huts can also be rented for $25 to $30 per person, per night.

WHERE TO STAY

Bronze Antler Bed and Breakfast ⚜   This beautifully restored Craftsman bun-galow is Joseph's finest B&B and has by far the best view of any lodging in the area. Throughout the 1925-vintage home, you'll see lots of beautiful architectural details, and furnishings are in keeping with the style of the period. Guest rooms have fluffy down comforters and European antiques collected by the innkeepers Bill Finney and Heather Tyreman during travels in Europe. Joseph's restaurants and art galleries are within a few blocks of the inn, which makes this a very convenient place to stay if you're in town to soak up Joseph's artistic atmosphere.

309 S. Main St. (P.O. Box 74), Joseph, OR 97846. © **866/520-9769** or 541/432-0230. Fax 541/432-6219. www.bronze antler.com. 3 units. $75–$140 double. Rates include full breakfast. AE, DISC, MC, V. Children over 12 are welcome. **Amenities:** Concierge. *In room:* A/C, hair dryer, no phone.

Eagle Cap Chalets ⚜ *Kids*   Set under tall pines just a short walk from hiking trails and the lake, Eagle Cap Chalets has a wide variety of rooms, as well as an indoor pool and Jacuzzi, and a miniature golf course. Consequently, this place is very popular with families and groups. The rooms here vary from motel style to rustic-though-renovated cabins, and most have phones. Siding on all the buildings makes them appear to be built of logs. Cabins and condos have kitchens. In the early fall, there always seem to be deer hanging out on the lawns.

59879 Wallowa Lake Hwy., Joseph, OR 97846. © **541/432-4704** or 541/432-8800. www.eaglecapchalets.com. 35 units. $50–$95 double; $75–$150 cabin; $85–$140 1- and 2-bedroom condos. DISC, MC, V. Pets accepted in off season only ($20). **Amenities:** Indoor pool; Jacuzzi. *In room:* TV.

Imnaha River Inn ⌖   Located 35 miles northeast of Joseph on the edge of Hell's Canyon, this remote log inn is set deep in the Imnaha River Canyon. The sprawling modern inn is filled with animal hides and trophy heads, and the log construction conjures up the wild pioneering spirit of this region. The lofty, high-ceilinged living room, with its big stone fireplace, is the perfect place to relax after a day in the outdoors. However, the deck overlooking the river is equally enticing. Fishing, hunting, rafting, and hiking are the primary pursuits, but if you just want to get away from it all in an awe-inspiring setting, this is the best choice in all of eastern Oregon. Lunches ($6) and dinners ($15) are available.

73946 Rimrock Rd., Imnaha, OR 97842. © **866/601-9214** or 541/577-6002. www.imnahariverinn.com. 7 units (all with shared bathroom). $100–$110 double. Rates include full breakfast. No credit cards. **Amenities:** Dining room; game room. *In room:* A/C, no phone.

Wallowa Lake Lodge ⌖   This rustic two-story lodge at the south end of Wallowa Lake was built in 1923 and is surrounded by big pines and a wide expanse of lawn that attracts deer in late summer and early fall. Big comfortable chairs fill the lobby, where folks often sit by the stone fireplace in the evening. The guest rooms are divided between those with carpeting and modern bathrooms and those with hardwood floors, original bathroom fixtures, and antique furnishings (our favorites). All but two of the latter have two bedrooms each, and two rooms have balconies overlooking the lake. The cabins are rustic but comfortable and have full kitchens. The dining room is the best place in the area for dinner.

60060 Wallowa Lake Hwy., Joseph, OR 97846. © **541/432-9821.** Fax 541/432-4885. www.wallowalakelodge.com. 30 units (including 8 cabins). May to mid-Oct $89–$150 double, $120–$195 cabin; mid-Oct to Apr $75–$115 double, $95–$135 cabin. DISC, MC, V. **Amenities:** Restaurant (American); lounge. *In room:* No phone.

A GUEST RANCH IN THE WILDERNESS

Minam Lodge ⌖   Located on the Minam River and surrounded by the Eagle Cap Wilderness, Minam Lodge is 8½ miles from the nearest road and is accessible only on foot, on horseback, or by small plane, which makes this rustic and very remote getaway one of the most unusual lodges in the state. Horseback riding, hiking, fishing, and hunting are guests' primary pursuits. The rustic log cabins are set atop a low hill and have wood stoves for warmth; good-size windows let in the sunshine and the views. Horseback rides to and from the lodge are $65 each way, and horse rentals are available ($40 for 2 hr.; $80 for a full day). Guided overnight pack trips and packages are also available.

Minam Lodge Outfitters, 13716 S. Rock Creek Lane, Haines, OR 97833. © **541/519-8414** or 541/856-3617. www.minam lodgeoutfitters.com. 9 units. $112–$145 per person per night (children under 12 half price); $100 per night in dormitory. Rates include all meals. DISC, MC, V. Pets accepted. **Amenities:** Dining room; hot tub; sauna. *In room:* No phone. Closed Nov–Apr.

CAMPGROUNDS

At the south end of Wallowa Lake, you'll find a campground under the trees at **Wallowa Lake State Park** (© **541/432-4185**). In addition to campsites, the park has yurts and cabins for rent. For campsite reservations, contact **ReserveAmerica** (© 800/ 452-5687; www.reserveamerica.com).

WHERE TO DINE

If you're just looking for some baked goodies or a light lunch, check out the **Wild-flour Bakery,** 600 N. Main St., Joseph (© 541/432-7225), which is set behind an attractive perennial garden and has a deck out front and wooden booths inside.

Terminal Gravity Brewery & Pub ☆ INTERNATIONAL   Although it's small, this brewery on the east side of Enterprise gets raves across the state for its excellent beers. The beer alone would be worth a stop, but this little place, housed in an old Craftsman bungalow, also serves some of the best food in this corner of the state. There are only a couple of tables and a few barstools in the main dining room, but there are a few more tables upstairs and out on the veranda, plus some picnic tables in the front yard. Expect a couple of dinner specials each night; the menu itself has only a handful of basic dishes on the menu.

803 School St., Enterprise. © 541/426-0158. Main courses $7–$17. MC, V. Wed–Sat 11am–10pm; Sun–Mon 4–9pm.

Vali's Alpine Restaurant and Delicatessen ☆ EASTERN EUROPEAN   Just past the Wallowa Lake Lodge you'll find this little restaurant, which specializes in the hearty fare of Eastern Europe. Only one dish is served each evening, so if you like to have options, you won't want to eat here. Stuffed cabbage or Hungarian goulash (Wed), chicken paprikas (Thurs), beef kabobs (Fri), steak (Sat), and schnitzel (Sun) should help you stay warm on cold mountain evenings. Hungarian gypsy music plays on the stereo, and at breakfast there are fresh homemade doughnuts.

59811 Wallowa Lake Hwy. © 541/432-5691. Reservations required. Main courses $10–$12. No credit cards. Memorial Day to Labor Day Wed–Fri 5–8pm, Sat–Sun 9–11am and 5–8pm; Labor Day to Oct and mid-Mar to Memorial Day Sat–Sun 9–11am and 5–8pm. Closed Nov to mid-Mar.

Wallowa Lake Lodge Dining Room ☆ AMERICAN   This historic lodge at the far end of Wallowa Lake from Joseph is the quintessential Wallowa Mountains dining experience. There's often live music in the lobby of the lodge, and in the fall, you'll usually see deer on the lawns surrounding the hotel. Although the prime rib (served Fri and Sat nights only) is probably the most popular item on the menu, the halibut with marionberry glaze is also very good. Hazelnut pancakes with marionberry butter are a breakfast specialty.

60060 Wallowa Lake Hwy. © 541/432-9821. www.wallowalakelodge.com. Reservations recommended. Main courses $13–$28. DISC, MC, V. Daily 8–11am and 5:30–8pm.

4 Hells Canyon & the Southern Wallowas

South access: 70 miles NE of Baker City; North access: 20 to 30 miles E of Joseph

Sure, the Grand Canyon is an impressive sight, but few people realize that it isn't the deepest canyon in the United States. That distinction goes to **Hells Canyon,** which forms part of the border between Oregon and Idaho. Carved by the Snake River and bounded on the east by the Seven Devils Mountains and on the west by the Wallowa Mountains, Hells Canyon is as much as 8,000 feet deep. Although it's not quite as spectacular a sight as the Grand Canyon, neither is it as crowded. Because there is so little road access to Hells Canyon, it is one of the least-visited national recreation areas in the West.

The Hells Canyon area boasts a range of outdoor activities, but because of blazing hot temperatures in summer, when this rugged gorge lives up to its name, spring and fall are the best times to visit. Despite the heat, though, boating, swimming, and fishing are all popular in the summer.

ESSENTIALS

GETTING THERE   The south access to Hells Canyon National Recreation Area is reached off of Ore. 86 between 9 and 48 miles northeast of the town of Halfway, depending on which route you follow. Northern sections of the national recreation area, including the Hat Point Overlook, are reached from Joseph on Ore. 82, which begins in La Grande.

VISITOR INFORMATION   For more information, contact the **Hells Canyon National Recreation Area,** 88401 Ore. 82, Enterprise, OR 97828 (© **541/426-4978;** www.fs.fed.us/hellscanyon).

EXPLORING THE REGION

Much of **Hells Canyon** ⌖ is wilderness and is accessible only by boat, on horseback, or on foot. Few roads lead into the canyon, and most of these are recommended only for four-wheel-drive vehicles. If you are driving a car without high clearance, you'll have to limit your exploration of this region to the road to Hells Canyon Dam and the scenic byway that skirts the eastern flanks of the Wallowa Mountains. If you don't mind driving miles on gravel, you can also head out to the **Hat Point Overlook** east of Joseph.

Southern river-level access begins in the community of Oxbow, but the portion of the Snake River that has been designated a National Wild and Scenic River starts 27 miles farther north, below Hells Canyon Dam. Below the dam, the Snake River is turbulent with white water and provides thrills for jet boaters and rafters. To get this bottom-up view of the canyon, take Ore. 86 to Oxbow, cross the river into Idaho, and continue 22 miles downriver to **Hells Canyon Creek Visitor Center** (© **541/785-3395**), which is located 1 mile past the Hells Canyon Dam. This center has informative displays on the natural history of Hells Canyon and is open daily 8am to 4pm from Memorial Day weekend to the first week of October. The Stud Creek Trail leads 1 mile down the river from the visitor center and is an easy way to get a sense of what it's like to hike in the canyon.

To get a top-down overview of the canyon, drive to the **Hells Canyon Overlook,** 30 miles northeast of Halfway on Forest Road 39. From here you can gaze down into the canyon, but you won't be able to see the river.

You'll find many miles of **hiking trails** within the national recreation area, but summer heat, rattlesnakes, and poison oak keep all but the most dedicated hikers at bay. However, in early June, the wildflowers in Hells Canyon can be spectacular. For information on trails here, contact the information center for the recreation area (see above).

The best way to see Hells Canyon is by **white-water raft** or in a **jet boat.** Both sorts of trips can be arranged through **Hells Canyon Adventures,** 4200 Hells Canyon Dam Rd. (P.O. Box 159), Oxbow, OR 97840 (© **800/422-3568** or 541/785-3352; www. hellscanyonadventures.com). Jet-boat tours range from $32 to $442 per adult for a 2-hour tour to $110 per adult for a 6-hour tour. Children pay half price or less. A day of white-water rafting runs $165.

Multiday horseback trips into the southern Wallowas are offered by **Cornucopia Wilderness Pack Station,** P.O. Box 568, Union, OR 97883 (© **866/562-8075** or 541/562-1181; www.cornucopiapackstation.com), which charges around $175 per day for most of its trips. Hourly rides can also be arranged ($15 per hour).

You can also opt to explore the southern Wallowas with a llama carrying your gear. Contact **Wallowa Llamas,** 36678 Allstead Lane, Halfway, OR 97834 (© **541/742-2961;** www.wallowallamas.com), for more information. Trips range in price from $395 to $1,595.

WHERE TO STAY & DINE

Pine Valley Lodge 🌟🌟 *(Finds)*   This little lodge, composed of four old buildings in downtown Halfway, is a Wild West fantasy of an inn and is owned by a local cattle ranch. With handmade furniture and Western collectibles scattered about, the main lodge is a fascinating place to wander around. The main house has a large suite on the ground floor and two smaller rooms upstairs. Next door is the Blue Dog, a four-bedroom cottage. Outdoorsy types will like the Main Street Shack and Bunkhouse, which truly is a shack, albeit a charming one.

163 N. Main St. (P.O. Box 609), Halfway, OR 97834. © 541/742-2027. Fax 541/742-2028. www.pvlodge.com. 8 units (7 with private bathroom). $80–$160 double. Rates include continental breakfast. MC, V. Pets accepted ($10). **Amenities:** Business center; laundry service. *In room:* A/C, no phone.

5 Ontario & the Owyhee River Region

Ontario: 72 miles SE of Baker City, 63 miles NW of Boise, 130 miles NE of Burns

Ontario, the easternmost town in Oregon, lies in the Four Rivers region, at the confluence of the Owyhee, Snake, Malheur, and Payette rivers. Irrigated by waters from the massive Owyhee Reservoir, these wide, flat valleys are prime agricultural lands that produce onions, sugar beets, and, as in Idaho, plenty of potatoes. This region is also where most of the world's zinnia seeds are grown. During the summer, zinnia fields color the landscape in bold swaths. If you're curious to see the flower fields, head south out of Ontario on Ore. 201.

The biggest attraction in the region is the **Four Rivers Cultural Center,** which focuses on the various cultures that have made the region what it is today. However, there is also some Oregon Trail history to be seen nearby, and south of Ontario lies one of Oregon's most rugged and remote regions. This corner of the state is a vast untracked high desert, and along the banks of the Owyhee River and Succor Creek, you can see canyons and cliffs that seem far more suited to a Southwestern landscape.

ESSENTIALS

GETTING THERE   Ontario is on the Idaho line at the junction of I-84 and U.S. 20/26, all of which link the town to western Oregon.

VISITOR INFORMATION   For more information on the Ontario area, contact the **Ontario Chamber of Commerce,** 676 SW Fifth Ave., Ontario, OR 97914 (© **888/889-8012** or 541/889-8012; www.ontariochamber.com).

Note: Ontario follows Mountain Time, not Pacific Time.

A CULTURAL MUSEUM

Four Rivers Cultural Center & Museum 🌟   Although this remote corner of Oregon may seem an unlikely place for a multicultural museum, that is exactly what you'll find at the Four Rivers Cultural Center & Museum. The museum focuses on four very distinct cultures that have called this region home. The Paiutes were the original inhabitants of the area, and an exploration of their hunting-and-gathering culture is the first exhibit. In the mid–19th century, the first pioneers began arriving in the area and quickly displaced the Paiutes. By the late 19th century, many Mexican cowboys, known as *vaqueros* or *buckaroos*, had come north to the region to work the large cattle ranches. At the same time, Basque shepherds settled in the area and tended large herds of sheep in the more remote corners of the region. The fourth culture is that of the Japanese, who were forced to live in internment camps in the area during World War II. The museum is currently adding a Japanese garden.

676 SW Fifth Ave. ℂ 541/889-8191. www.4rcc.com. Admission $4 adults, $3 seniors and children 6–14. Mon–Sat 10am–5pm. Closed all national holidays.

MORE TO SEE & DO: EXPLORING THE REGION

For more Oregon Trail history, head 18 miles west of Ontario to the small farming community of **Vale.** Here you'll find the **Rinehart Stone House Museum,** 255 Main St. S. (ℂ **541/473-2070**), which was built in 1872 and was a stage stop and an important wayside along the route of the Oregon Trail. Today, it houses a small historical museum that is open from March through October Tuesday through Saturday from 12:30 to 4pm; admission is free. Six miles south of Vale, at Keeney Pass, you can see **wagon ruts** left by pioneers traveling the Oregon Trail.

South of Ontario 15 miles, you'll find **Nyssa,** the "Thunderegg Capital of Oregon." **Rockhounding** is the area's most popular pastime, and thundereggs (also known as *geodes*) are the prime find. These round rocks look quite plain until they are cut open to reveal the agate or crystals within. You'll find plenty of cut-and-polished thundereggs in the rock shops around town. If you'd like to do a bit of rockhounding yourself, you can head south to **Succor Creek State Natural Area** 🀫, a rugged canyon where you'll find a campground, picnic tables, and thundereggs waiting to be unearthed.

If you have a four-wheel-drive or high-clearance vehicle, you can continue another 30 minutes to **Leslie Gulch** 🀫🀫, an even more spectacular canyon with walls of naturally sculpted sandstone. If you're lucky, you might even see bighorn sheep here. Few places in Oregon have more of the feel of the desert than these two canyons, and just as in the desert Southwest, here, too, rivers have been dammed to provide irrigation waters and aquatic playgrounds. **Lake Owyhee,** 45 miles south of Ontario off Ore. 201, is the longest lake in Oregon and offers boating, fishing, and camping. The Owyhee River above the lake is a designated State Scenic Waterway and is popular for **white-water rafting** 🀫🀫. If you're interested in running this remote stretch of river, contact **Destination Wilderness** (ℂ **800/423-8868** or 541/549-1336; www.wildernesstrips.com), or **Oregon Whitewater Adventures** (ℂ **800/820-RAFT** or 541/746-5422; www.oregon whitewater.com), both of which occasionally run this river. Expect to pay $675 to $990 for a 5-day trip. Below the Owyhee Dam, 12 miles southwest of the town of Adrian, you'll find a signposted WATCHABLE WILDLIFE **area** that offers excellent bird-watching. You may also spot beavers, porcupines, mule deer, and coyotes.

WHERE TO STAY

For the most part, Ontario is a way station for people traveling along I-84, and as such, the city's accommodations are strictly off-ramp budget motels. Motel options include a **Best Western Inn,** 251 Goodfellow St., Ontario, OR 97914 (ℂ **800/828-0364** or

541/889-2600), charging $56 to $169 double; a **Super 8 Motel,** 266 Goodfellow St., Ontario, OR 97914 (© **800/800-8000** or 541/889-8282), charging $51 to $66 double; and a **Motel 6,** 275 NE 12th St., Ontario, OR 97914 (© **800/466-8356** or 541/889-6617), charging $38 to $45 double.

At nearby **Farewell Bend State Recreation Area** (© **541/869-2365**), 25 miles northwest of Ontario on I-84, you'll find not only campsites but also covered wagons that can be rented for overnight stays ($29 per night). Don't look for horses to hitch up, though; these wagons stay put. The park also rents teepees ($29 per night) and cabins ($38 per night). For campsite, covered-wagon, and teepee reservations, contact **ReserveAmerica** (© **800/452-5687;** www.reserveamerica.com).

WHERE TO DINE

In downtown Ontario, you'll find a couple of basic Mexican restaurants and some places specializing in steaks, but that's about it.

6 Southeastern Oregon: Land of Marshes, Mountains & Desert

Burns: 130 miles SE of Bend, 130 miles SW of Ontario, 70 miles S of John Day

Southeastern Oregon, the most remote and least populated region of the state, is a region of extremes. Vast marshlands, the most inhospitable desert in the state, and a mountain topped with aspen groves and glacial valleys are among the most prominent features of this landscape. Although cattle outnumber human inhabitants, and the deer and the antelope play, it's birdlife that's the region's number-one attraction. At **Malheur National Wildlife Refuge,** birds abound almost any month of the year, attracting flocks of bird-watchers, binoculars and bird books in hand.

Because this is such an isolated region (Burns and Lakeview are the only towns of consequence), it is not an area to be visited by the unprepared. Always keep your gas tank topped off and carry water for both you and your car. Two of the region's main attractions, **Steens Mountain** and the **Hart Mountain National Antelope Refuge,** are accessible only by way of gravel roads more than 50 miles long. A visit to the Alvord Desert will also require spending 60 or more miles on a gravel road.

ESSENTIALS

GETTING THERE   The town of Burns is midway between Bend and Ontario on U.S. 20. Malheur National Wildlife Refuge, Steens Mountain, and Hart Mountain National Antelope Refuge are all located south of Burns off Ore. 205.

VISITOR INFORMATION   For more information on this area, contact the **Harney County Chamber of Commerce,** 76 E. Washington St., Burns, OR 97720 (© **541/573-2636;** www.harneycounty.com).

EXPLORING THE REGION

Because water is scarce here in the high desert, it becomes a magnet for wildlife wherever it appears. Three marshy lakes—Malheur, Harney, and Mud—south of Burns cover such a vast area and provide such an ideal habitat for birdlife that they have been designated the **Malheur National Wildlife Refuge** ⊀. The shallow lakes, surrounded by thousands of acres of marshlands, form an oasis that annually attracts more than 300 species of birds, including waterfowl, shorebirds, songbirds, and raptors. Some of the more noteworthy birds that are either resident or migratory at Malheur are trumpeter swans, sandhill cranes, white pelicans, great blue herons, and great horned owls.

Of the more than 58 mammals that live in the refuge, the most visible are mule deer, pronghorn antelope, and coyotes, but I once saw a bobcat near the visitor center.

The refuge headquarters is 32 miles south of Burns on Ore. 205, but the refuge stretches for another 30 miles south to the crossroads of Frenchglen. The refuge is open daily from dawn to dusk. The **visitor center,** where you can find out about recent sightings and current birding hot spots, is open weekdays and most weekends during the spring and summer, while a **museum** housing a collection of nearly 200 stuffed-and-mounted birds is open daily. About 6 miles north of the visitor center, you can visit **Historic Sod House Ranch,** which at one time was the northern headquarters for the huge ranch created by 19th-century rancher Peter French (for whom the nearby community of Frenchglen is named). The ranch preserves several historic buildings including a 116-foot-long barn. The ranch, which is part of the wildlife refuge, is open August 15 to October 31 daily from 8am to 4pm, and there are interpretive tours between 9am and 3pm. Camping is available at two campgrounds near Frenchglen. For more information on the refuge, contact Refuge Manager, **Malheur National Wildlife Refuge,** HC 72 Box 245, Princeton, OR 97721 (© **541/493-2612;** www.fws.gov/malheur).

Steens Mountain, at 9,733 feet high, is a different sort of desert oasis. This mountain rises so high that it creates its own weather, and on the upper slopes the sagebrush of the high desert gives way to juniper and aspen forests. From Frenchglen, there's a 66-mile loop road that leads to the summit and back down by a different route. Due to early snows and lingering snow in the spring, this road is usually open only between July and October. Even then the road is not recommended for cars with low clearance, but if you have the appropriate vehicle, the mountain is well worth a visit.

Steens Mountain is a fault-block mountain that was formed when the land on the west side of a geological fault line rose in relationship to the land on the east side of the fault. This geologic upheaval caused the east slope of Steens Mountain to form a precipitous escarpment that falls away to the Alvord Desert a mile below. From the summit of Steens Mountain, the panorama across southeastern Oregon is spectacular. The road leads almost to the summit, but then you'll have to walk 5 or 10 minutes to the very top of the peak. Stretched out below you when you stand on the summit, or at the nearby East Rim Overlook, are four glacier-carved gorges—Kiger, Little Blitzen, Big Indian, and Wildhorse. From near the summit, a steep and strenuous trail leads down into Wildhorse Gorge to Wildhorse Lake. Although the round-trip hike is only 2.6 miles in length, it involves descending and then ascending 1,100 feet to and from the floor of the gorge. And, yes, there are wild horses in the area; they are known as Kiger mustangs.

For more information on Steens Mountain, contact the **Bureau of Land Management (BLM),** Burns District Office, HC74, 12533 U.S. 20 W., Hines, OR 97738 (© **541/573-4400**).

More wildlife-viewing opportunities are available at the **Hart Mountain National Antelope Refuge** ⚐, which is a refuge for both pronghorns, the fastest land mammal in North America, and California bighorn sheep. The most accessible location for viewing pronghorns is the refuge headquarters, 49 miles southwest of Frenchglen. For more information, contact the **Sheldon-Hart Mountain National Wildlife Refuge Complex,** P.O. Box 111, Lakeview, OR 97630 (© **541/947-3315;** www. fws.gov/sheldonhartmtn).

Appendix:
Oregon in Depth

1 The Natural Environment

At 97,073 square miles (roughly 1½ times the size of New England), Oregon is the 10th-largest state in the Union, and it encompasses within its vast area an amazing diversity of natural environments— not only lush forests, but also deserts, glacier-covered peaks, grasslands, alpine meadows, sagebrush-covered hills, sand beaches, and rugged ocean shores. Together, these diverse environments support a surprisingly wide variety of natural life.

The **Oregon coast** stretches for nearly 300 miles from the redwood country of Northern California north to the mouth of the Columbia River, and for most of this length is only sparsely populated. Consequently, this coastline provides habitat not only for large populations of seabirds—such as cormorants, tufted puffins, and pigeon guillemots—but also for several species of marine mammals, including Pacific gray whales, Steller's sea lions, California sea lions, and harbor seals.

Each year between December and April, more than 20,000 **Pacific gray whales** pass by the Oregon coast as they make their annual migration south to their breeding grounds off Baja California. These whales can often be seen from shore at various points along the coast, and numerous whale-watching tour boats operate out of different ports. Many gray whales also spend the summer in Oregon's offshore waters, and it is possible to spot these leviathans any month of the year. More frequently spotted, however,

are **harbor seals** and Steller's and California **sea lions,** which are frequently seen lounging on rocks. The Newport bayfront, Sea Lion Caves, and Cape Arago State Park, all on the central Oregon coast, are the best places to spot sea lions.

The **Coast Range,** which in places rises directly from the waves, gives the coastline its rugged look. However, even more than the mountains, it is **rain** that gives this coastline its definitive character. As moist winds from the Pacific Ocean rise up and over the Coast Range, they drop their moisture as rain and snow. The tremendous amounts of rain that fall on these mountains have produced dense forests that are home to some of the largest trees on earth. Although the south coast is the northern limit for the coast redwood, the **Douglas firs,** which are far more common and grow throughout the region, are almost as impressive in size, sometimes reaching 300 feet tall. Other common trees of these coastal forests include Sitka spruce, Western hemlocks, Port Orford cedars, Western red cedars, and, along the southern Oregon coast, evergreen myrtle trees. The wood of these latter trees is used extensively for carving, and myrtle-wood shops are common along the south coast.

More than a century of intensive **logging** has, however, left the state's forests of centuries-old trees shrunken to remnant groves scattered in largely remote and rugged areas. How much exactly is still left is a matter of hot debate between the timber industry and environmentalists, and the battle to save the remaining old-growth forests continues, with both sides claiming victories and losses with each passing year.

Among this region's most celebrated and controversial wild residents is the **Northern spotted owl,** which, because of its requirements for large tracts of undisturbed old-growth forest and its listing as a federally endangered species, brought logging of old-growth forests to a virtual halt in the 1990s. Concern next focused on the **marbled murrelet,** a small bird that feeds on the open ocean but nests exclusively in old-growth forests. Destruction of forests has also been partially blamed for the demise of trout, salmon, and steelhead populations throughout the region.

Roosevelt elk, the largest commonly encountered land mammal in the Northwest, can be found throughout the Coast Range, and there are even designated elk-viewing areas along the coast (one off U.S. 26 near Jewell and one off Ore. 38 near Reedsport).

To the east of the northern section of the Coast Range lies the **Willamette Valley,** which, because of its mild climate and fertile soils, was the first region of the state to be settled by pioneers. Today, the Willamette Valley remains the state's most densely populated region and is home to Oregon's largest cities. It also still contains the most productive farmland in the state.

To the east of the Willamette Valley rise the mountains of the 700-mile-long **Cascade Range,** which stretches from Northern California to southern British Columbia. The most prominent features of the Oregon's Cascades are its **volcanic peaks:** Hood, Jefferson, Three Fingered Jack, Washington, the Three Sisters, Broken Top, Thielsen, and McLoughlin. The eruption of Washington's Mount St. Helens on May 18, 1980, reminded

Northwesterners that this is still a volcanically active region. However, here in Oregon, it is the remains of ancient Mount Mazama, which erupted with unimaginable violence 7,000 years ago, that provide the most dramatic reminder of the potential power of Cascade volcanoes. Today, the waters of **Crater Lake** fill the shell of this long-gone peak. Near the town of Bend, geologically recent volcanic activity is also visible in the form of cinder cones, lava flows, lava caves, and craters. Much of this volcanic landscape near Bend is now preserved as **Newberry National Volcanic Monument.**

The same moisture-laden clouds that produce the near rainforest conditions in the Coast Range frequently leave the Cascades with heavy snows and, on the highest peaks (Mount Hood, Mount Jefferson, the Three Sisters), numerous glaciers. The most readily accessible glaciers are on **Mount Hood,** where ski lifts keep running right through the summer, carrying skiers and snowboarders to slopes atop the Palmer Glacier, high above the historic Timberline Lodge.

East of the Cascades, less than 200 miles from the damp Coast Range forests, the landscape becomes a desert. The **Great Basin,** which reaches its northern limit in central and eastern Oregon, comprises a vast, high-desert region that stretches east to the Rockies. Through this desolate landscape flows the **Columbia River,** which, together with its tributary, the Snake River, forms the second-largest river drainage in the United States. During the last ice age, roughly 13,000 years ago, glaciers repeatedly blocked the flow of the Columbia, forming huge lakes behind dams of ice. These vast prehistoric lakes repeatedly burst the ice dams, sending massive and devastating walls of water flooding down the Columbia. These floodwaters were sometimes 1,000 feet high and carried with them ice and rocks, which scoured out the **Columbia Gorge.** Today, the gorge's many waterfalls are the most evident signs of these prehistoric floods.

Today, it is numerous large, modern **dams,** not ice, that impound the Columbia, and these dams have become the focus of another of the region's environmental battles. The large dams, mostly built during the middle part of the 20th century, present a variety of barriers both to adult salmon heading upstream and to young salmon headed downstream to the Pacific. Though many of the dams have fish ladders to allow **salmon** to return upriver to spawn, salmon must still negotiate an obstacle course of degraded spawning grounds, slower river flows in the reservoirs behind the dams, turbines that kill fish by the thousands, and irrigation canals that often confuse salmon into swimming out of the river and into farm fields. Overfishing for salmon canneries in the late 19th century struck the first major blow to salmon populations, and for more than a century, these fish have continued to struggle against man-made and natural obstacles. Compounding the problems faced by wild salmon has been the use of fish hatcheries to supplement the wild fish

populations (hatchery fish tend to be less vigorous than wild salmon). A salmon recovery plan was adopted in the 1990s to attempt to save threatened runs of native salmon, but farmers, electricity producers, shipping companies, and major users of hydroelectric power have continued to fight the requirements of the recovery plan, which include lowering water levels in reservoirs to speed the downstream migration of young salmon.

South-central and southeastern Oregon are the most remote and unpopulated regions of the state. However, this vast desert area does support an abundance of wildlife. The **Hart Mountain National Antelope Refuge** shelters herds of pronghorn antelopes, which are the fastest land mammals in North America. This refuge also protects a small population of California bighorn sheep. At **Malheur National Wildlife Refuge,** more than 300 bird species frequent large shallow lakes and wetlands, and at the **Lower Klamath National Wildlife Refuge,** large numbers of bald eagles gather each winter. Several other of the region's large lakes, including Summer Lake and Lake Abert, also attract large populations of birds.

2 Oregon Today

Oregon is a state dominated by a **love of the outdoors,** and this isn't surprising when you realize just how much nature dominates beyond the city limits. From almost anywhere in Oregon, it's possible to look up and see green forests and snow-capped mountains, and a drive of less than 2 hours from any Willamette Valley city will get you to the mountains or the Pacific Ocean's beaches.

Oregonians don't let the weather stand between them and the outdoors. The temptation is too great to head for the mountains, the river, or the beach—no matter what the forecast. Consequently, life in Oregon's cities tends to revolve less around cultural venues and shopping

than around parks, gardens, waterfronts, rivers, mountains, and beaches. Portland has its Forest Park, Rose Garden, Japanese Garden, Classical Chinese Garden, and Waterfront Park. Eugene has its miles of riverside parks, bike paths, and even a park just for rock climbing. In Hood River, the entire Columbia River has become a playground for windsurfers and kiteboarders, and when the wind doesn't blow, there are always the nearby mountain-bike trails and rivers for kayaking. In Bend, mountain biking, downhill skiing, and snowboarding are a way of life. These outdoor areas are where people find tranquillity, where summer festivals are held, where locals take their visiting friends and relatives, and where Oregonians tend to live their lives when they aren't being interrupted by such inconveniences as work and sleep.

This is not to say, however, that the region is a cultural wasteland. Both Portland and Eugene have large, modern, and active **performing arts centers.** During the summer months, numerous **festivals** take music, theater, and dance outdoors. Most impressive of these are the Oregon Shakespeare Festival and the Britt Festivals, both of which are staged in southern Oregon. Many other festivals feature everything from chamber music to alternative rock.

Word of the state's natural beauty and the Oregon good life has been spreading far and wide in recent years, and the state has been experiencing unprecedented growth. As the population in urban areas of the Willamette Valley has expanded, a pronounced urban-rural **political split** has developed in Oregon. Citizens from the eastern part of the state argue that Salem and Portland are dictating to rural regions that have little in common with the cities, while urban dwellers, who far outnumber those living outside the Willamette Valley, argue that majority rule is majority rule. This split has pitted conservative voters (often from rural regions) against liberal voters (usually urban) on a wide variety of issues, and the reality of Oregon politics is now quite a bit different from the popular perception of a state dominated by liberal, forward-thinking environmentalists and former hippies. Medical use of marijuana and assisted suicide, both of which were legalized in Oregon in the late 1990s, have both continued to generate controversy and court cases.

Some areas outside of Oregon's urban population centers have also been experiencing rapid growth. Hood River in the Columbia Gorge, Bend in central Oregon, and the Ashland/Medford area of southern Oregon have all been attracting large numbers of wealthy retirees and other transplants. These areas have all seen lots of development in the past few years, and along with this development has come a proliferation of high-end restaurants. So, for anyone visiting the state, Oregon's popularity as a place to live has also made the state a great place to visit.

3 Oregon History 101

EARLY HISTORY   The oldest known inhabitants of what is now the state of Oregon lived along the shores of huge lakes in the Klamath Lakes Basin some 10,000 years ago. Here they fished and hunted ducks and left records of their

Dateline

- **13,000 B.C.** Massive floods, as much as 1,200 feet deep, rage down Columbia River and carve the Columbia Gorge.
- **10,000 B.C.** Earliest known human inhabitation of Oregon.
- **5,000 B.C.** Mount Mazama erupts violently, creating a caldera that will later fill with water and become known as Crater Lake.
- **A.D. 1542** Spanish exploratory ship reaches what is now the southern Oregon coast.
- **1579** Englishman Sir Francis Drake reaches the mouth of the Rogue River.
- **1602** Spain's Martín de Aguilar explores the coast of Oregon, probably as far as Coos Bay.
- **1792** Robert Gray becomes the first explorer to sail a ship into a great river he names the Columbia, in honor of his ship the *Columbia Rediviva.*
- **1805–06** Expedition led by Meriwether Lewis and William Clark crosses the continent and spends the winter at the mouth of the Columbia River.

continued

passing in several caves. These peoples would have witnessed the massive eruption of Mount Mazama, which left a vast caldera that eventually filled with water and was named Crater Lake. Along the coast, numerous small tribes subsisted on salmon and shellfish. In the northeast corner of the state, the Nez Perce Indians became experts at horse breeding even before Lewis and Clark passed through the region at the start of the 19th century. In fact, the appaloosa horse derives its name from the nearby Palouse Hills of Washington.

However, it was the **Columbia River tribes** that became the richest of the Oregon tribes through their control of Celilo Falls, which was historically the richest salmon-fishing area in the Northwest. These massive falls on the Columbia River, east of present-day The Dalles, witnessed the annual passage of millions of salmon, which were speared and dipnetted by Native Americans, who then smoked the fish to preserve it for the winter. Today, Native Americans still fish for salmon as they once did, perched on precarious wooden platforms with dip nets in hand. However, Celilo Falls are gone, inundated by the water impounded behind The Dalles Dam, which was completed in 1957. Today, little remains of what was once the Northwest's most important Native American gathering ground, a place where tribes from hundreds of miles away congregated each year to fish and trade.

Even before this amazing fishing ground was lost, a far greater tragedy had been visited upon Northwest tribes. Between the 1780s, when white explorers and traders began frequenting the Northwest coast, and the 1830s, when the first settlers began arriving, the Native American population of the Northwest was reduced to perhaps a 10th of its historic numbers. These people were not wiped out by war but by European diseases—smallpox, measles, malaria, and influenza. The Native Americans had no resistance to these diseases, and entire tribes were soon wiped out by fast-spreading epidemics.

THE AGE OF EXPLORATION

Though a Spanish ship reached what is now southern Oregon in 1542, the Spanish had no interest in the gray and rainy coast. Nor did famed British buccaneer Sir Francis Drake, who in 1579 sailed his ship the *Golden Hind* as far north as the mouth of the Rogue River. Drake called off his explorations in the face of what he described as "thicke and stinking fogges."

However, when the Spanish found out that Russian fur traders were establishing themselves in Alaska and along the North Pacific coast, Spain took a new interest in the Northwest. Several **Spanish expeditions** sailed north from Mexico to

- **1810** Americans attempt first settlement at the Columbia River's mouth.
- **1819** Spain cedes all lands above 42-degree north latitude.
- **1824–25** Russia gives up claims to land south of Alaska; Fort Vancouver founded by Hudson's Bay Company on Columbia River near present-day Portland.
- **1834** Methodist missionary Jason Lee founds Salem,

which later becomes the state capital.
- **1840** First settlers move to what is now Oregon.
- **1842** Jason Lee founds first school of higher learning west of the Mississippi.
- **1843** First wagons cross the continent on the Oregon Trail; Asa Lovejoy and William Overton stake claim on land that will soon become Portland.

- **1844** Oregon City becomes the first incorporated town west of the Mississippi.
- **1846** The 49th parallel is established as the boundary between American and British territories in the Northwest.
- **1848** Oregon becomes first U.S. territory west of the Rockies.
- **1851** Portland is incorporated; gold is discovered in southern Oregon.

reassert the Spanish claim to the region. In 1775, Spanish explorers Bruno de Heceta and Francisco de la Bodega y Quadra charted much of the Northwest coast, and though they found the mouth of the Columbia River, they did not enter it. To this day, four of the coast's most scenic headlands—Cape Perpetua, Heceta Head, Cape Arago, and Cape Blanco—bear names from these early Spanish explorations.

It was not until 1792 that an explorer, American trader Robert Gray, risked a passage through treacherous sandbars that guarded the mouth of the long-speculated-upon Great River of the West. Gray named this newfound river Columbia's River, in honor of his ship, the *Columbia Rediviva.* This discovery established the first American claim to the region. When news of the *Columbia's* discovery reached the United States and England, both countries began speculating on a northern water route across North America. Such a route, if it existed, would facilitate trade with the Northwest.

In 1793, Scotsman Alexander Mac-Kenzie made the first overland trip across North America north of New Spain. Crossing British Canada on foot, MacKenzie arrived somewhere north of Vancouver Island. After reading MacKenzie's account of his journey, Thomas Jefferson decided that the United States needed to find a better route overland to the Northwest. To this end, he commissioned Meriwether Lewis and William Clark to lead an expedition up the Missouri River in hopes of finding a single easy portage that would lead to the Columbia River.

Beginning in 1804, the members of the **Lewis and Clark expedition** paddled up the Missouri, crossed the Rocky Mountains on foot, and then paddled down the Columbia River to its mouth. A French Canadian trapper and his Native American wife, Sacagawea, were enlisted as interpreters, and it was the presence of Sacagawea that helped the expedition gain acceptance among Western tribes. After spending the wet and dismal winter of 1805 to 1806 at the mouth of the Columbia at a spot they named **Fort Clatsop,** the expedition headed back east. Discoveries made by the expedition added greatly to the scientific and geographical knowledge of the continent. A replica of Fort Clatsop in the newly designated Lewis and Clark National and State Historical Park burned down in late 2005, just prior to the park's bicentennial celebrations, but at press time, work was already underway to rebuild the fort, which was one of the most interesting historical sites in the state. Outside of The Dalles, a campsite used by Lewis and Clark has also been preserved.

- **1915** Columbia Gorge scenic highway is constructed.
- **1935** Angus Bowmer stages *As You Like It* in Ashland and plants the seed of the Oregon Shakespeare Festival.
- **1940s** Kaiser shipyards in the Portland area become the world's foremost shipbuilders.
- **1945** Oregon becomes the only state with civilian war casualties when a Japanese balloon bomb kills six children.
- **1957** The Dalles Dam is completed; backwaters inundate Celilo Falls, the region's most productive Native American salmon-fishing grounds.
- **1974** In a bold step toward making Portland a more livable city, a freeway along the city's downtown waterfront is removed.
- **2005** The replica of Lewis and Clark's Fort Clatsop near Astoria burns down only months prior to planned bicentennial celebrations.

Did You Know?

- Oregon was home to America's first policewoman, Lola Greene Baldwin, who joined the Portland force in 1908.
- Matt Groening, creator of *The Simpsons,* got his start in Portland.
- Portland is home to the world's smallest dedicated park—Mill Ends Park—measuring only 24 inches in diameter.
- Oregon is one of the few states with no sales tax.
- Astoria, in the very northwest corner of the state, is the oldest American community west of the Mississippi.
- Oregon's Crater Lake is the deepest lake in the U.S.
- Hells Canyon is the deepest gorge in North America.

In 1819, the Spanish relinquished all claims north of the present California-Oregon state line, and the Russians gave up their claims to all lands south of Alaska. This left only the British and Americans dickering for control of the Northwest.

SETTLEMENT Fur Traders, Missionaries & the Oregon Trail Only 6 years after Lewis and Clark spent the winter at the mouth of the Columbia, employees of John Jacob Astor's Pacific Fur Company managed to establish themselves at a nearby spot they called **Fort Astoria.** This was the first permanent settlement in the Northwest, but with the War of 1812 being fought on the far side of the continent, the fur traders at Fort Astoria, with little protection against the British, chose to relinquish control of their fort. In the wake of the war, the fort returned to American control, though the United States and Britain produced no firm decision about possession of the Northwest. The British still dominated the region, but American trade was tolerated.

With the decline of the sea-otter population, British fur traders turned to beaver and headed inland up the Columbia River. For the next 30 years or so, fur-trading companies would be the sole authority in the region. Fur-trading posts were established throughout the Northwest, though most were on the eastern edge of the territory in the foothills of the Rocky Mountains. The powerful Hudson's Bay Company (HBC) eventually became the single fur-trading company in the Northwest.

In 1824, the HBC established its Northwest headquarters at **Fort Vancouver,** 100 miles up the Columbia near the mouth of the Willamette River; and in 1829, the HBC founded **Oregon City** at the falls of the Willamette River. Between 1824 and 1846, when the 49th parallel was established as the boundary between British and American northwestern lands, Fort Vancouver was the most important settlement in the region. A replica of the fort now stands in the city of Vancouver, Washington, across the Columbia River from Portland. In Oregon City, several homes from this period are still standing, including that of John McLoughlin, who was chief factor at Fort Vancouver and aided many of the early pioneers who arrived in the area after traveling the Oregon Trail.

By the 1830s, the future of the Northwest had arrived in the form of **American missionaries.** The first was Jason Lee, who established his mission in the Willamette Valley near present-day Salem.

(Today, the site is Willamette Mission State Park.) Two years later, in 1836, Marcus and Narcissa Whitman, along with Henry and Eliza Spaulding, made the overland trek to Fort Vancouver, then backtracked into what is now eastern Washington and Idaho, to establish two missions. This journey soon inspired other settlers to make the difficult overland crossing.

In 1840, a slow trickle of American settlers began crossing the continent, a 2,000-mile journey. Their destination was the Oregon country, which had been promoted as a veritable Eden where land was waiting to be claimed. In 1843, Marcus Whitman, after traveling east to plead with his superiors not to shut down his mission, headed back west, leading 900 settlers on the **Oregon Trail.** Before these settlers ever arrived, the small population of retired trappers, missionaries, and HBC employees who were living at Fort Vancouver and in nearby Oregon City had formed a provisional government in anticipation of the land-claim problems that would arise with the influx of settlers to the region. Today, the best places to learn about the experiences of the Oregon Trail emigrants are at the Oregon Trail Interpretive Center outside Baker City and the End of the Oregon Trail Interpretive Center in Oregon City. In many places in the eastern part of the state, **Oregon Trail wagon ruts** can still be seen.

In 1844, Oregon City became the first incorporated town west of the Rocky Mountains. This outpost in the wilderness, a gateway to the fertile lands of the Willamette Valley, was the destination of the wagon trains that began traveling the Oregon Trail, each year bringing more and more settlers to the region. As the land in the Willamette Valley was claimed, settlers began fanning out to different regions of the Northwest so that during the late 1840s and early 1850s many new towns, including Portland, were founded.

Though the line between American and British land in the Northwest had been established in 1846 at the 49th parallel (the current U.S.–Canada border), Oregon was not given U.S. territorial status until 1848. It was the massacre of the missionaries at the Whitman mission in Walla Walla (now in Washington state) and the subsequent demand for territorial status and U.S. military protection that brought about the establishment of the first U.S. territory west of the Rockies.

The discovery of **gold** in eastern Oregon in 1860 set the stage for one of the saddest chapters in Northwest history. With miners pouring into eastern Oregon and Washington, conflicts with Native Americans over land were inevitable. Since 1805, when Lewis and Clark had first passed this way, the **Nez Perce tribes** (the name means "pierced nose" in French) had been friendly to the white settlers. However, in 1877 a disputed treaty caused friction. Led by Chief Joseph, 700 Nez Perce, including 400 women and children, began a march from their homeland to their new reservation. Along the way, several angry young men, in revenge for the murder of an older member of the tribe, attacked a white settlement and killed several people. The U.S. Army took up pursuit of the Nez Perce, who fled across Idaho and Montana, only to be caught 40 miles from the Canadian border and sanctuary.

INDUSTRIALIZATION & THE 20TH CENTURY

From the very beginning of white settlement in the Northwest, the region based its growth on an extractive economy. **Lumber** and **salmon** were exploited ruthlessly. The history of the timber and salmon-fishing industries ran parallel for more than a century and led to similar results in the 1990s.

The trees in Oregon grew to gigantic proportions. Nurtured on steady rains, such trees as Douglas fir, Sitka spruce, Western red cedar, Port Orford cedar, and hemlock grew tall and straight, sometimes as tall as 300 feet. The first sawmill in the Northwest began operation near present-day Vancouver, Washington, in 1828, and between the 1850s and the 1870s, Northwest sawmills supplied the growing California market as well as a limited foreign market. When the transcontinental railroads arrived in the 1880s, a whole new market opened up, and mills began shipping to the eastern states.

Lumber companies developed a cut-and-run policy that leveled the forests. By the turn of the century, the government had gained more control over public forests in an attempt to slow the decimation of forestlands, and sawmill owners began buying up huge tracts of land. At the outbreak of World War I, more than 20% of the forestland in the Northwest was owned by three companies—Weyerhaeuser, the Northern Pacific Railroad, and the Southern Pacific Railroad—and more than 50% of the workforce labored in the timber industry.

The timber industry, which has always been extremely susceptible to fluctuations in the economy, experienced a roller-coaster ride of boom and bust throughout the 20th century. Boom times in the 1970s brought on record-breaking production that came to a screeching halt in the 1980s, first with a nationwide recession and then with the listing of the **Northern spotted owl** as a threatened species. When the timber industry was born in the Northwest, there was a belief that the forests of the region were endless. However, by the latter half of this century, big lumber companies had realized that the forests were dwindling. Tree farms were planted with increasing frequency, but the large old trees continued

to be cut faster than younger trees could replenish them. By the 1970s, environmentalists, shocked by the vast clear-cuts, began trying to save the last **old-growth trees.** The battle between the timber industry and environmentalists is today still one of the state's most heated debates, and tree-sitters continue to attract media attention as they attempt to stop the cutting of old-growth forests.

In the Northwest, salmon was the mainstay of the Native American diet for thousands of years before the first whites arrived in the Oregon country, but within 10 years of the opening of the first salmon cannery in the Northwest, the fish population was decimated. In 1877, the first fish hatchery was developed to replenish dwindling runs of salmon, and by 1895, salmon canning had reached its peak on the Columbia River. Later, in the 20th century, salmon runs would be further decimated by the construction of numerous dams on the Columbia and Snake rivers. Though fish ladders help adult salmon make their journeys upstream, the young salmon heading downstream have no such help, and the turbines of hydroelectric dams kill a large percentage of fish. One solution to this problem has been barging and trucking young salmon downriver. Today the **salmon populations** of the Northwest have been so diminished that entire runs of salmon have been listed as threatened or endangered under the Endangered Species Act. Talk in recent years has focused on the removal of certain dams that pose insurmountable barriers to salmon. There is great resistance to this, and long, drawn-out legal battles continue to wend their way through the courts.

The dams that have proved such a detriment to salmon populations have, however, provided irrigation water and cheap electricity that have fueled both industry and farming. Using irrigation water, potato and wheat farms flourished in northeastern Oregon after the middle of the 20th century. The reservoirs behind the Columbia and Snake River dams have also turned these rivers into waterways that can be navigated by huge barges, which often carry wheat downriver from ports in Idaho. Today, the **regional salmon recovery plan** is attempting to strike a balance between saving salmon runs and meeting all the other needs that have been created since the construction of these dams.

Manufacturing began gaining importance during and after World War II. In the Portland area, the Kaiser Shipyards employed tens of thousands of people in the construction of warships, but the postwar years saw the demise of the Kaiser facilities. In the 1980s and 1990s, there was a diversification into **high-tech industries,** with such major manufacturers as Intel, Epson, and Hewlett-Packard operating manufacturing facilities in the Willamette Valley.

However, it is in the area of **sportswear manufacturing** that Oregon businesses have gained the greatest visibility. With outdoor recreation a way of life in this state, it comes as no surprise that a few regional companies have grown into international giants. Chief among these is Nike, which is headquartered in the Portland suburb of Beaverton. Other familiar names include Jantzen, one of the nation's oldest swimwear manufacturers; Pendleton Woolen Mills, maker of classic wool shirts, Indian-design blankets, and other classic wool fashions; and Columbia Sportswear, which in recent years has become one of the country's biggest sports-related outerwear manufacturers. If you like to play outside, you probably own some article of clothing that originated in Oregon.

4 Eat, Drink & Be Merry

Although there is no cuisine that can be specifically identified as Oregon cuisine, there is a regional Northwest cooking style that can be distinguished by its pairings of meats and seafood with local fruits and nuts. This cuisine features such regional produce as salmon, oysters, halibut, raspberries, blackberries, apples, pears, and hazelnuts. A classic Northwest dish might be raspberry chicken or halibut with a hazelnut crust.

Salmon is king of Oregon fish and has been for thousands of years, so it isn't surprising that in one shape or another, it shows up on plenty of menus throughout the state. It's prepared in seemingly endless ways, but the most traditional method is what's known as **alder-planked salmon.** Traditionally, this Native American cooking style entailed preparing a salmon as a single filet, splaying it on readily available alder wood, and slow-cooking it over hot coals. The result is a cross between grilling and smoking. Today, however, it's hard to find salmon prepared this traditional way. Much more readily available, especially along the Oregon coast, is traditional **smoked salmon.** Smoked oysters are usually also available at smokehouses and are a treat worth trying.

With plenty of clean cold waters in many of its bays and estuaries, Oregon raises large numbers of **oysters,** especially in Tillamook and Coos Bays. If you see an oyster burger listed on a menu, give it a try; there's no beef, just oysters. Plenty of mussels and clams also come from these waters. Of particular note are **razor clams,** which can be tough and chewy if not prepared properly, but which are eagerly sought after along north-coast beaches when the clamming season is open. After salmon, though, **Dungeness crab** is the region's other top seafood offering. Though not as large as an

Alaskan king crab, the Dungeness is usually big enough to make a meal for one or two people. Crab cakes are also ubiquitous on Oregon restaurant menus, and along the coast, you can find old-fashioned crab shacks that boil up crabs on a daily basis.

The Northwest's combination of climate and abundant irrigation waters has also helped make this one of the nation's major fruit-growing regions. The Hood River Valley and the Medford area are two of the nation's top **pear-growing regions,** and just a few miles east of Hood River, around The Dalles, cherries reign supreme, with the blushing **Rainier cherry** a regional treat rarely seen outside the Northwest. The Willamette Valley, south of Portland, has become the nation's center for the production of **berries,** including strawberries, raspberries, and numerous varieties of blackberries. All these fruits show up in the summer months at farm stands, making a drive through the Willamette Valley at that time of year a real treat. Pick-your-own farms are also fairly common throughout the Northwest. So famed are Oregon's fruits that the Harry and David's company ships regional produce all over the country.

When hunger strikes on the road, Oregon offers what seems to be a regional potato preparation known as **jo-jos.** Consisting of potato wedges dipped in batter and fried, jo-jos are traditionally served with ranch dressing. These belly bombs are usually purchased as an accompaniment to fried or baked chicken.

One last Northwest food we should mention is the **wild mushroom.** As you'd expect in such a rainy climate, mushrooms abound here. The most common wild mushrooms are morels, which are harvested in spring, and chanterelles, which are harvested in autumn. You'll find wild mushrooms on menus of better restaurants throughout the state, so by all means try to have some while you're here.

Oregon's thriving wine industry has for several decades now been producing **award-winning varietal wines.** Oregon is on the same latitude as the French wine regions of Burgundy and Bordeaux and produces similar wines. Oregon pinot noirs rank up there with those from France, and local pinot gris and other varietals are getting good press as well. Wineries throughout the state are open to the public for tastings, with the greatest concentrations to be found southwest of Portland in Yamhill County, just west of Salem, northwest of Roseburg, and west of Jacksonville.

Oregon is at the center of the national obsession with **craft beers,** and new brewpubs continue to open across the state. Such Oregon breweries as Bridgeport, Full Sail, and Widmer, which have long been at the forefront of the state's craft brewing industry, have grown so large that the term "microbrewery" no longer applies to them. Although Portland is still the state's (and the nation's) microbrewery mecca, brewpubs can now be found throughout the state.

Local wines may be the state's preferred accompaniment to dinner, and microbrews the favorite social drink, but it's **coffee** that keeps Oregonians going through long gray winters—and even through hot sunny summers, for that matter. Although Seattle gets all the press for its espresso obsession, this dark and flavorful style of coffee is just as popular in Oregon. There may still be a few small towns in the state where you can't get an espresso, but you certainly don't have to worry about falling asleep at the wheel for want of a decent cup of java. In parking lots throughout the state, tiny espresso stands dispense all manner of coffee concoctions to the state's caffeine addicts.

Index

A AA (American Automobile
  Association), 48–49
A&T Myrtlewood (Port Orford),
  225
AARP, 25
Abacela Winery (Roseburg),
  303
Abbey Bach Festival
  (Mt. Angel), 146
Access-Able Travel Source, 24
Access America, 23
Accessible Journeys, 24
Accommodations
  best, 9–12
  money-saving tips, 38–39
  surfing for, 26–27
  tipping, 53
A.C. Gilbert Discovery Village
  (Salem), 144
Active vacations, 31–36
Adelman Peony Gardens
  (Brooks), 147
Adelsheim Vineyard (Newberg),
  125–126
Adler House Museum
  (Baker City), 334
Aerial tours, Tillamook, 185
Agate Beach, 200
AIDSinfo, 42
Ainsworth State Park, 240
Airfares, 26, 30–31, 47
Airlie Winery (Monmouth), 151
Airlines, 29, 47, 48
Airport security, 29–30
Air travel, 29–31, 37
Aladdin Theater (Portland), 116
Alameda Brewhouse (Portland),
  119
Albany, 149–154
Albany Regional Museum, 151
Alder Dune Campground, 214
Alder House III (Lincoln City),
  192
Alder Springs Campground, 264
Alfred A. Loeb State Park,
  230–232

Almeda Park, 298
Alpenfest, 340
Alton Baker Park (Eugene), 157
American Automobile
  Association (AAA), 48–49
American Express, 39
  Portland, 70
  traveler's checks, 18
American Foundation for the
  Blind (AFB), 24–25
Amity, 131–132, 134, 138–139
Amity Vineyards, 131–132
Amnesia Brewing Company
  (Portland), 120
Amtrak, 31, 47, 48
Andrea's Cha-Cha Club
  (Portland), 117
Angus Bowmer Theatre
  (Ashland), 276–277
Ankeny National Wildlife
  Refuge, 143
Ankeny Vineyard (Salem),
  146–147
Anne Amie Vineyards (Carlton),
  129
Annz Panz (Hood River), 244
Antique Motorcycle & Auto
  Museum (Port Orford), 225
Antique Powerland Museum
  (Brooks), 146
Applegate Trail Interpretive
  Center (Sunny Valley), 296
Apple Valley Country Store
  (near Hood River), 243
Aquariums, 8, 173, 199
Arcadia Beach Wayside, 176
Archery Summit (Dayton), 126
Arch Rock Viewpoint, 228
Area codes, 39
Argyle Winery (Dundee), 126
Arlene Schnitzer Concert Hall
  (Portland), 114
Art galleries
  Ashland, 280
  Astoria, 168
  Bandon, 221
  Bend, 322

  Cannon Beach, 177
  Eugene, 159
  Grants Pass, 295
  Hood River, 244
  Jacksonville, 290
  Lincoln City, 192
  Neskowin, 188
  Newport, 201
  North Willamette Valley, 134
  Portland, 109
  Port Orford, 225
  Seal Rock, 202
  Silverton, 145
  Yachats, 206
Artists Repertory Theatre
  (Portland), 115
Ashland, 56, 57, 275–287
  accommodations, 281–283
  exploring the area, 277–278
  nightlife, 287
  Oregon Shakespeare Festival,
    276–277
  outdoor activities, 279–280
  restaurants, 284–287
  shopping, 280
  wineries, 278–279
Ashland Art Works, 280
Ashland Hardwood Gallery,
  280
Ashland Vineyards, 278
Aspen Point Campground, 274
Astoria, 2, 55, 57, 61, 164–171
Astoria Column, 167
Astoria Regatta, 166
Astoria Riverfront Trolley, 168
Astoria Visual Arts, 168
Astor Street Opry Company
  (Astoria), 171
Astro Lounge (Bend), 327
ATMs (automated teller
  machines), 17–18, 39, 45–46
Aufderheide National Scenic
  Byway, 262
Augen Gallery (Portland), 109
August Cellars (Newberg), 126
Aurora, 134
Azalea Park, 231

Bachelor, Mount, 319–320
Backpacking, 33–34
Bagdad Theater (Portland), 120
Baker City, 333–338
Bandon, 3, 6, 219–224
Bandon Cranberry Festival, 22
Bandon Glass Art Studio, 221
Bandon Marsh National
  Wildlife Refuge, 220–221
Bandon State Natural Area, 220
Barlow Trail, 254
Bar Pastiche (Portland), 118
Bartini (Portland), 117
Baseball, Portland, 108
Basketball, Portland, 108
Basket Slough National Wildlife
  Refuge, 143–144
Bastendorff Beach County
  Park, 216, 219
Battle Rock Park, 225
The Bayfront (Newport),
  200–201
Beaches. *See also specific
  beaches*
  best, 6
  Brookings, 228
  Cannon Beach, 176–177
  the Coos Bay area, 216
  Lincoln City, 190–191
  Manzanita, 182
  Newport, 201
  Newport area, 200
  Oceanside, 186
  Seaside, 173
  south of Yachats, 208
Beachside State Recreation
  Site (Yachats), 207
Beacon Rock State Park,
  238, 240
Bear Creek Artichokes
  (near Tillamook), 185
Bear Creek Winery (Cave
  Junction), 300
Bear Valley National Wildlife
  Refuge (near Worden), 273
Beaverton wineries, 130
Bed-and-breakfasts (B&Bs),
  best, 9–10
Beekman House (Jacksonville),
  289
Beer, 361
Belknap Resort and Hot
  Springs, 262
Bend, 3, 56, 58–59, 316–327
  accommodations, 322–324
  campgrounds, 325
  exploring, 317–322
  festivals, 317

nightlife, 327
outdoor activities, 319–321
restaurants, 325–326
scenic drives, 321–322
transportation, 317
traveling to, 316
visitor information, 316
Bend Brewing Co., 327
Bendistillery (Bend), 327
Benham Falls, 319
Benton County Courthouse
  (Corvallis), 150
Benton-Lane Winery (near
  Corvallis), 151
Berbati's Pan (Portland), 116
The Berry Botanic Garden
  (Portland), 103
Bethel Heights Vineyards
  (Salem), 132
Beverly Beach State Park,
  196, 203
Big Horse Brew Pub
  (Hood River), 248
Biking and mountain biking,
  31–32
  Ashland, 280
  Astoria, 168
  Bend/Sunriver area, 5, 321
  Cannon Beach, 176
  Corvallis, 150
  Hood River, 242
  Klamath Falls area, 273
  McKenzie River area, 262
  Mount Hood, 256
  the Oregon Coast, 5, 172
  Portland, 96, 106
  Seaside, 173
  Sisters area, 313
  Willamette National Forest,
    265
Billy Chinook, Lake, 309
Bird-watching, 32
  Bandon, 220–221
  Garibaldi, 184
  Klamath Falls area, 272–273
  Ladd Marsh Wildlife Area, 335
  Malheur National Wildlife
    Refuge, 348
  Owyhee River region, 347
  Twilight Creek Eagle Sanctu-
    ary (near Astoria), 169
  Willamette Mission State
    Park, 143–144
  William L. Finley National
    Wildlife Refuge, 152
Blackfish Gallery (Artistbn),
  109
The Black Sheep (Ashland), 287
Blue Basin, 310

The Blue Giraffe (Ashland), 278
Blue Heron Cheese & Wine
  Company (Tillamook), 185
Blue Mountains, 333, 334, 336,
  337
Boating (boat rentals). *See also*
  Canoeing; Kayaking; White-
  water rafting
  Garibaldi, 184
  Lincoln City, 191
  Newport, 201
Boatnik (Grants Pass), 20, 294
Boat tours and cruises. *See
  also* Whale-watching
  Crater Lake National Park,
    270
  Grants Pass, 295
  Klamath Lake, 273
  Portland, 105
  Rogue River, 227
Boiler Bay State Scenic
  Viewpoint, 196
Bonneville Fish Hatchery, 237
Bonneville Hot Springs Resort,
  238
Bonneville Lock and Dam, 237
Bookstores, Portland, 110
Bradford Island Visitors Center,
  237
Brandy Peak Distillery
  (Brookings), 231
The Brazen Bean (Portland),
  117
Breach the Moon Gallery
  (Newport), 201
Breitenbush Hot Springs
  Retreat and Conference
  Center, 261
Brewpubs
  Ashland, 287
  Bend, 327
  Eugene, 162
  Hood River, 248
  Portland, 119–120
Bridge of the Gods, 237
Bridgeview (near Cave
  Junction), 301
Bridgeview Applegate
  Tasting Room (Grants Pass),
  290–291
Brigittine Monastery (Amity),
  134
Britt Festivals (Jacksonville),
  21, 287–289
Broadway in Portland, 115
Brookings, 7, 228, 230–232
Brooks, 146
Bullards Beach State Park,
  220, 222

The Bullseye Connection Gallery (Portland), 110
Burns, 348
Bush Barn Art Center (Salem), 142
Bush House Museum (Salem), 142
Business hours, 39, 49
Bus travel, 48
Butte Creek Mill (Jacksonville), 289

Calendar of events, 20–22
Camelot Theatre Company (Ashland), 287
Camping and campgrounds, 32–33
   Bandon, 222
   Bend and Cascade Lakes Highway area, 325
   Brookings, 232
   Cannon Beach, 179
   Cape Blanco State Park, 226
   the Columbia Gorge, 240
   Coos Bay area, 219
   Crater Lake National Park, 271
   the Dalles, 251–252
   Devil's Lake State Recreation Area, 194
   Elkhorn National Scenic Byway, 338
   Farewell Bend State Recreation Area, 348
   Florence area, 214
   Fort Stevens State Park, 170
   between Gold Beach and Agness, 229
   Hood River, 246
   Klamath Falls area, 274
   lower Deschutes River, 311
   McKenzie River area, 264
   near Oregon Caves National Monument, 301
   Nehalem Bay State Park, 184
   Newport area, 203
   North Umpqua River, 268
   reservations, 32
   Rogue River Valley, 298
   Sisters area, 315
   south of Cape Perpetua, 209
   Three Capes Loop area, 187
   visitor information, 17
   Wallowa Lake, 343–344
   Willamette Pass route, 266
   Yachats, 207
Camp Sherman Campground, 315

Cannon Beach, 2, 6, 55, 61, 175–181
Cannon Beach Gallery, 177
Cannon Beach Historical Society, 177
Cannon Beach Sand Castle Festival, 20
Cannon Beach Spa, 177
Canoeing, 34
   Klamath Falls area, 273
   Upper Klamath Canoe Trail, 273
Cape Arago State Park, 216
Cape Blanco, 224
Cape Blanco Lighthouse, 225
Cape Blanco State Park, 225, 226
Cape Ferrelo Viewpoint, 228
Cape Kiwanda, 186
Cape Lookout State Park, 186, 187
Cape Lookout Trail, 6
Cape Meares Lighthouse, 186
Cape Meares State Scenic Viewpoint, 186
Cape Perpetua Campground, 207
Cape Perpetua Interpretive Center, 205
Cape Perpetua Scenic Area, 205–206
Cape Sebastian, 228
Carl G. Washburne Memorial State Park, 209
Carlton, 2, 60
   restaurants, 139–140
   wineries, 128–130
Car rentals, 36, 48
   for customers with special travel needs, 24
   surfing for, 27
Carson Hot Springs Resort, 238
Carter Dunes Trail, 211
Carter Lake Campground, 211, 214
Car travel, 31, 36–37, 48–49
   driving safety, 46
Cascade Cliffs Vineyard & Winery (Wishram), 251
Cascade Festival of Music (Bend), 21, 317
Cascade Head, 188
Cascade Head Music Festival, 190
Cascade Lakes Highway, 7, 321–322
Cascade Locks, 237–238
Cascade Locks Historical Museum, 238

The Cascades, 16, 19, 253–274, 351
Cascade-Siskiyou National Monument, 280
Casinos, 191–192, 218, 331
Cathedral Ridge Winery (near Hood River), 243
Cat Ski Mt. Bailey, 268
Cave Creek Campground, 301
C.C. Slaughters Nightclub & Lounge (Portland), 120
Cellphones, 28–29
Central Oregon, 3, 5, 16–17, 306–327
Chamber Music Northwest (Portland), 115
Champagne Creek Cellars (Roseburg), 303
Champoeg State Park, 134
Changes (Portland), 112
Chateaulin Wine Shoppe (Ashland), 280
Chateau Lorane (Lorane), 157
Chief Joseph Days Rodeo, 340
Children. See Families with children
Chinatown (Portland), 67
Chinook Winds Casino (Lincoln City), 191–192
Clamming, 163, 186, 220, 227, 228, 360
Clarno Unit, 310
Clear Lake, 262
Climate, 19
The Coast Range, 350
Coffee, 360
Coldwater Cove Campground, 264
Colliding Rivers Viewpoint, 267
Columbia Art Gallery (Hood River), 244
The Columbia Gorge, 3, 14, 16, 233–252, 352
Columbia Gorge Discovery Center (The Dalles), 249
Columbia Gorge Interpretive Center Museum (Stevenson), 236
The Columbia Gorge National Scenic Area, 4, 234–241
Columbia Gorge (sternwheeler), 238
Columbia Hills State Park, 251, 252
Columbia River, 37, 238, 351–352
Columbia River Maritime Museum (Astoria), 8, 166

Columbia Sportswear Company (Portland), 111
Columbia Sportswear Company Factory Outlet Store (Portland), 112
Connie Hansen Garden (Lincoln City), 191
Contemporary Crafts Museum & Gallery (Portland), 111
Cook Gallery (Port Orford), 225
Cooley's Gardens (Silverton), 147
Cooper Mountain Vineyards (Beaverton), 130
Coos Art Museum (Coos Bay), 218
The Coos Bay area, 215–219
Coquille Point, 220
Coquille River Lighthouse, 220
Corvallis, 149–154
Corvallis Arts Center, 150
Cougar Crossing Campground, 264
Cove Palisades State Park, 309–311
Covered bridges
    Albany, 152
    Lane County, 156
    near Lincoln City, 191
Crabbing, 163, 183, 184, 186, 201, 220, 227
Crane Prairie Reservoir, 322
Craterian Ginger Rogers Theater (Medford), 289
Crater Lake National Park, 5, 56–58, 269–271
Crater Lake Rim Drive, 7, 270
Credit cards, 18–19, 45
Crescent Lake, 265
Cristom Vineyards (Salem), 132
Crooked River Railroad Company Dinner Train (Redmond), 313–314
Cross-country skiing, 35
    Crater Lake National Park, 270
    Hoodoo Nordic Center, 261
    Mount Bachelor, 319
    Mount Hood, 258
    Wallowa Mountains, 342
Crown Point, 236
Crush Bar (Portland), 120–121
Crystal Ballroom (Portland), 116
Crystal Springs Rhododendron Garden (Portland), 103
Cuisine, 359–360
Cultus Lake, 322

Cuneo Cellars (Carlton), 129
Curry County Historical Museum (Gold Beach), 227
Customs regulations, 43–44

Dalles, The, 248–252
The Dalles Lock and Dam, 250–251
Darcelle's XV (Portland), 117
Darlingtonia State Natural Site, 208
David Hill Winery (Forest Grove), 130
DaVinci Days (Corvallis), 21, 150
Davis & Cline (Ashland), 280
Daylight saving time, 52
Day spas
    Ashland, 277–278
    Portland, 108
Dayton, restaurant, 138–139
Dean Creek Elk Viewing Area (Reedsport), 213
Del Rio Vineyards (Gold Hill), 296
Delta Campground, 264
Department of Theatre Arts at Southern Oregon University (Ashland), 287
Depoe Bay, 3, 195–198
Depoe Bay State Park, 196
Deschutes River, 306
    lower, 307–309
Deschutes River State Recreation Area, 251
Deschutes River Trail, 7, 320
Destinations (Eugene), 159
Devil's Churn, 206
Devils Garden, 322
Devil's Lake, 190–191
Devil's Lake Campground, 325
Devil's Lake State Recreation Area, 191
Devil's Punchbowl State Natural Area, 196
Devitt Winery & Vineyards (Jacksonville), 291
Diamond Lake, 266–269
Diamond Lake RV Park, 269
Disabilities, travelers with, 24–25
Doe Point Campground, 274
Dogsled rides, 319
Do Jump! Extremely Physical Theatre (Portland), 115
Domaine Drouhin Oregon (Dayton), 126–127

Domaine Serene (Dayton), 127
Doug Fir Lounge (Portland), 1, 116
Douglas County Museum of History & Natural History (Roseburg), 302
Down to Earth (Eugene), 159
Drift Creek Bridge, 191
Drift Creek Falls Trail, 191
Drinking laws, 49
Driver's licenses, foreign, 42
Duck Pond Cellars (Dundee), 127
Dundee, 32, 60
    restaurants, 137–138
    wineries, 125–128
Dune Musher's Mail Run, 212
Dutchman Flat, 322

Eagle Bar (Portland), 121
Eagle Cap Excursion Train, 340
Eagle Cap Wilderness, 342
Eagle Creek Campground, 240
Eagle Creek Trail, 6, 237
Eagle Point Museum (Jacksonville), 289
Earthworks Gallery (Lincoln City), 192
Earthworks Gallery (Yachats), 206
Eastbank Esplanade (Portland), 98
Eastern Oregon, 17, 328–349
Eastern Oregon Museum (Haines), 337
Ecola State Park, 6, 173, 176
Eden Hall (Lincoln City), 192
EdenVale Wines (Medford), 278
Edgefield Theater (Portland), 120
Eel Creek Campground, 211, 214
Elderhostel, 25
ElderTreks, 25
Electricity, 49
Elgin, 334
Elgin Opera House, 334
Elizabethan Theatre (Ashland), 276
Elk Cove Vineyards (Gaston), 130
Elkhorn Mountain Scenic Loop, 336–337
Elkhorn Wildlife Area (North Powder), 335–336
Elk Lake, 322

Elk Rock Garden of the Bishop's Close (Portland), 103–104
Elliot Glacier Public House (Parkdale), 243
Elowah Falls, 237
Elsinore Theater (Salem), 149
Embassies and consulates, 49–50
The Embers Avenue (Portland), 120
Emergencies, 50
Enchanted Forest (Salem), 144
End of the Oregon Trail Interpretive Center (Oregon City), 121
Enterprise, 340, 342, 344
Entry requirements, 41–42
Eola Hills
  accommodations, 137
  wineries, 131–133
Eola Hills Wine Cellars (Rickreall), 132
Erath Vineyards (Dundee), 127
Ernest Bloch Music Festival (Newport), 199
Eugene, 2, 154–162
  accommodations, 159–160
  festivals, 155
  nightlife, 161–162
  outdoor activities, 158
  parks and gardens, 157
  restaurants, 160–161
  shopping, 158–159
  sightseeing, 155–157
  transportation, 154
  traveling to, 154
  visitor information, 154
Eugene Celebration, 22, 155
Europ Assistance, 44
Evergreen Aviation Museum (McMinnville), 7, 133

Faber Farms (Bandon), 221
Face Rock Viewpoint, 220
Fall Kite Festival (Lincoln City), 22
Families with children
  best family attractions, 8
  information and resources, 25–26
  Portland
    hotels, 78
    restaurants, 90
    sights and attractions, 104–105
  Salem attractions, 144
  suggested itinerary, 58–59

Family Travel Forum, 26
Family Travel Network, 26
Fareless Square (Portland), 65, 67–68, 97
Farewell Bend Campground, 269
Farewell Bend State Recreation Area, 348
Farmer John's Produce & Nursery (McMinnville), 134
Favell Museum of Western Art and Indian Artifacts (Klamath Falls), 8, 272
Fax machines, 52
Ferguson Ridge, 342
Festivals and special events, 20–22
Fifth Street Public Market (Eugene), 159
Finnegan's Toys and Gifts (Portland), 113
Fire House Gallery (Grants Pass), 295
Fire's Eye Gallery (near Sheridan), 134
Firestone Farms (near Dundee), 134
First Friday Artwalk (Eugene), 159
Fisher Poets Gathering (Astoria), 166
Fishing, 33
  Astoria, 168
  Brookings, 230
  Cape Kiwanda, 186
  the Columbia Gorge, 239
  the Coos Bay area, 218
  Depoe Bay, 196
  Deschutes River, 309, 320
  Gold Beach, 227
  Grants Pass, 295
  Hood River, 242
  Jacksonville/Medford area, 290
  Newport, 201
  North Umpqua River, 5, 267
  the Oregon coast, 163
  Reedsport, 213
  Sisters area, 312
  Tillamook, 185
  Wallowa Mountains, 342
  Yachats, 206
Fish Lake, 273
Fish Lake Campground, 274
Flavel House Museum (Astoria), 166
Fleet of Flowers (Depoe Bay), 195

Florence, 3, 209–215
Flying Dutchman Winery (Depoe Bay), 196
Flying Wheels Travel, 24
Fogarty Creek State Recreation Area, 196
Forest Grove, 137, 140
Forest Park (Portland), 100, 107
Foris (Cave Junction), 301
Fort Astoria, 167–168, 356
Fort Clatsop, 355
Fort Dalles Museum (the Dalles), 250
Fort Stevens Museum (Astoria), 168
Fort Stevens State Park, 168, 170
Fossil (town), 310
Fossils, 200, 310
Four Rivers Cultural Center & Museum (Ontario), 346–347
Fourth of July Fireworks (Vancouver), 21
Freed Gallery (Lincoln City), 192
French Pete Campground, 264
French Quarter (Eugene), 159
Frissell Crossing Campground, 264
Frommers.com, 27
Full Sail Tasting Room & Pub (Hood River), 248

Garibaldi, 184
Gasoline, 50
Gaston, restaurant, 140
Gay and lesbian travelers, 25
  Portland, 120–121
Gay Men's Health Crisis, 42
GeBzz Gallery (Jacksonville), 290
Geiser Grand Hotel (Baker City), 334
Girardet Wine Cellars & Vineyard (Roseburg), 303
Glacier View Sno-Park, 258
Gleneden Beach, 190–194
Glider flights, McMinnville, 133
Gold Beach, 7, 227–230
Golden Access Passport, 24
Golden Age Passport, 25
Gold Lake Campground, 266
The Gold Post Grocery & Mercantile/Museum (Sumpter), 336

Golf, 33
  Bandon, 221
  Bend, 320
  Brookings, 230
  Florence, 212
  Gold Beach, 227
  Lincoln City, 191
  McKenzie River area, 262
  Manzanita, 182
  Portland, 106–107
  Seaside, 173
  Sisters area, 312–313
Governor Tom McCall Preserve, 248
Granite, 336–337
Grants Pass, 294–299
Grants Pass Museum of Art, 295
Grape Escape, 133
Grayback Campground, 301
The Great Basin, 317, 351
Great Cats World Park, 299–300
Great Springs, 262
Green Lakes, trail head for, 322
Greer Gardens (Eugene), 157
Greyhound/Trailways, 48

Hallie Ford Museum of Art (Salem), 142–143
The Hall of Fame (Pendleton), 330
Hamaker Campground, 269
Hanson Howard Gallery (Ashland), 280
Happy Canyon Dance Hall (Pendleton), 330
Harbor Vista County Park, 214
Harris Beach State Park, 228–229, 232
Harry and David's Country Village (Medford), 289
Hart Mountain National Antelope Refuge, 348, 349
Hatfield Marine Science Center (Newport), 199
Hat Point Overlook, 345
Hawk Creek Gallery (Neskowin), 188
Hayward Field (Eugene), 158
Health concerns, 23–24
Health insurance, 23, 44–45
Heceta Head Lighthouse, 208
Heceta Head Lighthouse State Scenic Viewpoint, 208
Hellgate Canyon, 295
Hells Canyon, 5, 344–346
Hells Canyon Creek Visitor Center, 345

Hells Canyon Overlook, 345
Hendricks Park and Rhododendron Garden (Eugene), 157
Henry Estate Winery (Umpqua), 303
Heritage Museum (Astoria), 166
Heritage Station/Umatilla County Historical Society Museum (Pendleton), 331
High Cascade Descent, 321
The High Desert Museum (Bend), 8, 317–318
Hiking, 33–34
  Ashland, 280
  Bend, 320
  best hikes, 6
  Cannon Beach, 176–177, 180–181
  Cascade Head, 188
  Coos Bay area, 216
  Crater Lake National Park, 270
  Deschutes River State Recreation Area, 251
  Gold Beach, 228
  Hells Canyon area, 345
  Hood River, 242
  Illinois Valley, 300
  Jacksonville/Medford area, 290
  Klamath Falls area, 273
  Lincoln City, 191
  Mount Hood, 256
  Portland, 107
  Sisters area, 313
  Wallowa Mountains, 342
Hillcrest Vineyard (Roseburg), 303
Hillsboro, wineries, 130
Historical sites, best, 8
Historic Columbia River Highway, 7, 236–238
Historic Columbia River Highway State Trail, 237, 248
Historic Deepwood Estate (Salem), 143
Historic Sod House Ranch (near Burns), 349
History of Oregon, 353–359
HIV-positive visitors, 42
Hoffman Gallery (Portland), 111
Holiday Festival of Lights (Ashland), 22, 276
Holiday Lights and Open House at Shore Acres State Park (Charleston), 22
Holiday Parade of Ships (Willamette and Columbia rivers), 22

Holidays, 50
Holmes Road Park (Lincoln City), 191
Homestead Campground, 264
Honeywood (Salem), 147
Hood, Mount, 4–5, 59, 254–260, 352
Hoodoo Nordic Center, 261
Hoodoo Ski Area, 261
Hood River, 241–248
  windsurfing, 5, 242
Hood River County Historical Museum, 244
Hood River Valley Blossom Festival, 20
Hood River Valley Harvest Fest, 22
Hood River Vineyards, 243
Hood to Coast Run (Seaside), 172
Horseback riding
  Ashland, 280
  Bandon, 221
  Cannon Beach, 176
  Florence, 212
  Gold Beach, 227
  Silverton, 145
  Sisters area, 313
  Sunriver, 321
Horse packing, Wallowa Mountains, 342, 346
Horseshoe Bend Campground, 268–269
Horsetail Falls, 237
Hosmer Lake, 322
Hot-air ballooning, 133
Hot springs, 238, 261, 262, 265, 267, 308, 332, 335
House Rock Viewpoint, 228
Hoyt Arboretum (Portland), 100
Hughes House Museum (Cape Blanco), 225
Hug Point State Recreation Site, 176
Hult Center for the Performing Arts (Eugene), 161
Humbug Mountain State Park, 225
Hutson Museum (Parkdale), 243

Icefire Glassworks (Cannon Beach), 177
Illahee Campground, 229
Illinois Valley, 299, 300–301
Imago Theatre (Portland), 115
Imbibe (Portland), 1, 116
Indian Mary Park, 298

Insurance, 22–23
International Ameripass, 48
International Gay and Lesbian Travel Association (IGLTA), 25
International Museum of Carousel Art (Hood River), 244
International Pinot Noir Celebration (North Willamette Valley), 124
International Rose Test Garden (Portland), 100, 101–102
International visitors, 41–53
  customs regulations, 43–44
  entry requirements, 41–42
  immigration and customs clearance, 47
  money matters, 45–46
  passports, 42–43
  safety, 46
  traveling around the U.S., 48
  traveling to the U.S., 47
Internet access, 28
Irvington (Portland), 67
Islet Campground, 266
Itineraries, suggested, 54–61

Jackson and Perkins rose test garden (Medford), 290
Jacksonville, 3, 8–9, 57, 287–294
  sights and attractions, 289–290
Jacksonville Museum of Southern Oregon History, 289
Jake's Famous Crawfish (Portland), 117
James Cant Ranch, 310
Japanese Garden (Portland), 96, 100, 102
Jensen Arctic Museum (Monmouth), 7, 146
Jerry's Rogue River Museum (Gold Beach), 227
Jessie M. Honeyman Memorial State Park, 211, 214
Jewell Meadows Wildlife Area, 180
Jimmy Mak's (Portland), 116
Jo Federigo's Café & Bar (Eugene), 162
John Day Fossil Beds National Monument, 310
John Dellenback Dunes Trail, 6, 211
Jordan Schnitzer Museum of Art (Eugene), 156

Joseph, 339–344
Junction City's Scandinavian Festival, 155

Kam Wah Chung & Co. Museum (John Day), 9, 339
K&R Drive Inn (near Roseburg), 305
Kayaking, 34
  Bandon, 221
  Cove Palisades State Park, 309
  Deschutes River, 321
  Grants Pass, 295
  Mount Hood, 257
  North Umpqua River, 267
  Portland, 96, 107
  Wheeler, 183
Keller Auditorium (Portland), 114
Kennedy School Theater (Portland), 120
Kerbyville Museum (Kerby), 300
Kiahanie Campground, 264
Kinetic Sculpture Race (Corvallis), 150
King Estate (near Eugene), 157
Kite boarding, 36
Kite flying, 175, 176, 190
Klamath County Museum, 272
Klamath Falls area, 271–274
Koosah Falls, 262
Kramer Vineyards (Gaston), 131
Kristin Hill Winery (Amity), 132

Ladd Marsh Wildlife Area, 335
Lafayette Schoolhouse Antique Mall, 134
Lagoon Campground, 214
La Grande, 333–338
Lake Basin, 342
Lake of the Woods, 273
Lake Oswego, accommodations, 80
Lange Estate Winery & Vineyards (Dundee), 127
Langlitz Leathers (Portland), 112
La Pine State Park, 325
Latourell Falls, 236
The Laura Russo Gallery (Portland), 110
Laurelhurst Theater (Portland), 120
Laurel Ridge Winery (Carlton), 129

Lava Butte, 318–319
Lava Camp Lake Campground, 264
Lava Cast Forest, 319
Lava Lake, 322, 325
Lava Lands Visitor Center, 318
Lava River Cave, 319
LaVelle Vineyards (Elmira), 157
Lawrence Gallery (near Sheridan), 134
Legal aid, 51
Lehman Hot Springs, 335
Leslie Gulch, 347
Les Schwab Amphitheater (Bend), 327
Let It Rain (Astoria), 168
Lewis and Clark expedition, 172, 173, 176, 177, 234, 249, 341, 355
Lewis and Clark National and State Historical Park (Astoria), 8, 166–167
Lewis and Clark Salt Works (Seaside), 172–173
Lewis & Clark State Park, 236
Liberty Theater (Astoria), 171
Lincoln City, 3, 188–195
Liquor laws, 39
Lithia Artisan's Market of Ashland, 280
Lithia Park (Ashland), 279
Little Lava Lake, 322, 325
Little Log Church by the Sea (Yachats), 206
Little Redwood Campground, 232
Living History Park (The Dalles), 249
Llama trekking, the southern Wallowas, 346
The Lobby Court (Portland), 116
Lobster Creek Campground, 229
The Lodge at Cascade Lakes Brewing Co. (Bend), 327
Logging and lumber, 350–351, 357–358
Lolo Pass Road, 256
Lone Ranch Viewpoint, 228
Lost and found, 39–40
Lost Creek Campground, 271
Lost Lake, 256
Lost-luggage insurance, 23
The Lucky Labrador Brew Pub (Portland), 119
Lumber, 357–358
Luna (Eugene), 162
Lunar Boy Gallery (Astoria), 168
Lunaria Gallery (Silverton), 145

MacTarnahan's Tap Room (Portland), 119
Made in Oregon (Portland), 112–113
Mail, 51
Malheur National Wildlife Refuge, 348
Mallard Marsh Campground, 325
Manzanita, 182–183
Market District (Eugene), 159
Marshal's Winery (Dallesport), 251
MarshAnne Landing Winery (Oakland), 303–304
Maryhill Museum of Art, 251
Maryhill Winery, 251
Mary's Peak, 152
MasterCard traveler's checks, 18
Mazama Campground, 271
McCormick and Schmick's Harborside Pilsner Room (Portland), 117
McCredie Hot Springs, 265
McKenzie Pass, 7, 261–263
McKenzie River, 261, 262–263
McKenzie River Trail to Tamolitch Pool, 6–7, 262
McLoughlin House (Oregon City), 121
McMenamin's Kennedy School (Portland), 120
McMenamin's Old St. Francis School Hotel (Bend), 327
McMenamin's Ringlers Pub (Portland), 119
McMinnville
  accommodations, 136–137
  restaurants, 139–140
  wineries, 128

MEDEX Assistance, 23
Medford, 287–294
Medford Jazz Jubilee, 289
MedicAlert identification tag, 24
Medical insurance, 23, 44–45
Medical requirements for entry, 42
Meier and Frank (Portland), 111
Melrose Vineyards (Roseburg), 304
Memaloose State Park, 246
Memorial Day Wine Tastings (Portland area), 20

Metolius River, headwaters of the, 312
Meyers Creek, 228
Mid-Willamette Valley, 140–149
Mill Ends Park (Portland), 104
Mint/820 (Portland), 2, 117
Mirror Lake, 256
Mirror Pond Gallery (Bend), 322
Mission Mill Museum (Salem), 143
Mission Theater (Portland), 120
Money matters, 17–19, 45–46
Monmouth, 146
Monteith House (Albany), 151
Montinore Vineyards (Forest Grove), 131
Monty Campground, 311
Moss Rehab, 24
Mossy Creek Pottery (Lincoln City), 192
Mother's Day Rhododendron Show (Portland), 20
Mountain biking. See Biking and mountain biking
Mountaineering, 34–35
Mt. Angel, 22, 146
Mount Angel Abbey, 146
Mt. Angel Oktoberfest, 22, 142
Mt. Ashland Ski & Snowboard Resort, 280
Mount Hood Jazz Festival (Gresham), 21
Mount Hood Meadows, 256, 257–258
Mount Hood Meadows Nordic Center, 258
Mount Hood National Forest, 237
Mount Hood Railroad, 244
Mt. Hood Skibowl, 257
Mt. Hood Skibowl Action Park, 256
Mt. Hood Winery (near Hood River), 243
Mount Pisgah Arboretum (Eugene), 157
Multnomah Falls, 236–237
Murdock Sky Theater (Portland), 98
The Museum at Warm Springs, 8, 309
Museums, best, 7–8
Myrtle Tree Trail, 228
Myrtlewood, 218, 230–231
Mystic Wines (Amity), 132

National Historic Oregon Trail Interpretive Center at Flagstaff Hill (Baker City), 8, 334
National Recreation Reservation Service, 32
Native Americans
  The Dalles, 249
  Favell Museum of Western Art and Indian Artifacts (Klamath Falls), 272
  Four Rivers Cultural Center & Museum (Ontario), 346–347
  Heritage Museum (Astoria), 166
  history of, 353–354
  Klamath County Museum (Klamath Falls), 272
  The Museum at Warm Springs, 309
  Pendleton area, 331
  pictographs (Devils Garden), 322
  Sunbird Gallery (Bend), 322
  TamKaLiks Celebration (Wallowa), 340
  Wallowa County Museum (Joseph), 340
Natural Bridge Campground, 269
Natural Bridge Viewpoint, 228
Natural environment, 350–352
Nature of the Northwest Information Center (Portland), 34
Nehalem Bay State Park, 182, 184
Nesika Illahee, 190
Neskowin, 188
Neskowin Beach State Recreation Site, 188
Netarts Bay, 186
Newberg, 32, 135–138
  wineries, 125, 126, 128
Newberry Caldera, 319
Newberry National Volcanic Monument, 318, 351
Newport, 3, 55–56, 61, 198–205
Newport Performing Arts Center, 201
Newport Seafood and Wine Festival, 20
Newport Visual Arts Center, 201
New Theatre (Ashland), 277
New Theater Building (Portland), 114
New Twist (Eugene), 159

Nez Perce Indians, 340, 341, 354, 357
Nez Perce National Historical Park (Spalding, Idaho), 341
Nez Perce Wallowa Homeland Photography Exhibit (Joseph), 341
Nike Factory Company Store (Portland), 112
Nike Store (Eugene), 158, 159
NIKETOWN Portland, 112
Noble Rot (Portland), 118
Nordstrom (Portland), 111
Norm Thompson (Portland), 112
North central Oregon, 307–311
North Fork Campground, 274
North Umpqua River, 5, 267, 268
North Umpqua Trail, 267
North Umpqua–Upper Rogue River Scenic Byway, 266–269
North Waldo Campground, 266
Northwest by Northwest (Cannon Beach), 177
North Willamette Valley Wine Country, 2, 122–140
    accommodations, 135–137
    outdoor activities, 133–134
    restaurants, 137–140
    shopping, 134
    traveling to, 124
    visitor information, 124
    wineries, 124–133
        Eola Hills area, 131–133
        Gaston and Forest Grove area, 130–131
        Hillsboro and Beaverton area, 130
        McMinnville McMinnvilleae, 128
        Newberg and Dundee area, 125–128
Nye Beach, 201
Nye Beach Gallery (Newport), 201
Nyssa, 347

Oak Knoll Winery (Hillsboro), 130
Oakland, 302–303, 305
Oakland Museum, 303
Oakridge, 264–266
Oaks Park Amusement Center (Portland), 105
¡Oba! (Portland), 117
Observatories, 318
Oceanic Arts (Newport), 201
Oceanside, 186, 187

Odell Creek Campground, 266
Odell Lake, 265
Old Aurora Colony Museum, 134
The Old Church (Portland), 114
Old Mill District (Bend), 322
Old St. Peter's Landmark church (the Dalles), 250
Old Town (Florence), 212
Old Town Bandon, 221
Ona Beach State Park, 200
Oneonta Falls, 237
Oneonta Gorge, 237
One World Performing Arts series (Ashland), 287
Ontario, 346–348
Oregon Air and Space Museum (Eugene), 155–156
Oregon Bach Festival (Eugene), 21, 155
Oregon Ballet Theatre (Portland), 115
Oregon Brewers Festival (Portland), 21
Oregon Cabaret Theatre (Ashland), 287
Oregon Candy Farm (Sandy), 258
Oregon Caves National Monument, 299–302
Oregon City, 121, 356
The Oregon Coast, 4, 14, 163–232, 350
    suggested itinerary, 60–61
    what's new in, 2–3
Oregon Coast Aquarium (Newport), 8, 199
Oregon Coast Explorer, 184
Oregon Coast History Center (Newport), 202
Oregon Coast Passport, 164
Oregon Coast Trail, 228
Oregon Country Fair (Eugene), 21
Oregon Country Fair (Veneta), 155
Oregon Dune Mushers' Mail Run (Florence), 20
Oregon Dunes National Recreation Area, 61, 209, 210–212
Oregon Dunes Overlook, 211
Oregon Electric Station (Eugene), 162
Oregon Festival of American Music (Eugene), 155
Oregon Fossil Guy (Newport), 200
The Oregon Garden (Silverton), 145

Oregon Historical Society Museum (Portland), 97–98
Oregon Islands National Wildlife Refuge, 220
Oregon Museum of Science and Industry (OMSI; Portland), 8, 98–99
Oregon River Sports (Eugene), 158
Oregon Shakespeare Festival (Ashland), 20, 276–277
Oregon Stage Works (Ashland), 287
Oregon State Capitol (Salem), 143
Oregon State Fair (Salem), 21, 142
Oregon Symphony (Portland), 114
Oregon Trail, 331, 334, 357
    Rinehart Stone House Museum (Vale), 347
    wagon ruts, 9, 328, 331, 333, 334, 347, 357
Oregon Trail Interpretive Park at Blue Mountain Crossing (near Baker City), 334
Oregon Trail Regional Museum (Baker City), 334
Oregon Trail Wagon Ruts (Baker City), 9
Oregon Vortex (Gold Hill), 296
Oregon Wines on Broadway (Portland), 113, 118
Oregon Wine Warehouse (Eugene), 157
Oregon Zoo (Washington Park Zoo; Portland), 97, 102, 115
Oswald West State Park, 6, 176–177, 179
Otter Crest State Scenic Loop, 196
Outdoor activities, 31–36
    best, 5
    visitor information, 17
Owen Memorial Rose Garden (Eugene), 157
Owyhee, Lake, 347
Owyhee River region, 346–348

Pacific City, 186–187
Pacific Northwest Truck Museum (Brooks), 146
Painted Hills Unit, 310
Palotai Vineyard and Winery (Roseburg), 304
Panorama Point, 243

Panther Creek Cellars
(McMinnville), 128
Paradise Point State Recreation
Site, 225
Parks Bronze (Joseph), 340
Paschal (Talent), 278
Passports, 42–43
The Pearl District (Portland),
67, 99
restaurants, 86–89
shopping, 109
Pendleton, 328–333
Pendleton Center for the Arts,
331
Pendleton Round-Up and
Happy Canyon Pageant,
22, 328, 330
Pendleton Underground Tours,
331
Pendleton Woolen Mills,
328, 330–331
Peninsula Park Rose Garden
(Portland), 103
Penner-Ash Wine Cellars
(Newberg), 129
Pentacle Theatre (Salem), 149
Perry South Campground, 311
Petersen Rock Gardens &
Museum, 314
Peter's Walking Tours of
Portland, 106
Petrol, 50
Pets, traveling with, 40
Pheasant Valley Vineyard &
Winery (near Hood River),
243
The Phoenix (Ashland),
277–278
Pilot Butte, 318, 320
Pine Mountain Observatory,
318
Pinot Station Tasting Room
(Dundee), 127
Pioneer Courthouse Square
(Portland), 96, 108–109
Pioneer Place (Portland), 113
Pistol River State Scenic
Viewpoint, 228
Pittock Mansion (Portland),
102–103
Police, 40
Ponzi Vineyards (Beaverton),
130
Ponzi Vineyards/Ponzi Wine Bar
(Dundee), 127
Portland, 1, 62–121
accommodations, 1, 72–81
American Express, 70
area codes, 70

arriving in, 63–64
average monthly tempera-
tures and rainfall, 20
babysitters, 70
bakeries and pastry shops,
93–94
bars and pubs, 117–120
brewpubs, 119–120
cafes, 93
car rentals, 69
Chinatown, 67
day spas, 108
doctors and dentists, 70
downtown (including the
Skidmore Historic District
and Chinatown), 66–67
accommodations, 74–77
Cultural District, 96–98
restaurants, 81, 84–86
sights and attractions,
96–100
emergencies, 70
finding an address in, 65–66
Frommer's favorite experiences, 96–97
gay and lesbian nightlife,
120–121
Hawthorne/Belmont
District, 67
hospitals, 70
Internet access, 71
Irvington, 67
accommodations, 78–79
for kids, 104
layout of, 64–65
main arteries and streets, 65
neighborhoods, 66–67
newspapers and maga-
zines, 71
nightlife, 1–2, 113–121
Northwest (including
the Pearl District and
Nob Hill), 67
accommodations, 77–78
restaurants, 86–89
shopping, 109
organized tours, 105–106
outdoor activities, 106–107
parking, 69
the Pearl District, 67
performing arts, 114
pharmacies, 71
post offices, 71
restaurants, 1, 81–94
smoking, 71
southeast, 90–93
southwest, 89
restrooms, 71
safety, 71

Sellwood/Westmoreland,
67, 109
shopping, 108–113
sights and attractions,
1, 94–104
spectator sports, 108
street maps, 66
suggested itineraries, 54, 56,
58, 60
taxes, 71
taxis, 70
transit info, 72
transportation, 67–70
visitor information, 64
weather information, 72
what's new in, 1–2
Portland Art Museum, 1, 7, 98,
115
Portland Audubon Society,
100–101
Portland Beavers Baseball
Club, 108
Portland Building, 97
Portland Center for the
Performing Arts (PCPA), 114
Portland Center Stage, 115
Portland Children's Museum,
104
Portland City Grill, 117
Portland Classical Chinese
Garden, 99–100
Portlandia (Portland), 97
Portland International Airport
(PDX), 63
accommodations near, 80
The Portland International
Film Festival, 20
Portland International
Raceway, 108
Portland Opera, 114–115
Portland Oregon Visitors Asso-
ciation (POVA) Information
Center, 64
Portland Outdoor Store, 112
The Portland Pendleton Shop,
112
Portland Rose Festival, 21
Portland Saturday Market,
97, 100, 113
Portland Trail Blazers, 108
Portland Underground Tours,
106
Portland Women's Forum State
Scenic Viewpoint, 236
Port of Cascade Locks Visitors
Center, 238
Port Orford, 224–227
Port Orford Heads State Park,
225

Port Orford Lifeboat Station, 225

Powell's City of Books (Portland), 96, 110

Prehistoric Gardens (near Port Orford), 226

Prescription medications, 24

Pre's Trail (Eugene), 158

Promenade (Seaside), 172

Proxy Falls, 263

Puffin Kite Festival (Cannon Beach), 175

Pulliam Deffenbaugh Gallery (Portland), 110

Quintana Galleries (Portland), 110

Quosatana Campground, 229

Rafting. *See also* Whitewater rafting
    Grants Pass, 295
    North Umpqua River, 267
    White Salmon River, 242

Rainbow Rock Viewpoint, 228

Rasmussen Fruit & Flower Farm (near Hood River), 243

The Real Mother Goose (Portland), 111

Red Ridge Farms (Dayton), 134

Redwood Nature Trail, 231

Reedsport, 212–213

Regatta Grounds Park (Lincoln City), 191

Regions in brief, 14–17

Reservations, campgrounds and lodges, 32

Restaurants
    best, 12–13
    tipping, 53

Restrooms, 53

Rex Hill Vineyards (Newberg), 128

Rinehart Stone House Museum (Vale), 347

Ripley's Believe It or Not (Newport), 201

Rising Sun Farms (Phoenix), 278

RiverSea Gallery (Astoria), 168

Riverside Park (Grants Pass), 296

Rock climbing, 35
    Sisters area, 313

Rock Creek Campground, 209

Rock Fort, 249–250

Rockhounding, 347

Rocky Creek State Scenic Viewpoint, 196

Rocky Mountain elk, 335–336

Rodeos, 312, 330, 340

Rogue Ales Public House (Portland), 119

Rogue Creamery (Medford), 290

Rogue River, 5, 227

Rogue River Gorge, 268

Rogue River Valley, 294–299

Roosevelt elk, 180, 352

Rooster Rock State Park, 238, 239

Roseburg, 266, 302–305

Roseland Theater & Grill (Portland), 116

Ross Island, 96

Ross Ragland Theater & Cultural Center (Klamath Falls), 272

RoxyAnn Winery (Medford), 278

RVs (recreational vehicles), 38

Ryan Gallery (Lincoln City), 192

Saddle Mountain State Natural Area, 180–181

Safety, 46

Sahalie Falls, 262

Sahalie Wine Cellars (Corvallis), 151

St. Innocent Winery (Salem), 147

St. Mary's Church (Albany), 151

Salem, 2, 58, 140–149
    accommodations, 148
    festivals, 142
    for kids, 144
    nearby towns and attractions, 144–146
    nightlife, 149
    restaurants, 148–149
    sights and attractions, 142–144
    traveling to, 141
    visitor information, 142

Salem Arts Festival, 21, 142

Salmon, 353, 357, 358–359

Salmon Bake (Depoe Bay), 195

Salt Creek Falls, 265

Samuel H. Boardman State Scenic Corridor, 6, 228

Sandcastle Building Contest (Lincoln City), 190

Sand Castle Day (Cannon Beach), 175–176

Sand Dunes Frontier (near Florence), 211

Sandland Adventures (Florence), 211

Sand Master Park, 212

Sand Point Park (Lincoln City), 191

Santiam Pass, 7, 261

SATH (Society for Accessible Travel & Hospitality), 25

Saturday Market
    Eugene, 154, 158–159
    Hood River, 244
    Portland, 97, 100, 113

Saucebox (Portland), 118

Scandal's & The Otherside Lounge (Portland), 121

Scenic drives
    Aufderheide National Scenic Byway, 262
    best, 7
    Cascade Lakes Highway, 321–322
    the Columbia Gorge National Scenic Area, 236–238
    Crater Lake Rim Drive, 270
    Depoe Bay area, 196
    Elkhorn Mountain Scenic Loop, 336–337
    Hood River Valley, 243
    North Umpqua–Upper Rogue River Scenic Byway, 266–269

Schneider Museum of Art (Ashland), 277

Schrader Old-Growth Trail, 228

Schreiner's Iris Gardens (Salem), 147

Science Works Hands-On Museum (Ashland), 278

Scott Lake Campground, 264

Sea Lion Caves (near Florence), 8, 208

Seal Rock State Recreation Site, 200

Sea Ranch R.V. Park & Stables (Cannon Beach), 179

Seaside, 171–175

Seaside Aquarium (Seaside), 173

Seasons, 19

Secret House Vineyards Winery (Veneta), 157–158

Senior travelers, 25

Shadow Bay Campground, 266

Shafer Vineyard Cellars (Forest Grove), 131
Shallon Winery (Astoria), 168
Shaniko, 309–310
Shedd Institute for the Arts (Eugene), 161–162
Sheep Rock Unit, 310
Shelton-McMurphey-Johnson House (Eugene), 156
Sherar's Falls, 308–309
Sherwood Campground, 246
Shore Acres State Park, 216
Shrewsbury Renaissance Faire (Kings Valley), 22, 150
Silvan Ridge/Hinman Vineyards (Eugene), 158
Silver Falls State Park, 145
Silverton, 144–146
Simpson Beach, 216
Simpson Reef Viewpoint, 216
Siskiyou Mountains, 299, 300
Sisters area, 312–316
Sisters Folk Festival, 312
Sisters in Sisters Celebration, 312
Sisters Outdoor Quilt Show, 21, 312
Sisters Rodeo and Parade, 20, 312
Sitka Center for Art and Ecology, 188
Siuslaw National Forest, 152
Sixth Street Viewing Dock (Astoria), 168
Ski Anthony Lakes, 335
Skidmore Historic District (Portland), 66–67
Skiing, 35. See also Cross-country skiing
    Cat Ski Mt. Bailey, 268
    Hoodoo Ski Area, 261
    Mount Bachelor, 5, 319
    Mount Hood, 257–258
    Mt. Ashland, 280
    Ski Anthony Lakes, 335
    Willamette Pass Ski Area, 265
Skinner Butte Park (Eugene), 157
Ski tours, Wallowa Mountains, 342
Smelt Sands State Recreation Site, 206
Smith Rock State Park, 313
Sno-Park permit, 257
Snowshoeing, 319
Sokol Blosser Winery (Dundee), 128

Soléna Cellars (Carlton), 129
Sorosis Park (the Dalles), 250
South Beach State Park, 200, 203
South Campground (Hosmer Lake), 325
Southeastern Oregon, 348–349
Southern Oregon, 3, 16, 275–305
The Southern Oregon Coast, 57, 224–232
Southpark Seafood Grill & Wine Bar (Portland), 118
South Slough National Estuarine Research Reserve, 216
Spangler Vineyards (Roseburg), 304
Sparks Lake, 322
Special events and festivals, 20–22
Spirit Mountain Casino (Grand Ronde), 140
Springhill Cellars (Albany), 151
Standing Stone Brewing (Ashland), 287
Stangeland Vineyards (Salem), 132
Steel Information Center (Crater Lake National Park), 269
Steens Mountain, 348, 349
Stonehenge Monument, 251
Storm-watching, 223
Stormy Weather Arts Festival (Cannon Beach), 22, 176
Sturgeon Viewing Center, 237
Succor Creek State Natural Area, 347
Sumpter, 336
Sumpter Valley Dredge State Heritage Area, 336
Sumpter Valley Railroad, 336
Sunbird Gallery (Bend), 322
Sundance River Center (near Grants Pass), 34
Sunriver, 58, 324–327
Sunriver Music Festival (Bend), 317
Sunriver Nature Center & Observatory, 318
Sunset Bay State Park, 6, 216, 219
Sunset Beach State Recreation Area, 168
Sunset Campground, 274
Surfing, 173, 191, 196

Susan Creek Campground, 268
Sutton Campground, 214
Sweet Oregon Berry Farm (between Dundee and Lafayette), 134
Swimming, Illinois River, 300

Tabu (Ashland), 287
Tahkenitch Campground, 214
Tahkenitch Trail Head, 211
Tamástslikt Cultural Institute, 331
TamKaLiks Celebration (Wallowa), 340
Tamolitch Pool, 6–7, 262
Tanger Outlet Center (Lincoln City), 192
Taxes, 51
Teacup Lake, 258
Telegraph and telex services, 52
Telephone, 51–52
Territorial Vineyards & Wine Company (Eugene), 158
Terwilliger Hot Springs, 262
Theater
    Ashland, 276–277, 287
    Astoria, 171
    Portland, 114, 115
Theater (Medford), 289
Thomas Condon Paleontology Center, 310
Thomas Creek Bridge, 228
Three Arch Rocks, 186
Three Capes Scenic Loop, 55, 57, 61, 185–186
Three Sisters Wilderness, 320
Thrill-Ville USA (Salem), 144
Thursday Art Walk (Portland), 97
Tillamook, 185
Tillamook Air Museum, 185
Tillamook Cheese Factory, 185
Tillamook County, 2–3, 181–188
Tillamook Head Trail, 173
Tillamook Rock Lighthouse, 176
Timberline Lodge (Mount Hood), 254, 256, 257
Timberline Ski Area, 256, 257
Timberline Trail, 6, 256
Time zones, 40, 52
Tipping, 53
Todd Lake, 322
Todd Lake Campground, 325
Toilets, 53

Toketee Falls, 267
Toketee Lake Campground, 269
Toledo, art galleries, 202
Toll Bridge Park, 246
Tom McCall Waterfront Park (Portland), 98
Torii Mor Winery (Dundee), 128
Toujours (Newport), 201
Trail Bridge Campground, 264
Trains and railways, 31, 47, 48
   Crooked River Railroad Company Dinner Train (Redmond), 313–314
   Eagle Cap Excursion Train, 340
   Mount Hood Railroad, 244
   Oregon Coast Explorer, 184
   Sumpter Valley Railroad, 336
Travel Assistance International, 23
Traveler's Aid Society, 50
Traveler's checks, 18, 45
Travelex Insurance Services, 23
Travel Guard International, 23
Travel insurance, 22–23
Travel Insured International, 23
Triad Gallery (Seal Rock), 202
Trip-cancellation insurance, 22–23
Troon Vineyard (Grants Pass), 291
Tryon Creek State Park (Portland), 107
Tualatin Estate Vineyards, 131
Tucker Park, 246
Tulip Festival (Woodburn), 20
Tumalo State Park, 325
Turtle Rock Wayside, 228
Twin Lakes, 322
Twist (Portland), 111
Tyee Wine Cellars (Corvallis), 151–152
Tyrus Evan/The Depot (Carlton), 129

Umpqua Discovery Center (Reedsport), 212–213
Umpqua Hot Springs, 267
Umpqua Lighthouse State Park, 213
Umpqua River Lighthouse, 213
Undersea Gardens (Newport), 201
Union Creek Campground, 269, 338

Union Station (Portland), 31, 64
University of Oregon Museum of Natural History (Eugene), 156
Upper Klamath Canoe Trail, 273
Upper Klamath Lake, 271
Urban Wineworks (Portland), 118
USA Rail Pass, 48
U.S. Bank (Baker City), 334–335

Vale, 347
Valley Bronze of Oregon (Joseph), 340
Valley of the Rogue State Park, 297
Valley View Vineyard (Ruch), 291
Vancouver, Washington, accommodations, 79–80
Van Duzer Vineyards (Dallas), 132–133
Vault Martini (Portland), 118
Viento State Park, 239, 246
Viento Wines (near Hood River), 243
Vietnam Veterans Living Memorial (Portland), 100
Vino Mercato (Bend), 327
Vino Paradiso (Portland), 118
Visas, 41–42
Visa traveler's checks, 18
Visitor information, 17
Visit USA, 48
Vista House, 236

Wagon ruts, Oregon Trail, 9, 328, 331, 333, 334, 347, 357
Wahclella Falls, 237
Waldo Lake, 265
Wallowa County Museum (Joseph), 340
Wallowa Lake Marina, 340
Wallowa Lake State Park, 340, 343–344
Wallowa Lake Tramway, 340–341
Wallowa Mountains, 17, 328, 339, 341
Wallowa-Whitman National Forest, 335
Wasco County Courthouse (the Dalles), 250
Wasco County Historical Museum (The Dalles), 249

Washington Park (Portland), 100
Washington Park and Zoo Railway (Portland), 102
Washington Park Zoo (Oregon Zoo; Portland), 97, 102, 115
Wasson Brothers wine tasting room (Sandy), 258
Waterfront Blues Festival (Portland), 21
Waterstone Mineral Springs Spa (Ashland), 278
Waxmyrtle Campground, 214
Wax Works Museum (Newport), 201
Weather Machine (Portland), 96
The Websters (Ashland), 280
Weisinger's (Ashland), 279
West Coast Game Park (Bandon), 8, 221
Westfir, 264–266
Whalehead Beach Viewpoint, 228
Whalen Island County Park, 187
Whale-watching, 35, 350
   Bandon, 220
   Depoe Bay, 196–197
   Garibaldi, 184
   Newport, 201
   Reedsport, 213
   Yachats, 206
Wheelchair accessibility, 24
Wheeler, 183–184
White Bird (Portland), 115
White Bird Gallery (Cannon Beach), 177
White River Falls State Park, 309
White River Sno-Park, 258
Whitespires Church (Albany), 151
White-water kayaking, 34
White-water rafting, 5, 35–36.
   See also Rafting
   Ashland, 279–280
   Deschutes River, 308, 321
   Grants Pass, 295
   Hells Canyon area, 345
   Jacksonville/Medford area, 290
   McKenzie River, 262
   Mount Hood, 257
   Owyhee River, 347
Widmer Brewing and Gasthaus (Portland), 120
Wildflowers, 16, 181, 248, 290, 345
Wildhorse Casino Resort, 331

Wildlife Images Rehabilitation and Education Center (Grants Pass), 296
Wildlife Safari (Winston), 8, 302
Wildlife viewing. *See also* Birdwatching; Whale-watching
   Ankeny National Wildlife Refuge, 143
   Elkhorn Wildlife Area (North Powder), 335–336
   Hart Mountain National Antelope Refuge, 349
   The High Desert Museum (Bend), 317–318
   Jewell Meadows Wildlife Area, 180
   Ladd Marsh Wildlife Area, 335
   Malheur National Wildlife Refuge, 348–349
   the Oregon coast, 163
   Owyhee River region, 347
   Wildlife Images Rehabilitation and Education Center (Grants Pass), 296
   Wildlife Safari (Winston), 8, 302
Wildwood Recreation Site, 256–257
Willakenzie Estate (Yamhill), 130
Willamette Falls overlook (Oregon City), 121
Willamette Mission State Park, 143–144
Willamette Pass Route (Ore. 58), 264–266
Willamette Pass Ski Area, 265
Willamette Queen (Salem), 142
Willamette Shore Trolley (Portland), 105–106

The Willamette Valley, 2, 14, 122–162, 351. *See also* Mid-Willamette Valley; North Willamette Valley Wine Country
Willamette Valley Vineyards (Salem), 147–148
The Willamette Valley Wine Country. *See also* The North Willamette Valley Wine Country
   suggested itinerary, 59–60
William L. Finley National Wildlife Refuge, 152
William M. Tugman State Park, 214
Winchester Bay, 215
Wind River Cellars (Husum), 243
Windsurfing, 36
   the Columbia Gorge, 239
   Hood River, 5, 242
Wine Country Thanksgiving (Willamette Valley), 22
Wineries. *See also* North Willamette Valley wine country, wineries
   Ashland area, 278–279
   Astoria, 168
   Cave Junction area, 300–301
   Corvallis–Albany area, 151–152
   Eugene area, 157–158
   Hood River Valley, 243
   Jacksonville/Medford area, 290–291
   near the Dalles, 251
   Roseburg area, 303
   Salem area, 132, 133, 146–148

Wines, 360
Wiseman Gallery (Grants Pass), 295
Witness Tree Vineyard (Salem), 133
Wooden Shoe Bulb Company (Woodburn), 147
Wood Gallery (Newport), 201
Wooldridge Creek Vineyard & Wines (Grants Pass), 291
World Forestry Center Discovery Museum (Portland), 1, 103
Worldwide Assistance Services, 23, 44
WOW Hall (Eugene), 162
Wright's for Camping (Cannon Beach), 179
Wyeth Campground, 240

Yachats, 205–209
Yachats Ocean State Park Wayside, 206
Yachats State Park, 206
Yamhill County wineries, 2, 128–130
Yamhill Valley Vineyards (McMinnville), 128
Yaquina Bay Lighthouse, 199, 200
Yaquina Bay State Recreation Site, 200
Yaquina Head Interpretive Center, 200
Yaquina Head Lighthouse, 199–200
Yaquina Head Outstanding Natural Area, 200
Your Northwest (Dundee), 134

THE NEW TRAVELOCITY GUARANTEE

EVERYTHING YOU BOOK WILL BE RIGHT, OR WE'LL WORK WITH OUR TRAVEL PARTNERS TO MAKE IT RIGHT, RIGHT AWAY.

*To drive home the point,
we're going to use the word "right" in every single sentence.*

Let's get right to it. Right to the meat! Only Travelocity guarantees everything about your booking will be right, or we'll work with our travel partners to make it right, right away. Right on!

Here's a picture taken smack dab right in the middle of Antigua, where the guarantee also covers you.

The guarantee covers all but one of the items pictured to the right.

Now, you may be thinking, "Yeah, right, I'm so sure." That's OK; you have the right to remain skeptical. That is until we mention help is always right around the corner. Call us right off the bat, knowing that our customer service reps are there for you 24/7. Righting wrongs. Left and right.

For example, what if the ocean view you booked actually looks out at a downright ugly parking lot? You'd be right to call – we're there for you. And no one in their right mind would be pleased to learn the rental car place has closed and left them stranded. Call Travelocity and we'll help get you back on the right track.

Now if you're guessing there are some things we can't control, like the weather, well you're right. But we can help you with most things – to get all the details in righting,* visit **travelocity.com/guarantee**.

*Sorry, spelling things right is one of the few things not covered under the guarantee.

I'd give my right arm for a guarantee like this, although I'm glad I don't have to.

*** travelocity®
You'll never roam alone.™

IF YOU BOOK IT, IT SHOULD BE THERE.

Only Travelocity guarantees it will be, or we'll work
with our travel partners to make it right, right away.
So if you're missing a balcony or anything else you
booked, just call us 24/7. 1-888-TRAVELOCITY

travelocity

You'll never roam alone